The Editor

JASON P. ROSENBLATT is Professor of English at Georgetown University, where he has taught since 1974. He is coeditor of *"Not in Heaven": Coherence and Complexity in Biblical Narrative* and author of *Renaissance England's Chief Rabbi: John Selden, Torah and Law in "Paradise Lost,"* and many essays on seventeenth-century English literature. He is currently working on an annotated edition of John Selden's *Table Talk*.

A NORTON CRITICAL EDITION

MILTON'S SELECTED POETRY AND PROSE

AUTHORITATIVE TEXTS
BIBLICAL SOURCES
CRITICISM

Edited by

JASON P. ROSENBLATT
GEORGETOWN UNIVERSITY

W · W · NORTON & COMPANY · *New York* · *London*

W. W. Norton & Company has been independent since its founding in 1923, when William Warder Norton and Mary D. Herter Norton first published lectures delivered at the People's Institute, the adult education division of New York City's Cooper Union. The firm soon expanded its program beyond the Institute, publishing books by celebrated academics from America and abroad. By midcentury, the two major pillars of Norton's publishing program—trade books and college texts—were firmly established. In the 1950s, the Norton family transferred control of the company to its employees, and today—with a staff of four hundred and a comparable number of trade, college, and professional titles published each year—W. W. Norton & Company stands as the largest and oldest publishing house owned wholly by its employees.

Library of Congress Cataloging-in-Publication Data

Milton, John, 1608–1674.
  [Selections. 2010]
  Milton's selected poetry and prose : authoritative texts, biblical sources, criticism / edited By Jason P. Rosenblatt. — 1st ed.
        p. cm. — (A Norton critical edition)
  Includes bibliographical references.
  ISBN 978-0-393-97987-9 (pbk.)
  I. Rosenblatt, Jason Philip, 1941–   II. Title.
  PR3553.R67 2010
  821' .4—dc22

                                                              2010041084

W. W. Norton & Company, Inc., 500 Fifth Avenue, New York, N.Y. 10110-0017
www.wwnorton.com
W. W. Norton & Company Ltd., Castle House, 75/76 Wells Street,
London W1T 3QT

4 5 6 7 8 9 0

For Tehila, Zachary, Gabriel, and Eitan

Contents

Preface and Acknowledgments

Editions of Milton that modernize spelling and punctuation, remove italics, drop most of the capitalizations, and add quotation marks to spoken passages begin defensively, and this one is no exception. And the same justification is meekly offered: these are all of Milton's words, set down in the same order as in the more scholarly editions but more readable for the student and the sought-after amateur. The base text of *Paradise Regained* and *Samson Agonistes* is the first edition of 1671, and most of the shorter poems derive from the 1645 edition. But anyone who is looking for a faithful old-spelling edition will be no happier with this book than those poor readers who were expecting to find *Paradise Lost* between its covers.

The aim has been to facilitate understanding but not at the expense of what one imagines to be the Miltonic intention or of those ambiguities that enrich the poetry. Students can look to the annotations for help, but they will still have work to do. Thus, for example, the Bible uses the same word to denote "angel" and "messenger" in both the Hebrew and the Greek (*mal'akh, angelos*). Milton assumed everyone's familiarity with this identity, but the memory of one's own first perplexed encounter with Sonnet 19 suggests that perhaps he shouldn't have: "thousands at his bidding speed / And post o'er land and ocean without rest." It is obvious that *thousands* requires an explanation. But in the same sonnet, the one-talent servant fears lest his master

> returning chide,
> "Doth God exact day-labor, light denied?"
> I fondly ask;

Some undergraduates find it difficult to discern the source of the question, and most at least momentarily assume that it is the master. It would be easy to substitute a semicolon for the comma after *chide,* but in this instance, and in many others, it has seemed preferable to follow the other editors (except for Raffel, whose aim is perfect clarity) and retain the comma and the momentary perplexity.

Some decisions are easy, such as retaining elisions for the sake of meter and archaic spelling for a variety of reasons, including rhyme (e.g., *shew* instead of "show" in *A Masque* [512] to chime with *true*) and allusiveness (e.g., *lickerish*, which suggests both liquor and lechery, instead of "liquorish" [700]). But numerous discussions with Nathan Stogdill, my first and only graduate assistant, betray the anxiety behind even the most minor ad hoc decisions about punctuation. The more one broods over them, the harder they are to decide: "Why prithee shepherd" or "Why, prithee, shepherd"? And some of the decisions, of course, affect meaning. Here are the lines from the 1671 edition describing the procession leading Samson to the temple of Dagon:

> before him Pipes
> And Timbrels, on each side went armed guards,
> Both horse and foot before him and behind
> Archers, and Slingers, Cataphracts and Spears.
> (1616–19)

Line 1618 seems to require additional punctuation for the sake of clarity, but does one place a comma after *him* and not after *behind*? That would position all of the guards in front of Samson. Or after *behind* but not after *him*? That would position the armed guards both in front of him and behind him. Or does one follow the 1671 first edition and omit punctuation entirely from the line. One must choose, but even at present the line feels like a Miltonic crux:

> before him pipes
> And timbrels; on each side went armèd guards,
> Both horse and foot before him and behind,
> Archers, and slingers, cataphracts and spears.

Milton's prose as well as poetry has been modernized, also for the sake of clarity, with very long sentences and paragraphs broken up into more manageable units. What is lost is the pleasure of encountering the full force of those headlong sentences and of meeting the challenge of parsing them. What remains, one hopes, is the intellectual and aesthetic pleasure of "untwisting all the chains that tie / The hidden soul of harmony." That harmony resides in the best prose tracts as well as in the poetry, and this edition reprints *The Doctrine and Discipline of Divorce* (the longer second edition of 1644), *Of Education*, the *Areopagitica*, *The Tenure of Kings and Magistrates*, and the longer second edition of *The Ready and Easy Way*. Like the major poems *Paradise Regained* and *Samson Agonistes*, each of these prose treatises is sufficiently diverse to merit a separate introduction. The same principle of printing complete works instead of snippets from a lot of them (the prose fills nineteen of the twenty-one volumes of the Columbia edition of the complete works) applies to the selection of critical essays. Choos-

ing from among the many superior works available has been the
hardest part of editing this volume, and some of the decisions were
made, reluctantly, only days before sending it off, with a full understanding that favorite essays of many readers (including me!) have
been omitted. Although more of those essays could have been
included if they had been radically abridged, the only way to allow
authors to develop their ideas at their own pace is to reprint substantial portions of their essays. And, of course, even without *Paradise Lost*, to reprint the poetry, major prose, and criticism in a volume
with page limits that keep it truly affordable requires triage.

Although, as noted, the diversity of the works in this edition makes
individual introductions more appropriate than a general one, I
would like to discuss only briefly (because it is taken up again in
some of this edition's introductions) a general quality in Milton's
greatest works of poetry and prose that bears on all of the classical
and biblical references and allusions addressed only superficially in
the annotations. Milton's monistic belief in the continuity of body,
mind, and spirit finds passionate expression in his greatest works.
The right order of ascending value includes the lower in the higher,
without any turning away or disparagement. This principle of monist
continuity applies as well to the Greek and Latin cultures, the
Hebrew Bible, and the New Testament. Milton's greatest works
assume continuity among the natural law of virtuous pagans, the
Mosaic law, and the Gospel, with the last transposing the values of
the others into a higher key. The aesthetic counterpart of this theological principle of transposition is the tripartite crescendo movement in Milton's poetry: the development of the idea of *katharos*
(pure) in the successive quatrains of the twenty-third sonnet, which
begin with Euripides' *Alcestis*, extend to the Levitical rites of purification after childbirth under "the old" Mosaic law, and conclude
with a vision of absolute purity in a Christian heaven (see Spitzer);
and the continuous but developing meanings of the words *pastoral* and *pastor* in *Lycidas*, which measure the consolation of the
shepherd-narrator. This great poem progresses from pagan classical aesthetics (64–84), through Hebraic-prophetic ethics (113–31),
to the limitless reward of a Christian heaven purged of evil (165–85).
The sources range from Theocritus, Bion, Moschus, and Virgil,
through Psalms ("The Lord is my shepherd"), Isaiah, and Jeremiah,
to the Book of Revelation. Because of Milton's ability to weight this
poem with the gravity of endless implication, all of these sources
can converge powerfully in a single verse paragraph.

Critics who disparage *Samson Agonistes* compare it invidiously
with *Paradise Regained*, Samson with Christ, Manoa with God (Samson's *real* father), and even Judges 13–16 (the ostensible source of the
story) with Hebrews 11:32 (the real source). A monistic reading of

Samson Agonistes, in accord with classical, Hebraic, and Christian thought, would acknowledge the humanity of the Chorus, its capacity for fellow-feeling, and its considerable spiritual and intellectual development, instead of rejecting it, as many critics have, as a narrow, obsolete, erroneous "chorus of enslaved Hebrews," representing "the whole Hebrew people, bound by the law of Moses in its service to Jehovah."

One can occasionally discern the spirit of rejection not only in the critics but even in some of Milton's own less successful work. Passages in books 11 and 12 of *Paradise Lost* employ the negative typology of the Epistle to the Hebrews, emphasizing disparity rather than congruity (12.285–314) and the Pauline distinction between children of loins and children of faith (12.446–50). Perhaps the most disturbing example of all, despite attempts to explain it away, is Jesus' long and vehement rejection of Greek culture—especially its philosophy and literature—in book 4 of *Paradise Regained* (286–364). Jesus' triumphalist claims about "our Hebrew songs" as the source of Greek poetry, and his insistence on the inherent unworthiness of that poetry, jar against the reader's knowledge that Milton is the most cultured of the great English poets, nurtured by the classics that his hero dismisses peremptorily.

Milton's first polemical writings, five substantial antiprelatical treatises published in 1641 and 1642, trace the decline of the church from the perfect pattern of scripture clearly revealed, "backslid[ing] one way into the Jewish beggery, of old cast rudiments, and stumbl[ing] forward another way into the new-vomited Paganisme of sensuall Idolatry" (*YP*, 1:520). In these treatises, only Presbyterianism (later repudiated) is "the one right discipline" (605), and Milton's language is at times racist and hierarchical.

Three of the five prose tracts reprinted in this edition were published between 1643 and 1645, when Milton employed a radically monist hermeneutic of inclusiveness, strikingly different from the exclusivity of the early antiprelatical pamphlets. (His wife's desertion may have made him more compassionate toward human weakness and less certain of his own elect status.) Milton's divorce tracts include *Tetrachordon*, which attempts to harmonize passages from the Hebrew and Greek Bibles. And in *The Doctrine and Discipline of Divorce*, Milton argues strenuously for the compatibility of universal natural law, the Mosaic law, and the Gospel. He can even speak with a measure of sympathy about Anabaptists, Familists, and Antinominans, "of life . . . not debauched," attributing their excess zeal to "the restraint of some lawful liberty which ought to be given men and is denied them."

The topics of Milton's five prose treatises reprinted in this edition differ from one another: arguing, against an apparent New Testament prohibition, for freedom to divorce on grounds of incompatibility; proposing to reform the educational system; trying to persuade Parliament to rescind a licensing order that would have imposed prepublication censorship; justifying the execution of Charles I; warning his countrymen days before the Restoration of the dangers of monarchy. But all of them affirm the authority of Greek and Roman learning, the Hebrew Bible, and the New Testament. One hopes that there is a correlation between such intellectual inclusiveness and political, religious, and social toleration.

My debts to other scholars are so heavy that this is an edition nearly anonymous. The most profound of all are to Milton's editors and annotators, beginning with Patrick Hume. There is an almost irresistible impulse to devote individual sentences to each of them, pointing out the qualities that distinguish their editions: H. J. Todd, David Masson, John Leonard, Douglas Bush (both his edition of the poetry and volume two of the *Milton Variorum*, with A. S. P. Woodhouse), John Carey, Merritt Hughes, Frank Allen Patterson, Don M. Wolfe, Ernest Sirluck, and, in the later stages, William Kerrigan, John Rumrich, and Stephen Fallon. Although John Leonard, with characteristic thoroughness, had already checked every English word in Milton's poems against the OED, which should have made looking up words unnecessary, at least for the poetry, that dictionary was the default page on my computer screen. Barbara Lewalski, scholar and lifelong teacher, provides the opportunity to shift from the more impersonal debts to the heavy personal ones. One of the pleasures of editing this volume has been the opportunity to reread and make use of her magnificent biography of Milton.

The personal debts are few but substantial. From beginning to end, Carol Bemis at Norton has been extraordinarily patient and generous. Former Georgetown graduate student Nathaniel Stogdill was my co-worker in establishing a text for the major poems. More recently I have benefited from Rivka Genesen's prompt helpfulness and from Candace Levy's perspicacity. William Shullenberger, Professor of Literature at Sarah Lawrence College, has provided a new verse translation as well as annotation of the three Latin poems included here: *Elegia V*, *Ad Patrem*, and *Epitaphium Damonis*. Whatever work on this edition I managed to do while chairing a large department is thanks to the competence of Karen Lautman, Georgetown English Department administrator. Finally, Zipporah Marton Rosenblatt, my darling helpmate, extended her able assistance to this project.

A note to readers of Milton's prose in this edition: Norton policy is to combine originally individual footnotes into a composite one, which works backward by defining the last word in the group first. Readers encountering a perplexing word or phrase in the prose should find it defined or explained in the next footnote, sometimes occurring several lines later.

Abbreviations

Aen.	Virgil, *Aeneid*
Apol.	*Apology for Smectymnuus*
A. V.	Authorized Version of the Bible (1611)
Bush	Douglas Bush, ed., *Milton: Poetical Works* (London: Oxford University Press, 1966)
DDC	*De Doctrina Christiana*
DDD	*The Doctrine and Discipline of Divorce*
DNB	*The Oxford Dictionary of National Biography*
Dzelzainis	Martin Dzelzainis, ed., *Milton: Political Writings* (Cambridge: Cambridge University Press, 1991)
FQ	*The Faerie Queene*
Gr.	Greek
Haskin	Dayton Haskin, *Milton's Burden of Interpretation* (Philadelphia: University of Pennsylvania Press, 1994)
Heb.	Hebrew
Honigmann	E. A. J. Honigmann, ed., *Milton's Sonnets* (London, Melbourne: Macmillan, 1966)
Il.	Homer, *Iliad*
Ital.	Italian
KJV	King James Version of the Bible (Authorized Version), 1611
L.	Latin
Leonard	John Leonard, ed., *John Milton: The Complete Poems* (London and New York: Penguin, 1998)
Lewalski	Barbara Lewalski, *The Life of John Milton: A Critical Biography* (Oxford: Blackwell, 2000)

lit.   literally

Lutaud   Olivier Lutaud, ed. and trans., *For the Liberty of Unlicensed Printing: Areopagitica*, (Paris: Aubier-Flammarion, 1956)

Lyc.   *Lycidas*

Masque   *A Masque Presented at Ludlow Castle, 1634* (*Comus*)

Met.   Ovid, *Metamorphoses*

Mod Lib   William Kerrigan, John Rumrich, and Stephen M. Fallon, eds., *The Complete Poetry and Essential Prose of John Milton* (New York: The Modern Library, 2007)

MS   Milton Studies

Norbrook   David Norbrook, *Writing the English Republic: Poetry, Rhetoric, and Politics, 1627–1660* (Cambridge: Cambridge University Press, 1999)

Od.   Homer, *Odyssey*

Patrick   J. Max Patrick, gen. ed., *The Prose of John Milton* (Garden City, N.Y.: Anchor, 1967)

pl.   plural

PL   *Paradise Lost*

PR   *Paradise Regained*

RCG   *The Reason of Church-Government*

Rep.   Plato's *Republic*

Silv.   *Silvae*

Sirluck   Ernest Sirluck, ed., *Areopagitica*, in YP:2

Spitzer   Leo Spitzer, "Understanding Milton," in his *Essays on English and American Literature*, ed. Anna Hatcher (Princeton, N.J.: Princeton University Press, 1962), pp. 116–31.

TKM   *The Tenure of Kings and Magistrates*

TMS   Poems, a letter to a friend, and notes on themes for projected tragedies, all (except for late sonnets composed when he was blind) in Milton's own hand, from the Manuscript in Trinity College, Cambridge

Var.   A. S. P. Woodhouse and Douglas Bush, eds., *A Variorum Commentary on The Poems of John Milton*, vol. 2 (New York: Columbia University Press, 1972)

YP   Don M. Wolfe, gen. ed., *The Complete Prose Works of John Milton*, 8 vols. (New Haven, Conn.: Yale University Press, 1953–82)

MILTON'S SELECTED
POETRY AND PROSE

ON THE MORNING OF CHRIST'S NATIVITY In December 1629, when he turned twenty-one, Milton attained his poetic majority with his *Ode on the Morning of Christ's Nativity*. In his *Elegy VI, To Charles Diodati, Staying in the Country*, written a few days after Christmas, he outlines for his best friend the poem he has just been writing:

> But if you would know what I do now, at least
> If you think it fit to know if I do anything,
> We sing the king who bears our peace, the seed of heaven,
> The blessed ages promised in the sacred books,
> God's wailing, and his stabling beneath a humble roof,
> Who with his father dwells in heaven supreme;
> The star-bearing sky, hosts warbling in the ethereal sphere,
> And gods expelled at once from their own fanes.
> These gifts have we offered for Christ's nativity,
> Gifts which the dawn's first light on me bestowed.
> —From William Shullenberger's new verse translation

The Nativity Ode, Milton's first great English poem, can be seen as a triptych, with the left flanking panel representing peace and silence, the right one violence and cacophony, and the main central panel celebrating as musical harmony the blending of the human and divine. For the correlatives of that music in Christian doctrine, see Christopher's essay on p. 465. And for what a great twentieth-century poet can do with a single line from the ode, see Anthony Hecht's "Lizards and Snakes" (p. 465).

To see changes in Milton's sensibility, it might be worth comparing the flight of the pagan gods in the third section (stanzas 19–25, lines 173–228) with the catalog of pagan deities in *Paradise Lost* (1.376–521), composed more than thirty years later. With one magnificent exception (1.419–31), Milton's voice in the latter catalog is shrill in its fierce denunciation of the pagan gods who incarnated the fallen angels, demon idols who audaciously got themselves worshiped in God's holy city. The tone in the Nativity Ode is far more ambivalent, at times sympathetic and even nostalgic for the lost beauty of pagan myth.

On The Morning of Christ's Nativity

I

This is the month, and this the happy morn,
Wherein the son of Heav'n's eternal King,
Of wedded maid and virgin mother born,
Our great redemption from above did bring;
5   For so the holy sages° once did sing,   *Hebrew prophets*
    That he our deadly forfeit° should release,   *crime, penalty*
And with his Father work us a perpetual peace.

II

That glorious form, that light unsufferable,°   *unendurable*
And that far-beaming blaze of majesty
10 Wherewith he wont° at Heav'n's high   *was accustomed*
        council-table
To sit the midst of trinal Unity,°   *the Trinity*
He laid aside; and here with us to be
    Forsook the courts of everlasting day,
And chose with us a darksome house of
        mortal clay.[1]

III

15 Say, Heav'nly Muse,[2] shall not thy sacred vein°   *style, particular*
Afford a present to the infant God?   *strain of talent*
Hast thou no verse, no hymn, or solemn strain
To welcome him to this his new abode,
Now while the heav'n, by the sun's team[3] untrod,
20   Hath took no print of the approaching light,
And all the spangled host keep watch in
        squadrons bright?[4]

IV

See how from far upon the eastern road
The star-led wizards° haste with odors sweet: *Magi*
O run, prevent[5] them with thy humble ode,
25 And lay it lowly at his blessèd feet;
Have thou the honor first thy Lord to greet,
    And join thy voice unto the angel choir,
From out his secret altar touched with
        hallowed fire.[6]

---

1. the body, alluding to *kenosis*, Christ's self-renunciation in the incarnation.
2. possibly Urania (Gr. "heavenly"), the muse of astronomy and of the Miltonic bard in *PL* (7.1–39); associated in the Renaissance with exalted and religious inspiration.
3. Horses pulling the sun god's chariot.
4. "The stars above London become the angelic host above the shepherds. Throughout the Hymn the mixture of tenses telescopes past and present" (Bush).
5. Come before (L. *praevenire*).
6. A symbol of inspiration. In Isa. 6:6–7, a seraph touches the prophet's lips with a burning coal taken from God's altar. In *RCG* (*YP*, 1:820–21), Milton as Christian poet urges "devout prayer to that eternal spirit who . . . sends out his seraphim with the hallowed fire of his altar to touch and purify the lips of whom he pleases."

THE HYMN

I

It was the winter wild,
30 While the Heav'n-born-child
    All meanly wrapped in the rude manger lies;
    Nature in awe to him
    Had doffed her gaudy trim,
      With her great Master so to sympathize;
35 It was no season then for her
    To wanton with the sun her lusty paramour.

II

    Only with speeches fair
    She woos the gentle air
      To hide her guilty front with innocent snow,
40 And on her naked shame,
    Pollute with sinful blame,
      The saintly veil of maiden white to throw,
    Confounded that her Maker's eyes
    Should look so near upon her foul deformities.[7]

III

45 But He her fears to cease
    Sent down the meek-eyed Peace;
      She, crowned with olive green, came softly
        sliding
    Down through the turning sphere,[8]
    His ready harbinger
50   With turtle° wing the amorous clouds   *turtledove*
        dividing,
    And waving wide her myrtle[9] wand,
    She strikes a universal peace through sea and land.[1]

---

7. "I counsel thee to buy . . . white raiment, that thou mayest be clothed, and that the
   shame of thy nakedness do not appear" (Rev. 3:18). Evokes the shame, "sin-bred," of the
   Fall, which Christ's redemption will annul.
8. According to the old Ptolemaic astronomy, the starry globe of the heavens turning
   daily about the earth.
9. The tree of Venus and thus of love.
1. Like Truth, Justice, and Mercy (lines 141–46), Peace resembles a figure in a contemporary court masque.

IV

No war or battle's sound
Was heard the world around:
55   The idle spear and shield were high uphung;
The hookèd[2] chariot stood
Unstained with hostile blood,
   The trumpet spake not to the armèd throng;[3]
And kings sat still with awful eye
60 As if they surely knew their sovereign Lord was by.

V

But peaceful was the night
Wherein the Prince of Light
   His reign of peace upon the earth began:
The winds with wonder whist°   *hushed*
65 Smoothly the waters kissed,
   Whispering new joys to the mild ocëan,
Who now hath quite forgot to rave,
While birds of calm[4] sit brooding on the
     charmèd wave.

VI

The stars with deep amaze
70 Stand fixed in steadfast gaze,
   Bending one way their precious influence,[5]
And will not take their flight
For all the morning light,
   Or Lucifer° that often warned them thence;   *morning star, Venus*
75 But in their glimmering orbs did glow,
Until their Lord himself bespake, and bid
     them go.

VII

And though the shady gloom
Had given day her room,

---

2. I.e., with projecting blades.
3. Christ, born in the *pax Romana*, was seen to fulfill Isaiah's prophecy: "they shall beat their swords into plowshares, and their spears into pruninghooks: nation shall not lift up sword against nation, neither shall they learn war any more (2:4)." But here war seems ready to break out at any moment.
4. Halcyons (kingfishers), who sit brooding on their floating nests during the winter solstice; associated with fair weather at sea.
5. The power exerted on humans by the heavenly bodies.

The sun himself withheld his wonted speed,
80 And hid his head for shame,
  As his inferior flame
    The new-enlightened world no more should need;
  He saw a greater Sun appear
  Than his bright throne or burning axle-tree
      could bear.

VIII

85 The shepherds on the lawn,
  Or ere° the point of dawn,   *before*
    Sat simply chatting in a rustic row;
  Full little thought they then
  That the mighty Pan
90   Was kindly[6] come to live with them below;
  Perhaps their loves, or else their sheep,
  Was all that did their silly° thoughts so busy   *innocent*
      keep.

IX

  When such music sweet
  Their hearts and ears did greet
95   As never was by mortal finger strook,
  Divinely-warbled voice
  Answering the stringèd noise,
    As all their souls in blissful rapture took;
  The air such pleasure loath to lose,
100 With thousand echoes still prolongs each
      heav'nly close.[7]

X

  Nature that heard such sound
  Beneath the hollow round°   *sphere of the moon*
    Of Cynthia's seat, the airy region thrilling,
  Now was almost won
105 To think her part was done,
    And that her reign had here its last fulfilling;
  She knew such harmony alone
  Could hold all heav'n and earth in happier unïon.

---

6. (1) lovingly, (2) as one of their kind—i.e., human.
7. Conclusion of a musical phrase.

XI

At last surrounds their sight
110   A globe° of circular light,   *troop, sphere*
  That with long beams the shame-faced
   night arrayed;
The helmèd Cherubim
And sworded Seraphim
  Are seen in glittering ranks with wings displayed,
115   Harping in loud and solemn choir
With unexpressive° notes to Heaven's   *beyond human*
  new-born heir.   *expression*

XII

Such music (as 'tis said)
Before was never made,
  But when of old the sons of morning[8] sung,
120   While the Creator great
His constellations set,
  And the well-balanced world on hinges hung,
And cast the dark foundations deep,
And bid the welt'ring waves their oozy channel keep.

XIII

125   Ring out ye crystal spheres,
Once bless our human ears
  (If ye have power to touch our senses so),[9]
And let your silver chime
Move in melodious time,
130   And let the bass of Heav'n's deep organ blow;
And with your ninefold harmony
Make up full consort° to th'angelic symphony.[1]   *harmony, company*
                  of musicians

XIV

For if such holy song
Enwrap our fancy long,

---

8. The angels at creation: "Where wast thou when I laid the foundations of the earth ? . . . When the morning stars sang together, and all the sons of God shouted for joy?" (Job 38:4, 7).
9. In this Christian adaptation of the Pythagorean-Platonic tradition, the music made by the planets as they turn were audible only to sinless souls and not to unpurged faculties after the Fall.
1. "The music of the nine spheres blending with that of the nine orders of angels" (Bush).

135   Time will run back and fetch the age of gold,[2]
And speckled Vanity
Will sicken soon and die,
    And lep'rous Sin will melt from earthly mold,°   *the human body*
And Hell itself will pass away,
140   And leave her dolorous mansions to the
            peering day.

XV

Yea, Truth and Justice then
Will down return to men,
    Orbed in a rainbow; and, like glories wearing,
Mercy will sit between,[3]
145   Throned in celestial sheen,
    With radiant feet the tissued[4] clouds down steering,
And Heav'n, as at some festival,
Will open wide the gates of her high palace hall.

XVI

But wisest Fate° says no,   *God's will*
150   This must not yet be so,
    The babe lies yet in smiling infancy[5]
That on the bitter cross
Must redeem our loss,
    So both himself and us to glorify;
155   Yet first to those ychained in sleep,°   *death*
The wakeful trump of doom° must thunder   *judgment*
            through the deep,

XVII

With such a horrid clang
As on Mount Sinai rang
    While the red fire and smold'ring clouds out brake:[6]
160   The agèd Earth aghast
With terror of the blast
    Shall from the surface to the center shake,
When at the world's last sessïon

---

2. The reign of Cronos or Saturn, a classical parallel to the state of innocence.
3. Combines the classical Astraea or Justice with Ps. 85:10: "Mercy and truth are met together; righteousness and peace have kissed each other."
4. I.e., woven with gold or silver thread.
5. Lit., not speaking.
6. When Moses received the Ten Commandments (Exod. 19:16–18).

The dreadful Judge in middle air shall spread
    his throne.[7]

XVIII

165 And then at last our bliss
Full and perfect is,
    But now begins; for from this happy day
Th' old Dragon° under ground   *Satan*
In straiter° limits bound   *narrower*
170   Not half so far casts his usurpèd sway,
And wroth to see his kingdom fail,
Swinges° the scaly horror of his folded tail.   *Lashes about*

XIX

The oracles are dumb,[8]
No voice or hideous hum
175   Runs through the archèd roof in words deceiving.
Apollo[9] from his shrine
Can no more divine,
    With hollow shriek the steep of Delphos leaving.
No nightly trance or breathèd spell
180 Inspires the pale-eyed priest from the prophetic cell.

XX

The lonely mountains o'er
And the resounding shore
    A voice of weeping heard and loud lament;[1]
From haunted spring, and dale
185 Edged with poplar pale,
    The parting genius° is with sighing sent.   *local guardian spirit*
With flow'r-inwoven tresses torn
The nymphs in twilight shade of tangled
    thickets mourn.

---

7. 1 Thess. 4:17: "Then we which are alive and remain shall be caught up together with them in the clouds, to meet the Lord in the air: and so shall we ever be with the Lord."
8. Milton draws on the tradition that the ancient oracles of Greece and Rome, who practiced divination, fell silent at the birth of Christ, the true prophet-priest.
9. God of light, music, poetry, prophecy, and healing; driver of the sun chariot daily across the heavens.
1. John Selden's *De Diis Syris* (2nd ed. 1629), an important source of information about false gods both here and in *PL* (1.376–521), quotes Macrobius on the Venus of the Ascalonites: "The image of this goddess was made on Mt. Lebanon, with her head veiled and with a sorrowful countenance. . . . Tears are believed to flow from her eyes at the sight of spectators."

XXI

In consecrated earth
190 And on the holy hearth
    The lars and lemures[2] moan with midnight plaint.
In urns and altars round,
A drear and dying sound
    Affrights the flamens° at their service quaint;   *ancient Roman*
195 And the chill marble seems to sweat,   *priests*
While each peculiar° power forgoes his wonted seat.   *distinct*

XXII

Peor and Baälim[3]
Forsake their temples dim,
    With that twice-battered god of Palestine;[4]
200 And moonèd Ashtaroth,[5]
Heav'n's queen and mother both,
    Now sits not girt with tapers' holy shine.
The Libyc Hammon[6] shrinks his horn;
In vain the Tyrian maids their wounded
        Thammuz[7] mourn.

XXIII

205 And sullen Moloch,[8] fled,
Hath left in shadows dread
    His burning idol all of blackest hue;
In vain with cymbals' ring
They call the grisly king,

---

2. Roman household gods and spirits of the departed, respectively.
3. Plural of *Baal*, worshiped in various local manifestations, such as Baal-Zebub (Beelzebub), Baal-Berith, Baal-Zephon. (See *PL*, 1.419–31.) Peor, or Baal-Peor, Canaanite sun god condemned in the Bible. (See *PL*, 1.406–18.) Selden repeats numerous accounts of both priapic and scatological rites associated with his worship, although he eventually denies their validity.
4. Dagon, Philistine maritime deity (Heb., *dag*, "fish"), whose idol, kept in the presence of the captured ark of the covenant, was twice thrown down (1 Sam. 5:3–4).
5. Plural of Astoreth (Astarte), female counterpart of Baal, fertility goddess associated with Aphrodite and Venus as well as with Diana, goddess of the moon. According to Selden, she is called *regina caeli* and *mater deum* ("Heav'n's queen and mother both").
6. Ammon, Egyptian deity represented as a ram; associated with Jove.
7. Dying god; Phoenician version of Adonis, killed by a boar.
8. God of the Ammonites. His hollow idol, with the body of an enthroned king (Heb. *Moloch*, "king") and the head of a bull, was a furnace used to incinerate the infants brought as sacrifices. According to Selden, the name Tophet (*PL*, 1.404), a site of worship, derives from Heb. *toph* ("a drum"), "which was beaten and loudly sounded in the vicinity to prevent the parents from hearing the most grievous lamentations and wailings of their children while the sacred rites were being performed."

₂₁₀ In dismal dance about the furnace blue;
The brutish gods of Nile as fast,
Isis and Orus, and the dog Anubis[9] haste.

XXIV

Nor is Osiris[1] seen
In Memphian grove or green,
₂₁₅   Trampling the unshow'red° grass with   *without rain*
        lowings loud;
Nor can he be at rest
Within his sacred chest,
    Naught but profoundest hell can be his
        shroud;°   *(1) a shelter, (2)*
In vain with timbrelled° anthems dark   *winding sheet /*
₂₂₀ The sable-stolèd° sorcerers bear his worshiped   *accompanied by*
    ark.   *tambourines /*
                                                            black-robed

XXV

He feels from Judah's land
The dreaded infant's hand,
    The rays of Bethlehem blind his dusky eyn;°   *eyes (archaic)*
Nor all the gods beside
₂₂₅ Longer dare abide,
    Not Typhon[2] huge ending in snaky twine:
Our babe, to show his Godhead true,
Can in his swaddling bands control the
    damnèd crew.[3]

XXVI

So when the sun in bed,
₂₃₀ Curtained with cloudy red,
    Pillows his chin upon an orient° wave,   *(1) eastern, (2) bright*
The flocking shadows pale
Troop to th' infernal jail,
    Each fettered ghost slips to his several grave,

---

9. Son of Osiris; represented with a dog's or jackal's head. Isis, Egyptian moon goddess,
wife of Osiris; represented with a cow's horns. Orus, or Horus, Egyptian sky god, son
of Isis and Osiris; represented with a hawk's head.
1. The chief Egyptian sun god, whose idol took the form of a bull. Selden associates him
with the golden calf worshiped by the idolatrous Israelites.
2. The Egyptian Typhon slew his brother Osiris. The Greek Typhon was the most dangerous opponent of the Olympian gods, and his vast body terminated in vipers.
3. These lines suggest the infant Hercules strangling the two serpents sent by Juno to kill
him in his cradle.

235 And the yellow-skirted fays°   *fairies*
    Fly after the night-steeds,° leaving their   *horses drawing Night's*
        moon-loved maze.°   *chariot / fairy ring*

XXVII

    But see, the virgin blest
    Hath laid her babe to rest;
        Time is our tedious song should here have
            ending;
240 Heav'n's youngest-teemèd° star   *latest-born*
    Hath fixed her polished car,°   *chariot*
        Her sleeping Lord with handmaid lamp
            attending;
    And all about the courtly stable
    Bright-harnessed° angels sit in order   *armored*
        serviceable.

A Paraphrase on Psalm 114[1]

    When the blest seed of Terah's faithful son°   *Abraham*
    After long toil their liberty had won,
    And passed from Pharian° fields to Canaan   *Egyptian*
        land,
    Led by the strength of the Almighty's hand,
5   Jehovah's wonders were in Israel shown,
    His praise and glory was in Israel known.
    That saw the troubled sea, and shivering fled,
    And sought to hide his froth-becurlèd head
    Low in the earth; Jordan's clear streams recoil,
10 As a faint host that hath receiv'd the foil.°   *repulse, defeat*
    The high, huge-bellied mountains skip like rams

---

1. Milton adds a note: "This and the following Psalm [#136] were done by the author at fifteen years old" [i.e., 1624], which would make them his earliest surviving poetic compositions. Both read like school exercises, which is why only this very first one is included here. But there were many competitors of all ages hoping that their metrical psalms might be adopted for congregational singing. Milton's father had contributed tunes to Ravenscroft's *Whole Book of Psalms* of 1621. According to Milton's anonymous biographer, "David's Psalms were in esteem with him above all poetry," as they were for Jesus in *Paradise Regained* (4.335–37), who paraphrases Psalm 137 even as he declares their superiority over Greek poetry. According to John Aubrey's *Minutes of the Life of Mr. John Milton*, "He was an early riser. yea, after he had lost his sight. He had a man read to him. the first thing he read was the Hebrew bible, & that was at [4:30 A.M.]. Then he contemplated." Nineteen of Milton's Psalm paraphrases survive: Psalms 114 and 136, Psalms 80–88 (1648), and Psalms 1–8 (1653; a year after he completely lost his sight). See his paraphrase of Psalm 6 on page 76, and compare his paraphrases with the King James Version on page 458.

Amongst their ewes, the little hills like lambs.
Why fled the ocean? And why skipped the mountains?
Why turnèd Jordan toward his crystal fountains?
15 Shake, earth, and at the presence be aghast
Of him that ever was, and aye shall last,
That glassy floods from rugged rocks can crush,
And make soft rills from fiery flint-stones gush.

On the Death of a Fair Infant Dying of a Cough[1]

I

O fairest flower no sooner blown° but blasted,   *in bloom*
Soft silken primrose fading timelessly,°   *unseasonably*
Summer's chief honor if thou hadst outlasted
Bleak Winter's force that made thy blossom dry;
5   For he being amorous on that lovely dye
   That did thy cheek envermeil,° thought to kiss   *tinge with vermilion*
But killed alas, and then bewailed his fatal bliss.

II

For since grim Aquilo[2] his charioteer
By boist'rous rape th' Athenian damsel got,
10 He thought it touched his deity full near,
If likewise he some fair one wedded not,
Thereby to wipe away th' infamous blot
   Of long-uncoupled bed, and childless eld,°   *old age*
Which 'mongst the wanton gods a foul
    reproach was held.

III

15 So mounting up in icy-pearlèd car,°   *hailstone-covered*
Through middle empire of the freezing air   *chariot*
He wandered long, till thee he spied from far;
There ended was his quest, there ceased his care.

---

1. This is the first truly original English poem by Milton (not a translation, not in Latin).
   According to Edward Phillips, Milton's nephew, it was occasioned by the death of Anne
   Phillips, infant daughter of the poet's sister Anne, and Edward's own sister. Although
   Milton added the caption "*Anno aetatis 17*" ([composed] "at the age of 17"), the infant
   was buried in January 1628, when Milton was nineteen. Milton did not publish it in his
   1645 poems, and when he did, in 1673, he might have had a lapse of memory. It
   wouldn't be the only time that Milton predated a poem (see, e.g., Sonnet VII), perhaps
   out of a sense of belated accomplishment.
2. The north wind (Gr. Boreas), who carried off the Athenian princess Orithyia (*Met.*,
   682–710). This incites the lust of Winter, who is portrayed as clumsy and heavy handed.

Down he descended from his snow-soft chair,
20   But all unwares with his cold-kind embrace
Unhoused thy virgin soul from her fair
    biding-place.

IV

Yet art thou not inglorious in thy fate;
For so Apollo, with unweeting° hand   *unwitting,*
Whilom did slay his dearly-lovèd mate,   *unknowing*
25 Young Hyacinth born on Eurotas'[3] strand,
Young Hyacinth the pride of Spartan land;
  But then transformed him to a purple flower;
Alack that so to change thee Winter had no power.

V

Yet can I not persuade me thou art dead
30 Or that thy corse° corrupts in earth's dark womb,   *corpse*
Or that thy beauties lie in wormy bed,
Hid from the world in a low delvèd tomb;
Could Heav'n for pity thee so strictly doom?
  O no! for something in thy face did shine
35 Above mortality that showed thou wast divine.

VI

Resolve me° then, O soul most surely blest   *Answer my questions*
(If so it be that thou these plaints dost hear),
Tell me bright spirit where'er thou hoverest,
Whether above that high first-moving sphere[4]
40 Or in the Elysian fields[5] (if such there were).
  O say me true if thou wert mortal wight,°   *creature*
And why from us so quickly thou didst take
    thy flight.

VII

Wert thou some star which from the ruined roof
Of shaked Olympus by mischance didst fall;
45 Which careful Jove in nature's true behoof°   *benefit, advantage*

3. River flowing past the city of Sparta. Apollo, god of light, music, poetry, prophecy, and healing, accidentally killed his beloved Hyacinthus, a Spartan prince. The hyacinth flower sprang from his blood (*Met.* 10.162–219).
4. The outermost sphere in the Ptolemaic universe, the *primum mobile*, which communicated motion to the inner spheres.
5. Home of the blessed dead.

Took up, and in fit place did reinstall?
Or did of late Earth's sons[6] besiege the wall
  Of sheeny° Heav'n, and thou some goddess fled   *shining*
Amongst us here below to hide thy nectared head?

VIII

50 Or wert thou that just maid[7] who once before
Forsook the hated earth, O tell me sooth,
And cam'st again to visit us once more?
Or wert thou [Mercy],[8] that sweet smiling youth?
Or that crowned matron, sage white-robèd Truth?
55   Or any other of that heav'nly brood
Let down in cloudy throne to do the world
          some good?

IX

Or wert thou of the golden-wingèd host,°   *angels*
Who having clad thy self in human weed,°   *garment (of flesh)*
To earth from thy prefixèd° seat didst post,   *preordained*
60 And after short abode fly back with speed,
As if to show what creatures Heav'n doth breed,
    Thereby to set the hearts of men on fire
To scorn the sordid world, and unto Heav'n aspire?

X

But O why didst thou not stay here below
65 To bless us with thy Heav'n-loved innocence,
To slake his° wrath whom sin hath made our foe,   *God's*
To turn swift-rushing black perdition hence,
Or drive away the slaughtering pestilence,[9]
    To stand 'twixt us and our deserved smart?°   *pain, punishment*
70 But thou canst best perform that office where
          thou art.

XI

Then thou the mother of so sweet a child
Her false imagined loss cease to lament,

---

6. The Giants, who warred against the gods.
7. Astraea, goddess of justice, who left the earth after the corruption of humankind and became Virgo in the zodiac.
8. The line is short by a metrical foot, and editors insert *mercy* or *virtue* to fill it out.
9. Alluding to the plague of 1625–26, around the time of the infant's birth.

And wisely learn to curb thy sorrows wild;
Think what a present thou to God hast sent,
75 And render° him with patience what he lent;   *give back*
    This if thou do he will an offspring give,
    That till the worlds last end shall make thy
       name to live.[1]

From At a Vacation Exercise in the College[1]

Hail native language, that by sinews weak
Didst move my first-endeavoring tongue to speak,
And mad'st imperfect words with childish trips,
Half unpronounced, slide through my infant lips,
5 Driving dumb Silence from the portal door,
Where he had mutely sat two years before:
Here I salute thee and thy pardon ask,
That now I use thee in my latter° task: *later*
Small loss it is that thence can come unto thee,
10 I know my tongue but little grace can do thee.
Thou need'st not be ambitious to be first,
Believe me, I have thither[2] packed the worst:
And, if it happen as I did forecast,
The daintiest dishes shall be served up last.
15 I pray thee then deny me not thy aid,
For this same small neglect that I have made;
But haste thee straight to do me once a pleasure,
And from thy wardrobe bring thy chieftest treasure;

1. Anne Phillips gave birth to another child, Elizabeth, baptized April 9, 1628. Contemporary editors hear an allusion to God's promise of immortality to the eunuchs in Isa. 56:5: "unto them will I give . . . a place and a name better than of sons and daughters: I will give them an everlasting name, that shall not be cut off." (The original Hebrew of "a place and a name," is *yad vashem*, the name of the Holocaust History Museum in Jerusalem, itself an allusion to the sterilization of concentration camp inmates by the Nazis.)
1. Milton composed these lines for delivery at his college's assembly just before the long summer vacation, in July 1628, when he was nineteen. His fellow students had chosen him to be "Father" or "Dictator" at this festive academic event. These verses were preceded by a two-part Latin prolusion: a mock oration on the topic "Sportive exercises on occasion are not inconsistent with philosophical studies," and the prolusion proper, with coarse undergraduate humor, although it betrays the hurt feelings of a sensitive scholar when Milton wittily broaches the topic of his nickname, "The Lady of Christ's," comparing his transformation from 'Lady' to 'Father' to that of Tiresias, and commenting on his schoolmates: 'How I wish that their asininity could be shed as easily as my femininity!'" In these verses, which follow the Prolusion, Milton, most of whose poetic efforts so far have been in Latin, addresses the English language as his muse and describes in lines 29–52 the poems on "some graver subject" that he plans to write.
2. In the Latin oration.

Not those new-fangled toys° and trimming   *idle tales*
    slight
20 Which takes° our late° fantastics[3] with delight,   *captivates / recent*
But cull those richest robes and gay'st attire
Which deepest spirits and choicest wits desire.
I have some naked thoughts that rove about
And loudly knock to have their passage out,
25 And weary of their place do only stay
Till thou hast decked them in thy best array;
That so they may without suspect° or fears   *suspicion*
Fly swiftly to this fair assembly's ears;
Yet I had rather, if I were to choose,
30 Thy service in some graver subject use,
Such as may make thee search thy coffers°   *treasury*
    round,
Before thou clothe my fancy° in fit sound: *imagination*
Such where the deep° transported mind may soar   *high*
Above the wheeling poles,[4] and at Heav'n's door
35 Look in, and see each blissful deity
How he before the thunderous throne[5] doth lie,
Listening to what unshorn Apollo sings
To th' touch of golden wires,° while Hebe[6]   *harp or lyre strings*
    brings
Immortal nectar to her kingly sire;
40 Then passing through the spheres of watchful fire,[7]
And misty regions of wide air next under,
And hills of snow and lofts° of pilèd thunder,°   *upper regions /*
May tell at length how green-eyed Neptune   *stockpiled*
    raves,   *thunderbolts*
In heaven's defiance mustering all his waves;
45 Then sing of secret things that came to pass
When beldam° Nature in her cradle was;   *grandmother, aged*
And last of kings and queens and heroes old,   *woman*
Such as the wise Demodocus[8] once told
In solemn songs at King Alcinous' feast,
50 While sad Ulysses' soul and all the rest

3. Those who indulge in fanciful ideas.
4. Axes of the rotating Ptolemaic universe.
5. Of Jove.
6. Goddess of youth and cupbearer of the gods.
7. Various interpretations: (1) the angels assigned to the spheres of the Ptolemaic universe; (2) the sphere of fire (the fourth element) between the sphere of air and the sphere of the moon; (3) the sun, moon, and planets created to guard the numbers of time (Plato, *Timaeus*, 38c); (4) the axes that turn the Ptolemaic spheres.
8. In the *Od.* (8.487–543), the blind bard who often visits the court of King Alcinous. His song recounting the fall of Troy moves Odysseus to tears.

Are held with his melodious harmony
In willing chains and sweet captivity.
But fie, my wand'ring Muse,[9] how thou dost stray!
Expectance calls thee now another way.
55 Thou know'st it must be now thy only bent°   *aim*
To keep in compass° of thy Predicament:[1]   *within limits*
Then quick about thy purposed business come,
That to the next I may resign my room.°   *office*

The Passion[1]

I

Erewhile of music and ethereal mirth,
Wherewith the stage of air and earth did ring,
And joyous news of Heav'nly infant's birth,
My muse with angels did divide[2] to sing;
5 But headlong joy is ever on the wing,
    In wintry solstice like the shortened light[3]
Soon swallowed up in dark and long outliving night.

II

For now to sorrow must I tune my song,
And set my harp to notes of saddest woe,
10 Which on our dearest Lord did seize ere long,
Dangers, and snares, and wrongs, and worse than so,
Which he for us did freely undergo.
    Most perfect hero, tried in heaviest plight
Of labors[4] huge and hard, too hard for human wight.°   *creature*

9. In abruptly returning to the occasion, Milton echoes Horace's *quo, Musa, tendis?* (Muse, where are you going?)
1. In the lines that follow, Milton as "Father," representing *Ens*, or absolute being, gives to his ten "sons" names corresponding to the categories, or predicaments, of Aristotle. (Milton preserved only four of them from this performance: Substance, Quantity, Quality, and Relation. These are classes into which fell whatever could be predicated of any particular entity.)
1. Milton's only self-acknowledged failure was intended as a companion to the Nativity Ode of 1629 and was probably composed at Easter 1630. Birth and creation are the themes closest to Milton's heart, but the crucifixion never had a strong hold on his emotions.
2. (1) Share (with the angels); (2) to execute divisions—i.e., rapid melodic passages.
3. Like shortened daylight at the winter solstice.
4. Alluding to Hercules, compared to Christ in the Nativity Ode, lines 227–28.

III

15 He sov'reign priest[5] stooping his regal head
That dropped with odorous oil[6] down his fair eyes,
Poor fleshly tabernacle° enterèd,   *Christ's body*
His starry front° low-roofed beneath the skies;   *forehead*
O what a mask was there, what a disguise!
20   Yet more: the stroke of death he must abide,
Then lies him meekly down fast by his
            brethren's side.

IV

These latest scenes confine my roving verse,
To this horizon is my Phoebus[7] bound;
His godlike acts, and his temptations fierce,
25 And former sufferings otherwhere are found;
Loud o'er the rest Cremona's trump[8] doth sound;
        Me softer airs befit, and softer strings
Of lute, or viol still, more apt for mournful things.

V

Befriend me, Night, best patroness of grief,
30 Over the pole° thy thickest mantle throw,   *sky*
And work my flattered fancy to belief
That heav'n and earth are colored with my woe;
My sorrows are too dark for day to know.
        The leaves should all be black whereon I write,
35 And letters where my tears have washed a
            wannish white.[9]

VI

See, see the chariot and those rushing wheels
That whirled the prophet[1] up at Chebar flood;

---

5. In *DDC* (1.15), Milton describes Christ's threefold mediatorial office as prophet, priest, and king. As priest he offers himself as the perfect sacrifice.
6. The word *Christ* is a Greek translation of the Hebrew *moshiach* (messiah), which means "anointed." Both high priests and kings were anointed with oil.
7. Apollo, who drove the chariot of the sun daily across the sky. As god of poetry, he is identified with poetic inspiration.
8. Milton admired the Neo-Latin *Christiad* by Marco Girolamo Vida, born in Cremona, Italy.
9. Some 17th-century funeral poems are reported to have been written in white letters on black paper.
1. Ezekiel, who saw the mystical vision of the throne chariot (source of Milton's Chariot of Paternal Deity in *PL*, 6 and 7) "by the river of Chebar" (Ezek. 1:1).

My spirit some transporting cherub feels,
   To bear me where the towers of Salem° stood,   *Jerusalem*
40 Once glorious towers, now sunk in guiltless blood;
      There doth my soul in holy vision sit
   In pensive trance, and anguish, and ecstatic° fit.   *outside-the-body*

VII

   Mine eye hath found that sad sepulchral rock°   *Holy Sepulchre*
   That was the casket of Heav'n's richest store,°   *treasure*
45 And here though grief my feeble hands uplock
   Yet on the softened quarry would I score°   *cut*
   My plaining verse as lively° as before;   *vividly, feelingly*
      For sure so well instructed are my tears,
   That they would fitly fall in ordered characters.°   *letters*

VIII

50 Or should I thence hurried on viewless° wing   *invisible*
   Take up a weeping on the mountains wild,
   The gentle neighborhood of grove and spring
   Would soon unbosom° all their echoes mild,   *disclose*
   And I (for grief is easily beguiled)
55   Might think th' infection of my sorrows loud
   Had got° a race of mourners on some pregnant   *begotten*
      cloud.[2]

This subject the author finding to be above the years he had when he wrote it, and nothing satisfied with what was begun, left it unfinished.

On Time[1]

   Fly, envious Time, till thou run out thy race,
   Call on the lazy leaden-stepping° hours,   *slow-moving*
   Whose speed is but the heavy plummet's[2] pace;
   And glut thyself with what thy womb° devours,   *stomach*
5 Which is no more than what is false and vain,
   And merely mortal dross;
   So little is our loss,
   So little is thy gain.

2. Zeus, to protect Hera from rape by Ixion, fashioned a cloud in her shape, and on it the deceived Ixion begot a race of centaurs.
1. In the Trinity Manuscript, the poem was originally headed "set on a clock case."
2. Not a pendulum but the lead weight affixed to the newly invented lantern clock, whose graduated descent drove the movement.

For when as each thing bad thou hast entombed,
10 And last of all thy greedy self consumed,
Then long Eternity shall greet our bliss
With an individual° kiss;   *indivisible,*
And joy shall overtake us as a flood,   *everlasting*
When everything that is sincerely° good   *wholly*
15 And perfectly divine,
With Truth and Peace, and Love shall ever shine
About the supreme throne
Of Him t' whose happy-making sight° alone,   *beatific vision*
When once our Heav'nly-guided soul shall climb,
20 Then all this earthy grossness quit,°   *having been left*
Attired° with stars, we shall forever sit,   *behind / Crowned*
   Triumphing over Death, and Chance, and
    thee, O Time.

Upon the Circumcision

Ye flaming Powers,[1] and wingèd warriors bright,
That erst° with music and triumphant song   *formerly*
First heard by happy watchful shepherds' ear,
So sweetly sung your joy the clouds along
5 Through the soft silence of the list'ning night;
Now mourn, and if sad share with us to bear
Your fiery essence can distill no tear,
Burn in your sighs, and borrow
Seas wept from our deep sorrow;[2]
10 He who with all Heav'ns heraldry° whilere°   *heraldic pomp / a*
Entered the world, now bleeds to give us ease;   *while ago*
Alas, how soon our sin
   Sore doth begin
    His Infancy to seize!
15 O more exceeding love or law more just?
Just law indeed, but more exceeding love!
For we by rightful doom° remédiless   *judgment*
Were lost in death, till he that dwelt above
High-throned in secret bliss, for us frail dust
20 Emptied his glory, ev'n to nakedness;
And that great cov'nant° which we still transgress   *Mosaic law*
Entirely satisfied,

1. One of the nine orders of angels.
2. I.e., If you angels can't cry, you can burn and, sunlike, draw up to Heaven the seas of
human tears.

And the full wrath beside
Of vengeful Justice bore for our excess,[3]
25 And seals obedience first with wounding smart
This day, but O ere long
   Huge pangs and strong
      Will pierce more near his heart.[4]

At a Solemn Music[1]

Blest pair of Sirens, pledges° of Heav'n's joy,   *offspring, assurances*
Sphere-borne[2] harmonious sisters, Voice and
    Verse,
Wed your divine sounds, and mixed power employ
Dead things with inbreathed sense able to pierce,
5 And to our high-raised fantasy present
That undisturbèd song of pure concent,°   *harmony, concord*
Ay° sung before the sapphire-colored throne   *forever*
To him° that sits thereon,   *God*
With saintly shout and solemn jubilee,
10 Where the bright Seraphim in burning row
Their loud uplifted angel-trumpets blow,
And the Cherubic host in thousand choirs
Touch their immortal harps of golden wires,
With those just spirits that wear victorious palms,
15 Hymns devout and holy psalms
Singing everlastingly;
That° we on earth with undiscording voice   *So that*
May rightly answer that melodious noise;
As once we did, till disproportioned° sin   *disharmonious*
20 Jarred against Nature's chime, and with harsh din
Broke the fair music that all creatures made
To their great Lord, whose love their motion swayed
In perfect diapason,° whilst they stood   *complete concord*
In first obedience and their state of good.
25 O may we soon again renew that song
And keep in tune with Heav'n, till God ere long
To his celestial consort[3] us unite,
To live with him and sing in endless morn of light.

---

3. Sin, perhaps symbolized by the foreskin that circumcision removes.
4. Alludes to the spear that pierced Christ's side at the crucifixion (John 19:34).
1. Sacred concert
2. Carried by the spheres, but could also mean heavenly born.
3. Harmony of voices or company of musicians.

On Shakespeare[1]

What needs my Shakespeare for his honored bones
The labor of an age in pilèd stones,
Or that his hallowed relics should be hid
Under a star-ypointing[2] pyramid?
5 Dear son of memory, great heir of fame,
What need'st thou such weak witness of thy name?
Thou in our wonder and astonishment
Hast built thyself a live-long monument.
For whilst to th' shame of slow-endeavoring art
10 Thy easy numbers° flow, and that each heart   *verses*
Hath from the leaves of thy unvalued° book   *invaluable*
Those Delphic[3] lines with deep impression took,
Then thou, our fancy of itself bereaving,
Dost make us marble with too much conceiving;
15 And so sepúlchred in such pomp dost lie,
That kings for such a tomb would wish to die.

L'ALLEGRO AND IL PENSEROSO These "graceful, urbane companion poems" (Lewalski, 48) explore the ideal pleasures of mirth and
contemplation or, more literally, *L'Allegro* (Ital. "the joyful man") and *Il
Penseroso* ("the pensive man"). These are two different approaches to
life, "heart-easing Mirth" and "divinest Melancholy," and each has its
distinctive pleasures. L'Allegro's are mostly those of the daytime, while
Il Penseroso's are nocturnal. Each poem begins by banishing a travesty of the goddess who symbolizes the state of mind celebrated in the
other. Among the most beautiful lines in each of the poems are those
devoted to music (especially lines 135–44 in *L'Allegro* and 161–66 in *Il
Penseroso*). Both of the poems are best appreciated if read aloud, thus
revealing "the hidden soul of harmony." The poems inspired Handel to
create a pastoral ode (1740) of the same name, using Milton's words, although he added a third movement called "*Il Moderato*." And that work
in turn inspired the great contemporary choreographer Mark Morris,
whose *L'Allegro, Il Penseroso et Moderato* (1988) combines ideas, music,
and dance in new ways while still acknowledging its debt to Milton.

1. Milton's first published English poem appeared anonymously in the Second Folio of
   Shakespeare (1632) under the title "An Epitaph on the admirable Dramaticke Poet, W.
   Shakespeare."
2. Pointing. An inaccurate imitation of Spenserian archaism because the Middle English
   y is a prefix of the past participle, not the present.
3. Apollo, god of poetry, had his oracle at Delphi.

L'Allegro[1]

Hence loathèd Melancholy,[2]
  Of Cerberus[3] and blackest Midnight born,
In Stygian[4] cave forlorn
  'Mongst horrid shapes and shrieks and sights unholy,
5 Find out some uncouth° cell   *desolate*
    Where brooding Darkness spreads his
      jealous wings,
And the night-raven sings;
    There under ebon shades° and low-browed°   *trees / beetling*
      rocks,
As ragged° as thy locks,   *rugged*
10   In dark Cimmerian[5] desert ever dwell.
But come thou goddess fair and free,
In Heav'n yclept° Euphrosyne,[6]   *called*
And by men heart-easing Mirth,
Whom lovely Venus at a birth
15 With two sister Graces more
To ivy-crownèd Bacchus bore;
Or whether (as some sager sing)
The frolic wind that breathes the spring,
Zephyr,° with Aurora° playing,   *West Wind / Dawn*
20 As he met her once a-Maying,
There on beds of violets blue,
And fresh-blown roses washed in dew,
Filled her with thee a daughter fair,
So buxom, blithe, and debonair.°   *affable, courteous*
25 Haste thee nymph and bring with thee
Jest and youthful Jollity,
Quips and Cranks and wanton Wiles,[7]
Nods and Becks° and wreathèd Smiles,   *upward nods,*
Such as hang on Hebe's[8] cheek,   *come-ons*
30 And love to live in dimple sleek;
Sport that wrinkled Care derides,

---

1. Ital. the happy person.
2. Not the contemplative state celebrated in *Il Penseroso* but a pathological condition of sullenness and depression thought to result from an excess of black bile in the body.
3. Three-headed watchdog of Hades. Lit. heart-eating. (Cf. "eating cares," line 135).
4. Relating to the river Styx; infernal.
5. Belonging to a mythical land of perpetual darkness.
6. Mirth, one of the three Graces. She and her sisters Aglaia (Brilliance) and Thalia (Bloom) personify the refinements of life.
7. Unrestrained, playful tricks. "Quips": witty sayings. "Cranks": verbal tricks, odd turns of speech.
8. Goddess of youth.

And Laughter holding both his sides.
Come and trip it° as ye go   *dance*
On the light fantastic° toe,   *making elaborate*
35 And in thy right hand lead with thee   *movements*
The mountain nymph, sweet Liberty;
And if I give thee honor due,
Mirth, admit me of thy crew,
To live with her and live with thee,
40 In unreprovèd° pleasures free;   *blameless*
To hear the lark begin his flight,
And singing startle the dull night,
From his watch-tower in the skies,
Till the dappled dawn doth rise.
45 Then to come[9] in spite of° sorrow,   *in defiance of*
And at my window bid good morrow,
Through the sweet-briar or the vine,
Or the twisted eglantine;
While the cock with lively din
50 Scatters the rear° of darkness thin,   *like an army in*
And to the stack or the barn door   *retreat*
Stoutly struts his dames before;
Oft list'ning how the hounds and horn
Cheerly rouse the slumb'ring morn
55 From the side of some hoar° hill,   *gray with frost or mist*
Through the high wood echoing shrill;
Some time walking not unseen
By hedge-row elms, on hillocks green,
Right against the eastern gate,
60 Where the sun begins his state,[1]
Robed in flames and amber light,
The clouds in thousand liveries dight;°   *clothed*
While the ploughman near at hand
Whistles o'er the furrowed land,
65 And the milkmaid singeth blithe,
And the mower whets his scythe,
And every shepherd tells his tale[2]
Under the hawthorn in the dale.
Straight mine eye hath caught new pleasures,
70 Whilst the landscape round it measures:

---

9. The subject of "to come" is disputed, earlier editors assuming that it was the lark, more
   recent ones favoring L'Allegro.
1. I.e., the royal progress of Phoebus, the sun god.
2. Either "counts his sheep" or "tells his story" (of love).

Russet lawns and fallows³ gray,
Where the nibbling flocks do stray;
Mountains on whose barren breast
The laboring clouds do often rest;
75 Meadows trim with daisies pied,°   *variegated*
Shallow brooks and rivers wide.
Towers and battlements it sees
Bosomed high in tufted° trees,   *growing in clusters*
Where perhaps some beauty lies,°   *dwells*
80 The cynosure⁴ of neighboring eyes.
Hard by a cottage chimney smokes
From betwixt two agèd oaks,
Where Corydon and Thyrsis⁵ met
Are at their savory dinner set
85 Of herbs and other country messes,
Which the neat-handed Phyllis dresses;
And then in haste her bower she leaves,
With Thestylis⁶ to bind the sheaves;
Or if the earlier season lead,
90 To the tanned° haycock in the mead.   *sun-dried*
Sometimes with secure° delight   *carefree*
The upland hamlets will invite,
When the merry bells ring round,
And the jocund rebecks° sound   *fiddles*
95 To many a youth and many a maid
Dancing in the chequered shade;
And young and old come forth to play
On a sunshine holiday,
Till the livelong daylight fail;
100 Then to the spicy nut-brown ale,
With stories told of many a feat,
How fairy Mab the junkets⁷ eat:
She was pinched and pulled, she said,
And he,⁸ by friar's lantern° led,   *will-o'-the-wisp*
105 Tells how the drudging goblin° sweat   *Robin Goodfellow,*
To earn his cream-bowl duly set,   *Puck*
When in one night, ere glimpse of morn,
His shadowy flail hath threshed the corn

---

3. Plowed but unseeded. "Russet lawns": Unplowed lands scorched reddish brown by the sun.
4. Guiding star, center of attraction.
5. Two men.
6. A woman.
7. Cream cheeses or other dishes made with cream. Mab is queen of the fairies, as in Mercutio's famous speech (*Romeo and Juliet*, 1.4.54 ff.).
8. In lines 103 and 104 "she" and "he" are members of the storytelling group.

That ten day-laborers could not end;
110 Then lies him down the lubber° fiend,   *(1) lout, (2) drudge*
And stretched out all the chimney's° length,   *fireplace's*
Basks at the fire his hairy strength;
And crop-full° out of doors he flings,   *completely full*
Ere the first cock his matin rings.
115 Thus done the tales, to bed they creep,
By whispering winds soon lulled asleep.
Towered cities please us then,
And the busy hum of men,
Where throngs of knights and barons bold
120 In weeds of peace° high triumphs hold,   *courtly garments*
With stores of ladies whose bright eyes
Rain influence,[9] and judge the prize
Of wit or arms, while both contend
To win her grace whom all commend.
125 There let Hymen[1] oft appear
In saffron robe, with taper clear,
And pomp and feast and revelry,
With masque and antique pageantry;
Such sights as youthful poets dream
130 On summer eves by haunted stream.
Then to the well-trod stage anon,°   *at once, instantly*
If Jonson's learnèd sock[2] be on,
Or sweetest Shakespeare, Fancy's child,
Warble his native wood-notes wild.
135 And ever against eating cares,
Lap me in soft Lydian airs,°   *sensuous, relaxing*
Married to immortal verse,   *music*
Such as the meeting soul may pierce
In notes with many a winding bout[3]
140 Of linkèd sweetness long drawn out,
With wanton heed and giddy cunning,
The melting voice through mazes running,
Untwisting all the chains that tie
The hidden soul of harmony;
145 That Orpheus' self may heave his head
From golden slumber on a bed

---

9. Eyes are imagined as stars with their supposed power to affect human destiny.
1. God of marriage.
2. The low-heeled slipper of ancient comic actors, a symbol of comedy.
3. Circuit. The soul-piercing music turns or circles back on itself, as in the solo air or Italian aria.

Of heaped Elysian[4] flow'rs, and hear
Such strains as would have won the ear
Of Pluto, to have quite set free
His half-regained Eurydice.[5]
These delights, if thou canst give,
Mirth with thee, I mean to live.

Il Penseroso[1]

Hence vain deluding Joys,
 The brood of Folly without father bred,
How little you bestead,°   *help*
 Or fill the fixèd mind with all your toys;° *idle fancies*
Dwell in some idle brain,
 And fancies fond° with gaudy shapes possess, *foolish*
As thick and numberless
 As the gay motes that people the sunbeams,
Or likest hovering dreams,
 The fickle pensioners° of Morpheus'[2] train. *attendants*
But hail thou goddess sage and holy,
Hail divinest Melancholy,[3]
Whose saintly visage is too bright
To hit° the sense of human sight,   *suit, agree with*
And therefore to our weaker view
O'erlaid with black, staid Wisdom's hue;[4]
Black, but[5] such as in esteem
Prince Memnon's sister[6] might beseem,
Or that starred Ethiop queen[7] that strove
To set her beauty's praise above
The sea nymphs, and their powers offended.
Yet thou art higher far descended:

4. According to Ovid (*Met.*, 11.61–66), Orpheus and Eurydice were reunited in the Elysian fields, the classical abode of the blessed after death.
5. Orpheus won his wife, Eurydice, back from Pluto, though he lost her again by looking back.
1. The pensive person.
2. God of dreams.
3. Not the pathological condition dismissed in *L'Allegro*. "The affectation of melancholy was a fashionable mark of intellectual or aesthetic refinement" (OED). Sentimental reflection as a source of aesthetic pleasure: "Wrapped in a pleasing fit of melancholy" (*Comus*, 546).
4. Cf. *PL*, 3.377–82: "Dark with excessive bright thy skirts appear."
5. "I am black but comely, O ye daughters of Jerusalem" (Song of Sol. 1:5).
6. Memnon, "handsomest of men" (*Od.*, 11.522), was a black Ethiopian king who fought for Troy. Later versions of the Troy story gave him a beautiful sister, Himera.
7. Cassiopea, wife of the Ethiopian king Cephalus, transformed into a constellation ("starred") for claiming to be more beautiful than the Nereids ("sea nymphs," line 21).

Thee bright-haired Vesta[8] long of yore
To solitary Saturn[9] bore;
25 His daughter she (in Saturn's reign
Such mixture was not held a stain).
Oft in glimmering bow'rs and glades
He met her, and in secret shades
Of woody Ida's inmost grove,
30 While yet there was no fear of Jove.[1]
Come, pensive nun, devout and pure,
Sober, steadfast, and demure,
All in a robe of darkest grain,°   °dye
Flowing with majestic train,
35 And sable stole of cypress lawn°   fine black linen
Over thy decent shoulders drawn.
Come, but keep thy wonted state,
With even step and musing gait,
And looks commercing° with the skies,   communicating
40 Thy rapt soul sitting in thine eyes;
There held in holy passion still,
Forget thyself to marble,[2] till
With a sad leaden downward cast[3]
Thou fix them on the earth as fast.°   fixedly
45 And join with thee calm Peace and Quiet,
Spare Fast, that oft with gods doth diet,
And hears the Muses in a ring
Ay° round about Jove's altar sing.   Continually
And add to these retired Leisure,
50 That in trim gardens takes his pleasure;
But first, and chiefest, with thee bring
Him that yon soars with golden wing,
Guiding the fiery-wheelèd throne,[4]
The cherub Contemplatïon;
55 And the mute Silence hist° along,   summoned silently
'Less Philomel[5] will deign a song,
In her sweetest, saddest plight,
Smoothing the rugged brow of Night,

8. Roman goddess of the hearth, Saturn's virgin daughter. Milton invents the story of
Vesta as mother of Melancholy.
9. In astrology, associated with contemplation and with melancholy (saturnine temperament).
1. Zeus (Jupiter), brought up on Mount Ida in Crete, later dethroned his father Cronos
(Saturn).
2. Become so enraptured that your body is like a statue. Cf. "On Shakespeare," 14.
3. Glance, expression. "Leaden": in alchemy, Saturn was associated with lead.
4. God's chariot (Ezek. 1).
5. Nightingale. Cf. Comus, 234n.

While Cynthia[6] checks her dragon yoke
60 Gently o'er th' accustomed oak;
Sweet bird that shunn'st the noise of folly,
Most musical, most melancholy!
Thee chantress oft the woods among
I woo to hear thy even-song;
65 And missing thee, I walk unseen
On the dry smooth-shaven green,
To behold the wandering moon
Riding near her highest noon,°   *apogee*
Like one that had been led astray
70 Through the heav'n's wide pathless way;
And oft, as if her head she bowed,
Stooping through a fleecy cloud.
Oft on a plat° of rising ground,   *plot, patch*
I hear the far-off curfew[7] sound
75 Over some wide-watered shore,
Swinging slow with sullen° roar;   *deep or mournful*
Or if the air° will not permit,   *weather, climate*
Some still removèd place will fit,
Where glowing embers through the room
80 Teach light to counterfeit a gloom,
Far from all resort of mirth,
Save the cricket on the hearth,
Or the bellman's drowsy charm,[8]
To bless the doors from nightly harm.
85 Or let my lamp at midnight hour
Be seen in some high lonely tower,
Where I may oft outwatch the Bear,[9]
With thrice-great Hermes, or unsphere[1]
The spirit of Plato to unfold
90 What worlds or what vast regions hold
The immortal mind that hath forsook
Her mansion in this fleshly nook;
And of those daemons[2] that are found
In fire, air, flood, or under ground,
95 Whose power hath a true consent°   *accord*

6. Goddess of the moon, given the dragon-drawn chariot of Hecate, Thracian goddess associated with witchcraft and magical rites.
7. Evening bell rung as a sign to extinguish or cover fire (*couvre feu*).
8. Both song (Lat. *carmen*) and spell. "Bellman": night watchman calling the hours.
9. I.e., stay up all night, since Ursa Major (the Great Bear) does not set.
1. Call down from his planetary sphere. Hermes Trismegistus, supposed ancient author of the *Corpus Hermeticum*, mystical writings now thought to date back to only around 300 C.E.
2. In Hermetic philosophy, spiritual beings corresponding to the four elements inhabit the cosmos.

With planet or with element.
Sometime let gorgeous Tragedy
In sceptered pall° come sweeping by,   *robe*
Presenting Thebes,[3] or Pelops' line,[4]
100 Or the tale of Troy divine,[5]
Or what (though rare) of later age
Ennobled hath the buskined[6] stage.
But, O sad Virgin, that thy power
Might raise Musaeus[7] from his bower,
105 Or bid the soul of Orpheus sing
Such notes as, warbled to the string,
Drew iron tears down Pluto's cheek
And made hell grant what love did seek.[8]
Or call up him[9] that left half told
110 The story of Cambuscan bold,
Of Camball and of Algarsife,
And who had Canace to wife,[1]
That owned the virtuous° ring and glass,   *magical*
And of the wondrous horse of brass,
115 On which the Tartar king did ride;
And if aught else great bards beside
In sage and solemn tunes have sung,
Of tourneys and of trophies hung,
Of forests and enchantments drear,
120 Where more is meant than meets the ear.
Thus, Night, oft see me in thy pale career,°   *moonlit course*
Till civil-suited° Morn[2] appear,   *plainly dressed*
Not tricked° and frounced° as she was wont,   *adorned / with hair*
With the Attic boy to hunt,   *curled*
125 But kerchiefed in a comely cloud,
While rocking winds[3] are piping loud,
Or ushered with a shower still,°   *quiet*

3. Thebes was the city of Oedipus and site of tragedies by Aeschylus, Sophocles, and Euripides.
4. Pelops's descendants include the tragic characters Atreus and Thyestes, Agamemnon, Orestes, Electra, and Iphigenia.
5. Sophocles and Euripides set tragedies in Troy, and Homer calls the city "divine" (*Od.*, 11.86).
6. The buskin was a high thick-soled boot worn by ancient tragic actors. Cf. the comic "sock" of *L'Allegro*, 132.
7. A mythical Greek poet.
8. See *L'Allegro*, 145–50, for the story of Orpheus, the archetypal poet, whose music won his wife back from Pluto. Here Milton omits any mention of the unhappy ending.
9. Chaucer, who left his "Squire's Tale" unfinished.
1. Echoing Spenser's words (*FQ*, 4.3.52) in his continuation of "The Squire's Tale."
2. Aurora, who loved the young Athenian Cephalus ("the Attic boy," line 124), an ardent hunter (*Met.*, 7.690–865).
3. That cause to rock.

When the gust hath blown his fill,
Ending on the rustling leaves,
130   With minute drops from off the eaves.
And when the sun begins to fling
His flaring beams, me goddess bring
To archèd walks of twilight groves,
And shadows brown that Sylvan[4] loves
135   Of pine and monumental oak,
Where the rude axe with heavèd stroke
Was never heard the nymphs to daunt,
Or fright them from their hallowed haunt.
There in close covert by some brook,
140   Where no profaner eye may look,
Hide me from day's garish eye,
While the bee with honeyed thigh,
That at her flow'ry work doth sing,
And the waters murmuring
145   With such consort° as they keep,   *musical harmony*
Entice the dewy-feathered Sleep;
And let some strange mysterious dream
Wave at his wings in airy stream
Of lively portraiture displayed,
150   Softly on my eyelids laid.[5]
And as I wake, sweet music breathe
Above, about, or underneath,
Sent by some spirit to mortals good,
Or th' unseen Genius° of the wood.   *protective spirit*
155   But let my due feet never fail
To walk the studious cloister's pale,°   *enclosure*
And love the high embowèd° roof,   *vaulted*
With antique pillars' massy proof,°   *proven massive strength*
And storied° windows richly dight,°   *pictorial stained glass /*
160   Casting a dim religious light.   *decorated*
There let the pealing organ blow
To the full-voiced choir below,
In service high and anthems clear,
As may with sweetness, through mine ear,
165   Dissolve me into ecstasies,
And bring all Heav'n before mine eyes.
And may at last my weary age
Find out some peaceful hermitage,
The hairy gown and mossy cell,

4. Sylvanus, Roman wood god.
5. Come floating with the wings of Sleep as they settle on my eyes.

170 Where I may sit and rightly spell°   *learn*
    Of every star that heav'n doth shew,
    And every herb that sips the dew,
    Till old experience do attain
    To something like prophetic strain.
175 These pleasures Melancholy give,
    And I with thee will choose to live.

Arcades[1]

*Part of an entertainment presented to the Countess
Dowager of Derby at Harefield by some noble persons of her
family, who appear on the scene in pastoral habit, moving
toward the seat of state, with this song.*

I. SONG

Look, nymphs, and shepherds, look,
What sudden blaze of majesty
Is that which we from hence descry,
Too divine to be mistook:
5   This, this is she
To whom our vows° and wishes bend;   *prayers, sacred*
Here our solemn search hath end.   *promises*

Fame, that her high worth to raise°   *extol, exalt*
Seemed erst° so lavish and profuse,   *formerly*
10 We may justly now accuse
Of detraction from her praise:
    Less than half[2] we find expressed,
    Envy bid conceal the rest.

Mark what radiant state[3] she spreads
15 In circle round her shining throne,
Shooting her beams like silver threads:
This, this is she alone,

---

1. Arcadian, ideally rural or rustic. The poem is probably the opening of a larger entertainment honoring the aged countess of Derby, born Alice Spencer, who enjoyed many
   literary associations. Edmund Spenser dedicated poems to her and her sisters. She
   performed in Jacobean masques at court, such as Jonson's *Masque of Beauty*. Her
   daughter married Sir John Egerton, later earl of Bridgewater, whose investiture as lord
   president of Wales Milton would later celebrate in *A Masque*.
2. The queen of Sheba to Solomon: "and, behold, the half was not told me: thy wisdom
   and prosperity exceedeth the fame which I heard" (1 Kings 10:7).
3. Exalted position; canopy over a throne.

Sitting like a goddess bright
In the center of her light.

20 Might she the wise Latona[4] be,
Or the tow'rèd Cybele,[5]
Mother of a hundred gods?
Juno dares not give her odds;°   *compete with her*
Who had thought this clime had held
25   A deity so unparalleled?

As they come forward, the Genius[6] *of the Wood appears,*
and turning toward them, speaks.

Genius. Stay, gentle swains, for though in this disguise,
I see bright honor sparkle through your eyes;
Of famous Arcady ye are, and sprung
Of that renownèd flood, so often sung,
30 Divine Alphéus,[7] who by secret sluice
Stole under seas to meet his Arethuse;
And ye, the breathing° roses of the wood,   *fragrant human*
Fair silver-buskined° nymphs as great and good,   *wearing high boots*
I know this quest of yours and free° intent   *noble, generous*
35 Was all in honor and devotion meant
To the great mistress of yon princely shrine,
Whom with low reverence° I adore as mine,   *deep bow*
And with all helpful service will comply
To further this night's glad solemnity,°   *festive ceremony*
40 And lead ye where ye may more near behold
What shallow-searching Fame hath left untold,
Which I full oft amidst these shades alone
Have sat to wonder at and gaze upon.
For know by lot from Jove I am the power
45 Of this fair wood, and live in oaken bower,
To nurse the saplings tall, and curl the grove
With ringlets quaint, and wanton windings
        wove.
And all my plants I save from nightly ill
Of noisome° winds and blasting° vapors chill,   *noxious / withering*

---

4. Mother of Apollo and Diana.
5. Phrygian goddess, identified with Rhea, Jove's mother. Virgil describes her as *turrita*,
   "turret-crowned" (towered), *Aen.*, 6.784–87. In Roman mythology, her equivalent is
   Magna Mater ("Great Mother").
6. Protective local deity.
7. Both a river and a river god. He pursues Arethusa (line 85), a nymph who bathed in his
   waters before her metamorphosis into a stream. The river meets up with the fountain
   Arethusa in Sicily. See *Lyc.*, lines 85, 132–33.

50 And from the boughs brush off the evil dew,°   *mildew*
And heal the harms of thwarting thunder° blue,   *lightning*
Or what the cross dire-looking planet[8] smites,
Or hurtful worm with cankered venom bites.
When evening gray doth rise, I fetch my round°   *walk my circuit*
55 Over the mount and all this hallowed ground,
And early ere the odorous breath of morn
Awakes the slumbering leaves, or tasseled horn°   *hunting horn*
Shakes the high thicket, haste I all about,
Number my ranks,[9] and visit every sprout
60 With puissant words° and murmurs made to   *powerful magic*
    bless.   *charms*
But else in deep of night, when drowsiness
Hath locked up mortal sense, then listen I
To the celestial Sirens' harmony,[1]
That sit upon the nine enfolded spheres,
65 And sing to those[2] that hold the vital shears,
And turn the adamantine spindle round,
On which the fate of gods and men is wound.
Such sweet compulsion doth in music lie,
To lull the daughters of Necessity,
70 And keep unsteady Nature to her law,
And the low world in measured motion draw
After the heavenly tune, which none can hear
Of human mold° with gross unpurgèd ear;   *earth, body*
And yet such music worthiest were to blaze°   *proclaim*
75 The peerless height of her immortal praise,
Whose luster leads us, and for her most fit,
If my inferior hand or voice could hit°   *imitate exactly*
Inimitable sounds; yet as we go,
Whate'er the skill of lesser gods can show,
80 I will assay, her worth to celebrate,
And so attend ye toward her glittering state;°   *chair of state*
Where ye may all that are of noble stem
Approach, and kiss her sacred vesture's hem.

8. Saturn, of evil aspect in the astrological sense.
9. Count my trees in a row, like an officer inspecting soldiers.
1. The passage follows Plato (*Rep.*, 10.16–17), whose universe consists of eight concentric whorls threaded on a spindle of adamant, which is turned on the knees of Necessity. Milton, describing a Ptolemaic cosmos, describes nine celestial spheres, each of them governed by a one-note Siren. Their combined notes constitute the music of the spheres, inaudible to fallen human beings with unpurged faculties.
2. The three fates, daughters of Necessity, who hold the shears that cut life's thread. Only the Sirens' music can bring their destructive power under control.

II. SONG

O'er the smooth enamelled[3] green
85 Where no print of step hath been,
   Follow me as I sing,
   And touch the warbled string.
Under the shady roof
Of branching elm star-proof,°   *impenetrable by*
90   Follow me;   *starlight*
I will bring you where she sits,
Clad in splendor as befits
   Her deity.
Such a rural Queen
95 All Arcadia hath not seen.

III. SONG

Nymphs and shepherds, dance no more
   By sandy Ladon's[4] lilied banks;
On old Lycaeus or Cyllene hoar,
   Trip no more in twilight ranks;
100 Though Erymanth your loss deplore,
   A better soil shall give ye thanks.
From the stony Maenalus,[5]
Bring your flocks and live with us;
Here ye shall have greater grace,
105 To serve the Lady of this place.
   Though Syrinx[6] your Pan's mistress were,
   Yet Syrinx well might wait on her.
      Such a rural Queen
   All Arcadia hath not seen.

A MASQUE PRESENTED AT LUDLOW CASTLE [COMUS] *A Masque* was presented at Ludlow Castle in Shropshire, on September 29, 1634, to celebrate the installation of John Egerton, first earl of Bridgewater (1579–1649), as lord president of Wales. Drafts of the work in *TMS*, revealing Milton's process of revision, suggest that the poet may have begun the work earlier. Egerton had been a noted classical scholar during his student years at Brasenose College, Oxford, and he would have appreciated Milton's use of Platonic ideas and pagan

---

3. Beautified with various colors (of flowers).
4. A river in Arcadia that flows into the Alpheus.
5. Lycaeus, Cyllene, Erymanth, and Maenalus are all mountains in Arcadia.
6. A chaste nymph, fleeing amorous Pan, arrived at the river's edge and was transformed into hollow water reeds (*Met.*, 1.689 ff.).

mythology to provide a Christian allegory. And in this Platonic and Christian allegorical celebration of the love of the good, the *dramatis personae* are idealized versions of the Egerton household. The stars of the *Masque* are Egerton's three children: Lady Alice Egerton, fifteen years old (the Lady), John Egerton, Viscount Brackley, eleven (the Elder Brother), and Thomas Egerton, nine (the Younger Brother). (Incidentally, Milton's position in his own family was that of the Elder Brother in *A Masque*, with an older sister, Ann, and a younger brother, Christopher.) Thyrsis, who incarnates the Attendant Spirit, is enacted by Henry Lawes, music tutor of the children. *A Masque* reunites Milton and Lawes, who had written the words and music, respectively, for *Arcades*, as well as the Egerton children, who had taken part in the performance at Harefield, probably in 1633. *Arcades* had celebrated Alice Spencer, dowager countess of Derby, mother of Lady Frances Stanley and both stepmother and mother-in-law to the earl of Bridgewater.

One can see from the names dropped in the preceding paragraph that masques, which were expensive to mount, were entertainments for royalty and nobility and could flourish only in rigidly hierarchical societies. They exist mainly to voice compliments, to provide a spectacle, and to present a moral allegory. Beginning in the early 1640s, Milton the political activist would play a role in making the genre obsolete. But see also the essay by Norbrook (p. 485), who demonstrates that in *A Masque* Milton felt and recorded the incipient revolutionary vibrations of his age, even if, as a deferential young man, he spoke more softly.

Very different but equally brilliant is Kerrigan's Freudian reading of the work (p. 507). For the best—indeed, indispensable—introduction to Milton's youthful conception of the ideal of chastity and the literature that nurtured it, see the autobiographical excerpt from *An Apology for Smectymnuus* on p. 227.

A Masque Presented at Ludlow Castle, 1634, Before the Earl of Bridgewater, Then President of Wales [Comus]

The Persons

The Attendant Spirit, afterwards in the habit of Thyrsis.
Comus with his crew.
The Lady.
1. Brother.
2. Brother.
Sabrina the Nymph.

The chief persons which presented were
The Lord Brackley

Mr. Thomas Egerton his Brother
The Lady Alice Egerton

> *The first scene discovers° a wild wood.*   reveals
> *The Attendant° Spirit descends or enters.*   guardian

Before the starry threshold of Jove's court
My mansion is, where those immortal shapes
Of bright aërial Spirits live insphered
In regions mild of calm and serene air,
5 Above the smoke and stir of this dim spot
Which men call earth, and with low-thoughted care,
Confined and pestered in this pinfold° here,   pen for animals
Strive to keep up a frail and feverish being,
Unmindful of the crown that Virtue gives,
10 After this mortal change, to her true servants
Amongst the enthroned gods on sainted seats.
Yet some there be that by due steps aspire
To lay their just hands on that golden key
That opes the palace of eternity:
15 To such my errand is, and but for such
I would not spoil these pure ambrosial weeds°   divine garments
With the rank vapors of this sin-worn mold.°1   (1) earth (2) flesh
    But to my task. Neptune, besides the sway
Of every salt flood and each ebbing stream,
20 Took in by lot 'twixt high and nether Jove
Imperial rule of all the sea-girt isles,2
That like to rich and various gems inlay
The unadornèd bosom of the deep,
Which he, to grace his tributary gods,
25 By course commits to several° government,   separate
And gives them leave to wear their sapphire crowns
And wield their little tridents. But this isle,
The greatest and the best of all the main,°   ocean
He quarters to his blue-haired deities;

1. The opening lines fuse classical and Christian images and themes, as does the rest of
the masque. The language is Platonic, evoking the mansions of the True Earth (*Phaedo*
109–10), which is distinguished from what human beings call earth. We think we live
on the upper surface of the earth, but in fact we merely inhabit one of its hollows, "into
which the water and mist and air have run together. . . . But the earth itself is pure, and
is situated in the pure heaven in which the stars are." At the same time, the allegory is
Christian: Jove is God, his court is heaven, and the attendant spirit is a guardian angel,
willing to soil his ambrosial weeds, just as Christ, in the *Nativity Ode*, "Forsook the
courts of everlasting day, / And chose with us a darksome house of mortal clay" (13–14).
2. After defeating the titans, Jove and his brothers divided their rule of the universe by
drawing lots, Jove taking the heavens, Pluto the underworld, and Neptune the sea (*Il.*,
15.187–93).

30 And all this tract[3] that fronts the falling sun
    A noble peer[4] of mickle° trust and power   *great*
    Has in his charge, with tempered awe to guide
    An old and haughty nation proud in arms;
    Where his fair offspring, nursed in princely lore,
35 Are coming to attend their father's state°   *(1) throne,*
    And new-entrusted scepter. But their way   *(2) high rank*
    Lies through the perplexed paths of this drear
        wood,[5]
    The nodding horror of whose shady brows
    Threats the forlorn and wand'ring passenger.
40 And here their tender age might suffer peril,
    But that by quick command from sovereign Jove
    I was dispatched for their defense and guard;
    And listen why, for I will tell ye now
    What never yet was heard in tale or song
45 From old or modern bard in hall or bow'r.
        Bacchus, that first from out the purple grape
    Crushed the sweet poison of misusèd wine,
    After the Tuscan mariners transformed,[6]
    Coasting the Tyrrhene shore,[7] as the winds
        listed,°   *wished*
50 On Circe's island fell. (Who knows not Circe,
    the daughter of the Sun? whose charmèd cup
    Whoever tasted, lost his upright shape,
    And downward fell into a groveling swine.)[8]
    This nymph that gazed upon his clust'ring locks,
55 With ivy berries wreathed, and his blithe youth,
    Had him, ere he parted thence, a son
    Much like his father, but his mother more,
    Whom therefore she brought up and Comus[9]
        named;
    Who, ripe and frolic° of his full-grown age,   *merry, sportive*
60 Roving the Celtic and Iberian[1] fields,
    At last betakes him to this ominous wood,
    And, in thick shelter of black shades imbow'red,
    Excels his mother at her mighty art,

---

3. Wales and the Welsh–English border.
4. I.e., earl of Bridgewater.
5. A symbol of life and its hazards.
6. I.e., after the transformation of. Bacchus, kidnapped by pirates, turned them into dol-
    phins (*Met.*, 3.605–86).
7. The west coast of Italy.
8. Circe changed Odysseus' men into swine (*Od.* 10.238).
9. From Gr. *kommos*, "revelry."
1. France and Spain.

Off'ring to every weary traveler
65 His orient liquor in a crystal glass,
To quench the drought of Phoebus,° which as   *sun thirst*
    they taste
(For most do taste through fond° intemperate thirst),   *foolish*
Soon as the potion works, their human count'nance,
Th' express resemblance of the gods,[2] is changed
70 Into some brutish form of wolf, or bear,
Or ounce,° or tiger, hog, or bearded goat,   *lynx*
All other parts remaining as they were;
And they, so perfect is their misery,
Not once perceive their foul disfigurement,
75 But boast themselves more comely than before,[3]
And all their friends and native home forget,
To roll with pleasure in a sensual sty.
Therefore when any favored of high Jove
Chances to pass through this advent'rous glade,
80 Swift as the sparkle of a glancing° star   *shooting, gleaming*
I shoot from Heav'n to give him safe convoy,
As now I do. But first I must put off
These my sky-robes, spun out of Iris' woof,°   *woven fabric of the*
And take the weeds° and likeness of a swain°   *rainbow / garments /*
85 That to the service of this house belongs,   *shepherd, attendant*
Who with his soft pipe and smooth-dittied song
Well knows to still the wild winds when they roar,
And hush the waving woods; nor of less faith,°   *no less loyal (than*
And in this office of his mountain watch   *skillful)*
90 Likeliest,° and nearest to the present aid   *best fitted*
Of this occasion. But I hear the tread
Of hateful steps; I must be viewless now.

> *Comus enters with a charming-rod in one hand, his glass in the other; with him a rout of monsters headed like sundry sorts of wild beasts, but otherwise like men and women, their apparel glistering. They come in making a riotous and unruly noise, with torches in their hands.*

COMUS. The star[4] that bids the shepherd fold°   *pen their sheep*
    Now the top of heav'n doth hold,
95 And the gilded car° of day   *sun's chariot*

---

2. "So God created man in his own image" (Gen. 1:27).
3. "The early editions have no comma after 'before' and have one after 'friends.' Most editors reverse the punctuation to make more obvious sense, though the original reading [*friends* parallel to *themselves* as objects of *boast*] was probably Milton's intention; the 'friends' are fellow victims of Comus" (Bush).
4. Hesperus (Venus).

His glowing axle doth allay°   *cool down*
In the steep Atlantic stream;
And the slope° sun his upward beam   *descending*
Shoots against the dusky pole,°   *sky*
100 Pacing toward the other goal
Of his chamber in the east.
Meanwhile welcome joy and feast,
Midnight shout and revelry,
Tipsy dance and jollity.
105 Braid your locks with rosy twine° *intertwined roses*
Dropping odors, dropping wine.
Rigor now is gone to bed,
And Advice with scrupulous head,
Strict Age, and sour Severity,
110 With their grave saws° in slumber lie.   *maxims*
We that are of purer fire
Imitate the starry choir,[5]
Who in their nightly watchful spheres
Lead in swift round the months and years.
115 The sounds° and seas with all their finny *narrow channels /*
   drove°   *crowd*
Now to the moon in wavering morris° move, *Moorish dance*
And on the tawny sands and shelves° *sandbanks*
Trip the pert fairies and the dapper elves;
By dimpled brook and fountain brim
120 The wood-nymphs, decked with daisies trim,
Their merry wakes° and pastimes keep: *nighttime revels*
What hath night to do with sleep?
Night hath better sweets to prove,
Venus now wakes, and wakens Love.
125 Come, let us our rites begin;
'Tis only daylight that makes sin,
Which these dun shades will ne'er report.
Hail, goddess of nocturnal sport,
Dark-veiled Cotytto,[6] t' whom the secret flame
130 Of midnight torches burns; mysterious dame,
That ne'er art called but when the dragon womb
Of Stygian[7] darkness spits her thickest gloom,
And makes one blot of all the air,

5. Comus's claim to imitate the orderly movement and music of the spheres is false since he is drunk, and his unsteadiness leads to eccentric, grotesque movement ("fantastic," line 144).
6. Thracian earth goddess celebrated in secret licentious rituals.
7. Infernal (from the river Styx).

Stay thy cloudy ebon chair
135　Wherein thou rid'st with Hecat',[8] and befriend
　　Us thy vowed priests, till utmost end
　　Of all thy dues be done, and none left out,
　　Ere the blabbing eastern scout,
　　The nice Morn on th' Indian steep,
140　From her cabined loop-hole° peep,　　　　　　*small window*
　　And to the tell-tale sun descry°　　　　　　　*reveal*
　　Our concealed solemnity.
　　Come, knit hands, and beat the ground,
　　In a light fantastic° round.°　　　　　*grotesque / ring*
　　　　　　　　　　　　　　　　　　　　　　dance

THE MEASURE.

145　Break off, break off, I feel the different pace
　　Of some chaste footing near about this ground.
　　Run to your shrouds° within these brakes°　　*hiding places /*
　　　and trees;　　　　　　　　　　　　　　　　*thickets*
　　Our number may affright: some virgin sure
　　(For so I can distinguish by mine art)
150　Benighted in these woods. Now to my charms
　　And to my wily trains;° I shall ere long　　*allurements*
　　Be well stocked with as fair a herd as grazed
　　About my mother Circe. Thus I hurl
　　My dazzling spells into the spongy° air,　　*absorbing*
155　Of power to cheat the eye with blear illusion,
　　And give it false presentments,° lest the place　　*pictures*
　　And my quaint habits° breed astonishment,　*unfamiliar garments*
　　And put the damsel to suspicious flight,
　　Which must not be, for that's against my course;
160　I, under fair pretense of friendly ends,
　　And well-placed words of glozing° courtesy　　*flattering*
　　Baited with reasons not unplausible,
　　Wind me into the easy-hearted man,
　　And hug him into snares. When once her eye
165　Hath met the virtue° of this magic dust,　　*power*
　　I shall appear some harmless villager
　　Whom thrift keeps up about his country
　　　gear.°　　　　　　　　　　　　　　　　　　*doings*
　　But here she comes; I fairly° step aside,　　*quietly*
　　And hearken, if I may, her business here.
　　　　The Lady enters.

8. Hecate was the goddess of witchcraft.

170 LADY. This way the noise was, if mine ear be true,
        My best guide now. Methought it was the sound
        Of riot and ill-managed merriment,
        Such as the jocund flute or gamesome pipe
        Stirs up among the loose unlettered hinds,°   *dissolute, uneducated*
175   When for their teeming flocks and granges°   *farm workers / barns*
          full
        In wanton dance they praise the bounteous Pan,[9]
        And thank the gods amiss. I should be loath
        To meet the rudeness and swilled insolence
        Of such late wassailers; yet O where else
180   Shall I inform° my unacquainted feet   *direct*
        In the blind mazes of this tangled wood?
        My brothers, when they saw me wearied out
        With this long way, resolving here to lodge
        Under the spreading favor of these pines,
185   Stepped as they said to the next thicket side
        To bring me berries, or such cooling fruit
        As the kind hospitable woods provide.
        They left me then when the gray-hooded Ev'n,
        Like a sad votarist in palmer's weed,[1]
190   Rose from the hindmost wheels of Phoebus' wain.° *sun's chariot*
        But where they are, and why they came not back,
        Is now the labor of my thoughts; 'tis likeliest
        They had engaged their wand'ring steps too far,
        And envious darkness, ere they could return,
195   Had stole them from me. Else, O thievish Night,
        Why shouldst thou, but for some felonious end,
        In thy dark lantern thus close up the stars
        That Nature hung in heav'n, and filled their lamps
        With everlasting oil, to give due light
200   To the misled and lonely traveller?
        This is the place, as well as I may guess,
        Whence even now the tumult of loud mirth
        Was rife,° and perfect in my listening ear,   *loud sounding*
        Yet naught but single° darkness do I find.   *absolute*
205   What might this be? A thousand fantasies
        Begin to throng into my memory
        Of calling shapes, and beck'ning shadows dire,
        And airy tongues that syllable men's names
        On sands and shores and desert wildernesses.
210   These thoughts may startle well, but not astound

9. The god of woods and shepherds.
1. A serious person under a religious vow, dressed like a pilgrim.

The virtuous mind, that ever walks attended
By a strong siding° champion, Consci̇ence.   *defending (taking*
O welcome, pure-eyed Faith, white-handed Hope,   *one's side)*
Thou hovering angel girt with golden wings,
215   And thou unblemished form of Chastity,
I see ye visibly, and now believe
That He, the supreme Good, t' whom all things ill
Are but as slavish officers of vengeance,
Would send a glist'ring guardian if need were
220   To keep my life and honor unassailed.
Was I deceived, or did a sable cloud
Turn forth her silver lining on the night?
I did not err, there does a sable cloud
Turn forth her silver lining on the night,
225   And casts a gleam over this tufted grove.
I cannot hallo to my brothers, but
Such noise as I can make to be heard farthest
I'll venture, for my new-enlivened spirits
Prompt me; and they perhaps are not far off.

SONG

230   *Sweet Echo,[2] sweetest nymph that liv'st unseen*
     Within thy airy shell[3]
     By slow Maeander's[4] margent green,
and in the violet-embroidered vale
     Where the lovelorn[5] nightingale
235   *Nightly to thee her sad song mourneth well:*
Canst thou not tell me of a gentle pair
     That likest thy Narcissus are?
          O if thou have
     Hid them in some flow'ry cave,
240   *Tell me but where,*
Sweet queen of parley,° daughter of the sphere;[6]   *speech*
So may'st thou be translated to the skies,
And give resounding grace to all heav'n's
     harmonies.

---

2. A nymph who died of unrequited love for beautiful Narcissus (line 237), but Aphrodite so loved her voice that she let it live on.
3. Either a vault of air or an actual cavern (TMS reads "cell").
4. A winding river in Anatolia.
5. Here, ruined through another's love. Alludes to the myth of Philomel, raped in a forest by her brother-in-law, Tereus, who cut out her tongue. She wove the story of his crime into a tapestry that she sent to her sister, Procne. Later the Olympian gods transformed her into a nightingale.
6. A Platonic siren or angelic intelligence that attends the celestial "nine enfolded spheres" of the Ptolemaic geocentric system. See *Arcades* 63 f. and *At a Solemn Music* 1–2.

COMUS. Can any mortal mixture of earth's mold°   *earth as human body*
245   Breathe such divine enchanting ravishment?
    Sure something holy lodges in that breast,
    And with these raptures moves the vocal air
    To testify his hidden residence;
    How sweetly did they float upon the wings
250   Of silence, through the empty-vaulted night,
    At every fall° smoothing the raven down°   *cadence / feathers*
    Of darkness till it smiled. I have oft heard
    My mother Circe with the Sirens[7] three,
    Amidst the flow'ry-kirtled° Naiades,[8]   *skirted*
255   Culling their potent herbs and baleful drugs,
    Who as they sung would take the prisoned soul
    And lap it in Elysium; Scylla[9] wept,
    And chid her barking waves into attention,
    And fell Charybdis[1] murmured soft applause.
260   Yet they in pleasing slumber lulled the sense,
    And in sweet madness robbed it of itself;
    But such a sacred and home-felt° delight,   *intimately felt*
    Such sober certainty of waking bliss,
    I never heard till now. I'll speak to her,
265   And she shall be my queen. Hail, foreign wonder,
    Whom certain these rough shades did never breed,
    Unless° the goddess that in rural shrine   *Unless you are*
    Dwell'st here with Pan or Sylvan,[2] by blest song
    Forbidding every bleak unkindly fog
270   To touch the prosperous growth of this tall wood.
LADY. Nay, gentle shepherd, ill is lost that praise
    That is addressed to unattending ears.
    Not any boast of skill, but extreme shift
    How to regain my severed company
275   Compelled me to awake the courteous Echo
    To give me answer from her mossy couch.
COMUS. What chance, good lady, hath bereft you such?[3]
LADY. Dim darkness and this leavy labyrinth.
COMUS. Could that divide you from near-ushering guides?
280 LADY. They left me weary on a grassy turf.

7. Sea nymphs whose singing put a spell on sailors (*Od.*, 12.47 f., 165 f.)
8. Freshwater nymphs.
9. A once-beautiful nymph beloved of the sea god Glaucus, transformed into a monster by
   Circe, who wanted Glaucus for herself. Even Scylla was enraptured by Circe's song. She
   ultimately became a rock dangerous to sailors. Elysium is a place of perfect happiness.
1. A whirlpool opposite Scylla.
2. A Roman wood god.
3. Dialogue in single lines is known as stichomythia in Greek drama.

COMUS. By falsehood, or discourtesy, or why?
LADY. To seek i' th' valley some cool friendly spring.
COMUS. And left your fair side all unguarded, lady?
LADY. They were but twain, and purposed quick return.
285 COMUS. Perhaps forestalling night prevented them.
LADY. How easy my misfortune is to hit!°   *guess*
COMUS. Imports their loss,° beside the present   *Does their loss*
   need?   *matter*
LADY. No less than if I should my brothers lose.
COMUS. Were they of manly prime, or youthful bloom?
290 LADY. As smooth as Hebe's[4] their unrazored lips.
COMUS. Two such I saw, what time° the   *(i.e., at evening)*
   labored ox
  In his loose traces from the furrow came,
  And the swinked hedger° at his supper sat;   *wearied hedge worker*
  I saw them under a green mantling° vine   *spreading, covering*
295 That crawls along the side of yon small hill,
  Plucking ripe clusters from the tender shoots;
  Their port° was more than human, as they stood.   *bearing*
  I took it for a faery visïon
  Of some gay creatures of the element,°   *sky*
300 That in the colors of the rainbow live
  And play i' th' plighted° clouds. I was awe-strook,   *folded*
  And as I passed, I worshiped; if those you seek,
  It were a journey like the path to heav'n
  To help you find them.
LADY.   Gentle villager,
305 What readiest way would bring me to that place?
COMUS. Due west it rises from this shrubby point.
LADY. To find out that, good shepherd, I suppose,
  In such a scant allowance of star-light,
  Would overtask the best land-pilot's art,
310 Without the sure guess of well-practiced feet.
COMUS. I know each lane and every alley green,
  Dingle° or bushy dell of this wild wood,   *wooded hollow*
  And every bosky bourn° from side to side,   *stream bordered by*
  My daily walks and ancient neighborhood;   *bushes*
315 And if your stray attendance° be yet lodged,   *attendants*
  Or shroud° within these limits, I shall know   *sheltered*
  Ere morrow wake or the low-roosted lark
  From her thatched pallet° rouse; if otherwise,   *straw nest*
  I can conduct you, lady, to a low

4. The goddess of youth.

320   But loyal cottage, where you may be safe
     Till further quest.
    LADY.   Shepherd, I take thy word,
     And trust thy honest-offered courtesy,
     Which oft is sooner found in lowly sheds
     With smoky rafters, than in tap'stry halls
325   And courts of princes, where it[5] first was named,
     And yet° is most pretended. In a place   *still*
     Less warranted than this, or less secure,
     I cannot be, that I should fear to change it.
     Eye me, blest Providence, and square° my trial   *adjust, adapt*
330   To my proportioned strength. Shepherd, lead on.
                          [*Exeunt.*]
      The two Brothers.
    ELD. BRO. Unmuffle, ye faint stars, and thou,
       fair moon,
     That wont'st° to love the traveler's benison,°   *are accustomed /*
     Stoop thy pale visage through an amber cloud   *blessing*
     And disinherit Chaos,° that reigns here   *dispossess primeval*
335   In double night of darkness and of shades;   *darkness*
     Or if your influence be quite dammed up
     With black usurping mists, some gentle taper,
     Though a rush-candle from the wicker hole[6]
     Of some clay habitation, visit us
340   With thy long leveled rule of streaming light,
     And thou shalt be our star of Arcady,
     Or Tyrian Cynosure.[7]
    SEC. BRO.   Or if our eyes
     Be barred that happiness, might we but hear
     The folded flocks penned in their wattled
       cotes,°   *sheepfolds made of*
345   Or sound of pastoral reed with oaten stops,[8]   *plaited branches*
     Or whistle from the lodge, or village cock
     Count the night-watches to his feathery dames,
     'Twould be some solace yet, some little cheering,
     In this close dungeon of innumerous boughs.
350   But O that hapless virgin, our lost sister,

---

5. I.e., courtesy.
6. A window filled with wicker-work instead of glass implied a poor dwelling. "Rush-candle": a candle made by dipping the stem of a rush in tallow or oil gave a weak light.
7. The Phoenicians, whose capital city was Tyre (hence "Tyrian"), navigated by Ursa Minor, the Little Bear, which has the North Star ("Cynosure") in its tail. Greek sailors steered by constellation Ursa Major, with the "star of Arcady."
8. The finger holes in a shepherd's pipe ("reed"), which was traditionally fashioned from oat stalks.

Where may she wander now, whither betake her
From the chill dew, amongst rude burs and thistles?
Perhaps some cold bank is her bolster now,
Or 'gainst the rugged bark of some broad elm
355 Leans her unpillowed head fraught with sad fears.
What if in wild amazement and affright,
Or, while we speak, within the direful grasp
Of savage hunger or of savage heat?

ELD. BRO. Peace, brother, be not over-exquisite°   *too careful*
360 To cast° the fashion of uncertain evils;   *forecast*
For grant they be so,° while they rest   *as you imagine them*
    unknown,
What need a man forestall° his date of grief,   *anticipate*
And run to meet what he would most avoid?
Or if they be but false alarms of fear,
365 How bitter is such self-delusïon?
I do not think my sister so to seek,°   *lacking*
Or so unprincipled in virtue's book,
And the sweet peace that goodness bosoms°   *carries in its bosom*
    ever,
As that the single° want of light and noise   *mere*
370 (Not being in danger, as I trust she is not)
Could stir the constant mood of her calm thoughts,
And put them into misbecoming° plight.   *unbecoming*
Virtue could see to do what Virtue would
By her own radiant light, though sun and moon
375 Were in the flat sea sunk. And Wisdom's self
Oft seeks to sweet retired solitude,
Where with her best nurse, Contemplatïon,
She plumes her feathers and lets grow her wings,
That in the various bustle of resort°   *concourse of people*
380 Were all to-ruffled,° and sometimes impaired.   *ruffled up*
He that has light within his own clear breast
May sit i' th' center[9] and enjoy bright day,
But he that hides a dark soul and foul thoughts
Benighted walks under the mid-day sun;
Himself is his own dungeon.

385 SEC. BRO.   'Tis most true
That musing meditation most affects°   *is drawn to*
The pensive secrecy of desert cell,
Far from the cheerful haunt of men and herds,
And sits as safe as in a senate-house;

9. Of the earth.

390   For who would rob a hermit of his weeds,
     His few books, or his beads,° or maple dish,   *rosary*
     Or do his gray hairs any violence?
     But beauty, like the fair Hesperian tree[1]
     Laden with blooming gold, had need the guard
395   Of dragon-watch with unenchanted eye
     To save her blossoms and defend her fruit
     From the rash hand of bold Incontinence.°   *Uncontrolled sexual*
     You may as well spread out the unsunned heaps   *passion*
     Of miser's treasure by an outlaw's den,
400   And tell me it is safe, as bid me hope
     Danger° will wink on° opportunity.   *Power / overlook*
     And let a single helpless maiden pass
     Uninjured in this wild surrounding waste.
     Of night or loneliness it recks me not;°   *I am not concerned*
405   I fear the dread events that dog them both,
     Lest some ill-greeting touch attempt the person
     Of our unowned° sister.   *lost*

ELD. BRO.   I do not, brother,
     Infer° as if I thought my sister's state   *Draw a conclusion*
     Secure without all doubt or controversy;
410   Yet where an equal poise° of hope and fear   *balancing, weighing*
     Does arbitrate th' event,° my nature is   *Decide the outcome*
     That I incline to hope rather than fear,
     And gladly banish squint suspicïon.
     My sister is not so defenseless left
415   As you imagine; she has a hidden strength
     Which you remember not.

SEC. BRO.   What hidden
       strength,
     Unless the strength of Heav'n, if you mean that?

ELD. BRO. I mean that too, but yet a hidden strength
     Which, if Heav'n gave it, may be termed her own:
420   'Tis chastity, my brother, chastity.
     She that has that is clad in complete steel,
     And like a quivered nymph[2] with arrows keen
     May trace huge forests and unharbored°   *shelterless*
      heaths,

---

1. A tree bearing golden apples, planted by Hera in the garden of the Hesperides, the three daughters of the evening star Hesperus. A dragon was set to guard it, and one of Hercules's twelve labors was to steal it. Often poets, including Shakespeare and Jonson, associated it with female beauty.
2. I.e., a nymph with a quiver of arrows, a follower of Diana, goddess of the hunt and of chastity.

Infamous hills and sandy perilous winds,
425 Where, through the sacred rays of chastity,
No savage fierce, bandit, or mountaineer°   *mountain wild men*
Will dare to soil her virgin purity.
Yea, there where very desolation dwells,
By grots and caverns shagged with horrid shades,
430 She may pass on with unblenched° majesty,   *fearless*
Be it not done in pride or in presumption.
Some say no evil thing that walks by night,
In fog or fire,° by lake or moorish fen,   *will-o'-the-wisp*
Blue meager hag, or stubborn unlaid³ ghost,
435 That breaks his magic chains at curfew time,
No goblin or swart° fairy of the mine,   *black*
Hath hurtful power o'er true virginity.
Do ye believe me yet, or shall I call
Antiquity from the old schools of Greece
440 To testify the arms of chastity?
Hence had the huntress Dian her dread bow,
Fair silver-shafted queen for ever chaste,
Wherewith she tamed the brinded° lioness   *tawny*
And spotted mountain-pard,° but set at   *panther, leopard*
    naught
445 The frivolous bolt of Cupid; gods and men
Feared her stern frown, and she was queen
    o' th' woods.
What was that snaky-headed Gorgon shield⁴
That wise Minerva wore, unconquered virgin,
Wherewith she freezed her foes to cóngealed stone,
450 But rigid looks of chaste austerity,
And noble grace that dashed brute violence
With sudden adoration and blank awe?
So dear to Heav'n is saintly chastity
That when a soul is found sincerely so,
455 A thousand liveried angels lackey her,
Driving far off each thing of sin and guilt,
And in clear dream and solemn visïon
Tell her of things that no gross ear can hear,
Till oft converse with heav'nly habitants
460 Begin to cast a beam on th' outward shape,
The unpolluted temple of the mind,

---

3. By exorcism.
4. Minerva, virgin goddess of wisdom and war, carried on her shield the head of Gorgon
Medusa, which turned those who looked upon it to stone.

And turns it by degrees to the soul's essence,
Till all be made immortal.[5] But when lust,
By unchaste looks, loose gestures, and foul talk,
465   But most by lewd and lavish act of sin,
Lets in defilement to the inward parts,
The soul grows clotted by contagion,
Embodies and imbrutes, till she quite lose
The divine property of her first being.
470   Such are those thick and gloomy shadows damp
Oft seen in charnel vaults and sepulchres
Lingering, and sitting by a new-made grave,
As loath to leave the body that it loved,
And linked itself by carnal sensualty
475   To a degenerate and degraded state.[6]
SEC. BRO. How charming is divine philosophy!
Not harsh and crabbed, as dull fools suppose,
But musical as is Apollo's lute,
And a perpetual feast of nectared sweets,
Where no crude surfeit reigns.
480   ELD. BRO. List, list, I hear
Some far-off hallo break the silent air.
SEC. BRO. Methought so too; what should it be?
ELD. BRO.   For certain,
Either some one like us night-foundered°   *engulfed in night*
   here,
Or else some neighbor woodman, or at worst,
485   Some roving robber calling to his fellows.
SEC. BRO. Heav'n keep my sister! Again, again,
   and near!
Best drawn, and stand upon our guard.
ELD BRO.   I'll hallo;
If he be friendly, he comes well; if not,
Defense is a good cause, and Heav'n be for us.
    The Attendant Spirit, habited like a shepherd.
490   That hallo I should know; what are you? Speak;
Come not too near, you fall on iron stakes° else.   *swords*
SPIR. What voice is that? my young lord? speak again.
SEC. BRO. O brother, 'tis my father's shepherd, sure.

---

5. The conversion of body to soul can't be literally true. It may owe something to neo-Platonism or to the ultimate state of glorification in the Pauline paradigm of salvation. The fantasy may also express indirectly the abhorrence felt by young Milton when contemplating bodily corruption.
6. A paraphrase of Plato's *Phaedo* 81, on the ultimate result of living in and for the body. Plato's body–soul dichotomy contrasts dramatically with the mature Milton's monism.

ELD. BRO. Thyrsis,[7] whose artful strains have
    oft delayed
495   The huddling° brook to hear his madrigal,   *hurrying*
    And sweetened every musk-rose of the dale,
    How cam'st thou here, good swain? Hath any ram
    Slipped from the fold, or young kid lost his dam,
    Or straggling wether the pent flock forsook?
500   How couldst thou find this dark sequestered nook?
SPIRIT. O my loved master's heir, and his next° joy,   *nearest*
    I came not here on such a trivial toy°   *trifle*
    As a strayed ewe, or to pursue the stealth
    Of pilfering wolf; not all the fleecy wealth
505   That doth enrich these downs is worth a thought
    To° this my errand, and the care it brought.   *Compared with*
    But O my virgin lady, where is she?
    How chance she is not in your company?
ELDER BROTHER. To tell thee sadly,° shepherd,   *in earnest*
    without blame
510   Or our neglect, we lost her as we came.
SPIRIT. Ay me unhappy, then my fears are true.
ELDER BROTHER. What fears, good Thyrsis?
      Prithee briefly shew.
SPIRIT. I'll tell ye. 'Tis not vain or fabulous
    (Though so esteemed by shallow ignorance)
515   What the sage poets, taught by the heavenly Muse,
    Storied of old in high immortal verse
    Of dire Chimeras[8] and enchanted isles,
    And rifted rocks whose entrance leads to hell,
    For such there be, but unbelief is blind.
520   Within the navel of this hideous wood,
    Immured in cypress shades, a sorcerer dwells,
    Of Bacchus and of Circe born, great Comus,
    Deep skilled in all his mother's witcheries,
    And here to every thirsty wanderer
525   By sly enticement gives his baneful cup,
    With many murmurs mixed, whose pleasing poison
    The visage quite transforms of him that drinks,
    And the inglorious likeness of a beast
    Fixes instead, unmolding reason's mintage
530   Charáctered° in the face; this have I learnt   *Engraved*

---

7. A singer in pastorals by Theocritus (*Idyll* 1) and Virgil (*Eclogue* 7), alluding to the composer and musician Henry Lawes, tutor of the Egerton children, who took the part.
8. A fire-breathing monster of Greek myth, with a lion's head, a goat's body, and a dragon's tail.

Tending my flocks hard by i' th' hilly crofts°   *enclosed fields*
That brow° this bottom glade, whence night   *overlook*
   by night
He and his monstrous rout are heard to howl
Like stabled wolves, or tigers at their prey,
535   Doing abhorrèd rites to Hecate[9]
In their obscurèd haunts of inmost bow'rs.
Yet have they many baits and guileful spells
T' inveigle and invite th' unwary sense
Of them that pass unweeting by the way.
540   This evening late, by then° the chewing flocks   *the time that*
Had ta'en their supper on the savory herb
Of knot-grass dew-besprent, and were in fold,
I sat me down to watch upon a bank
With ivy canopied, and interwove
545   With flaunting° honeysuckle, and began,   *gaily waving*
Wrapped in a pleasing fit of melancholy,
To meditate my rural minstrelsy,[1]
Till fancy had her fill. But ere a close°   *conclusion of a*
The wonted roar was up amidst the woods,   *musical phrase*
550   And filled the air with barbarous dissonance,
At which I ceased, and listened them a while,
Till an unusual stop of sudden silence
Gave respite to the drowsy frighted steeds
That draw the litter of close-curtained Sleep.
555   At last a soft and solemn-breathing sound
Rose like a steam of rich distilled perfumes,
And stole upon the air, that even Silence
Was took ere she was ware, and wished she might
Deny her nature and be never more,
560   Still to be so displaced.[2] I was all ear,
And took in strains that might create a soul
Under the ribs of Death. But O ere long
Too well I did perceive it was the voice
Of my most honored lady, your dear sister.
565   Amazed I stood, harrowed with grief and fear,
And "O poor hapless nightingale," thought I,
"How sweet thou sing'st, how near the
   deadly snare!"
Then down the lawns° I ran with headlong   *open spaces between*
   haste   *woods*

9. Underworld goddess of witchcraft; one aspect of the triune Diana.
1. Play on a shepherd's pipe.
2. No longer exist, if she could always be replaced by such music.

Through paths and turnings often trod by day,
570 Till guided by mine ear I found the place
Where that damned wizard hid in sly disguise
(For so by certain signs I knew) had met
Already, ere my best speed could prevent,
The aidless innocent lady, his wished prey,
575 Who gently asked if he had seen such two,
Supposing him some neighbor villager;
Longer I durst not stay, but soon I guessed
Ye were the two she meant; with that I sprung
Into swift flight, till I had found you here;
But further know I not.
580 SECOND BROTHER.   O night and shades,
How are ye joined with hell in triple knot
Against th' unarmed weakness of one virgin
Alone and helpless! Is this the confidence
You gave me, brother?
ELDER BROTHER.   Yes, and keep it still,
585 Lean on it safely; not a period°   *sentence*
Shall be unsaid for me. Against the threats
Of malice or of sorcery, or that power
Which erring men call chance, this I hold firm:
Virtue may be assailed, but never hurt,
590 Surprised by unjust force, but not enthralled;
Yea, even that which mischief meant most harm
Shall in the happy trial prove most glory.
But evil on itself shall back recoil
And mix no more with goodness, when at last,
595 Gathered like scum, and settled to itself,
It shall be in eternal restless change
Self-fed and self-consumed. If this fail,
The pillared firmament° is rottenness,   *heaven*
And earth's base built on stubble. But
    come, let's on.
600 Against th' opposing will and arm of Heav'n
May never this just sword be lifted up.
But for that damned magician, let him be girt
With all the grisly legïons that troop
Under the sooty flag of Acheron,[3]
605 Harpies and Hydras,[4] or all the monstrous forms
'Twixt Africa and Ind, I'll find him out

---

3. A river in Hades; here, Hell itself.
4. The hydra was a many-headed serpent killed by Hercules. Harpies had the faces of
women and the bodies and talons of birds.

And force him to restore his purchase back,
Or drag him by the curls to a foul death,
Cursed as his life.

SPIRIT.   Alas, good vent'rous youth,
610   I love thy courage yet, and bold emprise,°   *chivalric enterprise*
But here thy sword can do thee little stead;
Far other arms and other weapons must
Be those that quell the might of hellish charms.
He with his bare wand can unthread thy joints
And crumble all thy sinews.

615   ELDER BROTHER.   Why, prithee,
shepherd,
How durst thou then thyself approach so near
As to make this relation?

SPIRIT.   Care and utmost
shifts°   *expedients*
How to secure the lady from surprisal
Brought to my mind a certain shepherd lad,
620   Of small regard to see to,° yet well skilled   *Of unimpressive*
In every virtuous plant and healing herb   *appearance*
That spreads her verdant leaf to th' morning ray.
He loved me well, and oft would beg me sing,
Which when I did, he on the tender grass
625   Would sit, and hearken even to ecstasy,
And in requital ope his leathern scrip°   *small bag*
And show me simples° of a thousand names,   *medicinal herbs*
Telling their strange and vigorous faculties;
Amongst the rest a small unsightly root,
630   But of divine effect, he culled me out;
The leaf was darkish, and had prickles on it,
But in another country,[5] as he said,
Bore a bright golden flow'r, but not in this soil;
Unknown, and like esteemed,° and the dull swain   *unesteemed*
635   Treads on it daily with his clouted shoon,°   *hobnailed shoes*
And yet more med'cinal is it than that moly[6]
That Hermes once to wise Ulysses gave.
He called it haemony,[7] and gave it me,

5. Heaven (?).
6. The magical plant given by Hermes to Odysseus, which protected him from Circe's spells. It was allegorized as temperance in George Sandys's 1632 translation of Ovid's *Metamorphoses*.
7. Milton's invention, the meaning of which is much disputed. Haemonia is an old name for Thessaly, the land of witchcraft. "The plant apparently represents Platonic-Christian temperance; if it were religious faith or divine grace, its efficacy would surely be less limited than it proves to be" (Bush).

And bade me keep it as of sov'reign use
640 'Gainst all enchantments, mildew blast, or damp,
Or ghastly Furies' apparition;
I pursed it up, but little reck'ning made,
Till now that this extremity compelled,
But now I find it true; for by this means
645 I knew the foul enchanter though disguised,
Entered the very lime-twigs[8] of his spells,
And yet came off.° If you have this about you   escaped
(As I will give you when we go), you may
Boldly assault the necromancer's hall;
650 Where if he be, with dauntless hardihood
And brandished blade rush on him, break his glass,
And shed the luscious liquor on the ground,
But seize his wand. Though he and his
        cursed crew
Fierce sign of battle make, and menace high,
655 Or like the sons of Vulcan vomit smoke,[9]
Yet will they soon retire, if he but shrink.
ELDER BROTHER. Thyrsis, lead on apace, I'll
        follow thee,
And some good angel bear a shield before us.

> *The scene changes to a stately palace, set out with all manner
> of deliciousness: soft music, tables spread with all dainties.
> Comus appears with his rabble, and the Lady set in an
> enchanted chair, to whom he offers his glass, which she puts
> by[1] and goes about to rise.*

COMUS. Nay, lady, sit; if I but wave this wand,
660 Your nerves are all chained up in alabaster,
And you a statue, or as Daphne[2] was,
Root-bound, that fled Apollo.
LADY.   Fool, do not boast;
Thou canst not touch the freedom of my mind
With all thy charms, although this corporal rind
665 Thou hast immanacled, while Heav'n sees good.
COMUS. Why are you vexed, lady? why do you frown?
Here dwell no frowns, nor anger; from these gates
Sorrow flies far. See, here be all the pleasures

---

8. Traps. Twigs smeared with a sticky substance to catch birds (lit.).
9. Cacus, a son of Vulcan (the god of fire), "vomited smoke" when fighting Hercules (*Aen.*) 8.252–53).
1. Refuses.
2. A virgin nymph pursued by Apollo. She escaped by being transformed into a laurel (*Met.*, 1.547–52).

That fancy can beget on youthful thoughts
670 When the fresh blood grows lively, and returns
Brisk as the April buds in primrose season.
And first behold this cordial julep here
That flames and dances in his crystal bounds,
With spirits of balm and fragrant syrups mixed.
675 Not that nepenthes[3] which the wife of Thone
In Egypt gave to Jove-born Helena
Is of such power to stir up joy as this,
To life so friendly, or so cool to thirst.
Why should you be so cruel to yourself,
680 And to those dainty limbs which Nature lent
For gentle usage and soft delicacy?
But you invert the cov'nants of her trust,
And harshly deal like an ill borrower
With that which you received on other terms,
685 Scorning the unexempt condition
By which all mortal frailty must subsist,
Refreshment after toil, ease after pain,
That have been tired all day without repast,
And timely rest have wanted; but, fair virgin,
This will restore all soon.
690 LADY.   'Twill not, false traitor,
'Twill not restore the truth and honesty
That thou hast banished from thy tongue
    with lies.
Was this the cottage and the safe abode
Thou told'st me of? What grim aspécts° are   *faces and looks*
    these,
695 These ugly-headed monsters? Mercy guard me!
Hence with thy brewed enchantments, foul
    deceiver;
Hast thou betrayed my credulous innocence
With vizored falsehood and base forgery,
And wouldst thou seek again to trap me here
700 With lickerish° baits fit to ensnare a brute?   *pleasant-tasting,*
Were it a draught for Juno when she banquets,   *lustful*
I would not taste thy treasonous offer; none
But such as are good men can give good things,
And that which is not good is not delicious
705 To a well-governed and wise appetite.

3. A drug that banishes sorrow from the mind. Polydamna, wife of Thone, gave it to Helen of Troy, daughter of Zeus, who was visiting in Egypt; Helen in turn put it in Menelaus's drink (*Od.*, 4.219–32).

COMUS. O foolishness of men! that lend their ears
   To those budge doctors of the Stoic fur,
   And fetch their precepts from the Cynic tub,[4]
   Praising the lean and sallow Abstinence.
710   Wherefore did Nature pour her bounties forth
   With such a full and unwithdrawing hand,
   Covering the earth with odors, fruits, and flocks,
   Thronging the seas with spawn innumerable,
   But all to please and sate the curious° taste?   *fastidious*
715   And set to work millions of spinning worms
   That in their green shops weave the
      smooth-haired silk
   To deck her sons; and that no corner might
   Be vacant of her plenty, in her own loins
   She hutched° th' all-worshiped ore and   *stored in a coffer*
      precious gems
720   To store her children with. If all the world
   Should in a pet° of temperance feed on   *fit*
      pulse,°   *legume seeds*
   Drink the clear stream, and nothing wear
      but frieze,°   *rough wool*
   Th' All-giver would be unthanked, would be
      unpraised,
   Not half his riches known, and yet despised,
725   And we should serve him as a grudging master,
   As a penurious niggard of his wealth,
   And live like Nature's bastards, not her sons,
   Who would be quite surcharged with her own weight,
   And strangled with her waste fertility;
730   Th' earth cumbered, and the winged air
      darked with plumes,
   The herds would over-multitude their lords,
   The sea o'erfraught would swell, and th'
      unsought diamonds
   Would so emblaze the forehead of the deep,[5]
   And so bestud with stars, that they below[6]
735   Would grow inured to light, and come at last

4. A school of philosophy that scorned luxury as a distraction from the goal of self-knowledge. Diogenes, the Cynic philosopher of Athens, was said to have lived in a tub. "Budge": stiff, formal; alludes to the lamb's wool used on academic robes. "Stoic": a school of philosophy that advocated renunciation of worldly things and regarded the body as the soul's prison.
5. Either the earth or the vault of hell. "Forehead": top of the deep, the earth's crust as seen from its center.
6. The inhabitants of the underworld, whose exposure to the brilliant light of subterranean diamonds would embolden them to invade the surface of the earth.

To gaze upon the sun with shameless brows.
List, lady, be not coy,° and be not cozened°   *shy / duped*
With that same vaunted name Virginity.
Beauty is Nature's coin,[7] must not be hoarded,

740   But must be current,° and the good thereof   *in circulation, as*
       Consists in mutual and partaken° bliss,   *currency / shared*
       Unsavory in th' enjoyment of itself.[8]
       If you let slip time, like a neglected rose
       It withers on the stalk with languished head.
745   Beauty is Nature's brag, and must be shown
       In courts, at feasts, and high solemnities
       Where most may wonder at the workmanship;
       It is for homely creatures to keep home,
       They had their name thence; coarse complexïons
750   And cheeks of sorry grain° will serve to ply°   *color / work at*
       The sampler, and to tease° the housewife's wool. *comb out for spinning*
       What need a vermeil°-tinctured lip for that,   *scarlet*
       Love-darting eyes, or tresses like the morn?
       There was another meaning in these gifts,
755   Think what, and be advised; you are but young yet.
       LADY. I had not thought to have unlocked my lips
       In this unhallowed air, but that this juggler
       Would think to charm my judgment, as mine eyes,
       Obtruding false rules pranked° in reason's   *dressed up*
          garb.
760   I hate when vice can bolt° her arguments,   *sift, refine*
       And virtue has no tongue to check her pride.[9]
       Impostor, do not charge most innocent Nature,
       As if she would her children should be riotous
       With her abundance; she, good cateress,
765   Means her provision only to the good,
       That live according to her sober laws
       And holy dictate of spare Temperance.
       If every just man that now pines with want
       Had but a moderate and beseeming° share   *befitting*
770   Of that which lewdly pampered luxury
       Now heaps upon some few with vast excess,
       Nature's full blessings would be well dispensed
       In unsuperfluous even proportïon,

---

7. Comus's libertine plea for sexual license alludes to the parable of the talents (Matt. 25:14–30).
8. Celebrating the virtue of bilateral orgasm ("mutual and partaken bliss"), he makes virginity sound like masturbation ("Unsavory in th' enjoyment of itself").
9. Lines 756–61 were possibly spoken as an aside.

And she no whit encumbered with her store;
775   And then the Giver would be better thanked,
His praise due paid, for swinish gluttony
Ne'er looks to Heav'n amidst his gorgeous feast,
But with besotted base ingratitude
Crams, and blasphemes his Feeder. Shall I
    go on?
780   Or have I said enough? To him that dares
Arm his profane tongue with contemptuous words
Against the sun-clad power of Chastity
Fain would I something say, yet to what end?
Thou hast nor ear nor soul to apprehend
785   The sublime notion and high mystery[1]
That must be uttered to unfold the sage
And secret doctrine of Virginity,
And thou art worthy that thou shouldst not know
More happiness than this thy present lot.
790   Enjoy your dear wit and gay rhetoric
That hath so well been taught her dazzling
    fence;°   *fencing skill*
Thou art not fit to hear thyself convinced.
Yet should I try, the uncontrollèd° worth   *uncontrollable*
Of this pure cause would kindle my rapt spirits
795   To such a flame of sacred vehemence
That dumb things would be moved to sympathize,
And the brute earth would lend her nerves,°   *sinews*
    and shake,
Till all thy magic structures reared so high
Were shattered into heaps on thy false head.
800 COMUS. She fables not. I feel that I do fear
Her words set off by some superior power;
And though not mortal, yet a cold shudd'ring dew
Dips me all o'er, as when the wrath of Jove
Speaks thunder and the chains of Erebus
805   To some of Saturn's crew.[2] I must dissemble,
And try her yet more strongly. Come, no more,
This is mere moral babble, and direct
Against the canon laws[3] of our foundation;

1. A religious truth known only from divine revelation. See the excerpt from *Apology for Smectymnuus* (page 227), where Milton writes of "those chaste and high mysteries . . . that the body is for the Lord and the Lord for the body."
2. The rebel titans imprisoned in the underworld. Jove, son of Saturn, has a voice of thunder and pronounces a sentence of chains to the crew. Erebus—primeval darkness, son of Chaos, and husband and brother of Night—stands here for the underworld.
3. See Comus as priest in lines 93–144.

I must not suffer° this, yet 'tis but the lees°   *tolerate / dregs*
810 And settlings of a melancholy blood;
But this will cure all straight, one sip of this
Will bathe the drooping spirits in delight
Beyond the bliss of dreams. Be wise, and taste.—

> *The Brothers rush in with swords drawn, wrest his glass out of
> his hand, and break it against the ground. His rout⁴ make
> signs of resistance, but all are driven in. The Attendant Spirit
> comes in.*

SPIRIT. What, have you let the false enchanter scape?
815 O ye mistook, ye should have snatched his wand
And bound him fast; without his rod reversed,
And backward mutters of dissevering power,⁵
We cannot free the lady that sits here
In stony fetters fixed and motionless;
820 Yet stay, be not disturbed, now I bethink me,
Some other means I have which may be used,
Which once of Meliboeus⁶ old I learnt,
The soothest° shepherd that e'er piped on   *most truthful*
plains.
There is a gentle nymph not far from hence,
825 That with smooth curb sways° the smooth   *controls*
Severn stream,
Sabrina⁷ is her name, a virgin pure;
Whilom° she was the daughter of Locrine,   *Formerly*
That had the scepter from his father Brute.⁸
She, guiltless damsel, flying the mad pursuit
830 Of her enragèd stepdame Guendolen,
Commended° her fair innocence to the flood   *Entrusted*
That stayed° her flight with his cross-flowing   *hindered*
course;
The water-nymphs that in the bottom played
Held up their pearlèd wrists and took her in,
835 Bearing her straight to agèd Nereus'⁹ hall,

---

4. Disorderly crowd.
5. If the "rod" signifies persuasions of pleasure, its reversal signifies discipline. And, as a
verbal parallel to the reversal, Comus's spells can be undone by reciting them
backward.
6. Probably Edmund Spenser.
7. Milton adapts the story of Sabrina—a legend of the Severn River—from Spenser's
Faerie Queene 2.10.14–19. The daughter of King Locrine and his beloved mistress,
Estrildis, Sabrina is drowned at the command of Locrine's queen, Gwendolen, who
had defeated and killed her husband in battle. Milton's innocent Sabrina throws herself into the river and becomes a nymph. As an agent of supernatural assistance, she
may represent divine grace.
8. Brutus, great-grandson of Aeneas and legendary founder of Britain.
9. A benign sea god.

Who, piteous of her woes, reared her lank°   *drooping, languid*
    head
And gave her to his daughters[1] to imbathe
In nectared lavers° strewed with asphodel,°   *basins / the*
                                                 immortal flower
And through the porch and inlet of each
    sense
840 Dropped in ambrosial° oils, till she revived   *heavenly (thus*
And underwent a quick immortal change,   *restorative)*
Made goddess of the river. Still she retains
Her maiden gentleness, and oft at eve
Visits the herds along the twilight meadows,
845 Helping all urchin blasts[2] and ill-luck signs
That the shrewd meddling elf° delights to   *mischievous sprite*
    make,
Which she with precious vialed liquors heals;
For which the shepherds at their festivals
Carol her goodness loud in rustic lays,
850 And throw sweet garland wreaths into her stream
Of pansies, pinks, and gaudy daffodils.
And, as the old swain[3] said, she can unlock
The clasping charm and thaw the numbing spell,
If she be right invoked in warbled song;
855 For maidenhood she loves, and will be swift
To aid a virgin such as was herself
In hard-besetting need. This will I try
And add the power of some adjuring° verse.   *entreating*

SONG

Sabrina fair,
860   *Listen where thou art sitting*
Under the glassy, cool, translucent wave,
    In twisted braids of lilies knitting
The loose train of thy amber-dropping° hair;   *perfumed with*
    Listen for dear honor's sake,   *ambergris*
865   *Goddess of the silver lake,*
        Listen and save.

Listen and appear to us
In the name of great Oceanus,[4]
By th' earth-shaking Neptune's mace,

---

1. The Nereids.
2. Infections caused by evil spirits
3. Meliboeus.
4. Father of earth's rivers.

870 And Tethys'[5] grave majestic pace,
    By hoary Nereus' wrinkled look,
    And the Carpathian wizard's hook,[6]
    By scaly Triton's winding shell,[7]
    And old sooth-saying Glaucus'[8] spell,
875 By Leucothea's[9] lovely hands,
    And her son that rules the strands,
    By Thetis'[1] tinsel-slippered feet,
    And the songs of Sirens sweet,
    By dead Parthenope's dear tomb,
880 And fair Ligea's[2] golden comb,
    Wherewith she sits on diamond rocks
    Sleeking her soft alluring locks;
    By all the nymphs that nightly dance
    Upon thy streams with wily° glance,   *amorous, playful*
885 Rise, rise, and heave thy rosy head   *(not pejorative)*
    From thy coral-paven bed,
    And bridle° in thy headlong wave,   *curb, check, restrain*
    Till thou our summons answered have.
       Listen and save.

      Sabrina rises, attended by water-nymphs, and sings.

890   *By the rushy-fringèd bank,*
Where grows the willow and the osier dank,
     My sliding chariot stays,
Thick set with agate and the azurn sheen
Of turkis° blue, and emerald green,   *turquoise*
895   *That in the channel strays,*
Whilst from off the waters fleet
Thus I set my printless feet
O'er the cowslip's velvet head,
    That bends not as I tread.
900 *Gentle swain, at thy request*
    I am here.

SPIRIT. Goddess dear,

---

5. Wife of Oceanus
6. Staff of Proteus, the old man of the sea, prophet and shape-shifter, shepherd of Poseidon's seals.
7. Triton, Neptune's herald, blows through a huge conch shell. "Winding": (1) played like a trumpet, (2) twisting.
8. A fisherman who ate a magical herb and became a sea god and a prophet.
9. Gr. white goddess (lit.). The name of Ino when she became a sea goddess. She was mother of Melicertes (Palaemon), god of harbors.
1. A Nereid, Achilles' mother.
2. "The Attendant Spirit has so far invoked benign marine deities. Now he calls on the singers [Parthenope and Ligea] who accompany Circe and lure men to destruction" (Leonard).

We implore thy powerful hand
To undo the charmèd band°   *magic bond*
905   Of true virgin here distressed,
Through the force and through the wile
Of unblest enchanter vile.
SABRINA. Shepherd, 'tis my office best
To help ensnarèd chastity.
910   Brightest lady, look on me;
Thus I sprinkle on thy breast
Drops that from my fountain pure
I have kept of precious cure,
Thrice upon thy finger's tip,
915   Thrice upon thy rubied lip;
Next this marble venomed seat,
Smeared with gums of glutinous[3] heat,
I touch with chaste palms moist and cold.
Now the spell hath lost his hold;
920   And I must haste ere morning hour
To wait in Amphitrite's[4] bow'r.

    Sabrina descends, and the Lady rises out of her seat.

SPIRIT. Virgin, daughter of Locrine,
Sprung of old Anchises'[5] line,
May thy brimmèd waves for this
925   Their full tribute never miss
From a thousand petty rills,
That tumble down the snowy hills;
Summer drought or singèd air
Never scorch thy tresses fair,
930   Nor wet October's torrent flood
Thy molten crystal fill with mud;
May thy billows roll ashore
The beryl and the golden ore;
May thy lofty head° be crowned   *source of a river*
935   With many a tower and terrace round,
And here and there thy banks upon
With groves of myrrh and cinnamon.
    Come, lady, while Heaven lends us grace,
Let us fly this cursèd place,
940   Lest the sorcerer us entice
With some other new device.°   *trick*

---

3. Sticky, gluey. It may also suggest a pun on *gluteus* (buttock), implying sexual undercurrents in the phrase: "that was a dirty seat, if ever there was one" (E. Le Comte).
4. Wife of Neptune.
5. Father of Aeneas, ancestor of Brutus, Locrine, and Sabrina (see line 828).

Not a waste or needless sound
Till we come to holier ground;
I shall be your faithful guide
945 Through this gloomy covert wide,
And not many furlongs thence
Is your father's residence,
Where this night are met in state
Many a friend to gratulate
950 His wished presence, and beside
All the swains that there abide,
With jigs and rural dance resort;
We shall catch them at their sport,
And our sudden coming there
955 Will double all their mirth and cheer.
Come, let us haste, the stars grow high,
But Night sits monarch yet in the mid sky.

The scene changes, presenting Ludlow Town and the President's Castle; then come in country dancers, after them the Attendant Spirit, with the two Brothers and the Lady.

SONG

SPIRIT. *Back, shepherds, back, enough your play*
Till next sunshine holiday;
960 *Here be without duck° or nod°*   curtsy / bow
Other trippings to be trod
Of lighter toes, and such court guise
As Mercury did first devise
With the mincing Dryades°   wood nymphs dancing elegantly /
965 *On the lawn° and on the leas.°*   glades / meadows

This second song presents them to their father and mother.

Noble Lord, and Lady bright,
I have brought ye new delight;
Here behold so goodly grown
Three fair branches of your own;
970 *Heav'n hath timely° tried their youth,*   early
Their faith, their patience, and their truth,
And sent them here through long assays
With a crown of deathless praise,
To triumph in victorious dance
975 *O'er sensual folly and intemperance.*

The dances ended, the Spirit epiloguizes.

SPIRIT. To the ocean now I fly,
And those happy climes that lie

Where day never shuts his eye,
Up in the broad fields of the sky.
980 There I suck the liquid° air   *clear, bright*
All amidst the gardens fair
Of Hesperus, and his daughters three
That sing about the golden tree.
Along the crispèd shades° and bow'rs   *trees with curled leaves*
985 Revels the spruce° and jocund Spring;   *lively, elegant*
The Graces, and the rosy-bosomed Hours[6]
Thither all their bounties bring,
That there eternal summer dwells,
And west winds with musky wing
990 About the cedarn° alleys fling   *composed of cedars*
Nard and cassia's balmy smells.
Iris[7] there with humid bow
Waters the odorous banks that blow
Flowers of more mingled hue
995 Than her purfled° scarf can shew,   *multicolored*
And drenches with Elysian[8] dew
(List, mortals, if your ears be true)
Beds of hyacinth and roses,
Where young Adonis[9] oft reposes,
1000 Waxing well of his deep wound
In slumber soft, and on the ground
Sadly sits th' Assyrian queen;
But far above in spangled sheen
Celestial Cupid, her fair son advanced,
1005 Holds his dear Psyche[1] sweet entranced
After her wand'ring labors long,
Till free consent the gods among
Make her his eternal bride,

6. Three daughters of Zeus and Themis, goddesses of the seasons, especially the spring.
The Graces were three daughters of Zeus—Euphrosyne, Aglaia, and Thalia—who
were said to represent beauty, charm, and joy. They attended Venus and presided over
the joys of domestic life.
7. The rainbow.
8. The Elysian fields, the final resting place of the heroic and the virtuous, are associated
with the Christian heaven.
9. An archetypal life–death–rebirth deity in Greek mythology and a central cult figure in
various mystery religons. A hunter loved by Venus ("th' Assyrian queen" in line 1002),
Adonis died at the tusks of a boar but was restored to life in the garden of Adonis. In
this allegory, the love of Venus and Adonis seems to symbolize the perpetual cycle of
physical generation within the order of nature.
1. Apuleius, in *The Golden Ass* 4.28–6.24, tells how Cupid accidentally pricked himself
with his own golden arrow and fell in love with the beautiful mortal Psyche, whom he
visited in darkness. When Psyche, by the light of a lamp, discovered that her sleeping
lover was not a monster as she had been told but the god of love himself, a drop of oil
fell from the lamp and woke Cupid, who fled from her. She endured many trials until
Jove allowed her to marry Cupid.

And from her fair unspotted side
1010   Two blissful twins are to be born,
Youth and Joy;[2] so Jove hath sworn.
    But now my task is smoothly done,
I can fly, or I can run
Quickly to the green earth's end,
1015   Where the bowed welkin° slow doth bend,   *vaulted sky*
And from thence can soar as soon
To the corners° of the moon.   *horns*
    Mortals that would follow me,
Love virtue, she alone is free;[3]
1020   She can teach ye how to climb
Higher than the sphery chime;[4]
Or if Virtue feeble were,
Heav'n itself would stoop to her.

LYCIDAS In *TMS*, Milton dates *Lycidas* November 1637, a month before his twenty-ninth birthday, when he was engaged in private study at Horton. The occasion was the drowning three months earlier of a former Cambridge schoolmate, Edward King, in a shipwreck on the Irish Seas, as he sailed from Chester bound for home in Dublin at the start of a vacation from Cambridge. King was preparing for a career in the Anglican clergy, and it is said that after the ship struck a rock and others tried to save their lives, he remained kneeling on the deck in prayer. Milton accepted an invitation to contribute to a two-part memorial volume, the first part containing elegies in Latin and Greek, and the second, *Obsequies to the memory of Mr. Edward King,* with thirteen poems in English, of which *Lycidas* was the last. The Latin motto of the volume, from Petronius, translates as, "If you reckon rightly, shipwreck is everywhere."

The poem is a pastoral elegy, in which both the speaker and Lycidas are shepherds who were nurtured "upon the self-same hill" and fed "the same flock." The tradition goes back to ancient Greek and Latin poetry, with Virgil's fifth Eclogue as its great model. Dr. Johnson famously censured the poem: "Where there is leisure for fiction there is little grief." Among the reasons for his complaint are the artificiality and impersonality of the genre (Cambridge students aren't shepherds) and the mingling of pagan and Christian allusions. But for some readers, and certainly for many or even most of those who love Milton's poetry, *Lycidas* is one of the greatest short poems in the English language. And those among the sympathetic readers who have experienced loss through death of someone they loved understand well the depth of feeling in this poem.

There are many excellent essays on *Lycidas,* including those in two anthologies, Scott Elledge's *Milton's "Lycidas": Edited to Serve as an*

---

2. See Milton's *An Apology,* p. 229, for the Platonic allegory of knowledge and virtue as the "happy twins" produced by the union of divine love (Cupid) and the soul (Psyche).
3. "Comus, who claimed to be free, is a slave to sensuality" (Bush).
4. The music of the spheres. Above the spheres is heaven.

Introduction to Criticism (Harper & Row, 1966), and C. A. Patrides'
Milton's Lycidas: The Tradition and the Poem, 2nd edition (University
of Missouri Press, 1983).

Lycidas

*In this monody[1] the author bewails a learned friend,
unfortunately drowned in his passage from Chester
on the Irish Seas, 1637. And by occasion foretells the
ruin of our corrupted clergy, then in their height.*

Yet once more, O ye laurels, and once more
Ye myrtles brown, with ivy never sere,[2]
I come to pluck your berries harsh and crude,°   *unripe*
And with forced fingers rude°   *unskilled*
5 Shatter your leaves before the mellowing year.
Bitter constraint, and sad occasion dear,[3]
Compels me to disturb your season due;
For Lycidas is dead, dead ere his prime,[4]
Young Lycidas, and hath not left his peer.
10 Who would not sing for Lycidas? He knew
Himself[5] to sing, and build the lofty rhyme.
He must not float upon his wat'ry bier
Unwept, and welter° to the parching wind,   *be tossed about*
Without the meed° of some melodious tear.°   *reward / elegy*
15   Begin then, sisters of the sacred well[6]
That from beneath the seat of Jove doth spring,
Begin, and somewhat loudly sweep the string.
Hence° with denial vain and coy excuse;   *Take away*
So may some gentle Muse[7]
20 With lucky words favor my destined urn,
And as he passes turn,

1. "A poem in which a mourner bewails a person's death; an elegy" (OED). In 1638, when
   Lycidas first appeared, in a volume of memorial verses by Edward King's Cambridge
   acquaintances, there was no headnote. Milton added it in 1645, when Anglican censorship had fallen. It identifies the poet as a prophet in the passage denouncing the clergy
   (lines 113–31).
2. Evergreens ("never sere") associated, respectively, with Apollo (poetry), Venus (love),
   and Bacchus (frenzy, immortality, poetry, learning) and with crowns of honor, especially poetical honor.
3. Precious, also dire. Ps. 116:15: "Precious in the sight of the Lord is the death of his saints."
4. King was twenty-five years old when he drowned.
5. He himself knew how. King had written Latin poems of compliment, chiefly on members of the royal family.
6. The nine Muses, daughters of Zeus and Mnemosyne (memory), inspiring goddesses of
   poetry, arts, and sciences, called from the fountain Aganippe ("sacred well") on Mount
   Helicon. Here, a source of poetic power.
7. Here, some kindly poet.

And bid fair peace be to my sable shroud.
For we were nursed upon the self-same hill,
Fed the same flock, by fountain, shade, and rill.
25   Together both, ere the high lawns° appeared   *open spaces between*
Under the opening eyelids of the morn,   *woods*
We drove afield, and both together heard
What time° the gray-fly winds° her sultry horn,   *when / blows*
Batt'ning° our flocks with the fresh dews of   *Feeding, Fattening*
        night,
30 Oft till the star[8] that rose, at evening, bright
Toward heav'n's descent had sloped his
        westering wheel.
Meanwhile the rural ditties were not mute,
Tempered to th' oaten flute;[9]
Rough satyrs danced, and fauns[1] with clov'n heel
35 From the glad sound would not be absent long,
And old Damoetas[2] loved to hear our song.
    But O the heavy change, now thou art gone,
Now thou art gone, and never must return!
Thee, shepherd, thee the woods and desert caves,
40 With wild thyme and the gadding° vine o'ergrown,   *wandering*
And all their echoes mourn.
The willows and the hazel copses° green   *thickets of trees*
Shall now no more be seen
Fanning their joyous leaves to thy soft lays.
45 As killing as the canker° to the rose,   *cankerworm*
Or taint-worm[3] to the weanling herds that graze,
Or frost to flowers, that their gay wardrobe wear,
When first the white-thorn blows;°   *hawthorn blooms*
Such, Lycidas, thy loss to shepherd's ear.
50   Where were ye, nymphs, when the remorseless deep
Closed o'er the head of your loved Lycidas?
For neither were ye playing on the steep
Where your old bards, the famous Druids,[4] lie,
Nor on the shaggy top of Mona[5] high,

---

8. The evening star (Hesperus).
9. A musical pipe made of a straw or the stem of an oat.
1. Goat-legged woodland creatures. In regard to satyrs as attendants of Bacchus: "Notoriously boisterous and lecherous, they might be Cambridge undergraduates" (Leonard).
2. A conventional pastoral name; perhaps for some Cambridge don. Joseph Mead has
   been proposed, as closest in sound.
3. Intestinal parasite fatal only to newly weaned calves when they start grazing.
4. Priestly poet-kings of Celtic Britain; nature worshipers, buried on the mountain
   ("steep") of Bardsey Island ("bards"), which is off the tip of the Llŷn peninsula in
   northwest Wales. Milton, relying on contemporary authorities, believed mistakenly
   that it lay near King's tragic route.
5. Mona Insula (Isle of Anglesey, Wales) was the last outpost of the Druids.

55 Nor yet where Deva spreads her wizard stream.[6]
    Ay me! I fondly° dream—   *foolishly*
    Had ye been there—for what could that have done?
    What could the Muse herself that Orpheus[7] bore,
    The Muse herself, for her enchanting son
60 Whom universal nature did lament,
    When by the rout that made the hideous roar
    His gory visage down the stream was sent,
    Down the swift Hebrus to the Lesbian shore?
      Alas! What boots° it with uncessant care   *profits, avails*
65 To tend the homely slighted shepherd's trade,
    And strictly meditate the thankless Muse?[8]
    Were it not better done as others use,
    To sport with Amaryllis in the shade,
    Or with the tangles of Neaera's hair?[9]
70 Fame is the spur that the clear spirit[1] doth raise
    (That last infirmity of noble mind)
    To scorn delights, and live laborious days;
    But the fair guerdon° when we hope to find,   *reward*
    And think to burst out into sudden blaze,
75 Comes the blind Fury[2] with th' abhorrèd shears,
    And slits the thin-spun life. "But not the praise,"
    Phoebus[3] replied, and touched my trembling ears:[4]
    "Fame is no plant that grows on mortal soil,
    Nor in the glistering foil[5]
80 Set off to th' world, nor in broad rumor lies,
    But lives and spreads aloft by those pure eyes
    And perfect witness of all-judging Jove;
    As he pronounces lastly on each deed,
    Of so much fame in heav'n expect thy meed."°   *reward*

---

6. Changes of flow in the magic ("wizard") river Dee ("Deva") in Cheshire were considered good or bad omens for England and Wales.
7. The archetypal poet, son of Calliope, muse of epic poetry. His music charmed beasts, rivers, and trees. He was torn to pieces by Thracian Bacchantes (female followers of Bacchus) on the banks of the river Hebrus, which carried his head—still singing—to the island of Lesbos.
8. Study to write poetry.
9. Conventional ancient pastoral names, but also suggestive of less demanding and more popular contemporary erotic poetry.
1. Object of "doth raise."
2. Atropos, the Fate who cuts the thread of life. Here, described as a Fury, perhaps because of her ferocity, and as blind, because she chooses indiscriminately.
3. Apollo, god of poetic inspiration, who plucked Virgil's ears in *Eclogue* 6.3–4, warning him against impatient ambition.
4. "Shears" and "ears" might have reminded original readers of Bastwick, Prynne, and Burton, whose ears were cropped on Tower Hill, June 30, 1637, victims of the Laudian Church's persecution.
5. The bright setting (gold or silver leaf) of a jewel, to increase its brilliancy.

85   O fountain Arethuse,[6] and thou honored flood,
        Smooth-sliding Mincius,[7] crowned with vocal reeds,
        That strain I heard was of a higher mood.[8]
        But now my oat° proceeds,   *pastoral flute*
        And listens to the herald[9] of the sea
90   That came in Neptune's plea.
        He asked the waves, and asked the felon° winds,   *savage, wild*
        What hard mishap hath doomed this gentle swain?
        And questioned every gust of rugged° wings   *stormy*
        That blows from off each beakèd promontory;
95   They knew not of his story,
        And sage Hippotades[1] their answer brings,
        That not a blast was from his dungeon strayed;
        The air was calm, and on the level brine
        Sleek Panope[2] with all her sisters played.
100   It was that fatal and perfidious bark,
        Built in th' eclipse,[3] and rigged with curses dark,
        That sunk so low that sacred head of thine.
            Next Camus,[4] reverend sire, went footing slow,
        His mantle hairy, and his bonnet sedge,°   *formed of reeds*
105   Inwrought° with figures dim, and on the edge   *inscribed or*
        Like to that sanguine flower inscribed with   *embroidered*
            woe.[5]
        "Ah! who hath reft," quoth he, "my dearest pledge?"[6]
        Last came, and last did go,
        The pilot[7] of the Galilean lake;
110   Two massy keys he bore of metals twain
        (The golden opes, the iron shuts amain).°   *with full force*
        He shook his mitred locks, and stern bespake:
        "How well could I have spared for° thee,   *instead of*
            young swain,
        Enow° of such as for their bellies' sake   *Enough*

6. A fountain in Sicily, associated with Theocritus and with Greek pastoral poetry.
7. A river in Mantua, Virgil's birthplace, representing Latin pastoral.
8. The poet's invocation signals a return to the pastoral mode after the "higher mood" of
   Phoebus' speech.
9. Triton (see *Masque*, 873), who comes to gather evidence about the accident for Neptune's court.
1. Guardian of the winds, which he kept in a cave.
2. The chief Nereid, or sea nymph.
3. Ill-omened.
4. God of the river Cam, representing Cambridge University.
5. The hyacinth, supposedly inscribed "AI AI" with the blood of Hyacinthus, beloved of
   Apollo and accidentally killed by him.
6. "A child, esp. one considered as a token or evidence of mutual love and duty between
   parents" (OED). For pledges (*pignora*) as children, see Milton's Elegy 4.42.
7. St. Peter, a fisherman on the sea of Galilee when Christ called him (Luke 5:3–11);
   traditionally, the first bishop ("mitred locks," line 112), to whom were given the keys of
   heaven (Matt. 16:19).

115 Creep and intrude and climb[8] into the fold!
Of other care they little reck'ning make
Than how to scramble at the shearers' feast,
And shove away the worthy bidden guest.[9]
Blind mouths![1] that scarce themselves know
        how to hold
120 A sheep-hook, or have learned aught else the least
That to the faithful herdman's art belongs!
What recks it them? What need they? They
        are sped;[2]
And when they list,° their lean° and flashy   *choose (to play) /*
        songs   *meager*
Grate on their scrannel° pipes of wretched straw.   *harsh, unmelodious*
125 The hungry sheep look up, and are not fed,
But swoll'n with wind, and the rank mist they
        draw,°   *inhale*
Rot inwardly, and foul contagion spread;
Besides what the grim wolf[3] with privy° paw   *hidden, secret*
Daily devours apace, and nothing said.
130 But that two-handed engine[4] at the door
Stands ready to smite once, and smite no more.
        Return, Alphéus,[5] the dread voice is past
That shrunk thy streams; return, Sicilian Muse,
And call the vales, and bid them hither cast
135 Their bells° and flowrets of a thousand hues.   *bell-shaped flowers*
Ye valleys low where the mild whispers use°   *go frequently*
Of shades and wanton winds and gushing brooks,
On whose fresh lap the swart° star[6] sparely°   *blackened / seldom*
        looks,

8. John 10:1: "He that entereth not by the door into the sheepfold, but climbeth up some other way, the same is a thief and a robber."
9. The parable of the marriage feast (Matt. 22:1–14): "The wedding is ready, but they which were bidden were not worthy" (8).
1. Ruskin plays on the etymologies of *Episcopus*, "overseer," from Gr. σκοπός, "watcher," and *pastor*, "shepherd," from Lat. *pāscere*, "to feed." "A 'Bishop' means 'a person who sees.' A 'Pastor' means 'a person who feeds.' The most unbishoply character a man can have is therefore to be blind. The most unpastoral is, instead of feeding, to want to be fed—to be a Mouth" (*Sesames and Lilies*, 1.22).
2. What do they care? They are provided for.
3. A traditional term of abuse in anti-Catholic polemic.
4. The most notorious crux in Milton, apparently an instrument of God's justice. Suggestions include "the axe of God's reformation hewing at the old and hollow trunk of papacy" (*Of Reformation*, YP, 1.583) and the two-edged sword of Rev. 1:16, representing the word of God. See also Ps. 149:6, the "two-edged sword" in a context of executing judgment on kings and nobles.
5. Both a river and a river god. He pursues Arethusa (line 85), a nymph who bathed in his waters before her metamorphosis into a stream. The river meets up with the fountain Arethusa in Sicily, and both Alpheus and Arethusa stand for pastoral poetry, which receded during St. Peter's diatribe.
6. Sirius, the Dog Star, associated with the parched vegetation of late summer.

Throw hither all your quaint enameled eyes,
140 That on the green turf suck the honeyed showers,
And purple all the ground with vernal flowers.
Bring the rathe° primrose that forsaken dies,   *early*
The tufted crowtoe,° and pale jessamine,°   *wild hyacinth /*
    jasmine
The white pink, and the pansy freaked° with jet,   *flecked, streaked*
145 The glowing violet,
The musk-rose, and the well-attired woodbine,°   *honeysuckle*
With cowslips wan° that hang the pensive head,   *pale*
And every flower that sad embroidery wears.
Bid amaranthus[7] all his beauty shed,
150 And daffadillies fill their cups with tears,
To strew the laureate hearse where Lycid lies.
For so to interpose a little ease,
Let our frail thoughts dally with false surmise.
Ay me! Whilst thee the shores and sounding seas
155 Wash far away, where'er thy bones are hurled,
Whether beyond the stormy Hebrides,   *(1) filled with*
Where thou perhaps under the whelming tide   *monsters, (2)*
Visit'st the bottom of the monstrous° world;   *immense*
Or whether thou, to our moist vows° denied,   *tearful prayers*
160 Sleep'st by the fable of Bellerus[8] old,
Where the great Vision of the guarded mount
Looks toward Namancos and Bayona's hold;[9]
Look homeward, Angel, now, and melt with ruth;°   *pity*
And, O ye dolphins,[1] waft the hapless youth.
165   Weep no more, woeful shepherds, weep no more,
For Lycidas, your sorrow, is not dead,
Sunk though he be beneath the wat'ry floor;
So sinks the day-star° in the ocean bed,   *sun*
And yet anon repairs his drooping head,
170 And tricks° his beams, and with new-spangled ore   *adorns, trims*
Flames in the forehead of the morning sky:
So Lycidas sunk low, but mounted high,
Through the dear might of him[2] that walked
   the waves,

---

7. Gr., "unfading." An imaginary immortal flower (see *PL*, 3.353), here being asked to give over its exemption from mortality.
8. A giant invented to explain the origin of Bellerium, the Roman name of Land's End, Cornwall.
9. The archangel Michael was said to have appeared to fishermen on St. Michael's Mount, off the Cornish coast. He is asked to turn his gaze away from Roman Catholic Spain, represented by Nemancos and Bayona, a region and a fortress ("hold"), respectively.
1. Responsive to human beings, one carried to shore the drowned child Melicertes, who became the marine deity Palaemon. Another carried safely over water (i.e., wafted) the legendary poet Arion, who had jumped overboard to escape from murderous sailors.
2. Christ (Matt. 14:25–31).

Where, other groves and other streams[3] along,
175 With nectar pure his oozy° locks he laves,   *muddy, slimy*
And hears the unexpressive° nuptial song[4]   *inexpressible*
In the blest kingdoms meek of joy and love.
There entertain him all the saints above,
In solemn troops and sweet societies
180 That sing, and singing in their glory move,
And wipe the tears forever from his eyes.
Now, Lycidas, the shepherds weep no more;
Henceforth thou art the Genius° of the shore   *local guardian spirit*
In thy large recompense, and shalt be good
185 To all that wander in that perilous flood.
    Thus sang the uncouth swain° to th'oaks   *unskilled, unknown*
      and rills,   *shepherd*
While the still morn went out with sandals gray;
He touched the tender stops° of various quills,°   *finger holes /*
With eager thought warbling his Doric[5] lay.   *pipes*
190 And now the sun had stretched out all the hills,
And now was dropped into the western bay;
At last he rose, and twitched° his mantle blue: *pulled up*
Tomorrow to fresh woods, and pastures new.

On the New Forcers of Conscience under the Long Parliament[1]

Because you have thrown off your prelate lord,
And with stiff vows renounced his liturgy[2]

---

3. Rev. 22:1–2, on the "pure river of water of life" and the "tree of life, which bare twelve manner of fruits."
4. Sung by the faithful at the mystical "marriage of the Lamb" (Rev. 19:7–9). See the end of the excerpt from *An Apology for Smectymnuus* on p. 230.
5. The dialect of Theocritus, Moschus, and Bion; hence pastoral.
1. Dated 1646, when antagonists Edwards and Baillie were most active and when Milton believed that he had a chance to influence Parliament, which was about to draw up the rules of ordination by the Classical Presbyteries. In the early 1640s, Milton had ardently supported the Presbyterians in their fight against the Anglican clergy. Among the abuses he attacked were pluralities, the holding of two or more ministerial livings by one member of the clergy. Milton concludes *An Apology* (1642) by attacking the prelates, "who ingross many pluralities under a *non-resident* and slubbring [carelessly skimming] dispatch of soules" (*YP*, 1:952). Milton dedicated his *Doctrine and Discipline of Divorce* (1644) to Parliament and to the Westminster Assembly of Divines, which was appointed by the Long Parliament to reorganize the church. But by 1646, Milton could see that the Assembly (119 of its 149 members were divines, most of them Presbyterian) was guilty of the same abuses (pluralities, hierarchies) as the prelates that they replaced. Edwards, in *Gangraena* (1646), and Baillie, in *A Dissuasive* (November 1645), had attacked Milton and his views on divorce. The poem is a *sonetto caudato*, a sonnet with a tail, familiar to Milton from Italian verse. It has two half lines (tailed lines) and couplets after line 14.
2. The Assembly abolished Archbishop Laud's version of The Book of Common Prayer but adopted in its stead the Directory for Public Worship.

To seize the widowed whore Plurality
From them whose sin ye envied, not abhorred,
5   Dare ye for this adjure° the civil sword   *charge*
To force our consciences that Christ set free,
And ride us with a classic hierarchy[3]
Taught ye by mere A. S. and Rutherford?[4]
    Men whose life, learning, faith, and pure intent
10 Would have been held in high esteem with Paul
Must now be named and printed heretics
By shallow Edwards and Scotch
        What-d'ye-call:[5]
    But we do hope to find out all your tricks,
Your plots and packings° worse than those of   *fraudulent dealings*
        Trent,[6]
15 That so the Parliament
May with their wholesome and preventive shears
Clip your phylacteries, though balk your ears,[7]
    And succor our just fears
When they° shall read this clearly in your   *Parliament /*
        charge:°   *indictment*
20 "New *Presbyter* is but old *Priest* writ large."[8]

---

3. A *classis* in Presbyterian churches is "an inferior judicatory consisting of the elders or pastors of the parishes or churches of a district; a presbytery" (OED). Scotch Presbyterianism is organized by kirks, classes, and synods.
4. Samuel Rutherford was one of the Scots divines in the Assembly. Adam Stewart, a Scottish divine who signed his polemical treatises against the Independents with his initials.
5. Assumed by most editors to be Robert Baillie, the Scots commissioner on the Assembly, who also attacked Milton. Thomas Edwards was notorious as the author of *Gangraena*, which attacked various heresies, including those he found in Milton's divorce pamphlets.
6. The Council of Trent (1545–63) was convened to combat Protestantism. In the *Areopagitica*, Milton argues that it was the main inventor of censorship.
7. *TMS* originally had "Crop ye as close as marginal P—'s ears," alluding to the Presbyterian William Prynne, whose ears were first clipped and then removed in two separate punishments, one for supposedly defaming the queen, the other for attacking episcopacy. "Phylacteries": or tefillin, leather boxes containing texts from the Hebrew Bible, worn by Jews during weekday morning prayer but symbolizing pious ostentation and hypocrisy in the New Testament (Matt. 23:5). Parliament will spare or omit ("balk") clipping the ears of the hypocritical Presbyterians.
8. This famous line is an etymological play on words since the word *priest* derives from the post-classical Latin *presbyter* (elder).

A Paraphrase of Psalm 6[1]

Lord, in thine anger do not reprehend me,
Nor in thy hot displeasure me correct;
Pity me, Lord, for I am much deject,
Am very weak and faint; heal and amend me,
5 For all my bones, that even with anguish ache,
Are troubled, yea my soul is troubled sore.
And thou, O Lord, how long? turn, Lord, restore
My soul, O save me for thy goodness' sake,
For in death no remembrance is of thee;
10 Who in the grave can celebrate thy praise?
Wearied I am with sighing out my days,
Nightly my couch I make a kind of sea;
My bed I water with my tears; mine eye
Through grief consumes, is waxen old and dark
15 I' th' midst of all mine enemies that mark.
Depart all ye that work iniquity.
Depart from me, for the voice of my weeping
The Lord hath heard; the Lord hath heard my prayer;
My supplication with acceptance fair
20 The Lord will own, and have me in his keeping.
Mine enemies shall all be blank and dashed
With much confusion; then grow red with shame;
They shall return in haste the way they came
And in a moment shall be quite abashed.

1. Dated August 13, 1653, the month Milton paraphrased Psalms 1–8, a year and a half after he went totally blind. In his paraphrases of Ps. 80–88 (April 1648), he adds marginal transliterations and translations of the Hebrew words that he paraphrases, indicating that the rest "are the very words of the text, translated from the original." No such marginal additions accompany his paraphrases of Psalms 1–8. One imagines that they provided the poet with an opportunity for consolation as well as expression. In verse 7 (lines 13–15), alluding to his blindness, he adds "dark," which is missing from the KJV translation (see p. 458), although the Heb. *atqah*, translated as "waxeth old," can also mean "removed" or even more violently, "torn out."

The English Sonnets

Sonnet I

O nightingale, that on yon bloomy spray
    Warbl'st at eve when all the woods are still,
    Thou with fresh hope the lover's heart dost fill
    While the jolly Hours[1] lead on propitious May;
5 Thy liquid notes that close the eye of day,
    First heard before the shallow° cuckoo's bill,[2]   *thin, harsh*
    Portend success in love; O if Jove's will
    Have linked that amorous power to thy soft lay,°   *song*
Now timely sing, ere the rude bird of hate
10   Foretell my hopeless doom in some grove nigh:
    As thou from year to year hast sung too late
For my relief, yet hadst no reason why:
    Whether the Muse or Love call thee his mate,
    Both them I serve, and of their train am I.

Sonnet VII[1]

How soon hath Time, the subtle thief of youth,
    Stolen on his wing my three and twentieth year!
    My hasting days fly on with full career,°   *full speed*
    But my late spring no bud or blossom shew'th.
5 Perhaps my semblance° might deceived the truth,   *appearance*
    That I to manhood am arrived so near,
    And inward ripeness doth much less appear,
    That some more timely-happy spirits endu'th.°   *endows*

---

1. L. *Horae*, goddesses of the seasons, whose dance determined the course of the year.
2. The sound of the cuckoo ("the rude bird of hate," line 9), associated with cuckoldry, was a bad omen, while the song of the nightingale was a good one.
1. See Stephen Booth's extraordinarily close reading of this sonnet on p. 472. His insights on the relevance of the gospel parables of the talents and the workers in the vineyard can also be applied to Sonnet XIX. These two sonnets about a failure of achievement, one written at age twenty-three (or, as most editors agree, at twenty-four, since Milton liked to date his work in a way that would make him seem younger) and the other at age forty-four, can be profitably compared.

Yet be it° less or more, or soon or slow, — *inward ripeness*
10   It shall be still in strictest measure ev'n
    To° that same lot, however mean or high, — *Level with*
Toward which Time leads me, and the will of Heav'n;
    All is, if I have grace to use it so,
    As ever in my great Task-Master's eye.[2]

Sonnet VIII[1]

Captain or colonel,[2] or knight in arms,
   Whose chance on these defenseless doors may seize,
   If deed of honor did thee ever please,
   Guard them, and him within protect from harms;
5 He can requite thee, for he knows the charms
   That call fame on such gentle acts as these,
   And he can spread thy name o'er lands and seas,
   Whatever clime the sun's bright circle warms.
Lift not thy spear against the Muses' bow'r:
10   The great Emathian conqueror[3] bid spare
   The house of Pindarus, when temple and tow'r
Went to the ground; and the repeated air° — *recited chorus*
   Of sad Electra's poet[4] had the power
   To save th'Athenian walls from ruin bare.

Sonnet IX[1]

Lady that in the prime° of earliest youth — *springtime*
   Wisely hast shunned the broad way and the green,
   And with those few art eminently seen

2. One reading of the difficult last two lines (*Var.* 372): "All <that matters> is: whether I have grace to use it so, as ever <conscious of being> in my great Taskmaster's <enjoining> eye." Booth has much to say about these lines.
1. Composed in November 1642, three months after the outbreak of the civil war, when the citizens of London feared an assault from Charles's army. In the *TMS*, the sonnet is in the hand of an amanuensis, who titled it "On his door when the City expected an assault." Milton crossed out that title, substituting in his own hand "When the assault was intended to the City."
2. Trisyllabic; pronounced *cor-o-nel*.
3. Alexander the Great, who during the sack of Thebes spared the house where the poet Pindar had lived. Emathia is a district of Macedon.
4. After Athens was defeated by Sparta in the Peloponnesian War, a Theban proposed that it be razed to the ground. But a man from Phocis sang the first chorus from Euripides' *Electra*, and the council charged with the decision melted with compassion and refused to destroy a city that had produced such a poet.
1. Composed between 1642 and 1645. The identity of the lady, who has renounced earthly pleasure in order to serve God, is unknown.

That labor up the hill of heav'nly Truth,
5 The better part with Mary and with Ruth[2]
    Chosen thou hast; and they that overween,°   *presume*
    And at thy growing virtues fret° their   *irritate / ill-humor*
      spleen,°
    No anger find in thee, but pity and ruth.
Thy care is fixed and zealously attends
10   To fill thy odorous lamp[3] with deeds of light,
    And hope that reaps not shame. Therefore
      be sure,
    Thou, when the Bridegroom with his feastful° friends   *festive*
    Passes to bliss at the mid-hour of night,
    Hast gained thy entrance,[4] virgin wise and pure.

Sonnet X[1]

Daughter to that good Earl,[2] once President
    Of England's Council and her Treasury,
    Who lived in both unstained with gold or fee,
    And left them both, more in himself content,
5 Till the sad breaking of that Parliament
    Broke him, as that dishonest° victory   *shameful*
    At Chaeronea,[3] fatal to liberty,
    Killed with report that old man eloquent;
Though later born than to have known the days
10   Wherein your father flourished, yet by you,
    Madam, methinks I see him living yet:
So well your words his noble virtues praise,
    That all both judge you to relate them true,
    And to possess them, honored Margaret.

2. Ruth and Orpah were the two widowed Moabite daughters-in-law of the bereft Naomi, who entreated both to find new husbands. Orpah obeyed, but Ruth chose to stay with Naomi. Boaz blessed her for her kindness, married her, and she became the great-grandmother of David and thus part of the genealogy of Jesus. When Jesus visited the two sisters, Mary sat at his feet, while her sister Martha "was cumbered about much serving." When Martha complained, Jesus replied, "one thing is needful; and Mary hath chosen that good part" (Luke 10:39–42).
3. In the parable of the wise and foolish virgins (Matt. 25:1–13), the wise virgins trim their lamps and watch for the coming of the bridegroom Christ.
4. "I am the door: by me if any enter in, he shall be saved" (John 10:9).
1. Written between 1642 and 1645, when Milton was separated from Mary Powell, the sonnet praises Lady Margaret Ley, a married neighbor in Aldersgate Street, as the embodiment of her father's virtues.
2. Sir James Ley, former chief justice, lord high treasurer, and lord president of the council, who died six days after Charles dissolved Parliament on March 4, 1629.
3. According to a dubious tradition, the aged rhetorician Isocrates died of voluntary starvation four days after Philip of Macedon defeated the Athenian and Theban forces at Chaeronea in 338 B.C.E.

Sonnet XI[1]

A book was writ of late called *Tetrachordon*,
  And woven close, both matter, form, and style;
  The subject new: it walked the town a while,
  Numb'ring good intellects; now seldom
    pored on.
5 Cries the stall-reader, "Bless us! what a word on
  A title-page is this!"; and some in file°   *in a row*
  Stand spelling false,° while one might walk   *misspelling,*
    to Mile-   *misreading*
  End Green.[2] Why is it harder, sirs, than Gordon,
Colkitto, or Macdonnel, or Galasp?[3]
10   Those rugged names to our like° mouths *equally harsh / easy*
    grow sleek°
  That would have made Quintilian[4] stare and gasp.
Thy age, like ours, O soul of John Cheke,[5]
  Hated not learning worse than toad or asp,
  When thou taught'st Cambridge and King Edward Greek.

Sonnet XII[1]

I did but prompt the age to quit their clogs[2]
  By the known rules[3] of ancient liberty,
  When straight a barbarous noise environs me
  Of owls and cuckoos, asses, apes, and dogs;

1. The title in *TMS*: "On the detraction which followed upon my writing certain treatises." Written in the early months of 1646, the sonnet records Milton's disappointment at the ignorant reception afforded by Londoners to his *Tetrachordon*, one of his four treatises (five if we count the two different editions of *DDD*) arguing for freedom to divorce on grounds of incompatibility. A tetrachord is a four-stringed instrument, and the title alludes to the harmony within his densely argued treatise of four key biblical passages on marriage and divorce.
2. At the eastern limit of London.
3. The barbarous Scots names of the royalist General Montrose's officers: George, Lord Gordon (perhaps, since there were other Gordons as well), MacDonald, and Coll Keitache ("Colkitto"). George Gillespie ("Galasp") was a Presbyterian member of the Westminster Assembly.
4. Roman rhetorician (1st century C.E.), whose *Institutes* (1.5.8) condemns the use of barbarous (foreign) words.
5. Sir John Cheke (1514–57), first professor of Greek at Cambridge and tutor to Edward VI. While the meaning of lines 12–14 is disputed, the most probable one is: "Your age, in contrast to our age, did not hate learning." It could also mean that Cheke's age, like the poet's own, "hated not learning worse than toad or asp" (not worse, but as much).
1. Titled "On the Same," it is a companion to Sonnet XI, and in *TMS* it is given the same heading as that sonnet, "On the detraction . . ." The probable date is 1646.
2. Heavy pieces of wood attached to the legs or necks of prisoners or beasts to prevent escape. I.e., rid themselves of their encumbrances.
3. Mosaic law of divorce (Deut. 24:1–4).

5 As when those hinds that were transformed to frogs
      Railed at Latona's twin-born progeny
      Which after held the sun and moon in fee.[4]
      But this is got by casting pearl to hogs,[5]
    That bawl for freedom in their senseless mood,
10   And still revolt when truth would set them free.
      License they mean when they cry liberty;[6]
    For who loves that must first be wise and good:
      But from that mark° how far they rove we see   *target*
      For all° this waste of wealth and loss of blood.   *In spite of*

Sonnet XIII

To Mr. H. Lawes, on his Airs[1]

   Harry, whose tuneful and well-measured song
      First taught our English music how to span
      Words with just note and accent, not to scan[2]
      With Midas' ears, committing short and long,[3]
5   Thy worth and skill exempts° thee from the throng,   *singles out*
      With praise enough for envy to look wan;
      To after-age thou shalt be writ the man

---

4. Latona, mother of twins Apollo ("sun") and Diana ("moon") by Jove, fleeing the wrath of Juno, asked a group of peasants ("hinds") if she could quench her thirst at a small lake, asserting the natural right of all persons to sun, air, and water. When they prevented her by muddying the water, she turned them into frogs (*Met.*, 6.317–81). "Twin-born progeny": a possible allusion to twin tracts on divorce, *Tetrachordon* and *Colasterion*.
5. Christ, tempted by the Pharisees, did not cast his pearls before swine (Matt. 7:6): his was "not so much a teaching, as an intangling. . . . Neither was it seasonable to talke of honest and conscientious liberty among them who had abused legall and civil liberty to uncivil licence" (*Tetrachordon, YP*, 2:642–43). But Milton did cast his pearls before his swinish countrymen, hoping to free them through the Mosaic law of divorce.
6. As Christ accused the Pharisees of abusing legal liberty for the sake of uncivil license, so, perhaps, does Milton accuse contemporary libertines who mistake promiscuity for liberty, although the line echoes most strongly the numerous Presbyterian accusations against Milton's divorce tracts for introducing licentiousness ("license") under the guise of liberty. It may also allude to Milton's criticism in the *Areopagitica* of a Presbyterian Parliament that pretends to champion liberty while introducing a Licensing Order of prepublication censorship.
1. Songs. Addressed as "Harry," his familiar friend, Lawes, the tutor of the Egerton children, composed the music for *Masque* and played the part of the Attendant Spirit. He commissioned Milton to write the words for *Arcades* as well as *Masque*.
2. Determine the number and nature of poetic feet. Lawes, who "best" honored the English tongue (line 8), favored recitative and declamatory song and "accommodated musical stress and quantity to verbal values so as to set off the poet's words and sense" (Lewalski, 201).
3. Placing in a state of incongruity by matching a long syllable with a short note, or vice versa. King Midas was given ass's ears for preferring the music of Pan over that of Apollo.

That with smooth air couldst humor best
   our tongue.
Thou honor'st verse, and verse must lend her wing
10   To honor thee, the priest of Phoebus' choir,°   *poets*
   That tun'st their happiest lines in hymn or story.
Dante shall give Fame leave to set thee higher
   Than his Casella,[4] whom he wooed to sing,
   Met in the milder shades of Purgatory.

Sonnet XIV[1]

When Faith and Love,[2] which parted from
   thee never,
   Had ripened thy just soul to dwell with God,
   Meekly thou didst resign this earthy load
   Of death, called life, which us from life
   doth sever.
5 Thy works and alms and all thy good endeavor
   Stayed not behind, nor in the grave were trod;
   But as Faith pointed with her golden rod,
   Followed thee up to joy and bliss for ever.
Love led them on, and Faith who knew them
   best°   *best knew them*
10   Thy handmaids, clad them o'er with purple beams   *to be*
   And azure wings, that up they flew so dressed,
And spake the truth of thee on glorious themes
   Before the Judge, who thenceforth bid thee rest
   And drink thy fill of pure immortal streams.

Sonnet XV[1]

Fairfax, whose name in arms through Europe rings,
   Filling each mouth with envy or with praise,
   And all her jealous monarchs with amaze,

4. Dante met the shade of his composer friend, whom he addressed affectionately as "Casella mio," on the threshold of Purgatory (milder than Purgatory itself). When he asked for a song, Casella responded with one of Dante's *canzoni* that he had set to music.
1. In *TMS* this epigraph-sonnet bears the title (later crossed out), "On ye religious memorie of Mrs. Catharine Thomason my christian friend deceas'd 16 Decem. 1646." Widow of George Thomason, bookseller, whose great collection of civil war pamphlets is housed in the British Library, she was herself a lover of books and learning.
2. For a discussion of the importance to Milton of this dual principle of faith and charity, see pp. 320–21.
1. Titled in *TMS* "On ye Lord Gen. Fairfax at ye seige of Colchester," the sonnet was composed in either July or August 1648, when Fairfax was besieging some three thousand soldiers in that city. Sir Thomas Fairfax was the commander-in-chief of the New Model Army.

And rumors loud that daunt remotest kings,
5 Thy firm unshaken virtue° ever brings   *valor, courage*
   Victory home, though new rebellions raise
   Their Hydra[2] heads, and the false North displays
   Her broken league to imp their serpent wings:[3]
O yet a nobler task awaits thy hand;
10   For what can war but endless war still breed,
      Till truth and right from violence be freed,
And public faith[4] cleared from the shameful brand
   Of public fraud. In vain doth valor bleed
   While avarice and rapine share the land.

Sonnet XVI[1]

Cromwell, our chief of men, who through a cloud
   Not of war only, but detractions rude,
   Guided by faith and matchless fortitude
   To peace and truth thy glorious way hast ploughed,
5 And on the neck[2] of crownèd Fortune proud
   Hast reared God's trophies and his work pursued,
   While Darwen stream, with blood of Scots imbrued,°   *stained*
   And Dunbar field resounds thy praises loud,
And Worcester's[3] laureate wreath; yet more remains
10   To conquer still; peace hath her victories
      No less renowned than war; new foes[4] arise
Threat'ning to bind our souls with secular chains:
   Help us to save free conscience from the paw
   Of hireling wolves whose gospel is their maw.°   *belly*

2. A many-headed serpent, which grew two heads for each one cut off. Fairfax is compared to Hercules, one of whose twelve labors was to slay the hydra.
3. Milton regarded the Scottish invasion of England in July 1648 as a violation of the Solemn League and Covenant of 1643. In *PL*, Milton locates Satan's throne in the north. "Imp": to engraft feathers onto a bird's wings to improve its powers of flight.
4. Honigmann shows that this phrase was widely used to refer to a form of national debt and that Parliament's defaulting on such debts was an example of its greed and corruption. In light of the profusion of evils, Lewalski suggests that "Herculean Fairfax now needs to cleanse the English Augean stables."
1. Initially titled in *TMS* "To the Lord General Cromwell, May 1652 On the Proposals of Certain Ministers of the Committee for Propagation of the Gospel." Cromwell was a member of this Parliamentary committee, and the proposals included the establishment of a national church, a paid clergy, and an acceptance of fifteen fundamental doctrines. Milton passionately believed in the liberty of the individual conscience and in the separation of church and state, and he urges Cromwell to reject these proposals.
2. Alluding to the beheading of Charles I in January 1649.
3. Three battles in Scotland (against the Presbyterians) won by Cromwell. Milton doesn't mention battles in England and Ireland.
4. The Non-separating Congregationalists among the Independents who now join the Presbyterians in proposing a national church.

Sonnet XVII[1]

Vane, young in years, but in sage counsel old,
   Than whom a better senator ne'er held
   The helm of Rome, when gowns,[2] not arms,
      repelled
   The fierce Epirot and the African bold;[3]
5 Whether to settle peace or to unfold
   The drift of hollow states, hard to be spelled,[4]
   Then to advise how war may best, upheld,
   Move by her two main nerves, iron and gold,[5]
In all her equipage;° besides, to know   *apparatus of war*
10   Both spiritual power and civil, what each means,
   What severs each, thou hast learnt, which
      few have done.
The bounds of either sword° to thee we owe;   *church and state*
   Therefore on thy firm hand religion leans
   In peace, and reckons thee her eldest son.

Sonnet XVIII[1]

On the Late Massacre in Piedmont

Avenge, O Lord, thy slaughtered saints, whose bones
   Lie scattered on the Alpine mountains cold,
   Ev'n them who kept thy truth so pure of old

---

1. Initially titled in *TMS* "To Sir Henry Vane the younger," this panegyric sonnet was composed in 1652, when Vane was a member of the Council of State. He emigrated to New England in 1635 and became governor of the Massachusetts Bay Colony. Upon his return to England, he was appointed treasurer of the navy. Vane tried to protect religion by keeping it separate from the civil power. After the Restoration of Charles II, he was convicted of treason and executed.
2. Togas worn by Roman senators; a symbol of civil rather than military power.
3. Both Pyrrhus, king of Epirus, and Hannibal invaded Italy.
4. Discovered by close observation. "Drift": scheme, plot. "Hollow": insincere, false (with a pun on Holland, suggesting that Vane recognized the bad faith of Dutch ambassadors in diplomatic negotiations).
5. In his *Discourses* (2.10), Machiavelli argues that iron rather than money is the sinew of war.
1. Probably composed soon after the massacre of the Vaudois or Waldensians in the Italian Alps on April 24, 1655. According to the *Var.* (2:431), "The [sect] was thought by the Protestants of Milton's day to date back to patristic, even to apostolic, times, and actually to have preserved the primitive faith and practice which the Reformers sought, by their return to Scripture and the removal of current abuses, to restore." The duke of Savoy sent an army to remove the Vaudois from some of the villages in the Piedmont Valley. When the Vaudois fled to the hills, the army pursued and massacred 1,712 of them. Protestant Europe was shocked by the outrage, and Milton, on behalf of Cromwell, composed letters of protest. Honigmann cites passages from contemporary newsletter accounts that the sonnet reproduces, thus revealing the poet's fidelity to the details of the events. At the same time, the sonnet's prophetic power derives in part from its incorporation of phrases from Lamentations, Psalms, Isaiah, Jeremiah, and the Book of Revelation.

Sonnet XIX

When all our fathers worshiped stocks and
    stones,°   *wood and ston[e]*

5 Forget not; in thy book record their groans
    Who were thy sheep and in their ancient fold
    Slain by the bloody Piemontese that rolled
    Mother with infant down the rocks. Their moans
The vales redoubled to the hills, and they°   *the hills*
10   To Heav'n. Their martyred blood and ashes sow[2]
    O'er all th' Italian fields where still doth sway
The triple tyrant,[3] that from these may grow
    A hundredfold, who, having learnt thy way,
    Early may fly the Babylonian woe.[4]

Sonnet XIX[1]

When[2] I consider how my light° is spent,   *sight, inspiration*
    Ere half my days, in this dark world and wide,
    And that one talent which is death to hide
    Lodged with me useless,[3] though my soul
        more bent
5 To serve therewith my Maker, and present
    My true account, lest he returning chide,
    "Doth God exact day-labor, light denied?"[4]
I fondly° ask; but Patience to prevent°   *foolishly / forestall*
That murmur° soon replies: "God doth not need   *complaint*
10   Either man's work or his own gifts; who best
    Bear his mild yoke,[5] they serve him best.
       His state

2. Lines 10–13 combine the parable of the sower (Matt. 13:1–9), in which the seed of God's word "brought forth fruit, some a hundredfold," and Tertullian's maxim that "The blood of martyrs is the seed of the church." There is also a possible allusion to the myth of Cadmus, who sowed dragon's teeth that sprang up as armed men.
3. The pope wore a three-tiered crown.
4. Protestants often identified the Church of Rome with biblical Babylon, whose fall is predicted in Rev. 17–18. And see Jer. 51:6: "Flee out of the midst of Babylon, and deliver every man his soul: be not cut off in her iniquity; for this is the time of the Lord's vengeance."
1. Probably written in 1652, shortly after Milton's total loss of sight. As in Sonnet VII, the comforting parable of the vineyard (Matt. 20:1–16) and the threatening parable of the talents (Matt. 25:14–30), pp. 459–61, figure importantly. Much has been written (see especially Haskin) on the complexity and indeterminacy of individual words both in this masterpiece and in the parables. Thus, for example, the gospel text distinguishes between talent and ability ("he gave . . . talents . . . to every man according to his several abilities" [25:15]), thus leaving open the meaning of talents and how to spend them.
2. Whenever (possibly).
3. Possibly an allusion to the master's harsh judgment of the one-talent servant: "I should have received mine own with usury [interest]" (Matt. 25:27).
4. "I must work the works of him that sent me, while it is day: the night cometh, when no man can work" (John 9:4).
5. "My yoke is easy" (Matt. 11:30).

Is kingly: thousands[6] at his bidding speed
  And post o'er land and ocean without rest;
  They also serve who only stand and wait."

Sonnet XX[1]

Lawrence, of virtuous father[2] virtuous son,
  Now that the fields are dank and ways are mire,
  Where shall we sometimes meet, and by the fire
  Help waste° a sullen day, what may be won   *spend*
5 From the hard season° gaining? Time will run   *winter*
  On smoother, till Favonius[3] re-inspire
  The frozen earth, and clothe in fresh attire
  The lily and rose, that neither sowed nor spun.[4]
What neat° repast shall feast us, light and choice,   *elegant, tasteful,*
10   Of Attic taste,[5] with wine, whence we may rise   *simple*
  To hear the lute well touched, or artful voice
Warble immortal notes and Tuscan air?°   *Italian song*
  He who of those delights can judge, and spare[6]
  To interpose them oft, is not unwise.

Sonnet XXI[1]

Cyriack, whose grandsire[2] on the royal bench
  Of British Themis,[3] with no mean applause

6. I.e., of angels. Some are sent out on missions, while others wait for God's command.
1. Probably composed in the winter of 1655–56 for young Edward Lawrence, a virtuous and studious young man of promise who may have been Milton's former student as well as his friend. Elected to Parliament in 1656, he died in 1657 at age twenty-four.
2. Henry Lawrence (1600–64), powerful president of Cromwell's Council of State and keeper of the library at St. James House. Milton follows the Latin poet Horace by referring to the parentage of the addressee, and the sonnet as a whole was influenced by the Horatian short ode of invitation.
3. Zephyrus, the west wind.
4. "Consider the lilies of the field, how they grow; they toil not, neither do they spin: and yet I say unto you, That even Solomon in all his glory was not arrayed like one of these" (Matt. 6:28–29).
5. Such as the Athenians would have enjoyed.
6. A crux. Some read "spare" as "refrain" or "forbear," its more common meaning, which would set limits to Lawrence's good times, while others read it as "afford" (as in "Brother, can you spare a dime?"), which suggests that Lawrence should spare the time for such days, places, and repasts.
1. The probable date is 1655. A companion poem to Sonnet XX in advocating interludes of civilized pleasure.
2. Sir Edward Coke (1552–1634), chief justice of Common Pleas and Kings Bench, and the greatest legal authority of his age. Cyriack Skinner (1627–1700) may have been Milton's former student, and he frequently visited the poet in the 1650s in his house in Petty France. He is now believed to be the anonymous author of a brief life of Milton.
3. Greek goddess of justice.

Pronounced and in his volumes taught our laws,
   Which others[4] at their bar so often wrench,
5 Today deep thoughts resolve[5] with me to drench°   *drown in wine*
   In mirth that after no repenting draws;
   Let Euclid rest and Archimedes° pause,   *mathematics and physics*
   And what the Swede intends, and what the French.°   *politics*
To measure life learn thou betimes, and know
10   Toward solid good what leads the nearest way;
   For other things mild Heav'n a time ordains,
And disapproves that care, though wise in show,
   That with superfluous burden loads the day,
   And when God sends a cheerful hour, refrains.

Sonnet XXII[1]

Cyriack, this three years' day° these eyes,
      though clear   *for the past three years*
   To outward view of blemish or of spot,
   Bereft of light their seeing have forgot,
   Nor to their idle orbs doth sight appear
5 Of sun or moon or star throughout the year,
   Or man or woman.[2] Yet I argue not
   Against Heav'n's hand or will, nor bate° a jot   *abate, slacken*
   Of heart or hope, but still bear up° and steer   *helm up into the wind*
Right onward. What supports me, dost thou ask?
10   The conscience,° friend, to have lost them overplied   *consciousness*
   In liberty's defense,[3] my noble task,
Of which all Europe talks from side to side.
   This thought might lead me through the
      world's vain masque°   *masquerade, court masque*
   Content though blind, had I no better guide.

4. I.e., other judges.
5. An imperative.
1. The probable date is 1655. Milton writes a second sonnet on the subject of his blindness, very different in tone from the first.
2. Cf. *PL*, 3.40–44.
3. Alluding to Milton's first and second *Defence of the English People* (1651, 1654).

Sonnet XXIII[1]

Methought I saw my late espousèd saint[2]
   Brought to me like Alcestis[3] from the grave,
   Whom Jove's great son to her glad husband gave,
   Rescued from death by force, though pale
     and faint.
5 Mine as whom° washed from spot of child-bed   *as one whom*
   taint
   Purification in the old Law[4] did save,
   And such as yet once more I trust to have
   Full sight of her in Heaven without restraint,
Came vested all in white, pure as her mind.
10   Her face was veiled, yet to my fancied sight
   Love, sweetness, goodness in her person shined
So clear as in no face with more delight.
   But O as to embrace me she inclined,
   I waked, she fled, and day brought back my night.[5]

1. The date is probably 1658, the year that Katharine Woodcock, Milton's second wife, died. This is Milton's most poignant sonnet and "one of the greatest love poems in the language" (Lewalski, 355–56). Most critics believe that Katharine is the subject of the poem, which develops the idea of *katharos* ("pure") in its successive quatrains, beginning with Euripides' *Alcestis* (natural law), extending to the Levitical rites of purification under "the old Law" (Mosaic law), and concluding with a vision of absolute purity in a Christian heaven (Gospel). (See Spitzer on the tripartite crescendo movement.) But some hold that Mary Powell, Milton's first wife, who died in childbirth, is the subject, and that she and the poet lived together happily after their reconciliation.
2. Recently married saint? recently deceased wife?
3. Wife of King Admetus of Thessaly, who chose to die in place of her husband. Hercules visits Admetus, who is renowned for his hospitality and who will not upset his guest by telling him of his loss. But Hercules learns the news from a servant, and he battles Death and forces him to give up Alcestis. He brings her back, veiled, to her initially uncomprehending husband. The veil is lifted, but Alcestis cannot speak for three days, after which she undergoes purificatory rites and is restored fully to life.
4. Lev. 12:4–8 sets down the laws for the purification of women after childbirth. See also Luke 2:22–24, where, after the birth of Jesus, Mary offers the prescribed sacrifice "when the days of her purification according to the law of Moses were accomplished."
5. Cf. *PL*, 8.460–84.

Paradise Regained

Paradise Regained, published in one volume together with *Samson Ag-onistes* in 1671, is Milton's brief epic: four books, 2,070 blank-verse lines, most of them dialogue, presenting a three-day verbal battle in the wilderness between Jesus and Satan immediately after the baptism that inaugurates Jesus' public mission. Milton follows the sequence of Satanic temptations of Jesus in the gospel of Luke (4:1–12): to turn stones into bread, to rule the kingdoms of the world, and to cast him-self down from the pinnacle of the temple in Jerusalem. He also takes some details from the more often cited account of Matthew (4:1–11), who places the temptation in his gospel immediately after describing the baptism and who ends with angels ministering to the triumphant Jesus.

By giving his two epic poems the titles of *Paradise Lost* and *Paradise Regained*, Milton himself invites contrast as well as comparison. In his autobiography, Thomas Ellwood, a Quaker persecuted and imprisoned for his beliefs, takes some credit for inspiring the later epic. During the London plague of 1665, Ellwood, a former student of "Master" Milton, arranged for his occupancy of a cottage in the village of Chal-font St. Giles, Buckinghamshire. During his sojourn there, Milton gave Ellwood a draft of the manuscript of *Paradise Lost* to take home and read at his leisure and to return it when he had finished with his judgment of it:

> He asked me how I liked it, and what I thought of it; which I mod-estly but freely told him; and after some further discourse about it, I pleasantly said to him, Thou hast said much here of *Paradise lost*, but what hast thou to say of *Paradise found*? He made me no Answer, but sate some time in a Muse.[1]

Some time later, after Milton's return to London, Ellwood visited him. Milton showed him *Paradise Regained*, "and in a pleasant Tone said to me, *This is owing to you; for you put it into my Head by the Question you put to me at* Chalfont; *which before I had not thought of.*"[2]

Milton scholars justifiably love this story, which underscores the ma-ture poet's graciousness and the young student's naïveté. What Milton was actually thinking during the silence that followed the first response

---

1. Thomas Ellwood, *The History of the Life of Thomas Ellwood*, ed. Joseph Wyeth (Lon-don, 1714), p. 233.
2. Ellwood, *Life*, p. 314.

to his great epic Ellwood never knew, and we will never know. Certainly he never betrayed a trace of disappointment. And just as certainly, the gentle humor of his exaggerated compliment would have been lost on the earnest Ellwood, whom we can rely on to have reported what happened, even if he didn't fully understand it. He may not deserve the derision of contemporary scholars for not understanding that *Paradise Lost* tells the story of paradise both lost *and* found. If Ellwood believed that the Christian theme of redemption by "one greater man" is not as emotionally integrated into the great epic as the loss of paradise—indeed, that it is merely perfunctorily a part of it—such a view can at least be defended.[3]

From the beginning, readers have much preferred the stylistic magnificence of the great epic over the deliberate plainness of the brief one, although Milton himself, so patient with Ellwood, could not bear to hear the latter declared inferior to the former. The titles of the two epics, taken together, reveal a typological relationship between law and gospel, so perhaps Milton's preference for the more exalted subject was doctrinal rather than aesthetic. In the last book of *Paradise Lost*, the angel Michael describes Jesus' triumph as entry into the land of Canaan after long wandering in the desert and as a return to paradise (12.307–14). Adam and Moses are thus joined as sinners excluded from the sacred places that only Jesus can enter, yet granted by God's grace a consolatory vision. Reformation expositors contrasted Moses' ascent to the Pisgah height, which begins the last chapter of the Pentateuch (Deut. 34), with the kingdom temptation in the gospels. Where the mountaintop visions are consolatory for Adam in book 12 and for Moses in the Bible, the devil's ocular presentation of empire to Jesus is intended to subvert rather than to console. Milton's contemporary John Lightfoot notes a significant difference in "the Lords shewing to Moses from a high Mount all the kingdomes of *Canaan*, and saying, *All these will I give to the children of Israel*, and the Devils shewing to *Christ* all the kingdomes of the earth, and saying, *All these will I give thee*."[4] Henry Ainsworth amplifies this distinction and, in doing so, alludes to Hebrews 11, the principal biblical source for the vision framework of the last two books of *Paradise Lost*:

> God here sheweth Moses all the Kingdomes, and glory of Canaan, from an high mountaine, for his comfort and strengthening of his faith, who saw the promises a farre off, saluted them, and died, as did his godly forefathers. On the contrary, the Devill taketh Christ up into an exceeding high mountaine, & sheweth him all the kingdoms of the world, and the glory of them, to draw him (if he had been able) from the faith and service of God, unto the worship of Satan.[5]

3. See David Daiches, "The Opening of *Paradise Lost*," in *The Living Milton*, ed. Frank Kermode (London: Routledge & Kegan Paul, 1960), p. 59.
4. John Lightfoot, *The Harmony of the Foure Evangelists* (London, 1647), 2:29.
5. Henry Ainsworth, *Annotations Upon the Five Books of Moses, and the . . . Psalmes* (London, 1622), p. 166.

When Milton's Adam ascends the "Hill / Of Paradise the highest" (*PL*, 11.377–78), he is ignorant of the measure of grace he is receiving and of the trial which the Second Adam must undergo. The epic narrator makes certain that the reader is not:

> Not higher that Hill nor wider looking round,
> Whereon for different cause the Tempter set
> Our second *Adam* in the wilderness,
> To show him all Earth's Kingdoms and thir Glory. (11.381–84)

This is the poem's first indication that Adam's vision of the course of history is typologically related to the action of *Paradise Regained*, and Milton reminds his readers that Satan "took / The Son of God up to a mountain high" (*PR*, 3.251–52).

Typology is an important symbolic mode in the brief epic, since, as Barbara Lewalski has amply demonstrated, Satan tempts Jesus to define himself in relation to figures from classical and biblical history.[6] He refuses to do so, instead superseding the virtuous examples and reversing the effects of the sinful ones, such as our first parents, as when he rejects the Satanic banquet ("Alas, how simple, to these cates compared, / Was that crude apple that diverted Eve!" [*PR*, 2.348–49]), or, more important, when he regains the paradise that they lost. Of course the crucifixion, not the temptation in the wilderness, is the event that regained paradise; but, except for *The Passion*, an incomplete poem, and a self-described failure, Milton chooses never to describe Christ's death on the cross, his resurrection, or the traditional events in between: the descent into hell, the harrowing of hell, and the redemption of those worthies imprisoned there who lived before Christ. In an essay in this volume, Laura Knoppers suggests that Milton wants to avoid comparisons between Christ and the martyred King Charles, but there may be other reasons as well that the topic would have proved uncongenial to him. The question of soteriology might have been too emotionally intense to put into words. Or, at the other extreme, for so Pauline a theologian as Milton, the perceived cost of grace—of sacrificing a part of one's identity to live transplanted in Christ—might have proved to be unaffordable.

The problem may be related to the important question of Jesus' identity. (Milton never calls him Christ in either epic.) The temptation in the epic is not unrelated to the trial of Jesus in the gospels, where Caiaphas, the Roman-appointed Jewish high priest, adjures Jesus "by the living God, that thou tell us whether thou be the Christ, the Son of God" (Matt. 26:63):

> Jesus saith unto him, Thou hast said: nevertheless I say unto you,
> Hereafter shall ye see the Son of man sitting on the right hand of
> power, and coming in the clouds of heaven. Then the high priest
> rent his clothes, saying, He hath spoken blasphemy; what further

---

6. Barbara K. Lewalski, *Milton's Brief Epic: The Genre, Meaning, and Art of "Paradise Regained"* (Providence, R.I.: Brown University Press; London: Methuen, 1966). And see her essay in this volume, pp. 607–22.

need have we of witnesses? behold, now ye have heard his blasphemy." (Matt. 26:64–65)

Milton's Satan in *Paradise Regained*, as well as Milton's readers, share
Caiaphas' curiosity. All of them know that the term "Son of God" "bears
no single sense" (*PR*, 4.517). Present at the baptism, Satan heard the
voice from heaven pronounce Jesus "the Son of God beloved" (513), and
he kept Jesus under "narrower Scrutiny, that I might learn / In what
degree or meaning thou art called / The Son of God" (515–17):

> The Son of God I also am, or was,
> And if I was, I am; relation stands;
> All men are sons of God; yet thee I thought
> In some respect far higher so declared. (518–21)

Paul calls all who are led by the spirit of God Sons of God (Rom.
8:14; Gal. 4:4–7), and he also holds that people who have faith are Sons
of God (Gal. 3:26). The early Christians regarded the term much as
Milton's Satan does, as a high designation. Only in the passage in question does the Bible invest the term with a metaphysical meaning, when
Caiaphas asks Jesus if he is something more than human and follows
the question by shouting blasphemy when Jesus does not deny the title.
Milton's virtually Socinian depiction of Jesus in *Paradise Regained*
differs from the account of the self-affirming Christ in Matthew 26,
but that may make him more rather than less heroic. This more human
Jesus justifies his Father's faith in him:

> The Father knows the Son; therefore secure
> Ventures his filial virtue, though untried,
> Against whate'er may tempt, whate'er seduce,
> Allure, or terrify, or undermine. (1.176–79)

The opening invocation clearly indicates the result of the temptation:
Jesus is now "by proof [trial, proven or tested power, evidence such as
biblical testimonies or proof-texts] the undoubted Son of God" (1.11).
God calls him "This perfect man, by merit called my Son" (1.166). In
Paradise Lost, God the Father is similarly concise and resonant when
he praises the redeemer of humankind, "By Merit more than Birthright
Son of God" (3.309). The Miltonic coordinates of merit preferred over
birthright are limitless: good works (merit) over grace (birthright), free
will over determinism, republicanism over divine right monarchy, an
activist non-hireling clergy over an established, wealthy church. A concluding analog of merit and birthright that implicitly critiques its context within the great epic may be *praxis* and inherited doctrine—more
specifically, Jesus as a hero acting within historical time in *Paradise
Regained* and the Son in the heavenly theological dialogue of book 3
in *Paradise Lost*.
Jesus' final words in the epic are also its most famous crux, because
critics are divided over whether he discovers his divine identity at the
moment that he pronounces them: "Also it is written, / Tempt not the
Lord thy God" (4.560–61). Is this the citation of a proof-text or an over-

determined imperative? "Tempt not the Lord thy God" might be a dramatic correlative of the paradoxical Pauline doctrine that "Christ is the end of the law" (Rom. 10:4). Paul's audacious pun on "end" (both aim or purpose and termination or abolition) asserts that Christ fulfills the law by abrogating it. Submitting completely to God's law throughout the temptation, Jesus here orders Satan not to go beyond it either. His utterance is at once submissive and authoritative, both fulfilling the law and transcending it. Whatever Milton's original intention might have been, the pressure exerted over the centuries by Christian readers as well as its climactic position in the brief epic create a space within the statement that allows something more than mere repetition to take shape. There is a desire to turn a statement about a transcendent God the Father into an affirmation of immanent divinity. This is true even for most of those readers who understand that Jesus, quoting Deuteronomy 6:16 word for word, is not declaring his own divinity as Lord God, either in the poem or in its gospel sources (Matt. 4:7; Luke 4:12). An access of supernatural insight accompanies the declaration and the patient standing that follows it. In rebuking Satan, Jesus adheres to the tone set originally by Moses, when he reminds the wandering Israelites of their sins: "Ye shall not tempt the Lord your God, as ye tempted him in Massah" (Deut. 6:16; and see Exod. 17:7). The tone of Jesus' final reproach of Satan will be familiar to readers of the gospel. It resembles his frequent reproofs of the Pharisees, not for violating the law, as the biblical Israelites did, but for adhering to it too narrowly, as when he boldly justifies the disciples' plucking of grain on the Sabbath, declaring that the Sabbath was made for man, and not man for the Sabbath, and appointing himself in the bargain Lord also of the Sabbath (Mark 2:27–28).

Virtually all of the critics who assert that Jesus' final statement constitutes a revelation of his divinity also assert Satan's simultaneously full realization of that divinity. But the epic narrator states only that Satan is defeated and wounded, with a worse wound still to come (4.621–23). The torment of unrelieved perplexity might exceed that of understanding Jesus' identity at last, which would at least have provided the closure for which Satan had earlier expressed a strong desire, even if it meant the worst: "I would be at the worst; worst is my port, / My harbor and my ultimate repose, / The end I would attain" (3.209–11). This closure the poem withholds from Satan, whose impatience throughout the temptations contrasts strikingly with the Son's frequently underscored patience, exceeding even that of Job (1.426, 2.102, 3.92–95, 4.420). If patience is one of the virtues, both personal and political, that Milton wants to inculcate in his readers, perhaps Jesus' final words are as much a moral lesson as a crux, teaching us to be content with the mystery of his identity, without any irritable reaching after fact and reason.

Paradise Regained

The First Book

I who erewhile[1] the happy garden sung,
By one man's disobedience lost, now sing
Recovered Paradise to all mankind,
By one man's firm obedience fully tried[2]
5 Through all temptation, and the Tempter foiled
In all his wiles, defeated and repulsed,
And Eden raised in the waste wilderness.[3]
    Thou, Spirit,[4] who led'st this glorious Eremite°   *desert dweller*
Into the desert, his victorious field
10 Against the spiritual foe, and brought'st him thence
By proof the undoubted Son of God, inspire,
As thou art wont, my prompted song, else mute,
And bear through highth or depth of nature's bounds
With prosperous wing full summed° to tell of deeds   *in full plumage*
15 Above heroic, though in secret done,
And unrecorded° left through many an age,   *not told in full*
Worthy t' have not remained so long unsung.
    Now had the great proclaimer,° with a voice   *John the Baptist*
More awful than the sound of trumpet, cried
20 Repentance, and Heaven's kingdom nigh at hand
To all baptized. To his great baptism flocked
With awe the regions round, and with them came
From Nazareth the son of Joseph deemed[5]
To the flood Jordan, came as then obscure,
25 Unmarked, unknown; but him the Baptist soon
Descried,° divinely warned,[6] and witness bore   *Detected*

1. This retrospective proem recalls the first four lines of the *Aeneid* in most Renaissance editions, later excised: "I am he who once piped a song on a slender reed, / And then, leaving the woods, compelled the nearby fields / To provide amply for the greedy tiller of the soil—a work / Welcome to the farmers: But now of Mars' bristling. / Arms and the man I sing." Barbara Lewalski quotes other biblical epics that imitate this opening and adds that by echoing Virgil and alluding to *Paradise Lost* as a poem about a happy garden, "Milton seems to imply that he also has now graduated from pastoral apprentice work to the true epic subject."
2. Rom. 5:19: "For as by one man's disobedience many were made sinners, so by the obedience of one shall many be made righteous."
3. Isa. 51:3: "the Lord shall comfort Zion: he will comfort all her waste places; and he will make her wilderness like Eden."
4. Not the third person of the Trinity, who Milton says may not be invoked (*De Doctrina Christiana* 1.6), but, interpreted broadly, can include "a divine impulse, light, voice or word sent from above."
5. Luke 3:23: "Jesus . . . being (as was supposed) the son of Joseph."
6. John 1:33: "And I knew him not; but he that sent me to baptize with water, the same said unto me, Upon whom thou shalt see the Spirit descending, and remaining on him, the same is he which baptizeth with the Holy Ghost."

As to his worthier, and would have resigned
To him his heavenly office; nor was long
His witness unconfirmed: on him baptized
30 Heaven opened, and in likeness of a dove
The Spirit descended, while the Father's voice
From Heav'n pronounced him his belovèd Son.[7]
That heard the Adversary,[8] who, roving still°   *continually*
About the world, at that assembly famed
35 Would not be last, and with the voice divine
Nigh thunder-struck, th' exalted man, to whom
Such high attest° was giv'n, a while surveyed   *testimony*
With wonder; then with envy fraught and rage
Flies to his place, nor rests, but in mid-air[9]
40 To council summons all his mighty peers,
Within thick clouds and dark tenfold involved,
A gloomy cónsistory;[1] and them amidst
With looks aghast and sad he thus bespake:
"O ancient Powers of air and this wide world
45 (For much more willingly I mention air,
This our old conquest, than remember hell,
Our hated habitation), well ye know
How many ages, as the years of men,°   *by human*
This universe we have possessed, and ruled   *computation*
50 In manner at our will th' affairs of earth,
Since Adam and his facile° consort Eve   *easily led*
Lost Paradise, deceived by me, though since
With dread attending[2] when that fatal wound
Shall be inflicted by the seed of Eve
55 Upon my head.[3] Long the decrees of Heav'n
Delay, for longest time to him is short;
And now too soon for us the circling hours
This dreaded time have compassed, wherein we
Must bide the stroke of that long-threatened wound,
60 At least if so we can, and by the head

---

7. Matt. 3:16–17: "he saw the Spirit of God descending like a dove, and lighting upon
him: And lo a voice from heaven, saying, This is my beloved Son, in whom I am well
pleased."
8. Heb. *Satan.*
9. In Eph. 2:2, Satan is "prince of the power of the air."
1. *Aeneid* 2.679, *concilium horrendum*; refers ironically to the ecclesiastical senate in
which the pope presides over the whole body of cardinals and to the Anglican bishop's
court for ecclesiastical causes.
2. Awaiting (qualifies "me," line 52).
3. Gen. 3:15: God's punishment of the serpent, interpreted as the *protevangelium*, fore-
telling the defeat of Satan by Christ, the woman's seed: "And I will put enmity between
thee and the woman, and between thy seed and her seed; it shall bruise thy head, and
thou shalt bruise his heel."

Broken be not intended all our power
To be infringed,° our freedom and our being   *broken*
In this fair empire won of earth and air;
For this ill news I bring: the Woman's Seed,
65   Destined to this, is late of woman born.
His birth to our just fear gave no small cause;
But his growth now to youth's full flow'r, displaying
All virtue, grace and wisdom to achieve
Things highest, greatest, multiplies my fear.
70   Before him a great prophet, to proclaim
His coming, is sent harbinger, who all
Invites, and in the consecrated stream
Pretends[4] to wash off sin, and fit them so
Purified to receive him pure, or rather
75   To do him honor as their King. All come,
And he himself among them was baptized,
Not thence to be more pure, but to receive
The testimony of Heaven, that who he is
Thenceforth the nations may not doubt. I saw
80   The prophet do him reverence; on him rising
Out of the water, Heav'n above the clouds
Unfold her crystal doors; thence on his head
A perfect dove descend, whate'er it meant,
And out of Heav'n the Sov'reign Voice I heard,
85   'This is my Son beloved, in him am pleased.'
His mother then is mortal, but his Sire
He who obtains° the monarchy of Heav'n,   *holds*
And what will he not do to advance his Son?
His first-begot[5] we know, and sore have felt,
90   When his fierce thunder drove us to the deep;
Who this is we must learn, for man he seems
In all his lineaments, though in his face
The glimpses of his Father's glory shine.
Ye see our danger on the utmost edge
95   Of hazard, which admits no long debate,
But must with something sudden be opposed,
Not force, but well-couched° fraud, well-woven   *well-hidden,*
    snares,   *well-expressed*
Ere in the head of nations he appear
Their king, their leader, and supreme on earth.
100   I, when no other durst, sole undertook

4. Professes, with overtones of feigning.
5. In *PL*, 5.600–15, God's elevation of his "only son" above the other angels prompts Satan's
   rebellion.

The dismal expedition to find out
And ruin Adam,[6] and the exploit performed
Successfully; a calmer voyage now
Will waft me; and the way found prosperous once
105 Induces best to hope of like success."
     He ended, and his words impressions left
Of much amazement to th' infernal crew,
Distracted and surprised with deep dismay
At these sad tidings; but no time was then
110 For long indulgence to their fears or grief:
Unanimous they all commit the care
And management of this main° enterprise   *momentous*
To him their great dictator,[7] whose attempt
At first against mankind so well had thrived
115 In Adam's overthrow, and led their march
From hell's deep-vaulted den to dwell in light,
Regents and potentates, and kings, yea gods[8]
Of many a pleasant realm and province wide.
So to the coast of Jordan he directs
120 His easy steps, girded with snaky wiles,
Where he might likeliest find this new-declared,
This man of men, attested Son of God,
Temptation and all guile on him to try,
So to subvert whom he suspected raised
125 To end his reign on earth so long enjoyed;
But contrary unweeting he fulfilled
The purposed counsel preordained and fixed
Of the Most High, who in full frequence° bright   *assembly*
Of angels, thus to Gabriel smiling spake:
130 "Gabriel, this day by proof thou shalt behold,
Thou and all angels cónversant on earth
With man or men's affairs, how I begin
To verify that solemn message late,
On which I sent thee to the Virgin pure
135 In Galilee, that she should bear a son
Great in renown, and called the Son of God;
Then told'st her doubting how these things could be
To her a virgin, that on her should come
The Holy Ghost, and the power of the Highest

6. *PL,* 2.430–66, where Satan volunteers to travel from hell to earth to ruin humankind,
   a travesty of the Son's redemptive mission (3.236–65).
7. A temporary ruler invested with absolute authority, elected in seasons of emergency, a
   practice recommended by Machiavelli and English republican theorist James Harrington but opposed by Milton in his *Ready and Easy Way.*
8. *PL,* 1.376–505: fallen angels become the pagan gods condemned in the Hebrew Bible.

140 O'ershadow her. This man, born and now upgrown,
    To show him worthy of his birth divine
    And high prediction, henceforth I expose
    To Satan; let him tempt and now assay
    His utmost subtlety, because he boasts
145 And vaunts of his great cunning to the throng
    Of his apostasy;° he might have learnt   *apostate angels*
    Less overweening, since he failed in Job,
    Whose constant perseverance overcame
    Whate'er his cruel malice could invent.[9]
150 He now shall know I can produce a man
    Of female seed, far abler to resist
    All his solicitations, and at length
    All his vast force, and drive him back to hell,
    Winning by conquest what the first man lost
155 By fallacy surprised. But first I mean
    To exercise° him in the wilderness;   *subject to ascetic*
    There he shall first lay down the rudiments°   *discipline*
    Of his great warfare, ere I send him forth   *beginnings, first*
    To conquer Sin and Death the two grand foes,   *principles*
160 By humiliation and strong sufferance:
    His weakness shall o'ercome Satanic strength
    And all the world, and mass of sinful flesh;
    That all the angels and ethereal powers,
    They now, and men hereafter, may discern
165 From what consummate virtue I have chose
    This perfect man, by merit called my Son,
    To earn salvation for the sons of men."
        So spake the Eternal Father, and all Heaven
    Admiring stood a space, then into hymns
170 Burst forth, and in celestial measures moved,
    Circling the throne and singing, while the
            hand°   *instrumental music*
    Sung with the voice, and this the argument:°   *subject matter,*
    "Victory and triumph to the Son of God   *theme*
    Now ent'ring his great duel, not of arms,
175 But to vanquish by wisdom hellish wiles.
    The Father knows the Son; therefore secure°   *without anxiety*
    Ventures his filial virtue, though untried,
    Against whate'er may tempt, whate'er seduce,
    Allure, or terrify, or undermine.
180 Be frustrate all ye stratagems of hell,

9. Milton's reference in *Reason of Church Government* to Job as a "brief epic" suggests its
   possible structural influence on this poem. See also 1.369, 425, and 3.64, 67, 95.

And devilish machinations come to naught."
   So they in Heav'n their odes and vigils tuned.
Meanwhile the Son of God, who yet some days
Lodged in Bethabara[1] where John baptized,
185 Musing and much revolving in his breast
How best the mighty work he might begin
Of Saviour to mankind, and which way first
Publish° his godlike office now mature,   *Make public*
One day forth walked alone, the Spirit leading,
190 And his deep thoughts, the better to converse
With° solitude, till far from track of men,   *Keep company with*
Thought following thought, and step by step led on,
He entered now the bordering desert wild,
And with dark shades and rocks environed round,
195 His holy meditations thus pursued:
   "O what a multitude of thoughts at once
Awakened in me swarm, while I consider
What from within I feel myself, and hear
What from without comes often to my ears,
200 Ill sorting° with my present state compared.   *corresponding*
When I was yet a child, no childish play
To me was pleasing; all my mind was set
Serious to learn and know, and thence to do
What might be public good; myself I thought
205 Born to that end, born to promote all truth,
All righteous things. Therefore, above my years,
The Law of God I read, and found it sweet,
Made it my whole delight,[2] and in it grew
To such perfection, that ere yet my age
210 Had measured twice six years, at our great feast
I went into the Temple, there to hear
The teachers of our Law, and to propose
What might improve my knowledge or their own,
And was admired[3] by all; yet this not all
215 To which my spirit aspired. Victorious deeds
Flamed in my heart, heroic acts: one while
To rescue Israel from the Roman yoke,
Then to subdue and quell o'er all the earth
Brute violence and proud tyrannic pow'r,
220 Till truth were freed, and equity restored;
Yet held it more humane, more heavenly, first

1. Heb. "house of the ford" on the Jordan.
2. Milton's translation of Ps. 1:2: "Jehovah's Law is ever his delight."
3. Marveled at; Luke 2:42–49.

By winning words to conquer willing hearts,
And make persuasion do the work of fear,
At least to try, and teach the erring soul
225 Not wilfully misdoing, but unware
Misled; the stubborn only to subdue.[4]
These growing thoughts my mother soon perceiving
By words at times cast forth inly rejoiced,
And said to me apart: 'High are thy thoughts,
230 O son, but nourish them and let them soar
To what highth sacred virtue and true worth
Can raise them, though above example high;
By matchless deeds express° thy matchless Sire.   *manifest*
For know, thou art no son of mortal man,
235 Though men esteem thee low of parentage,
Thy Father is the Eternal King, who rules
All Heaven and earth, angels and sons of men.
A messenger from God foretold thy birth
Conceived in me a virgin; he foretold
240 Thou shouldst be great and sit on David's throne,
And of thy kingdom there should be no end.[5]
At thy nativity a glorious choir
Of angels in the fields of Bethlehem sung
To shepherds watching at their folds by night,
245 And told them the Messiah now was born,
Where they might see him; and to thee they came,
Directed to the manger where thou lay'st,
For in the inn was left no better room.
A star, not seen before, in heaven appearing
250 Guided the wise men thither from the east,
To honor thee with incense, myrrh, and gold,
By whose bright course led on they found the place,
Affirming it thy star new-grav'n° in heaven,   *(1) newly carved, (2)*
By which they knew thee King of Israel born.   *indelibly fixed*
255 Just Simeon and prophetic Anna,[6] warned
By vision, found thee in the Temple, and spake
Before the altar and the vested priest
Like things of thee to all that present stood.'
This having heard, straight I again revolved°   *studied, read*

4. Cf. Anchises' prophecy of Rome's destiny: "To pacify, to impose the rule of law, / To spare the conquered, battle down the proud" (*Aen.*, 6.852–53).
5. The angel (lit., "messenger") of annunciation. Luke 1:32–33: "He shall be great, and shall be called the Son of the Highest; and the Lord God shall give unto him the throne of his father David: and he shall reign over the house of Jacob forever; and of his kingdom there shall be no end."
6. See Luke 2:25–38.

260 The Law and Prophets, searching what was writ
    Concerning the Messiah, to our scribes
    Known partly, and soon found of whom they spake
    I am;[7] this chiefly, that my way must lie
    Through many a hard assay° even to the death,   *trial*
265 Ere I the promised kingdom can attain,
    Or work redemption for mankind, whose sins'
    Full weight must be transferred upon my head.
    Yet neither thus disheartened or dismayed,
    The time prefixed I waited; when behold
270 The Baptist (of whose birth I oft had heard,
    Not knew by sight) now come, who was to come
    Before Messiah and his way prepare.
    I as all others to his baptism came,
    Which I believed was from above; but he
275 Straight knew me, and with loudest voice proclaimed
    Me him (for it was shown him so from Heaven),
    Me him whose harbinger he was; and first
    Refused on me his baptism to confer,
    As much his greater, and was hardly won.°   *persuaded with*
280 But as I rose out of the laving stream,   *difficulty*
    Heaven opened her eternal doors, from whence
    The Spirit descended on me like a dove,
    And last, the sum of all, my Father's voice,
    Audibly heard from Heav'n, pronounced me his,
285 Me his belovèd Son, in whom alone
    He was well pleased; by which I knew the time
    Now full, that I no more should live obscure,
    But openly begin, as best becomes
    The authority which I derived from Heaven.
290 And now by some strong motion I am led
    Into this wilderness, to what intent
    I learn not yet, perhaps I need not know;
    For what concerns my knowledge God reveals."
       So spake our morning star then in his rise,
295 And looking round on every side beheld
    A pathless desert, dusk with horrid° shades.   *bristling*
    The way he came not having marked, return
    Was difficult, by human steps untrod;
    And he still on was led, but with such thoughts
300 Accompanied of things past and to come

---

7. Exod. 3:14: God's "I AM THAT I AM"; John 8:58: Jesus's transumptive affirmation, "Before Abraham was, I am."

Lodged in his breast, as well might
    recommend
Such solitude before choicest society.[8]
Full forty days he passed—whether on hill
Sometimes, anon in shady vale, each night
305 Under the covert of some ancient oak
Or cedar to defend him from the dew,
Or harbored in one cave, is not revealed;
Nor tasted human food, nor hunger felt
Till those days ended, hungered then at last
310 Among wild beasts; they at his sight grew mild,
Nor sleeping him nor waking harmed; his walk
The fiery serpent fled and noxious° worm;   *harmful*
The lion and fierce tiger glared aloof.
But now an aged man in rural weeds,
315 Following, as seemed, the quest of some stray ewe,
Or withered sticks to gather, which might serve
Against a winter's day when winds blow keen
To warm him wet returned from field at eve,
He saw approach, who first with curious eye
320 Perused him, then with words thus uttered spake:
    "Sir, what ill chance hath brought thee to
        this place
So far from path or road of men, who pass
In troop or caravan, for single none
Durst ever, who returned, and dropped not here
325 His carcass, pined° with hunger and with drouth?   *wasted away*
I ask the rather, and the more admire,°   *marvel*
For that° to me thou seem'st the man whom late   *Because*
Our new baptizing prophet at the ford
Of Jordan honored so, and called thee Son
330 Of God. I saw and heard, for we sometimes
Who dwell this wild, constrained by want,
    come forth
To town or village nigh (nighest is far),
Where aught we hear, and curious are to hear,
What happens new; fame° also finds us out."   *rumor*
335   To whom the Son of God: "Who brought me hither
Will bring me hence; no other guide I seek."
    "By miracle he may," replied the swain,°   *country laborer*
"What other way I see not; for we here
Live on tough roots and stubs, to thirst inured

8. Cicero's praise of Scipio Africanus: "Never less alone than when alone" (*De Offic.*
3.1.1).

340 More than the camel, and to drink go far,
    Men to much misery and hardship born.
    But if thou be the Son of God, command
    That out of these hard stones be made thee bread;
    So shalt thou save thyself and us relieve
345 With food, whereof we wretched seldom taste."
        He ended, and the Son of God replied:
    "Think'st thou such force in bread? Is it not written
    (For I discern thee other than thou seem'st),
    Man lives not by bread only, but each word
350 Proceeding from the mouth of God, who fed
    Our fathers here with manna? In the Mount
    Moses was forty days, nor eat[9] nor drank,
    And forty days Eliah without food
    Wandered this barren waste;[1] the same I now.
355 Why dost thou then suggest to me distrust,[2]
    Knowing who I am, as I know who thou art?"
        Whom thus answered th' Arch-Fiend now
            undisguised:
    "'Tis true, I am that Spirit unfortunate,
    Who leagued with millions more in rash revolt
360 Kept not my happy station, but was driv'n
    With them from bliss to the bottomless deep;
    Yet to that hideous place not so confined
    By rigor unconniving,[3] but that oft
    Leaving my dolorous prison I enjoy
365 Large liberty to round this globe of earth,
    Or range in th' air, nor from the Heav'n of Heav'ns
    Hath he excluded my resort sometimes.
    I came among the Sons of God when he
    Gave up into my hands Uzzean Job
370 To prove° him, and illustrate his high worth;[4]   *put to the test*
    And when to all his angels he proposed
    To draw the proud king Ahab into fraud°   *being defrauded*
    That he might fall in Ramoth, they
            demurring,°   *while they hesitated*

9. I.e., ate.
1. Moses to the Israelites, Deut. 8:3: "man doth not live by bread only, but by every word
   that proceedeth out of the mouth of the Lord doth man live." Exod. 24:18: "Moses was
   in the mount forty days and forty nights" to receive the tablets of the law. 1 Kings 19:1–
   8: Elijah traveled to Mt. Horeb for forty days and nights without food.
2. "In Reformation theology the essence of the first temptation was to inspire distrust of
   God's providence (cf. Giles Fletcher, *Christ's Victory on Earth* 20, marginal note)" (Bush).
3. Watchful, implying tacit permission.
4. Job 2: After asserting of Job that "there is none like him in the earth, a perfect and an
   upright man" (2:3), God allows Satan to test his faith by afflicting him.

I undertook that office, and the tongues
375 Of all his flattering prophets glibbed° with lies   *made glib*
To his destruction, as I had in charge.
For what he bids I do; though I have lost
Much luster of my native brightness, lost
To be beloved of God, I have not lost
380 To love, at least contémplate and admire,
What I see excellent in good, or fair,
Or virtuous; I should so have lost all sense.
What can be then less in me than desire
To see thee and approach thee, whom I know
385 Declared the Son of God, to hear attent°   *attentively*
Thy wisdom, and behold thy godlike deeds?
Men generally think me much a foe
To all mankind: why should I? They to me
Never did wrong or violence, by them
390 I lost not what I lost; rather by them
I gained what I have gained, and with them dwell
Copartner in these regions of the world,
If not disposer; lend them oft my aid,
Oft my advice by presages and signs,
395 And answers, oracles, portents and dreams,
Whereby they may direct their future life.
Envy they say excites me, thus to gain
Companions of my misery and woe.
At first it may be; but long since with woe
400 Nearer acquainted, now I feel by proof°   *experience, trial*
That fellowship in pain divides not smart,
Nor lightens aught each man's peculiar° load;   *particular,*
Small consolation then, were man adjoined.   *individual*
This wounds me most (what can it less?) that man,
405 Man fall'n, shall be restored, I never more."
     To whom our Saviour sternly thus replied:
"Deservedly thou griev'st, composed of lies
From the beginning, and in lies wilt end,
Who boast'st release from Hell, and leave to come
410 Into the Heav'n of Heavens. Thou com'st indeed,
As a poor miserable captive thrall
Comes to the place where he before had sat
Among the prime in splendor, now deposed,
Ejected, emptied, gazed, unpitied, shunned,
415 A spectacle of ruin or of scorn
To all the host of Heaven; the happy place
Imparts to thee no happiness, no joy,
Rather inflames thy torment, representing

Lost bliss, to thee no more communicable;
420 So never more in Hell than when in Heaven.
But thou art serviceable to Heaven's King!
Wilt thou impute to obedience what thy fear
Extorts, or pleasure to do ill excites?
What but thy malice moved thee to misdeem
425 Of righteous Job, then cruelly to afflict him
With all inflictions? But his patience won.
The other service⁵ was thy chosen task,
To be a liar in four hundred mouths;⁶
For lying is thy sustenance, thy food.
430 Yet thou pretend'st to truth; all oracles
By thee are giv'n, and what confessed more true
Among the nations? That hath been thy craft,
By mixing somewhat true to vent more lies.
But what have been thy answers, what but dark,
435 Ambiguous, and with double sense deluding,⁷
Which they who asked have seldom understood,
And not well understood, as good not known?
Who ever by consulting at thy shrine
Returned the wiser, or the most instruct°   *instructed*
440 To fly or follow what concerned him most,
And run not sooner to his fatal snare?
For God hath justly giv'n the nations up
To thy delusions; justly, since they fell
Idolatrous; but when his purpose is
445 Among them to declare his providence,
To thee not known, whence hast thou then thy truth,
But from him or his angels president°   *presiding*
In every province, who themselves disdaining
To approach thy temples, give thee in command
450 What to the smallest tittle thou shalt say
To thy adorers? Thou with trembling fear,
Or like a fawning parasite obey'st;
Then to thyself ascrib'st the truth foretold.
But this thy glory shall be soon retrenched;°   *cut short*
455 No more shalt thou by oracling abuse
The Gentiles; henceforth oracles are ceased,
And thou no more with pomp and sacrifice

5. See lines 371–76.
6. The number of Ahab's prophets that led him to destruction (1 Kings 22:20–35).
7. Since Milton believed that the fallen angels got themselves worshiped as the gods of
   heathen religions, it followed that the ambiguous and misleading Greek oracles, such
   as those of Apollo and Zeus, were of diabolical inspiration.

Shalt be inquired at Delphos[8] or elsewhere,
At least in vain, for they shall find thee mute.
460 God hath now sent his living Oracle
Into the world, to teach his final will,
And sends his Spirit of Truth henceforth to dwell
In pious hearts, an inward oracle
To all truth requisite for men to know."
465 So spake our Saviour; but the subtle Fiend,
Though inly stung with anger and disdain,
Dissembled, and this answer smooth returned:
"Sharply thou hast insisted on rebuke,
And urged me hard with doings which not will
470 But misery hath wrested from me; where
Easily canst thou find one miserable,
And not enforced ofttimes to part from truth,
If it may stand him more in stead to lie,
Say and unsay, feign, flatter, or abjure?
475 But thou art placed above me, thou art Lord;
From thee I can and must submiss[9] endure
Check or reproof, and glad to scape so quit.
Hard are the ways of truth, and rough to walk,
Smooth on the tongue discoursed, pleasing to th' ear,
480 And tuneable as sylvan° pipe or song;   woodland
What wonder then if I delight to hear
Her dictates from thy mouth? Most men admire
Virtue who follow not her lore. Permit me
To hear thee when I come (since no man comes),
486 And talk at least, though I despair to attain.
Thy Father, who is holy, wise and pure,
Suffers the hypocrite or atheous° priest   impious
To treat his sacred courts, and minister
About his altar, handling holy things,
490 Praying or vowing, and vouchsafed his voice
To Balaam reprobate, a prophet yet
Inspired;[1] disdain not such access to me."
To whom our Saviour, with unaltered brow:
"Thy coming hither, though I know thy scope,°   purpose
495 I bid not or forbid; do as thou find'st
Permission from above; thou canst not more."

---

8. Delphi, site of Apollo's oracle.
9. Submissively (lit. placed beneath).
1. Num. 22–24: Although Balak, king of Moab, ordered the prophet Balaam to curse the
   Israelites, he blessed them instead: "How goodly are thy tents, O Jacob, and thy taber-
   nacles, O Israel" (24:5).

He added not; and Satan, bowing low
His gray dissimulation, disappeared
Into thin air diffused: for now began
500 Night with her sullen° wing to double-shade   *gloomy*
The desert, fowls in their clay nests were couched;
And now wild beasts came forth the woods to roam.

The Second Book

Meanwhile the new-baptized, who yet remained
At Jordan with the Baptist, and had seen
Him whom they heard so late expressly called
Jesus Messiah,[1] Son of God declared,
5 And on that high authority had believed,
And with him talked, and with him lodged, I mean
Andrew and Simon, famous after known
With others though in holy writ not named,
Now missing him, their joy so lately found,
10 So lately found, and so abruptly gone,
Began to doubt, and doubted many days,
And as the days increased, increased their doubt.
Sometimes they thought he might be only shown,
And for a time caught up to God, as once
15 Moses was in the Mount, and missing long,[2]
And the great Thisbite who on fiery wheels
Rode up to heaven, yet once again to come.[3]
Therefore as those young prophets then with care
Sought lost Elia, so in each place these
20 Nigh to Bethabara—in Jericho
The city of palms, Aenon, and Salem old,[4]
Machaerus,[5] and each town or city walled
On this side the broad lake Genezaret,°   *Sea of Galilee*
Or in Peraea[6]—but returned in vain.
25 Then on the bank of Jordan, by a creek

1. Heb. the anointed one.
2. Exod. 32:1: "And when the people saw that Moses delayed to come down out of the mount, the people gathered themselves together unto Aaron, and said unto him, Up, make us gods, which shall go before us; for as for this Moses, the man that brought us up out of the land of Egypt, we wot not what is become of him."
3. 2 Kings 2:11: "behold, there appeared a chariot of fire, and horses of fire, . . . and Elijah went up by a whirlwind into heaven." Mal. 4:5: "Behold, I will send you Elijah the prophet before the coming of the great and dreadful day of the Lord."
4. John 3:23: John baptized in Aenon, near Salem [or Shalem], "because there was much water there." Old Shalem is mentioned in Gen. 33:18 as a dwelling-place of Jacob. "City of palms": Deut. 34:3.
5. A fortress east of the Dead Sea.
6. A region east of the Jordan.

Where winds with reeds and osiers°   *willows*
    whisp'ring play,
Plain fisherman (no greater men them call),
Close in a cottage low together got,
Their unexpected loss and plaints outbreathed:
30 "Alas, from what high hope to what relapse
Unlooked for are we fall'n! Our eyes beheld
Messiah certainly now come, so long
Expected of our fathers; we have heard
His words, his wisdom full of grace and truth.
35 'Now, now, for sure, deliverance is at hand,
The kingdom shall to Israel be restored:'[7]
Thus we rejoiced, but soon our joy is turned
Into perplexity and new amaze;
For whither is he gone, what accident
40 Hath rapt° him from us? Will he now retire   *snatched*
After appearance, and again prolong
Our expectation? God of Israel,
Send thy Messiah forth, the time is come;
Behold the kings of the earth how they oppress
45 Thy chosen, to what highth their pow'r unjust
They have exalted, and behind them cast
All fear of thee; arise and vindicate
Thy glory, free thy people from their yoke!
But let us wait; thus far he hath performed,
50 Sent his Anointed, and to us revealed him
By his great Prophet,° pointed at and shown,   *John the Baptist*
In public, and with him we have conversed.
Let us be glad of this, and all our fears
Lay on his providence; he will not fail,
55 Nor will withdraw him now, nor will recall,
Mock us with his blest sight, then snatch him hence;
Soon we will see our hope, our joy, return."
    Thus they out of their plaints new hope resume
To find whom at the first they found unsought.
60 But to his mother Mary, when she saw
Others returned from baptism, not her son,
Nor left at Jordan, tidings of him none,
Within her breast though calm, her breast
    though pure,
Motherly cares and fears got head, and raised

---

7. See Acts 1:6: the disciples ask the resurrected Jesus, "wilt thou at this time restore again the kingdom to Israel?"

65 Some troubled thoughts, which she in sighs
       thus clad:
   "O what avails me now that honor high
To have conceived of God, or that salute,
'Hail, highly favored, among women blest!'[8]
While I to sorrows am no less advanced,
70 And fears as eminent, above the lot
Of other women, by the birth I bore,
In such a season born when scarce a shed
Could be obtained to shelter him or me
From the bleak air. A stable was our warmth,
75 A manger his; yet soon enforced to fly
Thence into Egypt, till the murd'rous king[9]
Were dead, who sought his life, and missing filled
With infant blood the streets of Bethlehem;
From Egypt home returned, in Nazareth
80 Hath been our dwelling many years, his life
Private, unactive, calm, contemplative,
Little suspicious to any king; but now
Full grown to man, acknowledged, as I hear,
By John the Baptist, and in public shown,
85 Son owned from Heaven by his Father's voice;
I looked for some great change; to honor? no,
But trouble, as old Simeon plain foretold,
That to the fall and rising he should be
Of many in Israel, and to a sign
90 Spoken against, that through my very soul
A sword shall pierce.[1] This is my favored lot,
My exaltation to afflictions high;
Afflicted I may be, it seems, and blest;
I will not argue° that, nor will repine.   *find fault with*
95 But where delays he now? some great intent
Conceals him. When twelve years he scarce
       had seen,
I lost him, but so found, as well I saw
He could not lose himself, but went about
His father's business;[2] what he meant I
       mused,°   *wondered, pondered*

8. Gabriel's salutation in Luke 1:28.
9. Herod (see Matt. 2:1–8).
1. Luke 2:34–35:."And Simeon blessed them, and said unto Mary his mother, Behold, this child is set for the fall and rising again of many in Israel; and for a sign which shall be spoken against; (Yea, a sword shall pierce through thy own soul also)."
2. Luke 2:49,51: "wist ye not that I must be about my Father's business? . . . but his mother kept all these sayings in her heart."

100   Since understand; much more his absence now
     Thus long to some great purpose he obscures.°   *leaves unexplained*
     But I to wait with patience am inured;
     My heart hath been a storehouse long of things
     And sayings laid up, portending strange events."
105   Thus Mary pondering oft, and oft to mind
     Recalling what remarkably had passed
     Since first her salutation heard, with thoughts
     Meekly composed awaited the fulfilling;
     The while her son tracing the desert wild,
110   Sole but with holiest meditations fed,
     Into himself descended, and at once
     All his great work to come before him set:
     How to begin, how to accomplish best
     His end of being on earth, and mission high.
115   For Satan, with sly preface[3] to return,
     Had left him vacant,° and with speed was gone   *at leisure*
     Up to the middle region of thick air,
     Where all his Potentates in council sat;
     There without sign of boast, or sign of joy,
120   Solicitous and blank he thus began:
       "Princes, Heaven's ancient sons, Ethereal
         Thrones,
     Demonian Spirits° now, from the element   *element-inhabiting*
     Each of his reign allotted, rightlier called   *demons*
     Powers of fire, air, water, and earth beneath,
125   So may we hold our place and these mild seats
     Without new trouble; such an enemy
     Is risen to invade us, who no less
     Threatens than our expulsion down to Hell.
     I, as I undertook, and with the vote
130   Consenting in full frequence° was empow'red,   *assembly*
     Have found him, viewed him, tasted[4] him, but find
     Far other labor to be undergone
     Than when I dealt with Adam first of men,
     Though Adam by his wife's allurement fell,
135   However to this man inferior far,
     If he be man by mother's side at least,
     With more than human gifts from Heaven adorned,
     Perfections absolute, graces divine,

---

3. An earlier statement; see 1. 483–85.
4. Tested, examined as in Ps. 34:8.

And amplitude of mind[5] to greatest deeds.
140   Therefore I am returned, lest confidence
Of my success with Eve in Paradise
Deceive ye to persuasion over-sure
Of like succeeding here; I summon all
Rather to be in readiness, with hand
145   Or counsel to assist, lest I who erst
Thought none my equal, now be overmatched."
    So spake the old Serpent doubting, and from all
With clamor was assured their utmost aid
At his command; when from amidst them rose
150   Belial, the dissolutest Spirit that fell,
The sensualest, and after Asmodai[6]
The fleshliest incubus,[7] and thus advised:
    "Set women in his eye and in his walk,
Among daughters of men the fairest found;
155   Many are in each region passing fair
As the noon sky, more like to goddesses
Than mortal creatures, graceful and discreet,
Expért in amorous arts, enchanting tongues
Persuasive, virgin majesty with mild
160   And sweet allayed, yet terrible to approach,[8]
Skilled to retire, and in retiring draw
Hearts after them tangled in amorous nets.
Such object hath the power to soft'n and tame
Severest temper,° smooth the rugged'st brow,   *temperament,*
165   Enerve, and with voluptuous hope dissolve,   *character*
Draw out with credulous desire, and lead
At will the manliest, resolutest breast,
As the magnetic° hardest iron draws.   *magnet*
Women, when nothing else, beguiled the heart
170   Of wisest Solomon, and made him build,
And made him bow to the gods of his wives."[9]
    To whom quick answer Satan thus returned:
"Belial, in much uneven scale thou weigh'st

5. Aristotle's ideal of magnanimity, the virtue of a prince, and Cicero's *amplitudinem animi*, "which best shows itself in scorn and contempt of pain."
6. Heb. the destroyer. He lusted after Sarah and killed her successive husbands until Tobias, Tobit's son, following the angel Raphael's advice, drove him away with the smell of burning fish (Tob. 3).
7. An evil spirit or demon who descends on women in their sleep to seek sexual intercourse with them.
8. From the Song of Sol. (6:4): "Thou art beautiful, O my love . . . terrible, as an army with banners."
9. 1 Kings 11:4–8: Solomon's wives led him in old age into idolatry. See *PL*, 1:400–05, 442–46.

All others by thyself; because of old
175   Thou thyself dot'st on womankind, admiring
Their shape, their color, and attractive grace,
None are, thou think'st, but taken with such toys.
Before the Flood thou with thy lusty crew,
False-titled Sons of God, roaming the earth
180   Cast wanton eyes on the daughters of men,
And coupled with them, and begot a race.[1]
Have we not seen, or by relation heard,
In courts and regal chambers how thou lurk'st,[2]
In wood or grove by mossy fountain-side,
185   In valley or green meadow, to waylay
Some beauty rare, Callisto, Clymene,
Daphne, or Semele, Antiopa,
Or Amymóne, Syrinx,[3] many more
Too long,° then lay'st thy scapes° on names   *too many to mention /*
adored,   *escapades*
190   Apollo, Neptune, Jupiter, or Pan,
Satyr, or Faun, or Sylvan? But these haunts°   *habits*
Delight not all; among the sons of men,
How many have with a smile made small account
Of beauty and her lures, easily scorned
195   All her assaults, on worthier things intent?
Remember that Pelléan conqueror,[4]
A youth, how all the beauties of the East
He slightly viewed, and slightly overpassed;
How he surnamed of Africa dismissed
200   In his prime youth the fair Iberian maid.[5]
For° Solomon, he lived at ease, and full   *As for*
Of honor, wealth, high fare, aimed not beyond
Higher design than to enjoy his state;
Thence to the bait of women lay exposed.
205   But he whom we attempt is wiser far
Than Solomon, of more exalted mind,

1. Gen. 6:4: "when the sons of God came in unto the daughters of men, and they bare
children to them, the same became mighty men which were of old, men of renown."
2. *PL*, 1.490–92, 497: "Belial came last, than whom a Spirit more lewd / Fell not from
heaven, or more gross to love / Vice for itself. . . . In courts and palaces he also reigns."
3. All nymphs who were objects of the gods' lust, recalled by Ovid. Callisto, raped by Jupiter, who disguised himself as Diana. Clymene, mother of Phaethon by Apollo. Daphne,
loved and pursued by Apollo, changed into a laurel. Semele, consumed by lightning
when her lover, Jove, appeared to her in full splendor. Antiopa, a woman loved by Zeus.
Amymóne, loved by Neptune. Syrinx, pursued by Pan and changed into a reed.
4. Plutarch, in *Alexander* 21, tells of the sexual abstinence of Alexander the Great, born
at Pella in Macedonia. "Satan praises Alexander's restraint with women, but ignores
his homosexuality. Satan will include both women and youths in the banquet temptation, 2.351–61" (Leonard).
5. Scipio Africanus, who restored a beautiful captive woman to her fiancé.

Made and set wholly on the accomplishment
Of greatest things. What woman will you find,
Though of this age the wonder and the fame,
210 On whom his leisure will vouchsafe an eye
Of fond° desire? Or should she confident,   *foolish*
As sitting queen adored on Beauty's throne,
Descend with all her winning charms begirt
To enamor, as the zone of Venus[6] once
215 Wrought that effect on Jove (so fables tell),
How would one look from his majestic brow
Seated as on the top of Virtue's hill,
Discount'nance her despised, and put to rout
All her array; her female pride deject,°   *dejected, cast down*
220 Or turn to reverent awe? For Beauty stands
In the admiration only of weak minds
Led captive; cease to admire, and all her plumes
Fall flat and shrink into a trivial toy,
At every sudden slighting quite abashed.
225 Therefore with manlier objects we must try
His constancy, with such as have more show
Of worth, of honor, glory, and popular praise,
Rocks whereon greatest men have oftest wrecked;
Or that which only seems to satisfy
230 Lawful desires of nature, not beyond.
And now I know he hungers where no food
Is to be found, in the wide wilderness;
The rest commit to me; I shall let pass
No advantage, and his strength as oft assay."
235   He ceased, and heard their grant in loud acclaim;
Then forthwith to him takes a chosen band
Of Spirits likest to himself in guile
To be at hand, and at his beck appear,
If cause were to unfold some active scene
240 Of various persons, each to know his part;
Then to the desert takes with these his flight,
Where still from shade to shade[7] the Son of God
After forty days' fasting had remained,
Now hung'ring first, and to himself thus said:
245   "Where will this end? Four times ten days I
        have passed
Wand'ring this woody maze, and human food

---

6. The belt of Venus, or Aphrodite, which Hera wore when she seduced Zeus (*Il.* xiv, 214–17).
7. Either from shelter to shelter or from one night to the next.

Nor tasted, nor had appetite. That fast
To virtue I impute not, or count part
Of what I suffer here; if nature need not,
250 Or God support nature without repast,
Though needing, what praise is it to endure?
But now I feel I hunger, which declares
Nature hath need of what she asks; yet God
Can satisfy that need some other way,
255 Though hunger still remain: so° it remain   *so long as*
Without this body's wasting, I content me,
And from the sting of famine fear no harm,
Nor mind it, fed with better thoughts that feed
Me hung'ring more to do my Father's will."[8]
260   It was the hour of night, when thus the Son
Communed in silent walk, then laid him down
Under the hospitable covert nigh
Of trees thick interwoven; there he slept,
And dreamed, as appetite is wont to dream,
265 Of meats and drinks, nature's refreshment sweet.
Him thought° he by the brook of Cherith[9] stood   *It seemed to him*
And saw the ravens with their horny beaks
Food to Elijah bringing even and morn,
Though ravenous, taught to abstain from what
     they brought.
270 He saw the Prophet also how he fled
Into the desert, and how there he slept
Under a juniper; then how, awaked,
He found his supper on the coals prepared,
And by the angel was bid rise and eat,
275 And eat the second time after repose,
The strength whereof sufficed him forty days;
Sometimes that with Elijah he partook,
Or as a guest with Daniel at his pulse.°   *beans, lentils*
Thus wore out night, and now the herald lark
280 Left his ground-nest, high tow'ring to descry
The morn's approach, and greet her with his song;
As lightly from his grassy couch up rose
Our Saviour, and found all was but a dream:
Fasting he went to sleep, and fasting waked.
285 Up to a hill anon his steps he reared,

8. *PL*, 3.37: "Then feed on thoughts." In John 4:34, Christ tells his disciples, "My meat is to do the will of him that sent me."
9. See 1 Kings 17:2–6, where God commands Elijah to hide, and where ravens feed him; see also 1 Kings 19:4–8, where angels feed him twice before his forty-day fast.

From whose high top to ken the prospect round,
If cottage were in view, sheepcote or herd;
But cottage, herd or sheepcote none he saw,
Only in a bottom° saw a pleasant grove,   *valley*
290 With chant of tuneful birds resounding loud.
Thither he bent his way, determined there
To rest at noon, and entered soon the shade
High-roofed and walks beneath, and alleys
    brown°   *shaded, dark*
That opened in the midst a woody scene;
295 Nature's own work it seemed (nature taught art),
And to a superstitious eye the haunt
Of wood-gods and wood-nymphs. He viewed it round,
When suddenly a man before him stood,
Not rustic as before, but seemlier clad,
300 As one in city or court or palace bred,
And with fair speech these words to him addressed:
    "With granted leave officious[1] I return,
But much more wonder that the Son of God
In this wild solitude so long should bide
305 Of all things destitute, and well I know,
Not without hunger. Others of some note,
As story tells, have trod this wilderness:
The fugitive bond-woman with her son,
Outcast Nebaioth,[2] yet found he relief
310 By a providing angel; all the race
Of Israel here had famished, had not God
Rained from heaven manna;[3] and that
    Prophet bold,
Native of Thebez,[4] wand'ring here was fed
Twice by a voice inviting him to eat.
315 Of thee these forty days none hath regard,
Forty and more deserted here indeed."
    To whom thus Jesus: "What conclud'st thou hence?
They all had need, I as thou seest have none."
    "How hast thou hunger then?" Satan replied.
320 "Tell me, if food were now before thee set,
Wouldst thou not eat?" "Thereafter as I like
The giver," answered Jesus. "Why should that

1. Here, ready to serve; but the pejorative modern meaning (intrusive, meddling) was also
   current.
2. The name of Ishmael's son, here used for Ishmael himself, the son of the "bondwoman"
   Hagar (Gen. 21:9–19).
3. See Exod. 16:35.
4. I.e., Thisbe, City of Elijah in Gilead.

Cause thy refusal?" said the subtle Fiend,
"Hast thou not right to all created things,
325   Owe not all creatures by just right to thee
Duty and service, nor to stay till bid,
But tender all their power? Nor mention I
Meats by the Law unclean, or offered first
To idols[5]—those young Daniel could refuse;
330   Nor proffered by an enemy, though who
Would scruple that, with want oppressed? Behold
Nature ashamed, or better to express,
Troubled that thou shouldst hunger, hath purveyed
From all the elements her choicest store
335   To treat thee as beseems, and as her Lord
With honor; only deign to sit and eat."
      He spake no dream, for as his words had end,
Our Saviour lifting up his eyes beheld
In ample space under the broadest shade
340   A table richly spread, in regal mode,
With dishes piled, and meats of noblest sort
And savor, beasts of chase, or fowl of game,
In pastry built, or from the spit, or boiled,
Grisamber[6]-steamed; all fish from sea or shore,
345   Freshet,° or purling brook, of shell or fin,   *small stream*
And exquisitest name, for which was drained
Pontus, and Lucrine bay,[7] and Afric coast.
Alas, how simple, to these cates° compared,   *delicacies*
Was that crude apple that diverted° Eve!   *led astray, seduced*
350   And at a stately sideboard by the wine
That fragrant smell diffused, in order stood
Tall stripling youths rich-clad, of fairer hue
Than Ganymede or Hylas;[8] distant more
Under the trees now tripped, now solemn stood   *nymphs of rivers,*
355   Nymphs of Diana's train, and Naiades°   *streams, and springs*
With fruits and flowers of Amalthea's horn,°   *cornucopia, the*
And ladies of th' Hesperides,[9] that seemed   *horn of plenty*
Fairer than feigned of old, or fabled since

5. Satan lies, for shellfish (line 345) are forbidden under the ceremonial Mosaic law that
    Christ has not yet abrogated. Both 1 Cor. 10:20–21 and the Apostolic Decree in Acts
    (15:20) regard using food polluted by idolatry as a violation of minimum standards of
    decency and ethical practice binding on non-Jews as well as Jews.
6. Ambergris, used in perfumery and cooking.
7. A lagoon near Naples famous for its shellfish. Pontus is the Black Sea.
8. Beautiful youth beloved by Hercules. Ganymede was a Trojan youth abducted by Jove
    to be his cupbearer.
9. Nymphs who tend a blissful garden in a far western corner of the world. Here, the
    garden itself. See *A Masque*, 980–81.

Of fairy damsels met in forest wide
360 By knights of Logres, or of Lyonesse,[1]
Lancelot or Pelleas, or Pellenore;[2]
And all the while harmonious airs were heard
Of chiming strings or charming pipes, and winds
Of gentlest gale Arabian odors fanned
365 From their soft wings, and Flora's[3] earliest smells.
Such was the splendor, and the Tempter now
His invitation earnestly renewed:
   "What doubts° the Son of God to sit and eat?   *Why hesitates*
These are not fruits forbidden, no interdict
370 Defends° the touching of these viands pure;   *Forbids*
Their taste no knowledge works, at least of evil,
But life preserves, destroys life's enemy,
Hunger, with sweet restorative delight.
All these are Spirits of air, and woods, and springs,
375 Thy gentle ministers, who come to pay
Thee homage, and acknowledge thee their Lord.
What doubt'st thou Son of God? Sit down and eat."
   To whom thus Jesus temperately replied:
"Said'st thou not that to all things I had right?
380 And who withholds my pow'r that right to use?
Shall I receive by gift what of my own,
When and where likes° me best, I can   *pleases*
      command?
I can at will, doubt not, as soon as thou,
Command a table in this wilderness,[4]
385 And call swift flights of angels ministrant
Arrayed in glory on my cup to attend.
Why shouldst thou then obtrude this
      diligence°   *persistent effort to*
In vain, where no acceptance it can find,   *please*
And with my hunger what hast thou to do?
390 Thy pompous delicacies I contemn,
And count thy specious gifts no gifts but guiles."
   To whom thus answered Satan malcontent:
"That I have also power to give thou seest;
If of that pow'r I bring thee voluntary

1. A mythical region west of Cornwall. Logres is the middle region of Britain east of the
Severn.
2. King Arthur's amorous knights.
3. Goddess of flowers and springtime.
4. Ps. 78:19: "Can God furnish a table in the wilderness"? The psalm refers to Num.
11:4–5, where the wandering Israelites, murmuring against their heavenly diet of
manna, long for the delicacies they enjoyed in Egypt.

395 What I might have bestowed on whom I pleased,
And rather opportunely in this place
Chose to impart to thy apparent need,
Why shouldst thou not accept it? But I see
What I can do or offer is suspéct;
400 Of these things others quickly will dispose
Whose pains have earned the far-fet° spoil."   *far-fetched*
    With that
Both table and provision vanished quite
With sound of harpies' wings and talons heard;[5]
Only the impórtune° Tempter still remained,   *persistent*
405 And with these words his temptation pursued:
    "By hunger, that each other creature tames,
Thou art not to be harmed, therefore not moved;
Thy temperance invincible besides,
For no allurement yields to appetite,
410 And all thy heart is set on high designs,
High actions; but wherewith to be achieved?
Great acts require great means of enterprise;
Thou art unknown, unfriended, low of birth,
A carpenter thy father known, thyself
415 Bred up in poverty and straits at home,
Lost in a desert here and hunger-bit.
Which way or from what hope dost thou aspire
To greatness? whence authority deriv'st,
What followers, what retínue canst thou gain,
420 Or at thy heels the dizzy multitude,
Longer than thou canst feed them on thy cost?
Money brings honor, friends, conquest, and realms.
What raised Antipater the Edomite,[6]
And his son Herod placed on Judah's throne
425 (Thy throne), but gold that got him puissant
    friends?
Therefore, if at great things thou wouldst arrive,
Get riches first, get wealth, and treasure heap,
Not difficult, if thou hearken to me;
Riches are mine, fortune is in my hand;
430 They whom I favor thrive in wealth amain,°   *exceedingly*
While virtue, valor, wisdom sit in want."[7]

---

5. Recalls *The Tempest*, stage direction at 3.3.52: "Enter ARIEL like a Harpy; claps his
   wings upon the table; and, with a quaint device, the banquet vanishes."
6. Antipater the Idumaean (d. 43 B.C.E.), founder of the Herodian dynasty and father of
   Herod the Great, used wealth to curry favor with the Romans.
7. For contrast, see Milton, *First Defence*: "If you desire riches, liberty, peace, and empire,
   how much more excellent, how much more becoming yourselves would be, resolutely to

To whom thus Jesus patiently replied:
"Yet wealth without these three is impotent
To gain dominion or to keep it gained.
435   Witness those ancient empires of the earth,
In highth of all their flowing wealth dissolved;
But men endued with these have oft attained
In lowest poverty to highest deeds:
Gideon and Jephtha, and the shepherd lad[8]
440   Whose offspring on the throne of Judah sat
So many ages, and shall yet regain
That seat, and reign in Israel without end.
Among the heathen (for throughout the world
To me is not unknown what hath been done
445   Worthy of memorial) canst thou not remember
Quintius, Fabricius, Curius, Regulus?[9]
For I esteem those names of men so poor
Who could do mighty things, and could contemn
Riches though offered from the hand of kings.
450   And what in me seems wanting, but that I
May also in this poverty as soon
Accomplish what they did, perhaps and more?
Extol not riches then, the toil° of fools,   *(1) labor, (2) snare*
The wise man's cumbrance if not snare, more apt
455   To slacken virtue and abate° her edge   *blunt*
Than prompt her to do aught may merit praise.
What if with like aversion I reject
Riches and realms? Yet not for that° a crown,   *because*
Golden in show, is but a wreath of thorns,
460   Brings dangers, troubles, cares, and sleepless nights

---

seek all these by your own virtue, industry, prudence, and valor, than under a royal
despotism to hope for them in vain."
8. David, whom God took "from the sheepfolds" (Ps. 78:70). Gabriel prophesies Christ's
accession to David's throne (Luke 1:33). Gideon, a young man from a poor family and
unsure of himself, who was chosen by God to free the people of Israel (Judg. 6–8).
Jephtha, a harlot's son driven from his father's house, was recalled by the elders of Gilead to deliver his people from the Ammonites (Jud. 11–12).
9. Examples of plain integrity among leaders of the Roman republic. Lucius Quinctius
Cincinnatus left his farm, though his departure could have meant starvation for his
family, to deliver the Romans from the Aequi and Volscians. He resigned his dictator-
ship immediately after the crisis and returned home. Gaius Fabricius Luscinus was a
commander who, despite poverty, rejected the bribes and inducements of Pyrrhus to
change sides and fight against Rome. Manius Curius Dentatus (born with teeth—
hence the cognomen), a plebeian hero notable for ending the Samnite War, rejected
the expensive gifts proffered by the enemy, who found him sitting by a fire, roasting
turnips. Marcus Atilius Regulus, captured by the Carthaginians in the First Punic War,
was sent to Rome on parole to negotiate a peace or exchange of prisoners. Instead, he
urged the Roman senate to reject the proposals and to continue fighting. Despite all
persuasions, he honored his parole by returning to Carthage, where he was tortured to
death.

To him who wears the regal diadem,
When on his shoulders each man's burden lies;[1]
For therein stands the office of a king,
His honor, virtue, merit, and chief praise,
465   That for the public all this weight he bears.
Yet he who reigns within himself, and rules
Passions, desires, and fears, is more a king;
Which every wise and virtuous man attains;
And who attains not, ill aspires to rule
470   Cities of men, or headstrong multitudes,
Subject himself to anarchy within,
Or lawless passions in him which he serves.
But to guide nations in the way of truth
By saving doctrine, and from error lead
475   To know, and knowing worship God aright,
Is yet more kingly; this attracts the soul,
Governs the inner man, the nobler part,
That other o'er the body only reigns,
And oft by force, which to a generous mind
480   So reigning can be no sincere delight.
Besides, to give a kingdom hath been thought
Greater and nobler done, and to lay down
Far more magnanimous than to assume.[2]
Riches are needless then, both for themselves,
485   And for thy reason why they should be sought,
To gain a scepter, oftest better missed."

The Third Book

So spake the Son of God, and Satan stood
A while as mute, confounded what to say,
What to reply, confuted and convinced°   *overcome in*
Of his weak arguing and fallacious drift;   *argument*
5   At length collecting all his serpent wiles,
With soothing words renewed, him thus accosts:
"I see thou know'st what is of use to know,
What best to say canst say, to do canst do;
Thy actions to thy words accord, thy words
10   To thy large heart give utterance due, thy heart
Contains of good, wise, just, the perfect shape.
Should kings and nations from thy mouth consult,
Thy counsel would be as the oracle

1. Cf. 2 *Henry IV* 3.1: "Uneasy lies the head that wears the crown"; and *Henry V*, 4.1.235 ff.
2. Seneca, *Thyestes* 529: "To have a kingdom is chance; to give one, virtue."

Urim and Thummim,[1] those oraculous gems
On Aaron's breast, or tongue of seers old

15

Infallible; or wert thou sought to° deeds   *called on for*
That might require th' array of war, thy skill
Of conduct° would be such that all the world   *military leadership*
Could not sustain° thy prowess, or subsist   *withstand*

20

In battle, though against thy few in arms.
These godlike virtues wherefore dost thou hide?
Affecting private life, or more obscure
In savage wilderness, wherefore deprive
All earth her wonder at thy acts, thyself

25

The fame and glory, glory the reward
That sole excites to high attempts the flame
Of most erected° spirits, most tempered pure   *high-souled, noble*
Ethereal,[2] who all pleasures else despise,
All treasures and all gain esteem as dross,

30

And dignities and powers, all but the highest?
Thy years are ripe, and over-ripe; the son
Of Macedonian Philip had ere these
Won Asia and the throne of Cyrus held
At his dispose,[3] young Scipio had brought down

35

The Carthaginian pride,[4] young Pompey quelled
The Pontic king and in triumph had rode.[5]
Yet years, and to ripe years judgment mature,
Quench not the thirst of glory, but augment.
Great Julius, whom now all the world admires,

40

The more he grew in years, the more inflamed
With glory, wept that he had lived so long
Inglorious.[6] But thou yet art not too late."
    To whom our Saviour calmly thus replied:
"Thou neither dost persuade me to seek wealth

45

For empire's sake, nor empire to affect
For glory's sake, by all thy argument.
For what is glory but the blaze of fame,
The people's praise, if always praise unmixed?
And what the people but a herd confused,

50

A miscellaneous rabble, who extol

---

1. Traditionally, "light" and "perfection," two stones in Aaron's breastplate (Exod. 28:30) with oracular properties.
2. The most purely spiritual constitution.
3. By age twenty-six, Alexander had conquered the Persian Empire.
4. Scipio Africanus drove the Carthaginians from Spain while still in his twenties.
5. Although Pompey in his twenties received a triumph for his African victories, he was in his forties when he conquered "the Pontic king" Mithridates.
6. Plutarch reports that Caesar wept when he read of Alexander's youthful accomplishments, because at the same age he had not yet achieved a brilliant success.

Things vulgar, and well weighed, scarce worth
    the praise?
They praise and they admire they know not what,
And know not whom, but as one leads the other;
And what delight to be by such extolled,
55 To live upon their tongues and be their talk,
Of whom to be dispraised were no small praise?
His lot who dares be singularly good.
Th' intelligent among them and the wise
Are few, and glory scarce of few is raised.
60 This is true glory and renown, when God
Looking on the earth, with approbation marks
The just man, and divulges° him through Heaven   *proclaims publicly*
To all his angels, who with true applause
Recount his praises; thus he did to Job,
65 When to extend his fame through Heaven and earth,
As thou to thy reproach may'st well remember,
He asked thee, 'Hast thou seen my servant Job?'[7]
Famous he was in Heaven, on earth less known,
Where glory is false glory, attributed
70 To things not glorious, men not worthy of fame.
They err who count it glorious to subdue
By conquest far and wide, to overrun
Large countries, and in field great battles win,
Great cities by assault. What do these worthies
75 But rob and spoil, burn, slaughter, and enslave
Peaceable nations, neighboring or remote,
Made captive, yet deserving freedom more
Than those their conquerors, who leave behind
Nothing but ruin wheresoe'er they rove,
80 And all the flourishing works of peace destroy,
Then swell with pride, and must be titled gods,
Great benefactors of mankind, deliverers,
Worshiped with temple, priest, and sacrifice?
One is the son of Jove, of Mars[8] the other,
85 Till conqueror Death discover them scarce men,
Rolling in brutish vices,[9] and deformed,
Violent or shameful death their due reward.
But if there be in glory aught of good,

---

7. Job 1:8: "Hast thou considered my servant Job, that there is none like him in the earth,
   a perfect and an upright man, one that feareth God, and escheweth evil?" See also
   1.146–49, 369–70, 424–26, and 3.92–95.
8. Alexander and Romulus, respectively.
9. Alexander died after a bout of excessive drinking.

It may by means far different be attained
90 Without ambition, war, or violence;
By deeds of peace, by wisdom eminent,
By patience, temperance. I mention still
Him whom thy wrongs, with saintly patience borne,
Made famous in a land and times obscure:
95 Who names not now with honor patient Job?
Poor Socrates (who next more memorable?)
By what he taught and suffered for so doing,
For truth's sake suffering death unjust,[1] lives now
Equal in fame to proudest conquerors.
100 Yet if for fame and glory aught be done,
Aught suffered, if young African[2] for fame
His wasted country freed from Punic rage,
The deed becomes unpraised, the man at least,
And loses, though but verbal, his reward.
105 Shall I seek glory[3] then, as vain men seek
Oft not deserved? I seek not mine, but his
Who sent me, and thereby witness whence I am."
    To whom the Tempter murmuring thus replied:
"Think not so slight of glory, therein least
110 Resembling thy great Father: he seeks glory,
And for his glory all things made, all things
Orders and governs, nor content in Heaven
By all his angels glorified, requires
Glory from men, from all men good or bad,
115 Wise or unwise, no difference, no exemption;
Above all sacrifice or hallowed gift
Glory he requires, and glory he receives
Promiscuous° from all nations, Jew, or Greek,
Or barbarous,° nor exception hath declared;
120 From us, his foes pronounced, glory he exacts."
    To whom our Saviour fervently replied:
"And reason; since his word[4] all things produced,
Though chiefly not for glory as prime end,
But to show forth his goodness, and impart
125 His good communicable to every soul
Freely; of whom what could he less expect

*Without
discrimination
foreign,
non-Hellenic*

1. Accused of corrupting the youth of Athens and maligning the gods of the city-state, Socrates chose to die rather than to act unlawfully (Plato, *Crito*).
2. I.e., Scipio (see 3.34–35).
3. Majestic beauty and splendor; exalted honor, praise, or distinction accorded by common consent; renown.
4. Milton's Jesus uses "word" not to refer to himself (as in John 1:1 and *PL*, 7.163 f.) but rather to God's creative decree.

Than glory and benediction, that is thanks,
The slightest, easiest, readiest recompense
From them who could return him nothing else,
130 And not returning that, would likeliest render
Contempt instead, dishonor, obloquy?
Hard recompense, unsuitable return
For so much good, so much beneficence.
But why should man seek glory, who of his own
135 Hath nothing, and to whom nothing belongs
But condemnation, ignominy, and shame?
Who for so many benefits received
Turned recreant° to God, ingrate and false,　　　　　　　　*false, apostate*
And so of all true good himself despoiled,
140 Yet, sacrilegious, to himself would take
That which to God alone of right belongs;
Yet so much bounty is in God, such grace,
That who advance his glory, not their own,
Them he himself to glory will advance."
145 　　So spake the Son of God; and here again
Satan had not to answer, but stood struck
With guilt of his own sin, for he himself
Insatiable of glory had lost all:
Yet of another plea bethought him soon.
150 　　"Of glory as thou wilt," said he, "so deem;
Worth or not worth the seeking, let it pass.
But to a kingdom thou art born, ordained
To sit upon thy father David's throne,
By mother's side thy father, though thy right
155 Be now in powerful hands, that will not part
Easily from possession won with arms;
Judea now and all the Promised Land,
Reduced a province under Roman yoke,
Obeys Tiberius, nor is always ruled
160 With temperate sway; oft have they violated
The Temple,[5] oft the Law with foul affronts,
Abominations rather, as did once
Antiochus.[6] And think'st thou to regain
Thy right by sitting still or thus retiring?

5. Roman emperor Tiberius (14–37 C.E.) retained Pilate as procurator of Judea despite
tyrannical acts recorded by Josephus (*Antiquities*, 18.3). Pompey entered the Holy of
Holies in 63 B.C.E., and Pilate, violating the second commandment, brought into Jerusalem busts of the Roman Emperors.
6. Antiochus Epiphanes, king of Syria and oppressor of the Jews (1 Macc. 1:20–63).

165 So did not Machabeus:[7] he indeed
    Retired unto the desert, but with arms,
    And o'er a mighty king so oft prevailed
    That by strong hand his family obtained,
    Though priests, the crown, and David's
            throne usurped,
170 With Modin and her suburbs once content.
    If kingdom move thee not, let move thee zeal
    And duty; zeal and duty are not slow,
    But on Occasion's forelock[8] watchful wait.
    They themselves rather are occasion best—
175 Zeal of thy father's house,[9] duty to free
    Thy country from her heathen servitude;
    So shalt thou best fulfill, best verify
    The Prophets old, who sung thy endless reign,
    The happier reign the sooner it begins.
180 Reign then; what canst thou better do the while?"
        To whom our Saviour answer thus returned:
    "All things are best fulfilled in their due time,
    And time there is for all things,[1] Truth hath said.
    If of my reign prophetic writ hath told
185 That it shall never end, so when begin
    The Father in his purpose hath decreed,
    He in whose hand all times and seasons roll.[2]
    What if he hath decreed that I shall first
    Be tried in humble state, and things adverse,
190 By tribulations, injuries, insults,
    Contempts, and scorns, and snares, and violence,
    Suffering, abstaining, quietly expecting
    Without distrust or doubt, that he may know
    What I can suffer, how obey? Who best
195 Can suffer° best can do; best reign who first   *be acted on*
    Well hath obeyed; just trial ere I merit
    My exaltation without change or end.
    But what concerns it thee when I begin

---

7. Judas Maccabeus, born at Modin in Judea, was a Jewish leader against Antiochus (1 Macc. 2–9). Originally priests, his family later assumed royal power as the Hasmonean dynasty.
8. Occasion (Opportunity) was depicted as a woman bald except for one lock of hair hanging over her forehead, to illustrate the importance of seizing opportunity.
9. According to his disciples, Christ's zealous driving out of the money-changers from the temple fulfilled the prophecy, "the zeal of thine house hath eaten me up" (Ps. 69:9).
1. Eccles. 3:1: "To every thing there is a season, and a time to every purpose under the heaven."
2. Acts 1:7: "It is not for you to know the times or the seasons, which the Father hath put in his own power."

My everlasting kingdom? Why art thou
200 Solicitous? What moves thy inquisition?
Know'st thou not that my rising is thy fall,
And my promotion will be thy destruction?"
      To whom the Tempter, inly racked, replied:
"Let that come when it comes; all hope is lost
205 Of my reception into grace; what worse?
For where no hope is left, is left no fear.
If there be worse, the expectation more
Of worse torments me than the feeling can.
I would be at the worst; worst is my port,
210 My harbor and my ultimate repose,
The end I would attain, my final good.
My error was my error, and my crime
My crime, whatever° for itself condemned,   *whatever it was*
And will alike be punished, whether thou
215 Reign or reign not; though to that gentle brow
Willingly I could fly, and hope thy reign,
From that placíd aspéct and meek regard,
Rather than aggravate my evil state,
Would stand between me and thy Father's ire
220 (Whose ire I dread more than the fire of hell),
A shelter and a kind of shading cool
Interposition, as a summer's cloud.
If I then to the worst that can be haste,
Why move thy feet so slow to what is best,
225 Happiest both to thyself and all the world,
That thou who worthiest art shouldst be their king?
Perhaps thou linger'st in deep thoughts detained
Of the enterprise so hazardous and high;
No wonder, for though in thee be united
230 What of perfection can in man be found,
Or human nature can receive, consider
Thy life hath yet been private, most part spent
At home, scarce viewed the Galilean towns,
And once a year Jerusalem,[3] few days'
235 Short sojourn; and what thence couldst thou observe?
The world thou hast not seen, much less her glory,
Empires, and monarchs, and their radiant courts,
Best school of best experience, quickest insight
In all things that to greatest actions lead.
240 The wisest, unexperienced, will be ever

3. Luke 2:41: "Now his parents went to Jerusalem every year at the feast of the passover."

Timorous and loath, with novice modesty
(As he who seeking asses found a kingdom)[4]
Irresolute, unhardy, unadvent'rous.
But I will bring thee where thou soon shalt quit

245 Those rudiments,° and see before thine eyes   *initial stages*
The monarchies of the earth, their pomp and state,
Sufficient introduction to inform
Thee, of thyself so apt, in regal arts,
And regal mysteries; that thou may'st know

250 How best their opposition to withstand."
    With that (such power was giv'n him then) he took
The Son of God up to a mountain high.[5]
It was a mountain at whose verdant feet
A spacious plain outstretched in circuit wide

255 Lay pleasant; from his side two rivers° flowed,   *Tigris and Euphrates*
Th' one winding, the other straight, and left between
Fair champaign° with less rivers interveined,   *flat, open land*
Then meeting joined their tribute to the sea:
Fertile of corn the glebe,° of oil and wine;   *soil*

260 With herds the pastures thronged, with flocks
        the hills;
Huge cities and high-towered, that well might seem
The seats of mightiest monarchs; and so large
The prospect was that here and there was room
For barren desert fountainless and dry.

265 To this high mountain-top the Tempter brought
Our Saviour, and new train of words began:
    "Well have we speeded, and o'er hill and dale,
Forest and field, and flood, temples and towers,
Cut shorter many a league. Here thou behold'st

270 Assyria and her empire's ancient bounds,
Araxes[6] and the Caspian lake, thence on
As far as Indus east, Euphrates west,
And oft beyond; to south the Persian bay,
And inaccessible the Arabian drouth:°   *desert*

275 Here Nineveh,[7] of length within her wall
Several days' journey, built by Ninus[8] old,

---

4. Saul, looking for his father's stray asses, was anointed first king of Israel by the prophet
   Samuel (1 Sam. 9:3–10:1).
5. Probably Mt. Niphates, scene of Satan's soliloquy (*PL*, 4.32–113) and of Adam's final
   vision (11.381–84).
6 Armenian river flowing into the Caspian Sea.
7. The capital of Assyria.
8. In pagan tradition the eponymous founder of Nineveh and king of Assyria. In the Bible
   (Gen. 10:11), Asshur built Nineveh. See also Jon. 3:3: "Nineveh was an exceeding great
   city of three days' journey."

Of that first golden monarchy the seat,
And seat of Salmanassar,[9] whose success
Israel in long captivity still mourns;

280 There Babylon, the wonder of all tongues,
As ancient, but rebuilt by him° who twice   *Nebuchadnezzar*
Judah and all thy father David's house
Led captive and Jerusalem laid waste,
Till Cyrus set them free; Persepolis[1]

285 His city there thou seest, and Bactra[2] there;
Ecbatana[3] her structure vast there shows,
And Hecatompylos[4] her hundred gates;
There Susa by Choaspes,[5] amber stream,
The drink of none but kings; of later fame,

290 Built by Emathian,° or by Parthian hands,   *Macedonian*
The great Seleucia, Nisibis, and there
Artaxata, Teredon, Ctesiphon,[6]
Turning with easy eye thou may'st behold.
All these the Parthian (now some ages past

295 By great Arsaces led, who founded first
That empire) under his dominion holds,
From the luxurious kings of Antioch won.[7]
And just in time thou com'st to have a view
Of his great power; for now the Parthian king

300 In Ctesiphon hath gathered all his host
Against the Scythian, whose incursions wild
Have wasted Sogdiana;[8] to her aid
He marches now in haste. See, though from far,

9. Shalmaneser, king of Assyria, carried the ten northern tribes of Israel into captivity in 726 B.C.E. (2 Kings 17:3–6, 18:9–12).
1. In 538 B.C.E., Cyrus, founder of the Persian empire, took Babylon and released the captive Jews (2 Chron. 36:22–23). Persepolis ("city of Persians") Cyrus's summer capital, destroyed by a fire that broke out when Alexander's troops looted it in about 333 B.C.E.
2. The ancient capital of the Persian province of Bactria (modern Balkh, in Afghanistan).
3. Supposed by the Greeks to be the capital of Media, its massive fortifications are described in Jth. 1:2–4.
4. "Hundred gates," the Parthian capital.
5. A river east of the Tigris, famous for its pure water. Susa, the biblical Shushan (Esther 1, Dan. 8), was the winter residence of the Persian kings.
6. On the east bank of the Tigris, one of the great cities of Mesopotamia and capital of the Parthian Empire. Seleucia was a city on the Tigris, near modern Baghdad, founded by Alexander's general Seleucus Nicator (ca. 358–281 B.C.E.). Nisibis was a Macedonian city in northwestern Mesopotamia. Artaxata was the ancient capital of Armenia, on the Araxes (Aras) River. Teredon, a city near the confluence of the Tigris and Euphrates, was once the site of hanging gardens built by Nebuchadnezzar.
7. Arsaces founded the Parthian Empire, which lasted from ca. 240 B.C.E. until 224 C.E. At its greatest extent, it covered all of modern Iran as well as vast regions of the Middle East. It was the only military power capable of resisting Rome's eastward march of conquest.
8. Scythians, barbarian tribes who lived in what is now Russia and Siberia, overran the province of Sogdiana, whose territory corresponded to the modern districts of Samarkand and Bokhara in Uzbekistan as well as Tajikistan.

His thousands, in what martial equipage
305 They issue forth, steel bows and shafts their arms,
Of equal dread in flight or in pursuit,
All horsemen, in which fight they most excel;
See how in warlike muster they appear,
In rhombs and wedges,[9] and half-moons, and wings."
310   He looked and saw what numbers numberless°   *innumerable*
The city gates outpoured, the light-armèd troops
In coats of mail and military pride;
In mail their horses clad, yet fleet and strong,
Prancing their riders bore, the flower and choice
315 Of many provinces from bound to bound,
From Arachosia, from Candaor[1] east,
And Margiana to the Hyrcanian[2] cliffs
Of Caucasus, and dark Iberian[3] dales,
From Atropatia and the neighboring plains
320 Of Adiabéne, Media,[4] and the south
Of Susiana to Balsara's[5] hav'n.
He saw them in their forms of battle ranged,
How quick they wheeled, and flying behind
        them shot
Sharp sleet of arrowy showers against the face
325 Of their pursuers, and overcame by flight;
The field all iron cast a gleaming brown;
Nor wanted° clouds of foot,° nor on each horn°   *lacked / infantry /*
Cuirassiers° all in steel for standing fight,   *wing of an army*
Chariots or elephants endorsed° with towers   *Heavy-armored cavalry*
330 Of archers, nor of laboring pioneers°   *loaded on the back*
A multitude, with spades and axes armed   *military engineers*
To lay hills plain, fell woods, or valleys fill,
Or where plain was raise hill, or overlay
With bridges rivers proud, as with a yoke;
335 Mules after these, camels and dromedaries,
And wagons fraught with útensils of war.
Such forces met not, nor so wide a camp,

9. Triangular formations. "Rhombs": diamond-shaped formations.
1. Kandahar, a province and city in Afghanistan. Arachosia, west of the Indus river, was
the easternmost Parthian province.
2. Regions southeast of the Caspian Sea.
3. Mountains and a heavily wooded region, respectively, between the Black Sea and the
Caspian. Iberia is the modern Georgia.
4. The region known as Media Atropatia in northern Persia is the modern Azerbaijan.
Adiabéne was an ancient kingdom in Mesopotamia with its capital at Arbela (modern-
day Arbil, Iraq).
5. Modern Basra, the main port and second largest city in Iraq. Susiana is southernmost
Parthian province, on the Persian Gulf.

When Agrican[6] with all his northern powers
Besieged Albracca, as romances tell,
340 The city of Gallaphrone, from thence to win
The fairest of her sex, Angelica
His daughter, sought by many prowest° knights,   *most valiant*
Both paynim° and the peers of Charlemain.   *pagan*
Such and so numerous was their chivalry;°   *cavalry*
345 At sight whereof the Fiend yet more presumed,
And to our Saviour thus his words renewed:
    "That thou may'st know I seek not to engage
Thy virtue, and not every way secure
On no slight grounds thy safety,[7] hear, and mark
350 To what end I have brought thee hither and shown
All this fair sight. Thy kingdom, though foretold
By prophet or by angel, unless thou
Endeavor, as thy father David did,
Thou never shalt obtain; prediction still
355 In all things, and all men, supposes means;
Without means used, what it predicts revokes.
But say thou wert possessed of David's throne
By free consent of all, none opposite,°   *opposing*
Samaritan or Jew; how couldst thou hope
360 Long to enjoy it quiet and secure,
Between two such enclosing enemies,
Roman and Parthian? Therefore one of these
Thou must make sure thy own; the Parthian first
By my advice, as nearer and of late
365 Found able by invasion to annoy
Thy country, and captive lead away her kings
Antigonus and old Hyrcanus bound,[8]
Maugre° the Roman. It shall be my task   *In spite of*
To render thee the Parthian at dispose;
370 Choose which thou wilt, by conquest or by league.
By him thou shalt regain, without him not,
That which alone can truly reinstall thee
In David's royal seat, his true successor,
Deliverance of thy brethren, those ten tribes
375 Whose offspring in his territory yet serve
In Habor, and among the Medes dispersed;[9]

---

6. Tartar king in Boiardo's *Orlando Innamorato*, who besieged Albracca, stronghold of
   Gallaphrone, king of Cathay and father of Angelica, whom Agrican loves.
7. It is not my aim to arouse your courage without providing adequately for your safety.
8. According to Josephus (*Antiquities* 14.13–16), the Parthians invaded Judaea in ca. 40
   B.C.E., deposing and carrying off Hyrcanus II. But either Milton or Satan errs regarding Antiochus, an ally of the Parthians, made king by them.
9. See lines 278–79.

Ten sons of Jacob, two° of Joseph lost   *two of these being*
Thus long from Israel, serving as of old   *sons*
Their fathers in the land of Egypt served,
380 This offer sets before thee to deliver.
These if from servitude thou shalt restore
To their inheritance, then, nor till then,
Thou on the throne of David in full glory,
From Egypt to Euphrates and beyond
385 Shalt reign, and Rome or Caesar not need fear."
        To whom our Saviour answered thus, unmoved:
"Much ostentation vain of fleshly arm,
And fragile arms, much instrument of war,
Long in preparing, soon to nothing brought,
390 Before mine eyes thou hast set; and in my ear
Vented much policy,° and projects deep   *political cunning*
Of enemies, of aids, battles and leagues,
Plausible to the world, to me worth naught.
Means I must use, thou say'st, prediction else
395 Will unpredict and fail me of the throne:
My time I told thee (and that time for thee
Were better farthest off) is not yet come.
When that comes, think not thou to find me slack
On my part aught endeavoring, or to need
400 Thy politic maxims, or that cumbersome
Luggage° of war there shown me, argument   *baggage of an army*
Of human weakness rather than of strength.
My brethren, as thou call'st them, those ten tribes,
I must deliver, if I mean to reign
405 David's true heir, and his full scepter sway
To just extent over all Israel's sons;
But whence to thee this zeal? Where was it then
For Israel, or for David, or his throne,
When thou stood'st up his tempter to the pride
410 Of numb'ring Israel, which cost the lives
Of threescore and ten thousand Israelites
By three days' pestilence?[1] Such was thy zeal
To Israel then, the same that now to me.
As for those captive tribes, themselves were they
415 Who wrought their own captivity, fell off
From God to worship calves, the deities
Of Egypt, Baal next and Ashtaroth,[2]

---

1. 1 Chron. 21:1, 7, 14: "And Satan stood up against Israel, and provoked David to number
Israel. . . . And God was displeased with this thing; therefore he smote Israel. . . . So
the Lord sent pestilence upon Israel: and there fell of Israel seventy thousand men."
2. See *PL*, 1. 482–84.

And all the idolatries of heathen round,
Besides their other worse than heathenish crimes;[3]
420 Nor in the land of their captivity
Humbled themselves, or penitent besought
The God of their forefathers, but so died
Impenitent, and left a race behind
Like to themselves, distinguishable scarce
425 From Gentiles but by circumcision vain,
And God with idols in their worship joined.
Should I of these the liberty regard,
Who freed, as to their ancient patrimony,°   *legacy of idolatry*
Unhumbled, unrepentant, unreformed,
430 Headlong would follow, and to their gods perhaps
Of Bethel and of Dan? No, let them serve
Their enemies, who serve idols with God.
Yet he at length, time to himself best known,
Rememb'ring Abraham, by some wondrous call
435 May bring them back repentant and sincere,
And at their passing cleave the Assyrian°   *Euphrates*
      flood,[4]
While to their native land with joy they haste,
As the Red Sea and Jordan once he cleft,
When to the Promised Land their fathers passed;
440 To his due time and providence I leave them."
     So spake Israel's true King, and to the Fiend
Made answer meet, that made void all his wiles.
So fares it when with truth falsehood contends.

The Fourth Book

Perplexed and troubled at his bad success°   *result*
The Tempter stood, nor had what to reply,
Discovered in his fraud, thrown from his hope
So oft, and the persuasive rhetoric
5 That sleeked his tongue and won so much on° Eve   *gained such*
So little here, nay lost; but Eve was Eve,   *advantage over*
This° far his over-match, who° self-deceived   *Jesus / Satan*
And rash, beforehand had no better[1] weighed
The strength he was to cope with, or his own.
10 But as a man who had been matchless held

3. 2 Kings 17:7–20.
4. Isa. 11:16: "And there shall be a highway for the remnant of his people, which shall be left, from Assyria; like as it was to Israel in the day that he came up out of the land of Egypt."
1. I.e., no better than Eve.

In cunning, overreached where least he thought,
To salve his credit, and for very spite,
Still will be tempting him who foils him still,
And never cease, though to his shame the more;
15 Or as a swarm of flies in vintage-time,
About the wine-press where sweet must° is poured,   *new wine*
Beat off, returns as oft with humming sound;
Or surging waves against a solid rock,
Though all to shivers dashed, the assault renew,
20 Vain battery, and in froth or bubbles end;[2]
So Satan, whom repulse upon repulse
Met ever, and to shameful silence brought,
Yet gives not o'er though desperate of success,
And his vain importunity pursues.
25 He brought our Saviour to the western side
Of that high mountain, whence he might behold
Another plain,[3] long but in breadth not wide,
Washed by the southern sea, and on the north
To equal length backed with a ridge of hills
30 That screened the fruits of the earth and seats
          of men
From cold Septentrion° blasts; thence in the midst   *Northern*
Divided by a river, of whose banks
On each side an imperial city stood,
With towers and temples proudly elevate
35 On seven small hills, with palaces adorned,
Porches and theaters, baths, aqueducts,
Statues and trophies, and triumphal arcs,
Gardens and groves presented to his eyes,
Above the highth of mountains interposed.
40 By what strange parallax[4] or optic skill
Of vision multiplied through air, or glass
Of telescope, were curious° to inquire: *unduly inquisitive*
And now the Tempter thus his silence broke:
    "The city which thou seest no other deem
45 Than great and glorious Rome, queen of the earth
So far renowned, and with the spoils enriched
Of nations; there the Capitol thou seest

---

2. *Il.*, 15.618–22: "like some towering / huge sea-cliff that lies close along the grey salt
water / and stands up against the screaming winds and their sudden directions / and
against the waves that grow to bigness and burst up against it; / so the Danaans stood
steady against the Trojans, nor gave way."
3. Of Latium (Lazio) in central Italy, sheltered from the north winds by the Apennines,
and with Rome, on the Tiber, at its center.
4. Change in the apparent position of an object as seen from two different points.

Above the rest lifting his stately head
On the Tarpeian rock,[5] her citadel
50 Impregnable, and there Mount Palatine
The imperial palace, compass huge, and high
The structure, skill of noblest architects,
With gilded battlements, conspicuous far,
Turrets and terraces, and glittering spires.
55 Many a fair edifice besides, more like
Houses of gods (so well I have disposed
My airy microscope) thou may'st behold
Outside and inside both, pillars and roofs,
Carved work, the hand° of famed artificers   *handiwork*
60 In cedar, marble, ivory or gold.
Thence to the gates cast round thine eye, and see
What conflux issuing forth, or ent'ring in,
Praetors,° proconsuls° to their provinces   *magistrates /*
Hasting or on return, in robes of state;   *governors of*
65 Lictors and rods, the ensigns of their power;[6]   *senatorial provinces*
Legions and cohorts,[7] turms of horse° and   *troops of cavalry /*
    wings;°   *cavalry formations*
Or embassies from regions far remote
In various habits on the Appian road,[8]
Or on the Aemilian,[9] some from farthest south,
70 Syene,[1] and where the shadow both way falls,°   *at the equator*
Meroë,[2] Nilotic isle, and more to west,
The realm of Bocchus to the Blackmoor sea;[3]
From the Asian kings and Parthian among these,
From India and the golden Chersoness,[4]
75 And utmost Indian isle Tapróbanè,[5]
Dusk faces with white silken turbants° wreathed;   *turbans*
From Gallia,° Gades,° and the British west,   *Gaul (France) /*
Germans and Scythians, and Sarmatians[6] north   *Cadiz*

---

5. The steep cliffs of the Capitoline hill.
6. Officers attendant on magistrates ("lictors"), carrying a bundle of "rods" (*fasces*) as an emblem of power.
7. A legion is the largest body of infantry, up to six thousand soldiers. Ten cohorts made up a legion.
8. From Rome to Southern Italy.
9. The road from Rome to the north.
1. Aswan, in Egypt.
2. The ancient capital of the kingdom of Kush, on a peninsula (not an island) east of the Nile.
3. That part of the Mediterranean Sea bordering on Mauretania, by the Barbary coast. Bocchus was a king of ancient Mauretania (modern Morocco and coastal Algeria).
4. *Chersonesus Aurea* in Roman times. Possibly the Malay Peninsula, said by Josephus to have been the source of Solomon's gold.
5. Island identified with both Sri Lanka and Sumatra.
6. Barbarians related to the Scythians (see also p. 130, n. 8).

Beyond Danubius° to the Tauric pool.°   *the Danube / Sea*
80 All nations now to Rome obedience pay,   *of Azov*
To Rome's great Emperor,[7] whose wide domain
In ample territory, wealth and power,
Civility of manners, arts, and arms,
And long renown thou justly may'st prefer
85 Before the Parthian. These two thrones except,
The rest are barbarous, and scarce worth the sight,
Shared among petty kings too far removed;
These having shown thee, I have shown thee all
The kingdoms of the world, and all their glory.
90 The Emperor hath no son, and now is old,
Old and lascivious, and from Rome retired
To Capreae[8] an island small but strong
On the Campanian shore, with purpose there
His horrid lusts in private to enjoy,
95 Committing to a wicked favorite°   *Sejanus*
All public cares, and yet of him suspicious,
Hated of all, and hating; with what ease,
Endued with regal virtues as thou art,
Appearing, and beginning noble deeds,
100 Might'st thou expel this monster from his throne
Now made a sty, and in his place ascending,
A victor-people free from servile yoke!
And with my help thou may'st; to me the power
Is given, and by that right I give it thee.
105 Aim therefore at no less than all the world,
Aim at the highest, without the highest attained
Will be for thee no sitting, or not long
On David's throne, be prophesied what will."
     To whom the Son of God unmoved replied:
110 "Nor doth this grandeur and majestic show
Of luxury, though called magnificence,
More than of arms before, allure mine eye,
Much less my mind, though thou shouldst add to tell
Their sumptuous gluttonies, and gorgeous feasts
115 On citron° tables or Atlantic stone[9]   *citrus-wood*
(For I have also heard, perhaps have read),
Their wines of Setia, Cales, and Falerne,[1]

---

7. Tiberius (42 B.C.E.–37 C.E.).
8. Capri, south of Naples.
9. Quarried from the Atlas Mountains.
1. Districts south of Rome.

Chios and Crete,[2] and how they quaff in gold,
Crystal and myrrhine[3] cups embossed with gems
120 And studs of pearl—to me shouldst tell who thirst
And hunger still. Then embassies thou show'st
From nations far and nigh; what honor that,
But tedious waste of time to sit and hear
So many hollow compliments and lies,
125 Outlandish flatteries? Then proceed'st to talk
Of the Emperor, how easily subdued,
How gloriously; I shall, thou say'st, expel
A brutish monster: what if I withal
Expel a devil who first made him such?
130 Let his tormentor Conscience find him out;
For him I was not sent, nor yet to free
That people victor once, now vile and base,
Deservedly made vassal; who once just,
Frugal, and mild, and temperate, conquered well
135 But govern ill the nations under yoke,
Peeling° their provinces, exhausted all   *plundering,*
By lust and rapine; first ambitious grown   *stripping*
Of triumph, that insulting vanity;
Then cruel, by their sports to blood inured
140 Of fighting beasts, and men to beasts exposed;
Luxurious° by their wealth, and greedier still,   *Given to self-indulgence*
And from the daily scene° effeminate.   *theatrical performance*
What wise and valiant man would seek to free
These thus degenerate, by themselves enslaved,
145 Or could of inward slaves make outward free?[4]
Know therefore when my season comes to sit
On David's throne, it shall be like a tree
Spreading and overshadowing all the earth,
Or as a stone that shall to pieces dash
150 All monarchies besides throughout the world,
And of my kingdom there shall be no end.[5]
Means there shall be to this, but what the means
Is not for thee to know, nor me to tell."
     To whom the Tempter impudent replied:

---

2. Greek islands.
3. Possibly imported Chinese porcelain.
4. See *PL*, 12. 82–101.
5. Christ sees himself as the true fulfillment of Nebuchadnezzar's dreams: of a tree whose beautiful leaves provide shade, whose fruit nourishes all creatures, and whose height "reached unto heaven, and the sight thereof to the end of all the earth" (Dan. 4:10–12). Also of a stone that smashed a great idol and "became a great mountain, and filled the whole earth," which Daniel interprets as an everlasting kingdom established by God (Dan. 2:31–35, 44).

155　"I see all offers made by me how slight
　　　Thou valu'st, because offered, and reject'st.
　　　Nothing will please the difficult and nice,°   *hard to please,*
　　　Or nothing more than still° to contradict.   *fastidious / always*
　　　On the other side know also thou, that I
160　On what I offer set as high esteem,
　　　Nor what I part with mean to give for naught.
　　　All these which in a moment thou behold'st,
　　　The kingdoms of the world to thee I give;
　　　For giv'n to me, I give to whom I please,
165　No trifle; yet with this reserve, not else,
　　　On this condition, if thou wilt fall down,
　　　And worship me as thy superior lord,[6]
　　　Easily done, and hold them all of me;
　　　For what can less so great a gift deserve?"
170　　　Whom thus our Saviour answered with disdain:
　　　"I never liked thy talk, thy offers less,
　　　Now both abhor, since thou hast dared to utter
　　　The abominable terms, impious condition;
　　　But I endure the time, till which expired,
175　Thou hast permission on me. It is written
　　　The first of all commandments, 'Thou shalt worship
　　　The Lord thy God, and only him shalt serve';[7]
　　　And dar'st thou to the Son of God propound
　　　To worship thee accurst, now more accurst
180　For this attempt bolder than that on Eve,
　　　And more blasphémous? which expect to rue.
　　　The kingdoms of the world to thee were giv'n,
　　　Permitted rather, and by thee usurped;
　　　Other donation° none thou canst produce.   *bestowal of property*
185　If given, by whom but by the King of kings,
　　　God over all supreme? If giv'n to thee,
　　　By thee how fairly is the Giver now
　　　Repaid? But gratitude in thee is lost
　　　Long since. Wert thou so void of fear or shame
190　As offer them to me the Son of God,
　　　To me my own, on such abhorrèd pact,
　　　That I fall down and worship thee as God?
　　　Get thee behind me;[8] plain thou now appear'st
　　　That Evil One, Satan for ever damned."

6. Matt. 4:9: "All these things will I give thee, if thou wilt fall down and worship me." See also Luke 4:6–7.
7. See Exod. 20:3 and Deut. 6:13.
8. See Luke 4:8.

195   To whom the Fiend with fear abashed replied:
          "Be not so sore offended, Son of God,
          Though sons of God both angels are and men,
          If I, to try whether in higher sort
          Than these thou bear'st that title, have proposed
200   What both from men and angels I receive,
          Tetrarchs[9] of fire, air, flood, and on the earth
          Nations besides from all the quartered winds,
          God of this world[1] invoked and world beneath;
          Who then thou art, whose coming is foretold,
205   To me is fatal, me it most concerns.
          The trial hath endamaged thee no way,
          Rather more honor left and more esteem;
          Me naught advantaged, missing what I aimed.
          Therefore let pass, as they are transitory,
210   The kingdoms of this world; I shall no more
          Advise thee; gain them as thou canst, or not.
          And thou thyself seem'st otherwise inclined
          Than to a worldly crown, addicted more
          To contemplation and profound dispute,
215   As by that early action may be judged,
          When slipping from thy mother's eye thou went'st
          Alone into the Temple; there wast found
          Among the gravest Rabbis disputant
          On points and questions fitting Moses' chair,[2]
220   Teaching, not taught; the childhood shows the man,
          As morning shows the day. Be famous then
          By wisdom; as thy empire must extend,
          So let extend thy mind o'er all the world
          In knowledge, all things in it comprehend.
225   All knowledge is not couched in Moses' Law,
          The Pentateuch,[3] or what the Prophets wrote;
          The Gentiles also know, and write, and teach
          To admiration,° led by Nature's light;   *Admirably*
          And with the Gentiles much thou must converse,
230   Ruling them by persuasion as thou mean'st;
          Without their learning how wilt thou with them,
          Or they with thee hold conversation meet?
          How wilt thou reason with them, how refute

---

9. Subordinate rulers of a quarter of a country. Here, applied to demonic rulers of the
   four elements.
1. Satan's title in 2 Cor. 4:4.
2. Seat of judgment and legal interpretation in Exod. 18:13–16 and Matt. 23:2.
3. The five books of Moses; the first five books of the Hebrew Bible.

Their idolisms,° traditions, paradoxes?   *idolatries, fallacies*
235 Error by his own arms is best evinced.°   *overcome in*
Look once more, ere we leave this specular[4] mount,   *argument*
Westward, much nearer by southwest; behold
Where on the Aegean shore a city stands
Built nobly, pure the air, and light the soil,
240 Athens, the eye of Greece, mother of arts
And eloquence, native to famous wits
Or hospitable, in her sweet recess,°   *place of retirement*
City or suburban, studious walks and shades;
See there the olive grove of Academe,
245 Plato's retirement, where the Attic bird°   *nightingale*
Trills her thick-warbled notes the summer long;
There flow'ry hill Hymettus with the sound
Of bees' industrious murmur oft invites
To studious musing; there Ilissus rolls
250 His whispering stream. Within the walls then view
The schools of ancient sages: his who[5] bred
Great Alexander to subdue the world,
Lyceum there, and painted Stoa[6] next.
There thou shalt hear and learn the secret power
255 Of harmony in tones and numbers hit
By voice or hand, and various-measured verse,
Aeolian charms° and Dorian lyric odes,[7]   *songs*
And his who gave them breath, but higher sung,
Blind Melesigenes,[8] thence Homer called,
260 Whose poem Phoebus challenged for his own.[9]
Thence what the lofty grave tragedians taught
In chorus or iambic,[1] teachers best
Of moral prudence, with delight received
In brief sententious precepts, while they treat
265 Of fate, and chance, and change in human life,
High actions and high passions best describing.

---

4. Lat. *specula*, "watchtower."
5. Aristotle, Alexander's tutor.
6. The school of Zeno of Citium, who introduced stoic philosophy to Athens (ca. 301
   B.C.E.), took its name from the *stoa poikile* (the painted porch) where he taught.
   "Lyceum": an Athenian gymnasium and grove where Aristotle founded his famous
   school, the peripatetics (strollers), so named because he and his pupils strolled its
   grounds and its *stoae* (roofed colonnades).
7. The two chief Greek lyric modes. Sappho wrote in the Aeolian dialect; Pindar, in the
   Dorian.
8. An allusion to Homer's alleged birthplace on the banks of the Meles, in Ionia.
9. In an epigram in the *Greek Anthology* (9.455), envious Apollo ("Phoebus") says, "The
   song is mine, but divine Homer wrote it down."
1. In Greek tragedy, the chorus is written in various meters, and dialogue is usually in
   iambic trimeter.

Thence to the famous orators repair,
Those ancient, whose resistless eloquence
Wielded° at will that fierce democraty,°   *Ruled / democracy*
270   Shook the Arsenal[2] and fulmined° over Greece,   *thundered*
To Macedon, and Artaxerxes'[3] throne;
To sage philosophy next lend thine ear,
From heaven descended to the low-roofed house
Of Socrates, see there his tenement,
275   Whom well inspired the oracle pronounced
Wisest of men; from whose mouth issued forth
Mellifluous streams that watered all the schools
Of Academics old and new,[4] with those
Surnamed Peripatetics, and the sect
280   Epicurean, and the Stoic severe;
These here revolve,° or, as thou lik'st, at home,   *turn over in your*
Till time mature thee to a kingdom's weight;   *mind*
These rules will render thee a king complete
Within thyself, much more with empire joined."
285   To whom our Saviour sagely thus replied:
"Think not but that I know these things, or think
I know them not; not therefore am I short
Of knowing what I ought. He who receives
Light from above, from the Fountain of Light,
290   No other doctrine needs, though granted true;[5]
But these are false, or little else but dreams,
Conjectures, fancies, built on nothing firm.
The first° and wisest of them all professed   *Socrates*
To know this only, that he nothing knew;
295   The next° to fabling fell and smooth conceits;°   *Plato / fanciful*
A third sort[6] doubted all things, though plain sense;   *notions*
Others° in virtue placed felicity,   *Peripatetics*
But virtue joined with riches and long life;
In corporal pleasure he,° and careless ease;   *Epicurus*
300   The Stoic last in philosophic pride,
By him called virtue; and his virtuous man,
Wise, perfect in himself, and all possessing

2. A building at Piraeus, the Athenian harbor, on which construction was suspended in
    339 B.C.E. as a result of Demosthenes' oration that urged all civic resources be commit-
    ted to the war against Philip of Macedon.
3. King of Persia.
4. Philosophic schools deriving from Platonism but making it more syncretic, skeptical,
    and practical.
5. Jesus here prefers Jerusalem (the believer's faith in divine revelation) over Athens (self-
    sufficient human reason).
6. Skeptics, the followers of Pyrrho.

Equal to God, oft shames not to prefer,[7]
As fearing God nor man, contemning° all   *despising*
305 Wealth, pleasure, pain or torment, death and life,
Which when he lists,° he leaves, or boasts he can,   *pleases*
For all his tedious talk is but vain boast,
Or subtle shifts conviction to evade.
Alas what can they teach, and not mislead,
310 Ignorant of themselves, of God much more,
And how the world began, and how man fell
Degraded by himself, on grace depending?
Much of the soul they talk, but all awry,
And in themselves seek virtue, and to themselves
315 All glory arrogate, to God give none;
Rather accuse him under usual names,
Fortune and Fate, as one regardless° quite   *without concern for*
Of mortal things. Who therefore seeks in these
True wisdom finds her not, or by delusion
320 Far worse, her false resemblance only meets,
An empty cloud.[8] However, many books,
Wise men[9] have said, are wearisome; who reads
Incessantly, and to his reading brings not
A spirit and judgment equal or superior
325 (And what he brings, what needs he elsewhere seek?),
Uncertain and unsettled still remains,
Deep versed in books and shallow in himself,
Crude° or intoxicate, collecting toys   *Unable to digest*
And trifles for choice matters, worth a sponge,[1]
330 As children gathering pebbles on the shore.
Or if I would delight my private hours
With music or with poem, where so soon
As in our native language can I find
That solace? All our Law° and story strewed   *Torah*
335 With hymns, our Psalms with artful terms inscribed,
Our Hebrew songs and harps in Babylon,
That pleased so well our victors' ear,[2] declare
That rather Greece from us these arts derived;
Ill imitated while they loudest sing

7. I.e., to prefer himself over God.
8. "In spite of the context, Milton's classical instincts prompt an allusion to the myth of
   Ixion who, seeking to embrace Hera, clasped a cloud instead." (Bush)
9. Eccles. 12:12: "of making many books there is no end; and much study is a weariness of
   the flesh."
1. (1) of small value; (2) fit to be expunged, blotted out of existence.
2. Ps. 137:1–3: "By the rivers of Babylon, there we sat down, yea, we wept, when we
   remembered Zion. We hanged our harps upon the willows. . . . For there they that carried us away captive required of us a song . . . saying, Sing us one of the songs of Zion."

340 The vices of their deities, and their own,
In fable, hymn, or song, so personating
Their gods ridiculous, and themselves past shame.
Remove their swelling epithets, thick laid
As varnish on a harlot's cheek,[3] the rest,
345 Thin sown with aught of profit or delight,
Will far be found unworthy to compare
With Sion's songs, to all true tastes excelling,
Where God is praised aright and Godlike men,
The Holiest of Holies and his saints;
350 Such are from God inspired, not such from thee;
Unless[4] where moral virtue is expressed
By light of Nature not in all quite lost.
Their orators thou then extoll'st, as those
The top of eloquence, statists° indeed,   *statesmen*
355 And lovers of their country, as may seem;
But herein to our Prophets far beneath,
As men divinely taught, and better teaching
The solid rules of civil government
In their majestic unaffected style
360 Than all the oratory of Greece and Rome.
In them is plainest taught, and easiest learnt,
What makes a nation happy, and keeps it so,
What ruins kingdoms, and lays cities flat;
These only with our Law best form a king."
365   So spake the Son of God; but Satan now
Quite at a loss, for all his darts were spent,
Thus to our Saviour with stern brow replied:
    "Since neither wealth, nor honor, arms nor arts,
Kingdom nor empire pleases thee, nor aught
370 By me proposed in life contemplative,
Or active, tended on by glory, or fame,
What dost thou in this world? The wilderness
For thee is fittest place; I found thee there,
And thither will return thee. Yet remember
375 What I foretell thee: soon thou shalt have cause
To wish thou never hadst rejected thus
Nicely or cautiously my offered aid,
Which would have set thee in short time with ease
On David's throne, or throne of all the world,
380 Now at full age, fulness of time, thy season,
When prophecies of thee are best fulfilled.

---

3. *Hamlet*, 3.1.51: "The harlot's cheek, beautied with plast'ring art."
4. Refers to "unworthy" in line 346.

Now contrary, if I read aught in heaven,
Or heaven write aught of fate, by what the stars
Voluminous,° or single characters   *Collectively, as in a*
                                                                        book
385   In their conjunction met, give me to spell,°   *decipher*
Sorrows and labors, opposition, hate,
Attends thee, scorns, reproaches, injuries,
Violence and stripes, and lastly cruel death;
A kingdom they portend thee, but what kingdom,
390   Real or allegoric,° I discern not,   *figurative, hence*
Nor when; eternal sure, as without end,   *unreal*
Without beginning; for no date prefixed
Directs me in the starry rubric° set."   *red-letter chapter*
        So saying he took (for still he knew his power   *title*
395   Not yet expired) and to the wilderness
Brought back the Son of God, and left him there,
Feigning to disappear. Darkness now rose,
As daylight sunk, and brought in louring night,
Her shadowy offspring, unsubstantial both,
400   Privation mere° of light and absent day.   *absolute, entire*
Our Saviour meek and with untroubled mind
After his airy jaunt,° though hurried sore,   *fatiguing or*
Hungry and cold betook him to his rest,   *troublesome journey*
Wherever, under some concourse of shades
405   Whose branching arms thick intertwined
            might shield
From dews and damps of night his sheltered head;
But sheltered slept in vain, for at his head
The Tempter watched, and soon with ugly dreams
Disturbed his sleep. And either tropic° now   *northern or southern*
410   Gan thunder, and both ends of heav'n;° the   *skies / east and west*
            clouds
From many a horrid rift abortive poured
Fierce rain with lightning mixed, water with fire
In ruin reconciled; nor slept the winds
Within their stony caves, but rushed abroad
415   From the four hinges° of the world, and fell   *cardinal points of*
On the vexed wilderness, whose tallest pines,   *the compass*
Though rooted deep as high, and sturdiest oaks
Bowed their stiff necks, loaden with stormy blasts,
Or torn up sheer. Ill wast thou shrouded° then,   *sheltered*
420   O patient Son of God, yet only° stood'st   *solitary*
Unshaken; nor yet stayed the terror there:
Infernal ghosts, and hellish furies, round
Environed thee; some howled, some yelled,
            some shrieked,

Some bent at thee their fiery darts, while thou
425 Sat'st unappalled in calm and sinless peace.
Thus passed the night so foul till Morning fair
Came forth with pilgrim steps in amice[5] gray,
Who with her radiant finger stilled the roar
Of thunder, chased the clouds, and laid the winds
430 And grisly specters, which the Fiend had raised
To tempt the Son of God with terrors dire.
And now the sun with more effectual beams
Had cheered the face of earth, and dried the wet
From drooping plant, or dropping tree; the birds,
435 Who all things now behold more fresh and green,
After a night of storm so ruinous,
Cleared up their choicest notes in bush and
    spray°   *small twigs of trees*
To gratulate° the sweet return of morn.   *or shrubs / welcome*
Nor yet amidst this joy and brightest morn
440 Was absent, after all his mischief done,
The Prince of Darkness; glad would also seem
Of this fair change, and to our Saviour came,
Yet with no new device (they all were spent),
Rather by this his last affront resolved,
445 Desperate of better course, to vent his rage
And mad despite to be so oft repelled.
Him walking on a sunny hill he found,
Backed on the north and west by a thick wood;
Out of the wood he starts in wonted shape,
450 And in a careless mood thus to him said:
    "Fair morning yet betides thee, Son of God,
After a dismal night; I heard the wrack°   *crash, storm,*
As earth and sky would mingle, but myself   *destruction*
Was distant; and these flaws,° though mortals   *squalls*
    fear them
455 As dangerous to the pillared frame of heaven,
Or to the earth's dark basis underneath,
Are to the main° as inconsiderable,   *universe, the*
And harmless, if not wholesome, as a sneeze   *macrocosm*
To man's less universe,° and soon are gone.   *the human body,*
460 Yet as being ofttimes noxious where they light   *microcosm*
On man, beast, plant, wasteful and turbulent,
Like turbulencies in the affairs of men,
Over whose heads they roar, and seem to point,

5. A religious hood with gray fur.

They oft fore-signify and threaten ill:
465 This tempest at this desert most was bent;
Of men at thee, for only thou here dwell'st.
Did I not tell thee, if thou didst reject
The perfect season offered with my aid
To win thy destined seat, but wilt prolong
470 All to the push of Fate, pursue thy way
Of gaining David's throne no man knows when,
For both the when and how is nowhere told,
Thou shalt be what thou art ordained, no doubt,
For angels have proclaimed it, but concealing
475 The time and means: each act is rightliest done,
Not when it must, but when it may be best.
If thou observe not this, be sure to find
What I foretold thee, many a hard assay
Of dangers, and adversities and pains,
480 Ere thou of Israel's scepter get fast hold;
Whereof this ominous night that closed thee round,
So many terrors, voices, prodigies
May warn thee, as a sure foregoing sign."
     So talked he, while the Son of God went on
485 And stayed not, but in brief him answered thus:
     "Me worse than wet thou find'st not; other harm
Those terrors which thou speak'st of did me none.
I never feared they could, though noising loud
And threat'ning nigh; what they can do as signs
490 Betok'ning or ill boding I contemn
As false portents, not sent from God, but thee;
Who knowing I shall reign past thy preventing,
Obtrud'st thy offered aid, that I accepting
At least might seem to hold all power of thee,
495 Ambitious Spirit, and wouldst be thought my God,
And storm'st refused, thinking to terrify
Me to thy will; desist, thou art discerned
And toil'st in vain, nor me in vain molest."
     To whom the Fiend now swoll'n with rage replied:
500 "Then hear, O son of David, virgin-born,
For Son of God to me is yet in doubt:
"Of the Messiah I have heard foretold
By all the Prophets; of thy birth, at length
Announced by Gabriel, with the first I knew,
505 And of the angelic song in Bethlehem field,
On thy birth-night, that sung thee Saviour born.
From that time seldom have I ceased to eye
Thy infancy, thy childhood, and thy youth,

Thy manhood last, though yet in private bred;
Till at the ford of Jordan whither all
Flocked to the Baptist, I among the rest,
Though not to be baptized, by voice from Heav'n
Heard thee pronounced the Son of God beloved.
Thenceforth I thought thee worth my nearer view
515 And narrower scrutiny, that I might learn
In what degree or meaning thou art called
The Son of God, which bears no single sense;[6]
The Son of God I also am,[7] or was,
And if I was, I am; relation stands;
520 All men are sons of God;[8] yet thee I thought
In some respect far higher so declared.
Therefore I watched thy footsteps from that hour,
And followed thee still on to this waste wild,
Where by all best conjectures I collect°   *infer*
525 Thou art to be my fatal enemy.
Good reason then, if I beforehand seek
To understand my adversary, who
And what he is, his wisdom, power, intent;
By parle° or composition,° truce or league   *parley / agreement to*
530 To win him, or win from him what I can.   *cease hostilities*
And opportunity I here have had
To try thee, sift thee, and confess have found thee
Proof against all temptation as a rock
Of adamant,° and as a center firm,[9]   *alleged substance of*
535 To the utmost of mere man both wise and good,   *surpassing hardness*
Not more; for honors, riches, kingdoms, glory
Have been before contemned, and may again;
Therefore to know what more thou art than man,
Worth naming Son of God by voice from Heav'n
540 Another method I must now begin."
      So saying he caught him up, and without wing
Of hippogriff[1] bore through the air sublime
Over the wilderness and o'er the plain,
Till underneath them fair Jerusalem,

---

6. Paul calls all who are led by the spirit of God sons of God (Rom. 8:14; Gal. 4:4–7), and
   he also holds that people who have faith are sons of God (Gal. 3:26). Only in Matt.
   26:63–65, when Christ does not deny the title under interrogation by Caiaphas, does
   the Bible invest the term with a metaphysical meaning.
7. See Job 1:6: "Now there was a day when the sons of God came to present themselves
   before the Lord, and Satan came also among them."
8. Ps. 82:6: "you are all children of the most High."
9. Following Bush, who changes punctuation. The original is "center, firm / To the
   utmost."
1. Mythical creature that is half horse, half griffin.

545 The Holy City, lifted high her towers,
And higher yet the glorious Temple reared
Her pile, far off appearing like a mount
Of alabaster, topped with golden spires:
There on the highest pinnacle[2] he set
550 The Son of God, and added thus in scorn:
"There stand, if thou wilt stand; to stand upright
Will ask thee skill. I to thy Father's house
Have brought thee, and highest placed;
highest is best.
Now show thy progeny;° if not to stand,   lineage, parentage
555 Cast thyself down, safely if Son of God;
For it is written, 'He will give command
Concerning thee to his angels; in their hands
They shall uplift thee, lest at any time
Thou chance to dash thy foot against a stone.'"[3]
560 To whom thus Jesus: "Also it is written,
'Tempt not the Lord thy God'";[4] he said and stood.
But Satan smitten with amazement fell,
As when Earth's son Antaeus[5] (to compare
Small things with greatest) in Irassa[6] strove
565 With Jove's Alcides and oft foiled still rose,
Receiving from his mother Earth new strength,
Fresh from his fall, and fiercer grapple joined,
Throttled at length in the air, expired and fell;
So after many a foil the Tempter proud,
570 Renewing fresh assaults, amidst his pride
Fell whence he stood to see his victor fall.

2. The encounter on the pinnacle may be the strangest moment in Milton's poetry and, after the famous "two-handed engine" in line 130 of *Lycidas*, the second most puzzling question debated among critics. The disagreement over Jesus' humanity or divinity begins with differing interpretations of "a pinnacle of the temple" (Luke 4:9). If it is a parapet, a flat roof, or even the peak of the roof as it forms a ridge where two inclined planes meet (the meaning of the Gospel's *pterugion*), then Christ balances himself using only his human powers. If it is a point or spire, then his standing can be seen as miraculous.
3. Ps. 91:11–12: "For he shall give his angels charge over thee, to keep thee in all thy ways. They shall bear thee up in their hands, lest thou dash thy foot against a stone."
4. Jesus responds to this temptation to presumptuous action by quoting the warning of Deut. 6:16, "Ye shall not tempt [i.e., make trial of] the Lord your God, as ye tempted him in Massah," when the Israelites demanded a miracle (Exod. 17:7). Although Jesus seems to be saying that he has no right to expect God to deliver him from danger, just as Satan has no right to expect him to perform a miracle, a number of critics hear this apparent assertion of obedience as an assertion of divinity: "Do not tempt me, the Lord your God."
5. A wrestling giant, son of Poseidon and Gaia (the earth), he regained strength from his earth-mother whenever he was thrown to the ground. Hercules (Alcides, line 565) defeated him by strangling him while holding him aloft. Lines 563–68 and 572–75 are the only elaborate classical similes in the poem.
6. A district in Libya.

And as that Theban monster[7] that proposed
Her riddle, and him who solved it not devoured,
That once found out and solved, for grief and spite
575   Cast herself headlong from th' Ismenian steep,
So struck with dread and anguish fell the Fiend,
And to his crew, that sat consulting, brought
Joyless triumphals° of his hoped success,   *tokens of triumph*
Ruin, and desperation, and dismay,
580   Who durst so proudly tempt the Son of God.
So Satan fell, and straight a fiery globe
Of angels on full sail of wing flew nigh,
Who on their plumy vans° received him[8] soft   *wings*
From his uneasy station, and upbore
585   As on a floating couch through the blithe air,
Then in a flow'ry valley set him down
On a green bank, and set before him spread
A table of celestial food, divine,
Ambrosial, fruits fetched from the Tree of Life,
590   And from the Fount of Life ambrosial drink,
That soon refreshed him wearied, and repaired
What hunger, if aught hunger had impaired,
Or thirst, and as he fed, angelic choirs
Sung heavenly anthems of his victory
595   Over temptation and the Tempter proud:
    "True image of the Father, whether throned
In the bosom of bliss, and light of light
Conceiving, or remote from Heaven, enshrined
In fleshly tabernacle and human form,
600   Wand'ring the wilderness, whatever place,
Habit,° or state, or motion, still expressing   *outward form*
The Son of God, with God-like force endued
Against th' Attempter of thy Father's throne
And thief of Paradise; him long of old
605   Thou didst debel,° and down from Heav'n cast   *wear down in war*
With all his army; now thou hast avenged
Supplanted Adam, and by vanquishing
Temptation hast regained lost Paradise,
And frustrated the conquest fraudulent.
610   He never more henceforth will dare set foot

7. The Sphinx. She strangled anyone unable to answer her riddle, "Which creature in the
morning goes on four feet, at noon on two, and in the evening upon three?" When
Oedipus answered "Man"—who crawls on all fours as a baby, walks on two feet as an
adult, and walks with the help of a cane in old age—she threw herself from her high
rock and died.
8. I.e., Jesus, although Satan seems to be the antecedent. A similar syntactic confusion of
Jesus with Satan occurs in *PL*, 10.185.

In Paradise to tempt; his snares are broke.[9]

For though that seat of earthly bliss be failed,°   *be gone*

A fairer Paradise is founded now

For Adam and his chosen sons, whom thou

615   A Saviour art come down to reinstall;

Where they shall dwell secure, when time shall be

Of Tempter and temptation without fear.

But thou, Infernal Serpent, shalt not long

Rule in the clouds; like an autumnal star

620   Or lightning thou shalt fall from Heav'n trod down

Under his feet.[1] For proof, ere this thou feel'st

Thy wound, yet not thy last and deadliest wound,

By this repulse received, and hold'st in Hell

No triumph; in all her gates Abaddon° rues   *hell*

625   Thy bold attempt. Hereafter learn with awe

To dread the Son of God: he all unarmed

Shall chase thee with the terror of his voice

From thy demoniac holds, possession foul,

Thee and thy legions; yelling they shall fly,

630   And beg to hide them in a herd of swine,

Lest he command them down into the deep,

Bound, and to torment sent before their time.[2]

Hail, Son of the Most High, heir of both worlds,

Queller of Satan, on thy glorious work

635   Now enter, and begin to save mankind."

   Thus they the Son of God our Saviour meek

Sung victor, and from Heavenly feast refreshed

Brought on his way with joy; he unobserved

Home to his mother's house private returned.

---

9. Ps. 124:7.
1. Alluding to the judgment on the serpent of Gen. 3:15 (*PL*, 10.175–91). See also Luke 10:18: "I beheld Satan as lightning fall from heaven," and Rom. 16:20: "The God of peace shall bruise Satan under your feet."
2. In Matt. 8:29–33, Jesus meets two people possessed of devils who cry out, "art thou come hither to torment us before the time?" Jesus cures the demoniacs by permitting the devils to enter a herd of swine, who then plunge over a cliff into the sea and drown.

Samson Agonistes

John Milton's naming his tragedy *Samson Agonistes* (contestant or combatant in the public games) was both apt and prescient—apt because the title denotes its protagonist's agony both physical and spiritual, his *agon* or verbal dispute with his visitors, and his display of strength at the festival of Dagon; prescient because almost everything about the tragedy has been contested by scholars and critics, from its date of composition to the character of its protagonist. The volume in which it appeared was titled *PARADISE REGAIN'D . . . To which is added SAMSON AGONISTES* (1671). Some scholars, most notably William Riley Parker, interpret the title-page addendum as evidence that it may have been composed earlier, in the late 1640s or early 1650s, published at this time to augment the brief epic's mere 111 pages. Certainly the manifold afflictions of unhappy marriages portrayed in the divorce tracts of the 1640s appear newly addressed in the tragedy, in surprisingly varied contexts: in discussions of barrenness considered "[i]n wedlock a reproach" (353), servitude and slavery (410–13, 416–18), accepting offered freedom rather than enduring suffering as a trial of patience (503–06, 516), despair (594–97), divine providence (668–70), the errors committed even by "the best and wisest" (1034–40), and many others.

The strongest recent arguments of literary historians have favored a later date of composition, drawing persuasive parallels between the politics of exile and bondage in the tragedy and in post-Restoration England and between blind, defeated Samson's predicament and Milton's. One cannot read lines 692–96, on God's terrible ways with his faithful, without thinking of Royalist reprisals against champions of the "good old cause," including not only imprisoning and executing them but also exhuming and beheading their corpses. And the lines immediately following, 697–700, on the poverty and sickness endured by those who escaped such persecution, may well allude to Milton's personal situation. Comparisons abound: Samson in prison, forced to participate in idolatrous ceremonies, and Puritans ordered to attend Anglican services as a public gesture of uniformity. The large presence in the tragedy of Manoa's efforts to ransom his son (481 f., 601 f.), not found in the Bible, might recall the efforts made by persons of influence to secure a pardon for Milton after the Restoration. But Samson's refusal to accept ransom would be reminiscent of the refusal of Thomas Harrison and Henry Vane either to escape or to allow others to spend money on their behalf to secure their release.

153

It is at least possible to reconcile these different arguments by suggesting, as others already have, that Milton may have begun the work early and completed it after the Restoration. But it's not possible to square the traditional positive view of Samson's character with more recent, extremely negative ones. In the nineteenth century, David Masson completely identified Milton with Samson: —

> He also, in his veteran days, after the Restoration, was a champion at bay, a prophet-warrior left alone among men of a different faith and different manners—Philistines, who exulted in the ruin of his cause, and wreaked their wrath upon him for his past services to that cause by insults, calumnies, and jeers at his misfortunes and the cause itself.[1]

But as early as the 1970s, Joseph Wittreich separated "Samson the false prophet and destroyer from Milton the true prophet and creator."[2] Wittreich's reading of Milton's tragedy parallels post–World War II and post-Vietnam revaluations in classical studies that led to darker, colder views of Alexander and empire and of Virgil's relationship to Augustus. Wittreich deplores Samson's betrayal of the office of judge and the "pernicious casuistry" that would excuse his disregard of "God's laws." Writing on the first anniversary of the tragedies of 9/11, John Carey compares Samson with the hijackers: "Like them Samson sacrifices himself to achieve his ends. Like them he destroys many innocent victims, whose lives, hopes and loves are all quite unknown to him personally." Carey even suggests banning the work as "an incitement to terrorism."

The best way to negotiate between extreme positions would be to read the Bible's account of Samson in Judges 13–16 (pages 451–57), keeping in mind the changes that Milton made in his adaptation. Milton inherited the story of this primitive ruffian and, revering the Bible as he did, took pains to retain as many details of the original as possible; nevertheless, in addition to altering external details (making Dalila Samson's wife; changing Samson's last words), he attempted to transform the brutish champion of Judges into a person of conscience, integrity, and piety—at least in the unmediated words we hear before he leaves with the officer.

Samson Agonistes may be Milton's strangest major poem, a Hebraic narrative in a classical Greek framework, addressed to a Christian audience, with fault lines among those conflicting traditions exposed. Although it bears traces of Aeschylus' *Prometheus Unbound* and Euripides' *Herakles*, as well as of other Greek tragedies, its clearest classical

---

1. Introduction to *Samson Agonistes*, in *Milton's Poetical Works*, ed. David Masson (London: Macmillan, 1874), 2:91.
2. Joseph Wittreich, "Perplexing the Explanation: Marvell's 'On Mr. Milton's *Paradise Lost*,'" in *Approaches to Marvell: The York Tercentenary Lectures*, ed. C. A. Patrides (London: Routledge, 1978), p. 295. See also Wittreich's *Visionary Poetics: Milton's Tradition and His Legacy* (San Marino, Calif.: Huntington Library, 1978), pp. 197 ff., and, most important, his *Interpreting 'Samson Agonistes'* (Princeton, N.J.: Princeton University Press, 1986).

source is Sophocles' *Oedipus at Colonus*—evident in the assaults of successive interlocutors on the hero's resolve; in its handling of the chorus and the messenger; and especially in the pervasiveness of its irony. As many readers have noticed, irony, which expresses two meanings simultaneously, is a principal mode for expressing the paradoxes and polarities of Milton's tragedy. Samson's day of rest becomes the day of his most intense activity, and his three interlocutors achieve the opposite of their intentions: Manoa wants to help his son but throws him into his deepest depression; Dalila pleads for reconciliation but is instead decisively rejected; and Harapha, who has come to gloat and insult, leaves humiliated, having provided Samson with an occasion of both recreation and spiritual progress. Characters tend to express contingencies with either/or constructions: either Samson's strength is returning for a purpose or else he will soon die (587–98); Dalila is either a rich Philistian matron or Samson's wife (722–24); Samson is either triumphing over his enemies or being killed by them (1516–17). In every instance, the reality is both/and.

Although much in the tragedy can be accommodated within a generalized Judeo-Christian tradition, the conflict between the two elements of that tradition accounts for its most divergent readings. Critics who disparage Samson and believe that his "rousing motions" (1382) are merely instinctual rather than the result of divine inspiration often employ typology as a totalizing system that allows the amplitude of Milton's Hebraic poetry to shrink to the sharper focus of Christian doctrine. Submitting the Old Testament letter to the judgment of New Testament spirit, they may compare *Samson Agonistes* invidiously with *Paradise Regained*, Samson with Christ, Manoa with God (Samson's *real* father), and even Judges 13–16 (the ostensible source of the story) with Hebrews 11:32 (the real source).

Remembering a point made by Douglas Bush might lead to a more humane reading:

> Milton had spoken (in *Of Education*) of decorum as 'the grand masterpiece to observe,' and it is remarkable that so earnestly Christian a poet could so strictly maintain Hebraic decorum, avoiding overt reference to any specifically Christian belief or idea.[3]

A monistic reading that attempted to find common cause between Judaism and Christianity—instead of opposing them, as is usually the case—would not find in the chorus or Manoa or Samson easy objects of belittlement. It would not degrade the Torah that Samson defends with his last unmediated words (lines 1381–86, 1408–09, 1423–25). It would instead acknowledge the humanity of the chorus, its capacity for fellow feeling, and its considerable spiritual and intellectual development, instead of rejecting it in a spirit of Pauline dualism as a narrow, obsolete, erroneous chorus of enslaved Hebrews, representing an enslaved people bound by an oppressive law of Moses. The dominant

---

3. Douglas Bush, Introduction to *Samson Agonistes* in his *Milton: Poetical Works* (London: Oxford University Press, 1966), p. 514.

ironic Christian dualist reading of *Samson* presumes that Samson lived and died in vain, because he only "began to deliver Israel out of the hands of the Philistines" (Jud. 13:5), and neither he nor his surviving countrymen completed the act. But from an ampler biblical perspective, "he shall begin to deliver Israel . . . and the deliverance shall be carried on and perfected by others, as it was in part by *Eli*, and *Samuel*, and *Saul*, but especially by *David*."[4] Instead of merely disparaging Manoa for his parental inadequacies and for a crude ethnocentrism associated incorrectly with Judaism, a Hebraic reading compatible with Christianity would understand the love expressed by laying out money for one's child instead of laying it up for oneself and by preparing to devote the rest of one's life to nursing that child (lines 1485–89). And since devaluing the chorus and Manoa devalues their ethnicity, a corrective reading compatible with a charitable rather than a triumphalist Christianity would recognize Milton's employment of a positive typology (congruity rather than disparity) and his transfer of terms from the Hebrew Bible to the New Testament in order to emphasize God's continuous ways with all his creatures.

SAMSON AGONISTES[1]

A Dramatic Poem

OF THAT SORT OF DRAMATIC POEM WHICH IS CALLED TRAGEDY

Tragedy, as it was anciently composed, hath been ever held the gravest, moralest, and most profitable of all other poems: therefore said by Aristotle to be of power, by raising pity and fear, or terror, to purge the mind of those and suchlike passions, that is, to temper and reduce them to just measure with a kind of delight, stirred up by reading or seeing those passions well imitated.[2] Nor is Nature wanting in her own effects to make good his assertion; for so in physic, things of melancholic hue and quality are used against mel-

---

4. Matthew Poole, *Annotations upon the Holy Bible* (1683; 3rd ed. 1696), sig. Bbb3.
1. Greek for "a combatant or contestant in the games" and "actor," a reference to Samson's display of strength at the festival of Dagon but with overtones of "God's champion." The form of the title follows examples from ancient Greece, such as Aeschylus' *Prometheus Bound* and Sophocles' *Oedipus Coloneus* (*Oedipus at Colonus*), and from Renaissance Italy, including Ariosto's *Orlando Furioso* (Orlando Mad) and Tasso's *Gerusalemme Liberata* (Jerusalem Delivered). Milton's own epics have similar titles, and the title given to a projected tragedy on the subject of *Paradise Lost* was *Adam Unparadiz'd*.
2. The analogy between tragic catharsis and homeopathic medicine derives not from Aristotle but from Renaissance Italian theorists, such as Minturno and Guarini, although they maintain that tragedy drives out the passions of pity and fear rather than reducing them to a desirable and pleasurable mean.

ancholy, sour against sour, salt to remove salt humors. Hence philosophers and other gravest writers, as Cicero, Plutarch, and others,
frequently cite out of tragic poets, both to adorn and illustrate their
discourse. The Apostle Paul himself thought it not unworthy to
insert a verse of Euripides into the text of Holy Scripture, I Cor.
15.33; and Paraeus,[3] commenting on the Revelation, divides the
whole book as a tragedy, into acts distinguished each by a chorus of
heavenly harpings and song between. Heretofore men in highest
dignity have labored not a little to be thought able to compose a
tragedy. Of that honor Dionysius the elder[4] was no less ambitious
than before of his attaining to the tyranny. Augustus Caesar also
had begun his Ajax,[5] but unable to please his own judgment with
what he had begun, left it unfinished. Seneca the philosopher is by
some thought the author of those tragedies (at least the best of
them) that go under that name.[6] Gregory Nazianzen,[7] a Father of
the Church, thought it not unbeseeming the sanctity of his person
to write a tragedy, which he entitled Christ Suffering. This is mentioned to vindicate tragedy from the small esteem, or rather infamy,
which in the account of many it undergoes at this day with other
common interludes; happening through the poet's error of inter-
mixing comic stuff with tragic sadness and gravity, or introducing
trivial and vulgar persons, which by all judicious hath been counted
absurd, and brought in without discretion, corruptly to gratify the
people. And though ancient tragedy use no prologue,[8] yet using
sometimes, in case of self-defense, or explanation, that which Martial calls an epistle; in behalf of this tragedy, coming forth after the
ancient manner, much different from what among us passes for
best, thus much beforehand may be epistled: that chorus is here
introduced after the Greek manner, not ancient only but modern,

3. David Paraeus (1548–1622), a German Calvinist, whose commentary on Revelation
   Milton also cites approvingly in the Preface to Book II of The Reason of Church Government. 1 Cor. 15:33: "evil communications corrupt good manners," a proverbial
   phrase found in both Euripides and the comic poet Menander.
4. Dionysius I (431–367 B.C.E.), tyrant of Syracuse in Sicily, patron of the arts, whose
   poems were often derided but whose tragedy won a prize in Athens at the festival of
   Dionysus.
5. According to Suetonius (Caesars 2.85), Augustus began a tragedy called Ajax and, discovering his incompetence, gave it up.
6. The scholars of Milton's time were less certain than those of ours that Seneca the philosopher was also the tragedian.
7. Fourth-century bishop of Constantinople, his authorship of Christus Patiens (Christ
   Suffering) is now doubted.
8. An introductory speech, outside the play. Although Milton had earlier written dramatic poems, Arcades and A Masque Presented at Ludlow Castle (Comus), which had
   actually been performed for noble families of literary tastes, his attitude toward the
   English stage sounds entirely negative. His first published English poem, "On Shakespeare," appeared in the Second Folio (1632), but his reference to "the error of inter-
   mixing comic stuff with tragic sadness and gravity" seems to allude to Shakespeare as
   well as to Dryden and other post-Restoration playwrights.

and still in use among the Italians.[9] In the modeling therefore of
this poem, with good reason, the ancients and Italians are rather
followed, as of much more authority and fame. The measure of
verse used in the chorus is of all sorts, called by the Greeks *monostrophic*, or rather *apolelymenon*, without regard had to strophe,
antistrophe, or epode, which were a kind of stanzas framed only for
the music, then used with the chorus that sung; not essential to the
poem, and therefore not material; or, being divided into stanzas or
pauses, they may be called *alloeostropha*.[1] Division into act and
scene, referring chiefly to the stage (to which this work never was
intended), is here omitted.

It suffices if the whole drama be found not produced beyond the
fifth act.[2] Of the style and uniformity, and that commonly called
the plot, whether intricate or explicit[3]—which is nothing indeed
but such economy, or disposition of the fable, as may stand best
with verisimilitude and decorum—they only will best judge who
are not unacquainted with Aeschylus, Sophocles, and Euripides,
the three tragic poets unequaled yet by any, and the best rule to all
who endeavor to write tragedy. The circumscription of time wherein
the whole drama begins and ends is, according to ancient rule[4] and
best example, within the space of twenty-four hours.

The Argument

Samson, made captive, blind, and now in the prison at Gaza, there
to labor as in a common workhouse, on a festival day, in the general
cessation from labor, comes forth into the open air, to a place nigh,
somewhat retired, there to sit a while and bemoan his condition.
Where he happens at length to be visited by certain friends and
equals[5] of his tribe, which make the chorus, who seek to comfort
him what they can; then by his old father, Manoa, who endeavors
the like, and withal tells him his purpose to procure his liberty by
ransom; lastly, that this feast was proclaimed by the Philistines as a
day of thanksgiving for their deliverance from the hands of Sam-

---

9. In *Of Education* (and elsewhere), Milton shows his knowledge and respect for "the Italian Commentaries of Castelvetro, Tasso, Mazzoni, and others."
1. With strophes or paragraphs of varying form. "*Monostrophic*": consisting of one stanza.
"Apolelymenon": Gr. "freed" (from stanzaic pattern). "Strophe": the chorus sang the
strophe (lit. "turning") as it danced from right to left. "Antistrophe": the lines of choral
song in the returning movement, from left to right. "Epode": part of a lyric ode sung
while standing still, in a different meter, to a different tune.
2. Extended beyond the action that would be appropriate to the final act of a traditional
tragedy.
3. Complex or simple (Aristotle, *Poetics*, 6).
4. The brief time scheme of most Greek plays became one of the three unities in neoclassical criticism. Aristotle (*Poetics*, 5) mentions it as a general practice rather than as a
rule.
5. People of about the same age.

son, which yet more troubles him. Manoa then departs to prosecute his endeavor with the Philistian lords for Samson's redemption; who in the meanwhile is visited by other persons; and lastly by a public officer to require his coming to the feast before the lords and people, to play or show his strength in their presence. He at first refuses, dismissing the public officer with absolute denial to come; at length persuaded inwardly that this was from God, he yields to go along with him, who came now the second time with great threatenings to fetch him. The chorus yet remaining on the place, Manoa returns, full of joyful hope, to procure ere long his son's deliverance—in the midst of which discourse an Ebrew[6] comes in haste, confusedly at first and afterward more distinctly, relating the catastrophe, what Samson had done to the Philistines and by accident to himself, wherewith the tragedy ends.

Samson Agonistes

THE PERSONS

Samson	Harapha of Gath
Mánoa, the father of	Public officer
Samson	Messenger
Dálila, his wife	Chorus of Danites

The Scene, before the Prison in Gaza[7]

SAMSON. A little onward lend thy guiding hand
   To these dark steps,[8] a little further on,
   For yonder bank hath choice of sun or shade;
   There I am wont to sit, when any chance
5 Relieves me from my task of servile toil,
   Daily in the common prison else° enjoined me,   *otherwise*
   Where I, a prisoner chained, scarce freely draw
   The air imprisoned also, close and damp,
   Unwholesome draught.° But here I feel amends,   *inhaled air*
10 The breath of heav'n fresh-blowing, pure and sweet,
   With day-spring° born; here leave me to   *daybreak / breathe*
      respire.°
   This day a solemn feast the people hold

---

6. Milton's spelling of "Hebrew" throughout the tragedy, influenced perhaps by the title of John Selden's study of marriage laws, *Uxor Ebraica* (1646).
7. A major Philistine city.
8. In the opening scene of Sophocles' *Oedipus at Colonus*, the blind Oedipus is led by his daughter Antigone; the blind prophet Tiresias is also led by his daughter in the *Phoenissae* of Euripides (lines 834–35).

To Dagon[9] their sea-idol, and forbid
Laborious works; unwillingly this rest
15   Their superstition° yields me; hence with   *idolatrous religion*
        leave
Retiring from the popular° noise, I seek   *made by the*
This unfrequented place to find some ease;   *populace*
Ease to the body some, none to the mind
From restless thoughts, that like a deadly swarm
20   Of hornets armed, no sooner found alone,
But rush upon me thronging, and present
Times past, what once I was, and what am now.
O wherefore was my birth from Heaven foretold
Twice by an angel, who at last in sight
25   Of both my parents all in flames ascended
From off the altar, where an off'ring burned,
As in a fiery column charioting[1]
His godlike presence, and from some great act
Or benefit revealed to Abraham's race?
30   Why was my breeding ordered and prescribed
As of a person separate to God,[2]
Designed for great exploits, if I must die
Betrayed, captíved, and both my eyes put out,
Made of my enemies the scorn and gaze;°   *spectacle, gazing*
35   To grind in brazen fetters under task   *stock*
With this Heav'n-gifted strength? O
        glorious strength,
Put to the labor of a beast, debased
Lower than bondslave! Promise was that I
Should Israel from Philistian yoke deliver;
40   Ask for this great deliverer now, and find him
Eyeless in Gaza at the mill with slaves,
Himself in bonds under Philistian yoke;
Yet stay, let me not rashly call in doubt
Divine prediction; what if all foretold
45   Had been fulfilled but through° mine own default?   *were it not for*
Whom have I to complain of but myself?
Who this high gift of strength committed to me,

9. The chief Philistine god, "upward man / And downward fish" (*PL*, 1.462–63); his idol
was overcome by the ark of God (1 Sam. 5:1–5).
1. Josephus, *Antiquities*, 5.8, says that the angel ascended "by means of the smoke [of
Manoa's sacrifice] as by a vehicle." The image alludes to the chariot of fire that carried
Elijah heavenward (2 Kings 2:11).
2. Judg. 13:7: "the child shall be a Nazarite to God." Heb. *nazir*, "abstinent," one bound by
a vow to be set apart for the service of God and, as such, to abstain from wine and to let
his hair grow.

In what part lodged, how easily bereft me,
Under the seal of silence could not keep,
50 But weakly to a woman must reveal it,
O'ercome with importunity and tears.
O impotence of mind, in body strong!
But what is strength without a double share
Of wisdom? Vast, unwieldy, burdensome,
55 Proudly secure,° yet liable to fall   overconfident
By weakest subtleties; not made to rule
But to subserve where wisdom bears command.
God, when he gave me strength, to show withal
How slight the gift was, hung it in my hair.
60 But peace! I must not quarrel with the will
Of highest dispensation,° which herein   God's providence
Haply had ends above my reach to know:
Suffices° that to me strength is my bane,°   It suffices me to
And proves the source of all my miseries,   know / ruin
65 So many, and so huge, that each apart
Would ask a life to wail; but chief of all,
O loss of sight, of thee I most complain!
Blind among enemies, O worse than chains,
Dungeon, or beggary, or decrepit age!
70 Light, the prime work° of God, to me is   first creation
    extinct,
And all her various objects of delight
Annulled, which might in part my grief have eased,
Inferior to the vilest now become
Of man or worm; the vilest here excel me,
75 They creep, yet see; I, dark in light exposed
To daily fraud, contempt, abuse and wrong,
Within doors, or without, still as a fool,
In power of others, never in my own;
Scarce half I seem to live, dead more than half.
80 O dark, dark, dark, amid the blaze of noon,
Irrecoverably dark, total eclipse
Without all hope of day!
O first-created beam, and thou great Word,
"Let there be light,[3] and light was over all";
85 Why am I thus bereaved thy prime decree?
The sun to me is dark
And silent[4] as the moon,
When she deserts the night,

3. Gen. 1:3.
4. Not shining (sight applied to sound).

Hid in her vacant° interlunar cave.⁵   *empty, at leisure*
90   Since light so necessary is to life,
And almost life itself, if it be true
That light is in the soul,
She all in every part, why was the sight
To such a tender ball as th' eye confined?
95   So obvious° and so easy to be quenched,   *exposed*
And not, as feeling, through all parts diffused,
That she might look at will through every pore?
Then had I not been thus exiled from light,
As in the land of darkness, yet in light,
100   To live a life half dead, a living death,
And buried; but O yet more miserable!
Myself my sepulchre, a moving grave,
Buried, yet not exempt
By privilege of death and burial
105   From worst of other evils, pains and wrongs,
But made hereby obnoxious° more   *exposed, liable*
To all the miseries of life,
Life in captivity
Among inhuman foes.
110   But who are these? For with joint pace I hear
The tread of many feet steering this way;
Perhaps my enemies who come to stare
At my affliction, and perhaps to insult,
Their daily practice to afflict me more.
110   CHORUS. This, this is he; softly a while,
Let us not break in upon him.
O change beyond report, thought, or belief!
See how he lies at random, carelessly
    diffused,°   *sprawled*
With languished° head unpropped,   *drooping*
120   As one past hope, abandoned,
And by himself given over;
In slavish habit,⁶ ill-fitted weeds°   *clothes*
O'erworn and soiled;
Or do my eyes misrepresent? Can this be he,
125   That heroic, that renowned,
Irresistible Samson? whom unarmed
No strength of man, or fiercest wild beast
    could withstand;
Who tore the lion, as the lion tears the kid,

5. Where antiquity supposed the moon resided when not visible.
6. I.e., dressed like a slave.

Ran on embattled armies clad in iron,
130 And, weaponless himself,
Made arms ridiculous, useless the forgery° *(1) made of metal,*
Of brazen shield and spear, the hammered *(2) an imposture*
   cuirass,° *close-fitting*
Chalybean[7]-tempered steel, and frock of mail *defensive covering*
Adamantean proof;° *Resistant to the*
135 But safest he who stood aloof, *hardest substance*
When insupportably° his foot advanced, *irresistibly*
In scorn of their proud arms and warlike tools,
Spurned° them to death by troops. The bold *Trampled*
   Ascalonite[8]
Fled from his lion ramp,[9] old warriors turned
140 Their plated backs under his heel,
Or grov'ling soiled their crested helmets in the dust.
Then with what trivial weapon came to hand,
The jaw of a dead ass, his sword of bone,
A thousand foreskins° fell, the flower of Palestine, *uncircumcised*
145 In Ramath-lechi, famous to this day; *Philistines*
Then by main force pulled up, and on his
   shoulders bore
The gates of Azza,° post and massy bar, *Gaza*
Up to the hill by Hebron,[1] seat of giants old,
No journey of a Sabbath day,[2] and loaded
   so,
150 Like whom[3] the Gentiles feign to bear up heaven.
Which shall I first bewail,
Thy bondage or lost sight,
Prison within prison
Inseparably dark?
155 Thou art become (O worst imprisonment!)
The dungeon of thyself; thy soul
(Which men enjoying sight oft without
   cause complain)[4]
Imprisoned now indeed,

7. The Chalybes, a tribe on the Black Sea, were famous for their metal work.
8. Ascalon (Ashkelon), north of Gaza and south of Jaffa, was the oldest and largest sea-port in ancient Canaan and one of the five Philistine cities.
9. A threatening posture.
1. The city of Arba, father of Anak, whose children, the Anakim, were giants. See Num. 13:22, 33; Josh. 11:21–22, 15:13–14.
2. The distance that a Jew is permitted to walk on the Sabbath, fixed at one thousand cubits (one cubit is eighteen to twenty-two inches); cf: Acts 1:12, on the distance between Jerusalem and Mount Olivet, "a Sabbath day's journey."
3. I.e., Atlas.
4. They lament the soul's imprisonment in the body.

In real darkness of the body dwells,
160 Shut up from outward light
To incorporate° with gloomy night;   *become one body*
For inward light alas
Puts forth no visual beam.°   *beam of eyesight*
O mirror of our fickle state,
165 Since man on earth unparalleled!
The rarer thy example stands,
By how much from the top of wondrous glory,
Strongest of mortal men,
To lowest pitch of abject fortune thou art fall'n.
170 For him I reckon not in high estate
Whom long descent of birth
Or the sphere of fortune raises;
But thee whose strength, while virtue was her mate,
Might have subdued the earth,
175 Universally crowned with highest praises.
SAMSON. I hear the sound of words; their sense
   the air
Dissolves unjointed ere it reach my ear.
CHORUS. He speaks; let us draw nigh. Matchless
   in might,
The glory late of Israel, now the grief!
180 We come thy friends[5] and neighbors not unknown
From Eshtaol and Zora's[6] fruitful vale
To visit or bewail thee, or if better,
Counsel or consolation we may bring,
Salve to thy sores; apt words have power to swage°   *assuage*
185 The tumors of a troubled mind,
And are as balm to festered wounds.
SAMSON. Your coming, friends, revives me, for I learn
Now of my own experience, not by talk,
How counterfeit a coin they are who "friends"
190 Bear in their superscription° (of the most   *inscription on a coin*
I would be understood); in prosperous days
They swarm, but in adverse withdraw their head,
Not to be found, though sought. Ye see, O friends,
How many evils have enclosed me round;
195 Yet that which was the worst now least afflicts me,
Blindness, for had I sight, confused with shame,
How could I once look up, or heave the head,

5. Cf. friends in Job 2:11–13.
6. Danite cities: "And the Spirit of the Lord began to move him at times in the camp of Dan between Zorah and Eshtaol" (Judg. 13:25).

Who like a foolish pilot have shipwrecked
My vessel trusted to me from above,
200 Gloriously rigged; and for a word, a tear,
Fool, have divulged the secret gift of God
To a deceitful woman? Tell me, friends,
Am I not sung and proverbed for a fool
In every street, do they not say, "How well
205 Are come upon him his deserts"? Yet why?
Immeasurable strength they might behold
In me, of wisdom nothing more than mean;°   *average*
This with the other should, at least, have paired;
These two proportioned ill drove me transverse.[7]
210 CHORUS. Tax not divine disposal; wisest men
Have erred, and by bad women been deceived;
And shall again, pretend they ne'er so wise.
Deject not then so overmuch thyself,
Who hast of sorrow thy full load besides.
215 Yet truth to say, I oft have heard men wonder
Why thou shouldst wed Philistian women rather
Than of thine own tribe fairer, or as fair,
At least of thy own nation, and as noble.
SAMSON. The first I saw at Timna, and she pleased
220 Me, not my parents, that I sought to wed,
The daughter of an infidel: they knew not
That what I motioned was of God; I knew
From intimate° impúlse, and therefore urged   *inmost, deep-seated*
The marriage on; that by occasion hence
225 I might begin Israel's deliverance,
The work to which I was divinely called.
She proving false, the next I took to wife
(O that I never had! fond wish too late!)
Was in the vale of Sorec, Dalila,
230 That specious° monster, my accomplished   *deceptively attractive*
snare.
I thought it lawful from my former act,
And the same end, still watching to oppress
Israel's oppressors. Of what now I suffer
She was not the prime cause, but I myself,
235 Who vanquished with a peal of words (O weakness!)
Gave up my fort of silence to a woman.
CHORUS. In seeking just occasion to provoke
The Philistine, thy country's enemy,

---

7. Off course (continuing the ship metaphor).

Thou never wast remiss, I bear thee witness:
240 Yet Israel still serves° with all his sons.   *is in servitude*
SAMSON. That fault I take not on me, but transfer
On Israel's governors and heads of tribes,
Who seeing those great acts which God had done
Singly by me against their conquerors
245 Acknowledged not, or not at all considered,
Deliverance offered: I on th' other side
Used no ambition[8] to commend my deeds;
The deeds themselves, though mute, spoke
    loud the doer;
But they persisted deaf, and would not seem
250 To count them things worth notice, till at length
Their lords the Philistines with gathered powers
Entered Judea seeking me, who then
Safe to the rock of Etham[9] was retired,
Not flying, but forecasting° in what place   *planning*
255 To set upon them, what advantaged best;
Meanwhile the men of Judah, to prevent
The harass of their land, beset me round;
I willingly on some conditions came
Into their hands, and they as gladly yield me
260 To the uncircumcised a welcome prey,
Bound with two cords; but cords to me were threads
Touched with the flame: on their whole host I flew
Unarmed, and with a trivial weapon° felled   *jawbone of an ass*
Their choicest youth; they only lived who fled.
265 Had Judah that day joined, or one whole tribe,
They had by this possessed the towers of Gath,[1]
And lorded over them whom now they serve;
But what more oft in nations grown corrupt,
And by their vices brought to servitude,
270 Than to love bondage more than liberty,
Bondage with ease than strenuous liberty;
And to despise, or envy, or suspect
Whom God hath of his special favor raised
As their deliverer; if he aught begin,
275 How frequent to desert him, and at last
To heap ingratitude on worthiest deeds?
CHORUS. Thy words to my remembrance bring
How Succoth and the fort of Penuel

8. Soliciting of honors (L. *ambitio*).
9. Judg. 15:8.
1. Philistine city; here, for Philistia.

Their great deliverer contemned,
280 The matchless Gideon in pursuit
Of Madian and her vanquished kings:[2]
And how ingrateful Ephraim
Had dealt with Jephtha, who by argument,
Not worse than by his shield and spear,
285 Defended Israel from the Ammonite,
Had not his prowess quelled their pride
In that sore battle when so many died
Without reprieve adjudged to death,
For want of well pronouncing *Shibboleth*.[3]
290 SAMSON. Of such examples add me to the roll;
Me easily indeed mine° may neglect,   *my people*
But God's proposed deliverance not so.
CHORUS. Just are the ways of God,
And justifiable to men;
295 Unless there be who think° not God at all: *believe in*
If any be, they walk obscure;
For of such doctrine never was there school,
But the heart of the fool,
And no man therein doctor° but himself.   *teacher*
300 Yet more there be who doubt° his ways   *suspect*
not just,
As to his own edicts found contradicting,
Then give the reins to wand'ring thought,
Regardless of his glory's diminution;
Till by their own perplexities involved
305 They ravel° more, still less resolved,   *become tangled,*
But never find self-satisfying solution.   *perplexed*
As if they would confine th' Interminable,°   *Infinite*
And tie him to his own prescript,
Who made our laws to bind us, not himself,
310 And hath full right to exempt
Whom so it pleases him by choice
From national obstriction,[4] without taint
Of sin, or legal debt;
For with his own laws he can best dispense.

2. Judg. 8:1–17: The ungrateful Israelites refused to aid Gideon in pursuit of the kings of Midian ("Madian" in the Vulgate).
3. Judg. 11 and 12:1–6. The Ephraimites refused to aid Jephtha against the Ammonites and also threatened to burn him in his house. Jephtha then fought the Ephraimites and slaughtered those who tried to cross the Jordan. They revealed their identity by their inability to pronounce the word *shibboleth*. St. Paul names Gideon and Jephtha alongside Samson as heroes of faith (Heb. 11:32).
4. Obligation; in particular, the Mosaic law prohibiting marriage with Canaanite idolaters (Deut. 7:3). The Philistines were considered Canaanites.

315   He would not else, who never wanted means,
      Nor in respect of the enemy just cause
      To set his people free,
      Have prompted this heroic Nazarite,
      Against his vow of strictest purity,
320   To seek in marriage that fallacious° bride,   *deceitful*
      Unclean, unchaste.[5]
         Down Reason then, at least vain reasonings down,
      Though Reason here aver
      That moral verdict quits her of unclean:
325   Unchaste was subsequent; her stain, not his.
         But see, here comes thy reverend sire
      With careful° step, locks white as down,   *Full of care*
      Old Manoa: advise°   *consider*
      Forthwith how thou ought'st to receive him.
330 SAMSON. Ay me, another inward grief awaked
    With mention of that name renews th' assault.
   MANOA. Brethren and men of Dan, for such ye seem,
    Though in this uncouth place; if old respect,
    As I suppose, towards your once gloried friend,
335   My son now captive, hither hath informed
    Your younger feet, while mine cast back with age
    Came lagging after; say if he be here.
   CHORUS. As signal° now in low dejected state,   *conspicuous*
    As erst in highest, behold him where he lies.
340 MANOA. O miserable change! is this the man,
    That invincible Samson, far renowned,
    The dread of Israel's foes, who with a strength
    Equivalent to angels' walked their streets,
    None offering fight; who single combatant
345   Duelled° their armies ranked in proud array,   *Fought alone*
    Himself an army, now unequal match
    To save himself against a coward armed
    At one spear's length? O ever-failing trust
    In mortal strength! and oh what not in man
350   Deceivable and vain! Nay, what thing good
    Prayed for, but often proves our woe, our bane?
    I prayed for children, and thought barrenness
    In wedlock a reproach; I gained a son,
    And such a son as all men hailed me happy;
355   Who would be now a father in my stead?
    O wherefore did God grant me my request,

---

5. Samson's idolatrous ("unclean") first wife, the woman of Timna, was "given to his companion" (Judg. 14:20).

And as a blessing with such pomp adorned?
Why are his gifts desirable, to tempt
Our earnest prayers, then giv'n with solemn hand
360   As graces,° draw a scorpion's tail behind?   *favors*
For this did the angel twice descend? For this
Ordained thy nurture holy, as of a plant;
Select and sacred, glorious for a while,
The miracle of men; then in an hour
365   Ensnared, assaulted, overcome, led bound,
Thy foes' derision, captive, poor, and blind
Into a dungeon thrust, to work with slaves?
Alas, methinks whom God hath chosen once
To worthiest deeds, if he through frailty err,
370   He should not so o'erwhelm, and as a thrall
Subject him to so foul indignities,
Be it but for honor's sake of former deeds.
SAMSON. Appoint° not heavenly disposition, father.   *(1) blame, (2)*
Nothing of all these evils hath befall'n me   *prescribe*
375   But justly; I myself have brought them on,
Sole author I, sole cause: if aught seem vile,
As vile hath been my folly, who have profaned
The mystery of God giv'n me under pledge
Of vow, and have betrayed it to a woman,
380   A Canaanite, my faithless enemy.
This well I knew, nor was at all surprised,
But warned oft by experience: did not she
Of Timna first betray me, and reveal
The secret[6] wrested from me in her heighth
385   Of nuptial love professed, carrying it straight
To them who had corrupted her, my spies,°   *spies on me*
And rivals? In this other° was there found   *Dalila*
More faith? who also in her prime of love,
Spousal embraces, vitiated with gold,
390   Though offered only, by the scent° conceived   *the offer of money*
Her spurious first-born, treason against me.
Thrice she assayed with flattering prayers and sighs
And amorous reproaches to win from me
My capital° secret, in what part my strength   *(1) of the head, (2)*
395   Lay stored, in what part summed, that she might know: *fatal*
Thrice I deluded her, and turned to sport
Her importunity, each time perceiving
How openly, and with what impudence,

---

6. See Judg. 14:8–9, 12–18: the riddle of the lion and the honeycomb, which Samson's
wife wheedled out of him and then betrayed him by revealing it to her countrymen.

She purposed to betray me, and (which was worse
400   Than undissembled hate) with what
            contempt
        She sought to make me traitor to myself;
        Yet the fourth time, when must'ring all her wiles,
        With blandished parleys, feminine assaults,
        Tongue-batteries, she surceased not day nor night
405   To storm me over-watched[7] and wearied out,
        At times when men seek most repose and rest,
        I yielded, and unlocked her all my heart,
        Who with a grain of manhood well resolved
        Might easily have shook off all her snares;
410   But foul effeminacy held me yoked
        Her bondslave; O indignity, O blot
        To honor and religion! servile mind
        Rewarded well with servile punishment!
        The base degree to which I now am fall'n,
415   These rags, this grinding, is not yet so base
        As was my former servitude, ignoble,
        Unmanly, ignominious, infamous,
        True slavery, and that blindness worse than this,
        That saw not how degenerately I served.
420   MANOA. I cannot praise thy marriage choices, son,
        Rather approved them not; but thou didst plead
        Divine impulsion prompting how thou might'st
        Find some occasion to infest our foes.
        I state° not that; this I am sure: our foes   *give an opinion upon*
425   Found soon occasion thereby to make thee
        Their captive, and their triumph; thou the sooner
        Temptation found'st, or over-potent charms,
        To violate the sacred trust of silence
        Deposited within thee, which to have kept
430   Tacit was in thy power; true; and thou bear'st
        Enough, and more, the burden of that fault;
        Bitterly hast thou paid, and still art paying,
        That rigid score.° A worse thing yet remains: *debt*
        This day the Philistines a popular feast
435   Here celebrate in Gaza, and proclaim
        Great pomp, and sacrifice, and praises loud
        To Dagon, as their god who hath delivered
        Thee, Samson, bound and blind into their hands,
        Them out of thine, who slew'st them many a slain.

7. Tired from having to stay awake.

440 So Dagon shall be magnified, and God,
      Besides whom is no God, compared with idols,
      Disglorified, blasphemed, and had in scorn
      By th' idolatrous rout amidst their wine;
      Which to have come to pass by means of thee,
445 Samson, of all thy sufferings think the heaviest,
      Of all reproach the most with shame that ever
      Could have befall'n thee and thy father's house.
   SAMSON. Father, I do acknowledge and confess
      That I this honor, I this pomp have brought
450 To Dagon, and advanced his praises high
      Among the heathen round; to God have brought
      Dishonor, obloquy, and oped the mouths
      Of idolists and atheists; have brought scandal
      To Israel, diffidence° of God, and doubt   *distrust*
455 In feeble hearts, propense° enough before   *inclined*
      To waver, or fall off and join with idols:
      Which is my chief affliction, shame and sorrow,
      The anguish of my soul, that suffers not
      Mine eye to harbor sleep, or thoughts to rest.
460 This only hope relieves me, that the strife
      With me hath end; all the contést is now
      'Twixt God and Dagon; Dagon hath presumed,
      Me overthrown, to enter lists with° God,   *challenge to fight*
      His deity comparing and preferring
465 Before the God of Abraham. He, be sure,
      Will not connive,° or linger, thus provoked,   *shut eyes to wrong,*
      But will arise and his great name assert: *acquiesce*
      Dagon must stoop, and shall ere long receive
      Such a discomfit,° as shall quite despoil him   *defeat*
470 Of all these boasted trophies won on me,
      And with confusion blank° his worshipers.   *make pale,*
   MANOA. With cause this hope relieves thee,   *confound*
            and these words
      I as a prophecy receive; for God,
      Nothing more certain, will not long defer
475 To vindicate the glory of his name
      Against all competition, nor will long
      Endure it doubtful whether God be Lord,
      Or Dagon. But for thee what shall be done?
      Thou must not in the meanwhile, here forgot,
480 Lie in this miserable loathsome plight
      Neglected. I already have made way
      To some Philistian lords, with whom to treat
      About thy ransom: well they may by this°   *by now*

Have satisfied their utmost of revenge
485 By pains and slaveries, worse than death inflicted
On thee, who now no more canst do them harm.
SAMSON. Spare that proposal, father, spare the trouble
Of that solicitation; let me here,
As I deserve, pay on my punishment;
490 And expiate, if possible, my crime,
Shameful garrulity. To have revealed
Secrets of men, the secrets of a friend,
How heinous had the fact° been, how deserving   *deed*
Contempt, and scorn of all, to be excluded
495 All friendship, and avoided as a blab,
The mark of fool set on his front!° But I   *forehead*
God's counsel have not kept, his holy secret
Presumptuously have published, impiously,
Weakly at least, and shamefully: a sin
500 That Gentiles in their parables condemn[8]
To their abyss and horrid pains confined.
MANOA. Be penitent and for thy fault contrite,
But act not in thy own affliction, son;
Repent the sin, but if the punishment
505 Thou canst avoid, self-preservation bids;
Or th' execution leave to high disposal,
And let another hand, not thine, exact
Thy penal forfeit from thyself; perhaps
God will relent, and quit thee° all his debt;   *cancel*
510 Who evermore approves and more accepts
(Best pleased with humble and filial submission)
Him who imploring mercy sues for life,
Than who self-rigorous chooses death as due;
Which argues over-just, and self-displeased
515 For self-offense, more than for God offended.
Reject not then what offered means, who knows
But God hath set before us, to return thee
Home to thy country and his sacred house,[9]
Where thou may'st bring thy off'rings, to avert
520 His further ire, with prayers and vows renewed.
SAMSON. His pardon I implore; but as for life,
To what end should I seek it? When in strength

8. Alludes to the Greek myth of Tantalus, who was placed in Hades for revealing the secrets
of the gods. The biblical story places Samson under no obligation to keep the source of
his strength secret. Indiscretion is a fault that goes undenounced in the Bible.
9. The Tabernacle, the portable sanctuary of the Israelites during their wanderings in the
wilderness and afterward until the building of the Temple.

All mortals I excelled, and great in hopes
With youthful courage and magnanimous thoughts
525 Of birth from Heav'n foretold and high exploits,
Full of divine instinct, after some proof
Of acts indeed heroic, far beyond
The sons of Anak,[1] famous now and blazed,°   *celebrated*
Fearless of danger, like a petty god
530 I walked about admired of all and dreaded
On hostile ground, none daring my affront.
Then swoll'n with pride into the snare I fell
Of fair fallacious looks, venereal trains,°   *sexual traps*
Softened with pleasure and voluptuous life;
535 At length to lay my head and hallowed pledge[2]
Of all my strength in the lascivious lap
Of a deceitful concubine who shore me
Like a tame wether,° all my precious fleece,   *castrated ram*
Then turned me out ridiculous, despoiled,
540 Shav'n, and disarmed among my enemies.
CHOR. Desire of wine and all delicious drinks,
Which many a famous warrior overturns,
Thou couldst repress, nor did the dancing ruby
Sparkling outpoured, the flavor, or the smell,
545 Or taste that cheers the heart[3] of gods and men,
Allure thee from the cool crystálline stream.
SAMSON. Wherever fountain or fresh current flowed
Against the eastern ray, translucent, pure
With touch ethereal of heav'n's fiery rod,°   *sunbeam*
550 I drank, from the clear milky juice[4] allaying
Thirst, and refreshed; nor envied them the grape
Whose heads that turbulent liquor° fills with fumes.   *clear*
CHORUS. O madness, to think use of strongest wines
And strongest drinks our chief support of health,
555 When God with these forbidd'n made choice to rear
His mighty champion, strong above compare,
Whose drink was only from the liquid°   *clear, transparent*
    brook.
SAMSON. But what availed this temperance, not complete
Against another object more enticing?
560 What boots it° at one gate to make defense,   *What does it help*
And at another to let in the foe,

---

1. See p. 163, n. 1.
2. Sign (i.e., his hair).
3. Ps. 104:15: "wine that maketh glad the heart of man."
4. Water. See *PL*, 5. 306.

Effeminately vanquished? By which means,
Now blind, disheartened, shamed, dishonored,
　　quelled,
To what can I be useful, wherein serve
565　My nation, and the work from Heav'n imposed,
But to sit idle on the household hearth,
A burdenous drone; To visitants a gaze,
Or pitied object; these redundant° locks,
Robustious° to no purpose, clust'ring down,
570　Vain monument of strength; till length of years
And sedentary numbness craze my limbs
To a contemptible old age obscure.
Here rather let me drudge and earn my bread,
Till vermin or the draff° of servile food
575　Consume me, and oft-invocated death
Hasten the welcome end of all my pains.
MANOA. Wilt thou then serve the Philistines
　　with that gift
Which was expressly giv'n thee to annoy them?
Better at home lie bed-rid, not only idle,
580　Inglorious, unemployed, with age outworn.
But God, who caused a fountain at thy prayer
From the dry ground to spring, thy thirst to allay
After the brunt of battle,[5] can as easy
Cause light again within thy eyes to spring,
585　Wherewith to serve him better than thou hast;
And I persuade me so; why else this strength
Miraculous yet remaining in those locks?
His might continues in thee not for naught,
Nor shall his wondrous gifts be frustrate thus.
590　SAMSON. All otherwise to me my thoughts portend,
That these dark orbs no more shall treat with light,
Nor th' other light of life continue long,
But yield to double darkness nigh at hand:
So much I feel my genial[6] spirits droop,
595　My hopes all flat; nature within me seems
In all her functions weary of herself;
My race of glory run, and race of shame,
And I shall shortly be with them that rest.
MANOA. Believe not these suggestions, which proceed

(1) luxuriantly
flowing, (2)
superfluous /
Strong

garbage

---

5. Judg. 15:18–19.
6. Pertaining to *genius* or natural disposition; vital; generative (with a suggestion of
flaccidity).

600 From anguish of the mind and humors black,[7]
       That mingle with thy fancy.° I however   *imagination*
       Must not omit a father's timely care
       To prosecute° the means of thy deliverance   *pursue, persevere in*
       By ransom or how else: meanwhile be calm,
605 And healing words from these thy friends admit.
   SAMSON. O that torment should not be confined
       To the body's wounds and sores,
       With maladies innumerable
       In heart, head, breast, and reins;°   *kidneys or loins*
610 But must secret passage find
       To th' inmost mind,
       There exercise all his° fierce accidents,°   *its / symptoms of*
       And on her purest spirits prey,   *illness*
       As on entrails, joints, and limbs,
615 With answerable° pains, but more intense,   *corresponding*
       Though void of corporal sense.
           My griefs not only pain me
       As a ling'ring disease,
       But finding no redress, ferment and rage,
620 Nor less than wounds immedicable
       Rankle, and fester, and gangrene,
       To black mortification.°   *gangrene, necrosis*
       Thoughts, my tormentors, armed with
           deadly stings
       Mangle my apprehensive tenderest parts,°   *mind, conscience,*
625 Exasperate,° exulcerate,° and raise   *imagination / Irritate /*
       Dire inflammation which no cooling herb   *cause ulcers*
       Or med'cinal liquor can assuage,
       Nor breath of vernal air from snowy Alp.
       Sleep hath forsook and giv'n me o'er
630 To death's benumbing opium as my only cure.
       Thence faintings, swoonings of despair,
       And sense of Heav'n's desertion.
           I was his nursling once and choice delight,
       His destined from the womb,
635 Promised by Heavenly message twice descending.
       Under his special eye
       Abstemious° I grew up and thrived amain;°   *Abstaining from*
       He led me on to mightiest deeds   *wine / vigorously*
       Above the nerve of mortal arm
640 Against the uncircumcised, our enemies.
       But now hath cast me off as never known,

7. Black bile, a fluid associated with melancholy.

And to those cruel enemies,
Whom I by his appointment had provoked,
Left me all helpless with th' irreparable loss
645   Of sight, reserved alive to be repeated°   *made repeatedly*
The subject of their cruelty or scorn.
Nor am I in the list of them that hope;
Hopeless are all my evils, all remédiless;
This one prayer yet remains, might I be heard,
650   No long petition—speedy death,
The close of all my miseries, and the balm.
CHORUS. Many are the sayings of the wise
In ancient and in modern books enrolled,
Extolling patience as the truest fortitude;
655   And to the bearing well of all calamities,
All chances incident to man's frail life,
Consolatories writ
With studied argument, and much persuasion
      sought,
Lenient° of grief and anxious thought;   *Soothing*
660   But with th' afflicted in his pangs their sound
Little prevails, or rather seems a tune
Harsh, and of dissonant mood° from his   *(1) state of mind,*
      complaint,   *(2) musical mode*
Unless he feel within
Some source of consolation from above,
665   Secret refreshings that repair his strength,
And fainting spirits uphold.
      God of our fathers, what is man!
That thou towards him with hand so various,
Or might I say contrarious,
670   Temper'st° thy providence through his short   *Regulate, Control*
      course,
Not evenly, as thou rul'st
The angelic orders and inferior creatures mute,
Irrational and brute.
Nor do I name of men the common rout,
675   That wand'ring loose about
Grow up and perish, as the summer fly,
Heads without name no more remembered;
But such as thou hast solemnly elected,
With gifts and graces eminently adorned
680   To some great work, thy glory,
And people's safety, which in part they effect;
Yet toward these thus dignified, thou oft
Amidst their heighth of noon

Changest thy countenance and thy hand,
    with no regard
685 Of highest favors past
From thee on them, or them to thee of service.
    Nor only dost degrade them, or remit
To life obscured, which were a fair dismission,
But throw'st them lower than thou didst
    exalt them high,
690 Unseemly falls in human eye,
Too grievous for the trespass or omission;
Oft leav'st them to the hostile sword
Of heathen and profane, their carcasses
To dogs and fowls a prey, or else captived,
695 Or to the unjust tribunals, under change of times,
And condemnation of the ingrateful multitude.[8]
If these they scape, perhaps in poverty
With sickness and disease thou bow'st them down,
Painful diseases and deformed,
700 In crude° old age;   *premature*
Though not disordinate, yet causeless suff'ring
The punishment of dissolute days;[9] in fine,°   *in conclusion*
Just or unjust, alike seem miserable,
For oft alike, both come to evil end.
705   So deal not with this once thy glorious champion,
The image of thy strength, and mighty minister.
What do I beg? how hast thou dealt already?
Behold him in this state calamitous, and turn
His labors, for thou canst, to peaceful end.
710   But who is this, what thing of sea or land?
Female of sex it seems,
That so bedecked, ornate, and gay,
Comes this way sailing
Like a stately ship
715 Of Tarsus,[1] bound for th' isles

---

8. Perhaps the strongest evidence of the poem's late composition, these lines (678–696)
about God's terrible ways with his faithful throughout history can be read more specifically as an allusion to the Restoration government's reprisals upon Commonwealth
leaders. Milton's friend Henry Vane was beheaded on Tower Hill in June 1662, although
he was not a regicide, and despite the king's earlier assent to Parliament's petition to
spare him from death. The bodies of Cromwell, Henry Ireton, and John Bradshaw were
disinterred and mutilated; their heads were placed on poles on the top of Westminster
Hall, where they remained for several years.
9. Those who are not immoderate ("disordinate") suffer unjustly the same punishment as
those who have led dissolute lives.
1. The phrase *ships of Tarshish* occurs frequently in the Hebrew Bible, sometimes denot-
ing the specific type of vessel (large, intended for a long voyage) rather than the port.

Of Javan or Gadire,[2]
With all her bravery on, and tackle trim,
Sails filled, and streamers waving,
Courted by all the winds that hold them play,
720   An amber° scent of odorous perfume   ambergris (aromatic)
Her harbinger, a damsel train behind;
Some rich Philistian matron she may seem,
And now at nearer view, no other certain
Than Dálila thy wife.
725   SAMSON. My wife, my traitress, let her not come near.
CHORUS. Yet on she moves, now stands and
        eyes thee fixed,
About t' have spoke; but now, with head declined
Like a fair flower surcharged with dew, she weeps,
And words addressed seem into tears dissolved,
730   Wetting the borders of her silken veil;
But now again she makes address° to speak.   prepares
DALILA. With doubtful feet and wavering resolution
I came, still dreading thy displeasure, Samson,
Which to have merited,° without excuse,   deserved
735   I cannot but acknowledge; yet if tears
May expiate (though the fact° more evil drew   deed
In the perverse event° than I foresaw),   unexpected outcome
My penance hath not slackened, though my pardon
No way assured. But conjugal affection,
740   Prevailing over fear and timorous doubt,
Hath led me on, desirous to behold
Once more thy face, and know of thy estate;
If aught in my ability may serve
To lighten what thou suffer'st, and appease
745   Thy mind with what amends is in my power,
Though late, yet in some part to recompense
My rash but more unfortunate misdeed.
SAMSON. Out, out hyena![3] These are thy wonted arts,
And arts of every woman false like thee,
750   To break all faith, all vows, deceive, betray;
Then as repentant to submit, beseech,
And reconcilement move° with feigned remorse,   propose
Confess, and promise wonders in her change,

2. Cadiz in the western Mediterranean. Javan, Noah's grandson, was believed to have
been the progenitor of the Greeks.
3. According to a note on Eccles. 13:19 in the Geneva Bible (1560), the hyena "is a wilde
beaste that counterfaiteth the voyce of men, and so entiseth them out of their houses
and devoureth them."

Not truly penitent, but chief to try
755   Her husband, how far urged his patience bears,
His virtue or weakness which way to assail;
Then with more cautious and instructed skill
Again transgresses, and again submits;
That wisest and best men, full oft beguiled,
760   With goodness principled not to reject
The penitent, but ever to forgive,
Are drawn to wear out miserable days,
Entangled with a poisonous bosom snake,
If not by quick destruction soon cut off,
765   As I by thee, to ages an example.
DALILA. Yet hear me, Samson; not that I endeavor
To lesson or extenuate my offense,
But that on th' other side if it be weighed
By itself, with aggravations° not surcharged,°   *exaggerations /*
770   Or else with just allowance counterpoised,   *overburdened*
I may, if possible, thy pardon find
The easier towards me, or thy hatred less.
First granting, as I do, it was a weakness
In me, but incident to all our sex,
775   Curiosity, inquisitive, importune
Of secrets, then with like infirmity
To publish them, both common female faults;
Was it not weakness also to make known
For importunity, that is for naught,
780   Wherein consisted all thy strength and safety?
To what I did thou show'dst me first the way.
But I to enemies revealed, and should not.
Nor shouldst thou have trusted that to woman's frailty:
Ere I to thee, thou to thyself wast cruel.
785   Let weakness then with weakness come to parle,°   *parley*
So near related, or the same of kind;
Thine forgive mine, that men may censure thine
The gentler, if severely thou exact not
More strength from me than in thyself was found.
790   And what if love, which thou interpret'st hate,
The jealousy of love, powerful of sway
In human hearts, nor less in mine towards thee,
Caused what I did? I saw thee mutable
Of fancy, feared lest one day thou wouldst leave me

795 As her at Timna, sought by all means therefore
How to endear, and hold thee to me firmest:
No better way I saw than by impórtuning
To learn thy secrets, get into my power
Thy key of strength and safety. Thou wilt say,
800 "Why then revealed?" I was assured by those
Who tempted me that nothing was designed
Against thee but safe custody[4] and hold:
That made° for me; I knew that liberty   *decided it*
Would draw thee forth to perilous enterprises,
805 While I at home sat full of cares and fears,
Wailing thy absence in my widowed bed;
Here I should still enjoy thee day and night,
Mine and love's prisoner, not the Philistines',
Whole to myself, unhazarded abroad,
810 Fearless at home of partners in my love.
These reasons in love's law have passed for good,
Though fond° and reasonless to some perhaps;   *foolish*
And love hath oft, well meaning, wrought much woe,
Yet always pity or pardon hath obtained.
815 Be not unlike all others, not austere
As thou art strong, inflexible as steel.
If thou in strength all mortals dost exceed,
In uncompassionate anger do not so.

SAMSON. How cunningly the sorceress displays
820 Her own transgressions, to upbraid me mine!
That malice, not repentance, brought thee hither,
By this appears: I gave, thou say'st, th' example,
I led the way—bitter reproach, but true;
I to myself was false ere thou to me;
825 Such pardon therefore as I give my folly,
Take to thy wicked deed; which[5] when thou seest
Impartial, self-severe, inexorable,
Thou wilt renounce thy seeking, and much rather
Confess it feigned. Weakness is thy excuse,
830 And I believe it, weakness to resist
Philistian gold; if weakness may excuse,
What murderer, what traitor, parricide,
Incestuous, sacrilegious, but may plead it?
All wickedness is weakness: that plea therefore
835 With God or man will gain thee no remission.

4. But in Judg. 16:5, the Philistine lords urge Dalila to "Entice him . . . that we may bind
him to afflict him: and we will give thee every one of us eleven hundred pieces of
silver."
5. I.e., pardon.

But love constrained thee. Call it furious rage
To satisfy thy lust: love seeks to have love;
My love how couldst thou hope, who took'st the way
To raise in me inexpiable hate,
840 Knowing,[6] as needs I must, by thee betrayed?
In vain thou striv'st to cover shame with shame,
Or by evasions thy crime uncover'st more.
DALILA. Since thou determin'st weakness for no plea
In man or woman, though to thy own condemning,
845 Hear what assaults I had, what snares besides,
What sieges girt me round, ere I consented;
Which might have awed the best-resolved of men,
The constantest, to have yielded without blame.
It was not gold, as to my charge thou lay'st,
850 That wrought with me: thou know'st the magistrates
And princes of my country came in person,
Solicited, commanded, threatened, urged,
Adjured by all the bonds of civil duty
And of religion, pressed how just it was,
855 How honorable, how glorious to entrap
A common enemy, who had destroyed
Such numbers of our nation: and the priest
Was not behind, but ever at my ear,
Preaching how meritorious with the gods
860 It would be to ensnare an irreligious
Dishonorer of Dagon. What had I
To oppose against such powerful arguments?
Only my love of thee held long debate,
And combated in silence all these reasons
865 With hard contést. At length that grounded° maxim,   *established*
So rife and celebrated in the mouths
Of wisest men, that to the public good
Private respects must yield, with grave authority
Took full possession of me and prevailed;
870 Virtue, as I thought, truth, duty, so enjoining.
SAMSON. I thought where all thy circling wiles would end,
In feigned religion, smooth hypocrisy.
But had thy love, still odiously pretended,
Been, as it ought, sincere, it would have
        taught thee
875 Far other reasonings, brought forth other deeds.
I before all the daughters of my tribe
And of my nation chose thee from among

6. Knowing myself to be.

My enemies, loved thee, as too well thou knew'st,
Too well; unbosomed all my secrets to thee,
880   Not out of levity, but overpow'red
By thy request, who could deny thee nothing;
Yet now am judged an enemy. Why then
Didst thou at first receive me for thy husband,
Then, as since then, thy country's foe professed?
885   Being once a wife, for me thou wast to leave
Parents and country; nor was I their subject,
Nor under their protection but my own,
Thou mine, not theirs. If aught against my life
Thy country sought of thee, it sought unjustly,
890   Against the law of nature, law of nations,[7]
No more thy country, but an impious crew
Of men conspiring to uphold their state
By worse than hostile deeds, violating the ends
For which our country is a name so dear;
895   Not therefore to be obeyed. But zeal moved thee;
To please thy gods thou didst it. Gods unable
To acquit themselves° and prosecute their foes   *perform their offices*
But by ungodly deeds, the contradiction
Of their own deity, gods cannot be:
900   Less therefore to be pleased, obeyed, or feared.
These false pretexts and varnished colors failing,
Bare in thy guilt how foul must thou appear!
DALILA. In argument with men a woman ever
Goes by the worse, whatever be her cause.
905   SAMSON. For want of words, no doubt, or lack of breath;
Witness when I was worried° with thy peals.°   *assailed / noisy cries*
DALILA. I was a fool, too rash, and quite mistaken
In what I thought would have succeeded best.
Let me obtain forgiveness of thee, Samson;
910   Afford me place to show what recompense
Towards thee I intend for what I have misdone,
Misguided: only what remains past cure
Bear not too sensibly,° nor still insist   *intensely, grievously*
To afflict thy self in vain. Though sight be lost,
915   Life yet hath many solaces, enjoyed
Where other senses want° not their delights   *lack*
At home in leisure and domestic ease,
Exempt from many a care and chance to which

7. The title of John Selden's massive study of natural law, regarded as a series of divine universal moral imperatives, *De Jure Naturali et Gentium* (1640), cited by Milton in *DDD.*

Eyesight exposes daily men abroad.
920   I to the lords will intercede, not doubting
      Their favorable ear, that I may fetch thee
      From forth this loathsome prison-house, to abide
      With me, where my redoubled love and care
      With nursing diligence, to me glad office,
925   May ever tend about thee to old age
      With all things grateful° cheered, and so supplied,   *pleasing*
      That what by me thou hast lost thou least
            shalt miss.
SAMSON.   No, no, of my condition take no care;
      It fits not; thou and I long since are twain;
930   Nor think me so unwary or accursed
      To bring my feet again into the snare
      Where once I have been caught; I know thy trains,°   *traps, lures*
      Though dearly to my cost, thy gins,° and toils;°   *schemes, snares / nets*
      Thy fair enchanted cup[8] and warbling charms
935   No more on me have power, their force is nulled;
      So much of adder's wisdom[9] I have learnt
      To fence my ear against thy sorceries.
      If in my flower of youth and strength, when all men
      Loved, honored, feared me, thou alone could hate me
940   Thy husband, slight me, sell me, and forgo me,
      How wouldst thou use me now, blind, and thereby
      Deceivable, in most things as a child
      Helpless, thence easily contemned, and scorned,
      And last neglected? How wouldst thou insult°   *exult proudly or*
945   When I must live uxorious to thy will   *contemptuously*
      In perfect thraldom, how again betray me,
      Bearing my words and doings to the lords
      To gloss° upon, and censuring,° frown or   *comment / judging*
            smile?
      This jail I count the house of liberty
950   To° thine whose doors my feet shall never   *Compared to*
            enter.
DALILA.   Let me approach at least, and touch
            thy hand.
SAMSON.   Not for thy life, lest fierce remembrance
            wake
      My sudden rage to tear thee joint by joint.
      At distance I forgive thee, go with that.
955   Bewail thy falsehood, and the pious works

---

8. An allusion to Circe and an echo of *Comus* (50–53, 252–61).
9. Deafness (proverbial).

It hath brought forth to make thee memorable
Among illustrious women, faithful wives;
Cherish thy hastened widowhood with the gold
Of matrimonial treason: so farewell.
960   DALILA. I see thou art implacable, more deaf
To prayers than winds and seas; yet winds to seas
Are reconciled at length, and sea to shore:
Thy anger, unappeasable, still rages,
Eternal tempest never to be calmed.
965   Why do I humble thus my self, and suing
For peace, reap nothing but repulse and hate?
Bid go with evil omen¹ and the brand
Of infamy upon my name denounced?
To mix with thy concernments° I desist   *affairs*
970   Henceforth, nor too much disapprove my own.
Fame if not double-faced is double-mouthed,
And with contráry blast² proclaims most deeds;
On both his wings, one black, the other white,
Bears greatest names in his wild airy flight.
975   My name perhaps among the circumcised°   *Israelites*
In Dan, in Judah, and the bordering Tribes,
To all posterity may stand defamed,
With malediction mentioned, and the blot
Of falsehood most unconjugal traduced.
980   But in my country where I most desire,
In Ekron, Gaza, Asdod, and in Gath,³
I shall be named among the famousest
Of women, sung at solemn festivals,
Living and dead recorded, who to save
985   Her country from a fierce destroyer, chose
Above the faith of wedlock-bands; my tomb
With odors° visited and annual flowers: *incense*
Not less renowned than in Mount Ephraim
Jael, who with inhospitable guile
990   Smote Sisera sleeping through the temples nailed.⁴
Nor shall I count it heinous to enjoy
The public marks of honor and reward
Conferred upon me for the piety
Which to my country I was judged to have shown.

1. See lines 955–59.
2. As of a trumpet.
3. Philistine cities.
4. See Judg. 4: 17–22. Sisera, a Canaanite enemy of Israel, sought refuge after the defeat of his army in the tent of Jael, who gave him food and drink, but then, inhospitably, drove a tent peg into his temples as he slept. Deborah's renowned song celebrates this deed: "Blessed above women shall Jael be" (Judg. 5:24–31).

995   At this whoever envies or repines,
      I leave him to his lot, and like my own.
     CHORUS. She's gone, a manifest serpent by her sting
      Discovered in the end, till now concealed.
     SAMSON. So let her go; God sent her to debase me,

1000   And aggravate° my folly who committed   *make heavier*
      To such a viper his most sacred trust
      Of secrecy, my safety, and my life.
     CHORUS. Yet beauty, though injurious, hath
        strange power,
      After offense returning, to regain

1005   Love once possessed, nor can be easily
      Repulsed, without much inward passion felt
      And secret sting of amorous remorse.
     SAMSON. Love-quarrels oft in pleasing concord end,
      Not wedlock-treachery endangering life.

1010 CHORUS. It is not virtue, wisdom, valor, wit,
      Strength, comeliness of shape, or amplest merit
      That woman's love can win or long inherit;°   *possess*
      But what it is, hard is to say,
      Harder to hit,

1015   (Which way soever men refer° it),   *consider*
      Much like thy riddle,[5] Samson, in one day
      Or seven, though one should musing sit;
        If any of these, or all, the Timnian bride
      Had not so soon preferred

1020   Thy paranymph,° worthless to thee compared,   *best man*
      Successor in thy bed,
      Nor both° so loosely disallied°   *wives / dissolved*
      Their nuptials, nor this last so treacherously
      Had shorn the fatal harvest of thy head.

1025   Is it for that° such outward ornament   *because*
      Was lavished on their sex, that inward gifts
      Were left for haste unfinished, judgment scant,
      Capacity not raised to apprehend
      Or value what is best

1030   In choice, but oftest to affect° the wrong?   *prefer*
      Or was too much of self-love mixed,
      Of constancy no root infixed,
      That either they love nothing, or not long?
        Whate'er it be, to wisest men and best

1035   Seeming at first all heavenly under virgin veil,
      Soft, modest, meek, demure,

5. See p. 169, n. 6.

Once joined,° the contrary she proves, a thorn   *married*
Intestine,° far within defensive arms   *Internal, Domestic*
A cleaving mischief, in his way to virtue
1040   Adverse and turbulent; or by her charms
Draws him awry enslaved
With dotage, and his sense depraved
To folly and shameful deeds which ruin ends.
What pilot so expert but needs must wreck,
1045   Embarked with such a steers-mate at the helm?
   Favored of Heav'n who finds
   One virtuous rarely found,
   That in domestic good combines:
   Happy that house! his way to peace is smooth:[6]
1050   But virtue which breaks through all opposition,
   And all temptation can remove,
   Most shines and most is ácceptáble above.
   —Therefore God's universal Law
Gave to the man despotic power
1055   Over his female in due awe,
   Nor from that right to part an hour,
   Smile she or lour:
So shall he least confusion draw
On his whole life, not swayed
1060   By female usurpation, nor dismayed.
   But had we best retire? I see a storm.
SAMSON. Fair days have oft contracted° wind   *incurred, brought*
   and rain.
CHORUS. But this another kind of tempest brings.
SAMSON. Be less abstruse, my riddling days are past.
1065   CHORUS. Look now for no enchanting voice, nor fear
   The bait of honied words; a rougher tongue
   Draws hitherward; I know him by his stride,
   The giant Harapha[7] of Gath, his look
   Haughty as is his pile° high-built and proud.   *lofty mass*
1070   Comes he in peace? What wind hath blown him hither
   I less conjecture than when first I saw
   The sumptuous Dalila floating this way:
   His habit[8] carries peace, his brow defiance.

6. See the praise of a good wife in Prov. 31:10–12: "Who can find a virtuous woman? for her price is far above rubies. The heart of her husband doth safely trust in her. . . . She will do him good and not evil all the days of her life."
7. The A.V. of 2 Sam. 21:16 translates the Heb. *ha'rafa* as "the giant"; related to the Bible's *rephaim,* which denotes an old race of giants, extinct and powerless, from *rafa* ("enfeebled"). Milton based his Goliath-like invention in part on the *miles gloriosus* or braggart soldier of Roman and Renaissance comedies.
8. Clothing (not armed).

SAMSON. Or peace or not, alike to me he comes.

1075 CHORUS. His fraught° we soon shall know, he now arrives.   *freight,*
                                                                business
HARAPHA. I come not, Samson, to condole thy chance,

    As these perhaps, yet wish it had not been,

    Though for no friendly intent. I am of Gath,

    Men call me Harapha, of stock renowned

1080   As Og or Anak and the Emims[9] old

    That Kiriathaim[1] held; thou know'st me now,

    If thou at all art known. Much I have heard

    Of thy prodigious might and feats performed

    Incredible to me, in this displeased,

1085   That I was never present on the place

    Of those encounters where we might have tried

    Each other's force in camp° or listed field:°   *battlefield /*
                                                       tournament
    And now am come to see of whom such noise

    Hath walked about, and each limb to survey,

1090   If thy appearance answer loud report.

SAMSON. The way to know were not to see but taste.

HARAPHA. Dost thou already single° me? I   *challenge to single*
    thought   *combat*

    Gyves° and the mill had tamed thee; O that   *Shackles*
    fortune

    Had brought me to the field where thou art famed

1095   To have wrought such wonders with an ass's jaw;

    I should have forced thee soon wish other arms,

    Or left thy carcass where the ass lay thrown:

    So had the glory of prowess been recovered

    To Palestine, won by a Philistine

1100   From the unforeskinned race, of whom thou bear'st

    The highest name for valiant acts; that honor

    Certain to have won by mortal duel from thee,

    I lose, prevented by thy eyes put out.

SAMSON. Boast not of what thou wouldst have
    done, but do

1105 What then thou wouldst; thou seest it in
    thy hand.°   *within reach*

HARAPHA. To combat with a blind man I disdain,

    And thou hast need much washing to be touched.

SAMSON. Such usage as your honorable lords

    Afford me assassinated° and betrayed,   *treacherously*
                                                          attacked
1110 Who durst not with their whole united powers

---

9. Biblical giants. Og, King of Bashan, was one of the early victims of the Israelites on
  their way to Canaan. Emims (double plural from *Emim*) were a giant race of Moab (see
  Gen. 14:5, Deut. 2:10–11).
1. Moabite home of Emim.

In fight withstand me single and unarmed,
Nor in the house with chamber ambushes
Close-banded durst attack me, no, not sleeping,
Till they had hired a woman with their gold
1115   Breaking her marriage faith to circumvent me.
Therefore without feigned shifts° let be assigned   *evasions, excuses*
Some narrow place enclosed, where sight
   may give thee,
Or rather flight, no great advantage on me;
Then put on all thy gorgeous arms, thy helmet
1120   And brigandine of brass, thy broad habergeon,
Vant-brace and greaves, and gauntlet,[2] add
   thy spear,
A weaver's beam, and seven-times-folded shield;[3]
I only with an oaken staff will meet thee,
And raise such outcries on thy clattered iron,
1125   Which long shall not withhold me from thy head,
That in a little time while breath remains thee,
Thou oft shalt wish thyself at Gath to boast
Again in safety what thou wouldst have done
To Samson, but shalt never see Gath more.
1130   HARAPHA. Thou durst not thus disparage
   glorious arms
Which greatest heroes have in battle worn,
Their ornament and safety, had not spells
And black enchantments, some magician's art,
Armed thee or charmed thee strong, which
   thou from Heaven
1135   Feign'dst at thy birth was giv'n thee in thy hair,
Where strength can least abide, though all
   thy hairs
Were bristles ranged like those that ridge
   the back
Of chafed° wild boars, or ruffled porcupines.   *angered*
SAMSON. I know no spells, use no forbidden arts;[4]
1140   My trust is in the living God who gave me
At my nativity this strength, diffused

---

2. Glove of mail. "Brigandine": a metal-studded tunic. "Habergeon": sleeveless coat of mail. "Vant-brace": defensive armor for the forearm. "Greaves": armor for the leg below the knee.
3. Made of seven layers of hide, like the shield of Ajax (*Il.*, 7.220). "Weaver's beam": Goliath's spear in 1 Sam. 17:7 (the heavy roller on a loom).
4. "Samson's grand affirmation transcends the oath taken before medieval combats by contestants who swore that they used no magic but trusted only in God" (Bush).

No less through all my sinews, joints and bones,
Than thine, while I preserved these locks unshorn,
The pledge of my unviolated vow.
1145   For proof hereof, if Dagon be thy god,
Go to his temple, invocate his aid
With solemnest devotion, spread° before him   *lay*
How highly it concerns his glory now
To frustrate and dissolve these magic spells,
1150   Which I to be the power of Israel's God
Avow, and challenge Dagon to the test,
Offering to combat thee his champion bold,
With th' utmost of his godhead seconded:
Then thou shalt see, or rather to thy sorrow
1155   Soon feel, whose God is strongest, thine or mine.
HARAPHA. Presume not on thy God, whate'er he be,
Thee he regards not, owns not, hath cut off
Quite from his people, and delivered up
Into thy enemies' hand, permitted them
1160   To put out both thine eyes, and fettered send thee
Into the common prison, there to grind
Among the slaves and asses thy comrádes,
As good for nothing else, no better service
With those thy boist'rous locks, no worthy match
1165   For valor to assail, nor by the sword
Of noble warrior, so to stain his honor,
But by the barber's razor best subdued.
SAMSON. All these indignities, for such they are
From thine,° these evils I deserve and more,   *thy people*
1170   Acknowledge them from God inflicted on me
Justly, yet despair not of his final pardon
Whose ear is ever open, and his eye
Gracious to readmit the suppliant;
In confidence whereof I once again
1175   Defy thee to the trial of mortal fight,
By combat to decide whose god is God,
Thine or whom I with Israel's Sons adore.
HARAPHA. Fair honor that thou dost thy God,
     in trusting
He will accept thee to defend his cause,
1180   A murderer, a revolter, and a robber.
SAMSON. Tongue-doughty giant, how dost thou
     prove me these?

HARAPHA. Is not thy nation subject to our lords?
　　　Their magistrates confessed it, when they took thee
　　　As a league-breaker and delivered bound
1185　Into our hands:[5] for hadst thou not committed
　　　Notorious murder on those thirty men
　　　At Ascalon, who never did thee harm,
　　　Then like a robber stripp'dst them of their robes?
　　　The Philistines, when thou hadst broke the league,
1190　Went up with armèd powers thee only seeking,
　　　To others did no violence nor spoil.
SAMSON. Among the daughters of the Philistines
　　　I chose a wife, which argued me no foe,[6]
　　　And in your city held my nuptial feast;
1195　But your ill-meaning politician° lords,　　　　*plotting, scheming*
　　　Under pretense of bridal friends and guests,
　　　Appointed to await me thirty spies,[7]
　　　Who threatening cruel death constrained the bride
　　　To wring from me and tell to them my secret,
1200　That solved the riddle which I had proposed.
　　　When I perceived all set on enmity,
　　　As on my enemies, where ever chanced,
　　　I used hostility, and took their spoil
　　　To pay my underminers in their coin.
1205　My nation was subjected to your lords.
　　　It was the force of conquest; force with force
　　　Is well ejected when the conquered can.
　　　But I a private person, whom my country
　　　As a league-breaker gave up bound, presumed
1210　Single rebellion and did hostile acts:
　　　I was no private but a person raised
　　　With strength sufficient and command from Heav'n
　　　To free my country; if their servile minds
　　　Me their deliverer sent would not receive,
1215　But to their masters gave me up for naught,
　　　Th' unworthier they; whence to this day they serve.
　　　I was to do my part from Heav'n assigned,
　　　And had performed it if my known offense
　　　Had not disabled me, not all your force.
1220　These shifts refuted, answer thy appellant,°　　*challenger to combat*
　　　Though by his blindness maimed for high attempts,

5. 1185–1204. See Judg. 14.
6. See, however, lines 224–26, 231–35, and Judg. 14:4.
7. Not in Judges. But Josephus, *Antiquities*, 5.8.6, adds the detail that the thirty men were
offered to Samson "in pretense to be his companions, but in reality to be a guard upon
him."

Who now defies thee thrice to single fight,
As a petty enterprise of small enforce.°   *effort*
HARAPHA. With thee, a man condemned, a
       slave enrolled,
1225   Due by the law to capital punishment?
       To fight with thee no man of arms will deign.
SAMSON. Cam'st thou for this, vain boaster, to
       survey me,
       To descant° on my strength, and give thy   *comment at length*
          verdict?
       Come nearer, part not hence so slight informed;
1230   But take good heed my hand survey not thee.
HARAPHA. O Baal-zebub![8] can my ears unused
       Hear these dishonors, and not render death?
SAMSON. No man withholds thee, nothing from
       thy hand
       Fear I incurable; bring up thy van;[9]
1235   My heels are fettered, but my fist is free.
HARAPHA. This insolence other kind of answer fits.
SAMSON. Go, baffled° coward, lest I run upon thee,   *disgraced*
       Though in these chains, bulk without spirit vast,[1]
       And with one buffet lay thy structure low,
1240   Or swing thee in the Air, then dash thee down
       To the hazard of thy brains and shattered sides.
HARAPHA. By Astaroth,[2] ere long thou shalt lament
       These braveries in irons loaden on thee.
CHORUS. His giantship is gone somewhat crestfallen,
1245   Stalking with less unconscionable° strides,   *excessive*
       And lower looks, but in a sultry chafe.°   *rage*
SAMSON. I dread him not, nor all his giant brood,
       Though fame divulge him father of five sons
       All of gigantic size, Goliah[3] chief.
1250   CHORUS. He will directly to the lords, I fear,
       And with malicious counsel stir them up
       Some way or other yet further to afflict thee.
SAMSON. He must allege some cause, and
       offered fight

8. Lit., "Lord of the fly." A Canaanite deity worshiped in the Philistine city of Ekron (2 Kings 1:2); he appears as Beëlzebub in *PL*. John Selden, in *De Diis Syris* (1617), finds numerous explanations for the name, including the god's protection from flies. He cites the opinion of the "best scholars and ancient Arabic manuscripts" that read *Baal-Zebul* or *Dominus Stercoris*, "lord of dung," which would explain the flies.
9. Vanguard. I.e., start fighting.
1. Modifies *bulk*.
2. Plural of Ashtoreth or Astarte, a Phoenician fertility goddess, the female counterpart of Baal; identified with Aphrodite and Venus. Selden calls her "the mother of the gods."
3. Goliath, the giant killed by David (1 Sam. 17:4–51).

Will not dare mention, lest a question rise
1255 Whether he durst accept the offer or not,
And that he durst not plain enough appeared.
Much more affliction than already felt
They cannot well impose, nor I sustain,
If they intend advantage of my labors,
1260 The work of many hands, which earns my keeping
With no small profit daily to my owners.
But come what will, my deadliest foe will prove
My speediest friend, by death to rid me hence,
The worst that he can give, to me the best.
1265 Yet so it may fall out, because their end
Is hate, not help to me, it may with mine
Draw their own ruin who attempt the deed.
CHORUS. Oh how comely it is and how reviving
To the spirits of just men long oppressed,
1270 When God into the hands of their deliverer
Puts invincible might
To quell the mighty of the earth, th' oppressor,
The brute and boist'rous force of violent men,
Hardy and industrious to support
1275 Tyrannic power, but raging to pursue
The righteous and all such as honor truth!
He all their ammunition
And feats of war defeats
With plain heroic magnitude of mind
1280 And celestial vigor armed,
Their armories and magazines contemns,
Renders them useless, while
With winged expedition°   *speed*
Swift as the lightning glance he executes
1285 His errand on the wicked, who surprised
Lose their defense distracted° and amazed.   *crazed, mad*
    But patience is more oft the exercise
Of saints, the trial of their fortitude,
Making them each his own deliverer,
1290 And victor over all
That tyranny or fortune can inflict;
Either of these is in thy lot,
Samson, with might endued
Above the sons of men; but sight bereaved
1295 May chance to number thee with those
Whom patience finally must crown.
    This idol's day hath been to thee no day of rest,
Laboring thy mind

More than the working day thy hands;
1300   And yet perhaps more trouble is behind.°   *still to come*
       For I descry this way
       Some other tending, in his hand
       A scepter or quaint° staff he bears,   *skillfully made*
       Comes on amain,° speed in his look.   *at full speed*
1305   By his habit I discern him now
       A public officer, and now at hand.
       His message will be short and voluble.°   *rapid*
OFFICER. Ebrews, the pris'ner Samson here I seek.
CHORUS. His manacles remark° him, there he sits.   *mark him out*
1310 OFFICER. Samson, to thee our lords thus bid me say:
       This day to Dagon is a solemn feast,
       With sacrifices, triumph, pomp, and games;
       Thy strength they know surpassing human rate,
       And now some public proof thereof require
1315   To honor this great feast, and great assembly;
       Rise therefore with all speed and come along,
       Where I will see thee heartened° and fresh clad   *refreshed*
       To appear as fits before th' illustrious lords.
SAMSON. Thou know'st I am an Ebrew, therefore
           tell them
1320   Our Law forbids at their religious rites
       My presence; for that cause I cannot come.
OFFICER. This answer, be assured, will not
           content them.
SAMSON. Have they not sword-players, and every sort
       Of gymnic artists, wrestlers, riders, runners,
1325   Jugglers and dancers, antics,° mummers,°   *clowns / mimes*
           mimics,
       But they must pick me out with shackles tired,
       And over-labored at their public mill,
       To make them sport with blind activity?
       Do they not seek occasion of new quarrels
1330   On my refusal to distress me more,
       Or make a game of my calamities?
       Return the way thou cam'st; I will not come.
OFFICER. Regard thy self;° this will offend   *Look to your own*
           them highly.   *interests*
SAMSON. Myself? my conscience and internal peace.
1335   Can they think me so broken, so debased
       With corporal servitude, that my mind ever
       Will condescend to such absurd commands?
       Although their drudge, to be their fool or jester,
       And in my midst of sorrow and heart-grief

1340   To show them feats and play before their god,
        The worst of all indignities, yet on me
        Joined° with extreme contempt? I will not   *Enjoined, Imposed*
            come.
        OFFICER. My message was imposed on me with speed,
        Brooks° no delay; is this thy resolution?   *Puts up with*
1345   SAMSON. So take it with what speed thy
            message needs.
        OFFICER. I am sorry what this stoutness° will   *stubbornness,*
            produce.   *bravery*
        SAMSON. Perhaps thou shalt have cause to
            sorrow indeed.
        CHORUS. Consider, Samson: matters now are strained
        Up to the heighth, whether to hold or break;
1350   He's gone, and who knows how he may report
        Thy words by adding fuel to the flame?
        Expect another message more imperious,
        More lordly thund'ring than thou well wilt bear.
        SAMSON. Shall I abuse this consecrated gift
1355   Of strength, again returning with my hair
        After my great transgression, so requite
        Favor renewed, and add a greater sin
        By prostituting holy things to idols;[4]
        A Nazarite in place abominable
1360   Vaunting my strength in honor to their Dagon?
        Besides, how vile, contemptible, ridiculous,
        What act more execrably unclean, profane?
        CHORUS. Yet with this strength thou serv'st the
            Philistines,
        Idolatrous, uncircumcised, unclean.
1365   SAMSON. Not in their idol-worship, but by labor
        Honest and lawful to deserve my food
        Of those who have me in their civil power.
        CHORUS. Where the heart joins not, outward
            acts defile not.
        SAMSON. Where outward force constrains, the
            sentence holds;°   *maxim holds true*
1370   But who constrains me to the temple of Dagon,
        Not dragging? The Philistian lords command:
        Commands are no constraints. If I obey them,
        I do it freely, venturing to displease

---

4. "Prostituting" and "idols" suggest violation of the thrice-repeated Apostolic Decree (Acts 15:20, 15:29, and 21:25), which sets forth a minimum standard of decency and ethical practice binding on both Jews and non-Jews. Rejection of its moral requirements kept one outside the pale of salvation.

God for the fear of man, and man prefer,
1375 Set God behind; which in his jealousy
Shall never, unrepented, find forgiveness.
Yet that he may dispense with me or thee,
Present in temples at idolatrous rites[5]
For some important cause, thou need'st not doubt.
1380 CHORUS. How thou wilt here come off surmounts
  my reach.
 SAMSON. Be of good courage, I begin to feel
  Some rousing motions[6] in me which dispose
  To something extraordinary my thoughts.
  I with this messenger will go along,
1385 Nothing to do, be sure, that may dishonor
  Our Law, or stain my vow of Nazarite.
  If there be aught of presage in the mind,
  This day will be remarkable in my life
  By some great act, or of my days the last.
1390 CHORUS. In time thou hast resolved,[7] the man returns.
 OFFICER. Samson, this second message from our lords
  To thee I am bid say: art thou our slave,
  Our captive, at the public mill our drudge,
  And dar'st thou at our sending and command
1395 Dispute thy coming? Come without delay;
  Or we shall find such engines° to assail   *means or devices*
  And hamper thee, as thou shalt come of force,
  Though thou wert firmlier fastened than a rock.
 SAMSON. I could be well content to try their art,°   *skill*
1400 Which to no few of them would prove pernicious.
  Yet knowing their advantages too many,
  Because° they shall not trail me through   *So that*
   their streets
  Like a wild beast, I am content to go.
  Masters' commands come with a power resistless
1405 To such as owe them absolute subjection;
  And for a life who will not change his purpose?[8]
  (So mutable are all the ways of men!)
  Yet this be sure, in nothing to comply
  Scandalous or forbidden in our Law.

---

5. I.e., Grant a special dispensation for me or thee to be present at idolatrous rites.
6. Either workings of God in the soul or impulses, inner promptings.
7. The chorus misattributes Samson's change of heart to fear of the officer and self-interest.
8. Does Samson allude to God's resistless commands and to the eternal life of his soul? Is he merely professing plausible reasons for saving his skin by obeying the commands of his Philistine masters, even if his real reasons are quite different?

1410 OFFICER. I praise thy resolution; doff these links:
    By this compliance thou wilt win the lords
    To favor, and perhaps to set thee free.
    SAMSON. Brethren, farewell; your company along
    I will not wish, lest it perhaps offend them
1415 To see me girt with friends; and how the sight
    Of me as of a common enemy,
    So dreaded once, may now exasperate them
    I know not. Lords are lordliest in their wine;
    And the well-feasted priest then soonest fired
1420 With zeal, if aught° religion seem concerned;   *in any way*
    No less the people on their holy-days
    Impetuous, insolent, unquenchable.
    Happen what may, of me expect to hear
    Nothing dishonorable, impure, unworthy
1425 Our God, our Law, my nation, or myself;
    The last of me or no I cannot warrant.
    CHORUS. Go, and the Holy One
    Of Israel be thy guide
    To what may serve his glory best, and
      spread his name
1430 Great among the heathen round;
    Send thee the Angel of thy birth, to stand
    Fast by thy side, who from thy father's field
    Rode up in flames after his message told
    Of thy conception,[9] and be now a shield
1435 Of fire; that Spirit that first rushed on thee
    In the camp of Dan[1]
    Be efficacious in thee now at need.
    For never was from Heaven imparted
    Measure of strength so great to mortal seed,
1440 As in thy wondrous actions hath been seen.
    But wherefore comes old Manoa in such haste
    With youthful steps? Much livelier than erewhile
    He seems: supposing here to find his son,
    Or of him bringing to us some glad news?
1445 MANOA. Peace with you, brethren; my inducement
      hither
    Was not at present here to find my son,
    By order of the lords new parted hence
    To come and play before them at their feast.
    I heard all as I came, the city rings,

9. See Judg. 13:20.
1. Judg. 13:25.

1450 And numbers thither flock; I had no will,[2]
      Lest I should see him forced to things unseemly.
      But that which moved my coming now was chiefly
      To give ye part° with me what hope I have   *share with you*
      With good success° to work his liberty.   *outcome*
1455 CHORUS. That hope would much rejoice us to partake
      With thee. Say, reverend sire, we thirst to hear.
      MANOA. I have attempted one by one the lords
      Either at home, or through the high street passing,
      With supplication prone° and father's tears   *prostrating myself*
1460 To accept of ransom for my son their prisoner.
      Some much averse I found and wondrous harsh,
      Contemptuous, proud, set on revenge and spite;
      That part most reverenced Dagon and his priests;
      Others more moderate seeming, but their aim
1465 Private reward, for which both god and state
      They easily would set to sale; a third
      More generous far and civil, who confessed
      They had enough revenged, having reduced
      Their foe to misery beneath their fears;
1470 The rest was magnanimity to remit,[3]
      If some convenient ransom were proposed.
      What noise or shout was that? It tore the sky.
      CHORUS. Doubtless the people shouting to behold
      Their once great dread, captive and blind
          before them,
1475 Or at some proof of strength before them shown.
      MANOA. His ransom, if my whole inheritance
      May compass it, shall willingly be paid
      And numbered down;° much rather I shall choose   *paid out*
      To live the poorest in my tribe, than richest,
1480 And he in that calamitous prison left.
      No, I am fixed not to part hence without him.
      For his redemption all my patrimony,
      If need be, I am ready to forgo
      And quit: not wanting° him, I shall want   *lacking*
          nothing.
1485 CHORUS. Fathers are wont to lay up for their sons,
      Thou for thy son art bent to lay out all;
      Sons wont to nurse their parents in old age,

---

2. I.e., no desire to go there.
3. It would be generous to give up the rest of their revenge. The passage (lines 1461–71)
   alludes perhaps to the various attitudes held by Royalists after the Restoration toward
   leaders of the Commonwealth, including Milton.

Thou in old age car'st how to nurse thy son,
Made older than thy age through eyesight lost.
1490 MANOA. It shall be my delight to tend his eyes,
And view him sitting in the house, ennobled
With all those high exploits by him achieved,
And on his shoulders waving down those locks
That of a nation armed the strength contained.
1495 And I persuade me God had not permitted
His strength again to grow up with his hair
Garrisoned round about him like a camp
Of faithful soldiery, were not his purpose
To use him further yet in some great service,
1500 Not to sit idle with so great a gift
Useless, and thence ridiculous about him.
And since his strength with eyesight was not lost,
God will restore him eyesight to° his strength.   *in addition to*
CHORUS. Thy hopes are not ill-founded nor seem vain
1505 Of his delivery, and thy joy thereon
Conceived, agreeable to a father's love,
In both which we, as next,[4] participate.
MANOA. I know your friendly minds and—O
what noise!
Mercy of Heav'n, what hideous noise was that!
1510 Horribly loud, unlike the former shout.
CHORUS. Noise call you it, or universal groan,
As if the whole inhabitation° perished;   *population*
Blood, death, and deathful deeds are in that noise,
Ruin, destruction at the utmost point.
1515 MANOA. Of ruin° indeed methought I heard   *collapse*
the noise.
Oh it continues, they have slain my son.
CHORUS. Thy son is rather slaying them; that outcry
From slaughter of one foe could not ascend.
MANOA. Some dismal accident it needs must be;
1520 What shall we do, stay here or run and see?
CHORUS. Best keep together here, lest running thither
We unawares run into danger's mouth.
This evil on the Philistines is fall'n;
From whom could else a general cry be heard?
1525 The sufferers then will scarce molest us here;
From other hands we need not much to fear.
What if his eyesight (for to Israel's God

4. In kinship, as Danites.

Nothing is hard) by miracle restored,
He now be dealing dole° among his foes,   *(1) pain or grief, (2)*
1530   And over heaps of slaughtered walk his way?   *a portion*
MANOA. That were a joy presumptuous to be thought.
CHORUS. Yet God hath wrought things as incredible
       For his people of old; what hinders now?
MANOA. He can, I know, but doubt to think he will;
1535   Yet hope would fain subscribe,° and tempts belief.   *agree*
       A little stay° will bring some notice° hither.   *pause / news*
CHORUS. Of good or bad so great, of bad the sooner;
       For evil news rides post,° while good news baits.° *posthaste / pauses*
       And to our wish I see one hither speeding,
1540   An Ebrew, as I guess, and of our tribe.
MESSENGER. O whither shall I run, or which way fly
       The sight of this so horrid spectacle
       Which erst° my eyes beheld and yet behold;   *just now*
       For dire imagination still pursues me.
1545   But providence or instinct of nature seems,
       Or reason, though disturbed and scarce consulted,
       To have guided me aright, I know not how,
       To thee first, reverend Manoa, and to these
       My countrymen, whom here I knew remaining,
1550   As at some distance from the place of horror,
       So in the sad event too much concerned.
MANOA. The accident° was loud, and here   *occurrence*
       before thee
       With rueful cry, yet what it was we hear not;
       No preface needs, thou seest we long to know.
1555 MESSENGER. It would burst forth, but I recover breath
       And sense distract, to know well what I utter.
MANOA. Tell us the sum,° the circumstance defer.   *gist*
MESSENGER. Gaza yet stands, but all her sons are fall'n,
       All in a moment overwhelmed and fall'n.
1560 MANOA. Sad, but thou know'st to Israelites not saddest
       The desolation of a hostile city.
MESSENGER. Feed on that first, there may in
       grief be surfeit.
MANOA. Relate by whom.
MESSENGER.   By Samson.
MANOA.   That still lessens
       The sorrow, and converts it nigh to joy.
1565 MESSENGER. Ah, Manoa, I refrain, too suddenly
       To utter what will come at last too soon;
       Lest evil tidings with too rude irruption°   *bursting in*
       Hitting thy aged ear should pierce too deep.

MANOA. Suspense in news is torture, speak them out.
1570 MESSENGER. Then take the worst in brief:
    Samson is dead.
MANOA. The worst indeed, O all my hope's defeated
    To free him hence! But Death who sets all free
    Hath paid his ransom now and full discharge.
    What windy° joy this day had I conceived,   *empty*
1575   Hopeful of his delivery, which now proves
    Abortive as the first-born bloom of spring
    Nipped with the lagging rear of winter's frost.
    Yet ere I give the reins to grief, say first,
    How died he? Death to life is crown or shame.
1580   All by him fell, thou say'st; by whom fell he,
    What glorious hand gave Samson his death's
        wound?
MESSENGER. Unwounded of his enemies he fell.
MANOA. Wearied with slaughter then, or how? Explain.
MESSENGER. By his own hands.
MANOA.   Self-violence? what cause
1585   Brought him so soon at variance° with himself   *conflict*
    Among his foes?
MESSENGER. Inevitable cause
    At once both to destroy and be destroyed;
    The edifice where all were met to see him,
    Upon their heads and on his own he pulled.
1590 MANOA. O lastly over-strong against thy self!
    A dreadful way thou took'st to thy revenge.
    More than enough we know; but while
        things yet
    Are in confusion, give us, if thou canst,
    Eye-witness of what first or last was done,
1595   Relation more particular and distinct.
MESSENGER. Occasions° drew me early to this City,   *Business*
    And as the gates I entered with sunrise,
    The morning trumpets festival proclaimed
    Through each high street. Little I had
        dispatched°   *accomplished*
1600   When all abroad was rumored that this day
    Samson should be brought forth to show
        the people
    Proof of his mighty strength in feats and games;
    I sorrowed at his captive state, but minded°   *intended*
    Not to be absent at that spectacle.
1605   The building was a spacious theater
    Half round on two main pillars vaulted high,
    With seats where all the lords and each degree

Of sort° might sit in order to behold;   *high rank*
The other side was open, where the throng
1610 On banks° and scaffolds° under sky might stand;   *benches / platforms*
I among these aloof obscurely stood.
The feast and noon grew high, and sacrifice
Had filled their hearts with mirth, high
        cheer, and wine,
When to their sports they turned. Immediately
1615 Was Samson as a public servant brought,
In their state livery clad; before him pipes
And timbrels;° on each side went armèd   *tambourines*
        guards,
Both horse and foot before him and behind,
Archers, and slingers, cataphracts° and   *soldiers in full armor /*
        spears.°   *spearsmen*
1620 At sight of him the people with a shout
Rifted the air, clamoring their god with praise,
Who had made their dreadful enemy their thrall.
He patient but undaunted where they led him
Came to the place, and what was set before him,
1625 Which without help of eye might be assayed,
To heave, pull, draw, or break, he still°   *on each occasion*
        performed,
All with incredible, stupendious force,
None daring to appear antagonist.
At length for intermission sake they led him
1630 Between the pillars; he his guide requested
(For so from such as nearer stood we heard),
As over-tired to let him lean a while
With both his arms on those two massy pillars
That to the archèd roof gave main support.
1635 He unsuspicious led him; which when Samson
Felt in his arms, with head a while inclined
And eyes fast fixed he stood, as one who prayed,
Or some great matter in his mind revolved.
At last with head erect thus cried aloud:
1640 "Hitherto, lords, what your commands imposed
I have performed, as reason was, obeying,
Not without wonder or delight beheld.
Now of my own accord such other trial
I mean to show you of my strength, yet greater,
1645 As with amaze shall strike all who behold."
This uttered, straining all his nerves he bowed;
As with the force of winds and waters pent[5]

---

5. Earthquakes were attributed to the explosion of pent-up subterranean winds.

When mountains tremble, those two massy pillars
With horrible convulsion to and fro
1650 He tugged, he shook, till down they came and drew
The whole roof after them, with burst of thunder
Upon the heads of all who sat beneath,
Lords, ladies, captains, counselors, or priests,
Their choice nobility and flower, not only
1655 Of this but each Philistian city round,
Met from all parts to solemnize this feast.
Samson with these immixed, inevitably
Pulled down the same destruction on himself;
The vulgar only 'scaped who stood without.[6]
1660 CHORUS. O dearly-bought revenge, yet glorious!
Living or dying thou hast fulfilled
The work for which thou wast foretold
To Israel, and now li'st victorious
Among thy slain self-killed,
1665 Not willingly, but tangled in the fold
Of dire necessity, whose law in death conjoined
Thee with thy slaughtered foes in number more
Than all thy life had slain before.
SEMICHORUS. While their hearts were jocund
and sublime,°   *exalted*
1670 Drunk with idolatry, drunk with wine,
And fat regorged[7] of bulls and goats,
Chanting their idol, and preferring
Before our living Dread who dwells
In Silo[8] his bright sanctuary:
1675 Among them he a spirit of frenzy sent,
Who hurt their minds,
And urged them on with mad desire
To call in haste for their destroyer;
They only set on sport and play
1680 Unweetingly importuned
Their own destruction to come speedy upon them.
So fond° are mortal men   *foolish*
Fall'n into wrath divine,
As their own ruin on themselves to invite,
1685 Insensate left, or to sense reprobate,[9]

6. Milton organizes the temple architecture differently from the Bible, to allow the common people, placed outside on "banks and scaffolds" (line 1610), to escape.
7. Perhaps greedily devoured.
8. Shiloh, in the hill country of Ephraim (Judg. 21:9), site of the Ark of the Covenant, was the capital of Israel in the time of the judges.
9. Either without sense (stupid) or left to a depraved reason. Rom. 1:28: "God gave them over to a reprobate mind."

And with blindness internal struck.
SEMICHORUS. But he though blind of sight,
　　Despised and thought extinguished quite,
　　With inward eyes illuminated
1690　His fiery virtue° roused   *strength, courage*
　　From under ashes into sudden flame,
　　And as an evening dragon[1] came,
　　Assailant on the perchèd roosts
　　And nests in order[2] ranged
1695　Of tame villatic° fowl; but as an eagle   *farmyard*
　　His cloudless thunder bolted on their heads.
　　So virtue giv'n for lost,
　　Depressed, and overthrown, as seemed,
　　Like that self-begotten bird[3]
1700　In the Arabian woods embossed,°   *imbosked, hidden in*
　　That no second knows nor third,   *a wood*
　　And lay erewhile a holocaust,°   *sacrifice burnt whole*
　　From out her ashy womb now teemed,°   *born*
　　Revives, reflourishes, then vigorous most
1705　When most unactive deemed,
　　And though her body die, her fame survives,
　　A secular° bird ages of lives.   *lasting many ages*
MANOA. Come, come, no time for lamentation now,
　　Nor much more cause; Samson hath quit°   *acquitted himself*
　　himself
1710　Like Samson, and heroically hath finished
　　A life heroic, on his enemies
　　Fully revenged, hath left them years of mourning,
　　And lamentation to the sons of Caphtor[4]
　　Through all Philistian bounds. To Israel
1715　Honor hath° left, and freedom, let but them   *he hath*
　　Find courage to lay hold on this occasion;
　　To himself and father's house eternal fame;
　　And which is best and happiest yet, all this
　　With God not parted from him, as was feared,
1720　But favoring and assisting to the end.
　　Nothing is here for tears, nothing to wail
　　Or knock the breast, no weakness, no contempt,
　　Dispraise, or blame, nothing but well and fair,

1. Large snake (Lat. *draco*).
2. Like the Philistine aristocracy seated according to rank (line 1608).
3. The phoenix, according to Egyptian mythology, was an eagle-like bird, unique of its
   kind, that lived for five hundred years, then consumed itself in fire and rose from its
   own ashes.
4. The Philistines' original home; "Have not I brought up Israel out of the land of Egypt?
   And the Philistines from Caphtor?" (Amos 9:7).

And what may quiet us in a death so noble.
Let us go find the body where it lies
Soaked in his enemies' blood, and from the stream
With lavers° pure and cleansing herbs wash off   *washbasins*
The clotted gore. I with what speed° the while   *what speed I can*
(Gaza is not in plight° to say us nay)   *condition*
Will send for all my kindred, all my friends,
To fetch him hence and solemnly attend
With silent obsequy and funeral train
Home to his father's house: there will I build him
A monument, and plant it round with shade
Of laurel ever green, and branching palm,
With all his trophies hung, and acts enrolled
In copious legend,⁵ or sweet lyric song.
Thither shall all the valiant youth resort,
And from his memory inflame their breasts
To matchless valor and adventures high;
The virgins also shall on feastful days
Visit his tomb with flowers, only bewailing
His lot unfortunate in nuptial choice,
From whence captivity and loss of eyes.
CHORUS. All is best, though we oft doubt,
What th' unsearchable dispose°   *ordering of things*
Of highest wisdom brings about,
And ever best found in the close.
Oft he seems to hide his face,
But unexpectedly returns
And to his faithful champion hath in place°   *at hand*
Bore witness gloriously; whence Gaza mourns
And all that band them to resist
His uncontrollable intent;
His servants he with new acquist°   *acquisition*
Of true experience from this great event
With peace and consolation hath dismissed,
And calm of mind, all passion spent.

1725
1730
1735
1740
1745
1750
1755

5. I.e., fully written out.

Latin Poems

Newly translated in verse and annotated by William Shullenberger,
with assistance in annotations by Deanna Cachoian-Schanz

Elegy V[†]

AT THE AGE OF TWENTY

On the Advent of Spring

Revolving on itself in never-failing gyre,°	*circle, revolution*
Time calls forth Zephyrs° fresh with Spring's	*mild west winds*
warm glow,	
And Earth restored puts on the trim of her	
brief youth;	
Its frost dissolved, the humid mold° turns	*soil*
fragrant green.	

5 Am I deceived? Does vigorous song revive in me?
Does inspiration come, Spring's blessing unto me?
Spring's blessing unto me, it waxes° with the   *grows in strength*
   season strong
(Who would have thought?) and clamors for
   some worthy task.
Before my eyes, the cloven peak and Castaly[1] unfold,
10 And Pyrene[2] flows through my dreams by night.
By hidden motion stirred, my breast erupts in flame,
And furor° rouses me within, and holy sound.   *frenzied inspiration*
Delius[3] himself draws near—I see his radiant locks
With Penean laurel laced—Delius himself draws
   near![4]

---

† This gorgeous and exuberant poem was likely composed in spring 1629.
1. The sacred spring. "Cloven peak": refers to the twin-peaked Mount Parnassus sacred to Apollo and the Muses. At its foot lies the spring.
2. Located in Corinth, a fountain sacred to the Muses that sprung from the hoof of Pegasus.
3. Apollo's epithet refers to his birthplace, the island Delos.
4. According to Ovid, *Met.* 1.452–559, Apollo vowed to wear laurel leaves as a crown after Daphne, his beloved, had been turned into a laurel by her father Peneus, the river god, as she was pursued by her lover.

15 My mind upraised to high heaven's liquid air,
    From flesh set free, I soar through the wandering
        clouds.
    Through shades and caverns am I borne, through
        vatic° shrines,   *prophetic*
    And inmost fanes° divine unveil themselves to   *temples or shrines*
        me.
    My spirit apprehends all things Olympus holds,
20 Nor does blind Tartarus[5] find refuge from my sight.
    What does my full-voiced breath so loftily resound?
    What does this raging and this holy furor yield?
    Spring who inspires will now be sung by what
        she gave,
    And glory gain from her own gifts regiven.
25   Now, Philomela,[6] among fresh foliage hid,
            you flute
    Your modulations sweet till all the wood is still;
    In town and wood, let us as one begin,
    Let us as one the vernal advent lift in song.
    Io, Spring! Her change arrives, and let us celebrate
30 Spring's rites; let the Muse her perennial task begin.
    From Ethiopia and Tithonian fields[7] in flight, the sun
    Toward Arctic regions flicks his reins of gold.
    Brief is night's sojourn, her interrupt obscure is brief;
    She troops off into exile with her shadows grim.
35 And Lycaonian Bootes[8] now no more pursues
    The Wain celestial on its wearying long way;
    Across the sky immense, few stars still keep
    Their practiced watch about the courts of Jove;
    Mayhem, deceit, and violence with night recede,
40 And gods no longer dread the giants' blasphemy.[9]
    Perhaps some shepherd, in the rocky heights at ease,
    When dew-drenched earth glows red with the first sun,
    "Phoebus,"[1] exclaims, "this night you must
            have gone without

5. The lowest infernal depths of Greek and Roman mythology.
6. The nightingale. In *Met.* 4.424–674, Ovid describes Philomela's rape by Tereus and her
   subsequent transformation into a nightingale.
7. From Tithonus, husband of the dawn goddess Aurora; they represent the east. "Ethio-
   pia": the equator.
8. The Bear Keeper or Ox Driver (*Met.* 2.176) is the constellation surrounding the star
   Arcturus in the north. "Lycaonian": an Ovidian adjective meaning "northern," from
   the Arcadian king Lycaon, whose daughter Callisto was transformed to a bear by Juno.
   She was then turned into the constellation of the Great Bear by Jove. This constellation is sometimes called the Wain, or wagon (line 36).
9. Milton refers to *Met.*, 1.151–62, where Ovid describes earth-born giants who challenged the gods in warfare.
1. An epithet for Apollo, the sun god in the Greek pantheon.

Your girl, who would have curbed your
    swift-paced steeds."
45 Glad to retrace her wilds, her quiver to re-sling,
When from on high she sees the wheels of Lucifer,[2]
Cynthia[3] puts off her waning rays, well pleased,
    it seems,
To see her brother's work abbreviate her own.
"Aurora," Phoebus cries, "leave those decrepit arms;
50 What boots° it to recline in an exhausted bed?   *avails, matters*
In verdant fields Aeolides the hunter waits;
Arise, let your fires light the steeps of Hymmetus."[4]
With shamefast glance the shining goddess tells her sin,
And urges yet more swift the horses of the dawn.
55   Revivified, Earth sheds the scurf° of vile old age,   *desiccated skin*
And yearns to be entwined, Phoebus, in your embrace;
She yearns, most worthy she; who could be lovelier,
When she luxuriant reveals her fruitful breast,
Arabian fragrance breathes, and from her luscious mouth
60 Spills balsam sweet, with Paphian roses[5] mixed?
Behold her lofty brow, crowned with a sacred wood,
As towers of pine encincture° Idaean Ops;[6]   *encompass*
She braids her streaming hair with various flowers,
Flowers that seem to make her power to
    please more sweet,
65 As the Sicanian glory wreathed in her bright
    hair unbound
Flowers that pleased too well the grim
    Taenarian god.[7]
Phoebus, look now, how tender loves are
    urging you,
And vernal breezes swarm with honeyed pleas.
Now Zephyr[8] shakes fresh cinnamon from
    aery plumes,

2. The light bearer, the morning star.
3. The moon goddess Diana, sister of Apollo.
4. Aurora's husband Tithonus was given immortality but not lasting youth. As her husband endlessly decayed, Aurora fell in love with Cephalus, the son of Aeolus, or Aeolides (line 51). Aurora first sees Cephalus on Mount Hymmetus, preparing to catch deer,
in *Met.*, 7.700–13.
5. From Paphos, Venus's sacred city in Cyprus.
6. The Roman goddess of plenty, was originally worshiped near Troy as Cybele, a Phrygian earth goddess. Idaeus: reference to Ida, the pine-covered mountain near Troy. As
Cybele's lover, Attis, was turned to pine, the pine on Ida is sacred to her. Cybele wears
a crown of turrets, as she was the giver of towers to cities. Cybele's daughter, Ceres,
was goddess of agriculture.
7. *Taenarian* refers to Pluto, god of the underworld. Legend had it that the promontory
Taenarus, in Laconia, held an entrance to Pluto's domain. He captured Proserpina, the
"Sicanian glory" (line 65), in the flowering meadows of Sicania, Sicily.
8. God of the west wind.

70   And birds appear, to court you with their
           blandishments.°   *charms, attractions*
      Not without dowry does bold Earth pursue
           your love,
      Nor destitute, who pleads her longing for your bed.
      She tenders° for your healing skill medicinal   *gently offers*
           herbs,[9]
      And kindly magnifies the honors you receive.
75   If any bribe, if any glowing gifts to you
      Appeal (for love is often purchased with a gift),
      Before you she spreads forth whatever
           treasure hides
      Beneath the vast sea-swell, or scattered
           mountains high.
      Ah, often when you, worn from sheer Olympus'
           climb,
80   Would headlong plunge into the ocean's
           vesper° calm,   *evening*
      "Phoebus," she cries, "so languorous from your
           diurnal° course,   *daily*
      How can the blue-veiled mother swathe you in
           Hesperian[1] tides?
      What is Tethys to you? What the Tartessian streams?[2]
      Why should you bathe that face divine in
           swells of filth?
85   A sweeter chill will soothe you, Phoebus, in
           my shade.
      Draw near, and steep° your burning locks in   *soak, saturate*
           dew.
      Sleep more delicious waits you in my grasses cool,
      Draw near, and lay your radiance in my lap.
      And where you lie, a whispering breeze will
           lightly stroke
90   Our bodies, among moistened roses sweetly poured.
      Be sure, I do not dread the fate of Semele,[3]
      Nor Phaethon's[4] smoldering axletree° and   *chariot axle*
           furious team.

9. Phoebus Apollo was the god of healing.
1. Referring to the garden of Hesperus and his daughters at the western bound of the
   ocean. See *Comus*, 980ff., and *PL*, 4.250–51.
2. Identify the Atlantic Ocean by reference to the ancient Spanish city Tartessus. Tethys,
   a sea goddess and wife of Oceanus, was the mother of rivers.
3. Mother of Bacchus by Jove. She was destroyed by lightning after jealous Juno tricked
   her by urging her to ask Jove to come to her in his divine glory.
4. Apollo's son, who was struck dead by Jove's thunderbolt after he nearly destroyed earth
   by losing control of his father's chariot of the sun.

When you would spend your fire with greater
    sapience,°   *wisdom*
Phoebus, draw near, and lay your radiance in
    my lap."
95   So pants lascivious Earth, pleading her love,
And multitudes of loves swarm in the mother's train.
Indeed, across the wide world, Cupid vagrant strays,
And tips his failing torch in solar fire.
His lethal bow of horn resounds with sinew°   *bowstring of animal*
    fresh;   *tissue*
100 With iron new his ruthless arrows gleam.
He thinks to quell invincible Diana[5] now,
And Vesta[6] chaste, residing in the sacred hearth.
Venus[7] herself repairs her aging beauty with the year,
Seeming to rise afresh from the mild sea.
105 Youths surge through marble cities shouting *Hymenae*,
The shores cry *Io Hymen*,[8] and the rocky caves reply.
In splendor he comes on, with shining tunic fit,
His vestments rich with fumes of Punic crocuses.[9]
And girls crowd forth to taste the sweets of
    gaudy spring,
110 Their virgin breasts bound up with bands of gold.
The prayer of each is hers, yet one prayer joins
    them all:
That Cytherea grant the man whom she desires.
    And now the shepherd tunes his seven-stemmed
      pipe,
And Phyllis[1] has her songs she longs to join with his.
115 The sailor charms the stars with his nocturnal lays,
And dolphins gambol° in the wave-crests where   *frolic*
    he calls.
Jupiter on high Olympus revels with his bride,
And summons all the vassal° gods to share his   *subordinate*
    feasts.
As twilight rises late, quick bands of Satyrs[2] steal
120 Light-footed through the meadows thick with flowers,

---

5. Goddess of the hunt, dedicated to chastity.
6. Virgin goddess of the hearth.
7. Goddess of love and beauty, who was born from the sea near the island Cythera. The
epithet "Cytherea" (line 112) refers to her.
8. God of marriage.
9. Of a purple hue. Puniceus derives from *phoeniceus*, a purple or crimson shade associated with the rich purple dyes made by ancient Phoenicians from certain molluscs.
1. Common name for shepherdesses.
2. Woodland spirits of Greek and Roman mythology who had goat ears, tail, and hooves.

With Sylvanus, in Cyparissus'³ fronds enwreathed,
The deity half-goat, and goat half-deity.
Dryades⁴ who sheltered in the ancient trees
Come flocking over crags and solitary fields.
125 Maenalian Pan⁵ in field and copse° luxuriates;   *small dense wood*
Scarcely is mother Cybele safe, or Ceres⁶ safe,
      from him;
And Faunus lusts to plunder some poor Oread;⁷
With trembling steps the nymph would save herself;
She hides, and hiding scarcely veiled longs to be seen;
130 She flees, and hungers to be taken in her flight.
The gods forsake their native heavens for the groves,
And every forest boasts its local power.°   *spirit of place*
And long may every forest boast its local power,
Nor may you gods, I pray, leave your arboreal⁸ home.
135 Let the age of gold restore you, Jupiter,
To wretched earth; why seek the clouds
      embroiled with strife?
At least, Phoebus, as slowly as you can, drive on
Your fiery team, that spring's sweet prime may
      linger out her stay.
Let winter harsh bring in with tardy pace the
      lengthening nights;
140 Let shadow slow its sure encroachment on our pole.⁹

Ad Patrem

(*To His Father*)†

Now I long for Pierian springs¹ to press
Irriguous streams through my breast, and for
      the full flood-burst

---

3. Sylvanus, associated with satyrs, was the god of forests and uncultivated lands. He
   wore the leaves of cypress trees in remembrance of his love, the boy Cyparissus, who
   was transformed into a cypress after dying of grief.
4. Wood nymphs.
5. Greek god of nature, who was half man, half goat. Maenalus was a mountain in Arcadia sacred to Pan.
6. Goddess of agriculture. Her mother was Cybele (p. 207, n. 6).
7. A mountain nymph. Faunus, god of fields and woods, was protector of shepherds and
   agriculture.
8. Among trees.
9. The Northern Hemisphere and the portion of the heavens above it.
† Although the date of this personal *apologia pro sua vita poetica* has been subject to
   critical dispute, I find John Shawcross's proposal of late 1637 or early 1638 persuasive,
   because of Shawcross's correlation of the poem with the publication of *Lycidas* and of
   Comus, evidence of the poetic gifts and dedication that Milton here defends.
1. Fountains on Mount Pierus in Thessaly that were the birthplace and haunt of the Muses.

Released from the twin crests[2] to overflow my lips,
That my bold-winged Muse, her callow° cries   *immature*
        dispersed,
5   Might soar and sing a parent worthy to be praised.
However you are pleased, best Father, by this song,
Its thinking may seem slight, for I have not
        yet learned
How best to recompense you for your gifts unearned
For which my best would not be recompense
        in kind:
10 Your charities excel the reverence I own
In the fruitless gratitude of words alone.
Yet open on this page stands my account,
Summed in this leaf is all that I hold dear,
To me worth nothing if not golden Clio's[3] gift
15 For me grown ripe in distant caves of dream profound,
Parnassian shades and laurel-hallowed groves.
        You should not scorn the prophet's labor,
            holy verse;
Nothing displays more, by its origin,
The human mind's ethereal rising, seed of
        heaven,[4]
20 Rekindling embers of Promethean fire.[5]
The gods above love song, forceful to stir
Deep shuddering Tartarus,[6] to bind infernal powers,
And doleful shades to fix in threefold adamant.
The Phoebades,[7] and pale-lipped Sibyls
        trembling with song
25 Divulge those mysteries deep hid in days to come.
At altars purified by offering hymns, the priest
Strikes down with song-blessed hands the
        gold-horned thrashing bull;
His skilled eye scans the ribboned steaming
        flesh for clues,
And reads, in entrail heaps still warm, the
        word of Fate.
30 When we at last regain our Olympian fatherland,
And everlasting years in changeless order stand,

2. The double-peaked Mount Parnassus was a favored site sacred to Apollo and the
   Muses, thus a legendary source of poetic inspiration.
3. The guardian of lustration and the Muse of history.
4. The human mind, in Milton's Neo-Platonic conception.
5. Prometheus, the "forethinker," stole heaven's fire for man; thus allegorically bringing
   him philosophic and poetic insight.
6. The "deep pit" of Hades where the worst mortal sinners dwell.
7. Priestesses of Apollo who trembled under the god's possession at Delphi, like the
   Cumaean Sibyl did when escorting Aeneas to the underworld, in Aen. 6.

We will troop forth gold-crowned through
    heaven's bright shrines,
Mingling sweet airs with softly warbling strings,[8]
To which the starry vaults and heaven's twin
    poles° resound.   *North and South*
35 That fiery spirit circling the swift spheres[9]   *Poles*
Is circumfusing° even now the starry choir   *enveloping*
With strains sublime and timeless unexpressive°   *inexpressible*
    song,
As that old Serpent[1] glistering quells his torrid
    breath,
Orion[2] sheathes° his fierce obliterating sword,   *encases*
40 And Atlas[3] feels no more the burden of the stars.
    Time was when song graced banquet halls of kings
By luxury and gluttony's ruinous maw°   *greedy mouth*
    unspoiled,
While modest Lyaeus[4] sparkled at the wholesome
    board.
At festive gatherings the bard held honored place,
45 His flowing hair unshorn bound up in wreathes
    of oak;
Then feats of heroes would he sing, inspiring deeds,
Chaos, and the vast foundations of the
    well-poised world,
The great gods scrambling after acorns for
    their food,[5]
And that dread thunderbolt yet locked in
    Aetna's cave.[6]
50 Indeed, what empty lilt° of voice could give delight   *inflection*
Of words bereft, of sense, of numerous eloquence?

---

8. Milton references Rev. 4:4 and 5:8 where the elders of heaven are crowned with gold and strum their harps.
9. The identity of the *spiritus . . . igneus* has not been settled, although it has been nominated as Milton's own inspired imagination by John Carey. Perhaps it is best to associate it with the inspired "immortal mind that hath forsook / Her mansion in this fleshly nook" (*Il Penseroso* 91–92).
1. A constellation between the Greater and Lesser Bears.
2. The huntsman, who forms another major constellation, and in Statius (*Silv.* 1.1.44–45) frightens the stars with his sword.
3. He supported the heavens on his head and shoulders. Milton locates Atlas in ancient Mauritania (modern Morocco) with the Latin adjective *Maurusius*, but the epithet "Mauretanian" would have added two extra feet to an already overburdened line in this translation.
4. Or Bacchus, god of wine.
5. In this strangely comic line, Milton seems to be fusing classical ideas of the infancy of the gods with the gatherers' diet of the Golden Age under Saturn's rule.
6. In a cave under Mount Etna, the Cyclopes forged the thunderbolts Jupiter used to overthrow Saturn.

Let country choirs take up such song, not Orpheus,[7]
Who rivers held enthralled, gave ears to
    rugged oaks
With song, not plaintive lyre, and spellbound
    hosts of shades
55 Compelled to tears; such praises gained he
    from his song.
    Disdain no more the holy Muses' gifts, I pray,
Nor count them cheap or vain, who bless you
    with the skill
To wed harmonious numbers with a thousand tones,
Through endless change to lead the rapturous voice,
60 Which merits you a name as Arion's[8] heir.
Why wonder that I should be a poet born,
If we, by precious blood itself so dearly joined,
Should find ourselves to kindred arts and
    passions drawn?
Phoebus,[9] wishing to divide himself between
    the two,
65 To me gave certain gifts, and others to my sire;
Progenitor and child, we share the riven° God.   *divided*
    Although you seem to hate the lovely Camenae,[1]
I know you bear no hate; you never bid me go
Where the broad way spreads her lures, and
    easy pelf° is won,   *riches*
70 And gold hope gleams with promises of
    heaped up coin,
Nor do you bind me into law's bad custody
Of common right, nor blight my ears with
    harsh dispute.
Longing to cultivate the aspiring mind yet more,
Far from the strife of town, in lofty solitudes
75 You took me, to Aonian banks,[2] delicious in repose,
And blessed me there to walk by Phoebus' side
    as friend.
    Of a dear parent's common duties, I keep still,

---

7. The father of songs, who sang to the oak trees in Virgil's *Georgics* 4.510. Ovid, in *Met.* 10. 14–41, tells of Orpheus bringing the ghosts of the underworld to tears during his visit. See also *L'Allegro* 145–150; and *Il Penseroso* 105–109.
8. When cast overboard, he was saved by a dolphin that he charmed with his lyre (Herodotus 1. 23–24). See also *Lycidas* 164.
9. God of light as well as Apollo, Greek god of poetry and music.
1. Another Latin term for the Muses.
2. The Castalian stream at the foot of Mount Helicon in the Aonian hills is associated with Apollo and the Muses.

To higher calling charged; father, by your kind purse,
When eloquence in Romulus'[3] tongue opened to me
80 All Latium's[4] loveliness, and, fit for Jove's own lips,
Those words of grandeur thundered by the
          lofty Greeks,
You urged me then to cull° the flowers of   *select*
          which Gaul[5] boasts,
And what the fresh Italian with degenerate tongue
Pours forth, of old Barbarian[6] tumults vocal proof,
85 And mysteries the Palestinian sage proclaims.[7]
Lastly, whatever heaven holds, and under heaven
Our parent earth, and air, through earth and
          heaven in ceaseless flow,
Whatever tides conceal, and weltering foam seas,
Through you, I know; all I am pleased to
          know is due to you.
90 In glory knowledge steps forth from the
          parting cloud
And bends her naked face in splendor to my lips,
Unless, vexed by her sweet indulgences, I flee.
     Go now, hoard wealth, you who turn sick
          with longing for
Austria's hoary opulence, or Peruvian thrones.[8]
95 What more could a father grant, if even Jupiter[9]
Himself kept only heaven, and offered all the world?
He gave no gift more fine, however dear it proved,
Who trusted to his son the universal lamp,[1]
Hyperion's burning wheels, the glowing reins
          of dawn,
100 And orbed crown bristling with the spokes of
          radiant light.
     I therefore, least now in the host of learned men,

3. Said to be the forefather of the Romans.
4. The ancient homeland of the Latin people and thus of the language.
5. France.
6. Milton follows the suggestion of the Renaissance philologists that invasions and warfare by barbarians from the north had brought about the degeneration of classical
   Latin into modern Italian.
7. The mysteries of the Hebrew Bible told by a Hebrew prophet.
8. Milton references the ancient wealth accumulated in the Holy Roman Empire and the
   riches more recently acquired by Spain's expropriation of gold from its colonies in
   South America.
9. The supreme deity of the Roman pantheon.
1. Chariot of Hyperion, Titan god of the sun. Apollo gives in to his son Phaethon's pleading and grants him the chance to drive the solar chariot. Phaethon loses control of the
   vehicle and is blasted from the sky by Jupiter before he can devastate the earth and the
   heavens.

Will sit in triumph, ivy-wreathed and
    laurel-crowned;
No more obscure, to mingle with the uncouth crowd,
My step will turn aside from profane stares.
105 Get hence, you brooding cares, you grim
    complaints, get hence;
Warped thwarting glare of goat-foul Envy, go;
Gape° not your serpent-breeding maw, fierce   *Stretch wide*
    Calumny;[2]
Foul mob, you cannot touch my mind, for all you try,
Nor am I yours by right; with upright heart secure,
110 I shall tread forth uplifted from your serpent sting.
    Dear Father, it is not in my power to render back
What you deserve, or match your gifts with deeds;
Let recollection serve, with grateful mind to count
Your kindnesses, and keep them in a faithful heart.
115   And you, O sports, my youthful little songs,
If you dare hope at all for everlasting years
To thrive, and look on light when your
    master's ash is cold,
Unravished by oblivion black to Orcus'[3]
    swarming hold,
Perhaps these praises, and a parent's celebrated name
120 You will preserve, exemplary, for an age to come.

Damon's Epitaph[†]

Argument

(Thyrsis and Damon, shepherds of neighboring pastures, were dearest friends, following the same pursuits from boyhood. Progressing in the cultivation of his mind abroad, Thyrsis received word of Damon's death. Afterwards, having returned home, and finding this to be so, he lamented himself and his solitude with this song. Now under the figure of Damon is to be understood Charles Diodati,

2. Malicious slander; here, personified.
3. The underworld.
† Milton's dearest friend, Charles Diodati died in London in August 1638, while Milton was traveling in Italy. As the poet somewhat guiltily explains (lines 14–17), he composed the elegy shortly after his return to England in the late summer of 1639. Milton alludes to many of the characters and employs many of the features of classical pastoral elegy, including a recurring refrain, a procession (although not of mourners, but of friends who try to offer the poet consolation), and a search for comfort in nature; but as in *Lycidas*, Milton incorporates these features in an emerging Christian vision.

springing by paternal stock from the Etrurian city Lucca, but otherwise English; in genius, learning, and other most brilliant virtues,
while he lived, an exceptional youth.)

Himeridan nymphs—for you young Daphnis'[1]
    loss recall,
And Hylas, and the fate of Bion[2] long deplored—
Tell forth through cities of the Thames your
    Sicilian song,
What cries, what murmurs miserable Thyrsis[3] pourcd,
5 With what unceasing pleas he vexed the caves,
The streams, the vagrant° springs, and forest   *wandering*
    recesses,
While to himself he Damon mourned, untimely
    rapt;°   *seized, carried off*
He gave deep night his grief, wandering wastes
    forlorn.
Now twice up stood the grain shaft
    verdant°-eared,   *lush green*
10 As often granaries took count of golden yields,
Since his last day swept Damon[4] to the shades below,
Yet Thyrsis was not there; a Tuscan city kept[5]
That swain,° in truth, with love of the sweet   *young shepherd*
    Muse.
But when, with mind replete,° care for his   *abundantly filled*
    flock behind
15 Recalled him home, he took his seat beneath
    the old elm;
In truth then, he at last then felt his dear
    friend's loss,
And started to unburden his immense remorse.
  "Go home unfed, your lord has no time
    now, lambs.
Ai me! What powers should I profess on earth,
    in heaven,

1. Appears in Theocritus' *Idyl* 1 as a shepherd boy turned to stone by a jealous nymph.
   Himeridan nymphs, of the Sicilian river Himera, inspired Theocritus and Moschus.
2. Pastoral poet who wrote the "Lament for Adonis." Moschus uses Bion as the subject in
   his elegy "Lament for Bion." Hylas, who drank with Hercules' quiver bearer, is drowned
   by water nymphs in Theocritus's *Idyl,* 8.
3. Theocritus's shepherd (who symbolizes Milton in this elegy), mourns Daphnis's fate in
   Idyl 1.
4. A frequently appearing pastoral name.
5. Milton visited Florence in September and October of 1638, and March and April of
   1639. Italian crops would have been harvested twice since Diodati's death during Milton's sojourn, a fact that Milton notes in lines 9–11.

20 After they snatched you, Damon, in a bitter death;
Do you thus leave us, will your virtue nameless sink
Below, to mingle with the swarms of shades obscure?
Yet he whose golden wand divides the souls[6]
Would not wish this, but lead you to a worthy host,
25 And drive far off the mindless herd of the
    mute dead.
  "Go home unfed, your lord has no time
    now, lambs.
Whatever comes, unless a wolf spot me before,
You must not moulder° in a tomb unwept,   *decay*
Your honor will stand fixed and vigorous spread
30 Among the shepherds. Second to Daphnis,
    they will joy
To pay their vows to you, and after Daphnis speak
Your praise, while Pales blesses fields that
    Faunus[7] loves—
If to have nourished ancient faith is meet,°   *appropriate, fitting*
    and piety,
Palladian arts,[8] and to have held a friend in song.
35   "Go home unfed, your lord has no time
    now, lambs.
Certain are these rewards prepared for you, Damon,
But what will be my portion then? What
    bosom friend
Will cleave to me as you were wont to do
Through the harsh chills, when frost would
    blanket all the ground,
40 Or in the scorching sun, plants withering
    from thirst,
Whether the task was to charge huge lions
    from afar
Or frighten greedy wolves from the high sheepfolds?
Who will solace my day with converse sweet and song?
  "Go home unfed, your lord has no time
    now, lambs.
45 To whom shall I trust my heart? Who will
    teach me to ease

6. Milton references Mercury, the psychopomp, guide of the dead to the underworld in Homer and Virgil.
7. Protecting Roman deity of woodlands and pastures. Pales is the Roman protectress of flocks. In *PL*, 9.393, Milton compares the as-yet unfallen Eve to Pales in her fruitfulness and beauty.
8. Arts of the goddess Pallas Athena, goddess of learning and wisdom.

Eating cares, to while away the endless night
With pleasantries, when sizzles on a genial° fire   *warm*
The juicy pear, nuts crackle on the hearth,
    while foul south wind
Pummels the world without, thundering
    through the lofty elm.
50   "Go home unfed, your lord has no time now, lambs.
When summer's day-star° high on its mid-axis spins,   *the sun*
When Pan[9] retreating takes his rest in the
    oaken shade,
And nymphs revisit cherished seats beneath
    the waves,
Shepherds lie hid, and the plowman snores
    beneath the hedge,
55 Who will to me your tenderness, your laughter
    then restore
To me, your salt Cecropian quips,[1] your
    seasoned jests?
    "Go home unfed, your lord has no time
    now, lambs.
But now alone through fields, through
    pastures lone I stray,
And linger late in vales° where branching shades   *valleys*
60 Grow thick, while pelting rain above and
    southeast winds
Brood through the restless twilight of the
    shattered wood.
    "Go home unfed, your lord has no time
    now, lambs.
Alas! My once tilled fields are now with
    noxious weeds
Overgrown; the stately grain itself in ruin bows!
65 Neglected clusters wither on the vine unwed,[2]
Myrtle-groves delight no more; my very sheep
    grow tedious,
And sullen on their master cast a vacant gaze.
    "Go home unfed, your lord has no time
    now, lambs.
Tityrus to the hazel calls, Alphesiboeus to the
    mountain ash,

9. The goat god and shepherd, who slumbers at noontide in Theocritus's *Idyl* 1.
1. Cecrops was the first king of Athens. Athenian wit was proverbial.
2. The wedding of vines to the trees was a commonplace of Latin poetry. Milton adapts
   this commonplace to describe Adam and Eve's husbandry in *PL*, 5.215–19.

70 To the willow Aegon calls, fair Amyntas[3] to the rills,
       'Here are the cooling founts,° here turf   *springs*
          overspread with moss;
    Zephyrs are here, arbutus° here with murmuring   *wild strawberry*
          waves entwines.'
    They call to the deaf; I slink into the brush unseen.
       "Go home unfed, your lord has no time
          now, lambs.
75 Mopsus[4] came next, for he by chance marked
          my return;
    Mopsus, in stars and songs of birds well skilled.
    'Thyrsis, what's this,' he said, 'what bile
          perverse boils you?
    Either love wastes, or star malign possesses you.
    The star of Saturn[5] often grieves the swain,
80 Fixing the inmost heart with leaden shaft aslant.'[6]
       "Go home unfed, your lord has no time
          now, lambs.
    The nymphs, amazed, cry 'Thyrsis, what will
          become of you?
    What do you want? The brow of youth is not
    Accustomed to such gloom, fierce-eyed, with
          look severe;
85 Dances he seeks, and lightsome games, and
          always love,
    By right; twice miserable he who loves too late.'
       "Go home unfed, your lord has no time
          now, lambs.
    Then Hyas came, Dryope, and Baucis'
          daughter Aegle,[7]
    In measures taught, skilled with the lyre,
          ruined by pride;
90 Last Chloris, flowing Idumanus' neighbor,[8] came.
    No blandishments, no words of solace can move me,
    Not me, nothing, of what is now or any hope to be.

3. Tityrus, Alphesiboeus, Aegon, and Amyntas appear in various idylls of Theocritus and
   eclogues of Virgil.
4. A shepherd in Virgil's eclogues. He understands the language of birds in Tasso's
   Aminta.
5. Said to be the cause of pestilence. Anyone born under Saturn was said to have melancholic temperament.
6. Alchemists associated the metal lead with Saturn.
7. A beautiful Naiad in Virgil's *Eclogue* 6, who is never identified as Baucis's daughter.
   Hyas, a young hunter killed by a lioness, appears in Ovid's *Fasti*. Dryope and Baucis
   appear in the *Metamorphoses*.
8. Ptolemy's "Idumanian estuary" is identified by Camden in his *Britannia* (1607) as
   Blackwater Bay, the Chelmer River in Essex.

"Go home unfed, your lord has no time
   now, lambs.
Ai me! How young bulls all alike through
   pastures sport,
95 Companions all of one heart each to each by law,
Nor does one set this friend above another in
   the herd;
Thus bound together, wolves track down their prey;
Shaggy wild asses cleave in pairs by turns.
Such is the sea's law; Proteus[9] on his desert shore
100 Numbers his flock of seals; the sparrow vile
Has always his winged friend with whom
   around heaped grain
He gaily flits, late visiting his nest;
Whom if chance deathward hurls, whether a
   crook-beaked kite
Should carry off by fate, or swain with
   lime-twig snare,
105 He forthwith picks another from the airy crew.
We men are a hard race, by dire fates driven,
Estranged in mind, discordant° in the breast;   *conflicted*
Scarcely from thousands does one find a sole
   true friend,
Or if a fortune not unkind to vows should
   grant us one,
110 That one an unprepared-for day, and hour unforeseen
Seizes, condemning life to everlasting pain.
   "Go home unfed, your lord has no time
   now, lambs.
Ai, what reckless wandering drew me toward
   unknown shores
Across the airy steeps and snowy Alps?
115 Was it so great a thing sepulchral° Rome to   *dismal, tomb-like*
   see,
Even if it were such as when, it to behold,
Tityrus[1] himself left flocks and farm behind,
That I could absent me from your sweet fellowship,
That I could such high seas, so many mountains
   interpose,
120 So many forests, rocks, and sounding floods?

9. The shape-shifting sea god of Homer's *Odyssey* (4. 388–460) is called Shepherd of the
   Seas in Spenser's *Faerie Queene*, 3.8.30.1
1. Milton is most likely referring to Virgil's *Eclogue* 1, where Tityrus goes to Rome. In the
   eclogue, Tityrus represents Virgil himself, who traveled to Rome and appealed to Octa-
   vian in order to prevent the confiscation of his farm.

Ah! Surely I could have touched your right
    hand at the last,
And gently closed your eyes in dying calm,
And said, 'Farewell! Remembering me, you
    soar to the stars.'
   "Go home unfed, your lord has no time
    now, lambs.

125 Yet it will never shame me to remember you as well,
Shepherds of Tuscany, youths to the Muses pledged.
Here is grace, here wit, and Damon, you were
    Tuscan too,
Whence from the ancient city Lucca[2] you descend.
Oh, how great I felt, when stretched out to the murmurings
130 Of Arno[3] chill, in poplar glades, on the fresh grass,
I plucked now violets, now loftiest myrtle plucked,
And listened to Menalcas strive with Lycidas.[4]
I myself even dared the attempt, nor think I much
To have displeased, for your gifts are with me,
135 Baskets, and wicker bowls, and pipes with
    waxen seals;
Indeed both Dati and Francini[5] blazed my name
To their beech trees, men both for voices famed
And for their learning, both of Lydian[6] blood.
   "Go home unfed, your lord has no time
    now, lambs.
140 These things the dew-veiled moon would tell
    me in my joy
Alone, while tender kids I penned in wattled cotes.
Ah! How often have I said, even when black
    ash held you,
'He sings now; or Damon spreads his nets for
    rabbits now,
Osiers° he weaves, for various uses yet to be.'   *shoots of willow*

145 And then what things I hoped would be with
    facile mind

---

2. A small northern Italian republic in which Diodati's family was one of the oldest patrician families. While in Florence, Milton made an excursion to the republic.
3. Tuscan river that flows through Florence.
4. Menalcas and Lycidas competed, separately, in singing matches in Theocritus's *Idyls* 7 and 8. Milton alludes to these pastoral contests in describing poetic competitions at the academies in Florence, to which he contributed.
5. Milton befriended the Florentine poets Carlo Dati and Antonio Francini. Both provided commendatory lyrics that appeared in Milton's 1645 *Poems*.
6. According to Herodotus (1.94), the Lydians settled in the Etruscan hills after migrating from Asia Minor.

I caught with a light wish, and fixed as
    present fact:
'Whatever do you now, dear friend? Unless
    some chance detain,
Shall we go, shall we recline a while in
    melodious shades
Near Colne's waters, or where Cassivelaunus'[7]
    acres spread?
150 You will discourse to me of healing draughts
    and herbs,
Hellebore,[8] humble crocuses, and leaves of hyacinth,
What simples the marsh holds, and what
    medicinal arts.'[9]
Ah! Let simples perish, perish medicinal arts
And plants, for nothing could the master
    himself save.
155 For me, I know not what grand theme my pipes
Sounded, eleven nights since, and now
    another day;
I chanced to press my lips to my fresh pipes,
They shattered, bindings snapped, nor could
    they bear
Notes of such gravity; fearful lest I seem swollen
160 With pride, yet will I speak: forests, give way.[1]
    "Go home unfed, your lord has no time
      now, lambs.
I myself Dardanian sterns° through Rutupian   *helms or rear decks*
    seas[2]   *of a boat*
Shall sing, and the ancient reign of Inogene,
    Pandrasus' child,[3]
Brennus and Arviragus chiefs, Belinus old,[4]

---

7. British chieftain whose kingdom (mentioned by Caesar in the *Gallic War* 5.11) would
   have contained the Colne, a river near Horton that feeds into the Thames.
8. A genus of herbs in the lily family that can be prepared for toxic or medicinal uses.
9. Diodati studied medicine at Oxford.
1. In this startling transition, Milton announces his intention to pursue an epic subject,
   the gravity of which shatters the pipes of pastoral elegy, with its forest settings and
   associations.
2. The English Channel. Milton projects plans for his British epic, opening the account
   with the advance of the Trojans (Dardanians) under their leader Brutus, the legendary
   founder of Britain.
3. According to Spenser (*Faerie Queene*, 2.10.13.5) and Geoffrey of Monmouth, the
   Greek king Pandrasus gave his daughter Inogene as wife to Brutus, after Brutus's
   defeat of him.
4. Brennus and Belinus were legendary British warrior princes who conquered Rome. In
   his *History of Britain* (YP 5.30), Milton links Brennus to the Brennus who sacked Rome
   in 390 B.C.E. Arviragus, in some accounts the son of the British king Cymbeline, married the daughter of the Roman general Claudius, but eventually took up arms against
   the Roman occupation.

165 And Armorican settlers[5] under Britain's law at last;
    Then Igraine, heavy with Arthur by fatal fraud,
    The lying countenance and Gorlois' arms assumed,
    Merlin's device.[6] O then if any life remain to me,
    You pipes will on an aging pine be hung far off,[7]
170 Forgot by me, unless, by native muses changed,
    You shrill with British feats. What then? All is
                not fit for one,
    Nor ought one hope all things. Sufficient unto me
    The prize and honor great—though let me ever be
    Unknown to the world outside, and without
                any fame—
175 If golden Ouse read me, and he who drinks of Alne,
    Humber with freshets° rife, and all the groves   *freshwater eddies*
                of Trent,[8]   *and surges*
    And before all my Thames, and Tamar[9] stained
    With ores, and the Orkneys[1] me descant° to   *sing, discuss*
                the outmost waves.   *intensely*
        "Go home unfed, your lord has no time
                now, lambs.
180 These things I was preserving you in laurel's
                rippled bark,
    These and yet more as well: the chalices of Manso[2]—
    Manso no meanest glory of the Chalcidian[3] shore—
    He gave me two, work admirable, himself to
                be admired;
    With double argument he graved them round:
185 In the midst, the Red Sea swells, and
                fragrance-bearing Spring,
    And Araby's[4] long coasts, and forests dripping balm;

5. In the northwest coastal region of France, present-day Brittany. In *History of Britain*, Milton writes of this British colony established by Constantine the Great or Maximus.
6. Malory and Geoffrey of Monmouth recount how Uther Pendragon, by means of Merlin's magic, appeared to Igraine for a night in the form of her dead husband Gorlois, king of Cornwall, and produced a son, Arthur.
7. Traditionally, shepherd's instruments. Milton echoes Virgil and anticipates setting aside pastoral verse as he turns to write epic.
8. Rivers in England. The Ouse winds through the central shires and joins the sea. It was described by Camden on the East Riding as "very broad, swift and noisy." The river Alne, mentioned in Camden's *Brittania*, may refer to rivers flowing through Northumberland or Hampshire. The Trent meets the Humber between Yorkshire and Lincolnshire.
9. A river flowing between Cornwall and Devonshire, which is famous for the mines along its valley.
1. A remote cluster of islands off Scotland's northern coast.
2. Giovanni Battista Manso, a Neapolitan poet and patron of the arts whom Milton met on his journey to Italy. "Chalices": may symbolize the two volumes of his poems that he gave to Milton. They were also prizes for the winners of the pastoral singing contests in Florence.
3. The name the original Greek settlers gave to the Bay of Naples.
4. I.e., Arabia's.

Among them Phoenix,[5] bird divine, unique on earth,
Glistering cerulean° with many-colored wings,   *sky blue*
Looks toward Aurora[6] rising from the glassy seas.
190 In the other part, the vast unfolding sky,
     Olympus great,
Who could conceive? Here Cupid,[7] quivers
     bright, in clouds displayed,
Arms flashing, torches, arrows tipped in bronze;
Nor does he tenuous souls, or the crude
     rout's° ignoble breast   *mob's*
Pierce from above, but rolling round his
     flaming eyes,
195 Ever alert, he sprays his shafts° through all   *arrows*
     the spheres
At upright hearts, nor ever downward aims his bolts,
Whence hallowed minds catch fire, and even
     forms divine.
   "You Damon are among them too, no
     dubious hope;
You are among them sure; where else abides
     your sweet
200 Holy simplicity, your candid virtue bright?
Nor is it right to seek you in the Lethean[8] deep,
Nor do tears suit you; I shall weep no more.
Be gone now, tears, our Damon dwells in the
     aether° pure;   *sublime air of*
Pure, he pure aether breathes, and treads the   *heaven*
     rainbow with his step;
205 Among the souls of heroes and undying gods
He quaffs ethereal liquors and drinks joy
With hallowed lips. Since now the meed° of   *reward*
     heaven is yours,
Be near, and kindly favor me, o by what name
You now are called, whether our Damon, or if
     you rather hear
210 Diodati,[9] by which name divine the heavenly host
Shall know you now, while Damon through
     the forests sounds.

5. The bird of classical mythology, rising from the ashes of its periodic self-immolation, becomes for Christians a symbol of Christ and the resurrection promised in Christ.
6. Roman goddess of dawn.
7. Or Amor, the Roman equivalent to Eros. Milton depends here on the Neo-Platonic distinction between the heavenly Eros of spiritual love and the earthbound Eros of generative, material desire.
8. The Lethe, the infernal river of forgetfulness.
9. Lat. *Diodatus* means "God-given."

Since rosy modesty to you,[1] and spotless youth
Were sweet, and no taste of the pleasures of
    the bed,
Behold the virgin honors treasured up for you:[2]
215 Your brilliant head girt round with a radiant crown,
Bearing a joyous frond° of shady palm,[3]   *leaf*
You shall forever share the immortal marriage feast,[4]
Where songs and lyre in blissful dances join,
And Sion's thyrsus drives the festal orgy's rage."[5]

1. Reference to Plato's *Phaedrus* 254a, where he writes that the soul is restrained from incontinence through modesty.
2. Diodati's chastity merits him the visionary fulfillment assured to the host of 144,000 male virgins who rejoice in song before the Lamb of God, in Rev. 14:1–4.
3. In Rev. 7:9, heavenly hosts stand before the Lamb on his throne with palms in hand.
4. Rev. 19:6–8 celebrates the marriage of the lamb.
5. This startling and wonderful climactic image indicates that Milton, like Dante, understood the state of heaven to be a condition of perfected, consecrated, and fulfilled desire rather than a renunciation of desire. "Thyrsus": vine-wreathed staff carried by followers in Bacchic revels. "Sion's thyrsus" might fuse the Bacchic rod to the "potent rod / Of Amram's son" (*PL*, 1.338–39), the wonder-working staff of Moses.

Prose Treatises

From An Apology for Smectymnuus[1] (1642)

I had my time, readers, as others have who have good learning bestowed upon them, to be sent to those places where, the opinion was, it might be soonest attained; and as the manner is, was not unstudied in those authors which are most commended. Whereof some were grave orators and historians, whose matter methought I loved indeed, but as my age then was, so I understood them; others were the smooth elegiac poets, whereof the schools are not scarce, whom both for the pleasing sound of their numerous[2] writing, which in imitation I found most easy and most agreeable to nature's part in me, and for their matter, which what it is, there be few who know not, I was so allured to read that no recreation came to me better welcome. For that it was then those years with me which are excused though they be least severe, I may be saved the labor to remember ye. Whence having observed them to account it the chief glory of their wit, in that they were ablest to judge, to praise, and by that could esteem themselves worthiest to love those high perfections which under one or other name they took to celebrate; I thought with myself by every instinct and presage of nature, which is not wont to be false, that what emboldened them to this task might with such diligence as they used embolden me; and that what judgment, wit, or elegance was my share, would herein best appear, and best value itself, by how much more wisely and with more love of virtue I should choose (let rude ears be absent) the object of not unlike praises. For albeit these thoughts to some will seem virtuous and commendable, to others only pardonable, to a third sort perhaps idle; yet the mentioning of them now will end in serious.[3]

Nor blame it, readers, in those years to propose to themselves such a reward as the noblest dispositions above other things in this

---

1. The initials of five Presbyterian ministers ("ty" is Milton's former tutor Thomas Young). In this autobiographical excerpt from the fifth and last of his anti-prelatical tracts, Milton responds to an anonymous opponent's accusations of immorality.
2. Metrical. "Elegiac poets": Propertius, Tibullus, and especially Ovid, whose love poems were written in the elegiac meter.
3. Seriously (?); meaning unclear.

life have sometimes preferred—whereof not to be sensible when
good and fair in one person meet, argues both a gross and shallow
judgment, and withal an ungentle and swainish[4] breast. For by the
firm settling of these persuasions, I became, to my best memory, so
much a proficient that, if I found those authors[5] anywhere speaking
unworthy things of themselves or unchaste of those names which
before they had extolled, this effect it wrought with me, from that
time forward their art I still applauded, but the men I deplored; and
above them all preferred the two famous renowners of Beatrice and
Laura,[6] who never write but honor of them to whom they devote
their verse, displaying sublime and pure thoughts without transgression. And long it was not after when I was confirmed in this opinion, that he who would not be frustrate of his hope to write well
hereafter in laudable things ought himself to be a true poem, that
is, a composition and pattern of the best and honorablest things—
not presuming to sing high praises of heroic men or famous cities,
unless he have in himself the experience and the practice of all that
which is praiseworthy. These reasonings, together with a certain
niceness[7] of nature, an honest haughtiness, and self-esteem either
of what I was or what I might be (which let envy call pride), and
lastly that modesty whereof, though not in the title page, yet here I
may be excused to make some beseeming profession—all these,
uniting the supply of their natural aid together, kept me still above
those low descents of mind, beneath which he must deject and
plunge himself that can agree to saleable and unlawful prostitution.

   Next (for hear me out now, readers), that I may tell ye whither my
younger feet wandered, I betook me among those lofty fables and
romances,[8] which recount in solemn cantos the deeds of knighthood
founded by our victorious kings, and from hence had in renown over
all Christendom. There I read it in the oath of every knight that he
should defend to the expense of his best blood, or of his life if it so
befell him, the honor and chastity of virgin or matron. From whence
even then I learned what a noble virtue chastity sure must be, to the
defense of which so many worthies by such a dear adventure of themselves had sworn. And if I found in the story afterward any of them
by word or deed breaking that oath, I judged it the same fault of the
poet as that which is attributed to Homer, to have written indecent
things of the gods. Only this my mind gave me, that every free and
gentle spirit, without that oath, ought to be born a knight, nor
needed to expect the gilt spur or the laying of a sword upon his

4. Rustic, boorish. "Withal": in addition.
5. Ovid and other love poets.
6. Dante and Petrarch.
7. Fastidiousness.
8. Medieval Arthurian romances but especially Spenser's *Faerie Queene*.

shoulder to stir him up both by his counsel and his arm to secure and protect the weakness of any attempted[9] chastity. So that even those books which to many others have been the fuel of wantonness and loose living, I cannot think how, unless by divine indulgence, proved to me so many incitements, as you have heard, to the love and stead-fast observation of that virtue which abhors the society of bordellos.

Thus, from the laureate fraternity of poets, riper years and the ceaseless round of study and reading led me to the shady spaces of philosophy; but chiefly to the divine volumes of Plato and his equal,[1] Xenophon. Where, if I should tell ye what I learned of chastity and love, I mean that which is truly so, whose charming cup is only virtue, which she bears in her hand to those who are worthy (the rest are cheated with a thick intoxicating potion which a certain sorceress,[2] the abuser of love's name, carries about), and how the first and chiefest office of love begins and ends in the soul, producing those happy twins of her divine generation, knowledge and virtue[3]—with such abstracted sublimities as these, it might be worth your listening, readers, as I may one day hope to have ye in a still time, when there shall be no chiding; not in these noises, the adversary, as ye know, barking at the door or searching for me at the bordellos, where it may be he has lost himself, and raps up without pity the sage and rheumatic old prelatess, with all her young Corinthian laity,[4] to inquire for such a one.

Last of all, not in time, but as perfection is last, that care was ever had of me, with my earliest capacity, not to be negligently trained in the precepts of Christian religion. This that I have hitherto related hath been to show that, though Christianity had been but slightly taught me, yet a certain reservedness of natural disposition, and moral discipline learned out of the noblest philosophy, was enough to keep me in disdain of far less incontinences than this of the bordello. But having had the doctrine of Holy Scripture unfolding those chaste and high mysteries with timeliest care infused, that "the body is for the Lord, and the Lord for the body" [1 Cor. 6:13], thus also I argued to myself: that if unchastity in a woman, whom St. Paul terms the glory of man, be such a scandal and dishonor, then certainly in a man, who is both the image and glory of God, it must, though commonly not so thought, be much more deflowering and dishonorable—in that he sins both against his own body, which is the perfecter sex, and his own glory, which is in the woman, and that which is worst, against the image and glory of God, which is in

9. Attacked.
1. Contemporary.
2. Circe, mother of Comus in *A Masque*, who also tempts with a cup of intoxicating potion.
3. Cf. the "happy twins" of Cupid and Psyche in *A Masque*, lines 1003–11.
4. Prostitutes.

<u>himself.</u>[5] Nor did I slumber over that place[6] expressing such high rewards of ever accompanying the Lamb with those celestial songs to others inapprehensible, but not to those who were not defiled with women, which doubtless means fornication; for marriage must not be called a defilement.

Thus large I have purposely been, that if I have been justly taxed with this crime, it may come upon me, after all this my confession, with a tenfold shame.

THE DOCTRINE AND DISCIPLINE OF DIVORCE (1644)

Milton had both personal and political reasons for writing *The Doctrine and Discipline of Divorce* (1st ed., 1643; 2nd ed., much expanded, 1644, printed here). In June or July 1642, Milton, a thirty-three-year-old schoolmaster and householder ready to settle down, married Mary Powell, a girl of seventeen. A few months later, Mary left Milton's house to return to her parents, and she stayed away for three years. Although Milton was a deserted husband, his four divorce treatises (five if we count as separate the two different editions of *DDD*) emphasize not desertion but incompatibility as the primary justification for dissolving a marriage. A reader's response to these treatises depends in part on whether the relationship between Milton's personal situation and his published responses to it provoke a superior smile or arouse heartfelt sympathy. Those who see Milton's proper role as impartial judge will especially devalue the treatises' most personal passages. But others will regard him as a witness whose testimony is all the more credible because it is based on firsthand experience and subsequent reflection.

While Mary was away, between 1643 and 1645, Milton produced some of his greatest prose works, including the two editions of *The Doctrine and Discipline of Divorce, Tetrachordon, Of Education*, and the *Areopagitica*—which advocate, respectively, domestic liberty, educational reform, and "freedom to express oneself" (*YP*, 4:624). In these treatises Milton advocates freedom to divorce on grounds of incompatibility, religious toleration, and a rescinding by Parliament of a licensing order that would offend against both God and human reason by imposing prepublication censorship and thus preventing the discovery of the good.

Milton's first published writings—antiprelatical treatises (1641–42)—are marked by a Pauline absolutism that will not compound with human weakness as an inevitable condition lying within the bounds of divine forgiveness. Readers coming to *DDD* after reading those earliest works will be unprepared for the profound transformations in Milton's theology, philosophy, and politics, and in his attitude toward human weakness. A young poet who seems always to have had a sense of per-

---

5. 1 Cor. 11:7: "a man . . . is the image and glory of God: but woman is the glory of the man."
6. Rev. 14:4: "These are they which were not defiled with women; for they are virgins. These are they which follow the Lamb whithersoever he goeth."

sonal election might have begun to feel profoundly abandoned—and
not only by his wife. Beginning with the first divorce tract and extending through the *Areopagitica*, the former (and future) Pauline absolutist
confronts with compassion a life of mistake and the inseparability of
good and evil in this imperfect world. If Milton's prose provides the doctrinal underpinnings of his greatest poetry, then his first marriage and
separation constitute a major correlative of the Fall: like the prohibition,
marriage is a "mysterious Law" (*PL,* 4.750) instituted in paradise (Gen.
2:18), whose subjects find it at first easy to keep, then discover tragically
that it has become impossible. Arguing that spiritual incompatibility is
a more valid reason for dissolving a marriage than the physical causes
allowed by canon law (adultery, frigidity, impotence), Milton advocated
for a second chance—that is, for divorce with the right to remarry, a
position virtually none of his contemporaries was willing to maintain.
In this, the most passionate of his many prose treatises (prose takes up
sixteen of the eighteen volumes in the still-definitive Columbia edition
of his complete *Works*), Milton laments indifference in the face of "unreasonable wrong and burden" in the "perplexed life" of another human
being: "it is incredible how cold, how dull, and far from all fellow-feeling
we are, without the spur of self-concernment" (page 237).

The tone of the treatise is so intensely personal that it is sometimes
difficult to remember that the occasion of its composition is also political. The treatise is dedicated to both Parliament and the Westminster
Assembly of Divines. John Selden, a member of both bodies (and one
of the few lay members of the latter), who figures prominently in the
last chapter, is the only dedicatee of either to be named. In the last
chapter of this treatise and in the *Areopagitica*, Milton refers to *De Iure
Naturali et Gentium, Iuxta Disciplinam Ebraeorum* ("On the Law of
Nature and of Nations, According to the Teaching of the Jews") by "the
chief of learned men reputed in this land, Mr. *Selden*." "Our learned
Selden" published a half dozen works drawing on his knowledge not
only of biblical Hebrew but also on postbiblical rabbinica, including
the Babylonian-Aramaic texts of the Talmud. Selden amasses so many
sources that his arguments seem to turn of their own weight, without
being pushed; and he loves to bury his main point in a mere parenthesis, as he does on the last page of his treatise on the Jewish laws of
marriage and divorce. Like Milton in this treatise, Selden's aim is to
expose the anomaly of Protestant England still in thrall to "pontifical
teaching on divorce after the Reformation."

Milton's own most Hebraic prose flashes forth in this treatise.
Whereas the early antiprelatical tracts apotheosize the spiritual aristocrats of the Protestant Reformation, who emphasize dualism (us vs.
them, regenerate vs. reprobate), *DDD* owes much to the natural law
theorists Selden and his strong precursor Hugo Grotius, who emphasize the commonality of universal moral laws applicable in all dispensations. In the 1643 edition of this tract, Milton regards Christians as
superior in faith but not in virtue: "We find . . . by experience that the
Spirit of God in the Gospel hath been always more effectual in the illumination of our minds to the gift of faith, than in the moving of our

wills to any excellence of virtue, either above the *Jews* or the Heathen."
And in our edition, Milton advises Christians unhappily matched not
to presume upon the superior refinement of patience and suffering but
instead to accept the relief divorce affords them: "If we be worse [than
the Jews], or but as bad, which lamentable examples confirm we are,
then have we more, or at least as much, need of this permitted law, as
they to whom God therefore gave it (as they say) under a harsher covenant" (pages 316–17).

Against the argument that a partner in an inconvenient marriage
display Christian patience and submit to God's will as expressed in
Christ's uncompromising sentences of indissolubility in the gospels,
Milton bases his radical appeal to freedom on the law of divorce in
Deuteronomy (24:1–4). In this treatise, the Mosaic law rather than the
Son incarnates deity:

> The hidden ways of [God's] providence we adore and search not,
> but the law is his revealed will, his complete, his evident, and cer-
> tain will; herein he appears to us as it were in human shape, enters
> into covenant with us, swears to keep it, binds himself like a just
> lawgiver to his own prescriptions, gives himself to be understood
> by men, *judges and is judged*, measures and is commensurate to
> right reason. (page 280, emphasis added).

If even the heavenly king submits to human judgment, how dare King
Charles refuse? Although typology is the symbolic mode most often applied to Milton's poetry, this treatise reverses the direction of typology
from the New Testament to the Hebrew Bible. Of the relation between
Christ's words and the Mosaic law, Milton insists, "If we examine over
all [Christ's] sayings, we shall find him not so much interpreting the
Law with his words, as referring his own words to be interpreted by
the Law" (page 284). Milton's positive portrayal of Edenic-Mosaic law
in books 5 to 8 of *Paradise Lost* owes much to his divorce tracts. There
Milton presents in a favorable light the Mosaic law that will become
the source of Edenic polity, and there he provides a model of that law
as easy, charitable, and permissive—more charitable, in fact, than the
contemporary Christian interpretation of the law of divorce.

The biblical verses on divorce, and Milton's deconstruction of them,
constitute the best point of entry into the treatise: Deuteronomy 24:1–
2, the Hebrew Bible's law of divorce; Matthew 19:3–9, Mark 10:11–
12, and Luke 16:18, Jesus' explicit and categorical rejection of the
deuteronomic right; 1 Corinthians 7:9, Paul's "better to marry than
to burn" in lust and then in hell, which Milton reinterprets as a burning in blameless loneliness; Paul's reference to the unregenerate as
"children of wrath" (Eph. 2:3), which Milton applies to the children
of an unhappy marriage; the Gospel's allowing the dissolution of a
marriage on grounds of "fornication," which, under Miltonic pressure,
can mean almost anything, including spiritual or emotional faults or
even blameless incompatibility; Malachi 2:16, "For the Lord, the God
of Israel, saith that he hateth putting away," which Milton reads as
"he who hates let him divorce," and numerous other examples. Milton's

strong misreadings—or at least the differences between these verses
in their biblical contexts and in his prose—should reveal that the ostensible enemies in the divorce tracts, canon law and the Pharisees,
pose no real challenge. Indeed, despite his scapegoating of the latter
as "overweening" rabbis, whose "wild exorbitance" Christ intended to
curb, Milton's own juridical position on divorce is identical to that of
the most extreme Pharisee: "this law [of divorce] bounded no man; he
might put away whatever found not favor in his eyes." Milton's actual
enemies are the pronouncements of Christ and Paul against divorce
and Paul's message of death to the law.

For some readers, Milton's Malvolio-like attempts to make the New
Testament verses prohibiting divorce accord with the Hebrew Bible's
permission will appear unseemly. And one generally insightful critic
finds the divorce tracts "authentically ugly," largely because of their
"Old Testament sense of pollution." Moreover, Milton pays almost no
attention to the plight of the children of divorce, assuming, as he does
with abandoned wives, that they are better off than they would be had
the mismatched spouses remained together. Milton makes short work
of "what God hath joined together, let not man put asunder": if a couple
is unhappy, God simply must never have joined them. But what about
a couple that has been married for many years? Does their present
unhappiness mean that they were never meant to be together? Does it
cancel all meaning from their past?

For other readers, the brave and passionate argument for divorce on
grounds of incompatibility, with passages of undeniable brilliance, will
make this the most compelling of all of Milton's prose treatises. In the
1980s, the most powerful readings of Milton's gender politics in the
divorce tracts were overwhelmingly negative. But more recently, critics
and scholars have attempted to provide a more positive view. The ob-
verse of Milton's pained description of a bad marriage in this treatise is
his unmistakably heartfelt and poignant description of a good one. For
this great poet, there is no greater blessing in life than enduring love
based on spiritual harmony.

The Doctrine and Discipline of Divorce

THE Doctrine & Discipline of DIVORCE: Restor'd to the good of
both SEXES, from the Bondage of CANON LAW, and other mistakes, to the true meaning of Scripture in the Law and Gospel
compar'd.

Wherin also are set down the bad consequences of abolishing or
condemning of Sin, that which the Law of God allowes, and Christ
abolisht not.

Now the second time revis'd and much augmented,

In Two BOOKS:
To the Parlament of *England*, with the *Assembly*.
The Author J. M.

MATTH. 13. 52.

Every Scribe instructed to the Kingdome of Heav'n, is like the Maister of a house which bringeth out of his treasury things new and old.

Prov. 18. 13.

He that answereth a matter before he heareth it, it is folly and shame unto him.

LONDON

Imprinted in the yeare 1644.

To the Parliament of ENGLAND, with the Assembly.[1]

If it were seriously asked, and it would be no untimely question, renowned Parliament, select Assembly, who of all teachers and masters that have ever taught hath drawn the most disciples after him, both in religion and in manners, it might be not untruly answered, Custom. Though virtue be commended for the most persuasive in her theory, and conscience in the plain demonstration of the spirit finds most evincing, yet whether it be the secret of divine will or the original blindness we are born in,[2] so it happens for the most part that Custom still is silently received for the best instructor—except it be because the method is so glib and easy, in some manner like to that vision of Ezekiel,[3] rolling up her sudden book of implicit knowledge for him that will to take and swallow down at pleasure; which proving but of bad nourishment in the concoction[4] as it was heedless in the devouring, puffs up unhealthily a certain big face of pretended learning, mistaken among credulous men for the wholesome habit of soundness and good constitution, but is indeed no other than that swollen visage of counterfeit knowledge and literature, which not only in private mars our education but also in public is the common climber into every chair where either religion is preached or law reported, filling each estate of life and profession with abject and servile principles, depressing the high and heaven-born spirit of man far beneath the condition wherein either God created him or sin hath sunk him.[5]

To pursue the allegory, Custom being but a mere face, as Echo is a mere voice, rests not in her unaccomplishment until by secret incli-

---

1. The 149-member Westminster Assembly was the largest parliamentary committee of the English civil war, appointed soon after the formal abolition of Episcopacy in January 1643 to reorganize the church on the Presbyterian model. During its decade of operation, it regulated the church and the universities, instituting policies that Milton regarded as the encroachment of civil power on religious freedom. He registers his eventual disappointment in *Upon the New Forcers of Conscience under the Long Parliament* (1646).
2. The result of original sin. "Evincing": convincing.
3. God commands the prophet to eat the *megillah* (roll, scroll) that has been placed before him (Ezek. 2:9–3:3).
4. Digestion. "Implicit": unquestioning.
5. Although the blindness caused by the Fall has impaired the original wisdom, holiness, and righteousness enjoyed in paradise, Milton suggests here that the harm is limited.

nation she accorporate herself with Error, who being a blind and serpentine body without a head willingly accepts what he wants[6] and supplies what her incompleteness went seeking. Hence it is that Error supports Custom, Custom countenances Error;[7] and these two between them would persecute and chase away all truth and solid wisdom out of human life were it not that God, rather than man, once in many ages calls together the prudent and religious councils of men deputed to repress the encroachments and to work off the inveterate blots and obscurities wrought upon our minds by the subtle insinuating of Error and Custom; who with the numerous and vulgar train of their followers make it their chief design to envy and cry down the industry of free reasoning under the terms of humor[8] and innovation; as if the womb of teeming Truth were to be closed up if she presume to bring forth aught that sorts not with their unchewed notions and suppositions. Against which notorious injury and abuse of man's free soul to testify and oppose the utmost that study and true labor can attain, heretofore the incitement of men reputed grave hath led me among others; and now the duty and the right of an instructed Christian calls me through the chance of good or evil report to be the sole advocate of a discountenanced truth—a high enterprise, Lords and Commons, a high enterprise and a hard, and such as every seventh son of a seventh son[9] does not venture on.

Nor have I amidst the clamor of so much envy and impertinence whither to appeal but to the concourse of so much piety and wisdom here assembled—bringing in my hands an ancient and most necessary, most charitable, and yet most injured statute of Moses,[1] not repealed ever by him who only had the authority but thrown aside with much inconsiderate neglect under the rubbish of canonical ignorance, as once the whole Law was by some such like conveyance in Josiah's time.[2] And he who shall endeavor the amendment of any old neglected grievance in church or state or in the daily course of life, if he be gifted with abilities of mind that may raise him to so high an undertaking, I grant he hath already much whereof not to repent him. Yet let me aread[3] him not to be the foreman of any misjudged opinion unless his resolutions be firmly seated in a square

---

6. Lacks. "Accorporate": unite into one body.
7. Milton alludes to the serpentine body of Error in Spenser's *Faerie Queene*, 1.1.13–24.
8. Whimsical mood.
9. Proverbially destined for greatness.
1. Deut. 24:1, quoted in full in chapter one, allowing a husband to write "a bill of divorcement."
2. Like "good Josiah" (*PL*, 1.418), whose discovery and consequent implementation of the "book of the law of the Lord given by Moses" (2 Chron. 34; 2 Kings 22), after years of idolatrous neglect, made him an obvious symbolic figure to Protestant reformers, Milton sees himself as a moral archaeologist, picking up shards of truth buried for years in custom and error. "Conveyance": underhand dealing.
3. Advise, counsel.

and constant mind, not conscious to itself of any deserved blame, and regardless of ungrounded suspicions. For this let him be sure, he shall be boarded presently by the ruder sort, but not by discreet and well-nurtured men, with a thousand idle descants[4] and surmises—who when they cannot confute the least joint or sinew of any passage in the book, yet God forbid that truth should be truth, because they have a boisterous conceit of some pretenses in the writer. But were they not more busy and inquisitive than the Apostle[5] commends, they would hear him at least, *rejoicing so the truth be preached, whether of envy or other pretense whatsoever.* For Truth is as impossible to be soiled by any outward touch as the sunbeam, though this ill hap wait on her nativity, that she never comes into the world but like a bastard, to the ignominy of him that brought her forth—till Time, the midwife rather than the mother of Truth, have washed and salted the infant, declared her legitimate, and churched the father of his young Minerva from the needless causes of his purgation.[6] Yourselves can best witness this, worthy patriots, and better will no doubt hereafter, for who among ye of the foremost that have travailed in her behalf to the good of church or state hath not been often traduced to be the agent of his own by-ends, under pretext of Reformation?[7] So much the more I shall not be unjust to hope that however infamy or envy may work in other men to do her fretful will against this discourse, yet that the experience of your own uprightness misinterpreted will put ye in mind to give it free audience and generous construction.

What though the brood of Belial, the draff of men, to whom no liberty is pleasing but unbridled and vagabond lust without pale[8] or partition, will laugh broad perhaps to see so great a strength of Scripture mustering up in favor, as they suppose, of their debaucheries? They will know better when they shall hence learn that honest liberty is the greatest foe to dishonest license.[9] And what though others, out of a waterish and queasy conscience, because ever crazy and never yet sound, will rail and fancy to themselves that injury

---

4. Censorious criticisms, carpings. "Boarded": accosted.
5. Paul (Milton paraphrases Phil. 1:18).
6. The image mingles classical myth (Minerva born from the head of Jupiter) with the Anglican service of thanksgiving after childbirth known as churching, derived in part from the Hebrew Bible's laws of purification. Milton compares himself to Jupiter and this treatise to Minerva, or wisdom, but he also knows that his argument will be received initially as illegitimate and unclean.
7. John Selden (1584–1654), the only member of Parliament mentioned in this treatise, spent two years in prison as a result of his labors on behalf of individual rights and in opposition to constitutional violations by King Charles and Archbishop Laud. "Byends": secret selfish purposes.
8. Limit. "Belial": an abstract noun, from Heb. *b'li yaal*, "without value." In *PL*, 1.501–02, Milton associates "the Sons / Of Belial, flown with insolence and wine" with the libertine cavalier type. "Draff": dregs.
9. Sonnet 12: "License they mean when they cry liberty."

and license is the best of this book? Did not the distemper of their
own stomachs affect them with a dizzy megrim, they would soon
tie up their tongues and discern themselves like that Assyrian blasphemer all this while reproaching not man but the Almighty, the
holy one of Israel, whom they do not deny to have belawgiven his
own sacred people with this very allowance, which they now call
injury and license and dare cry shame on, and will do yet a while,
till they get a little cordial sobriety to settle their qualming[1] zeal.

But this question concerns not us perhaps. Indeed, man's disposition, though prone to search after vain curiosities, yet when
points of difficulty are to be discussed appertaining to the removal
of unreasonable wrong and burden from the perplexed life of our
brother, it is incredible how cold, how dull, and far from all fellow-
feeling we are, without the spur of self-concernment. Yet if the
wisdom, the justice, the purity of God be to be cleared from foulest
imputations, which are not yet avoided; if charity be not to be
degraded and trodden down under a civil ordinance; if matrimony
be not to be advanced like that exalted perdition written of to the
Thessalonians,[2] *above all that is called God* or goodness, nay against
them both; then I dare affirm there will be found in the contents of
this book that which may concern us all. You it concerns chiefly,
worthies in Parliament, on whom as on our deliverers all our grievances and cares, by the merit of your eminence and fortitude, are
devolved. Me it concerns next, having with much labor and faithful
diligence first found out, or at least with a fearless and communica-
tive candor first published to the manifest good of Christendom,
that which, calling to witness every thing mortal and immortal, I
believe unfeignedly to be true. Let not other men think their conscience bound to search continually after truth, to pray for enlightening from above, to publish what they think they have so obtained,
and debar me from conceiving myself tied by the same duties.

Ye have now, doubtless by the favor and appointment of God, ye
have now in your hands a great and populous nation to reform,
from what corruption, what blindness in religion ye know well; in
what a degenerate and fallen spirit from the apprehension of native
liberty and true manliness I am sure ye find; with what unbounded
license rushing to whoredoms and adulteries needs not long enquiry:
insomuch that the fears which men have of too strict a discipline
perhaps exceed the hopes that can be in others of ever introducing

1. Of the nature of a fit. "Megrim": migraine. "Assyrian blasphemer": King Sennacherib
of Assyria made threats against Jerusalem that were denounced as blasphemy against
"the Holy One of Israel" (2 Kings 19:22). "Belawgiven": legislated to.
2. To set the institution of marriage above Christian charity is to deserve the epithet "son
of perdition; Who opposeth and exalteth himself above all that is called God" (2 Thess.
2:3–4).

6

it with any great success. What if I should tell ye now of dispensations and indulgences,[3] to give a little the reins, to let them play and nibble with the bait a while, a people as hard of heart as that Egyptian colony that went to Canaan? This is the common doctrine that adulterous and injurious divorces were not connived[4] only but with eye open allowed of old for hardness of heart. But that opinion I trust, by then this following argument hath been well read, will be left for one of the mysteries of an indulgent Antichrist, to farm out incest by and those his other tributary pollutions. What middle way can be taken then, may some interrupt, if we must neither turn to the right nor to the left, and that the people hate to be reformed? Mark then, judges and lawgivers, and ye whose office it is to be our teachers, for I will utter now a doctrine, if ever any other, though neglected or not understood, yet of great and powerful importance to the governing of mankind. He who wisely would restrain the reasonable soul of man within due bound must first himself know perfectly how far the territory and dominion extends of just and honest liberty. As little must he offer to bind that which God hath loosened as to loosen that which he hath bound.[5] The ignorance and mistake of this high point hath heaped up one huge half of all the misery that hath been since Adam. In the Gospel[6] we shall read a supercilious crew of masters, whose holiness, or rather whose evil eye, grieving that God should be so facile to man, was to set straiter limits to obedience than God had set, to enslave the dignity of man, to put a garrison upon his neck of empty and over-dignified precepts. And we shall read our Savior never more grieved and troubled than to meet with such a peevish madness among men against their own freedom. How can we expect him to be less offended with us, when much of the same folly shall be found yet remaining where it least ought, to the perishing of thousands?

The greatest burden in the world is superstition, not only of ceremonies in the church but of imaginary and scarecrow sins at home. What greater weakening, what more subtle stratagem against our

3. Milton obliquely rejects the view that he presents: that divorce, like the Roman Catholic practice of selling indulgences, is corrupt, a dispensation granted only because of the hard-heartedness of the sinful Israelites ("that Egyptian colony"). He insists instead that divorce is a divinely instituted law.
4. Winked at, overlooked.
5. "Wherefore they are no more twain, but one flesh. What therefore God hath joined together, let not man put asunder" (Matt. 19:6). This verse, which seems to be an impediment to divorce, Milton cites directly and paraphrases frequently in this treatise, reinterpreting it—for example, if spouses are torn asunder by unhappiness, then God never joined them.
6. In Matt. 23:1–33, Milton condemns the Pharisees for laying burdens on peoples' shoulders "grievous to be borne." Later in the treatise (p. 275), Milton condemns the same Pharisees ("those over-weening Rabbis"), not, as here, for being overly strict, but rather for licentiousness so extreme that Christ forbade them to divorce in order to curb "their wild exorbitance." Milton doesn't advertise the fact that he and the Pharisees adopt an identical juridical position on divorce.

Christian warfare, when besides the gross body of real transgressions to encounter, we shall be terrified by a vain and shadowy men-
acing of faults that are not? When things indifferent shall be set to
over-front us under the banners of sin, what wonder if we be routed
and by this art of our adversary fall into the subjection of worst and
deadliest offenses? The superstition of the papist is, "touch not,
taste not" [Col. 2:21],[7] when God bids both; and ours is, part not,
separate not, when God and charity both permits and commands.
"Let all your things be done with charity," saith St. Paul [1 Cor.
16:14]; and his master saith, "She is the fulfilling of the Law" [Rom.
13:10]. Yet now a civil, an indifferent, a sometime dissuaded law of
marriage must be forced upon us to fulfill, not only without charity
but against her. No place in heaven or earth, except hell, where
charity may not enter; yet marriage, the ordinance of our solace and
contentment, the remedy of our loneliness, will not admit now either
of charity or mercy to come in and mediate or pacify the fierceness
of this gentle ordinance, the unremedied loneliness of this remedy.

Advise ye well, supreme Senate, if charity be thus excluded and
expulsed, how ye will defend the untainted honor of your own actions
and proceedings. He who marries intends as little to conspire his
own ruin as he that swears allegiance; and as a whole people is in
proportion to an ill government, so is one man to an ill marriage.[8] If
they, against any authority, covenant, or statute, may by the sovereign edict of charity save not only their lives but honest liberties
from unworthy bondage, as well may he against any private covenant, which he never entered to his mischief, redeem himself from
unsupportable disturbances to honest peace and just contentment:
And much the rather, for that to resist the highest magistrate though
tyrannizing God never gave us express allowance, only he gave us
reason, charity, nature, and good example to bear us out; but in this
economical misfortune thus to demean ourselves, besides the warrant of those four great directors, which doth as justly belong hither,
we have an express law of God, and such a law as whereof our Savior
with a solemn threat forbid the abrogating.[9] For no effect of tyranny
can sit more heavy on the commonwealth than this household unhappiness on the family. And farewell all hope of true reformation in
the state while such an evil as this lies undiscerned or unregarded

7. Paul rebukes those who still consider themselves "subject to ordinances," such as the
   Old Testament's dietary prohibitions. In the *Areopagitica*, Milton will develop the connection, based on appetite, between the freedom to eat anything and the freedom to
   read anything.
8. Both the family and other political institutions are subordinate to the purposes for
   which they were established, a principle invoked by Parliamentary supporters of resistance to the king.
9. The law of divorce in Deut. 24:1. Christ insists that "one jot or one tittle shall in no
   wise pass from the law (Matt. 5:18). "Economical": household, domestic. "Four great
   directors": the God-given gifts mentioned earlier in the sentence.

in the house—on the redress whereof depends not only the spiritful and orderly life of our grown men but the willing and careful education of our children.

Let this therefore be new examined, this tenure and freehold of mankind, this native and domestic charter given us by a greater lord than that Saxon king the Confessor.[1] Let the statutes of God be turned over, be scanned anew, and considered not altogether by the narrow intellectuals of quotationists and commonplacers but (as was the ancient right of councils) by men of what liberal profession soever,[2] of eminent spirit and breeding joined with a diffuse and various knowledge of divine and human things; able to balance and define good and evil, right and wrong, throughout every state of life; able to show us the ways of the Lord, straight and faithful as they are, not full of cranks and contradictions and pit-falling dispenses but with divine insight and benignity measured out to the proportion of each mind and spirit, each temper and disposition, created so different each from other and yet by the skill of wise conducting all to become uniform in virtue.

To expedite these knots were worthy a learned and memorable Synod, while our enemies expect to see the expectation of the Church tired out with dependencies and independencies, how they will compound and in what calends.[3] Doubt not, worthy senators, to vindicate the sacred honor and judgment of Moses your predecessor from the shallow commenting of scholastics and canonists. Doubt not after him to reach out your steady hands to the misinformed and wearied life of man to restore this his lost heritage into the household state. Wherewith be sure that peace and love, the best subsistence of a Christian family, will return home from whence they are now banished; places of prostitution will be less haunted, the neighbor's bed less attempted, the yoke of prudent and manly discipline will be generally submitted to; sober and well-ordered living will soon spring up in the Commonwealth.

Ye have an author great beyond exception, Moses, and one yet greater, he who hedged in from abolishing every smallest jot and tittle of precious equity contained in that Law with a more accurate and lasting Masoreth than either the synagogue of Ezra or the Galilean school at Tiberias[4] hath left us. Whatever else ye can enact will

1. Edward the Confessor (1002–66), last of the Saxon kings, widely remembered with affection.
2. More than once Milton reveals his preference for lay persons over the clergy in religious deliberations.
3. Days debts are settled. "Dependencies and independencies": Presbyterians and Independents.
4. A city on the west shore of the Sea of Galilee, a famous center of rabbinical scholarship. "Masoreth": the Masora are the body of rules relating to the text of the Hebrew Bible, developed by Jewish scholars in the 6th–9th centuries. In addition to establish-

scarce concern a third part of the British name, but the benefit and good of this your magnanimous example will easily spread far beyond the banks of Tweed and the Norman Isles.[5] It would not be the first or second time since our ancient Druids, by whom this island was the cathedral of philosophy to France, left off their pagan rites, that England hath had this honor vouchsafed from heaven, to give out reformation to the world. Who was it but our English Constantine[6] that baptized the Roman Empire? Who but the Northumbrian Willibrode and Winifride of Devon[7] with their followers were the first apostles of Germany? Who but Alcuin and Wycliffe[8] our countrymen opened the eyes of Europe, the one in arts, the other in religion? Let not England forget her precedence of teaching nations how to live.

Know, worthies, know and exercise the privilege of your honored country. A greater title I here bring ye than is either in the power or in the policy of Rome to give her monarchs: this glorious act will style ye the defenders of charity. Nor is this yet the highest inscription that will adorn so religious and so holy a defense as this. Behold here the pure and sacred law of God and his yet purer and more sacred name offering themselves to you first, of all Christian reformers, to be acquitted from the long suffered ungodly attribute of patronizing adultery. Defer not to wipe off instantly these imputative blurs and stains cast by rude fancies upon the throne and beauty itself of inviolable holiness, lest some other people more devout and wise than we bereave us this offered immortal glory, our wonted prerogative of being the first asserters in every great vindication.

For me, as far as my part leads me, I have already my greatest gain, assurance, and inward satisfaction to have done in this nothing unworthy of an honest life and studies well employed. With what event among the wise and right understanding handful of men, I am secure. But how among the drove of custom and prejudice this will be relished by such whose capacity, since their youth run ahead into the easy creek of a system or a medulla,[9] sails there at will under the blown physiognomy of their unlabored rudiments—for them, what

---

ing the text, the Masoretes added vowel points. Milton means that Christ's words are an even better interpretation of the Mosaic law.

5. The Channel islands.

6. Milton shared the mistaken belief that Constantine, the first Christian Roman emperor, was born in England.

7. Winfrid, Saint Boniface (675–754), an English missionary, monk, and martyr, called the Apostle of Germany. Saint Willibrord (658–739), a Northumbrian missionary, known as the Apostle to the Frisians in the modern Netherlands. He became the first bishop of Utrecht.

8. John Wycliffe (c. 1325–1384), the force behind the first translation of the Bible into English, opposed papal encroachments on secular power. He became known as "the Morning Star of the Reformation." Alcuin (735–804) was a scholar, ecclesiastic, poet, and teacher, from York, England. He became a leading intellectual figure in the court of Charlemagne.

9. Essential matter of a subject; an abridgement or summary.

their taste will be, I have also surety sufficient from the entire league that hath been ever between formal ignorance and grave obstinacy. Yet when I remember the little that our Savior could prevail about this doctrine of charity against the crabbed textuists of his time, I make no wonder but rest confident that who so prefers either matrimony or other ordinance before the good of man and the plain exigence of charity, let him profess papist or Protestant or what he will, he is no better than a Pharisee and understands not the Gospel—whom as a misinterpreter of Christ I openly protest against and provoke him to the trial of this truth before all the world; and let him bethink him withal how he will solder up the shifting flaws of his ungirt permissions, his venial and unvenial dispenses,[1] wherewith the law of God pardoning and unpardoning hath been shamefully branded, for want of heed in glossing, to have eluded and baffled out all faith and chastity from the marriage-bed of that holy seed with politic and judicial adulteries.

I seek not to seduce the simple and illiterate; my errand is to find out the choicest and the learnedest, who have this high gift of wisdom to answer solidly or to be convinced. I crave it from the piety, the learning, and the prudence which is housed in this place. It might perhaps more fitly have been written in another tongue: and I had done so, but that the esteem I have of my country's judgment, and the love I bear to my native language to serve it first with what I endeavor, made me speak it thus ere I assay the verdict of outlandish readers.[2] And perhaps also here I might have ended nameless, but that the address of these lines chiefly to the Parliament of England might have seemed ungrateful not to acknowledge by whose religious care, unwearied watchfulness, courageous and heroic resolutions, I enjoy the peace and studious leisure to remain,

The honorer and attendant of their noble worth and virtues,

John Milton.

THE
DOCTRINE AND DISCIPLINE
OF DIVORCE;
RESTORED TO THE GOOD OF BOTH SEXES.

---

1. Dispensations for minor and mortal sins.
2. A decade later, in his *Second Defence* (1654), Milton will regret his having published his divorce tracts in English: "One thing only I could wish, that I had not written it in the vernacular, for then I would not have met with vernacular readers, who are usually ignorant of their own good and laugh at the misfortune of others." "Outlandish": foreign.

Book I

THE PREFACE.

That man is the occasion of his own miseries in most of those
evils which he imputes to God's inflicting. The absurdity of our
canonists in their decrees about divorce. The Christian Imperial
laws framed with more equity. The opinion of Hugo Grotius and
Paulus Fagius; and the purpose in general of this discourse.

Many men, whether it be their fate or fond[3] opinion, easily persuade themselves, if God would but be pleased a while to withdraw
his just punishments from us and to restrain what power either the
devil or any earthly enemy hath to work us woe, that then man's
nature would find immediate rest and releasement from all evils.
But verily they who think so, if they be such as have a mind large
enough to take into their thoughts a general survey of human things,
would soon prove themselves in that opinion far deceived. For
though it were granted us by divine indulgence to be exempt from
all that can be harmful to us from without, yet the perverseness of
our folly is so bent that we should never lin[4] hammering out of our
own hearts, as it were out of a flint, the seeds and sparkles of new
misery to our selves till all were in a blaze again. And no marvel if
out of our own hearts, for they are evil;[5] but even out of those things
which God meant us either for a principal good or a pure contentment we are still hatching and contriving upon ourselves matter of
continued sorrow and perplexity. What greater good to man than
that revealed rule whereby God vouchsafes to show us how he would
be worshiped? And yet that not rightly understood became the cause
that once a famous man in Israel could not but oblige his conscience to be the sacrificer, or if not the jailer, of his innocent and
only daughter.[6] And was the cause ofttimes that armies of valiant
men have given up their throats to a heathenish enemy on the Sabbath day, fondly thinking their defensive resistance to be as then a
work unlawful.[7] What thing more instituted to the solace and delight
of man than marriage? And yet the misinterpreting of some Scripture directed mainly against the abusers of the law for divorce given
by Moses hath changed the blessing of matrimony not seldom into a
familiar and co-inhabiting mischief, at least into a drooping and

---

3. Foolish.
4. Cease.
5. "The imagination of man's heart is evil from his youth" (Gen. 8:21).
6. For the story of Jephthah and his vow, see Judg. 11:29–40. Some interpreters hold that
   he actually sacrificed his daughter as an offering, others that he dedicated her to a life
   of virginity.
7. Believing that to defend themselves would be to violate the Sabbath, the zealous followers of Mattathias were massacred by the forces of Antiochus (1 Macc. 2:31–38).

disconsolate household captivity, without refuge or redemption. So ungoverned and so wild a race doth superstition run us from one extreme of abused liberty into the other of unmerciful restraint. For although God in the first ordaining of marriage taught us to what end he did it, in words expressly implying the apt and cheerful conversation[8] of man with woman, to comfort and refresh him against the evil of solitary life, not mentioning the purpose of generation till afterwards, as being but a secondary end in dignity, though not in necessity; yet now, if any two be but once handed in the church and have tasted in any sort the nuptial bed, let them find themselves never so mistaken in their dispositions through any error, concealment, or misadventure, that through their different tempers, thoughts, and constitutions they can neither be to one another a remedy against loneliness nor live in any union or contentment all their days, yet they shall, so they be but found suitably weaponed to the least possibility of sensual enjoyment, be made, spite of antipathy, to fadge[9] together and combine as they may to their unspeakable wearisomeness and despair of all sociable delight in the ordinance which God established to that very end.

What a calamity is this, and as the wise man, if he were alive, would sigh out in his own phrase, what a "sore evil is this under the sun!"[1] All which we can refer justly to no other author than the canon law[2] and her adherents, not consulting with charity the interpreter and guide of our faith but resting in the mere element of the text; doubtless by the policy of the devil to make that gracious ordinance become unsupportable, that what with men not daring to venture upon wedlock, and what with men wearied out of it, all inordinate license might abound.

It was for many ages that marriage lay in disgrace with most of the ancient doctors as a work of the flesh, almost a defilement, wholly denied to priests and the second time dissuaded to all, as he that reads Tertullian or Jerome[3] may see at large. Afterwards it was thought so sacramental that no adultery or desertion could dissolve it; and this is the sense of our canon courts in England to this day, but in no other reformed church else; yet there remains in them also a burden on it as heavy as the other two were disgraceful or superstitious, and of as much iniquity, crossing a law not only written by Moses but charactered in us by nature, of more antiquity and deeper ground than marriage itself, which law is to force nothing against

8. Living together, society, intimacy.
9. Rub on, do with, put up with. "Antipathy": natural contrariety or incompatibility, the opposite of *sympathy*.
1. Eccles. 5:13; attributed to Solomon, the "wise man."
2. Ecclesiastical law, as laid down in decrees and the statutes of councils.
3. Saints Tertullian (160–230) and Jerome (240–420) prefer celibacy over marriage and reveal hostility toward sexuality.

the faultless proprieties of nature.[4] Yet that this may be colorably done, our Savior's words touching divorce are as it were congealed into a stony rigor inconsistent both with his doctrine and his office; and that which he preached only to the conscience is by canonical tyranny snatched into the compulsive censure of a judicial court where laws are imposed even against the venerable and secret power of nature's impression, to love, whatever cause be found to loathe— which is a heinous barbarism both against the honor of marriage, the dignity of man and his soul, the goodness of Christianity, and all the human respects of civility. Notwithstanding that some the wisest and gravest among the Christian emperors, who had about them to consult with those of the Fathers then living, who for their learning and holiness of life are still with us in great renown, have made their statutes and edicts concerning this debate far more easy and relenting in many necessary cases wherein the canon is inflexible. And Hugo Grotius,[5] a man of these times, one of the best learned, seems not obscurely to adhere in his persuasion of the equity of those Imperial decrees in his notes upon the Evangelists; much allaying the outward roughness of the text, which hath for the most part been too immoderately expounded; and excites the diligence of others to inquire further into this question as containing many points that have not yet been explained. Which ever likely to remain intricate and hopeless upon the suppositions commonly stuck to, the authority of Paulus Fagius,[6] one so learned and so eminent in England once, if it might persuade, would straight acquaint us with a solution of these differences no less prudent than compendious. He in his comment on the Pentateuch doubted not to maintain that divorces might be as lawfully permitted by the magistrate to Christians as they were to the Jews.

But because he is but brief and these things of great consequence not to be kept obscure, I shall conceive it nothing above my duty either for the difficulty or the censure that may pass thereon to communicate such thoughts as I also have had, and do offer them now in this general labor of reformation to the candid view both of church and magistrate, especially because I see it the hope of good men that those irregular and unspiritual courts have spun their utmost date in this land and some better course must now be

---

4. Milton seems to mean a natural disposition or temperament.
5. Hugo Grotius (1583–1645), the great Dutch polymath, whom Milton called "a most learned man . . . whom I ardently desired to meet." Grotius's *Annotationes in Quator Evangelia* (1641) directly influenced this divorce tract, and his important work on natural law, *De Jure Belli ac Pacis* (1625), may account in part for the religious toleration in this treatise, missing from Milton's five early antiprelatical works.
6. Paulus Fagius (1504–49), eminent scholar of biblical and postbiblical rabbinic Hebrew and Aramaic, dismissed from his position in Strasbourg as a result of the Counter-Reformation, was appointed professor of Hebrew at Cambridge University.

constituted.[7] This, therefore, shall be the task and period[8] of this discourse, to prove, first, that other reasons of divorce besides adultery were by the Law of Moses and are yet to be allowed by the Christian magistrate as a piece of justice, and that the words of Christ are not hereby contraried. Next, that to prohibit absolutely any divorce whatsoever except those which Moses excepted is against the reason of law, as in due place I shall show out of Fagius with many additions.

He, therefore, who by adventuring shall be so happy as with success to light the way of such an expedient liberty and truth as this, shall restore the much-wronged and over-sorrowed state of matrimony not only to those merciful and life-giving remedies of Moses but, as much as may be, to that serene and blissful condition it was in at the beginning, and shall deserve of all apprehensive men (considering the troubles and distempers which for want of this insight have been so oft in kingdoms, in states and families) shall deserve to be reckoned among the public benefactors of civil and human life, above the inventors of wine and oil. For this is a far dearer, far nobler, and more desirable cherishing to man's life, unworthily exposed to sadness and mistake, which he shall vindicate.

Not that license and levity and unconsented breach of faith should herein be countenanced, but that some conscionable and tender pity might be had of those who have unwarily, in a thing they never practiced before, made themselves the bondmen of a luckless and helpless matrimony. In which argument he whose courage can serve him to give the first onset must look for two several oppositions: the one from those who having sworn themselves to long custom and the letter of the text will not out of the road; the other from those whose gross and vulgar apprehensions conceit[9] but low of matrimonial purposes, and in the work of male and female think they have all. Nevertheless, it shall be here sought by due ways to be made appear that those words of God in the institution promising a meet help against loneliness[1] and those words of Christ that his yoke is easy and his burden light [Matt. 11:30] were not spoken in vain; for if the knot of marriage may in no case be dissolved but for adultery, all the burdens and services of the Law are not so intolerable.[2]

This only is desired of them who are minded to judge hardly of thus maintaining, that they would be still and hear all out, nor think it equal to answer deliberate reason with sudden heat and noise;

7. Although he would soon be disappointed, Milton based his hope on the recent termination of ecclesiastical courts.
8. Aim.
9. Conceive, imagine, think.
1. "And God said, 'It is not good that man should be alone; I will make him a help meet [suitable, fit] for him'" (Gen. 2:18).
2. An extreme statement: that the law of marriage can be a heavier burden than all of the positive and negative moral, ceremonial, and judicial laws of the Hebrew Bible.

remembering this, that many truths now of reverend esteem and credit had their birth and beginning once from singular and private thoughts, while the most of men were otherwise possessed, and had the fate at first to be generally exploded and exclaimed on by many violent opposers. Yet I may err perhaps in soothing myself that this present truth revived will deserve on all hands to be not sinisterly received, in that it undertakes the cure of an inveterate disease crept into the best part of human society; and to do this with no smarting corrosive but with a smooth and pleasing lesson, which received hath the virtue to soften and dispel rooted and knotty sorrows; and without enchantment, if that be feared, or spell used, hath regard at once both to serious pity and upright honesty; that tends to the redeeming and restoring of none but such as are the object of compassion, having in an ill hour hampered themselves to the utter dispatch of all their most beloved comforts and repose for this life's term.

But if we shall obstinately dislike this new overture of unexpected ease and recovery, what remains but to deplore the frowardness of our hopeless condition, which neither can endure the estate we are in nor admit of remedy either sharp or sweet. Sharp we our selves distaste; and sweet, under whose hands we are, is scrupled and suspected as too luscious. In such a posture Christ found the Jews, who were neither won with the austerity of John the Baptist, and thought it too much license to follow freely the charming pipe of him who sounded and proclaimed liberty and relief to all distresses. Yet Truth in some age or other will find her witness and shall be justified at last by her own children.[3]

CHAP. I.

The position. Proved by the Law of Moses. That Law expounded and asserted to a moral and charitable use, first by Paulus Fagius, next with other additions.

To remove therefore, if it be possible, this great and sad oppression which through the strictness of a literal interpreting hath invaded and disturbed the dearest and most peaceable estate of household society, to the overburdening if not the overwhelming of many Christians better worth than to be so deserted of the Church's considerate care, this position shall be laid down, first proving, then answering, what may be objected either from Scripture or light of reason:

That indisposition, unfitness, or contrariety of mind, arising from a cause in nature unchangeable, hindering and ever likely to hinder the main benefits of conjugal society, which are solace and peace, is a

---

3. "But wisdom is justified of all her children" (Luke 7:35).

greater reason of divorce than natural frigidity, especially if there be
no children, and that there be mutual consent.

This I gather from the Law in Deut. 24:1: *When a man hath taken*
a wife and married her, and it come to pass that she find no favor in his
eyes, because he hath found some uncleanness in her, let him write her
a bill of divorcement, and give it in her hand, and send her out of his
house, &c. This law, if the words of Christ may be admitted into our
belief, shall never, while the world stands, for him be abrogated.
First, therefore, I here set down what learned Fagius hath observed
on this law: *The Law of God,* saith he, *permitted divorce for the help*
of human weakness. For everyone that of necessity separates cannot live
single. That Christ denied divorce to his own hinders not, for what is
that to the unregenerate, who hath not attained such perfection? Let
not the remedy be despised which was given to weakness. And when
Christ saith, who marries the divorced commits adultery, it is to be
understood if he had any plot in the divorce. The rest I reserve until it
be disputed how the magistrate is to do herein. From hence we may
may plainly discern a twofold consideration of this law: first, the end
of the lawgiver and the proper act of the law to command or to allow
something just and honest or indifferent; secondly, his sufferance
from some accidental result of evil by this allowance, which the law
cannot remedy. For if this law have no other end or act but only the
allowance of sin, though never to so good intention, that law is no law
but sin muffled in the robe of law or law disguised in the loose garment of sin. Both which are two foul hypotheses to save the phenomenon of our Savior's answer to the Pharisees about this matter.[4] And
I trust anon by the help of an infallible guide to perfect such Prutenic
Tables[5] as shall mend the astronomy of our wide expositors.

The cause of divorce mentioned in the Law is translated "some
uncleanness," but in the Hebrew it sounds *"nakedness of ought* or
any real nakedness," which by all the learned interpreters is referred
to the mind as well as the body. And what greater nakedness or
unfitness of mind than that which hinders ever the solace and peaceful society of the married couple; and what hinders that more than
the unfitness and defectiveness of an unconjugal mind? The cause
therefore of divorce expressed in the position cannot but agree
with that described in the best and equallest sense of Moses' Law—

---

4. "Moses because of the hardness of your hearts suffered you to put away your wives: but
from the beginning it was not so. And I say unto you, Whosoever shall put away his
wife, except it be for fornication, and shall marry another, committeth adultery: and
whoso marrieth her which is put away doth commit adultery" (Matt. 19:8–9).
5. Or Prussian Tables of 1551, based on Copernican parameters, replaced the outmoded
Alphonsine tables. In *PL*, 8.75–84, Milton ridicules attempts by medieval astronomers
to save the phenomena of apparent irregularities in stellar motion by hypothesizing
"Cycle and epicycle." Like Copernicus and Galileo, Milton is a new scientist. He does
not seem to indicate awareness here of the Rudolphine Tables, published by Kepler in
1627, which superseded the Prutenic Tables.

which being a matter of pure charity is plainly moral and more now in force than ever, therefore surely lawful. For if under the Law such was God's gracious indulgence as not to suffer the ordinance of his goodness and favor through any error to be seared and stigmatized upon his servants to their misery and thraldom, much less will he suffer it now under the covenant of grace by abrogating his former grant of remedy and relief. But the first institution[6] will be objected to have ordained marriage inseparable. To that a little patience until this first part have amply discoursed the grave and pious reasons of this divorcive law, and then I doubt not but with one gentle stroking to wipe away ten thousand tears out of the life of man. Yet thus much I shall now insist on, that whatever the institution were, it could not be so enormous[7] nor so rebellious against both nature and reason as to exalt itself above the end and person for whom it was instituted.

CHAP. II.

The first reason of this Law grounded on the prime reason of matrimony. That no covenant whatsoever obliges against the main end both of itself and of the parties covenanting.

For all sense and equity reclaims[8] that any law or covenant, how solemn or strait soever, either between God and man or man and man, though of God's joining, should bind against a prime and principal scope of its own institution and of both or either party covenanting; neither can it be of force to engage a blameless creature to his own perpetual sorrow, mistaken for his expected solace, without suffering charity to step in and do a confessed good work of parting those whom nothing holds together but this of God's joining, falsely supposed against the express end of his own ordinance. And what his chief end was of creating woman to be joined with man his own instituting words declare and are infallible to inform us what is marriage and what is no marriage, unless we can think them set there to no purpose: *It is not good*, saith he, *that man should be alone; I will make him a help meet for him* [Gen. 2:18]. From which words so plain less cannot be concluded nor is by any learned interpreter than that in God's intention a meet and happy conversation is the chiefest and the noblest end of marriage: for we find here no expression so necessarily implying carnal knowledge as this prevention of loneliness to the mind and spirit of man. To

6. Of marriage in paradise.
7. Overgrown in power or importance.
8. Cries out in protest.

this Fagius, Calvin, Pareus, Rivetus[9] as willingly and largely assent
as can be wished.

And indeed it is a greater blessing from God, more worthy so
excellent a creature as man is and a higher end to honor and sanctify the league of marriage, whenas the solace and satisfaction of
the mind is regarded and provided for before the sensitive pleasing
of the body. And with all generous persons married thus it is, that
where the mind and person pleases aptly, there some unaccomplishment of the body's delight may be better borne with than when the
mind hangs off in an unclosing disproportion, though the body be
as it ought; for there all corporal delight will soon become unsavory
and contemptible. And the solitariness of man, which God had
namely and principally ordered to prevent by marriage, hath no remedy but lies under a worse condition than the loneliest single life.
For in single life the absence and remoteness of a helper might inure
him to expect his own comforts out of himself or to seek with hope:
but here the continual sight of his deluded thoughts without cure
must needs be to him, if especially his complexion[1] incline him to
melancholy, a daily trouble and pain of loss in some degree like that
which reprobates feel.

Lest therefore so noble a creature as man should be shut up
incurably under a worse evil by an easy mistake in that ordinance
which God gave him to remedy a less evil, reaping to himself sorrow
while he went to rid away solitariness, it cannot avoid to be concluded that if the woman be naturally so of disposition[2] as will not
help to remove but help to increase that same God-forbidden loneliness, which will in time draw on with it a general discomfort and
dejection of mind not beseeming either Christian profession or moral
conversation, unprofitable and dangerous to the commonwealth,
when the household estate, out of which must flourish forth the vigor
and spirit of all public enterprises, is so ill contented and procured at
home and cannot be supported—such a marriage can be no marriage whereto the most honest end is wanting; and the aggrieved
person shall do more manly to be extraordinary and singular in
claiming the due right whereof he is frustrated than to piece up his
lost contentment by visiting the stews or stepping to his neighbor's
bed, which is the common shift in this misfortune, or else by suffering his useful life to waste away and be lost under a secret affliction

9. David Paraeus (1548–1622) and André Rivet (1572–1651) were respected Calvinist
theologians and exegetes.
1. The combination of the four bodily humors in a certain proportion.
2. Encompassing both physical and moral attributes (natural constitution, temperament),
the word perfectly suits Milton, who keeps these two reasons for divorce side by side,
refusing to distinguish between immoral behavior and an unpleasing nature, "grossest
faults or disabilities," "wilfulness and inability."

of an unconscionable size to human strength. Against all which evils the mercy of this Mosaic Law was graciously exhibited.

CHAP. III.

The ignorance and iniquity of Canon law, providing for the right of the body in marriage but nothing for the wrongs and grievances of the mind. An objection—that the mind should be better looked to before contract—answered.

How vain therefore is it and how preposterous in the canon law to have made such careful provision against the impediment of carnal performance and to have had no care about the unconversing inability of mind, so defective to the purest and most sacred end of matrimony; and that the vessel of voluptuous enjoyment must be made good to him that has taken it upon trust, without any caution; whenas the mind, from whence must flow the acts of peace and love, a far more precious mixture than the quintessence of an excrement,[3] though it be found never so deficient and unable to perform the best duty of marriage in a cheerful and agreeable conversation, shall be thought good enough, however flat and melancholious it be, and must serve, though to the eternal disturbance and languishing of him that complains him. Yet wisdom and charity, weighing God's own institution, would think that the pining of a sad spirit wedded to loneliness should deserve to be freed as well as the impatience of a sensual desire so providently relieved. 'Tis read to us in the liturgy that we must not marry to satisfy the fleshly appetite like brute beasts that have no understanding,[4] but the canon so runs as if it dreamt of no other matter than such an appetite to be satisfied; for if it happen that nature hath stopped or extinguished the veins of sensuality, that marriage is annulled. But though all the faculties of the understanding and conversing part after trial appear to be so ill and so aversely met through nature's unalterable working as that neither peace nor any sociable contentment can follow, 'tis as nothing, the contract shall stand as firm as ever, betide what will. What is this but secretly to instruct us that however many grave reasons are pretended to the married life, yet that nothing indeed is thought worth regard therein but the prescribed satisfaction of an irrational heat. Which cannot be but ignominious to the state of marriage, dishonorable to the undervalued soul of man, and even to Christian doctrine itself—while it seems more moved at the disappointing of an impetuous nerve than at the ingenuous grievance of a mind unreasonably yoked, and to place more of marriage in the channel

---

3. The essential reproductive fluid as distinct from waste matter supposedly emitted with it.
4. Milton closely paraphrases from the exhortation at the beginning of the marriage service in the Anglican Book of Common Prayer.

of concupiscence than in the pure influence[5] of peace and love, whereof the soul's lawful contentment is the only fountain.

But some are ready to object that the disposition ought seriously to be considered before. But let them know again that for all the wariness can be used, it may yet befall a discreet man to be mistaken in his choice, and we have plenty of examples.[6] The soberest and best-governed men are least practiced in these affairs; and who knows not that the bashful muteness of a virgin may oft-times hide all the unliveliness and natural sloth which is really unfit for conversation; Nor is there that freedom of access granted or presumed as may suffice to a perfect discerning till too late. And where any indisposition is suspected, what more usual than the persuasion of friends that acquaintance as it increases will amend all? And lastly, it is not strange though many who have spent their youth chastely are in some things not so quick-sighted while they haste too eagerly to light the nuptial torch. Nor is it, therefore, that for a modest error a man should forfeit so great a happiness and no charitable means to release him, since they who have lived most loosely by reason of their bold accustoming prove most successful in their matches, because their wild affections unsettling at will have been as so many divorces to teach them experience. Whenas the sober man, honoring the appearance of modesty and hoping well of every social virtue under that veil, may easily chance to meet, if not with a body impenetrable, yet often with a mind to all other due conversation inaccessible, and to all the more estimable and superior purposes of matrimony useless and almost lifeless. And what a solace, what a fit help such a consort would be through the whole life of a man, is less pain to conjecture than to have experience.

CHAP. IV.

The second reason of this Law, because without it marriage as it happens oft is not a remedy of that which it promises, as any rational creature would expect. That marriage, if we pattern from the beginning as our Savior bids, was not properly the remedy of lust but the fulfilling of conjugal love and helpfulness.

And that we may further see what a violent and cruel thing it is to force the continuing of those together whom God and nature in the gentlest end of marriage never joined, diverse evils and extremities that follow upon such a compulsion shall here be set in view.

---

5. Flowing in. Milton contrasts carnal and spiritual flowing. "Ingenuous": without guile; honorable.
6. Milton added this clause to the second edition, perhaps because the rest of this paragraph so patently describes his own situation.

Of evils the first and greatest is that hereby a most absurd and rash imputation is fixed upon God and his holy laws of conniving and dispensing with open and common adultery among his chosen people—a thing which the rankest politician would think it shame and disworship that his laws should countenance. How and in what manner this comes to pass I shall reserve till the course of method brings on the unfolding of many Scriptures. Next, the Law and Gospel are hereby made liable to more than one contradiction, which I refer also thither. Lastly, the supreme dictate of charity is hereby many ways neglected and violated, which I shall forthwith address to prove. First, we know St. Paul saith, *It is better to marry than to burn* [1 Cor. 7:9]. Marriage, therefore, was given as a remedy of that trouble; but what might this burning mean? Certainly not the mere motion of carnal lust, not the mere goad of a sensitive desire; God does not principally take care for such cattle.[7] What is it then but that desire which God put into Adam in Paradise before he knew the sin of incontinence—that desire which God saw it was not good that man should be left alone to burn in, the desire and longing to put off an unkindly[8] solitariness by uniting another body (but not without a fit soul) to his in the cheerful society of wedlock. Which if it were so needful before the fall, when man was much more perfect in himself, how much more is it needful now against all the sorrows and casualties of this life to have an intimate and speaking help, a ready and reviving associate in marriage; whereof who misses, by chancing on a mute and spiritless mate, remains more alone than before and in a burning less to be contained than that which is fleshly and more to be considered, as being more deeply rooted even in the faultless innocence of nature.

As for that other burning, which is but as it were the venom of a lusty and over-abounding concoction, strict life and labor, with the abatement of a full diet, may keep that low and obedient enough; but this pure and more inbred desire of joining to itself in conjugal fellowship a fit conversing soul (which desire is properly called love) *is stronger than death*, as the spouse of Christ thought; *many waters cannot quench it, neither can the floods drown it.*[9] This is that rational burning that marriage is to remedy, not to be allayed with fasting nor with any penance to be subdued, which how can he assuage who by mishap hath met the unmeetest and most unsuitable mind? Who hath the power to struggle with an intelligible flame, not in

---

7. "Doth God take care for oxen?" (1 Cor. 9:9). Where Paul allegorizes Deut. 25:4, which prohibits the muzzling of an ox, Milton allegorizes Paul, whom he thinks cannot be referring merely to carnal lust in 1 Cor. 7:9.
8. Unnatural.
9. Song of Sol. 8:6–7; in a traditional Christian allegorical reading, the passage describes the love between Christ and his spouse, the Church.

Paradise to be resisted, become now more ardent by being failed of
what in reason it looked for; and even then most unquenched when
the importunity of a provender-burning[1] is well enough appeased,
and yet the soul hath obtained nothing of what it justly desires.
Certainly such a one forbidden to divorce is in effect forbidden to
marry and compelled to greater difficulties than in a single life. For
if there be not a more human burning which marriage must satisfy,
or else may be dissolved, than that of copulation, marriage cannot
be honorable for the mere reducing and terminating of lust between
two—seeing many beasts in voluntary and chosen couples live
together as unadulterously and are as truly married in that respect.

But all ingenuous men will see that the dignity and blessing of
marriage is placed rather in the mutual enjoyment of that which the
wanting soul needfully seeks than of that which the plenteous body
would jollily give away. Hence it is that Plato in his festival discourse
brings in Socrates relating what he feigned to have learned from the
Prophetess Diotima, how Love was the son of Penury, begot of
Plenty in the garden of Jupiter.[2] Which divinely sorts with that
which in effect Moses tells us, that Love was the son of Loneliness,
begot in Paradise by that sociable and helpful aptitude which God
implanted between man and woman toward each other. The same
also is that burning mentioned by St. Paul whereof marriage ought
to be the remedy; the flesh hath other mutual and easy curbs which
are in the power of any temperate man. When therefore this original
and sinless Penury or loneliness of the soul cannot lay itself down by
the side of such a meet and acceptable union as God ordained in
marriage, at least in some proportion, it cannot conceive and bring
forth Love but remains utterly unmarried under a formal wedlock
and still burns in the proper meaning of St. Paul. Then enters Hate,
not that hate that sins but that which only is natural dissatisfaction
and the turning aside from a mistaken object; if that mistake have
done injury, it fails not to dismiss with recompense; for to retain still
and not be able to love is to heap up more injury. Thence this wise
and pious law of dismission now defended took beginning.

He therefore who, lacking of his due in the most native and
humane end of marriage, thinks it better to part than to live sadly
and injuriously to that cheerful covenant (for not to be beloved and
yet retained is the greatest injury to a gentle spirit)—he, I say, who
therefore seeks to part, is one who highly honors the married life
and would not stain it: and the reasons which now move him to
divorce are equal to the best of those that could first warrant him to
marry; for, as was plainly shown, both the hate which now diverts

1. Human sexual desire is compared to an animal's appetite for hay or oats.
2. Diotima, in Plato's *Symposium*, 203, describes the union of Penia (poverty) and Poros
   (plenty), which produced Eros (love). Milton compares this to God's creation of Eve as
   a result of Adam's loneliness (Gen. 2:18–24).

him and the loneliness which leads him still powerfully to seek a fit help hath not the least grain of a sin in it, if he be worthy to understand himself.

The third Reason of this Law, because without it he who
hath happened where he find nothing but remediless
offenses and discontents is in more and greater temptations
than ever before.

Thirdly, yet it is next to be feared, if he must be still bound without reason by a deaf rigor, that when he perceives the just expectance of his mind defeated, he will begin even against law to cast about where he may find his satisfaction more complete, unless he be a thing heroically virtuous, and that are not the common lump of men, for whom chiefly the laws ought to be made—though not to their sins, yet to their unsinning weaknesses, it being above their strength to endure the lonely estate which while they shunned they are fallen into. And yet there follows upon this a worse temptation. For if he be such as hath spent his youth unblamably and laid up his chiefest earthly comforts in the enjoyment of a contented marriage, nor did neglect that furtherance which was to be obtained herein by constant prayers, when he shall find himself bound fast to an uncomplying discord of nature or, as it oft happens, to an image of earth and phlegm, with whom he looked to be the copartner of a sweet and gladsome society, and sees withal that his bondage is now inevitable, though he be almost the strongest Christian, he will be ready to despair in virtue and mutine[3] against divine providence. And this doubtless is the reason of those lapses and that melancholy despair which we see in many wedded persons, though they understand it not or pretend other causes, because they know no remedy, and is of extreme danger. Therefore when human frailty surcharged is at such a loss, charity ought to venture much and use bold physic, lest an over-tossed faith endanger to shipwreck.

The fourth reason of this law, that God regards love
and peace in the family more than a compulsive
performance of marriage, which is more broke by a
grievous continuance than by a needful divorce.

Fourthly, marriage is a covenant the very being whereof consists not in a forced cohabitation and counterfeit performances of duties

---

3. Mutiny. "Phlegm": one of the four bodily humors, an excess of which was thought to cause sluggishness and apathy.

but in unfeigned love and peace. And of matrimonial love no doubt
but that was chiefly meant which by the ancient sages was thus
parabled: that Love, if he be not twin-born, yet hath a brother wondrous like him called Anteros,[4] whom while he seeks all about, his
chance is to meet with many false and feigning desires that wander
singly up and down in his likeness. By them in their borrowed garb,
Love—though not wholly blind, as poets wrong him, yet having but
one eye, as being born an archer aiming, and that eye not the quickest in this dark region here below, which is not Love's proper sphere,
partly out of the simplicity and credulity which is native to him,
often deceived—embraces and consorts him with these obvious and
suborned striplings as if they were his mother's own sons, for so he
thinks them, while they subtly keep themselves most on his blind
side. But after a while, as his manner is, when soaring up into the
high tower of his *apogaeum*,[5] above the shadow of the earth, he
darts out the direct rays of his then most piercing eyesight upon the
impostures and trim disguises that were used with him and discerns
that this is not his genuine brother, as he imagined, he has no longer
the power to hold fellowship with such a personated mate. For
straight his arrows loose their golden heads and shed their purple
feathers, his silken braids[6] untwine and slip their knots, and that
original and fiery virtue given him by fate all on a sudden goes out
and leaves him undeified and despoiled of all his force; till finding
Anteros at last, he kindles and repairs the almost faded ammunition
of his deity by the reflection of a coequal and homogeneal fire.

Thus mine author sung it to me; and by the leave of those who
would be counted the only grave ones, this is no mere amatòrious
novel (though to be wise and skillful in these matters, men heretofore of greatest name in virtue have esteemed it one of the highest
arcs that human contemplation circling upward can make from the
glassy sea[7] whereon she stands), but this is a deep and serious verity, showing us that love in marriage cannot live nor subsist unless
it be mutual; and where love cannot be, there can be left of wedlock
nothing but the empty husk of an outside matrimony, as undelight-
ful and unpleasing to God as any other kind of hypocrisy. So far is
his command from tying men to the observance of duties which
there is no help for, but they must be dissembled. If Solomon's
advice be not over-frolic, *Live joyfully*, saith he, *with the wife whom*

---

4. Lit., "love returned," or reciprocated love. The son of Ares and Aphrodite, given to his
   lonely brother, Eros (or Cupid), as a playmate, the rationale being that love must be
   answered if it is to prosper.
5. Apogee, the point at which the moon or a planet is at its greatest distance from the earth.
6. Of his bowstring.
7. "And before the throne there was a sea of glass like unto crystal" (Rev. 4:6). "Mine
   author": no source has been found; perhaps Milton's own poetic insight.

thou lovest, all thy days, for that is thy portion [Eccles. 9:9]. How,
then, where we find it impossible to rejoice or to love, can we obey
this precept? How miserably do we defraud ourselves of that comfortable portion which God gives us by striving vainly to glue an
error together which God and nature will not join, adding but more
vexation and violence to that blissful society by our importunate
superstition that will not hearken to St. Paul, 1 Cor. 7, who speaking of marriage and divorce determines plain enough in general
that God therein hath called us to peace and not to bondage. Yea,
God himself commands in his Law more than once, and by his
Prophet Malachi, as Calvin and the best translations read, that he
who hates, let him divorce,[8] that is, he who cannot love. Hence is it
that the Rabbins, and Maimonides famous among the rest in a
book of his set forth by Buxtorfius,[9] tells us that divorce was permitted by Moses to preserve peace in marriage and quiet in the
family. Surely the Jews had their saving peace about them as well as
we, yet care was taken that this wholesome provision for household
peace should also be allowed them; and must this be denied to
Christians? O perverseness! that the Law should be made more
provident of peacemaking than the Gospel! That the Gospel should
be put to beg a most necessary help of mercy from the Law, but
must not have it; and that to grind in the mill of an undelighted and
servile copulation[1] must be the only forced work of a Christian
marriage, ofttimes with such a yoke-fellow from whom both love
and peace, both nature and religion, mourns to be separated.

I cannot therefore be so diffident as not securely to conclude that
he who can receive nothing of the most important helps in marriage, being thereby disenabled to return that duty which is his
with a clear and hearty countenance; and thus continues to grieve
whom he would not, and is no less grieved, that man ought even for
love's sake and peace to move divorce upon good and liberal conditions to the divorced. And it is a less breach of wedlock to part with

8. The elliptical Hebrew text of Mal. 2:16, which permits opposed readings, is a shibboleth dividing proponents of divorce from those who advocate Christian patience.
Rejecting the apparently more authoritative reading ("For the Lord, the God of Israel,
saith that he hateth putting away" [King James Version and most other translations]),
Milton chooses an alternative more to his liking.
9. Early modern Christian Hebraists, even those who disparaged other "Rabbins" (rabbis), always respected and sometimes revered Moses Maimonides (1135–1204), the
great codifier of rabbinic law and philosopher, whose *Guide of the Perplexed*, originally
written in Arabic, was translated into Latin as *Doctor Perplexorum* (Basel, 1629) by
Johannes Buxtorf the younger (1599–1664), who relied on the Hebrew translation of
the Arabic by Samuel Ibn-Tibbon (1160–1230).
1. Foreshadowing *Samson Agonistes*, whose protagonist, an unfortunate husband, grinds
"at the mill with slaves" (line 41). Milton refers in the last chapter of this treatise to
John Selden's *De Jure Naturali et Gentium* (1640), which includes an extensive philological analysis of "grind" in both Hebrew (*takhan*, in Job 31:10) and Latin (*permolere*,
in a threnody by Horace), a word that connects a female slave's grinding corn between
two millstones and grinding under her master as a sex slave.

wise and quiet consent betimes than still to soil and profane that mystery of joy and union with a polluting sadness and perpetual distemper; for it is not the outward continuing of marriage that keeps whole that covenant, but whosoever does most according to peace and love, whether in marriage or in divorce, he it is that breaks marriage least, it being so often written, that *Love only is the fulfilling of every commandment.*[2]

CHAP. VII.

The fifth reason, that nothing more hinders and disturbs the whole life of a Christian than a matrimony found to be uncurably unfit, and doth the same in effect that an Idolatrous Match.

Fifthly, as those priests of old were not to be long in sorrow, or if they were, they could not rightly execute their function,[3] so every true Christian in a higher order of priesthood is a person dedicate to joy and peace, offering himself a lively sacrifice of praise and thanksgiving, and there is no Christian duty that is not to be seasoned and set off with cheerfulness; which in a thousand outward and intermitting crosses may yet be done well, as in this vale of tears; but in such a bosom-affliction as this, crushing the very foundations of his inmost nature, when he shall be forced to love against a possibility and to use dissimulation against his soul in the perpetual and ceaseless duties of a husband, doubtless his whole duty of serving God must needs be blurred and tainted with a sad unpreparedness and dejection of spirit, wherein God has no delight. Who sees not therefore how much more Christianly it would be to break by divorce that which is more broken by undue and forcible keeping, rather than *to cover the altar of the Lord with continual tears, so that he regardeth not the offering any more* [Malachi 2:13]; rather than that the whole worship of a Christian man's life should languish and fade away beneath the weight of an immeasurable grief and discouragement? And because some think the children of a second matrimony succeeding a divorce would not be a holy seed, it hindered not the Jews from being so; and why should we not think them more holy than the offspring of a former ill-twisted wedlock, begotten only out of a bestial necessity, without any true love or contentment, or joy to their parents? So that in some sense we may call them the *children*

---

2. Although editors cite Rom. 13:10, on love as the fulfilling of the law, Milton himself declares about this passage, "I cited no particular Scripture, but spake a general sense, which might bee collected from many places" (*YP*, 2.750).
3. Jewish law imposed limits on periods of mourning by priests, who were "holy to the Lord" (Lev. 21:1–6).

of wrath[4] and anguish, which will as little conduce to their sanctifying as if they had been bastards. For nothing more than disturbance of mind suspends us from approaching to God—such a disturbance especially as both assaults our faith and trust in God's providence and ends, if there be not a miracle of virtue on either side, not only in bitterness and wrath, the canker of devotion, but in a desperate and vicious carelessness, when he sees himself (without fault of his) trained by a deceitful bait into a snare of misery, betrayed by an alluring ordinance,[5] and then made the thrall of heaviness and discomfort by an undivorcing law of God (as he erroneously thinks, but of man's iniquity, as the truth is). For that God prefers the free and cheerful worship of a Christian before the grievous and exacted observance of an unhappy marriage, besides that the general maxims of religion assure us, will be more manifest by drawing a parallel argument from the ground of divorcing an idolatress, which was, lest he should alienate his heart from the true worship of God. And what difference is there whether she pervert him to superstition by her enticing sorcery or disenable him in the whole service of God through the disturbance of her unhelpful and unfit society and so drive him at last, through murmuring and despair, to thoughts of atheism? Neither doth it lessen the cause of separating in that the one willingly allures him from the faith, the other perhaps unwillingly drives him; for in the account of God it comes all to one, that the wife loses him a servant; and therefore by all the united force of the Decalogue she ought to be disbanded, unless we must set marriage above God and charity, which is the doctrine of devils, no less than forbidding to marry.

CHAP. VIII.

That an idolatrous heretic ought to be divorced after a convenient space given to hope of conversion. That place of [1] Corinthians 7 restored from a two-fold erroneous exposition. And that the common expositors flatly contradict the moral law.

And here by the way to illustrate the whole question of divorce ere this treatise end, I shall not be loath to spend a few lines in hope to give a full resolve of that which is yet so much controverted, whether an idolatrous heretic ought be divorced—to the resolving whereof we must first know that the Jews were commanded to divorce an unbelieving Gentile for two causes: first, because all other nations, especially the Canaanites, were to them unclean; secondly, to avoid

---

4. Whereas St. Paul applies the term (Eph. 2:3) to unregenerate non-Christians, Milton applies it to the unhappy children of angry parents, whatever their religion.
5. The law of marriage.

seducement.[6] That other nations were to the Jews impure, even to
the separating of marriage, will appear out of Exod. 34.16. Deut. 7. 3,
6. compar'd with Ezra 9. 2. also Chap. 10. 10, 11. Nehem. 13. 30.
This was the ground of that doubt raised among the Corinthians by
some of the circumcision, whether an unbeliever were not still to be
counted an unclean thing, so as that they ought to divorce from such
a person. This doubt of theirs St. Paul removes by an evangelical
reason, having respect to that vision of St. Peter, wherein the distinction of clean and unclean being abolished, all living creatures were
sanctified to a pure and Christian use, and mankind especially now
invited by a general call to the covenant of grace [Acts 10:9–28].
Therefore, saith St. Paul, *the unbelieving wife is sanctified by the hus-*
band [1 Corinthians 7:14]—that is, made pure and lawful to his use,
so that he need not put her away for fear lest her unbelief should
defile him, but that if he found her love still towards him, he might
rather hope to win her. The second reason of that divorce was to
avoid seducement, as is proved by comparing those places of the Law
to that which Ezra and Nehemiah did by divine warrant in compelling the Jews to forgo their wives.[7] And this reason is moral and perpetual in the rule of Christian faith without evasion. Therefore, saith
the Apostle, 2 Cor. 6. *Mis-yoke not together with infidels,*[8] which is
interpreted of marriage in the first place. And although the former
legal pollution be now done off, yet there is a spiritual contagion in
idolatry as much to be shunned; and though seducement were not to
be feared, yet where there is no hope of converting, there always
ought to be a certain religious aversation and abhorring, which can
no way sort with marriage: Therefore, saith St. Paul, *What fellowship*
hath righteousness with unrighteousness? what communion hath light
with darkness? what concord hath Christ with Belial? what part hath
he that believeth with an Infidel? [2 Cor. 6:14–15]. And in the next
verse but one he moralizes and makes us liable to that command of
Isaiah, *Wherefore come out from among them and be ye separate, saith*
the Lord; touch not the unclean thing, and I will receive ye [2 Cor.
6:17; Isaiah 52:11]. And this command thus gospellized[9] to us hath
the same force with that whereon Ezra grounded the pious necessity
of divorcing. Neither had he other commission for what he did than
such a general command in Deut. as this, nay not so direct as this;

6. The case of an idolatrous spouse bears on Eve's idolatrous worship of the tree (*PL*,
9.795–804) and on Dalila's worship of Dagon.
7. Ezra 10:1–16 and Neh. 13:23–30 describe the people's divorce of foreign wives: "Ye
shall not give your daughters unto their sons, nor take their daughters unto your sons,
or for yourselves" (v. 25).
8. Milton's own translation of Paul's opening words lends domestic specificity to verses
that urge a general separation of righteousness from wickedness.
9. Imparted according to the spirit of the Gospel. (Milton places Paul's general statement
into a context of marriage.)

for he is bid there not to marry but not bid to divorce, and yet we see with what a zeal and confidence he was the author of a general divorce between the faithful and unfaithful seed.

The Gospel is more plainly on his side, according to three of the evangelists, than the words of the Law; for where the case of divorce is handled with such a severity as was fittest to aggravate the fault of unbounded license, yet still in the same chapter, when it comes into question afterwards whether any civil respect, or natural relation which is dearest, may be our plea to divide, or hinder, or but delay our duty to religion, we hear it determined that father and mother, and wife also, is not only to be hated but forsaken, if we mean to inherit the great reward there promised.[1] Nor will it suffice to be put off by saying we must forsake them only by not consenting or not complying with them, for that were to be done, and roundly too, though being of the same faith they should but seek out of a fleshly tenderness to weaken our Christian fortitude with worldly persuasions or but to unsettle our constancy with timorous and softening suggestions—as we may read with what a vehemence Job, the patientest of men, rejected the desperate counsels of his wife [Job 2:9–10]; and Moses, the meekest, being thoroughly offended with the profane speeches of Zipporah, sent her back to her father.[2] But if they shall perpetually at our elbow seduce us from the true worship of God, or defile and daily scandalize our conscience by their hopeless continuance in misbelief, then even in the due progress of reason and that ever-equal proportion which justice proceeds by, it cannot be imagined that this cited place commands less than a total and final separation from such an adherent, at least that no force should be used to keep them together—while we remember that God commanded Abraham to send away his irreligious wife and her son for the offenses which they gave in a pious family.[3] And it may be guessed that David for the like cause disposed of Michal in such a sort as little differed from a dismission.[4] Therefore, against reiterated scandals and seducements which never cease, much more can no other remedy or retirement be found but absolute departure. For what kind of matrimony can that remain to be, what one duty between such can be performed as it should be from the heart, when their thoughts and spirits fly asunder as far as heaven from hell, especially if the

1. "If any man come to me, and hate not his father, and mother, and wife, and children, and brethren, and sisters, yea, and his own life also, he cannot be my disciple" (Luke 14:26; cf. 18:29–30).
2. Milton seems to regard Zipporah's cryptic remark "Surely a bloody husband art thou to me" (Exod. 4:25) as offensive to her husband, Moses, whose life she has just saved. Exod. 18:2 states without explanation that Moses had sent her back to her father's house.
3. Milton shows less pity than God for the plight of Hagar and Ishmael (Gen. 21:9–20).
4. Although the Bible gives no reason for Michal's barrenness, Milton seems to attribute it to David's refusal to share her bed, which would resemble a "dismission." (2 Sam. 6:23).

time that hope should send forth her expected blossoms be passed in
vain. It will easily be true that a father or brother may be hated zealously[5] and loved civilly or naturally; for those duties may be performed at distance and do admit of any long absence. But how the
peace and perpetual cohabitation of marriage can be kept, how that
benevolent and intimate communion of body can be held with one
that must be hated with a most operative hatred, must be forsaken
and yet continually dwelt with and accompanied,[6] he who can distinguish hath the gift of an affection very oddly divided and contrived. While others both just and wise, and Solomon among the rest
[1 Kings 11:1–8)], if they may not hate and forsake as Moses enjoins
and the Gospel imports, will find it impossible not to love otherwise
than will sort with the love of God, whose jealousy brooks no co-
rival. And whether is more likely, that Christ bidding to forsake wife
for religion meant it by divorce as Moses meant it, whose Law,
grounded on moral reason, was both his office and his essence to
maintain; or that he should bring a new morality into religion, not
only new but contrary to an unchangeable command and dangerously derogating from our love and worship of God? As if when
Moses had bid divorce absolutely, and Christ had said, hate and forsake, and his Apostle had said, no communion with Christ and
Belial; yet that Christ after all this could be understood to say,
divorce not, no, not for religion, seduce or seduce not. What mighty
and invisible remora is this in matrimony able to demur and to contemn all the divorcive engines in heaven or earth—both which may
now pass away if this be true, for more than many jots or tittles, a
whole moral law is abolished.[7] But if we dare believe it is not,[8] then
in the method of religion and to save the honor and dignity of our
faith, we are to retreat and gather up ourselves from the observance
of an inferior and civil ordinance to the strict maintaining of a general and religious command, which is written, *Thou shalt make no
covenant with them,* Deut. 7. 2, 3; and that covenant which cannot
be lawfully made, we have directions and examples lawfully to dissolve. Also 2 Chron. 19. 2. *Shouldst thou love them that hate the
Lord?* No, doubtless: for there is a certain scale of duties, there is a
certain hierarchy of upper and lower commands, which for want of
studying in right order all the world is in confusion.

5. In the way of religious zeal or devotion.
6. Includes the meaning "cohabited with."
7. "Till heaven and earth pass, one jot or one tittle shall in no wise pass from the law"
   (Matt. 5:18). "Remora": the sucking fish believed by the ancients to have the power of
   controlling the course of a ship to which it has attached itself.
8. I.e., not true that Christ prohibited divorce.

Upon these principles I answer that a right believer ought to divorce an idolatrous heretic, unless upon better hopes: however, that it is in the believer's choice to divorce or not.

The former part will be manifest thus: first, that an apostate idolater, whether husband or wife seducing, was to die by the decree of God, Deut. 13. 6, 9. That marriage therefore God himself disjoins. For others born idolaters, the moral reason of their dangerous keeping and the incommunicable antagony that is between Christ and Belial will be sufficient to enforce the commandment of those two inspired reformers Ezra and Nehemiah to put an idolater away as well under the Gospel.

The latter part, that although there be no seducement feared, yet if there be no hope given the divorce is lawful, will appear by this: that idolatrous marriage is still hateful to God; therefore still it may be divorced by the pattern of that warrant that Ezra had and by the same everlasting reason. Neither can any man give an account wherefore, if those whom God joins no man can separate, it should not follow that whom he joins not, but hates to join, those man ought to separate. But, saith the lawyer, that which ought not to have been done, once done, avails. I answer, this is but a crotchet of the law, but that brought against it is plain Scripture. As for what Christ spake concerning divorce, 'tis confessed by all knowing men he meant only between them of the same faith. But what shall we say then to St. Paul, who seems to bid us not divorce an infidel willing to stay? We may safely say thus, that wrong collections have been hitherto made out of those words by modern divines. His drift, as was heard before, is plain: not to command our stay in marriage with an infidel—that had been a flat renouncing of the religious and moral Law—but to inform the Corinthians that the body of an unbeliever was not defiling, if his desire to live in Christian wedlock showed any likelihood that his heart was opening to the faith. And therefore advises to forbear departure so long till nothing have been neglected to set forward a conversion. This I say he advises, and that with certain cautions, not commands, if we can take up so much credit for him as to get him believed upon his own word. For what is this else but his counsel in a thing indifferent, *to the rest speak I, not the Lord* [1 Cor. 7:12]. For though it be true that the Lord never spake it, yet from St. Paul's mouth we should have took it as a command, had not himself forewarned us and disclaimed, which, notwithstanding, if we shall still avouch to be a command, he palpably denying it, this is not to expound St. Paul but to outface[9] him.

Neither doth it follow but that the Apostle may interpose his judgment in a case of Christian liberty without the guilt of adding

9. To maintain something false or shameful with boldness or effrontery.

to God's word. How do we know marriage or single life to be of choice but by such like words as these: *I speak this by permission, not of commandment; I have no command of the Lord, yet I give my judgment* [1 Cor. 7:6, 25]. Why shall not the like words have leave to signify a freedom in this our present question, though Beza deny?[1] Neither is the Scripture hereby less inspired because St. Paul confesses to have written therein what he had not of command; for we grant that the spirit of God led him thus to express himself to Christian prudence in a matter which God thought best to leave uncommanded. Beza therefore must be warily read when he taxes St. Austin of blasphemy for holding that St. Paul spake here as of a thing indifferent.[2]

But if it must be a command, I shall yet the more evince it to be a command that we should herein be left free, and that out of the Greek word used in the 12. v., which instructs us plainly, there must be a joint assent and good liking on both sides. He that will not deprave the text must thus render it: *If a brother have an unbelieving wife, and she join in consent to dwell with him* (which cannot utter less to us than a mutual agreement), let him not put her away for the mere surmise of Judaical uncleanness; and the reason follows: for the body of an infidel is not polluted, neither to benevolence nor to procreation. Moreover, this note of mutual complacency forbids all offer of seducement,[3] which to a person of zeal cannot be attempted without great offense. If therefore seducement be feared, this place hinders not divorce.

Another caution was put in this supposed command, of not bringing the believer into bondage hereby, which doubtless might prove extreme, if Christian liberty and conscience were left to the humor of a pagan staying at pleasure to play with or to vex and wound with a thousand scandals and burdens above strength to bear.[4] If therefore the conceived hope of gaining a soul come to nothing, then charity commands that the believer be not wearied out with endless waiting under many grievances sore to his spirit, but that respect be had rather to the present suffering of a true Christian than the uncertain winning of an obdured heretic. The counsel we have from St. Paul to hope cannot countermand the moral and evangelic charge we have from God to fear seducement, to separate from the misbeliever, the unclean, the obdurate. The Apostle wisheth us to hope

---

1. In his commentary on 1 Cor. 7:15, Theodore Beza (1519–1605), the great French Protestant scholar and theologian, insisted that Paul's statement, "If the unbeliever depart, let him depart," in no way altered Christ's pronouncement that adultery was the only cause of divorce.
2. Beza believes that Augustine distorts the word *permission* ("I speak this by permission, and not of commandment") in 7:6, but he does not accuse him of blasphemy.
3. I.e., to idolatry.
4. Cf. *Samson Agonistes*, lines 748–65.

but does not send us a wool-gathering after vain hope. He saith, *How knowest thou, O man, whether thou shalt save thy wife?* [1 Cor. 7:16]—that is, till he try all due means and set some reasonable time to himself, after which he may give over washing an Ethiope, if he will hear the advice of the Gospel: *Cast not pearls before swine* [Matthew 7:6], saith Christ himself. *Let him be to thee as a heathen* [18:7]. *Shake the dust off thy feet* [10:14]. If this be not enough, *hate and forsake*, what relation soever. And this also that follows must appertain to the precept, *Let every man wherein he is called therein abide with God* [1 Cor. 7:24]—that is, so walking in his inferior calling of marriage as not by dangerous subjection to that ordinance, to hinder and disturb the higher calling of his Christianity. Last, and never too oft remembered, whether this be a command or an advice, we must look that it be so understood as not to contradict the least point of moral religion that God hath formerly commanded; otherwise what do we but set the moral Law and the Gospel at civil war together, and who then shall be able to serve these two masters?

CHAP. IX.

*That adultery is not the greatest breach of matrimony;
that there may be other violations as great.*

Now whether idolatry or adultery be the greatest violation of marriage, if any demand, let him thus consider, that among Christian writers touching matrimony there be three chief ends thereof agreed on: Godly society, next civil, and thirdly, that of the marriage-bed.[5] Of these the first in name to be the highest and most excellent, no baptized man can deny, nor that idolatry smites directly against this prime end, nor that such as the violated end is, such is the violation; but he who affirms adultery to be the highest breach, affirms the bed to be the highest of marriage, which is in truth a gross and boorish opinion, how common soever—as far from the countenance of Scripture as from the light of all clean philosophy or civil nature. And out of question the cheerful help that may be in marriage toward sanctity of life is the purest and so the noblest end of that contract. But if the particular of each person be considered, then of those three ends which God appointed, that to him is greatest which is most necessary; and marriage is then most broken to him when he utterly wants the fruition of that which he most sought therein, whether it were religious, civil, or corporal society. Of which wants to do him right by divorce only for the last and meanest is a perverse injury,

---

5. Most religious writers on marriage would have also have mentioned having children.

and the pretended reason of it as frigid as frigidity itself, which the Code[6] and canon are only sensible of.

Thus much of this controversy. I now return to the former argument.[7] And having shown that disproportion, contrariety, or numbness of mind may justly be divorced, by proving already that the prohibition thereof opposes the express end of God's institution, suffers not marriage to satisfy that intellectual and innocent desire which God himself kindled in man to be the bond of wedlock, but only to remedy a sublunary and bestial burning, which frugal diet, without marriage, would easily chasten. Next, that it drives many to transgress the conjugal bed, while the soul wanders after that satisfaction which it had hope to find at home but hath missed. Or else it sits repining even to atheism, finding itself hardly dealt with, but misdeeming the cause to be in God's Law which is in man's unrighteous ignorance. I have shown also how it unties the inward knot of marriage, which is peace and love (if that can be untied which was never knit) while it aims to keep fast the outward formality; how it lets perish the Christian man, to compel impossibly the married man.

CHAP. X.

*The sixth reason of this law, that to prohibit divorce
sought for natural causes is against nature.*

The sixth place declares this prohibition to be as respectless of human nature as it is of religion and therefore is not of God. He teaches that an unlawful marriage may be lawfully divorced, and that those who having thoroughly discerned each other's disposition, which ofttimes cannot be till after matrimony, shall then find a powerful reluctance and recoil of nature on either side blasting all the content of their mutual society, that such persons are not lawfully married; to use the Apostle's words, *Say I these things as a man, or saith not the Law also the same? For it is written*, Deut. 22[:9–10]. *Thou shalt not sow thy vineyard with different seeds, lest thou defile both. Thou shalt not plow with an ox and an ass together*; and the like. I follow the pattern of St. Paul's reasoning: *Doth God care for asses and oxen, how ill they yoke together, or is it not said altogether for our sakes? For our sakes no doubt this is written* [1 Cor. 9:9–10].[8] Yea, the Apostle himself, in the fore-cited 2 Cor. 6. 14, alludes from that place of Deut. to forbid mis-yoking marriage, as by the Greek

6. The *Corpus Juris Civilis*, issued from 529 to 534 by order of the emperor Justinian, stands in here for the entire body of civil law.
7. Regarding marriage to an idolatrous heretic.
8. Milton's allegory would derive a law prohibiting marriage between incompatible partners from the Deuteronomic laws against sowing with diverse seeds and plowing with an ox and ass together.

word is evident, though he instance but in one example of mis-
matching with an infidel; yet next to that, what can be a fouler
incongruity, a greater violence to the reverend secret of nature, than
to force a mixture of minds that cannot unite and to sow the furrow
of man's nativity with seed of two incoherent and incombining dispositions. Which act being kindly and voluntary, as it ought, the
Apostle in the language he wrote called *eunoia* and the Latins
benevolence [1 Cor. 7:3], intimating the original thereof to be in the
understanding and the will. If not, surely there is nothing which
might more properly be called a malevolence rather, and is the most
injurious and unnatural tribute that can be extorted from a person
endowed with reason to be made pay out the best substance of his
body, and of his soul too, as some think,[9] when either for just and
powerful causes he cannot like, or from unequal causes finds not
recompense. And that there is a hidden efficacy of love and hatred
in man as well as in other kinds, not moral but natural, which
though not always in the choice yet in the success of marriage will
ever be most predominant, besides daily experience, the author of
Ecclesiasticus, whose wisdom hath set him next the Bible, acknowledges, 13. 16. *A man*, saith he, *will cleave to his like*. But what might
be the cause, whether each one's allotted genius or proper star, or
whether the supernal influence of schemes and angular aspects, or
this elemental crasis[1] here below, whether all these jointly or singly
meeting friendly or unfriendly in either party, I dare not, with the
men I am like to clash, appear so much a philosopher as to conjecture. The ancient proverb in Homer, less abstruse, entitles this work
of leading each like person to his like peculiarly to God himself:[2]
which is plain enough also by his naming of a meet or like help in
the first espousal instituted; and that every woman is meet for every
man, none so absurd as to affirm. Seeing then there is indeed a two-
fold seminary or stock in nature, from whence are derived the issues
of love and hatred distinctly flowing through the whole mass of created things, and that God's doing ever is to bring the due likenesses
and harmonies of his works together, except when out of two contraries met to their own destruction he molds a third existence, and
that it is error or some evil angel which either blindly or maliciously
hath drawn together in two persons ill embarked in wedlock the
sleeping discords and enmities of nature lulled on purpose with

9. This anticipates the materialist and monist philosophy (the unity of body/soul, matter/
   spirit) as spelled out in Milton's *De Doctrina Christiana*: "If the soul is wholly contained in all the body and wholly in any given part of that body, how can the human
   seed, that intimate and most noble part of the body, be imagined destitute and devoid
   of the soul of the parents, or at least of the father, when communicated to the son in
   the act of generation?" (1.7).
1. Blending of elements; in the human body, composition, temperament.
2. "God brings like unto like" (Od., 17.218). "Entitles": assigns.

some false bait, that they may wake to agony and strife later than prevention could have wished; if from the bent of just and honest intentions beginning what was begun and so continuing, all that is equal, all that is fair and possible hath been tried, and no accommodation likely to succeed, what folly is it still to stand combating and battering against invincible causes and effects, with evil upon evil, till either the best of our days be lingered out, or ended with some speeding sorrow. The wise Ecclesiasticus advises rather, 37. 27. *My son prove thy soul in thy life, see what is evil for it, and give not that unto it.* Reason he had to say so; for if the noisomeness[3] or disfigurement of body can soon destroy the sympathy of mind to wedlock duties, much more will the annoyance and trouble of mind infuse itself into all the faculties and acts of the body to render them invalid, unkindly, and even unholy against the fundamental lawbook of nature, which Moses never thwarts but reverences. Therefore he commands us to force nothing against sympathy[4] or natural order, no not upon the most abject creatures, to show that such an indignity cannot be offered to man without an impious crime. And certainly those divine meditating words of finding out a meet and like help to man have in them a consideration of more than the indefinite likeness of womanhood; nor are they to be made wastepaper on for the dullness of canon-divinity; no, nor those other allegoric precepts of beneficence fetched out of the closet of nature to teach us goodness and compassion in not compelling together unmatchable societies; or if they meet through mischance, by all consequence to disjoin them, as God and nature signifies and lectures to us not only by those recited decrees but even by the first and last of all his visible works, when by his divorcing command[5] the world first rose out of chaos, nor can be renewed again out of confusion but by the separating of unmeet consorts.

CHAP. XI.

The seventh reason, That sometimes continuance in marriage
may be evidently the shortening or endangering of life
to either party, both law and divinity concluding that life
is to be preferred before marriage, the intended solace of life.

Seventhly, The canon law and divines consent that if either party be found contriving against another's life, they may be severed by divorce, for a sin against the life of marriage is greater than a sin against the bed: the one destroys, the other but defiles. The same

---

3. Offensiveness.
4. An affinity between persons based in nature and beyond the will's control; the opposite of antipathy.
5. "God divided the light from the darkness" (Gen. 1:4).

may be said touching those persons who being of a pensive nature and course of life have summed up all their solace in that free and lightsome conversation which God and man intends in marriage; whereof when they see themselves deprived by meeting an unsociable consort, they ofttimes resent one another's mistake so deeply that long it is not ere grief end one of them. When therefore this danger is foreseen, that the life is in peril by living together, what matter is it whether helpless grief or willful practice be the cause? This is certain, that the preservation of life is more worth than the compulsory keeping of marriage; and it is no less than cruelty to force a man to remain in that state as the solace of his life which he and his friends know will be either the undoing or the disheartening of his life. And what is life without the vigor and spiritful exercise of life? How can it be useful either to private or public employment? Shall it therefore be quite dejected, though never so valuable, and left to moulder away in heaviness for the superstitious and impossible performance of an ill-driven bargain? Nothing more inviolable than vows made to God; yet we read in Numbers [30:7–9] that if a wife had made such a vow, the mere will and authority of her husband might break it. How much more may he break the error of his own bonds with an unfit and mistaken wife to the saving of his welfare, his life, yea his faith and virtue from the hazard of over-strong temptations? For if man be lord of the Sabbath to the curing of a fever [Matt. 12:8–12], can he be less than lord of marriage in such important causes as these?

CHAP. XII.

The eighth reason, It is probable, or rather certain, that everyone who happens to marry hath not the calling; and therefore, upon unfitness found and considered, force ought not to be used.

Eighthly, it is most sure that some even of those who are not plainly defective in body yet are destitute of all other marriageable gifts and consequently have not the calling to marry, unless nothing be requisite thereto but a mere instrumental body; which to affirm is to that unanimous[6] covenant a reproach. Yet it is as sure that many such, not of their own desire but by the persuasion of friends or not knowing themselves, do often enter into wedlock; where finding the difference at length between the duties of a married life and the gifts of a single life, what unfitness of mind, what wearisomness, what scruples and doubts to an incredible offense and displeasure are like to follow between may be soon imagined; whom thus to shut

6. Of one mind.

up and immure together, the one with a mischosen mate, the other in a mistaken calling, is not a course that Christian wisdom and tenderness ought to use. As for the custom that some parents and guardians have of forcing marriages, it will be better to say nothing of such a savage inhumanity but only this, that the law which gives not all freedom of divorce to any creature endued with reason so assassinated[7] is next in cruelty.

CHAP. XIII.

The ninth reason; Because marriage is not a mere carnal coition but a human society; where that cannot reasonably be had, there can be no true matrimony. Marriage compared with all other covenants and vows warrantably broken for the good of man. Marriage the papist's sacrament and unfit marriage the Protestant's idol.

Ninthly, I suppose it will be allowed us that marriage is a human society, and that all human society must proceed from the mind rather than the body, else it would be but a kind of animal or beastish meeting. If the mind, therefore, cannot have that due company by marriage that it may reasonably and humanly desire, that marriage can be no human society but a certain formality or gilding over of little better than a brutish congress, and so in very wisdom and pureness to be dissolved.

But marriage is more than human, *the covenant of God*, Prov. 2. 17; therefore, man cannot dissolve it. I answer, if it be more than human, so much the more it argues the chief society thereof to be in the soul rather than in the body, and the greatest breach thereof to be unfitness of mind rather than defect of body; for the body can have least affinity in a covenant more than human, so that the reason of dissolving holds good the rather. Again I answer that the Sabbath is a higher institution, a command of the first table,[8] for the breach whereof God hath far more and oftener testified his anger than for divorces, which from Moses to Malachi he never took displeasure at, nor then neither if we mark the text;[9] and yet as oft as the good of man is concerned, he not only permits but commands to break the Sabbath. What covenant more contracted with God and less in man's power than the vow which hath once passed his lips? Yet if it be found rash, if offensive, if unfruitful either to God's glory or the good of man, our doctrine forces not error and unwillingness irksomly to keep it but counsels wisdom and better

---

7. Treacherously attacked or destroyed.
8. "Remember the Sabbath day, to keep it holy" (Exod. 20:8) belongs to the *first* of the two tablets of the decalogue, which prescribe religious and moral duties, respectively.
9. See Milton's alternative translation of Mal. 2:16 in chapter 6.

thoughts boldly to break it; therefore, to enjoin the indi,
keeping of a marriage found unfit against the good of ma\
soul and body, as hath been evidenced, is to make an idol ot ...
riage, to advance it above the worship of God and the good of man,
to make it a transcendent command above both the second and first
table, which is a most prodigious doctrine.

Next, whereas they cite out of the Proverbs [2:17] that it is *the
covenant of God* and therefore more than human, that consequence
is manifestly false; for so the covenant which Zedekiah made with
the infidel king of Babel is called *the covenant of God*, Ezek. 17. 19,
which would be strange to hear counted more than a human covenant. So every covenant between man and man, bound by oath, may
be called the covenant of God, because God therein is attested. So
of marriage he is the author and the witness; yet hence will not follow any divine astriction[1] more than what is subordinate to the glory
of God and the main good of either party. For as the glory of God
and their esteemed fitness one for the other was the motive which
led them both at first to think without other revelation that God had
joined them together; so when it shall be found by their apparent
unfitness that their continuing to be man and wife is against the
glory of God and their mutual happiness, it may assure them that
God never joined them—who hath revealed his gracious will not
to set the ordinance above the man for whom it was ordained; not
to canonize marriage either as a tyranness or a goddess over the
enfranchised life and soul of man. For wherein can God delight,
wherein be worshiped, wherein be glorified by the forcible continuing of an improper and ill-yoking couple? He that loved not to see
the disparity of several cattle at the plow[2] cannot be pleased with
any vast unmeetness in marriage. Where can be the peace and love
which must invite God to such a house? May it not be feared that
the not divorcing of such a helpless disagreement will be the divorcing of God finally from such a place?

But it is a trial of our patience, they say. I grant it; but which of
Job's afflictions were sent him with that law that he might not use
means to remove any of them if he could? And what if it subvert our
patience and our faith too? Who shall answer for the perishing of all
those souls perishing by stubborn expositions of particular and inferior precepts against the general and supreme rule of charity? They
dare not affirm that marriage is either a sacrament[3] or a mystery,
though all those sacred things give place to man; and yet they invest

---

1. Obligation, binding.
2. The Deuteronomic prohibition against plowing with an ox and an ass together, which
Milton discusses in chapter 10.
3. Milton's opponents, anxious to avoid association with Roman Catholicism, "dare not"
call marriage a sacrament.

it with such an awful sanctity and give it such adamantine chains to bind with, as if it were to be worshipped like some Indian deity, when it can confer no blessing upon us but works more and more to our misery. To such teachers the saying of St. Peter at the Council of Jerusalem will do well to be applied: *Why tempt ye God to put a yoke upon the necks* of Christian men, which neither the *Jews,* God's ancient people, *nor we are able to bear* [Acts 15:10], and nothing but unwary expounding hath brought upon us?

CHAP. XIV.

Considerations concerning Familism, Antinomianism, and why it may be thought that such opinions may proceed from the undue restraint of some just liberty, than which no greater cause to contemn discipline.

To these considerations this also may be added as no improbable conjecture, seeing that sort of men who follow Anabaptism, Familism, Antinomianism, and other fanatic dreams (if we understand them not amiss)[4] be such most commonly as are by nature addicted to a zeal of religion, of life also not debauched, and that their opinions having full swing do end in satisfaction of the flesh, it may come with reason into the thoughts of a wise man whether all this proceed not partly, if not chiefly, from the restraint of some lawful liberty which ought to be given men and is denied them—as by physic we learn in menstruous bodies, where nature's current hath been stopped, that the suffocation and upward forcing of some lower part affects the head and inward sense with dotage and idle fancies. And on the other hand, whether the rest of vulgar men not so religiously professing do not give themselves much the more to whoredom and adulteries, loving the corrupt and venial discipline of clergy-courts but hating to hear of perfect reformation; whenas[5] they foresee that then fornication shall be austerely censured, adultery punished, and marriage, the appointed refuge of nature, though it hap to be never so incongruous and displeasing, must yet of force be worn out, when it can be to no other purpose

4. The condemnation of the first edition of this treatise may have caused Milton to add this clause in the second edition, which suggests sympathy with radical sectarians. "Anabaptists": insisted on adult baptism. "Familists": or the Family of Love, practiced a perfectionist theology, aspiring to a natural state of grace without sin. They, like many other radical Protestant sects (and like Milton in *De Doctrina Christiana,* but not in this treatise!), were antinomians, rejecting not only the ceremonial and judicial laws of Moses but also the moral law, including the decalogue, which some Reformed theologians identified with the law of nature innate and implanted in the hearts of all human beings.
5. Seeing that, supposing. This sentence may be corrupt. It seems to state that libertines dread perfect reformation, when they suppose that their sins will be punished and that even the unhappiest marriage will be indissoluble. Presumably, they might marry if they know that under a perfect reformation they would be allowed to divorce.

but of strife and hatred, a thing odious to God. This may be worth the study of skillful men in theology and the reason of things; and lastly to examine whether some undue and ill-grounded strictness upon the blameless nature of man be not the cause, in those places where already reformation is, that the discipline of the church, so often and so unavoidably broken, is brought into contempt and derision. And if it be thus, let those who are still bent to hold this obstinate literality so prepare themselves as to share in the account for all these transgressions, when it shall be demanded at the last day by one who will scan and sift things with more than a literal wisdom of equity. For if these reasons be duly pondered, and that the Gospel is more jealous of laying on excessive burdens than ever the Law was, lest the soul of a Christian, which is inestimable, should be over-tempted and cast away—considering also that many properties of nature, which the power of regeneration itself never alters, may cause dislike of conversing even between the most sanctified, which continually grating in harsh tune together may breed some jar and discord, and that end in rancor and strife, a thing so opposite both to marriage and to Christianity—it would perhaps be less scandal to divorce a natural disparity than to link violently together an unchristian dissension, committing two ensnared souls inevitably to kindle one another not with the fire of love but with a hatred irreconcilable, who, were they dissevered, would be straight friends in any other relation. But if an alphabetical[6] servility must be still urged, it may so fall out that the true Church may unwittingly use as much cruelty in forbidding to divorce as the Church of Antichrist doth wilfully in forbidding to marry.

Book II.

CHAP. I.

The ordinance of Sabbath and marriage compared. Hyperbole no unfrequent figure in the Gospel. Excess cured by contrary excess. Christ neither did nor could abrogate the law of divorce but only reprove the abuse thereof.

Hitherto the position undertaken hath been declared and proved by a law of God; that law proved to be moral and unabolishable for many reasons equal, honest, charitable, just, annexed thereto. It follows now that those places of Scripture which have a seeming to revoke the prudence of Moses, or rather that merciful decree of God, be forthwith explained and reconciled. For what are all these reasonings worth, will some reply, whenas the words of Christ are

6. Literal, strict.

plainly against all divorce, except in case of fornication [Matt. 5:32]? To whom he whose mind were to answer no more but this, *except also in case of charity*, might safely appeal to the more plain words of Christ in defense of so excepting. *Thou shalt do no manner of work*, saith the commandment of the Sabbath [Exod. 20:10]. Yes, saith Christ, works of charity. And shall we be more severe in paraphrasing the considerate and tender Gospel than he was in expounding the rigid and peremptory Law? What was ever in all appearance less made for man and more for God alone than the Sabbath? Yet when the good of man comes into the scales, we hear that voice of infinite goodness and benignity, that *Sabbath was made for man, not man for Sabbath* [Mark 2:27]. What thing ever was more made for man alone and less for God than marriage? And shall we load it with a cruel and senseless bondage utterly against both the good of man and the glory of God? Let who so will now listen, I want neither pall nor miter, I stay neither for ordination nor induction, but in the firm faith of a knowing Christian, which is the best and truest endowment of the keys,[7] I pronounce, the man who shall bind so cruelly a good and gracious ordinance of God hath not in that the spirit of Christ. Yet that every text of Scripture seeming opposite may be attended with a due exposition, this other part ensues and makes account to find no slender arguments for this assertion out of those very Scriptures which are commonly urged against it.

First, therefore, let us remember, as a thing not to be denied, that all places of Scripture wherein just reason of doubt arises from the letter are to be expounded by considering upon what occasion everything is set down and by comparing other texts. The occasion which induced our Savior to speak of divorce was either to convince the extravagance of the Pharisees in that point or to give a sharp and vehement answer to a tempting question.[8] And in such cases that we are not to repose all upon the literal terms of so many words, many instances will teach us, wherein we may plainly discover how Christ meant not to be taken word for word, but like a wise physician, administering one excess against another to reduce us to a perfect mean. Where the Pharisees were strict, there Christ seems remiss; where they were too remiss, he saw it needful to seem most severe. In one place he censures an unchaste look to be adultery already committed [Matt. 5:28]; another time he passes over actual adultery with less reproof than for an unchaste look [John 8:11], not so heavily condemning secret weakness as open malice. So here he may be justly thought to have given this rigid sentence against divorce, not

---

7. In *DDC* 1.29 (*YP*, 6:567), Milton insists that "the keys of the kingdom of heaven are not entrusted to Peter alone."
8. The Pharisees ask Christ if it is "lawful for a man to put away his wife for every cause" (Matthew 19:3).

to cut off all remedy from a good man who finds himself consuming away in a disconsolate and unenjoyed matrimony, but to lay a bridle upon the bold abuses of those over-weening Rabbis; which he could not more effectually do than by a countersway of restraint, curbing their wild exorbitance almost into the other extreme; as when we bow things the contrary way to make them come to their natural straightness. And that this was the only intention of Christ is most evident if we attend but to his own words and protestation made in the same sermon, not many verses before he treats of divorcing, that he came not to abrogate from the law *one jot or tittle* [Matt. 5:18], and denounces against them that shall so teach.

But St. Luke, the verse immediately before-going that of divorce, inserts the same caveat,[9] as if the latter could not be understood without the former, and as a witness to produce against this our wilful mistake of abrogating; which must needs confirm us that whatever else in the political law of more special relation to the Jews might cease to us, yet that of those precepts concerning divorce, not one of them was repealed by the doctrine of Christ—unless we have vowed not to believe his own cautious and immediate profession. For if these our Savior's words inveigh against all divorce and condemn it as adultery, except it be for adultery, and be not rather understood against the abuse of those divorces permitted in the Law, then is that law of Moses, Deut. 24. 1, not only repealed and wholly annulled against the promise of Christ and his known profession not to meddle in matters judicial, but, that which is more strange, the very substance and purpose of that law is contradicted and convinced both of injustice and impurity, as having authorized and maintained legal adultery by statute. Moses also cannot scape to be guilty of unequal and unwise decrees, punishing one act of secret adultery by death and permitting a whole life of open adultery by law. And albeit lawyers write that some political edicts, though not approved, are yet allowed to the scum of the people and the necessity of the times, these excuses have but a weak pulse. For first, we read not that the scoundrel people but the choicest, the wisest, the holiest of that nation have frequently used these laws, or such as these, in the best and holiest times. Secondly, be it yielded that in matters not very bad or impure a human lawgiver may slacken something of that which is exactly good to the disposition of the people and the times; but if the perfect, the pure, the righteous law of God—for so are all his statutes and his judgments—be found to have allowed smoothly, without any certain reprehension, that which Christ afterward declares to be

---

9. In Luke 16:17, Christ insists that "it is easier for heaven and earth to pass, than one tittle of the law to fail," but then immediately (v. 18), in an apparent rejection of the Deuteronomic law of divorce, condemns as an adulterer "Whosoever putteth away his wife and marrieth another."

adultery, how can we free this Law from the horrible indictment of being both impure, unjust, and fallacious?

[In chapter two, Milton argues that the Mosaic law of divorce is indeed a perfect law and neither an indulgence nor a permission: "Neither will it serve to say this was permitted for the hardness of their hearts in that sense as it is usually explained, for the law were then but a corrupt and erroneous schoolmaster, teaching us to dash against a vital maxim of religion, by doing foul evil in hope of some certain good." Milton interprets hardheartedness as a universal condition of infirmity resulting from the Fall.]

CHAP. III.

That to allow sin by law is against the nature of law, the end of the lawgiver, and the good of the people. Impossible therefore in the law of God. That it makes God the author of sin more than anything objected by the Jesuits or Arminians against predestination.

But let us further examine upon what consideration a law of license could be thus given to a holy people for the hardness of heart. I suppose all will answer that for some good end or other. But here the contrary shall be proved. First, that many ill effects but no good end of such a sufferance can be shown; next, that a thing unlawful can for no good end whatever be either done or allowed by a positive law. If there were any good end aimed at, that end was then good either as to the law or to the lawgiver licensing or as to the person licensed. That it could not be the end of the Law, whether moral or judicial, to license a sin, I prove easily out of Rom. 5. 20. *The Law entered that the offense might abound*, that is, that sin might be made abundantly manifest to be heinous and displeasing to God, that so his offered grace might be the more esteemed. Now if the Law, instead of aggravating and terrifying sin, shall give out license, it foils itself and turns recreant from its own end; it forestalls the pure grace of Christ, which is through righteousness, with impure indulgences, which are through sin. And instead of discovering sin, *for by the law is the knowledge thereof*, saith St. Paul [Rom. 3:20], and that by certain and true light for men to walk in safely, it holds out false and dazzling fires to stumble men; or like those miserable flies to run into with delight and be burnt; for how many souls might easily think that to be lawful which the law and magistrate allowed them? Again we read, 1 Tim. 1. 5. *The end of the commandment is charity, out of a pure heart, and of a good conscience, and of faith unfeigned*. But never could that be charity to allow a people what they could not use with a pure heart but with conscience and faith both deceived or else despised. The more particular end of the judicial Law is set forth to us clearly, Rom. 13 [3–4], that God hath given to that Law *a sword not in vain but to be a terror to evil works, a revenge to execute wrath upon him that doth evil.* If this terrible commission should but forbear to punish wickedness, were it other to be accounted than partial and unjust? But if it begin to write indulgence to vulgar uncleanness, can it do more to corrupt and shame the end of its own being? Lastly, if the Law allow sin, it enters into a kind of covenant with sin; and if it do, there is not a greater sinner in the world than the Law itself. The Law, to use an allegory something different from that in Philo Judaeus concerning Amalek,[1] though haply more significant, the Law is the Israelite, and hath this absolute charge given it, Deut. 25 [17–19], *To blot out the memory of* Sin *the Amalekite from under heaven, not to forget it.* Again, the Law is the Israelite and hath this express repeated command, *to make no covenant with* Sin, *the Canaanite* [Deut. 7:1–2], but to expel him, lest he prove a snare. And to say truth, it were too rigid and reasonless to proclaim such an enmity between man and man were it not the type of a greater enmity between Law and Sin.[2] I spake even now as if Sin were condemned in a perpetual villeinage[3] never to be free by Law, never to be manumitted; but sure Sin can have no tenure by Law at all but is rather an eternal outlaw and in hostility with Law past all atonement—both diagonial contraries, as much allowing one another as day and night together in one hemisphere. Or if it be possible that Sin with his darkness may come to composition, it cannot be without a foul eclipse and twilight to the Law, whose brightness ought to surpass the noon. Thus we see how this unclean permittance defeats the sacred and glorious end both of the moral and judicial Law.

As little good can the lawgiver propose to equity by such a lavish remissness as this. If to remedy hardness of heart, Paraeus and other divines confess, it more increases by this liberty than is lessened.[4] And how is it probable that their hearts were more hard in this, that it should be yielded to, than in any other crime? Their hearts were set upon usury and are to this day (no nation more), yet that which was the endamaging only of their estates was narrowly forbid;[5] this which is thought the extreme injury and dishonor of

---

1. In the battle between the Israelites and the Amalekites, Israel prevailed when Moses held up his hand, and when he let down his hand, Amalek prevailed (Exod. 17:11). Philo, in *Moses,* I, 217–18, associates the raised hand with heaven, the ethereal, and the Israelites, the lowered hand with earth, the lowest regions of the universe, and the Amalekites.
2. Cf. *PL,* 12.287–89: "And therefore was Law given them to evince / Their natural pravity, by stirring up / Sin against Law to fight."
3. Bond service rendered by a peasant to a lord.
4. According to Paraeus, in his commentary on Corinthians, divorce helped relieve the misery of wives but increased rather than diminished the hardheartedness of men.
5. See the prohibition against usury in Deut. 23:19–20.

their wives and daughters, with the defilement also of themselves, is bounteously allowed. Their hearts were as hard under their best kings to offer in high places, though to the true God; yet that, but a small thing, is strictly forewarned [Deut. 12:2]; this, accounted a high offense against one of the greatest moral duties, is calmly permitted and established. How can it be evaded but that the heavy censure of Christ should fall worse upon this lawgiver of theirs than upon all the Scribes and Pharisees? For they did but omit judgment and mercy to trifle in mint and cumin, yet all according to Law;[6] but this their lawgiver, altogether as punctual in such niceties, goes marching on to adulteries through the violence of divorce by Law against Law. If it were such a cursed act of Pilate, a subordinate judge to Caesar, over-swayed by those hard hearts with much ado to suffer one transgression of Law but once, what is it then with less ado to publish a Law of transgression for many ages?[7] Did God for this come down and cover the Mount of Sinai with his glory [Exod. 19:18], uttering in thunder those his sacred ordinances out of the bottomless treasures of his wisdom and infinite pureness, to patch up an ulcerous and rotten commonwealth with strict and stern injunctions, to wash the skin and garments for every unclean touch, and such easy permission given to pollute the soul with adulteries by public authority without disgrace or question? No, it had been better that man had never known Law or matrimony than that such foul iniquity should be fastened upon the Holy One of Israel, the judge of all the earth, and such a piece of folly as Beelzebub would not commit, to divide against himself and pervert his own ends. Or if he to compass more mischief might yield perhaps to feign some good deed, yet that God should enact a license of certain evil for uncertain good against his own glory and pureness is abominable to conceive. And as it is destructive to the end of Law and blasphemous to the honor of the lawgiver licensing, so is it as pernicious to the person licensed.[8] If a private friend admonish not, the Scripture saith, *he hates his brother and lets him perish* [Lev. 19:17]; but if he soothe him and allow him in his faults, the Proverbs [29:5; 26:28] teach us *he spreads a net for his neighbor's feet and worketh ruin*. If the magistrate or prince forget to administer due justice and restrain not sin, Eli himself could say *it made the Lord's people to transgress* [1 Sam. 2:22–24]. But if he countenance them against law by his own example, what havoc it makes both in religion and virtue among the

6. "Woe unto you, scribes and Pharisees, hypocrites! for ye pay tithe of mint and anise and cummin, and have omitted the weightier matters of the law, judgment, mercy, and faith" (Matt. 23:23).

7. Pilate's delivering Christ to be crucified (Matt. 27:26) is less deserving of outrage than Moses' promulgating the law of divorce, if that law permitted sin.

8. Falsely given permission to divorce. Milton rejects the view that divorce is a license or anything other than a law.

people may be guessed by the anger it brought upon Hophni and Phineas, not to be appeased with sacrifice nor offering forever [1 Sam. 3:14]. If the Law be silent to declare sin, the people must needs generally go astray, for the Apostle himself saith, *he had not known lust but by the law* [Rom. 7:7]; and surely such a nation seems not to be under the illuminating guidance of God's Law but under the horrible doom rather of such as despise the Gospel, *he that is filthy, let him be filthy still* [Rev. 22:11]. But where the Law itself gives a warrant for sin, I know not what condition of misery to imagine miserable enough for such a people, unless that portion of the wicked, or rather of the damned, on whom God threatens in 11 Psalm, *to rain snares*; but that questionless cannot be by any law, which the Apostle saith is a ministry ordained of God unto our good and not so many ways and in so high a degree to our destruction, as we have now been graduating. And this is all the good can come to the person licensed in his hardness of heart.

I am next to mention that which because it is a ground in divinity, Rom. 3, will save the labor of demonstrating, unless her given axioms be more doubted than in other arts (although it be no less firm in the precepts of philosophy) that a thing unlawful can for no good whatsoever be done, much less allowed by a positive law. And this is the matter[9] why interpreters upon that passage in Hos. [1:2–3] will not consent it to be a true story, that the prophet took a harlot to wife, because God, being a pure Spirit, could not command a thing repugnant to his own nature—no, not for so good an end as to exhibit more to the life a wholesome and perhaps a converting parable to many an Israelite. Yet that he commanded the allowance of adulterous and injurious divorces for hardness of heart, a reason obscure and in a wrong sense, they can very savorily persuade themselves, so tenacious is the leaven of an old conceit. But they shift it: he permitted only. Yet silence in the Law is consent, and consent is accessory; why, then, is not the Law being silent or not active against a crime accessory to its own conviction, itself judging? For though we should grant that it approves not, yet it wills; and the lawyers' maxim is that the will compelled is yet the will. And though Aristotle in his *Ethics* call this a mixed action, yet he concludes it to be voluntary and inexcusable if it be evil. How justly then might human law and philosophy rise up against the righteousness of Moses if this be true which our vulgar divinity fathers upon him—yea, upon God himself—not silently and only negatively to permit but in his law to divulge a written and general privilege to commit and persist in unlawful divorces with a high hand, with security and no ill fame. For this is more than permitting or conniving, this is maintaining, this is warranting, this

9. Reason, cause.

is protecting, yea, this is doing evil, and such an evil as that reprobate lawgiver did whose lasting infamy is engraven upon him like a
surname, *he who made Israel to sin*.[1] This is the lowest pitch contrary
to God that public fraud and injustice can descend.

If it be affirmed that God, as being Lord, may do what he will, yet
we must know that God hath not two wills but one will, much less
two contrary. If he once willed adultery should be sinful and to be
punished with death, all his omnipotence will not allow him to will
the allowance that his holiest people might, as it were by his own
antinomy or counter-statute, live unreproved in the same fact as he
himself esteemed it, according to our common explainers. The hidden ways of his providence we adore and search not, but the law is
his revealed will, his complete, his evident, and certain will; herein
he appears to us as it were in human shape, enters into covenant
with us, swears to keep it, binds himself like a just lawgiver to his
own prescriptions, gives himself to be understood by men, judges
and is judged, measures and is commensurate to right reason;[2] cannot require less of us in one cantle of his law than in another, his
legal justice cannot be so fickle and so variable, sometimes like a
devouring fire, and by and by connivent[3] in the embers, or, if I may
so say, oscitant and supine. The vigor of his Law could no more
remit than the hallowed fire on his altar could be let go out [Lev.
6:13]. The lamps that burnt before him might need snuffing, but
the light of his law never. Of this also more beneath, in discussing
a solution of Rivetus.

The Jesuits and that sect among us which is named of Arminius[4]
are wont to charge us of making God the author of sin in two
degrees especially, not to speak of his permissions: 1. Because we
hold that he hath decreed some to damnation and consequently to
sin, say they; next, because those means which are of saving knowledge to others, he makes to them an occasion of greater sin. Yet
considering the perfection wherein man was created and might
have stood, no decree necessitating his free will, but subsequent
though not in time yet in order to causes which were in his own
power, they might methinks be persuaded to absolve both God and

1. Manasseh, king of Judah (2 Kings 21:11).
2. In this resonant passage, the Mosaic law rather than Christ incarnates deity. Moreover,
   if God is a king willing to be judged, how dare Charles I refuse? For an example of legal
   rather than evangelical justification, see *PL*, 1.26: to justify the ways of God to men is to
   judge God as a king willing to be judged, who "gives himself to be understood to men."
3. Dozing, dormant. "Cantle": nook, corner.
4. Jacobus Arminius (1560–1609) was a Dutch Reformed theologian whose principal
   ideas opposed three points of doctrinaire Calvinism. He asserted conditional rather
   than absolute election, unlimited rather than limited atonement, and resistible rather
   than irresistible grace. Milton's mature position on grace and salvation, expressed
   especially in book 3 of *Paradise Lost* and in 1.3–4 of *De Doctrina Christiana*, is Arminian. In this treatise, and in this very sentence (the second "us"), Milton still writes as a
   Calvinist.

us.[5] When as the doctrine of Plato and Chrysippus, with their followers the Academics and the Stoics, who knew not what a consummate and most adorned Pandora was bestowed upon Adam to
be the nurse and guide of his arbitrary happiness and perseverance
(I mean his native innocence and perfection), which might have
kept him from being our true Epimetheus; and though they taught
of virtue and vice to be both the gift of divine destiny, they could
yet give reasons not invalid to justify the counsels of God and fate
from the insulsity[6] of mortal tongues: that man's own free will self-
corrupted is the adequate and sufficient cause of his disobedience
besides Fate; as Homer also wanted not to express, both in his *Iliad*
and *Odyssey*. And Manilius the poet, although in his fourth book he
tells of some *created both to sin and punishment*, yet without murmuring and with an industrious cheerfulness he acquits the deity.[7]
They were not ignorant in their heathen lore that it is most God-
like to punish those who of his creatures became his enemies with
the greatest punishments; and they could attain also to think that
the greatest when God himself throws a man farthest from him—
which then they held he did when he blinded, hardened, and stirred
up his offenders to finish and pile up their desperate work since
they had undertaken it. To banish forever into a local hell, whether
in the air or in the center, or in that uttermost and bottomless gulf
of Chaos, deeper from holy bliss than the world's diameter multiplied, they thought not a punishing so proper and proportionate for
God to inflict as to punish sin with sin. Thus were the common sort
of Gentiles wont to think, without any wry thoughts cast upon divine
governance. And therefore Cicero, not in his Tuscan or Campanian
retirements among the learned wits of that age but even in the Senate to a mixed auditory (though he were sparing otherwise to broach
his philosophy among statists[8] and lawyers), yet as to this point
both in his oration against Piso and in that which is about the
answers of the soothsayers against Clodius, he declares it publicly as
no paradox to common ears that God cannot punish man more nor
make him more miserable than still by making him more sinful.[9]

5. The corruption of human nature that began with original sin and extends to all human
   beings is neither the fault of God nor of the Calvinists. Milton's fallen Adam, after
   questioning why all of guiltless humankind should be condemned for his sin, concludes: "But from me what can proceed / But all corrupt, both mind and will depraved,
   / Not to do only but to will the same / With me" (*PL*, 10.824–26).
6. Stupidity, senselessness. Platonic and Stoic philosophers emphasized the element of
   human responsibility. "Arbitrary": dependent on one's own will or choice. Epimetheus,
   by opening Pandora's box, released evil upon human beings.
7. See Marcus Manilius, *Astronomicon*, 4.108–18. Despite fate, individuals justly deserve
   praise for virtue and blame for evil deeds.
8. Politicians.
9. In the oration *In Pisonem* (46), Cicero asserts that their own sin and guilt are the punishments ("the Avengers") that hound the wicked.

Thus we see how in this controversy the justice of God stood upright even among heathen disputers. But if anyone be truly and not pretendedly zealous for God's honor, here I call him forth before men and angels to use his best and most advised skill, lest God more unavoidably than ever yet, and in the guiltiest manner, be made the author of sin—if he shall not only deliver over and incite his enemies by rebukes to sin as a punishment, but shall by patent under his own broad seal[1] allow his friends whom he would sanctify and save, whom he would unite to himself and not disjoin, whom he would correct by wholesome chastening and not punish as he doth the damned by lewd sinning, if he shall allow these in his Law, the perfect rule of his own purest will and our most edified conscience, the perpetrating of an odious and manifold sin without the least contesting. 'Tis wondered how there can be in God a secret and a revealed will; and yet what wonder if there be in man two answerable causes. But here there must be two revealed wills grappling in a fraternal war with one another without any reasonable cause apprehended. This cannot be less than to engraft sin into the substance of the Law, which Law is to provoke sin by crossing and forbidding, not by complying with it. Nay, this is, which I tremble in uttering, to incarnate sin into the unpunishing and well-pleased will of God. To avoid these dreadful consequences that tread upon the heels of those allowances to sin will be a task of far more difficulty than to appease those minds which perhaps out of a vigilant and wary conscience except against predestination. Thus finally we may conclude that a law wholly giving license cannot upon any good consideration be given to a holy people for hardness of heart in the vulgar sense.

* * *

FROM *CHAP. IV*

[Milton rejects the position that divorce is only a dispensation rather than a law.]

[I]f we speak of a command in the strictest definition, then marriage itself is no more a command than divorce but only a free permission to him who cannot contain. But as to dispensation, I affirm the same as before of the law, that it can never be given to the allowance of sin. * * * Why should God enter covenant with a people to be holy, *as the command is holy, and just, and good, Ro. 7. 12*, and yet suffer an impure and treacherous dispense to mislead and betray them under the vizard[2] of Law to a legitimate practice of unclean-

---

1. Royal patents, or licenses, were issued under the "broad seal" of the English kings.
2. Mask, disguise.

ness. God is no covenant-breaker, he cannot do this. * * * God indeed in some ways of his providence is high and secret, past finding out; but in the delivery and execution of his Law, especially in the managing of a duty so daily and so familiar as this is whereof we reason, hath plain enough revealed himself, and requires the observance thereof not otherwise than to the law of nature and equity imprinted in us seems correspondent. And he hath taught us to love and to extol his Laws not only as they are his but as they are just and good to every wise and sober understanding. Therefore Abraham, even to the face of God himself, seemed to doubt of divine justice if it should swerve from that irradiation wherewith it had enlightened the mind of man and bound itself to observe its own rule. *Wilt thou destroy the righteous with the wicked? that be far from thee; shall not the Judge of the earth do right?*[3]—thereby declaring that God hath created a righteousness in right itself against which he cannot do.

*   *   *

FROM *CHAP. V.*

What a dispensation is.

* * * [A] dispensation most properly is some particular accident rarely happening and therefore not specified in the Law but left to the decision of charity even under the bondage of Jewish rites, much more under the liberty of the Gospel. Thus did *David enter into the house of God and did eat the shewbread, he and his followers, which was* ceremonially *unlawful* [1 Sam. 21:1–6; Matt. 12:3–4]. Of such dispenses as these it was that Verdun the French divine so gravely disputed in the Council of Trent against Friar Adrian, who held that the pope might dispense with any thing. *It is a fond persuasion,* saith Verdun, *that dispensing is a favor; nay, it is as good distributive justice as what is most, and the priest sins if he gives it not, for it is nothing else but a right interpretation of law.* Thus far that I can learn touching this matter wholesomely decreed. But that God, who is the giver of every good and perfect gift (James 1), should give out a rule and directory to sin by, should enact a dispensation as long-lived as a law whereby to live in privileged adultery for hardness of heart; and yet this obdurate disease cannot be conceived how it was the more amended by this unclean remedy, is the most deadly and scorpion-like gift that the enemy of mankind could have

3. Abraham's plea that God not destroy the sinful inhabitants of Sodom (Gen. 18:23–25), echoed by the Son on behalf of fallen humankind: "That be from thee far, / That far be from thee, Father, who art judge / Of all things made, and judgest only right" (*PL,* 3.153–55).

given to any miserable sinner, and is rather such a dispense as that was which the serpent gave to our first parents. God gave quails in his wrath [Num. 11:31–33] and kings in his wrath [1 Sam. 8:1–9], yet neither of these things evil in themselves; but that he whose eyes cannot behold impurity should in the book of his holy covenant, his most unpassionate Law, give license and statute for uncontrolled adultery, although it go for the received opinion, I shall ever dissuade my soul from such a creed, such an indulgence as the shop of Antichrist never forged a baser.

FROM *CHAP. VI.*

That the Jew had no more right to this supposed dispense than the Christian hath, and rather not so much.

But if we must needs dispense, let us for a while so far dispense with truth as to grant that sin may be dispensed;[4] yet there will be copious reason found to prove that the Jew had no more right to such a supposed indulgence than the Christian, whether we look at the clear knowledge wherein he lived or the strict performance of works whereto he was bound. Besides visions and prophecies, they had the Law of God, which in the Psalms and Proverbs is chiefly praised for sureness and certainty, both easy and perfect to the enlightening of the simple.[5] How could it be so obscure then, or they so sottishly blind, in this plain moral and household duty? They had the same precepts about marriage; Christ added nothing to their clearness, for that had argued them imperfect; he opens not the law but removes the Pharisaic mists raised between the law and the peoples' eyes. The only sentence which he adds, *What God hath joined let no man put asunder* [Matt. 19:6], is as obscure as any clause fetched out of Genesis and hath increased a yet undecided controversy of clandestine marriages. If we examine over all his sayings, we shall find him not so much interpreting the Law with his words as referring his own words to be interpreted by the Law, and oftener obscures his mind in short and vehement and compact sentences to blind and puzzle them the more who could not understand the Law. The Jews therefore were as little to be dispensed with for lack of moral knowledge as we.

Next, none, I think, will deny but that they were as much bound to perform the Law as any Christian. That severe and rigorous knife

4. This is an artificial argument, in which Milton, punningly, will "dispense with [do without, forgo] truth," in order to concede a position that he rejects: that divorce is merely a dispensation, a relaxation of the law due to the weakness and ignorance of the Jews.
5. "The law [lit. "Torah"] of the Lord is perfect, converting the soul: the testimony of the Lord is sure, making wise the simple" (Ps. 19:7).

not sparing the tender foreskin of any male infant, to carve upon his flesh the mark of that strict and pure covenant whereinto he entered [Gen. 17:10–14], might give us to understand enough against the fancy of dispensing. * * * Thus, if we consider the tenor of the Law, to be circumcised and to perform all, not pardoning so much as the scapes[6] of error and ignorance, and compare this with the condition of the Gospel, believe and be baptized [Mark 16:16], I suppose it cannot be long ere we grant that the Jew was bound as strictly to the performance of every duty as was possible, and therefore could not be dispensed with more than the Christian, perhaps not so much.

* * *

FROM CHAP. VIII.

The true sense how Moses suffered divorce for hardness of heart.

What may we do then to salve this seeming inconsistence?[7] I must not dissemble that I am confident that it can be done no other way than this.

Moses (Deut. 24:1) established a grave and prudent Law, full of moral equity, full of due consideration towards nature, that cannot be resisted, a Law consenting with the laws of wisest men and civilest nations, that when a man hath married a wife, if it come to pass he cannot love her by reason of some displeasing natural quality or unfitness in her, let him write her a bill of divorce—the intent of which law undoubtedly was this: that if any good and peaceable man should discover some helpless disagreement or dislike either of mind or body, whereby he could not cheerfully perform the duty of a husband without the perpetual dissembling of offense and disturbance to his spirit; rather than to live uncomfortably and unhappily both to himself and to his wife, rather than to continue undertaking a duty which he could not possibly discharge, he might dismiss her whom he could not tolerably and so not conscionably retain. And this Law the spirit of God by the mouth of Solomon (Prov. 30. 21, 23) testifies to be a good and a necessary Law, by granting it that *a hated woman* (for so the Hebrew word signifies, rather than odious, though it come all to one) *that a hated woman when she is married is a thing that the earth cannot bear.* What follows then but that the charitable Law must remedy what nature cannot undergo.

---

6. Transgressions due to thoughtlessness.
7. Between the Hebrew Bible's permitting divorce and the Gospel's apparent prohibition of it.

Now that many licentious and hard-hearted men took hold of this
Law to cloak their bad purposes is nothing strange to believe. And
these were they, not for whom Moses made the law, God forbid, but
whose hardness of heart taking ill advantage by this Law he held it
better to suffer as by accident, where it could not be detected, rather
than good men should lose their just and lawful privilege of remedy.
Christ therefore having to answer these tempting Pharisees, according as his custom was, not meaning to inform their proud ignorance what Moses did in the true intent of the Law, which they had
ill cited, suppressing the true cause for which Moses gave it and
extending it to every slight matter, tells them their own, what Moses
was forced to suffer by their abuse of his Law. Which is yet more
plain if we mark that our Savior in the fifth of Matth. cites not the
Law of Moses but the Pharisaical tradition falsely grounded upon
that Law. And in those other places, chap. 19 and Mark 10, the
Pharisees cite the Law but conceal the wise and human reason
there expressed, which our Saviour corrects not in them whose
pride deserved not his instruction, only returns them what is proper
to them: *Moses for the hardness of your heart suffered you*—that is,
such as you—*to put away your wives* [Matt. 19:8]; *and to you he
wrote this precept* [Mark 10:5] for that cause, which "to you" must be
read with an impression[8] and understood limitedly of such as covered ill purposes under that Law: for it was seasonable that they
should hear their own unbounded license rebuked but not seasonable for them to hear a good man's requisite liberty explained.

But us he hath taught better, if we have ears to hear. He himself
acknowledged it to be a Law, Mark 10, and being a Law of God, it
must have an undoubted *end of charity, which may be used with a
pure heart, a good conscience, and faith unfeigned* [1 Tim. 1:5], as
was heard; it cannot allow sin but is purposely to resist sin, as by
the same chapter to Timothy appears. There we learn also *that the
law is good, if a man use it lawfully* [1 Tim. 1:8]. Out of doubt then
there must be a certain good in this Law which Moses willingly
allowed; and there might be an unlawful use made thereof by hypocrites, and that was it which Moses unwillingly suffered, foreseeing
it in general but not able to discern it in particulars. Christ therefore mentions not here what Moses and the Law intended, for good
men might know that by many other rules; and the scornful Pharisees were not fit to be told until they could employ that knowledge
they had less abusively. Only he acquaints them with what Moses
by them was put to suffer.

---

8. Stress, emphasis.

FROM *CHAP. IX.*

The words of the institution how to be understood; and of our Savior's answer to his disciples.

And to entertain a little their overweening arrogance as best befitted and to amaze them yet further, because they thought it no hard matter to fulfill the Law, he draws them up to that unseparable institution which God ordained in the beginning before the fall, when man and woman were both perfect and could have no cause to separate— just as in the same chapter he stands not to contend with the arrogant young man who boasted his observance of the whole Law whether he had indeed kept it or not but screws him up higher to a task of that perfection which no man is bound to imitate [Matt. 19:16–22]. And in like manner that pattern of the first institution he set before the opinionative Pharisees to dazzle them and not to bind us. For this is a solid rule, that every command given with reason binds our obedience no otherwise than that reason holds. Of this sort was that command in Eden, *Therefore shall a man cleave to his wife, and they shall be one flesh* [Gen. 2:24], which we see is no absolute command but with an inference: "therefore." The reason then must be first considered, that[9] our obedience be not mis-obedience. The first is (for it is not single) because the wife is to the husband *flesh of his flesh*, as in the verse going before. But this reason cannot be sufficient of itself; for why then should he for his wife leave his father and mother, with whom he is far more *flesh of flesh and bone of bone*, as being made of their substance? And besides, it can be but a sorry and ignoble society of life whose unseparable injunction depends merely upon flesh and bones.[1] Therefore we must look higher, since Christ himself recalls us to the beginning, and we shall find that the primitive reason of never divorcing was that sacred and not vain promise of God to remedy man's loneliness by making him a *meet help for him* [Gen. 2:18], though not now in perfection as at first yet still in proportion as things now are. And this is repeated (verse 20) when all other creatures were fitly associated and brought to Adam, as if the divine power had been in some care and deep thought, because *there was not yet found an help meet for man*. And can we so slightly depress the all-wise purpose of a deliberating God, as if his consultation had produced no other good for man but to join him with an accidental companion of propagation, which his sudden word had already made for every beast? Nay, a far less good to man it will be found if she must at all adventures be fastened upon him

---

9. So that.
1. See Milton's addition in. *PL*, 8.499: "one flesh, one heart, one soul."

individually.[2] And therefore even plain sense and equity and, which is above them both, the all-interpreting voice of charity herself cries loud that this primitive reason, this consulted promise of God to make a meet help, is the only cause that gives authority to this command of not divorcing to be a command. And it might be further added that if the true definition of a wife were asked in good earnest, this clause of being *a meet help* would show itself so necessary and so essential in that demonstrative argument that it might be logically concluded, therefore, she who naturally and perpetually is no meet help can be no wife; which clearly takes away the difficulty of dismissing of such a one.

If this be not thought enough, I answer yet further that marriage, unless it mean a fit and tolerable marriage, is not inseparable neither by nature nor institution. Not by nature, for then those Mosaic divorces had been against nature, if separable and inseparable be contraries, as who doubts they be; and what is against nature is against Law, if soundest philosophy abuse us not. By this reckoning Moses should be most un-Mosaic, that is, most illegal, not to say most unnatural. Nor is it inseparable by the first institution, for then no second institution of the same Law for so many causes could dissolve it,[3] it being most unworthy a human (as Plato's judgment is in the fourth book of his Laws),[4] much more a divine lawgiver to write two several decrees upon the same thing. But what would Plato have deemed if the one of these were good, the other evil to be done? Lastly, suppose it be inseparable by institution, yet in competition with higher things, as religion and charity in mainest matters, and when the chief end is frustrate for which it was ordained, as hath been shown, if still it must remain inseparable it holds a strange and lawless propriety[5] from all other works of God under heaven.

From these many considerations we may safely gather that so much of the first institution as our Savior mentions (for he mentions not all) was but to quell and put to nonplus the tempting Pharisees and to lay open their ignorance and shallow understanding of the Scriptures. For, saith he, *have ye not read that he which made them at the beginning made them male and female, and said, for this cause shall a man cleave to his wife?* [Matt. 19:4–5]; which these blind usurpers of Moses' chair could not gainsay: as if this single respect of male and female were sufficient against a thousand inconveniences and mischiefs to clog a rational creature to his endless sorrow unre-

---

2. Indivisibly, inseparably.
3. The institution of marriage in paradise is part of the same Mosaic law as the deuteronomic law of divorce.
4. In *Laws* 4, 719d, Plato argues that the legislator must give not two rules about the same thing, but one only.
5. Particular character, idiosyncrasy.

linquishably, under the guileful superscription of his intended solace and comfort. What if they had thus answered: Master, if thou mean to make wedlock as inseparable as from the beginning, let it be made also a fit society, as God meant it, which we shall soon understand it ought to be if thou recite the whole reason of the Law. Doubtless our Savior had applauded their just answer. For then they had expounded his command of paradise even as Moses himself expounds it by his laws of divorce, that is, with due and wise regard to the premises and reasons of the first command, according to which, without unclean and temporizing permissions, he instructs us in this imperfect state what we may lawfully do about divorce.

But if it be thought that the disciples, offended at the rigor of Christ's answer, could yet obtain no mitigation of the former sentence pronounced to the Pharisees, it may be fully answered that our Savior continues the same reply to his disciples, as men leavened with the same customary license which the Pharisees maintained and displeased at the removing of a traditional abuse whereto they had so long not unwillingly been used. It was no time then to contend with their slow and prejudicial belief in a thing wherein an ordinary measure of light in Scripture, with some attention, might afterwards inform them well enough. And yet ere Christ had finished this argument, they might have picked out of his own concluding words an answer more to their minds and in effect the same with that which hath been all this while entreating audience: *All men*, saith he, *cannot receive this saying, save they to whom it is given; he that is able to receive it, let him receive it* [Matt. 19:11–12]. What saying is this which is left to a man's choice to receive or not receive? What but the married life. Was our Savior then so mild and favorable to the weakness of a single man, and is he turned on the sudden so rigorous and inexorable to the distresses and extremities of an ill-wedded man? Did he so graciously give leave to change the better single life for the worse married life? Did he open so to us this hazardous and accidental door of marriage to shut upon us like the gate of death without retracting or returning, without permitting to change the worst, most insupportable, most unchristian mischance of marriage for all the mischiefs and sorrows that can ensue, being an ordinance which was especially given as a cordial and exhilarating cup of solace, the better to bear our other crosses and afflictions? Questionless this were a hard-heartedness of divorcing worse than that in the Jews, which they say extorted the allowance from Moses, and is utterly dissonant from all the doctrine of our Savior.

After these considerations, therefore, to take a law out of paradise given in time of original perfection, and to take it barely without those just and equal inferences and reasons which mainly establish it, nor so much as admitting those needful and safe allowances wherewith Moses himself interprets it to the fallen condition of man, argues nothing in us but rashness and contempt of those means that God left us in his pure and chaste law, without which it will not be possible for us to perform the strict imposition of this command; or if we strive beyond our strength, we shall strive to obey it otherwise than God commands it. And lamented experience daily teaches the bitter and vain fruits of this our presumption, forcing men in a thing wherein we are not able to judge either of their strength or of their sufferance. Whom neither one vice nor other by natural addiction, but only marriage ruins, which doubtless is not the fault of that ordinance, for God gave it as a blessing, nor always of man's mis-choosing, it being an error above wisdom to prevent, as examples of wisest men so mistaken manifest. It is the fault therefore of a perverse opinion that will have it continued in despite of nature and reason, when indeed it was never truly joined. All those expositors upon the fifth of Matthew confess the law of Moses to be the law of the Lord, wherein no addition or diminution hath place; yet coming to the point of divorce, as if they feared not to be called least in the kingdom of heaven [Matt. 5:19], any slight evasion will content them to reconcile those contradictions which they make between Christ and Moses, between Christ and Christ.

* * *

CHAP. XI.

The other shift of saying divorce was permitted by law but not approved. More of the Institution.

But it was not approved. So much the worse that it was allowed—as if sin had overmastered the law of God to conform her steady and straight rule to sin's crookedness, which is impossible. Besides, what needed a positive grant of that which was not approved? It restrained no liberty to him that could but use a little fraud; it had been better silenced unless it were approved in some case or other. But still it was not approved. Miserable excusers! He who doth evil that good may come thereby approves not what he doth, and yet the grand rule forbids him and counts his damnation just if he do it [Rom. 3:8]. The sorceress Medea did not approve her own evil doings yet looked not to be excused for that;[6] and it is the constant opinion of Plato in *Protagoras* and other of his dialogues, agreeing with that proverbial sentence among the Greeks, that no man is wicked willingly, which also

---

6. See Euripides' *Medea*, contemplating the murder of her children: "I understand what evil I am about to do, / but my wrath is stronger even than my thoughts, / which is the cause of the greatest wrongs of humankind" (1078–80).

the Peripatetics do rather distinguish than deny. What great thank
then if any man reputed wise and constant will neither do nor permit
others under his charge to do that which he approves not, especially
in matter of sin. But for a judge, but for a magistrate the shepherd of
his people to surrender up his approbation against law and his own
judgment to the obstinacy of his herd, what more un-judge-like, more
un-magistrate-like, and in war more un-commander-like? Twice in a
short time it was the undoing of the Roman state, first when Pompey,
next when Marcus Brutus had not magnanimity enough but to make
so poor a resignation of what they approved to what the boisterous
tribunes and soldiers bawled for.[7] Twice it was the saving of two the
greatest commonwealths in the world, of Athens by Themistocles at
the sea fight of Salamis, of Rome by Fabius Maximus in the Punic
War, for that these two matchless generals had the fortitude at home
against the rashness and the clamors of their own captains and con-
federates to withstand the doing or permitting of what they could not
approve in the duty of their great command.[8] Thus far of civil prudence. But when we speak of sin, let us look again upon the old reverend Eli, who in his heavy punishment found no difference between
the doing and permitting of what he did not approve [1 Sam. 3:12–
13]. If hardness of heart in the people may be an excuse, why then is
Pilate branded through all memory? He approved not what he did, he
openly protested, he washed his hands and labored not a little ere he
would yield to the hard hearts of a whole people, both princes and
plebeians importuning and tumulting even to the fear of a revolt
[Matt. 27:22–26]. Yet is there any will undertake his cause? If therefore Pilate, for suffering but one act of cruelty against law, though
with much unwillingness testified, at the violent demand of a whole
nation, shall stand so black upon record to all posterity, alas for
Moses! What shall we say for him while we are taught to believe he
suffered not one act only both of cruelty and uncleanness in one
divorce but made it a plain and lasting law against law whereby ten
thousand acts accounted both cruel and unclean might be daily
committed, and this without the least suit or petition of the people
that we can read of.

And can we conceive without vile thoughts that the majesty and
holiness of God could endure so many ages to gratify a stubborn
people in the practice of a foul polluting sin? And could he expect
they should abstain, he not signifying his mind in a plain com-

<hr>

7. According to Plutarch's *Lives,* both Pompey's decision to fight against Caesar at Pharsa-
   lia and Brutus's to assassinate Caesar were made contrary to their own best judgment.
8. In deciding to provoke war with the Persians at the battle of Salamis (480 B.C.E.) Themistocles had to overcome the resistance of his allies, Eurybiades and the Spartans.
   Fabius Maximus' epithet, *Cunctator* (the Delayer), refers to his originally unpopular
   tactics in deploying the troops during the Second Punic War (218–01 B.C.E.).

mand, at such time especially when he was framing their laws and them to all possible perfection? But they were to look back to the first institution. Nay, rather why was not that individual institution brought out of paradise, as was that of the Sabbath, and repeated in the body of the Law,[9] that men might have understood it to be a command? For that any sentence that bears the resemblance of a precept, set there so out of place in another world, at such a distance from the whole law and not once mentioned there, should be an obliging command to us is very disputable, and perhaps it might be denied to be a command without further dispute. However, it commands not absolutely, as hath been cleared, but only with reference to that precedent promise of God which is the very ground of his institution. If that appear not in some tolerable sort, how can we affirm such a matrimony to be the same which God instituted? In such an accident it will best behoove our soberness to follow rather what moral Sinai prescribes equal to our strength than fondly to think within our strength all that lost Paradise relates.

CHAP. XII.

The third shift of them who esteem it a mere judicial law.
Proved again to be a law of moral equity.

Another while it shall suffice them that it was not a moral but a judicial law and so was abrogated. Nay, rather, *not* abrogated *because* judicial, which law the ministry of Christ came not to deal with. And who put it in man's power to exempt, where Christ speaks in general of not abrogating the least jot or tittle, and in special not that of divorce, because it follows among those laws which he promised expressly not to abrogate but to vindicate from abusive traditions, which is most evidently to be seen in the 16th of Luke [vss. 17–18], where this caution of not abrogating is inserted immediately and not otherwise than purposely, when no other point of the law is touched but that of divorce. And if we mark the 31 ver. of Mat. the 5, he there cites not the law of Moses but the licentious gloss which traduced the law;[1] that therefore which he cited, that he abrogated, and not only abrogated but disallowed and flatly condemned, which could not be the law of Moses, for that had been foully to the rebuke of his great servant. To abrogate a law made with God's allowance had been to tell us only that such a law was now to cease; but to refute it with an ignominious note of civilizing adultery casts the reproof, which was meant only to the Pharisees, even upon him who made

9. The Sabbath, described in Gen. 2:2–3, becomes a law in Exod. 20:8–11.
1. "It hath been said, Whosoever shall put away his wife, let him give her a writing of divorcement."

the law. But yet if that be judicial which belongs to a civil court, this law is less judicial than nine of the ten commandments; for antiquaries affirm that divorces proceeded among the Jews without knowledge of the magistrate, only with hands and seals under the testimony of some rabbis to be then present.[2] Perkins, in a *Treatise of Conscience*, grants that what in the judicial law is of common equity binds also the Christian, and how to judge of this prescribes two ways: if wise nations have enacted the same decree,[3] or if it maintain the good of family, church, or commonwealth. This therefore is a pure moral economical law, too hastily imputed of tolerating sin; being rather so clear in nature and reason that it was left to a man's own arbitrament to be determined between God and his own conscience—not only among the Jews, but in every wise nation; the restraint whereof, who is not too thick-sighted may see how hurtful and distractive it is to the house, the Church, and commonwealth. And that power which Christ never took from the master of family but rectified only to a right and wary use at home—that power the undiscerning canonist hath improperly usurped into his court-leet[4] and bescribbled with a thousand trifling impertinencies which yet have filled the life of man with serious trouble and calamity. Yet grant it were of old a judicial law, it need not be the less moral for that, being conversant as it is about virtue or vice. And our Savior disputes not here the judicature, for that was not his office, but the morality of divorce, whether it be adultery or no. If therefore he touch the law of Moses at all, he touches the moral part thereof, which is absurd to imagine that the covenant of grace should reform the exact and perfect law of works, eternal and immutable; or if he touch not the Law at all, then is not the allowance thereof disallowed to us.

2. The requirements under Jewish law—the writing of a bill of divorce at the husband's direction, its signing by two witnesses, and its delivery to the wife—keep divorce within private jurisdiction.
3. A judicial law of common equity ("equall, just, and necessary") accords with the natural reason and conscience of wise pagans and Jews as well as Christians. William Perkins (1558–1602), prolific despite his short life, was affiliated with the moderate-Puritan wing of the English Church. Although Milton refers to him three times in this treatise, neither he nor the other aristocrats of the Pauline renaissance mentioned—David Paraeus, Theodore Beza, and Andreas Rivetus—would have endorsed his main argument on divorce.
4. A district court with jurisdiction over petty offenses, here used disparagingly.

FROM *Chap. XIII.*

[Milton continues to maintain that divorce is a law rather than a mere dispensation or permission and adds: "it would be more religion to advise well, lest we make ourselves juster than God by censuring rashly that for sin which his unspotted Law without rebuke allows and his people without being conscious of displeasing him have used." He then turns to the institution of marriage in paradise.]

But still they fly back to the primitive institution and would have us re-enter Paradise against the sword that guards it. Whom I again thus reply to, that the place in Genesis contains the description of a fit and perfect marriage, with an interdict of ever divorcing such a union; but where nature is discovered to have never joined indeed but vehemently seeks to part, it cannot be there conceived that God forbids it—nay, he commands it both in the law and in the prophet Malachi, which is to be our rule. And Perkins upon this chapter of Mat. deals plainly that our Savior here confutes not Moses' Law but the false glosses that depraved the Law; which, being true, Perkins must need grant that something then is left to that Law which Christ found no fault with; and what can that be but the conscionable use of such liberty as the plain words import. So that by his own inference Christ did not absolutely intend to restrain all divorces to the only cause of adultery. This therefore is the true scope of our Savior's will, that he who looks upon the Law concerning divorce should also look back upon the institution, that he may endeavor what is perfectest; and he that looks upon the institution should not refuse as sinful and unlawful those allowances which God affords him in his following law, lest he make himself purer than his maker, and presuming above strength slip into temptations irrecoverably. For this is wonderful, that in all those decrees concerning marriage, God should never once mention the prime institution to dissuade them from divorcing, and that he should forbid smaller sins as opposite to the hardness of their hearts and let this adulterous matter of divorce pass ever unreproved. This is also to be marvelled, that seeing Christ did not condemn whatever it was that Moses suffered, and that thereupon the Christian magistrate permits usury and open stews, and here with us adultery to be so slightly punished which was punished by death to these hard-hearted Jews, why we should strain thus at the matter of divorce, which may stand so much with charity to permit, and make no scruple to allow usury, esteemed to be so much against charity. But this it is to embroil ourselves against the righteous and all-wise judgments and statutes of God, which are not variable and contrarious as we would make them, one while permitting and another while forbidding, but are most constant and most harmonious each to other. For how can the uncorrupt and majestic law of God, bearing in her hand the wages of life and death [Rom. 6:23], harbor such a repugnance within herself as to require an unexempted and impartial obedience to all her decrees, either from us or from our mediator, and yet debase herself to falter so many ages with circumcised adulteries by unclean and slubbering[5] permissions?

[In chapter fourteen, against Beza's opinion that some civil laws merely moderate sins that cannot be abolished, Milton takes the absolutist position that God's laws will not compound with human weakness as an inevitable human condition: "as for sin, the essence of it cannot consist with rule; and if the Law fall to regulate sin and not to take it utterly away, it necessarily confirms and establishes sin. To make a regularity of sin by law, either the Law must straiten sin into no sin, or sin must crook the Law into no law. * * * For what less indignity were this than as if Justice herself, the queen of virtues, descending from her sceptered royalty, instead of conquering should compound and treat with sin her eternal adversary and rebel upon ignoble terms? * * * Violence indeed and insurrection may force the law to suffer what it cannot mend; but to write a decree in allowance of sin, as soon can the hand of Justice rot off. Let this be ever concluded as a truth that will outlive the faith of those that seek to bear it down."]

In chapter fifteen, Milton rejects Beza's contention that divorce was a dispensation granted reluctantly by Moses only to release afflicted wives from their cruel husbands: "Whenas it could not be found how hardness of heart should be lessened by liberty of divorce, a fancy was devised to hide the flaw by commenting that divorce was permitted only for the help of wives. Palpably uxorious! Who can be ignorant that woman was created for man and not man for woman and that a husband may be injured as insufferably in marriage as a wife?"

Esteeming therefore to have asserted thus an injured law of Moses from the unwarranted and guilty name of a dispensation to be again a most equal and requisite law, we have the word of Christ himself that he came not to alter the least tittle of it; and signifies no small displeasure against him that shall teach to do so. On which relying, I shall not much waver to affirm that those words which are made to intimate as if they forbade all divorce but for adultery (though Moses have constituted otherwise)—those words taken circumscriptly,[6]

---

5. Sullying. "Circumcised": both "circumscribed, limited" and "committed by the Jewish people," who follow the Mosaic law of divorce.
6. In a circumscribed manner or sense.

without regard to any precedent law of Moses or attestation of Christ himself, or without care to preserve those his fundamental and superior laws of nature and charity to which all other ordinances give up their seals, are as much against plain equity and the mercy of religion as those words of *Take, eat, this is my body* [Matt. 26:26; Mark 14:22], elementally understood, are against nature and sense.

Milton concludes the chapter by insisting that Christ holds up to the Pharisees the perfection of paradise and the first institution of marriage to reprove them for abusing the freedom to divorce and not to oblige them to achieve prelapsarian perfection. The impossibility of regaining original righteousness makes divorce necessary: "for if the first institution must make wedlock, whatever happen, inseparable to us, it must make it also as perfect, as meetly helpful, and as comfortable as God promised it should be, at least in some degree; otherwise it is not equal or proportionable to the strength of man that he should be reduced into such indissoluble bonds to his assured misery, if all the other conditions of that covenant be manifestly altered."]

FROM *CHAP. XVI*

How to be understood that they must be one flesh;
and how that those whom God hath joined,
man should not sunder.

Next he saith, *they must be one flesh*; which, when all conjecturing is done, will be found to import no more but to make legitimate and good the carnal act, which else might seem to have something of pollution in it. And infers thus much over, that the fit union of their souls be such as may even incorporate them to love and amity; but that can never be where no correspondence is of the mind. Nay, instead of being one flesh, they will be rather two carcasses chained unnaturally together; or, as it may happen, a living soul bound to a dead corpse, a punishment too like that inflicted by the tyrant Mezentius,[7] so little worthy to be received as that remedy of loneliness which God meant us—since we know it is not the joining of another body will remove loneliness but the uniting of another compliable mind; and that it is no blessing but a torment, nay a base and brutish condition, to be one flesh, unless where nature can in some measure fix a unity of disposition. * * *

---

7. A cruel Etruscan king, who, according to Virgil (*Aen.*, 8.485–88), tortured his victims with lingering death by linking them to corpses.

Lastly, Christ himself tells who should not be put asunder: namely, those whom God hath joined. A plain solution of this great controversy, if men would but use their eyes; for when is it that God may be said to join, when the parties and their friends consent? No, surely, for that may concur to lewdest ends. Or is it when church rites are finished? Neither; for the efficacy of those depends upon the presupposed fitness of either party. Perhaps after carnal knowledge? Least of all; for that may join persons whom neither law nor nature dares join. 'Tis left that only then when the minds are fitly disposed and enabled to maintain a cheerful conversation, to the solace and love of each other, according as God intended and promised in the very first foundation of matrimony, *I will make him a help meet for him* [Gen. 2:18]. For surely what God intended and promised, that only can be thought to be his joining, and not the contrary. So likewise the Apostle witnesseth, 1 Cor. 7. 15, that in marriage God hath called us to peace. And doubtless in what respect he hath called us to marriage, in that also he hath joined us.

The rest, whom either disproportion or deadness of spirit or something distasteful and averse in the immutable bent of nature renders unconjugal, error may have joined, but God never joined against the meaning of his own ordinance. And if he joined them not, then is there no power above their own consent to hinder them from unjoining, when they cannot reap the soberest ends of being together in any tolerable sort. Neither can it be said properly that such twain were ever divorced but only parted from each other, as two persons unconjunctive and unmarriable together. But if, whom God hath made a fit help, frowardness[8] or private injuries hath made unfit, that being the secret of marriage God can better judge than man, neither is man indeed fit or able to decide this matter. However it be, undoubtedly a peaceful divorce is a less evil and less in scandal than a hateful, hardhearted, and destructive continuance of marriage, in the judgment of Moses and Christ; that justifies him in choosing the less evil, which if it were an honest and civil prudence in the Law, what is there in the Gospel forbidding such a kind of legal wisdom, though we should admit the common expositors?[9]

8. Perverseness; untowardness.
9. A term designating such Calvinist exegetes as Perkins, Beza, and Paraeus. "Admit": allow as valid; acknowledge.

*The sentence of Christ concerning divorce how to be
expounded. What Grotius hath observed. Other additions.*

Having thus unfolded those ambiguous reasons wherewith Christ,
as his wont was, gave to the Pharisees that came to sound him such
an answer as they deserved, it will not be uneasy[1] to explain the sentence itself that now follows: *Whosoever shall put away his wife,
except it be for fornication, and shall marry another, committeth adultery* [Matt. 19:9]. First, therefore, I will set down what is observed by
Grotius upon this point, a man of general learning. Next, I produce
what mine own thoughts gave me before I had seen his *Annotations*.[2]
Origen,[3] saith he, notes that Christ named adultery rather as one
example of other like cases than as one only exception; and that is
frequent not only in human but in divine laws to express one kind
of fact, whereby other causes of like nature may have the like plea,
as Exod. 21. 18, 19, 20, 26. Deut. 19. 5. And from the maxims of civil
law he shows that even in sharpest penal laws the same reason hath
the same right; and in gentler laws that from like causes to like the
law interprets rightly. But it may be objected, saith he, that nothing destroys the end of wedlock so much as adultery. To which he
answers that marriage was not ordained only for copulation but for
mutual help and comfort of life; and if we mark diligently the nature
of our Savior's commands, we shall find that both their beginning
and their end consists in charity, whose will is that we should so be
good to others as that we be not cruel to ourselves. And hence it
appears why Mark and Luke and St. Paul to the Corinthians, mentioning this precept of Christ, add no exception, because exceptions
that arise from natural equity are included silently under general
terms. It would be considered, therefore, whether the same equity
may not have place in other cases less frequent.

Thus far he.[4] From hence is what I add: First, that this saying of
Christ, as it is usually expounded, can be no law at all, that a man
for no cause should separate but for adultery, except it be a super-

---

1. Hard.
2. Hugo Grotius, *Annotationes in Quator Evangelia & Act Apostolorum* [1641], rpt. in
   Opera Theologicorum (Amsterdam, 1679), 2:53–54: "If we rightly consider the nature
   of all the precepts of Jesus Christ, we shall find that charity is their principle and perfection. Now charity requires we should procure the advantage of others, but so as to
   think of our own, and not be cruel to ourselves, as St. Paul teaches, 2 *Cor.* viii 13." This
   is the passage on charity, discussed below, that Grotius whispered to Milton: "*When I
   had almost finisht the first edition* [of The Doctrine and Discipline of Divorce], *I chanc't
   to read in the notes of* Hugo Grotius *upon the 5. Of Matth . . . and somthing he whisper'd
   rather than disputed about the law of charity, and the true end of wedlock*" (*The Judgement of Martin Bucer, YP*, 2:433–34).
3. A church father (185–254).
4. I.e., Grotius, whom Milton has been paraphrasing.

natural law, not binding us as we now are.[5] Had it been the law of
nature, either the Jews or some other wise and civil nation would
have pressed it. Or let it be so;[6] yet that law, Deut. 24. 1, whereby a
man hath leave to part whenas for just and natural cause discovered
he cannot love, is a law ancienter and deeper engraven in blameless
nature than the other; therefore, the inspired lawgiver Moses took
care that this should be specified and allowed; the other[7] he let van-
ish in silence, not once repeated in the volume of his law, even as
the reason of it vanished with paradise. Secondly, this can be no
new command, for the Gospel enjoins no new morality save only the
infinite enlargement of charity, which in this respect is called the
new commandment by St. John [13:34], as being the accomplishment of every command. Thirdly, it is no command of perfection
further than it partakes of charity, which is "the bond of perfection"
[Col. 3:14]. Those commands therefore which compel us to self-
cruelty above our strength so hardly will help forward to perfection
that they hinder and set backward in all the common rudiments of
Christianity, as was proved.

It being thus clear that the words of Christ can be no kind of command, as they are vulgarly taken, we shall now see in what sense
they may be a command, and that an excellent one, the same with
that of Moses and no other. Moses had granted that only for a natural annoyance, defect, or dislike, whether in body or mind (for so the
Hebrew words plainly note) which a man could not force himself to
live with, he might give a bill of divorce, thereby forbidding any
other cause wherein amendment or reconciliation might have place.
This law the Pharisees depraving extended to any slight contentious
cause whatsoever. Christ therefore, seeing where they halted,[8] urges
the negative part of that law, which is necessarily understood (for
the determinate permission of Moses binds them from further
license), and checking their supercilious drift, declares that no accidental, temporary, or reconcilable offence (except fornication) can
justify a divorce. He touches not here those natural and perpetual
hindrances of society, whether in body or mind, which are not to
be removed; for such, as they are aptest to cause an unchangeable
offense, so are they not capable of reconcilement because not of
amendment: they do not break, indeed, but they annihilate the bands
of marriage more than adultery. For that fault committed argues not
always a hatred either natural or incidental against whom it is committed; neither does it infer a disability of all future helpfulness or

5. Living in a fallen world.
6. Considered as a law of nature.
7. The law of marriage, instituted in paradise. "This": the law of divorce, instituted in a
   fallen world.
8. Fell short.

loyalty or loving agreement, being once past and pardoned, where it
can be pardoned. But that which naturally distastes and *finds no
favor in the eyes* of matrimony [Deut. 24:1] can never be concealed,
never appeased, never intermitted, but proves a perpetual nullity of
love and contentment, a solitude and dead vacation[9] of all acceptable conversing. Moses therefore permits divorce, but in cases only
that have no hands to join and more need separating than adultery.
Christ forbids it, but in matters only that may accord[1] and those less
than fornication. Thus is Moses' law here plainly confirmed, and
those causes which he permitted not a jot gainsaid.

And that this is the true meaning of this place I prove by no less
an author than St. Paul himself, 1 Cor. 7. 10, 11, upon which text
interpreters agree that the Apostle only repeats the precept of
Christ; where while he speaks of *the wife's reconcilement to her
husband,* he puts it out of controversy that our Savior meant chiefly
matters of strife and reconcilement, of which sort he would not that
any difference should be the occasion of divorce, except fornication. And that we may learn better how to value a grave and prudent law of Moses, and how unadvisedly we smatter with our lips
when we talk of Christ's abolishing any judicial law of his great
Father, except in some circumstances which are Judaical[2] rather
than judicial, and need no abolishing but cease of themselves, I say
again that this recited law of Moses contains a cause of divorce
greater beyond compare than that for adultery; and whoso cannot
so conceive it errs and wrongs exceedingly a law of deep wisdom for
want of well fathoming. For let him mark, no man urges the just
divorcing of adultery as it is a sin but as it is an injury to marriage;
and though it be but once committed, and that without malice,
whether through importunity or opportunity, the Gospel does not
therefore dissuade him who would therefore divorce; but that natural hatred whenever it arises is a greater evil in marriage than the
accident of adultery, a greater defrauding, a greater injustice, and
yet not blameable, he who understands not after all this representing, I doubt his will like a hard spleen draws faster than his understanding can well sanguify.[3] Nor did that man ever know or feel
what it is to love truly, nor ever yet comprehend in his thoughts what
the true intent of marriage is. And this also will be somewhat above
his reach but yet no less a truth for lack of his perspective, that as
no man apprehends what vice is so well as he who is truly virtuous,

9. Absence or cessation.
1. Be brought to reconciliation or agreement.
2. Involving the Jewish ceremonial law as opposed to the judicial law.
3. To produce blood, a function of the liver, according to Renaissance physiology. In Milton's figure, the understanding is the blood-producing liver, while the will is the spleen.
Anyone who doesn't understand that natural hatred is a more legitimate cause of
divorce than adultery is like a spleen laboring in vain without blood.

no man knows hell like him who converses most in heaven, so there is none that can estimate the evil and the affliction of a natural hatred in matrimony unless he have a soul gentle enough and spacious enough to contemplate what is true love.

And the reason why men so disesteem this wise-judging law of God and count hate, or *the not finding of favor* as it is there termed, a humorous,[4] a dishonest, and slight cause of divorce, is because themselves apprehend so little of what true concord means. For if they did, they would be juster in their balancing between natural hatred and casual adultery; this being but a transient injury and soon amended (I mean as to the party against whom the trespass is), but the other being an unspeakable and unremitting sorrow and offense, whereof no amends can be made, no cure, no ceasing but by divorce, which like a divine touch in one moment heals all, and like the word of God in one instant hushes outrageous tempests into a sudden stillness and peaceful calm [Matt. 8:26; Mark 4:39]. Yet all this so great a good of God's own enlarging to us is by the hard reins of them that sit us wholly diverted and embezzled from us. Maligners of mankind! But who hath taught ye to mangle thus and make more gashes in the miseries of a blameless creature with the leaden daggers of your literal decrees, to whose ease you cannot add the tithe of one small atom but by letting alone your unhelpful surgery? As for such as think wandering concupiscence to be here newly and more precisely forbidden than it was before, if the Apostle can convince them, we know that we are to *know lust by the law* [Rom. 7:7] and not by any new discovery of the Gospel. The Law of Moses knew what it permitted, and the Gospel knew what it forbid; he that under a peevish conceit of debarring concupiscence shall go about to make a novice of Moses (not to say a worse thing, for reverence sake) and such a one of God himself, as is a horror to think, to bind our Savior in the default of a downright promise breaking and to bind the disunions of complaining nature in chains together and curb them with a canon bit,[5] 'tis he that commits all the whoredom and adultery which himself adjudges, besides the former guilt so manifold that lies upon him. And if none of these considerations, with all their weight and gravity, can avail to the dispossessing him of his precious literalism, let some one or other entreat him but to read on in the same 19th of Matth. till he come to that place that says, *Some make themselves eunuchs for the kingdom of heaven's sake.* And if then he please to make use of Origen's knife, he may do well to be his own carver.[6]

4. Fanciful, capricious.
5. A pun, uniting the "canon bit" (a horse's restraining mouthpiece) with the canon law that forces unhappy couples to stay together.
6. Origen is said to have castrated himself after having read too literally Matt. 19:12.

Whether the words of our Savior be rightly expounded
only of actual fornication to be the cause of divorce.
The opinion of Grotius with other reasons.

But because we know that Christ never gave a judicial law and that
the word *fornication* is variously significant in Scripture, it will be
much right done to our Savior's words to consider diligently whether
it be meant here that nothing but actual fornication proved by witness can warrant a divorce, for so our canon law judges. Nevertheless, as I find that Grotius on this place hath observed, the Christian
emperors Theodosius the second and Justinian, men of high wisdom
and reputed piety, decreed it to be a divorsive fornication if the wife
attempted either against the knowledge or obstinately against the
will of her husband such things as gave open suspicion of adulteriz-
ing: as the wilful haunting of feasts, and invitations with men not of
her near kindred, the lying forth of her house without probable
cause, the frequenting of theaters against her husband's mind, her
endeavor to prevent or destroy conception.[7] Hence that of Jerome,
Where fornication is suspected, the wife may lawfully be divorced. Not
that every motion of a jealous mind should be regarded, but that it
should not be exacted to prove all things by the visibility of law-
witnessing or else to hoodwink the mind; for the law is not able to
judge of these things but by the rule of equity and by permitting a
wise man to walk the middle way of prudent circumspection, neither
wretchedly jealous nor stupidly and tamely patient. To this purpose
hath Grotius in his notes. He shows also that fornication is taken in
Scripture for such a continual headstrong behavior as tends to plain
contempt of the husband and proves it out of Judges 19. 2, where the
Levite's wife is said to have played the whore against him; which
Josephus and the Septuagint, with the Chaldean, interpret only of
stubbornness and rebellion against her husband; and to this I add
that Kimchi and the two other rabbis who gloss the text are in the
same opinion. Ben Gersom reasons that had it been whoredom, a
Jew and a Levite would have disdained to fetch her again.[8] And this

---

7. Grotius in his *Annotationes* on the Gospels, advocating "a just medium between too
   credulous jealousy and too stupid indolence," furnishes Milton with arguments for a
   broader conception of *fornication.*
8. Against the King James Bible's translation that reads the Hebrew word for fornication
   literally, "And his concubine played the whore" (Judg. 19:2), Milton appeals to the great
   medieval rabbinic commentaries of David Kimchi and Levi ben Gersom, which are
   found in the *Biblia Rabbinica* published by Johannes Buxtorf the Elder (1564–1629), in
   Basel. For Kimchi, the word designates the concubine's disdain of her husband,
   although he also notes that the word can indeed be taken literally: since the concubine
   was never given contracts of betrothal and marriage, she did indeed sleep with another
   man. Ben Gersom maintains that the concubine stayed away from her husband for
   sixteen months, and that if she had been unfaithful, her husband would have been
   forbidden to take her back. For Rashi, the word designates "going out."

I shall contribute, that had it been whoredom, she would have chosen any other place to run to than to her father's house, it being so infamous for an Hebrew woman to play the harlot and so opprobrious to the parents. Fornication, then, in this place of the Judges is understood for stubborn disobedience against the husband and not for adultery, a sin of that sudden activity as to be already committed when no more is done but only looked unchastely, which yet I should be loath to judge worthy a divorce, though in our Savior's language it be called adultery. Nevertheless, when palpable and frequent signs are given, the law of God, *Numbers* 5[:11-21] so far gave way to the jealousy of a man as that the woman, set before the sanctuary with her head uncovered, was adjured by the priest to swear whether she were false or no and constrained to drink that *bitter water* with an undoubted *curse of rottenness and tympany*[9] to follow, unless she were innocent. And the jealous man had not been guiltless before God, as seems by the last verse, if having such a suspicion in his head he should neglect this trial; which if to this day it be not to be used, or be thought as uncertain of effect as our antiquated law of *ordalium*,[1] yet all equity will judge that many adulterous demeanors which are of lewd suspicion and example may be held sufficient to incur a divorce, though the act itself hath not been proved. And seeing the generosity of our nation is so, as to account no reproach more abominable than to be nicknamed the husband of an adulteress, that our law should not be as ample as the law of God to vindicate a man from that ignoble sufferance is our barbarous unskilfulness, not considering that the law should be exasperated[2] according to our estimation of the injury. And if it must be suffered till the act be visibly proved, Solomon himself, whose judgment will be granted to surpass the acuteness of any canonist, confesses (Prov. 30. 19, 20) that for the act of adultery, it is as difficult to be found as the *track of an eagle in the air, or the way of a ship in the sea*; so that a man may be put to unmanly indignities ere it be found out. This therefore may be enough to inform us that divorsive adultery is not limited by our Savior to the utmost act, and that to be attested always by eyewitness, but may be extended also to diverse obvious actions which either plainly lead to adultery or give such presumption whereby sensible men may suspect the deed to be already done. And this the rather may be thought in that our Savior chose to use the word *fornication*, which word is found to signify other matrimonial transgressions of main breach to that covenant besides actual adultery. For that sin needed not the riddance of divorce but of death by the law, which

9. A morbid swelling.
1. Trial by ordeal, abolished in England about 1215.
2. Rendered more severe.

was active even till then by the example of the woman taken in adultery [John 8:3-11]; or if the law had been dormant, our Savior was
more likely to have told them of their neglect than to have let a capital crime silently scape into a divorce. Or if it be said his business
was not to tell them what was criminal in the civil courts but what
was sinful at the bar of conscience, how dare they then, having no
other ground than these our Savior's words, draw that into trial of
law which both by Moses and our Savior was left to the jurisdiction
of conscience? But we take from our Savior, say they, only that it was
adultery, and our law of itself applies the punishment. But by their
leave that so argue, the great lawgiver of all the world, who knew best
what was adultery both to the Jew and to the Gentile, appointed no
such applying and never likes when mortal men will be vainly presuming to outstrip his justice.

CHAP. XIX.

Christ's manner of teaching. St. Paul adds to this matter
of divorce without command to show the matter to be of
equity, not of rigor. That the bondage of a Christian
may be as much, and his peace as little, in some other
marriages besides idolatrous. If those arguments therfore
be good in that one case, why not in those other; therefore,
the Apostle himself adds ἐν τοῖς τοιούτοις.[3]

Thus at length we see, both by this[4] and by other places, that
there is scarce any one saying in the Gospel but must be read with
limitations and distinctions to be rightly understood; for Christ
gives no full comments or continued discourses but, as Demetrius
the Rhetorician phrases it, speaks oft in monosyllables, like a master[5] scattering the heavenly grain of his doctrine like pearls here
and there, which requires a skillful and laborious gatherer, who
must compare the words he finds with other precepts, with the end
of every ordinance, and with the general analogy of evangelic doctrine. Otherwise, many particular sayings would be but strange
repugnant riddles, and the church would offend in granting divorce
for frigidity, which is not here excepted with adultery but by them
added. And this was it undoubtedly which gave reason to St. Paul of
his own authority, as he professes, and without command from the
Lord, to enlarge the seeming construction of those places in the
Gospel by adding a case wherein a person deserted, which is some-

---

3. In such cases (1 Cor. 7:15).
4. Matt. 5:32: "whoever shall put away his wife, saving for the cause of fornication, causeth her to commit adultery."
5. Demetrius, *On Style* (4th century B.C.E.), distinguishes between the curt monosyllables
   of a master addressing a slave and the lengthier style of supplication.

thing less than divorced, may lawfully marry again. And having declared his opinion in one case, he leaves a further liberty for Christian prudence to determine in cases of like importance, using words so plain as are not to be shifted off, *that a brother or a sister is not under bondage in such cases*; adding also that *God hath called us to peace* in marriage [1 Cor. 7:15].

Now if it be plain that a Christian may be brought into unworthy bondage and his religious peace not only interrupted now and then but perpetually and finally hindered in wedlock by mis-yoking with a diversity of nature as well as of religion, the reasons of St. Paul cannot be made special to that one case of infidelity but are of equal moment to a divorce wherever Christian liberty and peace are without fault equally obstructed—that the ordinance which God gave to our comfort may not be pinned upon us to our undeserved thraldom, to be cooped up, as it were, in mockery of wedlock to a perpetual betrothed loneliness and discontent, if nothing worse ensue. There being naught else of marriage left between such but a displeasing and forced remedy against the sting of a brute desire—which fleshly accustoming,[6] without the soul's union and commixture of intellectual delight, as it is rather a soiling than a fulfilling of marriage-rites, so is it enough to embase the mettle of a generous spirit, and sinks him to a low and vulgar pitch of endeavor in all his actions, or (which is worse) leaves him in a despairing plight of abject and hardened thoughts; which condition, rather than a good man should fall into, a man useful in the service of God and mankind, Christ himself hath taught us to dispense with the most sacred ordinances of his worship—even, for a bodily healing, to dispense with that holy and speculative rest of Sabbath,[7] much more than with the erroneous observance of an ill-knotted marriage for the sustaining of an overcharged faith and perseverance.

CHAP. XX.

The meaning of St. Paul, that charity believeth all things. What is to be said to the license which is vainly feared will grow hereby. What to those who never have done prescribing patience in this case. The Papist most severe against divorce yet most easy to all license. Of all the miseries in marriage God is to be cleared and the faults to be laid on man's unjust laws.

And though bad causes would take license by this pretext, if that cannot be remedied, upon their conscience be it who shall so do.

---

6. Making oneself familiar with, cohabiting.
7. Mark 2:27: "The Sabbath was made for man, and not man for the Sabbath."

This was that hardness of heart and abuse of a good law which
Moses was content to suffer rather than good men should not have
it at all to use needfully. And he who to run after one lost sheep left
ninety-nine of his own flock at random in the wilderness [Matt.
18:12-13] would little perplex his thoughts for the obduring[8] of nine-
hundred and ninety such as will daily take worse liberties whether
they have permission or not. To conclude, as without charity God
hath given no commandment to men, so without it neither can men
rightly believe any commandment given. For every act of true faith,
as well that whereby we believe the law as that whereby we endeavor[9]
the law, is wrought in us by charity, according to that in the divine
hymn of St. Paul, 1 Cor. 13[:7], *Charity believeth all things*—not as if
she were so credulous, which is the exposition hitherto current, for
that were a trivial praise, but to teach us that charity is the high
governess of our belief, and that we cannot safely assent to any precept written in the Bible but as charity commends it to us. Which
agrees with that of the same Apostle to the Ephes[ians]. 4. 14, 15,
where he tells us that the way to get a sure undoubted knowledge of
things is to hold that for truth which accords most with charity—
whose unerring guidance and conduct having followed as a lodestar
with all diligence and fidelity in this question, I trust, through the
help of that illuminating Spirit which hath favored me, to have done
no every day's work in asserting[1] after many ages the words of Christ,
with other Scriptures of great concernment, from burdensome and
remorseless obscurity, tangled with manifold repugnances, to their
native luster and consent between each other; hereby also dissolving
tedious and Gordian[2] difficulties which have hitherto molested the
church of God and are now decided not with the sword of Alexander
but with the immaculate hands of charity, to the unspeakable good
of Christendom.

And let the extreme literalist sit down now and revolve[3] whether
this in all necessity be not the due result of our Savior's words. Or,
if he persist to be otherwise opinioned, let him well advise lest,
thinking to grip fast the Gospel he be found instead with the canon
law in his fist, whose boisterous[4] edicts, tyrannizing the blessed ordinance of marriage into the quality of a most unnatural and unchris-
tianly yoke, have given the flesh this advantage to hate it and turn
aside, oft-times unwillingly, to all dissolute uncleanness, even till

8. Becoming hardened in wrongdoing or sin.
9. Try to fulfill.
1. Rescuing.
2. A knot that could not be untied; Alexander the Great cut through it with his sword;
   figuratively, a matter of extreme difficulty.
3. Consider
4. Stiff, unyielding.

punishment itself is weary and overcome by the incredible frequency of trading lust and uncontrolled adulteries.

Yet men whose creed is custom I doubt not but will be still endeavoring to hide the sloth of their own timorous capacities with this pretext, that for all this 'tis better to endure with patience and silence this affliction which God hath sent. And I agree 'tis true if this be exhorted and not enjoined; but withal it will be wisely done to be as sure as may be that what man's iniquity hath laid on be not imputed to God's sending, lest under the color of an affected patience we detain ourselves at the gulf's mouth of many hideous temptations, not to be withstood without proper gifts, which, as Perkins well notes, God gives not ordinarily—no, not to most earnest prayers.[5] Therefore we pray, *Lead us not into temptation,* a vain prayer if, having led our selves thither, we love to stay in that perilous condition. God sends remedies as well as evils, under which he who lies and groans that may lawfully acquit himself is accessory to his own ruin; nor will it excuse him though he suffer, through a sluggish fearfulness to search thoroughly what is lawful, for fear of disquieting the secure falsity of an old opinion.

Who doubts not but that it may be piously said to him who would dismiss frigidity, "Bear your trial, take it as if God would have you live this life of continence." If he exhort this, I hear him as an angel, though he speak without warrant; but if he would compel me, I know him for Satan. To him who divorces an adulteress, piety might say, "Pardon her; you may show much mercy, you may win a soul"; yet the law both of God and man leaves it freely to him. For God loves not to plow out the heart of our endeavors with over-hard and sad tasks. God delights not to make a drudge of virtue, whose actions must be all elective and unconstrained. Forced virtue is as a bolt over-shot:[6] it goes neither forward nor backward and does no good as it stands.

Seeing therefore that neither Scripture nor reason hath laid this unjust austerity upon divorce, we may resolve that nothing else hath wrought it but that letter-bound servility of the canon doctors, supposing marriage to be a sacrament, and out of the art they have to lay unnecessary burdens upon all men, to make a fair show in the fleshly observance of matrimony, though peace and love with all other conjugal respects fare never so ill. And indeed the papists, who are the strictest forbidders of divorce, are the easiest libertines to admit of grossest uncleanness; as if they had a design, by making wedlock a supportless yoke, to violate it most under color of pre-

---

5. William Perkins, in his *Christian Oeconomie* (1609), distinguishes between "proper" gifts of God, "which are given onely to some certaine men," withheld from most even "though they be often and earnestely asked," and general gifts, which "are such as God giveth generally to all."
6. Probably a jammed lock.

serving it most inviolable; and withal delighting, as their mystery[7] is, to make men the day-laborers of their own afflictions, as if there were such a scarcity of miseries from abroad that we should be made to melt our choicest home blessings and coin them into crosses, for want whereby to hold commerce with patience.

If any, therefore, who shall hap to read this discourse, hath been through misadventure ill engaged in this contracted evil here complained of, and finds the fits and workings of a high impatience frequently upon him, of all those wild words which men in misery think to ease themselves by uttering, let him not open his lips against the providence of heaven or tax the ways of God and his divine truth,[8] for they are equal, easy, and not burdensome; nor do they ever cross the just and reasonable desires of men, nor involve this our portion of mortal life into a necessity of sadness and malcontent by laws commanding over the unreducible antipathies of nature, sooner or later found; but allow us to remedy and shake off those evils into which human error hath led us through the midst of our best intentions, and to support our incident extremities by that authentic precept of sovereign charity, whose grand commission is to do and to dispose over all the ordinances of God to man, that love and truth may advance each other to everlasting. While we, literally superstitious through customary faintness of heart, not venturing to pierce with our free thoughts into the full latitude of nature and religion, abandon ourselves to serve under the tyranny of usurped opinions, suffering those ordinances which were allotted to our solace and reviving to trample over us and hale us into a multitude of sorrows which God never meant us. And where he set us in a fair allowance of way, with honest liberty and prudence to our guard, we never leave subtilizing and casuisting[9] till we have straitened and pared that liberal path into a razor's edge to walk on, between a precipice of unnecessary mischief on either side; and starting at every false alarm, we do not know which way to set a foot forward with manly confidence and Christian resolution, through the confused ringing in our ears of panic scruples and amazements.

---

7. Secret purpose. "Supportless": insupportable, unbearable.
8. A prose theodicy, evoking the great argument of the opening invocation of *Paradise Lost* (1.25–26), asserting providence and justifying the ways of God but with a big difference: in this instance, sadness and evils become remediable through both human action and the divine institution of divorce.
9. Practicing false moral reasoning. (Reflecting Milton's anti-Catholic prejudice against casuistry, which examines morally difficult cases of conscience, often involving conflicting duties.)

CHAP. XXI.

*That the matter of divorce is not to be tried by law
but by conscience, as many other sins are. The magistrate
can only see that the condition of divorce be just and equal.
The opinion of Fagius and the reasons of this assertion.*

Another act of papal encroachment it was to pluck the power and arbitrament of divorce from the master of family, into whose hands God and the law of all nations had put it, and Christ so left it, preaching only to the conscience and not authorizing a judicial court to toss about and divulge the unaccountable and secret reasons of disaffection between man and wife as a thing most improperly answerable to any such kind of trial. But the popes of Rome, perceiving the great revenue and high authority it would give them, even over princes, to have the judging and deciding of such a main consequence in the life of man as was divorce, wrought so upon the superstition of those ages as to divest them of that right which God from the beginning had entrusted to the husband; by which means they subjected that ancient and naturally domestic prerogative to an external and unbefitting judicature. For although differences in divorce about dowries, jointures, and the like, besides the punishing of adultery, ought not to pass without referring, if need be, to the magistrate, yet that the absolute and final hindering of divorce cannot belong to any civil or earthly power against the will and consent of both parties, or of the husband alone, some reasons will be here urged as shall not need to decline the touch.

But first I shall recite what hath been already yielded by others in favor of this opinion. Grotius and many more agree that notwithstanding what Christ spake therein to the conscience, the magistrate is not thereby enjoined aught against the preservation of civil peace, of equity, and of convenience. Among these Fagius is most remarkable and gives the same liberty of pronouncing divorce to the Christian magistrate as the Mosaic had. *For whatever,* saith he, *Christ spake to the regenerate, the judge hath to deal with the vulgar;*[1] *if therefore any through hardness of heart will not be a tolerable wife to her husband, it will be lawful as well now as of old to pass the bill of divorce, not by private but by public authority. Nor doth man separate them but God by his law of divorce given to Moses. What can hinder the magistrate from so doing, to whose government all outward things are subject, to separate and remove from perpetual vexation and no small danger those bodies whose minds are already separate; it being his office to procure peaceable and convenient living in the commonwealth; and being as certain also that they so necessarily separated can-*

---

1. The common people.

not all receive a single life.[2] And this I observe, that our divines do generally condemn separation of bed and board without the liberty of second choice; if that therefore in some cases be most purely necessary, as who so blockish to deny, then is this also as needful.

Thus far by others is already well stepped, to inform us that divorce is not a matter of law but of charity. If there remain a furlong yet to end the question, these following reasons may serve to gain it with any apprehension not too unlearned or too wayward. First because ofttimes the causes of seeking divorce reside so deeply in the radical and innocent affections of nature as is not within the diocese of law to tamper with. Other relations may aptly enough be held together by a civil and virtuous love. But the duties of man and wife are such as are chiefly conversant in that love which is most ancient and merely[3] natural, whose two prime statutes are to join itself to that which is good and acceptable and friendly, and to turn aside and depart from what is disagreeable, displeasing, and unlike. Of the two this latter is the strongest and most equal to be regarded; for although a man may often be unjust in seeking that which he loves, yet he can never be unjust or blameable in retiring from his endless trouble and distaste, whenas his tarrying can redound to no true content on either side. Hate is of all things the mightiest divider—nay, is division itself. To couple hatred therefore, though wedlock try all her golden links and borrow to her aid all the iron manacles and fetters of law, it does but seek to twist a rope of sand,[4] which was a task, they say, that posed the devil. And that sluggish fiend in hell, Ocnus, whom the poems tell of, brought his idle cordage to as good effect, which never served to bind with but to feed the ass that stood at his elbow.[5] And that the restrictive law against divorce attains as little to bind anything truly in a disjointed marriage, or to keep it bound, but serves only to feed the ignorance and definitive impertinence of a doltish canon, were no absurd allusion.

To hinder therefore those deep and serious regresses of nature in a reasonable soul parting from that mistaken help which he justly seeks in a person created for him, recollecting[6] himself from an unmeet help which was never meant, and to detain him by compulsion in such an unpredestined misery as this, is in diameter against[7] both nature and institution. But to interpose a jurisdictive power over the inward and irremediable disposition of man, to command love and sympathy, to forbid dislike against the guiltless instinct of

---

2. Paulus Fagius, in *Thargum* (1546).
3. Entirely.
4. A proverbial expression for an attempt to do the impossible.
5. Ocnus, a mythological figure, was condemned to spend eternity in the underworld, weaving a rope of straw, which his donkey ate as fast as it was made.
6. Withdrawing.
7. Directly opposed to.

nature, is not within the province of any law to reach, and were indeed an uncommodious rudeness, not a just power. For that law may bandy with nature and traverse her sage motions was an error in Callicles the rhetorician, whom Socrates from high principles confutes in Plato's *Gorgias*.[8] If therefore divorce may be so natural, and that law and nature are not to go contrary, then to forbid divorce compulsively is not only against nature but against law.

Next, it must be remembered that all law is for some good that may be frequently attained without the admixture of a worse inconvenience; and therefore many gross faults, as ingratitude and the like, which are too far within the soul to be cured by constraint of law, are left only to be wrought on by conscience and persuasion—which made Aristotle, in the 10th of his *Ethics* to Nicomachus, aim at a kind of division of law into private or persuasive and public or compulsive.[9] Hence it is that the law forbidding divorce never attains to any good end of such prohibition but rather multiplies evil. For if nature's resistless sway in love or hate be once compelled, it grows careless of itself, vicious, useless to friend, unserviceable and spiritless to the commonwealth, which Moses rightly foresaw, and all wise lawgivers that ever knew man, what kind of creature he was. The Parliament also and clergy of England were not ignorant of this when they consented that Harry the 8th might put away his Q. Anne of Cleve, whom he could not like, after he had been wedded half a year; unless it were that contrary to the proverb they made a necessity of that which might have been a virtue in them to do. For even the freedom and eminence of man's creation gives him to be a law in this matter to himself, being the head of the other sex which was made for him;[1] whom therefore though he ought not to injure, yet neither should he be forced to retain in society to his own overthrow, nor to hear any judge therein above himself. It being also an unseemly affront to the sequestered and veiled modesty of that sex to have her unpleasingness and other concealments bandied up and down, and aggravated in open court by those hired masters of tongue-fence.

Such uncomely exigences it befell no less a majesty than Henry the 8th to be reduced to; who finding just reason in his conscience to forgo his brother's wife, after many indignities of being deluded and made a boy of by those his two cardinal judges, was constrained at last, for want of other proof that she had been carnally known by Prince Arthur, even to uncover the nakedness of that virtuous lady

---

8. Against the Sophist Callicles, who argues that justice is a mere convention, Socrates maintains that it is inherent in the nature of things (*Gorgias*, 482–510). In *Paradise Lost*, "God and Nature bid the same" (6.176), and in the divorce tracts the divine Mosaic law accords with human desire.
9. *Nichomachean Ethics* 10.9, on public regulation and private persuasion.
1. 1 Cor. 11:3: "The head of the woman is the man."

and to recite openly the obscene evidence of his brother's chamberlain.[2] Yet it pleased God to make him see all the tyranny of Rome by discovering this which they exercised over divorce, and to make him the beginner of a reformation to this whole kingdom by first asserting into his familiary[3] power the right of just divorce. 'Tis true, an adulteress cannot be shamed enough by any public proceeding; but that woman whose honor is not appeached is less injured by a silent dismission, being otherwise not illiberally dealt with, than to endure a clamoring debate of utterless[4] things in a business of that civil secrecy and difficult discerning as not to be overmuch questioned by nearest friends. Which drew that answer from the greatest and worthiest Roman of his time, Paulus Emilius, being demanded why he would put away his wife for no visible reason: *This shoe* (said he, and held it out on his foot) *is a neat shoe, a new shoe, and yet none of you know where it wrings me*.[5] Much less by the unfamiliar cognizance of a fee'd gamester can such a private difference be examin'd, neither ought it.

Again, if law aim at the firm establishment and preservation of matrimonial faith, we know that cannot thrive under violent means but is the more violated. It is not when two unfortunately met are by the canon forced to draw in that yoke an unmerciful day's work of sorrow till death unharness 'em, that then the law keeps marriage most unviolated and unbroken; but when the law takes order that marriage be accountant and responsible to perform that society, whether it be religious, civil, or corporal, which may be conscionably required and claimed therein, or else to be dissolved if it cannot be undergone. This is to make marriage most indissoluble by making it a just and equal dealer, a performer of those due helps which instituted the covenant, being otherwise a most unjust contract, and no more to be maintained under tuition[6] of law than the vilest fraud or cheat or theft that may be committed. But because this is such a secret kind of fraud or theft as cannot be discerned by law but only

---

2. Milton takes a Henrician stance toward the "great matter" of the divorce from Catherine of Aragon, in accordance with Tudor myth, endorsing a teleological reading of Henry VIII's divorce from Rome, which was actually motivated less by *conscience* than by lust for Anne Boleyn. The "two cardinal judges," Campeggio and Wolsey, were delegated by Pope Clement VII to hear Henry's plea for the annulment of his marriage, but they also connived with the king against Catherine. The queen was the widow of Henry's brother, Prince Arthur, and the king's belated claim that he had violated the prohibition in Leviticus (18:16) against marriage to a brother's wife ("Thou shalt not uncover the *nakedness* of thy brother's wife") depended in part on whether sickly Arthur had ever consummated the union. The chamberlain reported that on the first morning of his marriage Arthur declared that he had spent a hot night in Spain.
3. Pertaining to the control of a family; domestic.
4. Unutterable. "Appeached": impeach, cast aspersion upon.
5. Plutarch records the story in *Aemilius Paulus* 5.1–2, attributing it to an anonymous Roman and applying it to the situation of Aemilius. Milton might be following John Selden's *Uxor Ebraica*, where the remark itself is mistakenly attributed to Aemilius.
6. Protection.

by the plaintiff himself, therefore to divorce was never counted a political or civil offense neither to Jew nor Gentile, nor by any judicial intendment of Christ further than could be discerned to transgress the allowance of Moses, which was of necessity so large that it doth all one as if it sent back the matter undeterminable at law and intractable by rough dealing, to have instructions and admonitions bestowed about it by them whose spiritual office is to adjure and to denounce, and so left to the conscience.

The law can only appoint the just and equal conditions of divorce, and is to look how it is an injury to the divorced, which in truth it can be none as a mere separation: for if she consent, wherein has the law to right her? Or consent not, then is it either just, and so deserved, or if unjust, such in all likelihood was the divorcer, and to part from an unjust man is a happiness and no injury to be lamented. But suppose it be an injury, the law is not able to amend it, unless she think it other than a miserable redress to return back from whence she was expelled, or but entreated to be gone, or else to live apart, still married without marriage, a married widow. Last, if it be to chasten the divorcer, what law punishes a deed which is not moral but natural, a deed which cannot certainly be found to be an injury? Or how can it be punished by prohibiting the divorce, but that the innocent must equally partake both in the shame and in the smart? So that which way soever we look the law can to no rational purpose forbid divorce; it can only take care that the conditions of divorce be not injurious. Thus then we see the trial of law how impertinent it is to this question of divorce, how helpless next, and then how hurtful.

CHAP. XXII.

The last reason why divorce is not to be restrained by law, it being against the law of nature and of nations. The larger proof whereof referred to Mr. Selden's Book De Jure Naturali & Gentium. An objection of Paraeus answered. How it ought to be ordered by the church. That this will not breed any worse inconvenience nor so bad as is now suffered.

Therefore, the last reason why it should not be[7] is the example we have, not only from the noblest and wisest commonwealths, guided by the clearest light of human knowledge, but also from the divine testimonies of God himself, law-giving in person to a sanctified people. That all this is true, who so desires to know at large with least pains and expects not here over-long rehearsals of that which is by others already so judiciously gathered, let him hasten to be

---

7. *Should not be* restrained by law.

acquainted with that noble volume written by our learned Selden, *Of the Law of Nature & of Nations*,[8] a work more useful and more worthy to be perused, whosoever studies to be a great man in wisdom, equity, and justice than all those decretals and sumless sums which the pontifical clerks have doted on ever since that unfortunate mother famously sinned thrice[9] and died impenitent of her bringing into the world those two misbegotten infants, and for ever infants, Lombard and Gratian, him the compiler of canon iniquity, t'other the Tubalcain[1] of scholastic sophistry, whose overspreading barbarism hath not only infused their own bastardy upon the fruitfulest part of human learning, not only dissipated and dejected the clear light of nature in us, & of nations, but hath tainted also the fountains of divine doctrine and rendered the pure and solid Law of God unbeneficial to us by their calumnious dunceries.

Yet this Law, which their unskilfulness hath made liable to all ignominy, the purity and wisdom of this Law shall be the buckler of our dispute. Liberty of divorce we claim not, we think not, but from this Law; the dignity, the faith, the authority thereof is now grown among Christians (O astonishment!) a labor of no mean difficulty and envy[2] to defend. That it should not be counted a faltering dispense, a flattering permission of sin, the bill of adultery, a snare, is the expense of all this apology. And all that we solicit is that it may be suffered to stand in the place where God set it, amidst the firmament of his holy Laws, to shine, as it was wont, upon the weaknesses and errors of men perishing else in the sincerity of their honest purposes. For certain there is no memory of whoredoms and adulteries left among us now, when this warranted freedom of God's own giving is made dangerous and discarded for a scroll of license. It must be your suffrages and votes, O Englishmen, that this exploded[3] decree of God and Moses may scape and come off fair without the censure of a shameful abrogating—which, if yonder sun ride sure and mean not

8. In the 847 folio pages of *De Jure Naturali et Gentium juxta Disciplinam Ebraeorum* (1640), John Selden (1584–1654), the most learned person in 17th-century England, discusses the rabbinic identification of natural law with the divinely pronounced Adamic and Noachide laws, the *praeceptem Noachidarum*, considered by rabbinic tradition as the minimal moral duties enjoined upon all of humankind. Milton dedicates *The Doctrine and Discipline of Divorce* to Parliament and the Westminster Assembly, and Selden, a member of both bodies, is the only dedicatee of either to be named in the treatise.
9. Alluding to the unfounded medieval legend that Peter Lombard, Johannes Gratian, and Peter Comestor, reputed to be the founders of canon law, theology, and biblical scholarship, respectively, were the illegitimate offspring of an unrepentant mother. Milton would have found the legend in John Selden's *Titles of Honor* (1614), sig. D4v. "Decretals": collections of papal decrees, forming part of canon law, which Milton disparages. "Sumless sums": endless *summas*, or digests, such as Aquinas's *Summa Theologica*. "Famously": notoriously.
1. "An instructor of every artificer in brass and iron" (Gen. 4:22).
2. Unpopularity; inciting ill-will.
3. Disused, held in contempt.

to break word with us tomorrow, was never yet abrogated by our Savior. Give sentence, if you please, that the frivolous canon may reverse the infallible judgment of Moses and his great Director.

Or if it be the reformed writers whose doctrine persuades this rather, their reasons I dare affirm are all silenced, unless it be only this: Paraeus, on the Corinthians, would prove that hardness of heart in divorce is no more now to be permitted but to be amerced with fine and imprisonment.[4] I am not willing to discover the forgettings of reverend men, yet here I must. What article or clause of the whole new covenant can Paraeus bring to exasperate[5] the judicial Law upon any infirmity under the Gospel? (I say infirmity, for if it were the high hand of sin, the Law as little would have endured it as the Gospel.) It would not stretch to the dividing of an inheritance;[6] it refused to condemn adultery[7]—not that these things should not be done at Law, but to show that the Gospel hath not the least influence upon judicial courts, much less to make them sharper and more heavy, least of all to arraign before a temporal judge that which the law without summons acquitted. But, saith he,[8] the Law was the time of youth, under violent affections; the Gospel in us is mature age and ought to subdue affections. True, and so ought the Law too, if they be found inordinate and not merely natural and blameless.

Next, I distinguish that the time of the Law is compared to youth and pupilage in respect of the ceremonial part, which led the Jews as children through corporal and garish rudiments, until the fullness of time should reveal to them the higher lessons of faith and redemption. This is not meant of the moral part; therein it soberly concerned them not to be babies but to be men in good earnest. The sad and awful majesty of that Law was not to be jested with. To bring a bearded nonage[9] with lascivious dispensations before that throne had been a lewd affront, as it is now a gross mistake. But what discipline is this, Paraeus, to nourish violent affections in youth by cockering[1] and wanton indulgences and to chastise them in mature age with a boyish rod of correction? How much more coherent is it to Scripture that the Law as a strict schoolmaster should have punished every trespass without indulgence so baneful to youth, and that the Gospel should now correct that by admonition

---

4. Milton paraphrases Paraeus in *Operum Theologicorum*, on 1 Cor. 7:10–11, where he claims that the hardness of heart which made divorce necessary among the Israelites is not to be permitted among Christians. He advocates excommunication and amercement, the imposition of penalty and fine.
5. Render more severe.
6. See Luke 12:13–14.
7. See John 8:3–11.
8. Paraeus, on 1 Cor.
9. Youth. Milton rejects as grotesque Paraeus's view of the Jews under the ancient Mosaic law.
1. Indulgent, pampering.

and reproof only, in free and mature age, which was punished with
stripes in the childhood and bondage of the Law.[2] What therefore it
allowed then so fairly, much less is to be whipped now, especially in
penal courts: and if it ought now to trouble the conscience, why did
that angry accuser and condemner Law reprieve it?

So then, neither from Moses nor from Christ hath the magistrate
any authority to proceed against it. But what? Shall then the disposal of that power return again to the master of family? Wherefore
not? Since God there put it, and the presumptuous canon thence
bereft it. This only must be provided, that the ancient manner be
observed in the presence of the minister and other grave selected
elders, who after they shall have admonished and pressed upon him
the words of our Savior, and he shall have protested, in the faith of
the eternal Gospel and the hope he has of happy resurrection, that
otherwise than thus he cannot do, and thinks himself and this his
case not contained in that prohibition of divorce which Christ pronounced, the matter not being of malice but of nature and so not
capable of reconciling. To constrain him further were to unchristen
him, to unman him, to throw the mountain of Sinai upon him, with
the weight of the whole Law to boot, flat against the liberty and
essence of the Gospel, and yet nothing available either to the sanctity of marriage, the good of husband, wife, or children, nothing
profitable either to church or commonwealth but hurtful and pernicious in all these respects.

But this will bring in confusion.[3] Yet these cautious mistrusters
might consider that what they thus object lights not upon this book
but upon that which I engage against them, the book of God and
Moses,[4] with all the wisdom and providence which had forecast the
worst of confusion that could succeed and yet thought fit of such a
permission. But let them be of good cheer. It wrought so little disorder among the Jews that from Moses till after the captivity not
one of the prophets thought it worth rebuking; for that of Malachi
well looked into will appear to be not against divorcing but rather
against keeping strange concubines, to the vexation of their Hebrew
wives.[5] If therefore we Christians may be thought as good and tractable as the Jews were, and certainly the prohibiters of divorce presume us to be better, then less confusion is to be feared for this
among us than was among them. If we be worse, or but as bad,
which lamentable examples confirm we are, then have we more, or

---

2. See Gal. 3:24–25.
3. Milton anticipates his opponents' objection.
4. I.e., an attack on this treatise is really an attack on the Pentateuch (the five books of
   Moses), and specifically on Deut. 24:1–3.
5. See Mal. 2:16 and p. 257, n. 8.

at least as much, need of this permitted law as they to whom God therefore gave it (as they say) under a harsher covenant.

Let not therefore the frailty of man go on thus inventing needless troubles to itself, to groan under the false imagination of a strictness never imposed from above, enjoining that for duty which is an impossible and vain supererogating. *Be not righteous overmuch* is the counsel of Ecclesiastes [7:16]; *why shouldest thou destroy thyself?* Let us not be thus over-curious to strain at atoms[6] and yet to stop every vent and cranny of permissive liberty, lest nature, wanting those needful pores and breathing-places which God hath not debarred our weakness, either suddenly break out into some wide rupture of open vice and frantic heresy or else inwardly fester with repining and blasphemous thoughts, under an unreasonable and fruitless rigor of unwarranted law. Against which evils nothing can more beseem the religion of the church or the wisdom of the state than to consider timely and provide. And in so doing let them not doubt but they shall vindicate the misreputed honor of God and his great Lawgiver, by suffering him to give his own laws according to the condition of man's nature best known to him, without the unsufferable imputation of dispensing legally with many ages of ratified adultery. They shall recover the misattended words of Christ to the sincerity of their true sense from manifold contradictions and shall open them with the key of charity. Many helpless Christians they shall raise from the depth of sadness and distress, utterly unfitted as they are to serve God or man. Many they shall reclaim from obscure and giddy sects, many regain from dissolute and brutish license, many from desperate hardness, if ever that were justly pleaded. They shall set free many daughters of Israel, not wanting much of her sad plight *whom Satan had bound eighteen years* [Luke 13:16]. Man they shall restore to his just dignity and prerogative in nature, preferring the soul's free peace before the promiscuous draining of a carnal rage. Marriage, from a perilous hazard and snare, they shall reduce to be a more certain haven and retirement of happy society, when they shall judge according to God and Moses (and how not then according to Christ?), when they shall judge it more wisdom and goodness to break that covenant seemingly and keep it really, than by compulsion of law to keep it seemingly and by compulsion of blameless nature to break it really, at least if it were ever truly joined. The vigor of discipline they may then turn with better success upon the prostitute looseness of the times, when men finding in themselves the infirmities of former ages shall not be constrained above the gift of God in them to unprofitable and impossible observances never required from the civilest, the wisest, the holiest nations, whose other excellencies in moral virtue they never yet

6. Motes or particles of dust; see Matt. 23:24: "Ye blind guides, which strain at a gnat."

could equal. Last of all, to those whose mind still is to maintain textual restrictions, whereof the bare sound cannot consist sometimes with humanity, much less with charity, I would ever answer by putting them in remembrance of a command above all commands, which they seem to have forgot, and who spake it; in comparison whereof this which they so exalt is but a petty and subordinate precept. *Let them go* therefore with whom I am loath to couple them (yet they will needs run into the same blindness with the Pharisees), *let them go therefore* and consider well what this lesson means, *I will have mercy and not sacrifice;*[7] for on that *saying all the law and prophets depend* [Matt. 22:40], much more the Gospel, whose end and excellence is mercy and peace. Or if they cannot learn that, how will they hear this, which yet I shall not doubt to leave with them as a conclusion: that God the Son hath put all other things under his own feet, but his commandments he hath left all under the feet of charity.

OF EDUCATION *Of Education* (1644) consists of eight quarto sheets in the form of a letter to Samuel Hartlib, who had solicited Milton's views on the subject. Its brevity and the absence of a title page, author's or publisher's name, and date of publication suggest that Milton intended it for limited circulation. Hartlib (c. 1600–1662), an educational reformer and "intelligencer" (an agent for disseminating news, books, and manuscripts), was a disciple of the Czech educationist John Amos Comenius (1592–1670), and he hoped to enlist Milton in the cause.

Although Milton at this time would have been sympathetic to Comenius's dual civic and religious goals, serving the public good and achieving the coming of the millennium through the dissemination of knowledge, he would have been skeptical of his pansophical scheme for creating a universal encyclopedia of human knowledge. Milton distances himself from Comenius at the outset with a slightly disparaging reference to two of his books, the *Janua Linguarum Reserata* (The Door of Languages Unlocked) and the *Didacta Magna* (Great Instruction): "to search what many modern *Januas* and *Didactics*, more than ever I shall read, have projected, my inclination leads me not." Having dedicated himself to years of arduous study at Cambridge (1625–32), and then at Hammersmith (1632–35) and Horton (1635–38), Milton had no use for digests and compendia. And where Comenius was a proponent of universal education, for girls as well as boys, Milton's vision of a male public citizen is less liberal.

But if there were no important pro-Comenian elements in the treatise, Milton would not have accepted the assignment, especially since it required an interruption in the writing of his more urgent divorce

---

7. Christ, quoting from the Hebrew Bible (Hos. 6:6), in his reply to the Pharisees (Matt. 9:13).

treatises. Milton agreed with Comenius on the need for educational reform, "for the want whereof this nation perishes." Both Hartlib and Comenius would have concurred with Milton's educational scheme, which has students beginning with "arts most easy," "most obvious to the sense," and progressing to "things invisible." The treatise is sympathetic to the practical nature of a Comenian education, which was influenced by Francis Bacon's scientific empiricism and inductive logic. The *organum* in Bacon's influential *Novum Organum* (1620) translates as instrument or implement, used of military or architectonic engines, and Milton conceives of logic and rhetoric as "organic arts," serving as means to an end: "language is but the instrument conveying to us things useful to be known." He advocates supplementing book learning with "the helpful experiences of hunters, fowlers, fishermen, shepherds, gardeners, apothecaries, and in the other sciences, architects, engineers, mariners, anatomists."

But even in these latter instances, Milton departs from Comenius by including poetry, defined as "simple, sensuous, and passionate," alongside the organic arts of logic and rhetoric. And he buttresses his argument for the study of agriculture with references to classical Latin treatises on the subject and with Pliny's allegorical reading of Hercules' cleansing of the Augean stables as introducing the manuring of Italian soil. Contemporary readers are bound to be struck by the sheer volume of books and authors cited and by what appears to be a schoolmaster's unrealistic expectations. He introduces Italian as an afterthought, and as if a teacher were unnecessary: students "may have easily learnt at any odd hour the Italian tongue." The tone throughout the treatise is confident, perhaps because Milton has only superior students in mind, but one wonders if such assurance is justified when he notes that "the Hebrew tongue at a set hour might have been gained," along with two Aramaic dialects.

The comprehensiveness, if not the universality, of Milton's educational scheme derives in part from his unusually ambitious combination (as in the example of agriculture) of the new system of education with Renaissance humanism. Other systems of education at the time would have chosen one and rejected the other. Although the treatise derides scholasticism, it is most notable for its inclusiveness, a foreshadowing of the monist aesthetic of Milton's greatest poetry, such as the middle books of *Paradise Lost*, in which classical, Hebraic, and Christian traditions coexist. This treatise and that poetry accommodate both historical continuity and change. Milton's large vision in *Of Education* encompasses "all the offices, both private and public, of peace and war." The primal creative vision of paradise in the middle books of his great epic can be understood in relation to all of the pamphlets written between 1643 and 1645, advocating, respectively, domestic liberty, educational reform, and "freedom to express oneself" (*YP,* 4:624). Though in important ways models of paradise, these tracts address themselves to problems of the present and the immediate future, not to nostalgic evocations of an irrecoverable past.

In both of Milton's epics, fallen human beings, bankrupt of virtue,

are powerless to work their own salvation and only a perfect Christ can
recover paradise by his suffering and death. God describes his Son and
his mission as "This perfect man, by merit called my Son, / To earn
salvation for the sons of men" (*PR*, 1.166–67). Even the adversary Satan of *Paradise Regained* acknowledges that he has discovered in Jesus
"What of perfection can in man be found" (3.230). But in *Of Education*, human beings are capable of achieving "the highest perfection"
through education and hence, in accord with pansophy, of recovering
the knowledge that humankind had lost when expelled from paradise:

> The end then of learning is to repair the ruins of our first parents
> by regaining to know God aright, and out of that knowledge to
> love him, to imitate him, to be like him, as we may the nearest by
> possessing our souls of true virtue, which being united to the
> heavenly grace of faith makes up the highest perfection.

Although the treatise spends a great deal of time on a secular curriculum and on the civic humanist purpose of education, its opening sentence identifies the religious motive and purpose of informed
human activity as "simply the love of God and of mankind." This
may well be for Milton the most important principle of all, and he
enunciates it in his major works of poetry and prose, transferring
terms from one dispensation to another to emphasize God's continuous ways with all of his creatures. "Faith and virtue" and "love of
God and of mankind" appear in Milton's *De Doctrina Christiana* (*YP*,
6:353) as the two divine commands in paradise beyond natural law:
those concerning the tree of knowledge and marriage. These are
precise Edenic counterparts to postlapsarian dispensations.

The ends of natural law are wisdom and virtue, as Plato attests in
a passage that Milton knew well. In the *Symposium* (209A), Socrates
distinguishes between those people whose creative instinct is physical and those whose creative desire is of the soul. The latter "long
to beget spiritually, not physically, the progeny which it is the
nature of the soul to create and bring to birth. If you ask what that
progeny is, it is wisdom and virtue in general." Writing in *An Apology* of happiness both individual and communal, Milton places
these remarks in a framework of platonic idealism and ethical doctrine: "the first and chiefest office of love, begins and ends in the
soule, producing those happy twins of her divine generation knowledge and vertue" (p. 229).

The tree of knowledge, a pledge of the relationship between
humankind and God, and marriage, a pledge of the relationship
between human beings, are the Edenic prototypes of knowledge
and virtue. Under the Mosaic law, the counterparts of the two
pledges (Edenic) and the twin progeny of the soul (natural law) are
the two tables of the decalogue, which reduce the commandments
to faith and performance. The chronology of *Paradise Lost* begins

with the metaphorical begetting of the Son as ruler over the angels, which Raphael narrates as Sinai theophany. God's emphatically legal declaration compresses into just two lines the two tables of the law, the Ten Commandments, the love of God ("Under his great Vice-gerent reign" [5.609]) and of our neighbor ("abide / United as one individual Soul" [609–10]). Milton asserts that the law and the gospel, correctly understood, are entirely compatible: "The works of the faithful are the works of the Holy Spirit itself. These never run contrary to the love of God and of our neighbor . . . which is the sum of the law" (*YP*, 6:640). With the advent of Christ, the two tables of the law are in turn transposed to a higher key. To begin the second book of *De Doctrina Christiana*, Milton defines the two parts of Christian theology: "The first book dealt with FAITH and THE KNOWLEDGE OF GOD. This second book is about THE WORSHIP OF GOD and CHARITY" (*YP*, 6:637). The two commands that extend beyond natural law, concerning the tree of knowledge and marriage, constitute an Edenic equivalent for Milton of the central imperatives of natural law, the Mosaic law, and the gospel, resembling most closely "the love of God and of our neighbor."

What might appear to contemporary readers of this treatise to be merely an ostentatious display of one's learning is, in reality, the result of Milton's passionate commitment to reform a nation that he regards as a second Israel. And the fountainhead from which everything in the treatise flows is "simply the love of God and of mankind."

Of Education

To Master Samuel Hartlib

Master Hartlib

I am long since persuaded that to say or do aught worth memory and imitation, no purpose or respect should sooner move us than simply the love of God and of mankind. Nevertheless, to write now the reforming of education, though it be one of the greatest and noblest designs that can be thought on, and for the want whereof this nation perishes, I had not yet at this time been induced but by your earnest entreaties and serious conjurements; as having my mind for the present half-diverted in the pursuance of some other assertions, the knowledge and the use of which cannot but be a great furtherance both to the enlargement of truth and honest living, with much more peace.

Nor should the laws of any private friendship have prevailed with me to divide thus or transpose my former thoughts, but that I see those aims, those actions which have won you with me the esteem of a person sent hither by some good providence from a far country[1] to be the occasion and the incitement of great good to this island. And, as I hear, you have obtained the same repute with men of most approved wisdom and some of the highest authority among us; not to mention the learned correspondence which you hold in foreign parts, and the extraordinary pains and diligence which you have used in this matter both here and beyond the seas, either by the definite will of God so ruling or the peculiar sway of nature, which is also God's working. Neither can I think that, so reputed and so valued as you are, you would, to the forfeit of your own discerning ability, impose upon me an unfit and over-ponderous argument, but that the satisfaction which you profess to have received from those incidental discourses which we have wandered into hath pressed and almost constrained you into a persuasion that what you require from me in this point I neither ought nor can in conscience defer beyond this time both of so much need at once and so much opportunity[2] to try what God hath determined.

I will not resist, therefore, whatever it is either of divine or human obligement that you lay upon me, but will forthwith set down in writing, as you request me, that voluntary[3] idea which hath long in silence presented itself to me of a better education, in extent and comprehension far more large, and yet of time far shorter, and of attainment far more certain, than hath been yet in practice. Brief I shall endeavor to be; for that which I have to say, assuredly this nation hath extreme need should be done sooner than spoken. To tell you, therefore, what I have benefited herein among old renowned authors, I shall spare; and to search what many modern *Januas* and *Didactics*,[4] more than ever I shall read, have projected, my inclination leads me not. But if you can accept of these few observations which have flowered off[5] and are as it were the burnishing of many studious and contemplative years altogether spent in the search of religious and civil knowledge, and such as pleased you so well in the relating, I here give you them to dispose of.

The end then of learning is to repair the ruins of our first parents[6] by regaining to know God aright, and out of that knowledge to love him, to imitate him, to be like him, as we may the nearest by possess-

---

1. A Cambridge-educated resident of London, Hartlib was born in Elbing, the Baltic town that was then part of western Poland. Before matriculating at Cambridge, he may have studied at the University of Königsberg.
2. In June 1641, the House of Commons resolved to use lands taken from the prelates for the advancement of education.
3. Purely spontaneous, without external constraint.
4. A disparaging reference to two books by the Czech educationist John Amos Comenius: the *Janua Linguarum Reserata* (The door of languages unlocked) and the *Didacta Magna* (Great instruction). Hartlib was an enthusiastic proponent of Comenius's pansophical projects. But Milton had no use for digests and compendia.
5. Arisen spontaneously in the treatment of a subject.
6. I.e., the consequences of Adam and Eve's Fall.

ing our souls of true virtue, which being united to the heavenly grace
of faith makes up the highest perfection. But because our understanding cannot in this body found itself but on sensible things, nor
arrive so clearly to the knowledge of God and things invisible as by
orderly conning over the visible and inferior creature,[7] the same
method is necessarily to be followed in all discreet teaching. And
seeing every nation affords not experience and tradition enough for
all kind of learning, therefore we are chiefly taught the languages of
those people who have at any time been most industrious in wisdom;
so that language is but the instrument conveying to us things useful
to be known. And though a linguist should pride himself to have all
the tongues that Babel cleft the world into, yet if he have not studied
the solid things in them as well as the words and lexicons, he were
nothing so much to be esteemed a learned man as any yeoman or
tradesman competently wise in his mother dialect only.

Hence appear the many mistakes which have made learning generally so unpleasing and so unsuccessful. First, we do amiss to
spend seven or eight years merely in scraping together so much miserable Latin and Greek as might be learned otherwise easily and
delightfully in one year. And that which casts our proficiency therein
so much behind is our time lost partly in too oft idle vacancies given
both to schools and universities, partly in a preposterous exaction,
forcing the empty wits of children to compose themes, verses, and
orations, which are the acts of ripest judgment, and the final work of
a head filled by long reading and observing with elegant maxims and
copious invention.[8] These are not matters to be wrung from poor
striplings like blood out of the nose or the plucking of untimely
fruit. Besides the ill habit which they get of wretched barbarizing
against the Latin and Greek idiom with their untutored Anglicisms,
odious to be read, yet not to be avoided without a well-continued
and judicious conversing among pure authors digested, which they
scarce taste; whereas, if after some preparatory grounds of speech
by their certain forms got into memory, they were led to the praxis[9]
thereof in some chosen short book lessoned thoroughly to them,
they might then forthwith proceed to learn the substance of good
things and arts in due order, which would bring the whole language
quickly into their power. This I take to be the most rational and
most profitable way of learning languages, and whereby we may best
hope to give account to God of our youth spent herein.

---

7. Visible creation; the material world. "Conning over": studying.
8. In classical rhetoric, *inventio* refers to research: discovering and selecting materials
pertinent to any topic of discussion. "Vacancies": vacations, holidays. "preposterous":
placing last what should be first (and placing first what should be last, hence
premature).
9. Practice. "Conversing": familiar engagement.

And for the usual method of teaching arts, I deem it to be an old error of universities not yet well recovered from the scholastic grossness[1] of barbarous ages, that instead of beginning with arts most easy, and those be such as are most obvious to the sense, they present their young unmatriculated[2] novices at first coming with the most intellective abstractions of logic and metaphysics. So that they having but newly left those grammatic flats and shallows where they stuck unreasonably to learn a few words with lamentable construction, and now on the sudden transported under another climate to be tossed and turmoiled with their unballasted wits in fathomless and unquiet deeps of controversy, do for the most part grow into hatred and contempt of learning, mocked and deluded all this while with ragged notions and babblements while they expected worthy and delightful knowledge; till poverty or youthful years call them importunately their several ways and hasten them with the sway of friends either to an ambitious and mercenary or ignorantly zealous divinity;[3] some allured to the trade of law, grounding their purposes not on the prudent and heavenly contemplation of justice and equity, which was never taught them, but on the promising and pleasing thoughts of litigious terms, fat contentions, and flowing fees; others betake them to state affairs, with souls so unprincipled in virtue and true generous breeding that flattery and court-shifts and tyrannous aphorisms[4] appear to them the highest points of wisdom, instilling their barren hearts with a conscientious slavery if, as I rather think, it be not feigned. Others, lastly, of a more delicious and airy[5] spirit, retire themselves (knowing no better) to the enjoyments of ease and luxury, living out their days in feast and jollity; which indeed is the wisest and the safest course of all these, unless they were with more integrity undertaken. And these are the errors, and these are the fruits of misspending our prime youth at the schools and universities as we do, either in learning mere words or such things chiefly as were better unlearned.

I shall detain you now no longer in the demonstration of what we should not do, but straight conduct ye to a hill-side, where I will point ye out the right path of a virtuous and noble education— laborious indeed at the first ascent, but else so smooth, so green, so full of goodly prospect and melodious sounds on every side that the

---

1. Milton is characteristically scornful of the backwardness of contemporary universities, which retained vestiges of the theological and philosophical teachings of the Schoolmen (1000–1500 C.E.).
2. Not yet admitted by enrollment to university. "Arts": fields of knowledge.
3. Career in the clergy. "Controversy": school exercises in the form of debate. "Sway": influence.
4. Maxims accepted by custom, untested by reason. "Litigious terms": times when the law courts were (profitably) in session. "Shifts": fraudulent or evasive behavior; machinations.
5. Insubstantial; superficial. "Delicious": sensual.

harp of Orpheus was not more charming. I doubt not but ye shall
have more ado to drive our dullest and laziest youth, our stocks and
stubs, from the infinite desire of such a happy nurture, than we
have now to hale and drag our choicest and hopefullest wits to that
asinine feast of sow-thistles and brambles which is commonly set
before them as all the food and entertainment of their tenderest
and most docible[6] age. I call therefore a complete and generous[7]
education that which fits a man to perform justly, skillfully, and
magnanimously all the offices, both private and public, of peace
and war. And how all this may be done between twelve and one and
twenty (less time than is now bestowed in pure trifling at grammar
and sophistry) is to be thus ordered.

First, to find out a spacious house and ground about it fit for an
academy, and big enough to lodge a hundred and fifty persons, whereof
twenty or thereabout may be attendants, all under the government
of one who shall be thought of desert sufficient and ability either to
do all or wisely to direct and oversee it done. This place should be at
once both school and university, not needing a remove to any other
house of scholarship, except it be some peculiar college of law or
physic where they mean to be practitioners; but as for those general
studies which take up all our time from Lily to the commencing, as
they term it, Master of Art, it should be absolute.[8] After this pattern,
as many edifices may be converted to this use as shall be needful
in every city throughout this land, which would tend much to the
increase of learning and civility[9] everywhere. This number, less or
more thus collected, to the convenience of a foot company,[1] or inter-
changeably two troops of cavalry, should divide their day's work
into three parts as it lies orderly: their studies, their exercise and
their diet.

For their studies: first, they should begin with the chief and necessary rules of some good grammar, either that now used or any
better; and while this is doing, their speech is to be fashioned to a
distinct and clear pronunciation, as near as may be to the Italian,
especially in the vowels. For we Englishmen, being far northerly, do
not open our mouths in the cold air wide enough to grace a southern
tongue, but are observed by all other nations to speak exceeding

6. Teachable. In Greek myth, Orpheus is the singer-musician who represents for Milton
   culture as well as poetry. When he sang, even "woods and rocks had ears / To rapture"
   (*PL*, 7.35–36). "Stocks and stubs": logs and stumps; blockheads.
7. Appropriate to one of noble birth or spirit.
8. Complete. "Peculiar": specialized. William Lily (1468?–1522/3), grammarian, was the
   first headmaster of St. Paul's School, Milton's alma mater. The definitive form of "Lily's
   Grammar" (1548–49), a posthumous compilation and revision of three earlier works,
   represents two complete grammars, one in English for beginners and one in Latin.
9. Good citizenship.
1. The number (around one hundred) appropriate for an infantry company.

close and inward, so that to smatter Latin with an English mouth is as ill a hearing as law French.[2]

Next, to make them expert in the usefullest points of grammar, and withal to season them and win them early to the love of virtue and true labor ere any flattering seducement or vain principle seize them wandering, some easy and delightful book of education would be read to them, whereof the Greeks have store, as Cebes, Plutarch, and other Socratic discourses.[3] But in Latin we have none of classic authority extant except the two or three first books of Quintilian[4] and some select pieces elsewhere. But here the main skill and groundwork will be to temper them such lectures and explanations, upon every opportunity, as may lead and draw them in willing obedience, inflamed with the study of[5] learning and the admiration of virtue, stirred up with high hopes of living to be brave men and worthy patriots, dear to God and famous to all ages. That they may despise and scorn all their childish and ill-taught qualities to delight in manly and liberal exercises, which he who hath the art and proper eloquence to catch them with—what with mild and effectual persuasions, and what with the intimation of some fear, if need be, but chiefly by his own example—might in short space gain them to an incredible diligence and courage, infusing into their young breasts an ingenuous[6] and noble ardor as would not fail to make many of them renowned and matchless men.

At the same time, some other hour of the day, might be taught them the rules of arithmetic and soon after the elements of geometry, even playing,[7] as the old manner was. After evening repast, till bedtime, their thoughts will be best taken up in the easy grounds of religion and the story of Scripture. The next step would be to the authors of agriculture, Cato, Varro, and Columella,[8] for the matter is most easy; and if the language be difficult, so much the better: it is not a difficulty above their years. And here will be an occasion of inciting and enabling them hereafter to improve the tillage of their country, to recover the bad soil, and to remedy the waste that is made of good; for this was one of Hercules' praises.[9] Ere half these authors be read, which will soon be with plying hard and daily, they cannot

---

2. A degenerate form of Norman French, used in English legal reports. "Smatter": besmirch; talk without proper knowledge or proficiency; dabble.
3. Platonic dialogues. *The Tablet of Cebes*, erroneously attributed to Cebes of Thebes, a disciple of Socrates, asserts that true education consists not in mere erudition but in the formation of character. Plutarch, author of *On the Education of Children* and *Moralia*.
4. The *Institutes*, a treatise on education and rhetoric.
5. Zeal for; devotion to. "Temper": adapt for.
6. High-minded. "Liberal": worthy of a free person; becoming to a gentleman.
7. Both Plato and Quintilian recommend games as an educational tool.
8. Each wrote a Latin agricultural treatise with the title *De Re Rustica*.
9. Pliny's *Natural History* reads Hercules' cleansing of the Augean stables allegorically, as introducing the manuring of Italian soil.

choose but be masters of any ordinary prose. So that it will be then seasonable for them to learn in any modern author the use of the globes and all the maps, first with the old names and then with the new;[1] or they might be then capable to read any compendious method of natural philosophy.

And at the same time might be entering into the Greek tongue, after the same manner as was before prescribed in the Latin, whereby the difficulties of grammar being soon overcome, all the historical physiology of Aristotle and Theophrastus are open before them and, as I may say, under contribution.[2] The like access will be to Vitruvius, to Seneca's *Natural Questions*, to Mela, Celsus, Pliny, or Solinus.[3] And having thus passed the principles of arithmetic, geometry, astronomy, and geography, with a general compact of physics, they may descend in mathematics to the instrumental science of trigonometry, and from thence to fortification, architecture, enginery,[4] or navigation. And in natural philosophy they may proceed leisurely from the history of meteors, minerals, plants, and living creatures, as far as anatomy. Then also in course might be read to them, out of some not tedious writer, the institution of physic, that they may know the tempers, the humors, the seasons, and how to manage a crudity;[5] which he who can wisely and timely do is not only a great physician to himself and to his friends, but also may at some time or other save an army by this frugal and expenseless means only, and not let the healthy and stout bodies of young men rot away under him for want of this discipline, which is a great pity and no less a shame to the commander.

To set forward all these proceedings in nature and mathematics, what hinders but that they may procure, as oft as shall be needful, the helpful experiences of hunters, fowlers, fishermen, shepherds, gardeners, apothecaries; and in the other sciences, architects, engineers, mariners, anatomists; who doubtless would be ready, some

1. Place names in both Latin and the vernacular.
2. Forced to contribute; rendered tributary. Milton refers to the biological works of Aristotle and the botanical works of his pupil Theophrastus.
3. Gaius Julius Solinus (3rd century), whose *Collectanea Rerum Memorabilium* described the known world geographically arranged. Vitruvius (1st century B.C.E.), Roman authority on engineering and architecture. Leon Battista Alberti's use of his rediscovered *De architectura* in his own seminal treatise on architecture, *De re aedificatoria* (c. 1450) made him influential in the Italian Renaissance. Seneca's (1st century) *Natural Questions* was a collection of material from earlier Greek and Roman writers on the natural world. Mela (1st century), author of the earliest surviving Latin geography. Celsus (1st century), author of an encyclopedic work, of which eight books on medicine have survived. Pliny the Elder (1st century), author of a thirty-seven-volume work of natural history.
4. Military engineering.
5. Indigestion. "Institution of physic": introduction to medicine. The traditional four elements of fire, air, earth, and water correspond to the personality types or "tempers" (choleric, sanguine, phlegmatic, melancholic), and these in turn correspond to the four bodily "humors" (yellow bile, blood, phlegm, black bile). Ancient authors found seasonal correspondences as well (e.g., an increase of phlegm in winter).

328   Prose Treatises

for reward and some to favor such a hopeful seminary. And this will
give them such a real tincture of natural knowledge as they shall
never forget but daily augment with delight. Then also those poets
which are now counted most hard will be both facile and pleasant:
Orpheus, Hesiod, Theocritus, Aratus, Nicander, Oppian, Dionysius;
and in Latin, Lucretius, Manilius, and the rural part of Virgil.[6]

By this time, years and good general precepts will have furnished
them more distinctly with that act of reason which in ethics is
called *proairesis*,[7] that they may with some judgment contemplate
upon moral good and evil. Then will be required a special reinforcement of constant and sound indoctrinating to set them right
and firm, instructing them more amply in the knowledge of virtue
and the hatred of vice, while their young and pliant affections are
led through all the moral works of Plato, Xenophon, Cicero, Plutarch, Laertius, and those Locrian remnants; but still to be reduced
in their nightward studies, wherewith they close the day's work
under the determinate sentence of David or Solomon, or the evan-
gels[8] and apostolic scriptures.

Being perfect in the knowledge of personal duty they may then
begin the study of economics.[9] And either now or before this they
may have easily learnt at any odd hour the Italian tongue. And soon
after, but with wariness and good antidote, it would be wholesome
enough to let them taste some choice comedies, Greek, Latin, or
Italian; those tragedies also that treat of household matters, such
as *Trachiniæ, Alcestis,*[1] and the like.

The next remove must be to the study of politics: to know the
beginning, end, and reasons of political societies, that they may not
in a dangerous fit of the commonwealth be such poor, shaken,
uncertain reeds of such a tottering conscience as many of our great
counselors have lately shown themselves, but steadfast pillars of the
state. After this they are to dive into the grounds of law and legal
justice, delivered first and with best warrant by Moses, and as far as
human prudence can be trusted, in those extolled remains of Gre-
cian lawgivers, Lycurgus, Solon, Zaleucus, Charondas,[2] and thence

---

6. Greek and Roman poets who depicted the natural world. *Lithica*, 770 lines setting
   forth the virtues, some of them magical, of various gems, was attributed to the mythical poet Orpheus.
7. Practical reasoning leading to choice.
8. Gospels. "Locrian remnants": texts attributed to Timaeus, a disciple of Plato, of Locri,
   in Italy. "Reduced": led back. "Determinate sentence": definitive judgment.
9. Household management.
1. Both Sophocles' *Trachiniae* and Euripides' *Alcestis* feature devoted wives: Deianira,
   who kills herself in remorse for having innocently caused the death of Hercules, and
   Alcestis, who chooses to die in place of her husband (see Milton's Sonnet XXIII).
2. Lawgivers, respectively, of Sparta, Athens, Locri Epizephyrii (a Greek colony near the
   southern tip of Italy), and Catana in Sicily.

to all the Roman edicts and tables with their Justinian,[3] and so down to the Saxon and common laws of England and the statutes.

Sundays also and every evening may be now understandingly spent in the highest matters of theology and church history ancient and modern; and ere this time the Hebrew tongue at a set hour might have been gained, that the Scriptures may be now read in their own original, whereto it would be no impossibility to add the Chaldee and the Syrian dialect.[4] When all these employments are well conquered, then will the choice histories, heroic poems, and Attic tragedies of stateliest and most regal argument, with all the famous political orations, offer themselves; which if they were not only read but some of them got by memory and solemnly pronounced with right accent and grace, as might be taught, would endue them even with the spirit and vigor of Demosthenes or Cicero, Euripides or Sophocles.

And now, lastly, will be the time to read with them those organic arts which enable men to discourse and write perspicuously, elegantly, and according to the fitted[5] style of lofty, mean or lowly. Logic, therefore, so much as is useful, is to be referred to this due place with all her well-couched heads and topics until it be time to open her contracted palm into a graceful and ornate rhetoric taught out of the rule of Plato, Aristotle, Phalereus, Cicero, Hermogenes, Longinus.[6] To which poetry would be made subsequent, or indeed rather precedent, as being less subtle[7] and fine but more simple, sensuous, and passionate. I mean not here the prosody of a verse, which they could not but have hit on before among the rudiments of grammar, but that sublime art which in Aristotle's *Poetics*, in Horace, and the Italian commentaries of Castelvetro, Tasso, Mazzoni, and others, teaches what the laws are of a true epic poem, what of a dramatic, what of a lyric, what decorum[8] is, which is the

3. Eastern Roman emperor (6th century), who ordered the codification of Roman law known as the *Corpus Juris Civilis* (Body of civil law). "Tables": i.e., the twelve tables; the ancient legislation (450 B.C.E.) that formed the centerpiece of the constitution of the Roman Republic.
4. A dialect of Middle Aramaic, which was the vehicle of eastern Christianity from the 4th to 8th centuries. "Chaldee": Aramaic, the Semitic language current during the Second Temple period (539 B.C.E.–70 C.E.), and thus spoken by Jesus; the main language of the Talmud. Portions of the biblical books of Daniel and Ezra are in Aramaic.
5. Appropriate to speaker, subject, and audience. "Organic arts": instrumental, serving as a means to an end, such as logic and rhetoric.
6. The references include the treatise *On Style*, attributed to Demetrius Phalereus (4th century B.C.E.); the rhetorical works of Hermogenes (1st century), Greek grammarian; and the treatise *On the Sublime*, long attributed to Longinus. "Well-couched": skillfully framed or expressed. "Contracted palm": the open palm of rhetoric, as opposed to the closed fist of logic.
7. Intricate, abstruse. "Subsequent": at a later point in the curriculum. "Precedent": higher in rank, taking precedence.
8. "That which is proper to a personage, place, time, or subject" in a literary composition (OED). Castelvetro (1505–71) translated Aristotle's *Poetics* into Italian and formulated the neoclassical three unities of time, place, and action. Tasso (1544–95), whom Mil-

grand masterpiece to observe. This would make them soon perceive
what despicable creatures our common rhymers and playwrights be
and show them what religious, what glorious and magnificent use
might be made of poetry both in divine and human things.

From hence, and not till now, will be the right season of forming
them to be able writers and composers in every excellent matter,
when they shall be thus fraught[9] with an universal insight into
things. Or whether they be to speak in parliament or council, honor
and attention would be waiting on their lips. There would then also
appear in pulpits other visages, other gestures, and stuff otherwise
wrought than what we now sit under, ofttimes to as great a trial of
our patience as any other that they preach to us.

These are the studies wherein our noble and our gentle youth
ought to bestow their time in a disciplinary way from twelve to one
and twenty, unless they rely more upon their ancestors dead than
upon themselves living. In which methodical course it is so supposed they must proceed, by the steady pace of learning, onward, as
at convenient times for memory's sake to retire back into the middleward and sometimes into the rear of what they have been taught,
until they have confirmed and solidly united the whole body of
their perfected knowledge, like the last embattling[1] of a Roman
legion. Now will be worth the seeing what exercises and recreations
may best agree and become these studies.

Their Exercise

The course of study hitherto briefly described is, what I can guess
by reading, likest to those ancient and famous schools of Pythagoras, Plato, Isocrates, Aristotle, and such others, out of which were
bred up such a number of renowned philosophers, orators, historians, poets, and princes all over Greece, Italy, and Asia, besides the
flourishing studies of Cyrene and Alexandria.[2] But herein it shall
exceed them and supply a defect as great as that which Plato noted
in the commonwealth of Sparta: whereas that city trained up their
youth most for war, and these in their academies and Lycæum all for
the gown,[3] this institution of breeding which I here delineate shall
be equally good both for peace and war. Therefore about an hour
and a half ere they eat at noon should be allowed them for exercise
and due rest afterwards; but the time for this may be enlarged at
pleasure, according as their rising in the morning shall be early.

---

    ton regarded as an exemplary epic poet, also wrote *Discourses on Epic Poetry.* Mazzoni
    (1548–98) defended Dante's poetic practices.
9. Fully supplied.
1. Arraying troops in order of battle. "Middleward": middle body of an army.
2. Ancient centers of Hellenistic learning.
3. Peacetime professions. "These": i.e., the Athenians.

The exercise which I commend first is the exact use of their weapon,[4] to guard and to strike safely with edge or point. This will keep them healthy, nimble, strong, and well in breath; is also the likeliest means to make them grow large and tall and to inspire them with a gallant and fearless courage, which being tempered with seasonable lectures and precepts to them of true fortitude and patience, will turn into a native and heroic valor and make them hate the cowardice of doing wrong. They must be also practiced in all the locks and grips of wrestling, wherein Englishmen are wont to excel, as need may often be in fight to tug, to grapple, and to close. And this perhaps will be enough wherein to prove and heat their single strength.[5]

The interim of unsweating themselves regularly, and convenient rest before meat, may both with profit and delight be taken up in recreating and composing their travailed spirits with the solemn and divine harmonies of music, heard or learnt; either while the skillful organist plies his grave and fancied descant in lofty fugues, or the whole symphony with artful and unimaginable touches adorn and grace the well-studied chords of some choice composer; sometimes the lute or soft organ-stop waiting on elegant voices either to religious, martial, or civil ditties; which, if wise men and prophets be not extremely out,[6] have a great power over dispositions and manners to smooth and make them gentle from rustic harshness and distempered passions. The like also would not be unexpedient after meat to assist and cherish nature in her first concoction[7] and send their minds back to study in good tune and satisfaction. Where having followed it close under vigilant eyes till about two hours before supper, they are by a sudden alarum or watchword to be called out to their military motions, under sky or covert[8] according to the season, as was the Roman wont; first on foot, then, as their age permits, on horseback to all the art of cavalry; that having in sport, but with much exactness and daily muster, served out the rudiments of their soldiership in all the skill of embattling, marching, encamping, fortifying, besieging, and battering, with all the helps of ancient and modern stratagems, tactics, and warlike maxims, they may as it were out of a long war come forth renowned and perfect commanders in the service of their country. They would not then, if they were trusted with fair and hopeful armies, suffer them, for want of just and wise discipline, to shed away from about them

4. Sword. (Milton's anonymous early biographer notes that "he wore a sword while he had his sight, and was skilled in using it.")
5. Test and exercise their strength unaided by weapons.
6. Mistaken. "Descant": an instrumental prelude, consisting of variations on a theme.
7. Foster or encourage the digestive process.
8. Cover.

like sick feathers, though they be never so oft supplied; they would not suffer their empty and unrecruitable colonels of twenty men in a company to quaff out or convey into secret hoards the wages of a delusive list[9] and a miserable remnant; yet in the meanwhile to be overmastered with a score or two of drunkards, the only soldiery left about them, or else to comply with all rapines and violences. No, certainly, if they knew aught of that knowledge that belongs to good men or good governors, they would not suffer these things.

But to return to our own institute: besides these constant exercises at home there is another opportunity of gaining experience to be won from pleasure itself abroad;[1] in those vernal seasons of the year when the air is calm and pleasant, it were an injury and sullenness against nature not to go out and see her riches and partake in her rejoicing with heaven and earth. I should not therefore be a persuader to them of studying much then, after two or three year that they have well laid their grounds, but to ride out in companies with prudent and staid guides to all the quarters of the land, learning and observing all places of strength, all commodities[2] of building and of soil for towns and tillage, harbors and ports for trade. Sometimes taking sea as far as to our navy to learn there also what they can in the practical knowledge of sailing and of sea-fight.

These ways would try all their peculiar[3] gifts of nature, and if there were any secret excellence among them would fetch it out and give it fair opportunities to advance itself by, which could not but mightily redound to the good of this nation and bring into fashion again those old admired virtues and excellencies with far more advantage now in this purity of Christian knowledge. Nor shall we then need the monsieurs of Paris to take our hopeful youth into their slight and prodigal custodies and send them over back again transformed into mimics, apes, and kickshaws.[4] But if they desire to see other countries at three or four and twenty years of age, not to learn principles but to enlarge experience and make wise observation, they will by that time be such as shall deserve the regard and honor of all men where they pass and the society and friendship of those in all places who are best and most eminent. And perhaps then other nations will be glad to visit us for their breeding or else to imitate us in their own country.

Now lastly for their diet there cannot be much to say, save only that it would be best in the same house—for much time else would

9. The colonel uses up (drinks dry) the wages of both the few real recruits who are left and the false names that he has added to the roster. "Shed away": desert. "Unrecruitable": incapable of getting recruits.
1. Outdoors.
2. Conveniences.
3. Distinctive.
4. Fantastical, frivolous persons (from Fr. *quelques choses*, "somethings").

be lost abroad and many ill habits got—and that it should be plain,
healthful, and moderate I suppose is out of controversy. Thus, Master Hartlib, you have a general view in writing, as your desire was,
of that which at several times I had discoursed with you concerning
the best and noblest way of education; not beginning, as some have
done, from the cradle, which yet might be worth many considerations, if brevity had not been my scope; many other circumstances
also I could have mentioned, but this,[5] to such as have the worth in
them to make trial, for light and direction may be enough. Only I
believe that this is not a bow for every man to shoot in that counts
himself a teacher, but will require sinews almost equal to those
which Homer gave Ulysses;[6] yet I am withal persuaded that it may
prove much more easy in the assay than it now seems at distance,
and much more illustrious; howbeit, not more difficult than I imagine, and that imagination presents me with nothing but very happy
and very possible according to best wishes, if God have so decreed
and this age have spirit and capacity enough to apprehend.

AREOPAGITICA (1644) In 1641–42, Milton had helped the Presbyterians by publishing five antiprelatical treatises, and when they came
to power, they abolished that notoriously comprehensive and repressive
instrument of censorship, King Charles' Star Chamber Decree of 1637.
But in June 1643, the mostly Presbyterian Parliament issued a licensing order that required all books, pamphlets, and papers to be licensed
by persons that it would appoint. Milton defied this order by failing to
register with the Stationers' Company either *The Doctrine and Discipline of Divorce* or the *Areopagitica*, the treatise in which he attempts,
unsuccessfully, to persuade his former allies to rescind that part of the
order that constituted prepublication censorship. (He supported the
part that required the name of the publisher and/or author and that
guaranteed copyright.) He also put his name to both treatises, "proudly
proclaiming his '*willingness to avouch what might be question'd*'" (Lewalski, 155; *YP*, 2.581).

Both treatises share many features, physically as well as conceptually.
Sublimity of style, learned content, and passionate emotion were embodied in pamphlets that as material objects reflected the poor production values of the period. (After the Star Chamber was abolished, printers with small presses rushed into business, a sign of the new freedom
of expression, and the number of annual printed items increased in the
early 1640s from the hundreds to the thousands.) Employing delibera-
tive rhetoric in both treatises, treating as choice what others before
him had treated as necessity, Milton exhorts radical change for the
improvement of the human condition and thus asserts faith in human

5. I.e., this treatise.
6. See *Od.*, 21 for the bow that only Odysseus could string. "In": with.

beings as agents capable in some measure of controlling their lives. In the divorce tracts, God is not the stern judge who demands the sacrifice of earthly pleasures, but a force of mercy who offers human beings who made bad marriage choices freedom from the misery that custom in the form of canon law would prevent them from exercising. A view of the world as imperfect but improvable carries over into the *Areopagitica* as well, where parliamentary legislation takes the place of the biblical law of divorce (Deut. 24) as the force to set things right: "For this is not the liberty which we can hope, that no grievance ever should arise in the commonwealth—that let no man in this world expect. But when complaints are freely heard, deeply considered, and speedily reformed, then is the utmost bound of civil liberty attained that wise men look for."

Laws granting permission to divorce and to publish would help good people but would also be susceptible to abuse by the wicked. The licentious, freed from mistaken Reformation interpretations of Christ's restricting words, could divorce at will, and, with no parliamentary licensing order to curb them, the vicious could publish scurrilities. But the deuteronomic law of divorce will disenthrall the hapless spouse, removing the desperate occasions of blasphemy; and freedom from prepublication censorship will allow the truth to circulate freely and thus to perfect the Reformation.

Although there are definite limits to Miltonic toleration in the *Areopagtica*, including especially his assertion that Roman Catholicism should be extirpated, in its general method this treatise shares with *The Doctrine and Discipline of Divorce* an inclusiveness that diverges from the exclusivity of the antiprelatical tracts. The great church father Tertullian famously asked, "What has Athens to do with Jerusalem?" (*De praescriptione*, vii). But in this treatise, Milton finds the teachings of philosophy and of scripture to be compatible. And, like John Selden, the Erastian MP invoked as "the chief of learned men reputed in this land," Milton joins politics and religion, asking England's legislative body to advance the cause of the Reformation.

The very title *Areopagitica* embodies this inclusiveness. It alludes to the *Areopagitic Discourse* of Isocrates (436–338 B.C.E.), an oration intended to be read rather than delivered in person, in which a private citizen urges a change in policy in Athens's highest judicial body, the Council of the Areopagus (lit. "the hill of Ares," or Mars' Hill). Besides its allusion to a pre-Christian culture, the title also alludes to St. Paul's great sermon on Mars' Hill (Acts 17:22–31), in which the apostle, preaching to the Athenians, actually quotes from the invocation to Zeus in the didactic poem *Phaenomena*, by Aratus, one "of your own poets": "in him we live, and move, and have our being" (v. 28). Milton appeals to scripture as well as Isocrates in ranking written over spoken discourse. He defends the "textual Chetiv," the original transcription of the Masoretic text of the Hebrew Bible, against the "marginal Keri," the amended text to be read aloud. He distinguishes between *keri* and his own *chetiv*, proclamation and writing, in the opening sentence, setting those who "direct their speech" over against those, like himself, who "write that which they foresee may advance the public good." Later he adds that "writing is more public than preaching and more easy to refutation, if need be."

In this classical oration, the single sentence setting forth the four-part *confirmation*, or adducing of proofs, is the fountainhead from which the main arguments flow (p. 340). Olivier Lutaud (see also Sirluck, 164–70, and Lewalski, 193–96) classifies them as the historical, intellectual, pragmatic, and moral. Milton lays before his audience "first, the inventors of it to be those whom ye will be loath to own." Calling the parliamentary order an "authentic Spanish policy of licensing books," he links it to the Spanish Inquisition as well as to the "apishly Romanizing" episcopal church of William Laud, archbishop of Canterbury. In this historical argument, he condemns Roman Catholicism for imposing institutional authority on the freedom of the individual conscience.

The second argument is based on the fact of the external inseparability of good and evil in the field of this world. Both goodness and evil are within us, and we must freely exercise reason and temperance to recognize and choose the good: "Assuredly we bring not innocence into the world, we bring impurity much rather; that which purifies us is trial, and trial is by what is contrary." Recognizing that people have an appetite for knowledge as well as food, Milton argues that we should be free to read everything, just as we are free to eat everything. After all, works that at present are being condemned as heretical (such as his own treatises on divorce) may in the fullness of time be shown to have advanced the Reformation, while others, which would receive a licenser's *Imprimatur*, may eventually be revealed as false.

Milton cites at a key moment in this argument one Pauline verse that abolishes the dietary distinctions of the Jewish ceremonial law ("Rise *Peter*, kill and eat" [Acts 10:13]) and two additional verses that can be interpreted similarly: "Prove all things, hold fast that which is good" (1 Thes. 5:21); "To the pure all things are pure" (Titus 1:15), to which Milton adds, "not only meats and drinks, but all kind of knowledge whether of good or evil." Milton echoes Raphael's warning to Adam and Eve: "Knowledge is as food, and needs no less / Her Temperance over Appetite" (*PL*, 7.126–27). In paradise, food that is knowledge is forbidden by divine law; knowledge that is like food is subject to discretion in the form of temperance.

Milton finds bold conceptual force in the Pauline verses themselves, and his second argument adapts and extends a topic based on these verses in Reformation systematic theology. These verses turn up in chapters on "the Holy Scriptures," to reject the Roman Catholic distinction between the clergy, which is privileged to search the scriptures, and the laity, which is not. Pauline verses authorized to abolish distinctions between forbidden and permitted foods and, more important, between Jew and gentile are used by Reformers to abolish distinctions between clergy and laity and to proclaim throughout the land the liberty to search the scriptures. In his adaptation of this argument in the *Areopagitica*, Milton widens the freedom to read the Bible to include the freedom to read any text. The ability of any regenerate

Christian to interpret scripture with no aid except that of the Holy
Spirit and to arrive at a truth obscured and complicated by privileged
ecclesiasts is modified slightly to become an argument for individual
freedom against the imposition of censorship.

The third argument, pragmatic or practical, exposes the futility of
prepublication censorship. (Milton holds that books, like people, are
answerable for their faults and can be prosecuted, but the decision
to print should lie with the publisher, not with the censor.) Since we
contain evil within us, there is no use trying to quarantine it. Besides,
as Milton points out, licensers would have to control "all recreations
and pastimes," music and dancing, food, dress, conversation, and the
company one keeps. And people who are good enough to qualify for the
job of licenser wouldn't want it.

The fourth or moral argument is the most complex and the most
beautiful, embedded with major tropes—the building of Solomon's
temple, the Nazarite Samson, the city of refuge, the new Israel in
which all the Lord's people are prophets—that portray England as a
holy nation. The most evocative of all is the figure of truth as the mangled body of Osiris, and the friends of truth as Isis, "gathering up limb
by limb." This embedded myth can stand in for the cross-cultural references diffused throughout the treatise: the story of an Egyptian god,
found in Plutarch's *Moralia*, and adapted by an English Puritan.

Milton insists that truth may have more shapes than one. It has a
subjective as well as an objective aspect:

> Truth is compared in scripture to a streaming fountain; if her
> waters flow not in a perpetual progression they sicken into a
> muddy pool of conformity and tradition. A man may be a heretic
> in the truth; and if he believe things only because his pastor says
> so, or the [Westminster] Assembly so determines, without know-
> ing other reason, though his belief be true, yet the very truth he
> holds becomes his heresy.

This nationalistic argument makes frequent appeals to scripture: "the
favor and the love of Heaven, we have great argument to think in a peculiar manner propitious and propending towards us. Why else was this
nation chosen before any other, that out of her, as out of Sion, should be
proclaimed and sounded forth the first tidings and trumpet of reformation to all Europe?" Milton alludes to Isaiah 2:3 ("out of Zion shall go
forth the law, and the word of the Lord from Jerusalem"), comparing
England, the first nation to hear the trumpet of reformation, with Israel,
the first to hear the divine word. To submit the members of this holy
community, including its most learned, to the authority of a licenser is
to reduce them to children, to disappoint their faith in Parliament, to
insult their pastors, and to hinder the progress of the Reformation.

In 1651, Milton himself served as a licenser of books, a state censor,
and he concludes the *Areopagitica* by asking Parliament to regulate
publication by means of an earlier, less restrictive Order. In a sense,
then, he maintains the most important continuity with the divorce
tracts: urging Parliament not to abandon law altogether but to adopt
more humane regulations. This tract has generated widely divergent

readings. Milton is for some a poet of democratic liberalism and for others a prophet of revolutionary absolutism. Those who view liberty and authority as irreconcilable opposites might associate his Pauline Christian liberty with unrestrained tolerance and his defense of the law with authoritarianism. But throughout the treatise, despite its Pauline argument, Milton finds examples of freedom under the Mosaic law as well. The *Areopagitica* employs a monist hermeneutic in which universal natural law, the Mosaic law, and the gospel accord with a libertarian position on censorship. Milton uses a doctrinally unorthodox version of Christian liberty prevalent in Reformation texts on the Holy Scriptures to obliterate clerical privilege and to defend the universal right to read, a right that he is at pains to demonstrate also exists in the most enlightened pre-Christian and even polytheistic societies.

Areopagitica

A *Speech for the Liberty of Unlicensed Printing to the Parliament of England*

Τοὐλεύθερον δ' ἐκεῖνο, εἰ τις θέλει πόλει

Χρηστόν τι βούλευμ' εἰς μέσον φέρειν, ἔχων.

Καὶ ταῦθ ὁ χῄζων, λαμπρὸς ἐσθ᾽, ὁ μὴ θέλων,

Σιγᾷ, τί τούτων ἐστιν ἰσαίτερον πόλει;

Euripides. Hicetides.

This is true liberty, when free-born men,

Having to advise the public, may speak free,

Which he who can, and will, deserves high praise;

Who neither can, nor will, may hold his peace:

What can be juster in a state than this?

Euripides, The Suppliants

They who to states and governors of the commonwealth direct their speech, high court of Parliament, or, wanting such access in a private condition, write that which they foresee may advance the public good, I suppose them as at the beginning of no mean endeavor, not a little altered and moved inwardly in their minds: some with doubt of what will be the success, others with fear of what will be the censure,[1] some with hope, others with confidence of what they have to speak. And me perhaps each of these dispositions, as the subject was whereon I entered, may have at other times variously affected; and likely might in these foremost expressions now also disclose which of them swayed most, but that the very attempt of

---

1. Judgment.

this address thus made, and the thought of whom it hath recourse to, hath got the power within me to a passion far more welcome than incidental[2] to a preface.

Which though I stay not to confess ere any ask, I shall be blameless, if it be no other than the joy and gratulation which it[3] brings to all who wish and promote their country's liberty, whereof this whole discourse proposed will be a certain testimony, if not a trophy. For this is not the liberty which we can hope, that no grievance ever should arise in the commonwealth—that let no man in this world expect. But when complaints are freely heard, deeply considered, and speedily reformed, then is the utmost bound of civil liberty attained that wise men look for. To which if I now manifest by the very sound of this which I shall utter, that we are already in good part arrived, and yet from such a steep disadvantage of tyranny and superstition grounded into our principles as was beyond the manhood of a Roman recovery,[4] it will be attributed first, as is most due, to the strong assistance of God our deliverer, next to your faithful guidance and undaunted wisdom, Lords and Commons of England. Neither is it in God's esteem the diminution of his glory when honorable things are spoken of good men and worthy magistrates; which if I now first should begin to do, after so fair a progress of your laudable deeds and such a long obligement[5] upon the whole realm of your indefatigable virtues, I might be justly reckoned among the tardiest, and the unwillingest of them that praise ye.

Nevertheless, there being three principal things without which all praising is but courtship and flattery. First, when that only is praised which is solidly worth praise; next, when greatest likelihoods are brought that such things are truly and really in those persons to whom they are ascribed; the other, when he who praises, by showing that such his actual persuasion is of whom he writes, can demonstrate that he flatters not. The former two of these I have heretofore endeavored, rescuing the employment from him who went about to impair your merits with a trivial and malignant encomium;[6] the latter as belonging chiefly to mine own acquittal, that whom I so extolled I did not flatter, hath been reserved opportunely to this occasion.

---

2. Naturally likely to occur.
3. I.e., the very attempt of this address.
4. Having achieved a degree of liberty in state and church by overcoming King Charles I and the prelates, England has surpassed Rome, which could not recover the ancient republic that preceded the rule of emperors and popes.
5. Indebtedness for benefits. (The Long Parliament was ending its fourth year.)
6. Namely, the anonymous *Modest Confutation of a Slanderous and Scurrilous Libel* (1642), which Milton ascribed to Bishop Joseph Hall and attacked earlier (in his *Apology Against a Pamphlet*) for its covert royalist sympathies while pretending to praise the Parliament. *Malignant* was a stock term applied by anti-royalists to supporters of monarchy and episcopacy.

For he who freely magnifies what hath been nobly done, and fears not to declare as freely what might be done better, gives ye the best covenant of his fidelity; and that his loyalest affection and his hope waits on your proceedings. His highest praising is not flattery, and his plainest advice is a kind of praising. For though I should affirm and hold by argument that it would fare better with truth, with learning, and the commonwealth, if one of your published orders which I should name were called in, yet at the same time it could not but much redound to the luster of your mild and equal government whenas private persons are hereby animated to think ye better pleased with public advice than other statists[7] have been delighted heretofore with public flattery. And men will then see what difference there is between the magnanimity of a triennial Parliament, and that jealous haughtiness of prelates and cabin counselors[8] that usurped of late, whenas they shall observe ye in the midst of your victories and successes more gently brooking written exceptions against a voted order than other courts, which had produced nothing worth memory but the weak ostentation of wealth, would have endured the least signified dislike at any sudden proclamation.

If I should thus far presume upon the meek demeanor of your civil and gentle greatness, Lords and Commons, as what your published order hath directly said, that to gainsay, I might defend myself with ease, if any should accuse me of being new or insolent, did they but know how much better I find ye esteem it to imitate the old and elegant humanity of Greece than the barbaric pride of a Hunnish and Norwegian stateliness. And out of those ages, to whose polite wisdom and letters we owe that we are not yet Goths and Jutlanders, I could name him[9] who from his private house wrote that discourse to the Parliament of Athens that persuades them to change the form of democracy which was then established. Such honor was done in those days to men who professed the study of wisdom and eloquence, not only in their own country but in other lands, that cities and seigniories heard them gladly, and with great respect, if they had aught in public to admonish the state. Thus did Dion Prusaeus,[1] a stranger and a private orator, counsel the Rhodians against a former edict; and I abound with other like examples, which to set here would be superfluous.

7. Politicians.
8. When Charles consulted his Cabinet Council, between 1629 and 1640, no parliaments were summoned. "Triennial Parliament": An act of 1641 insured that Parliament would meet at least every three years.
9. Isocrates, physically incapacitated for public speaking, designed his *Areopagitic Discourse* (c. 355 B.C.E.) to be read. Its subject matter was the powers of the Court of the Areopagus, and it was addressed to the Athenian *ecclesia*, an assembly of the people, which Milton, exercising license, terms "the Parliament of Athens."
1. Dion Prusaeus (d. c. 117 C.E.), whose *Rhodian Discourse* urged repeal of a law that allowed new names to replace the original ones on public monuments.

But if from the industry of a life wholly dedicated to studious labors, and those natural endowments haply not the worst for two and fifty degrees of northern latitude,[2] so much must be derogated as to count me not equal to any of those who had this privilege, I would obtain to be thought not so inferior as yourselves are superior to the most of them who received their counsel. And how far you excel them, be assured, Lords and Commons, there can no greater testimony appear than when your prudent spirit acknowledges and obeys the voice of reason from what quarter soever it be heard speaking, and renders ye as willing to repeal any Act of your own setting forth as any set forth by your predecessors.

If ye be thus resolved, as it were injury to think ye were not, I know not what should withhold me from presenting ye with a fit instance wherein to show both that love of truth which ye eminently profess, and that uprightness of your judgment which is not wont to be partial to yourselves, by judging over again that order which ye have ordained *to regulate printing, that no book, pamphlet, or paper shall be henceforth printed, unless the same be first approved and licensed by such,* or at least one of such, as shall be thereto appointed. For that part which preserves justly every man's copy to himself, or provides for the poor, I touch not, only wish they be not made pretenses to abuse and persecute honest and painful[3] men, who offend not in either of these particulars. But that other clause of licensing books, which we thought had died with his brother quadragesimal and matrimonial when the prelates expired,[4] I shall now attend with such a homily as shall lay before ye: first, the inventors of it to be those whom ye will be loath to own; next, what is to be thought in general of reading, whatever sort the books be; and, that this order avails nothing to the suppressing of scandalous, seditious, and libelous books, which were mainly intended to be suppressed; last, that it will be primely to the discouragement of all learning, and the stop of truth, not only by disexercising and blunting our abilities in what we know already, but by hindering and cropping the discovery that might be yet further made both in religious and civil wisdom.[5]

I deny not but that it is of greatest concernment in the church and commonwealth to have a vigilant eye how books demean themselves as well as men, and thereafter to confine, imprison, and do sharpest

---

2. Believing that genius flourished in Mediterranean climate, Milton often blames "cold climate" (*PL*, 9.44–45) for English dullness.

3. Painstaking. "Copy": copyright.

4. In 1642, when Charles signed the bill excluding bishops from the House of Lords, although Presbyterianism was not established by law until 1645. Bishops had controlled dispensations from Lenten ("quadragesimal") dietary restrictions as well as from matrimonial matters, such as the publication of banns.

5. This sentence is the fountainhead from which the main arguments of the treatise flow: historical, intellectual, pragmatic, and moral.

justice on them as malefactors. For books are not absolutely dead things, but do contain a potency of life in them to be as active as that soul was whose progeny they are; nay, they do preserve as in a vial the purest efficacy and extraction of that living intellect that bred them. I know they are as lively and as vigorously productive as those fabulous dragon's teeth;[6] and being sown up and down, may chance to spring up armed men. And yet, on the other hand, unless wariness be used, as good almost kill a man as kill a good book. Who kills a man kills a reasonable creature, God's image; but he who destroys a good book kills reason itself, kills the image of God, as it were, in the eye. Many a man lives a burden to the earth, but a good book is the precious lifeblood of a master spirit, embalmed and treasured up on purpose to a life beyond life. 'Tis true, no age can restore a life, whereof perhaps there is no great loss; and revolutions of ages do not oft recover the loss of a rejected truth, for the want of which whole nations fare the worse. We should be wary therefore what persecution we raise against the living labors of public men, how we spill that seasoned life of man preserved and stored up in books, since we see a kind of homicide may be thus committed, sometimes a martyrdom, and if it extend to the whole impression, a kind of massacre, whereof the execution ends not in the slaying of an elemental life but strikes at that ethereal and fifth essence,[7] the breath of reason itself, slays an immortality rather than a life. But lest I should be condemned of introducing license while I oppose licensing, I refuse not the pains to be so much historical as will serve to show what hath been done by ancient and famous commonwealths against this disorder, till the very time that this project of licensing crept out of the Inquisition,[8] was catched up by our prelates, and hath caught some of our presbyters.

In Athens, where books and wits were ever busier than in any other part of Greece, I find but only two sorts of writings which the magistrate cared to take notice of: those either blasphemous and atheistical, or libelous. Thus the books of Protagoras[9] were by the judges of Areopagus commanded to be burnt, and himself banished the territory, for a discourse begun with his confessing not to know *whether there were gods, or whether not.* And against defaming, it was decreed that none should be traduced by name, as was the manner

---

6. Sown by Cadmus; the few survivors of the army that sprang from them helped him build Thebes (*Met.*, 3.101–30).
7. In classical and medieval philosophy, the quintessence, the substance of which the celestial bodies were composed; ethereal and eternal, not merely "elemental," like earth, air, fire, and water. "Spill": destroy.
8. A tribunal of the Roman Catholic Church for the discovery and suppression of heresy, organized in the 13th century under Innocent III.
9. Protagoras (c. 490–420 B.C.E.), credited by Plato with having invented the role of professional sophist or teacher of virtue.

of Vetus Comoedia,[1] whereby we may guess how they censured
libeling. And this course was quick enough, as Cicero writes, to
quell both the desperate wits of other atheists and the open way of
defaming, as the event showed. Of other sects and opinions, though
tending to voluptuousness and the denying of divine Providence,
they took no heed.

Therefore we do not read that either Epicurus, or that libertine
school of Cyrene, or what the Cynic impudence uttered,[2] was ever
questioned by the laws. Neither is it recorded that the writings of
those old comedians were suppressed, though the acting of them
were forbid; and that Plato commended the reading of Aristophanes, the loosest of them all, to his royal scholar Dionysius, is
commonly known and may be excused if holy Chrysostom,[3] as is
reported, nightly studied so much the same author and had the
art to cleanse a scurrilous vehemence into the style of a rousing
sermon.

That other leading city of Greece, Lacedaemon, considering that
Lycurgus[4] their lawgiver was so addicted to elegant learning as to
have been the first that brought out of Ionia the scattered works of
Homer, and sent the poet Thales from Crete to prepare and mollify
the Spartan surliness with his smooth songs and odes, the better to
plant among them law and civility, it is to be wondered how muse-
less and unbookish they were, minding naught but the feats of war.
There needed no licensing of books among them, for they disliked
all but their own laconic apophthegms and took a slight occasion to
chase Archilochus out of their city, perhaps for composing in a
higher strain than their own soldierly ballads and roundels could
reach to. Or if it were for his broad verses, they were not therein so
cautious, but they were as dissolute in their promiscuous conversing,[5]
whence Euripides affirms in *Andromache* that their women were all
unchaste. Thus much may give us light after what sort books were
prohibited among the Greeks.

The Romans also, for many ages trained up only to a military
roughness, resembling most the Lacedaemonian guise, knew of
learning little but what their twelve tables and the Pontific College

---

1. The Athenian Old Comedy regularly attacked public figures by name; a decree of 440
B.C.E. forbade the practice.
2. Diogenes is the most famous example of Cynic impudence. Asked why he carried a
lamp in broad daylight, he replied, "I am looking for a man, never having seen one; for
the Spartans are children, and the Athenians are women." Epicurus taught that pleasure and pain are the measures of what is good and bad. Aristippus, founder of a school
in Cyrene, taught that pleasure is the supreme good.
3. St. John Chrysostom (c. 347–407), one of the most influential of the Greek Church
Fathers.
4. According to Plutarch's semilegendary account, Lycurgus was the founder of Lacedaemon, or Sparta.
5. Socializing. "Promiscuous": Spartan men and women exercised naked together.

with their augurs and flamens[6] taught them in religion and law; so unacquainted with other learning that when Carneades and Critolaus, with the Stoic Diogenes coming ambassadors to Rome, took thereby occasion to give the city a taste of their philosophy, they were suspected for seducers by no less a man than Cato the Censor,[7] who moved it in the Senate to dismiss them speedily and to banish all such Attic babblers out of Italy. But Scipio and others of the noblest senators withstood him and his old Sabine austerity,[8] honored and admired the men, and the Censor himself at last, in his old age, fell to the study of that whereof before he was so scrupulous. And yet at the same time Naevius and Plautus,[9] the first Latin comedians, had filled the city with all the borrowed scenes of Menander and Philemon. Then began to be considered there also what was to be done to libelous books and authors, for Naevius was quickly cast into prison for his unbridled pen and released by the tribunes upon his recantation. We read also that libels were burnt and the makers punished by Augustus. The like severity no doubt was used if aught were impiously written against their esteemed gods. Except in these two points, how the world went in books the magistrate kept no reckoning.

And therefore Lucretius without impeachment versifies his Epicurism to Memmius, and had the honor to be set forth the second time by Cicero,[1] so great a father of the commonwealth, although himself disputes against that opinion in his own writings. Nor was the satirical sharpness or naked plainness of Lucilius, or Catullus, or Flaccus by any order prohibited. And for matters of state, the story of Titus Livius, though it extolled that part which Pompey held, was not therefore suppressed by Octavius Caesar of the other faction.[2] But that Naso was by him banished in his old age for the wanton poems of his youth was but a mere covert of state[3] over

6. Each of the fifteen performed sacrifices in the service of a particular deity. "Twelve tables": a codification of Roman laws made in 451 B.C.E. "Pontific College": the supreme religious institution of ancient Rome. "Augurs": priests who determined public policy by consulting natural omens.
7. Cato the Censor (234–149 B.C.E.) opposed the spread of Hellenic culture, preferring instead rugged Roman simplicity. Milton disapproves of his dismissal of the Greek intellectuals Carneades the skeptic, Critolaus the Aristotelian, and Diogenes the Stoic.
8. Cato returned periodically to the Sabine farm (in the central region of the Apennines) where he was raised. The great general and statesman Scipio Aemilianus Africanus (185–129 B.C.E.) was also noted for his refinement. His circle of friends included Greeks, among them the historian Polybius and the philosopher Panaetius.
9. Roman playwrights deeply influenced by the major authors of Athenian New Comedy.
1. Lucretius dedicated his poetic expression of Epicurean materialism, De Rerum Natura, to the praetor (elected magistrate) Memmius. Cicero was said to have edited the work.
2. According to Tacitus, regarding a section of Titus Livius's (Livy's) History that has not survived, Livy praised Pompey so highly that Pompey's opponent, Octavius Caesar (Augustus) called the historian "Pompeianus" but remained friendly with him.
3. Publius Ovidius Naso, or Ovid, was the author of Ars Amatoria. Milton believes that the licentiousness of the verse was only a "covert of state" (political pretext) for his banishment.

some secret cause; and besides, the books were neither banished
nor called in. From hence we shall meet with little else but tyranny
in the Roman Empire, that we may not marvel if not so often bad as
good books were silenced. I shall therefore deem to have been large
enough in producing what among the ancients was punishable to
write, save only which all other arguments were free to treat on.

By this time the emperors were become Christians, whose discipline in this point I do not find to have been more severe than what
was formerly in practice. The books of those whom they took to be
grand heretics were examined, refuted, and condemned in the general councils, and not till then were prohibited or burnt by authority
of the emperor. As for the writings of heathen authors, unless they
were plain invectives against Christianity, as those of Porphyrius and
Proclus, they met with no interdict that can be cited till about the
year 400 in a Carthaginian council, wherein bishops themselves
were forbid to read the books of gentiles,[4] but heresies they might
read; while others long before them, on the contrary, scrupled more
the books of heretics than of gentiles. And that the primitive councils and bishops were wont only to declare what books were not commendable, passing no further but leaving it to each one's conscience
to read or to lay by, till after the year 800, is observed already by
Padre Paolo,[5] the great unmasker of the Trentine Council.

After which time the popes of Rome, engrossing what they pleased
of political rule into their own hands, extended their dominion over
men's eyes as they had before over their judgments, burning and
prohibiting to be read what they fancied not; yet sparing in their
censures, and the books not many which they so dealt with; till
Martin the Fifth by his bull not only prohibited but was the first that
excommunicated the reading of heretical books, for about that time
Wickliffe and Huss,[6] growing terrible, were they who first drove the
Papal Court to a stricter polity of prohibiting. Which course Leo
the Tenth and his successors followed, until the Council of Trent[7]
and the Spanish Inquisition engendering together brought forth, or
perfected, those Catalogues and expurging Indexes that rake
through the entrails of many an old good author with a violation
worse than any could be offered to his tomb. Nor did they stay in

---

4. Non-Christians. Porphyrius (Porphyry) and Proclus were Neoplatonists hostile to Christianity. Constantine had Porphyry's treatise *Against the Christians* burned in public.
5. Pietro Sarpi (1552–1623), whom Milton, in *Of Reformation*, called "the great Venetian
   antagonist of the Pope." In the next few pages of this treatise, Milton draws heavily on
   his *Historie of the Council of Trent* (tr. 1620).
6. John Wycliffe (c. 1329–84) and John Huss (1369–1415) were, respectively, the great
   English and Bohemian precursors of the Protestant Reformation. Pope Martin V
   (1368–1431) issued a bull in 1418 condemning the reading of heretical works.
7. The council met from 1545 to 1563 to combat the threat of Protestantism and to
   reform doctrine and practices. It created the *Index of Prohibited Books* (1559) along
   with the *Index of Expurgations* from books otherwise allowed to be read.

matters heretical, but any subject that was not to their palate they either condemned in a prohibition or had it straight into the new purgatory of an index.

To fill up the measure of encroachment, their last invention was to ordain that no book, pamphlet, or paper should be printed (as if St. Peter had bequeathed them the keys of the press also out of Paradise) unless it were approved and licensed under the hands of two or three glutton friars. For example:

> "Let the Chancellor Cini be pleased to see if in this present work be contained aught that may withstand the printing."
> —Vincent Rabbatta, Vicar of Florence.

> "I have seen this present work, and find nothing athwart the Catholic faith and good manners: in witness whereof I have given, etc."   —Nicolo Cini, Chancellor of Florence.

> "Attending the precedent relation, it is allowed that this present work of Davanzati may be printed."   —Vincent Rabbatta, *etc.*

> "It may be printed, July 15."   —Friar Simon Mompei D'Amelia, Chancellor of the Holy Office in Florence.

Sure they have a conceit, if he of the bottomless pit had not long since broke prison, that this quadruple exorcism would bar him down. I fear their next design will be to get into their custody the licensing of that which they say Claudius intended but went not through with.[8] Vouchsafe to see another of their forms, the Roman stamp:

> "*Imprimatur*, If it seem good to the reverend Master of the holy Palace."   —Belcastro, Vicegerent.

> "Imprimatur."   —Friar Nicolò Rodolphi, Master of the Holy Palace.

Sometimes five *Imprimaturs* are seen together dialogue-wise in the piazza of one title-page complimenting and ducking each to other with their shaven reverences,[9] whether the author, who stands by in perplexity at the foot of his epistle, shall to the press or to the sponge. These are the pretty responsories, these are the dear antiph-

---

8. In the margin of the first edition, Milton quotes in Latin Suetonius on the emperor Tiberius (born Tiberius Claudius Nero), who, when told of a modest person who almost died of retention, considered publishing an edict making it lawful to break wind at table.
9. Bowing of their shaven heads, alluding to the tonsured Dominicans who often served as licensers.

onies, that so bewitched of late our prelates and their chaplains with the goodly echo they made; and besotted us to the gay imitation of a lordly *Imprimatur*, one from Lambeth House, another from the west end of Paul's;[1] so apishly Romanizing that the word of command still was set down in Latin, as if the learned grammatical pen that wrote it would cast no ink without Latin; or perhaps, as they thought, because no vulgar tongue was worthy to express the pure conceit of an *Imprimatur*; but rather, as I hope, for that our English, the language of men ever famous and foremost in the achievements of liberty, will not easily find servile letters enow to spell such a dictatory presumption English.

And thus ye have the inventors and the original of book-licensing ripped up and drawn as lineally as any pedigree. We have it not, that can be heard of, from any ancient state or polity or church, nor by any statute left us by our ancestors elder or later, nor from the modern custom of any reformed city or church abroad, but from the most antichristian council and the most tyrannous inquisition that ever inquired. Till then books were ever as freely admitted into the world as any other birth; the issue of the brain was no more stifled than the issue of the womb; no envious Juno sat cross-legged over the nativity of any man's intellectual offspring;[2] but if it proved a monster, who denies but that it was justly burnt or sunk into the sea? But that a book, in worse condition than a peccant soul, should be to stand before a jury ere it be born to the world, and undergo yet in darkness the judgment of Rhadamanth and his colleagues ere it can pass the ferry backward into light, was never heard before, till that mysterious iniquity,[3] provoked and troubled at the first entrance of Reformation, sought out new limbos and new hells wherein they might include our books also within the number of their damned. And this was the rare morsel so officiously snatched up and so ill-favoredly imitated by our inquisiturient bishops and the attendant minorites,[4] their chaplains. That ye like not now these most certain authors of this licensing order, and that all sinister intention was far distant from your thoughts when ye were importuned the passing it, all men who know the integrity of your actions and how ye honor truth will clear ye readily.

1. Lambeth Palace is the London residence of the archbishop of Canterbury. The palace of the bishop of London was near St. Paul's cathedral. "Responsories . . . antiphonies": responsive parts of a church service.
2. Hercules was the son of Jove by the mortal Alcmena. When he was about to be born, Juno, Jove's jealous wife, sent the goddess of childbirth to hinder the delivery by sitting before the mother's door with legs and fingers crossed.
3. The Roman Catholic Church; see Rev. 17:1-5, which Protestant Milton applied to Rome and the Papacy. Rhadamanthus, Minos, and Aeacus judged the dead. Emphasizing the absurdity of prepublication censorship by reversing the usual progressions, Milton has them judging the unborn instead before they can be ferried backward across the river Styx to the world of the living.
4. Milton links Anglican chaplains with the Franciscans, who adopted the name Friars Minor as a sign of humility but whom Puritans nevertheless regarded as arrogant.

But some will say, what though the inventors were bad, the thing for all that may be good? It may be so; yet if that thing be no such deep invention, but obvious and easy for any man to light on, and yet best and wisest commonwealths through all ages and occasions have forborne to use it, and falsest seducers and oppressors of men were the first who took it up, and to no other purpose but to obstruct and hinder the first approach of Reformation, I am of those who believe it will be a harder alchemy than Lullius ever knew to sublimate[5] any good use out of such an invention. Yet this only is what I request to gain from this reason, that it may be held a dangerous and suspicious fruit, as certainly it deserves, for the tree that bore it, until I can dissect one by one the properties it has. But I have first to finish, as was propounded, what is to be thought in general of reading books, whatever sort they be, and whether be more the benefit or the harm that thence proceeds.

Not to insist upon the examples of Moses, David, and Paul, who were skillful in all the learning of the Egyptians, Chaldeans, and Greeks, which could not probably be without reading their books of all sorts; in Paul especially, who thought it no defilement to insert into holy scripture the sentences of three Greek poets, and one of them a tragedian.[6] The question was notwithstanding sometimes controverted among the primitive doctors, but with great odds on that side which affirmed it both lawful and profitable, as was then evidently perceived when Julian the Apostate[7] and subtlest enemy to our faith made a decree forbidding Christians the study of heathen learning; for, said he, they wound us with our own weapons, and with our own arts and sciences they overcome us. And indeed the Christians were put so to their shifts by this crafty means and so much in danger to decline into all ignorance, that the two Apollinarii were fain, as a man may say, to coin all the seven liberal sciences out of the Bible, reducing it into diverse forms of orations, poems, dialogues, even to the calculating of a new Christian grammar. But, saith the historian Socrates, the providence of God provided better than the industry of Apollinarius and his son[8] by taking away that illiterate law with the life of him who devised it. So great an injury they then held it to be deprived of Hellenic learn-

---

5. Ramon Llull (c. 1232–1315), famous alchemical theorist. Sublimation was the alchemical process of refining base material by chemical fire.
6. "Moses was learned in all the wisdom of the Egyptians" (Acts 7:22). God gave Daniel "knowledge and skill in all learning and wisdom" (Dan. 1:17). Paul cites texts attributed to Greek authors Aratus (Acts 17:28), Epimenides (Titus 1:12), and the tragedian Euripides (1 Cor. 15:33).
7. The name given to Roman emperor Flavius Claudius Iulianus (332–363) because of his rejection of Christianity in favor of a form of Neo-Platonic paganism and his attempt to rid the empire of Christianity.
8. Apollinaris of Alexandria and his son adapted biblical texts to classical forms of grammar and rhetoric. The Greek historian Socrates Scholasticus (380–450) recounts the story of the Apollinarii and of Julian's early death in battle.

ing, and thought it a persecution more undermining and secretly decaying the church than the open cruelty of Decius or Diocletian.[9]

And perhaps it was the same politic drift that the devil whipped St. Jerome in a Lenten dream, for reading Cicero; or else it was a phantasm bred by the fever which had then seized him.[1] For had an angel been his discipliner, unless it were for dwelling too much upon Ciceronianisms, and had chastised the reading, not the vanity, it had been plainly partial; first to correct him for grave Cicero and not for scurril Plautus, whom he confessed to have been reading, not long before; next to correct him only, and let so many more ancient fathers wax old in those pleasant and florid studies without the lash of such a tutoring apparition; insomuch that Basil teaches how some good use may be made of *Margites*, a sportful poem, not now extant, writ by Homer; and why not then of *Morgante*, an Italian romance much to the same purpose?[2]

But if it be agreed we shall be tried by visions, there is a vision recorded by Eusebius far ancienter than this tale of Jerome to the nun Eustochium, and besides, has nothing of a fever in it. Dionysius Alexandrinus was, about the year 240, a person of great name in the church for piety and learning, who had wont to avail himself much against heretics by being conversant in their books; until a certain presbyter laid it scrupulously to his conscience how he durst venture himself among those defiling volumes. The worthy man, loath to give offense, fell into a new debate with himself what was to be thought, when suddenly a vision sent from God (it is his own epistle that so avers it) confirmed him in these words: *Read any books whatever come to thy hands, for thou art sufficient both to judge aright and to examine each matter.* To this revelation he assented the sooner, as he confesses, because it was answerable to that of the apostle to the Thessalonians, *Prove all things, hold fast that which is good.* And he might have added another remarkable saying of the same author: *To the pure, all things are pure*; not only meats and drinks, but all kind of knowledge whether of good or evil; the knowledge cannot defile, nor consequently the books, if the will and conscience be not defiled.[3]

For books are as meats and viands are: some of good, some of evil substance; and yet God, in that unapocryphal vision, said without exception, *Rise, Peter, kill and eat,* leaving the choice to each man's

---

9. Roman emperors who persecuted the Christians.
1. During Lent, while suffering from a fever, Jerome fell into a dreamlike state, in which, despite his affirming that he was a Christian, an angel whipped him for his excessive devotion to Cicero. He insisted that the marks of the lash on his body proved that he had not merely been asleep.
2. Both mock-heroic poems: The first, ascribed to Homer, of which only fragments survive; the second, by Luigi Pulci (1431–87), in which French chivalric material is infused with an Italian comic spirit.
3. The apostle Paul in 1 Thess. 5:21 and Titus 1:15.

discretion.[4] Wholesome meats to a vitiated stomach differ little or nothing from unwholesome; and best books to a naughty mind are not unappliable to occasions of evil. Bad meats will scarce breed good nourishment in the healthiest concoction;[5] but herein the difference is of bad books, that they to a discreet and judicious reader serve in many respects to discover, to confute, to forewarn, and to illustrate. Whereof what better witness can ye expect I should produce than one of your own now sitting in Parliament, the chief of learned men reputed in this land, Mr. Selden,[6] whose volume of natural and national laws proves, not only by great authorities brought together but by exquisite reasons and theorems almost mathematically demonstrative, that all opinions, yea errors, known, read, and collated, are of main service and assistance toward the speedy attainment of what is truest.

I conceive, therefore, that when God did enlarge the universal diet of man's body, saving ever the rules of temperance, he then also, as before, left arbitrary the dieting and repasting of our minds, as wherein every mature man might have to exercise his own leading capacity. How great a virtue is temperance, how much of moment through the whole life of man! Yet God commits the managing so great a trust, without particular law or prescription, wholly to the demeanor of every grown man. And therefore when he himself tabled the Jews from heaven, that omer, which was every man's daily portion of manna, is computed to have been more than might have well sufficed the heartiest feeder thrice as many meals.[7] For those actions which enter into a man, rather than issue out of him, and therefore defile not,[8] God uses not to captivate under a perpetual childhood of prescription, but trusts him with the gift of reason to be his own chooser. There were but little work left for preaching, if law and compulsion should grow so fast upon those things which heretofore were governed only by exhortation. Solomon informs us that much reading is a weariness to the flesh;[9] but neither he nor

4. Acts 10:9–16; the voice orders hungry Peter to eat for the first time food prohibited by Jewish dietary law. This vision is canonical ("unapocryphal"), as opposed to the visions just discussed of Jerome and Dionysius Alexandrinus.
5. Digestion.
6. John Selden (1584–1654), the most learned person in England in the 17th century, served as MP beginning in the 1620s and in the Long Parliament for Oxford University in the 1640s. Milton refers here to his *De Jure Naturali et Gentium juxta Disciplinam Ebraeorum* (1640), in which he asserts that the collation of all opinions, including errors, on philosophical, theological, and legal disputations, is the method of the Talmud. His ultimate proof-text is biblical: "In the multitude of counselors there is safety" (Prov. 11:14 and 24:6).
7. Exod. 16. This passage includes an extraordinary insistence on dietary freedom under the Mosaic ceremonial law and on continuity between Gospel ("then") and Torah ("as before") in the matter of intellectual freedom ("the dieting and repasting of our minds").
8. An allusion, contrary in spirit to the preceding passage, to Jesus' attack on Jewish sacred food hygiene (Mark 7:15).
9. Eccles. 12:12.

other inspired author tells us that such or such reading is unlawful; yet certainly had God thought good to limit us herein, it had been much more expedient to have told us what was unlawful than what was wearisome. As for the burning of those Ephesian books by St. Paul's converts, 'tis replied the books were magic, the Syriac[1] so renders them. It was a private act, a voluntary act, and leaves us to a voluntary imitation: the men in remorse burnt those books which were their own; the magistrate by this example is not appointed; these men practiced the books; another might perhaps have read them in some sort usefully.

Good and evil we know in the field of this world grow up together almost inseparably; and the knowledge of good is so involved and interwoven with the knowledge of evil, and in so many cunning resemblances hardly to be discerned, that those confused seeds which were imposed upon Psyche as an incessant labor to cull out and sort asunder were not more intermixed.[2] It was from out the rind of one apple tasted that the knowledge of good and evil, as two twins cleaving together, leaped forth into the world.[3] And perhaps this is that doom which Adam fell into of knowing good and evil, that is to say, of knowing good by evil. As therefore the state of man now is, what wisdom can there be to choose, what continence to forbear without the knowledge of evil? He that can apprehend and consider vice with all her baits and seeming pleasures, and yet abstain, and yet distinguish, and yet prefer that which is truly better, he is the true warfaring[4] Christian.

I cannot praise a fugitive and cloistered virtue, unexercised and unbreathed, that never sallies out and sees her adversary, but slinks out of the race where that immortal garland is to be run for, not without dust and heat. Assuredly we bring not innocence into the world, we bring impurity much rather; that which purifies us is trial, and trial is by what is contrary. That virtue therefore which is but a youngling in the contemplation of evil and knows not the utmost that vice promises to her followers, and rejects it, is but a blank virtue, not a pure; her whiteness is but an excremental[5] whiteness. Which was the reason why our sage and serious poet Spenser, whom

---

1. A version of Acts 19:19.
2. Venus, jealous of Psyche's beauty and of Cupid's love for her, set her the impossible task of separating mixed seeds before sundown. Helpful ants accomplished the task.
3. Since the theme is the difficulty of distinguishing good from evil, the twins Milton has in mind are probably Jacob and Esau (Gen. 27). Jacob, the ostensibly good brother, obtains by trickery the blessing from his father Isaac to which Esau was entitled. His thorough knowledge of the habits, appearances, and tricks of speech peculiar to his evil brother allowed him to impersonate him successfully, but the deception was morally ambiguous. Is the reader of this biblical episode wiser than Isaac, who always preferred Esau and in his blindness was unable to discern his favorite son?
4. The printed text's "wayfaring," in four copies that Milton presented to friends, is corrected by hand to "warfaring," which suggests that he approved of the change.
5. External, superficial.

I dare be known to think a better teacher than Scotus or Aquinas,[6]
describing true temperance under the person of Guyon, brings him
in with his palmer through the cave of Mammon and the bower of
earthly bliss that he might see and know and yet abstain.[7] Since
therefore the knowledge and survey of vice is in this world so necessary to the constituting of human virtue, and the scanning of error
to the confirmation of truth, how can we more safely and with less
danger scout into the regions of sin and falsity than by reading all
manner of tractates and hearing all manner of reason? And this is
the benefit which may be had of books promiscuously read.

But of the harm that may result hence, three kinds are usually
reckoned. First is feared the infection that may spread. But then all
human learning and controversy in religious points must remove
out of the world, yea the Bible itself, for that ofttimes relates blasphemy not nicely; it describes the carnal sense of wicked men not
unelegantly, it brings in holiest men passionately murmuring against
providence through all the arguments of Epicurus;[8] in other great
disputes it answers dubiously and darkly to the common reader. And
ask a Talmudist what ails the modesty of his marginal Keri, that
Moses and all the prophets cannot persuade him to pronounce the
textual Chetiv.[9] For these causes we all know the Bible itself put by
the papist into the first rank of prohibited books. The ancientest
fathers must be next removed, as Clement of Alexandria, and that
Eusebian book of evangelic preparation, transmitting our ears
through a hoard of heathenish obscenities to receive the Gospel.[1]
Who finds not that Irenaeus, Epiphanius, Jerome, and others discover[2] more heresies than they well confute, and that oft for heresy
which is the truer opinion?

Nor boots it to say for these and all the heathen writers of greatest infection, if it must be thought so, with whom is bound up the
life of human learning, that they writ in an unknown tongue, so

6. Milton disparages medieval scholastic philosophy and theology as exemplified by John
Duns Scotus (1265–1308) and St. Thomas Aquinas (1225–74).
7. Although the palmer, representing prudence or reason, accompanies Guyon to the
Bower of Bliss (*Faerie Queene*, 2), Guyon, representing temperance, enters the Cave of
Mammon alone. For Spenser, the habit of temperance suffices to resist material temptation, but for Milton, who misremembers Spenser, perhaps significantly, both active
reason and the habit of virtue are required.
8. Even the holiest figures in the Bible (as Solomon in Ecclesiastes) may express opinions
as skeptical as those of Epicurus. "Not nicely": not squeamishly.
9. "Keri": a marginal word in the Hebrew text of the Bible, to be substituted for that found
in the written text ("Chetiv"), which might be considered corrupted by manuscript
transmission or otherwise unintelligible or erroneous. Milton is probably thinking of
the substitution of a euphemism for a frankly explicit word, which occurs infrequently.
"Talmudist": a student of the Talmud—in normative Judaism, the codified oral law as
decisive interpretation of the Hebrew Bible.
1. The great church father Clement of Alexandria, in his *Hortatory Address to the Greeks*,
and Eusebius, Milton's favorite church historian, in his *Praeparatio Evangelica*, describe
obscene pagan rites in order to discourage Christians from participating in them.
2. Expose, and, in doing so, introduce their readers to them.

long as we are sure those languages are known as well to the worst
of men, who are both most able and most diligent to instill the poi-
son they suck, first into the courts of princes, acquainting them
with the choicest delights and criticisms of sin. As perhaps did that
Petronius whom Nero called his Arbiter, the master of his revels,
and the notorious ribald of Arezzo,[3] dreaded and yet dear to the
Italian courtiers. I name not him for posterity's sake, whom Harry
the 8 named in merriment his vicar of hell.[4] By which compendious way all the contagion that foreign books can infuse will find a
passage to the people far easier and shorter than an Indian voyage,
though it could be sailed either by the north of Cataio[5] eastward or
of Canada westward while our Spanish licensing gags the English
press never so severely.

But on the other side that infection which is from books of controversy in religion is more doubtful and dangerous to the learned
than to the ignorant, and yet those books must be permitted
untouched by the licenser. It will be hard to instance where any
ignorant man hath been ever seduced by papistical book in English,
unless it were commended and expounded to him by some of that
clergy; and indeed all such tractates, whether false or true, are as
the prophecy of Isaiah was to the eunuch, not to be *understood without a guide.*[6] But of our priests and doctors how many have been
corrupted by studying the comments of Jesuits and Sorbonists,[7] and
how fast they could transfuse that corruption into the people, our
experience is both late and sad. It is not forgot, since the acute and
distinct Arminius[8] was perverted merely by the perusing of a nameless discourse written at Delft, which at first he took in hand to
confute.

Seeing therefore that those books, and those in great abundance
which are likeliest to taint both life and doctrine, cannot be suppressed without the fall of learning and of all ability in disputation;
and that these books of either sort are most and soonest catching to
the learned, from whom to the common people whatever is heretical or dissolute may quickly be conveyed; and that evil manners are

---

3. Pietro Aretino (1492–1556), born in Arezzo, wrote lewd and vicious satires. He was
   "dear" (precious) but also expensive for those courtiers who paid him off to avoid being
   attacked. Petronius (d. 66), author of the *Satyricon* and supervisor of entertainments
   for Nero, who called him his *arbiter elegantiae* (judge of matters of taste).
4. Sir Francis Bryan, a notorious libertine, cousin of Anne Boleyn.
5. Cathay (China).
6. Acts 8:27–31.
7. The Sorbonne in Paris was a center of Roman Catholic polemic.
8. Named for the Dutch Reformed theologian Jacobus Arminius (1560–1609), Arminianism dissents from orthodox Calvinism, in particular regarding human free will, holding
   that God's election and human salvation are conditional on continued human faith and
   that grace is resistible. The unintended irony of Milton's word "perverted" is that he will
   convert to Arminianism, which is evident in book 3 of *PL* as well as in *De Doctrina
   Christiana* 1.4.

as perfectly learned without books a thousand other ways which
cannot be stopped; and evil doctrine not with books can propagate
except a teacher guide, which he might also do without writing,
and so beyond prohibiting, I am not able to unfold how this cau-
telous[9] enterprise of licensing can be exempted from the number of
vain and impossible attempts. And he who were pleasantly disposed
could not well avoid to liken it to the exploit of that gallant man
who thought to pound up the crows by shutting his park gate.

Besides another inconvenience, if learned men be the first receiv-
ers out of books and dispreaders both of vice and error, how shall
the licensers themselves be confided in unless we can confer upon
them, or they assume to themselves above all others in the land, the
grace of infallibility and uncorruptedness? And again, if it be true
that a wise man like a good refiner can gather gold out of the drossiest volume, and that a fool will be a fool with the best book, yea
or without book, there is no reason that we should deprive a wise
man of any advantage to his wisdom, while we seek to restrain
from a fool that which being restrained will be no hindrance to his
folly. For if there should be so much exactness always used to keep
that from him which is unfit for his reading, we should, in the judgment of Aristotle not only, but of Solomon and of our Savior, not
vouchsafe him good precepts, and by consequence not willingly
admit him to good books, as being certain that a wise man will
make better use of an idle pamphlet than a fool will do of sacred
scripture.[1]

'Tis next alleged we must not expose ourselves to temptations
without necessity, and, next to that, not employ our time in vain
things. To both these objections one answer will serve out of the
grounds already laid, that to all men such books are not temptations, nor vanities, but useful drugs and materials wherewith to
temper and compose effective and strong medicines which man's
life cannot want.[2] The rest, as children and childish men who have
not the art to qualify[3] and prepare these working materials, well
may be exhorted to forbear, but hindered forcibly they cannot be by
all the licensing that sainted inquisition could ever yet contrive.
Which is what I promise to deliver next—that this order of licensing conduces nothing to the end for which it was framed—and hath
almost prevented[4] me by being clear already while thus much hath

---

9. Deceitful, crafty.
1. All three advise against attempting to impart wisdom, to inexperienced young men
   who are led by their passions (Aristotle, *Nicomachean Ethics* 1.3. [1095a]), to a fool
   (Solomon in Prov. 23), and to swine ("Give not that which is holy to dogs, neither cast
   ye your pearls before swine" [Matt. 7:6]).
2. Cannot be without.
3. Modify, control the strength of.
4. Come before, anticipated.

been explaining. See the ingenuity[5] of Truth, who, when she gets a free and willing hand, opens herself faster than the pace of method and discourse can overtake her.

It was the task which I began with to show that no nation or well-instituted state, if they valued books at all, did ever use this way of licensing; and it might be answered that this is a piece of prudence lately discovered. To which I return that as it was a thing slight and obvious to think on, so if it had been difficult to find out, there wanted not among them long since who suggested such a course, which they, not following, leave us a pattern of their judgement that it was not the not knowing but the not approving which was the cause of their not using it.

Plato, a man of high authority indeed, but least of all for his commonwealth, in the book of his *Laws*, which no city ever yet received, fed his fancy by making many edicts to his airy burgomasters, which they who otherwise admire him wish had been rather buried and excused in the genial cups of an Academic night sitting.[6] By which laws he seems to tolerate no kind of learning but by unalterable decree, consisting most of practical traditions, to the attainment whereof a library of smaller bulk than his own dialogues would be abundant. And there also enacts that no poet should so much as read to any private man what he had written until the judges and law-keepers had seen it and allowed it. But that Plato meant this law peculiarly to that commonwealth which he had imagined and to no other is evident. Why was he not else a lawgiver to himself, but a transgressor, and to be expelled by his own magistrates both for the wanton epigrams and dialogues which he made and his perpetual reading of Sophron Mimus and Aristophanes, books of grossest infamy, and also for commending the latter of them, though he were the malicious libeler of his chief friends, to be read by the tyrant Dionysius[7] who had little need of such trash to spend his time on? But that he knew this licensing of poems had reference and dependence to many other provisos there set down in his fancied republic which in this world could have no place. And so neither he himself nor any magistrate or city ever imitated that course, which taken apart from those other collateral injunctions must needs be vain and fruitless. For if they fell upon one kind of strictness, unless their care were equal to regulate all other things

5. Openness, candor; also liberality, generosity.
6. Alludes to the drinking and general conviviality described in Plato's *Symposium*. "Commonwealth": not Plato's *Republic*, describing an ideal state, but his *Laws*, intended for an actual state, although Milton disparages even them as impractical.
7. Even though Aristophanes had mocked Socrates in the *Clouds*, Plato sent his writings to Dionysius, ruler of Syracuse, who had wanted to learn about the Athenian constitution. "Wanton": probably the homoeroticism celebrated in the *Symposium* and the *Phaedrus*. Sophron (5th century B.C.E.) wrote mimes, dramatic sketches of everyday life.

of like aptness to corrupt the mind, that single endeavor they knew
would be but a fond labor, to shut and fortify one gate against corruption and be necessitated to leave others round about wide open.

If we think to regulate printing, thereby to rectify manners, we
must regulate all recreations and pastimes, all that is delightful to
man. No music must be heard, no song be set or sung, but what is
grave and Doric.[8] There must be licensing dancers, that no gesture,
motion, or deportment be taught our youth but what by their allowance shall be thought honest; for such Plato was provided of. It will
ask more than the work of twenty licensers to examine all the lutes,
the violins, and the guitars in every house; they must not be suffered to prattle as they do, but must be licensed what they may say.
And who shall silence all the airs and madrigals that whisper soft-
ness in chambers? The windows also and the balconies must be
thought on—there are shrewd books with dangerous frontispieces
set to sale[9]—who shall prohibit them, shall twenty licensers? The
villages also must have their visitors to inquire what lectures the
bagpipe and the rebeck reads even to the balladry and the gamut of
every municipal fiddler, for these are the countryman's Arcadias,
and his Montemayors.[1]

Next, what more national corruption for which England hears ill
abroad, than household gluttony; who shall be the rectors of our
daily rioting? And what shall be done to inhibit the multitudes that
frequent those houses where drunkenness is sold and harbored?
Our garments also should be referred to the licensing of some more
sober workmasters to see them cut into a less wanton garb. Who
shall regulate all the mixed conversation of our youth, male and
female together, as is the fashion of this country? Who shall still
appoint what shall be discoursed, what presumed, and no further?
Lastly, who shall forbid and separate all idle resort, all evil company? These things will be, and must be; but how they shall be least
hurtful, how least enticing, herein consists the grave and governing
wisdom of a state.

To sequester out of the world into Atlantic and Utopian[2] polities
which never can be drawn into use will not mend our condition,
but to ordain wisely as in this world of evil, in the midst whereof
God hath placed us unavoidably. Nor is it Plato's licensing of books

---

8. Described by Plato (*Republic* 3.398–99) as a manly and militaristic musical mode.
9. Lewd pictures to entice buyers, with an allusion to prostitutes displaying themselves in
front windows (as they do in contemporary Amsterdam). "Shrewd": depraved.
1. These musical entertainments are to ordinary villagers what Sidney's *Arcadia* and
Jorge de Montemayor's *Diana* are to the relatively elite consumers of romances. "Visitors": alluding to Archbishop of Canterbury William Laud's hated ecclesiastical censors. "Rebeck": a three-stringed fiddle.
2. Imaginary political systems such as those of Plato's island kingdom of Atlantis in *Cri-
tias*, Bacon's *New Atlantis*, and More's *Utopia*.

will do this, which necessarily pulls along with it so many other kinds of licensing as will make us all both ridiculous and weary, and yet frustrate, but those unwritten or at least unconstraining laws of virtuous education, religious and civil nurture, which Plato there[3] mentions as the bonds and ligaments of the commonwealth, the pillars and the sustainers of every written statute. These they be which will bear chief sway in such matters as these, when all licensing will be easily eluded. Impunity and remissness for certain are the bane of a commonwealth, but here the great art lies, to discern in what the law is to bid restraint and punishment and in what things persuasion only is to work.

If every action which is good or evil in man at ripe years were to be under pittance and prescription and compulsion, what were virtue but a name, what praise could be then due to well-doing, what gramercy[4] to be sober, just, or continent? Many there be that complain of divine providence for suffering Adam to transgress. Foolish tongues! When God gave him reason, he gave him freedom to choose, for reason is but choosing; he had been else a mere artificial Adam, such an Adam as he is in the motions.[5] We ourselves esteem not of that obedience, or love, or gift, which is of force. God therefore left him free, set before him a provoking object, ever almost in his eyes; herein consisted his merit, herein the right of his reward, the praise of his abstinence. Wherefore did he create passions within us, pleasures round about us, but that these rightly tempered are the very ingredients of virtue? They are not skillful considerers of human things who imagine to remove sin by removing the matter of sin. For besides that it is a huge heap increasing under the very act of diminishing, though some part of it may for a time be withdrawn from some persons, it cannot from all, in such a universal thing as books are; and when this is done, yet the sin remains entire. Though ye take from a covetous man all his treasure, he has yet one jewel left, ye cannot bereave him of his covetousness. Banish all objects of lust, shut up all youth into the severest discipline that can be exercised in any hermitage, ye cannot make them chaste that came not thither so; such great care and wisdom is required to the right managing of this point.

Suppose we could expel sin by this means; look how much we thus expel of sin, so much we expel of virtue; for the matter of them both is the same; remove that, and ye remove them both alike. This justifies the high providence of God, who though he command us temperance, justice, continence, yet pours out before us, even to a

---

3. Plato's *Laws* 1.643–44.
4. Thanks.
5. Puppet shows.

profuseness, all desirable things and gives us minds that can wander beyond all limit and satiety. Why should we then affect a rigor contrary to the manner of God and of nature by abridging or scanting those means which books freely permitted are, both to the trial of virtue and the exercise of truth? It would be better done to learn that the law must needs be frivolous which goes to restrain things uncertainly and yet equally working to good and evil. And were I the chooser, a dram of well-doing should be preferred before many times as much the forcible hindrance of evil-doing. For God sure esteems the growth and completing of one virtuous person more than the restraint of ten vicious.

And albeit whatever thing we hear or see, sitting, walking, traveling, or conversing may be fitly called our book, and is of the same effect that writings are; yet grant the thing to be prohibited were only books, it appears that this order hitherto is far insufficient to the end which it intends. Do we not see—not once or oftener, but weekly—that continued court-libel[6] against the Parliament and city printed, as the wet sheets can witness, and dispersed among us, for all that licensing can do? Yet this is the prime service, a man would think, wherein this order should give proof of itself. If it were executed, you'll say. But certain, if execution be remiss or blindfold now, and in this particular, what will it be hereafter and in other books? If then the order shall not be vain and frustrate, behold a new labor, Lords and Commons, ye must repeal and proscribe all scandalous and unlicensed books already printed and divulged, after ye have drawn them up into a list, that all may know which are condemned and which not; and ordain that no foreign books be delivered out of custody till they have been read over. This office will require the whole time of not a few overseers, and those no vulgar men. There be also books which are partly useful and excellent, partly culpable and pernicious; this work will ask as many more officials to make expurgations and expunctions, that the commonwealth of learning be not damnified.[7] In fine, when the multitude of books increase upon their hands, ye must be fain to catalogue all those printers who are found frequently offending and forbid the importation of their whole suspected typography. In a word, that this your order may be exact and not deficient, ye must reform it perfectly according to the model of Trent and Seville,[8] which I know ye abhor to do.

Yet though ye should condescend to this, which God forbid, the order still would be but fruitless and defective to that end whereto

---

6. *Mercurius Aulicus* (The court mercury), a Royalist underground newspaper with wide circulation, published between 1642 and 1645.
7. Injured.
8. Milton has already discussed censorship imposed by the Council of Trent and the Spanish Inquisition, whose headquarters were in Seville.

ye meant it. If to prevent sects and schisms, who is so unread or so uncatechized in story[9] that hath not heard of many sects refusing books as a hindrance and preserving their doctrine unmixed for many ages only by unwritten traditions? The Christian faith, for that was once a schism, is not unknown to have spread all over Asia ere any Gospel or Epistle was seen in writing. If the amendment of manners be aimed at, look into Italy and Spain, whether those places be one scruple the better, the honester, the wiser, the chaster, since all the inquisitional rigor that hath been executed upon books.

Another reason, whereby to make it plain that this order will miss the end it seeks, consider by the quality which ought to be in every licenser. It cannot be denied but that he who is made judge to sit upon the birth or death of books, whether they may be wafted into this world or not, had need to be a man above the common measure, both studious, learned, and judicious. There may be else no mean mistakes in the censure of what is passable or not, which is also no mean injury. If he be of such worth as behooves him, there cannot be a more tedious and unpleasing journey-work, a greater loss of time levied upon his head, than to be made the perpetual reader of unchosen books and pamphlets, ofttimes huge volumes. There is no book that is acceptable unless at certain seasons; but to be enjoined the reading of that at all times, and in a hand scarce legible, whereof three pages would not down[1] at any time in the fairest print, is an imposition which I cannot believe how he that values time and his own studies, or is but of a sensible nostril, should be able to endure. In this one thing I crave leave of the present licensers to be pardoned for so thinking; who doubtless took this office up, looking on it through their obedience to the Parliament, whose command perhaps made all things seem easy and unlaborious to them; but that this short trial hath wearied them out already, their own expressions and excuses to them who make so many journeys to solicit their license are testimony enough. Seeing therefore those who now possess the employment by all evident signs wish themselves well rid of it, and that no man of worth, none that is not a plain unthrift of his own hours, is ever likely to succeed them except he mean to put himself to the salary of a press corrector, we may easily foresee what kind of licensers we are to expect hereafter, either ignorant, imperious, and remiss, or basely pecuniary. This is what I had to show wherein this order cannot conduce to that end whereof it bears the intention.

9. History.
1. Go down, be swallowed or endured.

I lastly proceed from the no good it can do, to the manifest hurt it causes, in being first the greatest discouragement and affront that can be offered to learning and to learned men.

It was the complaint and lamentation of prelates, upon every least breath of a motion to remove pluralities[2] and distribute more equally church revenues, that then all learning would be for ever dashed and discouraged. But as for that opinion, I never found cause to think that the tenth part of learning stood or fell with the clergy, nor could I ever but hold it for a sordid and unworthy speech of any churchman who had a competency left him.[3] If therefore ye be loath to dishearten utterly and discontent, not the mercenary crew of false pretenders to learning, but the free and ingenuous sort of such as evidently were born to study and love learning for itself, not for lucre or any other end but the service of God and of truth, and perhaps that lasting fame and perpetuity of praise which God and good men have consented shall be the reward of those whose published labors advance the good of mankind, then know, that so far to distrust the judgment and the honesty of one who hath but a common repute in learning, and never yet offended, as not to count him fit to print his mind without a tutor and examiner, lest he should drop a schism or something of corruption, is the greatest displeasure and indignity to a free and knowing spirit that can be put upon him.

What advantage is it to be a man over it is to be a boy at school, if we have only escaped the ferular to come under the fescue[4] of an *Imprimatur*; if serious and elaborate writings, as if they were no more than the theme of a grammar-lad under his pedagogue, must not be uttered without the cursory eyes of a temporizing and extemporizing licenser? He who is not trusted with his own actions, his drift not being known to be evil, and standing to the hazard of law and penalty, has no great argument to think himself reputed in the commonwealth wherein he was born for other than a fool or a foreigner. When a man writes to the world, he summons up all his reason and deliberation to assist him; he searches, meditates, is industrious, and likely consults and confers with his judicious friends; after all which done he takes himself to be informed in what he writes as well as any that writ before him. If in this the most consummate act of his fidelity and ripeness, no years, no industry, no former proof of his abilities can bring him to that state of maturity as not to be still mistrusted

---

2. The practice among clergymen of possessing more than one church living.
3. The spirit of John Selden broods over the anti-clerical sentiments in this sentence. His controversial *Historie of Tithes* (1618) decisively rejects the view that tithes were due by divine law, and he reiterated the view that "laymen have best interpreted the hard places of the Bible, such as Joannes Picus [Pico], Scaliger, Grotius, Salmasius, Heinsius, &c." "Tenth part": alluding to the controversy over tithing to support the clergy. "Competency": income sufficient to live modestly.
4. A teacher's pointer. "Ferular": rod or cane used for beating.

and suspected, unless he carry all his considerate diligence, all his midnight watchings and expense of Palladian oil, to the hasty view of an unleisured licenser, perhaps much his younger, perhaps far his inferior in judgment, perhaps one who never knew the labor of book-writing; and if he be not repulsed or slighted, must appear in print like a puny[5] with his guardian and his censor's hand on the back of his title to be his bail and surety that he is no idiot or seducer; it cannot be but a dishonor and derogation to the author, to the book, to the privilege and dignity of learning.

And what if the author shall be one so copious of fancy as to have many things well worth the adding come into his mind after licensing, while the book is yet under the press, which not seldom happens to the best and diligentest writers, and that perhaps a dozen times in one book. The printer dares not go beyond his licensed copy. So often then must the author trudge to his leave-giver, that those his new insertions may be viewed; and many a jaunt will be made ere that licenser, for it must be the same man, can either be found or found at leisure. Meanwhile, either the press must stand still, which is no small damage, or the author lose his accuratest thoughts and send the book forth worse than he had made it, which to a diligent writer is the greatest melancholy and vexation that can befall. And how can a man teach with authority, which is the life of teaching, how can he be a doctor in his book as he ought to be (or else had better be silent), whenas all he teaches, all he delivers, is but under the tuition, under the correction of his patriarchal licenser to blot or alter[6] what precisely accords not with the hidebound humor which he calls his judgment? When every acute reader upon the first sight of a pedantic license will be ready with these like words to ding the book a quoit's distance[7] from him: "I hate a pupil teacher, I endure not an instructor that comes to me under the wardship of an overseeing fist. I know nothing of the licenser but that I have his own hand here for his arrogance; who shall warrant me his judgment?" "The State, sir," replies the stationer, but has a quick return: "The state shall be my governors but not my critics; they may be mistaken in the choice of a licenser as easily as this licenser may be mistaken in an author; this is some common stuff"; and he might add from Sir Francis Bacon, that "such authorized books are but the language of the

---

5. A person younger or more junior than another; from Fr. *puis-né*, "born later." "Palladian": scholarly; pertaining to Pallas Athena, goddess of wisdom.
6. At the recent trial of Laud (1644), he was accused of trying to reconcile Anglicanism to the Roman Catholic Church on condition that the pope appoint him patriarch of the western church. Sirluck points out that the House of Commons had also accused Laud's licensers not only of blotting out but also of changing texts of which they disapproved (YP, 2:533).
7. The distance that a flat metal ring is thrown in the horseshoes-like game of quoits; a common measure, like a stone's throw. "Ding": fling.

times." For though a licenser should happen to be judicious more than ordinary, which will be a great jeopardy of the next succession, yet his very office and his commission enjoins him to let nothing pass but what is vulgarly received already.

Nay, which is more lamentable, if the work of any deceased author, though never so famous in his lifetime and even to this day, come to their hands for license to be printed or reprinted, if there be found in his book one sentence of a venturous edge, uttered in the height of zeal (and who knows whether it might not be the dictate of a divine spirit?), yet not suiting with every low decrepit humor of their own, though it were Knox himself, the reformer of a kingdom, that spake it, they will not pardon him their dash.[8] The sense of that great man shall to all posterity be lost for the fearfulness or the presumptuous rashness of a perfunctory licenser. And to what an author this violence hath been lately done, and in what book of greatest consequence to be faithfully published, I could now instance but shall forbear till a more convenient season.

Yet if these things be not resented seriously and timely by them who have the remedy in their power, but that such iron molds[9] as these shall have authority to gnaw out the choicest periods of exquisitest books and to commit such a treacherous fraud against the orphan remainders of worthiest men after death, the more sorrow will belong to that hapless race of men whose misfortune it is to have understanding. Henceforth let no man care to learn or care to be more than worldly-wise; for certainly in higher matters to be ignorant and slothful, to be a common steadfast dunce, will be the only pleasant life, and only in request.

And as it is a particular disesteem of every knowing person alive, and most injurious to the written labors and monuments of the dead, so to me it seems an undervaluing and vilifying of the whole nation. I cannot set so light by all the invention, the art, the wit, the grave and solid judgment which is in England, as that it can be comprehended in any twenty capacities how good soever, much less that it should not pass except their superintendence be over it, except it be sifted and strained with their strainers, that it should be uncurrent without their manual stamp. Truth and understanding are not such wares as to be monopolized and traded in by tickets[1] and statutes and standards. We must not think to make a staple commodity of all the knowledge in the land, to mark and license it

---

8. Line drawn through a word or passage. Some passages from John Knox's *History of the Reformation in Scotland* (1584) were cut from the 1644 edition.
9. Discolorations, stains; here identified with the work of the licensers.
1. Certificates of special trading rights. "Monopolized": Parliament's resentment of the king's granting of monopolies was a cause of the revolution; truth and understanding can't be commodified.

like our broadcloth and our woolpacks. What is it but a servitude like that imposed by the Philistines, not to be allowed the sharpening of our own axes and coulters, but we must repair from all quarters to twenty licensing forges?[2] Had anyone written and divulged erroneous things and scandalous to honest life, misusing and forfeiting the esteem had of his reason among men, if after conviction this only censure were adjudged him, that he should never henceforth write but what were first examined by an appointed officer, whose hand should be annexed to pass his credit for him that now he might be safely read, it could not be apprehended less than a disgraceful punishment. Whence to include the whole nation, and those that never yet thus offended, under such a diffident and suspectful prohibition, may plainly be understood what a disparagement it is. So much the more whenas debtors and delinquents may walk abroad without a keeper, but unoffensive books must not stir forth without a visible jailer in their title.

Nor is it to the common people less than a reproach. For if we be so jealous over them as that we dare not trust them with an English pamphlet, what do we but censure them for a giddy, vicious, and ungrounded people, in such a sick and weak state of faith and discretion as to be able to take nothing down but through the pipe[3] of a licenser? That this is care or love of them we cannot pretend, whenas in those popish places where the laity are most hated and despised, the same strictness is used over them. Wisdom we cannot call it, because it stops but one breach of license, nor that neither whenas those corruptions which it seeks to prevent break in faster at other doors which cannot be shut.

And in conclusion, it reflects to the disrepute of our ministers also, of whose labors we should hope better, and of the proficiency which their flock reaps by them, than that after all this light of the Gospel which is and is to be, and all this continual preaching, they should be still frequented with such an unprincipled, unedified, and laic[4] rabble as that the whiff of every new pamphlet should stagger them out of their catechism and Christian walking. This may have much reason to discourage the ministers, when such a low conceit is had of all their exhortations and the benefiting of their hearers as that they are not thought fit to be turned loose to three sheets of paper without a licenser; that all the sermons, all the lectures preached, printed, vented in such number and such volumes as have now well nigh made all other books unsaleable,

---

2. The Philistines did not allow smiths and forges in Israel, so the captive Israelites had to go to their captors in order to sharpen their axes and plow blades (1 Sam. 13:19–20).
3. Feeding-tube.
4. Nonclerical, secular, with the implication of irreligious.

should not be armor enough against one single enchiridion without the castle of St. Angelo[5] of an *Imprimatur.*

And lest some should persuade ye, Lords and Commons, that these arguments of learned men's discouragement at this your order are mere flourishes and not real, I could recount what I have seen and heard in other countries where this kind of inquisition tyrannizes; when I have sat among their learned men, for that honor I had, and been counted happy to be born in such a place of philosophic freedom as they supposed England was, while themselves did nothing but bemoan the servile condition into which learning amongst them was brought; that this was it which had damped the glory of Italian wits; that nothing had been there written now these many years but flattery and fustian. There it was that I found and visited the famous Galileo, grown old, a prisoner to the Inquisition, for thinking in astronomy otherwise than the Franciscan and Dominican licensers thought.[6] And though I knew that England then was groaning loudest under the prelatical yoke, nevertheless I took it as a pledge of future happiness that other nations were so persuaded of her liberty.

Yet was it beyond my hope that these worthies were then breathing in her air who should be her leaders to such a deliverance as shall never be forgotten by any revolution of time that this world hath to finish. When that was once begun, it was as little in my fear that what words of complaint I heard among learned men of other parts uttered against the Inquisition, the same I should hear by as learned men at home uttered in time of Parliament against an order of licensing; and that so generally that, when I had disclosed myself a companion of their discontent, I might say, if without envy, that he whom an honest quaestorship had endeared to the Sicilians was not more by them importuned against Verres,[7] than the favorable opinion which I had among many who honor ye, and are known and respected by ye, loaded me with entreaties and persuasions that I would not despair to lay together that which just reason should bring into my mind toward the removal of an undeserved thraldom upon learning. That this is not therefore the disburdening of a particular fancy, but the common grievance of all those who had prepared their minds and studies above the vulgar pitch to

---

5. Castel Sant Angelo, a papal prison in Rome, once a fortress. "Enchiridion": handbook, but also dagger.
6. Milton visited Italy during his European tour of 1638–39. The Inquisition forced Galileo to recant heresies found in his *Dialogue on the Two Principal Systems of the World*, and to spend the rest of his life under house arrest in a villa near Florence.
7. The Sicilians, remembering that Cicero had been an honest *quaestor* (treasurer), asked Cicero to prosecute their extortionate governor Verres, which he did successfully in his Verrine Orations.

advance truth in others, and from others to entertain it, thus much
may satisfy.

And in their name I shall for neither friend nor foe conceal what
the general murmur is: that if it come to inquisitioning again and
licensing, and that we are so timorous of ourselves and so suspicious of all men as to fear each book and the shaking of every leaf
before we know what the contents are; if some who but of late were
little better than silenced from preaching shall come now to silence
us from reading except what they please, it cannot be guessed what
is intended by some but a second tyranny over learning, and will
soon put it out of controversy that bishops and presbyters are the
same to us, both name and thing.[8] That those evils of prelaty, which
before from five or six and twenty sees[9] were distributively charged
upon the whole people, will now light wholly upon learning is not
obscure to us, whenas now the pastor of a small unlearned parish
on the sudden shall be exalted archbishop over a large diocese of
books, and yet not remove but keep his other cure too, a mystical
pluralist.[1] He who but of late cried down the sole ordination of
every novice Bachelor of Art, and denied sole jurisdiction over the
simplest parishioner, shall now at home in his private chair assume
both these over worthiest and excellentest books and ablest authors
that write them.[2] This is not—ye covenants and protestations that
we have made!—this is not to put down prelaty; this is but to chop
an episcopacy; this is but to translate the Palace Metropolitan from
one kind of dominion into another; this is but an old canonical
sleight of commuting our penance.[3]

To startle thus betimes at a mere unlicensed pamphlet will after
a while be afraid of every conventicle[4] and a while after will make a
conventicle of every Christian meeting. But I am certain that a state
governed by the rules of justice and fortitude, or a church built and
founded upon the rock of faith and true knowledge, cannot be so

---

8. Milton turns against the Presbyterians their own contention that "bishop" and "presbyter" refer to the same ecclesiastical office, that of priest (lit., "elder"). Although his
earlier antiprelatical tracts had helped the Presbyterian cause, he now intimates a fear
of tyranny that he will state more directly in the sonnet "On the New Forcers of Conscience": "New Presbyter is but old Priest writ large."
9. A bishop's seat or center of authority.
1. One who mysteriously manages to be in two places at once.
2. The same Presbyterian who only recently denounced the Laudian church's restrictive
policies regarding the ordination of ministers and the exercise of spiritual jurisdiction
now adopts similar policies toward books and authors.
3. Accepting money instead of requiring some other form of penance, a charge leveled
against Laud. "Covenants and protestations": various parliamentary proclamations
opposing episcopacy and defending the rights of the people. In spite of these, the
Licensing Order would "chop an episcopacy" (exchange one church hierarchy for
another). "Palace Metropolitan": Lambeth Palace, London residence of the Archbishop of
Canterbury.
4. An illegal religious assembly of dissenters from the established church. "To startle thus
betimes": one who is so quickly alarmed.

pusillanimous. While things are yet not constituted in religion,[5] that freedom of writing should be restrained by a discipline imitated from the prelates, and learnt by them from the Inquisition to shut us up all again into the breast of a licenser, must needs give cause of doubt and discouragement to all learned and religious men. Who cannot but discern the fineness[6] of this politic drift, and who are the contrivers, that while bishops were to be baited down then all presses might be open; it was the people's birthright and privilege in time of Parliament; it was the breaking forth of light.

But now, the bishops abrogated and voided out of the Church, as if our Reformation sought no more but to make room for others into their seats under another name, the episcopal arts begin to bud again, the cruse of truth must run no more oil,[7] liberty of printing must be enthralled again under a prelatical commission of twenty, the privilege of the people nullified, and, which is worse, the freedom of learning must groan again, and to her old fetters; all this the Parliament yet sitting. Although their own late arguments and defenses against the prelates might remember them that this obstructing violence meets for the most part with an event utterly opposite to the end which it drives at: instead of suppressing sects and schisms, it raises them and invests them with a reputation. *The punishing of wits enhances their authority*, saith the Viscount St. Albans,[8] *and a forbidden writing is thought to be a certain spark of truth that flies up in the faces of them who seek to treat it out.* This order, therefore, may prove a nursing mother to sects, but I shall easily show how it will be a stepdame to Truth, and first by disenabling us to the maintenance of what is known already.

Well knows he who uses to consider, that our faith and knowledge thrives by exercise as well as our limbs and complexion.[9] Truth is compared in scripture to a streaming fountain;[1] if her waters flow not in a perpetual progression they sicken into a muddy pool of conformity and tradition. A man may be a heretic in the truth; and if he believe things only because his pastor says so, or the Assembly[2] so determines, without knowing other reason, though his belief be true, yet the very truth he holds becomes his heresy.

There is not any burden that some would gladlier post off to another than the charge and care of their religion. There be—who

5. The Westminster Assembly was still debating the new church discipline to replace episcopacy.
6. Subtlety, cunning.
7. See 1 Kings 17:8–16: Elijah, helping a poor widow, miraculously produced an abundance of oil from a single "cruse" (jar).
8. Sir Francis Bacon.
9. Bodily constitution.
1. See Ps. 85:11, Prov. 18:4, and Song of Sol. 4:15 ("a fountain of gardens, a well of living waters").
2. The Westminster Assembly of Divines.

knows not that there be?—of Protestants and professors who live
and die in as arrant an implicit faith as any lay papist of Loretto.[3] A
wealthy man addicted to his pleasure and to his profits finds religion to be a traffic so entangled and of so many piddling accounts
that of all mysteries[4] he cannot skill to keep a stock going upon that
trade. What should he do? Fain he would have the name to be religious, fain he would bear up with his neighbors in that. What does
he, therefore, but resolves to give over toiling and to find himself
out some factor[5] to whose care and credit he may commit the whole
managing of his religious affairs; some divine of note and estimation that must be. To him he adheres, resigns the whole warehouse
of his religion with all the locks and keys into his custody; and
indeed makes the very person of that man his religion; esteems his
associating with him a sufficient evidence and commendatory of
his own piety. So that a man may say his religion is now no more
within himself but is become a dividual movable[6] and goes and
comes near him according as that good man frequents his house.
He entertains him, gives him gifts, feasts him, lodges him; his religion comes home at night, prays, is liberally supped, and sumptu-
ously laid to sleep, rises, is saluted, and after the malmsey or some
well-spiced brewage, and better breakfasted than he whose morning appetite would have gladly fed on green figs between Bethany
and Jerusalem,[7] his religion walks abroad at eight and leaves his
kind entertainer in the shop trading all day without his religion.

Another sort there be who, when they hear that all things shall
be ordered, all things regulated and settled, nothing written but
what passes through the custom-house of certain publicans that
have the tunnaging and poundaging[8] of all free-spoken truth, will
straight give themselves up into your hands, make 'em and cut 'em
out what religion ye please. There be delights, there be recreations
and jolly pastimes that will fetch the day about from sun to sun,
and rock the tedious year as in a delightful dream. What need they
torture their heads with that which others have taken so strictly
and so unalterably into their own purveying? These are the fruits
which a dull ease and cessation of our knowledge will bring forth

3. It was believed that angels transported Mary and Jesus' house from Nazareth to this
Italian shrine. "Professors": Puritans who publicly profess their faith. "Implicit faith":
subordinating one's own belief to the general belief of the church.
4. Trades, professions, occupations.
5. Agent.
6. Separable commodity.
7. The fig tree disappoints hungry Jesus: "when he came to it, he found nothing but
leaves; for the time of figs was not yet" (Mark 11:13).
8. An allusion to the king's having collected an excise tax on wine (*tun*, "barrel") and
wool, respectively, without specific statutory authorization by Parliament. His continued collection violated the petition of right. John Selden, whom Milton praises in this
treatise and in *DDD*, went to prison over this matter. "Publicans": tax collectors.

among the people. How goodly and how to be wished were such an obedient unanimity as this; what a fine conformity would it starch us all into! Doubtless a staunch and solid piece of framework as any January could freeze together.

Nor much better will be the consequence even among the clergy themselves. It is no new thing never heard of before for a parochial minister, who has his reward and is at his Hercules' pillars[9] in a warm benefice, to be easily inclinable, if he have nothing else that may rouse up his studies, to finish his circuit in an English concordance and a topic folio, the gatherings and savings of a sober graduateship, a harmony and a catena, treading the constant round of certain common doctrinal heads, attended with their uses, motives, marks, and means; out of which, as out of an alphabet or sol-fa, by forming and transforming, joining and disjoining variously, a little bookcraft, and two hours' meditation, might furnish him unspeakably to the performance of more than a weekly charge of sermoning—not to reckon up the infinite helps of interlinearies,[1] breviaries, synopses, and other loitering gear.

But as for the multitude of sermons ready and printed and piled up on every text that is not difficult, our London trading St. Thomas in his vestry, and add to boot St. Martin and St. Hugh, have not within their hallowed limits more vendible ware of all sorts ready made; so that penury he never need fear of pulpit provision, having where so plenteously to refresh his magazine.[2] But if his rear and flanks be not impaled,[3] if his back door be not secured by the rigid licenser, but that a bold book may now and then issue forth and give the assault to some of his old collections in their trenches, it will concern him then to keep waking, to stand in watch, to set good guards and sentinels about his received opinions, to walk the round and counter-round with his fellow inspectors, fearing lest any of his flock be seduced, who also then would be better instructed, better exercised and disciplined. And God send that the fear of this diligence which must then be used do not make us affect the laziness of a licensing church.

For if we be sure we are in the right and do not hold the truth guiltily, which becomes not, if we ourselves condemn not our own weak and frivolous teaching, and the people for an untaught and

---

9. Limits of aspiration, named after the pillars Hercules was said to have set, marking the western limit of the ancient world.
1. Line-by-line translations. Milton disparages these shortcuts. "Topic folio": commonplace book. "Harmony": books reconciling scriptural passages on the same topic, especially from the four gospels. "Catena": a chain or string of extracts from the church fathers, proving the existence of a continuous tradition. "Sol-fa": musical scale.
2. Storehouse. Milton puns on "vestry" (clothing), sold in the vicinity of St. Thomas Apostle, and on "boot" (shoes), sold in the precincts of St. Martin le Grand. St. Hugh was the patron saint of shoemakers.
3. Protected by a fence.

irreligious gadding rout, what can be more fair than when a man judicious, learned, and of a conscience, for aught we know, as good as theirs that taught us what we know, shall not privily from house to house, which is more dangerous, but openly by writing publish to the world what his opinion is, what his reasons, and wherefore that which is now thought cannot be sound. Christ urged it as wherewith to justify himself that he preached in public;[4] yet writing is more public than preaching and more easy to refutation, if need be, there being so many whose business and profession merely it is to be the champions of truth, which if they neglect, what can be imputed but their sloth or unability?

Thus much we are hindered and disinured[5] by this course of licensing toward the true knowledge of what we seem to know. For how much it hurts and hinders the licensers themselves in the calling of their ministry, more than any secular employment, if they will discharge that office as they ought, so that of necessity they must neglect either the one duty or the other, I insist not because it is a particular, but leave it to their own conscience how they will decide it there.

There is yet behind[6] of what I purposed to lay open, the incredible loss and detriment that this plot of licensing puts us to; more than if some enemy at sea should stop up all our havens and ports and creeks, it hinders and retards the importation of our richest merchandise, Truth. Nay, it was first established and put in practice by antichristian malice and mystery on set purpose to extinguish, if it were possible, the light of reformation and to settle falsehood, little differing from that policy wherewith the Turk upholds his Alcoran,[7] by the prohibition of printing. 'Tis not denied, but gladly confessed, we are to send our thanks and vows to heaven louder than most of nations for that great measure of truth which we enjoy, especially in those main points between us and the Pope, with his appurtenances the prelates. But he who thinks we are to pitch our tent here, and have attained the utmost prospect of reformation that the mortal glass[8] wherein we contemplate can show us till we come to beatific vision, that man by this very opinion declares that he is yet far short of truth.

 Truth indeed came once into the world with her divine Master and was a perfect shape most glorious to look on; but when he ascended and his apostles after him were laid asleep, then straight

---

4. John 18:19–20.
5. Deprived of use or practice.
6. Still to show.
7. The Koran.
8. Mirror. "For now we see through [by means of] a glass darkly; but then face to face" (1 Cor. 13:12).

arose a wicked race of deceivers who, as that story goes of the
Egyptian Typhon with his conspirators, how they dealt with the
good Osiris, took the virgin Truth, hewed her lovely form into a
thousand pieces, and scattered them to the four winds.[9] From that
time ever since, the sad friends of Truth, such as durst appear, imitating the careful search that Isis made for the mangled body of
Osiris, went up and down gathering up limb by limb still as they
could find them. We have not yet found them all, Lords and Commons, nor ever shall do, till her Master's second coming; he shall
bring together every joint and member and shall mold them into an
immortal feature[1] of loveliness and perfection. Suffer not these
licensing prohibitions to stand at every place of opportunity, forbidding and disturbing them that continue seeking, that continue to
do our obsequies[2] to the torn body of our martyred saint.

We boast our light, but if we look not wisely on the sun itself, it
smites us into darkness. Who can discern those planets that are oft
combust,[3] and those stars of brightest magnitude that rise and set
with the sun, until the opposite motion of their orbs bring them to
such a place in the firmament where they may be seen evening or
morning? The light which we have gained was given us, not to be
ever staring on, but by it to discover onward things more remote
from our knowledge. It is not the unfrocking of a priest, the
unmitering of a bishop, and the removing him from off the Presbyterian shoulders that will make us a happy nation. No, if other
things as great in the church and in the rule of life both economical
and political be not looked into and reformed, we have looked so
long upon the blaze that Zwinglius and Calvin[4] hath beaconed up
to us that we are stark blind.

There be who perpetually complain of schisms and sects, and
make it such a calamity that any man dissents from their maxims.
'Tis their own pride and ignorance which causes the disturbing,
who neither will hear with meekness nor can convince, yet all must
be suppressed which is not found in their syntagma.[5] They are the
troublers, they are the dividers of unity, who neglect and permit not
others to unite those dissevered pieces which are yet wanting to the
body of Truth. To be still searching what we know not by what we
know, still closing up truth to truth as we find it (for all her body is

9. There are cross-cultural implications in the story of an Egyptian god, found in Greek
   Plutarch's *Moralia* ("On Isis and Osiris"), and adapted by an English Puritan.
1. Shape.
2. Funeral rites or ceremonies.
3. Burned up—that is, their light unapparent because of their nearness to the sun.
4. Two principal theologians of the Reformation. Ulrich Zwingli (1484–1531) first established Protestantism in Switzerland, in Zürich, thus preceding the French John Calvin
   (1509–1564), who established it in Geneva.
5. A systematically arranged treatise.

homogeneal and proportional), this is the golden rule[6] in theology as well as in arithmetic and makes up the best harmony in a church, not the forced and outward union of cold and neutral and inwardly divided minds.

Lords and Commons of England, consider what nation it is whereof ye are and whereof ye are the governors: a nation not slow and dull but of a quick, ingenious, and piercing spirit, acute to invent, subtle and sinewy to discourse, not beneath the reach of any point the highest that human capacity can soar to. Therefore the studies of learning in her deepest sciences have been so ancient and so eminent among us that writers of good antiquity and ablest judgment have been persuaded that even the school of Pythagoras and the Persian wisdom[7] took beginning from the old philosophy of this island. And that wise and civil Roman, Julius Agricola,[8] who governed once here for Caesar, preferred the natural wits of Britain before the labored studies of the French. Nor is it for nothing that the grave and frugal Transylvanian sends out yearly from as far as the mountainous borders of Russia and beyond the Hercynian wilderness,[9] not their youth but their staid men, to learn our language and our theological arts.

Yet that which is above all this, the favor and the love of Heaven, we have great argument to think in a peculiar manner propitious and propending[1] towards us. Why else was this nation chosen before any other, that out of her, as out of Sion,[2] should be proclaimed and sounded forth the first tidings and trumpet of reformation to all Europe? And had it not been the obstinate perverseness of our prelates against the divine and admirable spirit of Wycliffe, to suppress him as a schismatic and innovator, perhaps neither the Bohemian Huss and Jerome,[3] no, nor the name of Luther or of Calvin, had been ever known; the glory of reforming all our neighbors had been completely ours. But now, as our obdurate clergy have with violence demeaned the matter, we are become hitherto the latest and the backwardest scholars of whom God offered to have made us the teachers. Now once again by all concurrence of signs and by the general instinct of holy and devout men as they daily and

6. In arithmetic, the rule of proportion or the rule of three, a method for finding an unknown fourth quantity when three quantities are known.
7. The occult, magic. "School of Pythagoras": an ultra-nationalistic assertion that the ancient Pythagorean belief in the transmigration of souls derives from the British Druids ("old philosophy").
8. Proconsul in Britain, 78–85 C.E.
9. Wooded area in central and southern Germany. Protestant Transylvania (in present-day Romania) sent scholars to England to study theology.
1. Inclining.
2. "For out of Zion shall go forth the law (lit., "Torah"), and the word of the Lord from Jerusalem" (Isa. 2:3). Milton sees England as a holy community, a new Israel.
3. Jerome of Prague (1370–1416) and his friend Huss were disciples of Wycliffe burned to death for heresy.

solemnly express their thoughts, God is decreeing to begin some
new and great period in his church, even to the reforming of reformation itself. What does he then but reveal himself to his servants,
and, as his manner is, first to his Englishmen? I say as his manner
is, first to us, though we mark not the method of his counsels and
are unworthy.

Behold now this vast city, a city of refuge,[4] the mansion house of
liberty, encompassed and surrounded with his protection. The shop
of war hath not there more anvils and hammers waking to fashion
out the plates and instruments of armed justice in defense of belea-
guered truth than there be pens and heads there, sitting by their
studious lamps, musing, searching, revolving new notions and ideas
wherewith to present, as with their homage and their fealty, the
approaching reformation; others as fast readying, trying all things,[5]
assenting to the force of reason and convincement. What could a
man require more from a nation so pliant and so prone to seek after
knowledge? What wants there to such a towardly and pregnant soil
but wise and faithful laborers to make a knowing people, a nation
of prophets, of sages, and of worthies? We reckon more than five
months yet to harvest; there need not be five weeks; had we but
eyes to lift up, the fields are white already.[6] Where there is much
desire to learn, there of necessity will be much arguing, much writing, many opinions; for opinion in good men is but knowledge in
the making. Under these fantastic[7] terrors of sect and schism, we
wrong the earnest and zealous thirst after knowledge and understanding which God hath stirred up in this city. What some lament
of, we rather should rejoice at, should rather praise this pious forwardness among men to reassume the ill-deputed care of their
religion into their own hands again. A little generous prudence, a
little forbearance of one another, and some grain of charity might
win all these diligences to join and unite in one general and brotherly search after truth, could we but forgo this prelatical tradition
of crowding free consciences and Christian liberties into canons
and precepts of men. I doubt not, if some great and worthy stranger
should come among us, wise to discern the mold and temper of a
people and how to govern it, observing the high hopes and aims,
the diligent alacrity of our extended thoughts and reasonings in the
pursuance of truth and freedom, but that he would cry out as

4. God commands the Jews to establish cities of refuge to protect unintentional killers
from avengers (Num. 35). Perhaps Milton considers London to be a refuge from
revengeful royalists.
5. "Prove all things; hold fast that which is good" (1 Thess. 5:21).
6. "Say not ye, There be yet four months, and then cometh harvest? behold, I say unto
you, Lift up your eyes, and look on the fields: for they are white already to harvest"
(John 4:35).
7. Imaginary.

Pyrrhus[8] did, admiring the Roman docility and courage: "If such were my Epirots, I would not despair the greatest design that could be attempted to make a church or kingdom happy."

Yet these are the men cried out against for schismatics and sectaries; as if, while the temple of the Lord was building, some cutting, some squaring the marble, others hewing the cedars, there should be a sort of irrational men who could not consider there must be many schisms and many dissections made in the quarry and in the timber ere the house of God can be built.[9] And when every stone is laid artfully together, it cannot be united into a continuity, it can but be contiguous in this world; neither can every piece of the building be of one form; nay rather the perfection consists in this, that out of many moderate varieties and brotherly dissimilitudes that are not vastly disproportional arises the goodly and the graceful symmetry that commends the whole pile and structure.

Let us therefore be more considerate builders, more wise in spiritual architecture, when great reformation is expected. For now the time seems come, wherein Moses the great prophet may sit in Heaven rejoicing to see that memorable and glorious wish of his fulfilled, when not only our seventy elders but all the Lord's people are become prophets. No marvel then though some men, and some good men too perhaps, but young in goodness, as Joshua then was, envy them.[1] They fret and out of their own weakness are in agony lest these divisions and subdivisions will undo us. The adversary again applauds and waits the hour. "When they have branched themselves out, saith he, small enough into parties and partitions, then will be our time." Fool! He sees not the firm root out of which we all grow, though into branches; nor will beware until he see our small divided maniples cutting through at every angle of his ill-united and unwieldy brigade.[2] And that we are to hope better of all these supposed sects and schisms, and that we shall not need that solicitude—honest, perhaps, though over-timorous—of them that vex in this behalf, but shall laugh in the end at those malicious applauders of our differences, I have these reasons to persuade me.

8. King of Epirus, who praised the Romans after defeating them at the battle of Heraclea (280 B.C.E.).
9. "A remarkable example of Milton's technique of reversing a damaging received inference from a scriptural text by enlarging the scope of its reference" (*YP*, 2:555). Suppressors of religious dissent interpreted the silence within the precincts of Solomon's temple as a sign that God dislikes the noise of controversy: "there was neither hammer nor axe nor any tool of iron heard in the house, while it was in building" (1 Kings 6:7). But Milton echoes words from the larger context of 1 Kings 5–7 that describe the necessary sounds of construction.
1. When Joshua asks his master Moses to forbid Eldad and Medad from prophesying, he replies, "Enviest thou for my sake? would God that all the Lord's people were prophets, and that the Lord would put his spirit upon them" (Num. 11:29).
2. A large division of troops. "Maniples": small bands of soldiers.

First, when a city shall be as it were besieged and blocked about, her navigable river infested, inroads and incursions round, defiance and battle oft rumored to be marching up even to her walls and suburb trenches, that then the people, or the greater part, more than at other times, wholly taken up with the study of highest and most important matters to be reformed, should be disputing, reasoning, reading, inventing, discoursing, even to a rarity and admiration,[3] things not before discoursed or written of, argues first a singular goodwill, contentedness, and confidence in your prudent foresight and safe governments, Lords and Commons. And from thence derives[4] itself to a gallant bravery and well-grounded contempt of their enemies, as if there were no small number of as great spirits among us as his was, who, when Rome was nigh besieged by Hannibal, being in the city, bought that piece of ground at no cheap rate whereon Hannibal himself encamped his own regiment.[5]

Next, it is a lively and cheerful presage of our happy success and victory. For as in a body when the blood is fresh, the spirits pure and vigorous, not only to vital but to rational faculties, and those in the acutest and the pertest operations of wit and subtlety, it argues in what good plight and constitution the body is; so when the cheerfulness of the people is so sprightly up as that it has not only wherewith to guard well its own freedom and safety, but to spare, and to bestow upon the solidest and sublimest points of controversy and new invention, it betokens us not degenerated nor drooping to a fatal decay, but casting off the old and wrinkled skin of corruption to outlive these pangs and wax young again, entering the glorious ways of truth and prosperous virtue destined to become great and honorable in these latter ages.

Methinks I see in my mind a noble and puissant nation rousing herself like a strong man after sleep and shaking her invincible locks.[6] Methinks I see her as an eagle mewing[7] her mighty youth and kindling her undazzled eyes at the full midday beam, purging and unscaling her long-abused sight at the fountain itself of heavenly radiance, while the whole noise of timorous and flocking birds, with those also that love the twilight, flutter about, amazed at what she means, and in their envious gabble[8] would prognosticate a year of sects and schisms.

---

3. Provoking wonder.
4. Conducts.
5. Livy's *History* (26.11) tells of a Roman citizen who paid full price for the field where Hannibal's army was then encamped.
6. A reference to Samson's triumphs over Delilah's first three attempts to learn the secret of his strength (Judg. 16:6–20).
7. Renewing by molting.
8. Inarticulate noises.

What should ye do then? should ye suppress all this flowery crop of knowledge and new light sprung up and yet springing daily in this city? Should ye set an oligarchy of twenty engrossers[9] over it to bring a famine upon our minds again, when we shall know nothing but what is measured to us by their bushel? Believe it, Lords and Commons, they who counsel ye to such a suppressing do as good as bid ye suppress yourselves, and I will soon show how. If it be desired to know the immediate cause of all this free writing and free speaking, there cannot be assigned a truer than your own mild and free and humane government. It is the liberty, Lords and Commons, which your own valorous and happy counsels have purchased us, liberty which is the nurse of all great wits; this is that which hath rarefied and enlightened our spirits like the influence of heaven; this is that which hath enfranchised, enlarged, and lifted up our apprehensions degrees above themselves. Ye cannot make us now less capable, less knowing, less eagerly pursuing of the truth, unless ye first make yourselves, that made us so, less the lovers, less the founders of our true liberty. We can grow ignorant again, brutish, formal, and slavish, as ye found us; but you then must first become that which ye cannot be, oppressive, arbitrary, and tyrannous, as they were from whom ye have freed us. That our hearts are now more capacious, our thoughts more erected to the search and expectation of greatest and exactest things, is the issue of your own virtue propagated in us; ye cannot suppress that unless ye reinforce an abrogated and merciless law, that fathers may dispatch at will their own children.[1] And who shall then stick closest to ye and excite others? Not he who takes up arms for coat and conduct and his four nobles of Danegelt.[2] Although I dispraise not the defense of just immunities, yet love my peace better if that were all.[3] Give me the liberty to know, to utter, and to argue freely according to conscience, above all liberties.

What would be best advised then, if it be found so hurtful and so unequal[4] to suppress opinions for the newness or the unsuitableness to a customary acceptance, will not be my task to say. I only shall repeat what I have learned from one of your own honorable number, a right noble and pious lord who, had he not sacrificed his

9. Monopolizers.
1. The Roman law that gave a father power over the life and death of his children was abrogated in 318 C.E.
2. Ship money (opposed by John Hampden), a tax in support of the navy, originally raised to oppose or, as a bribe, to placate the Danes. If Parliament suppresses liberty, it will meet resistance from those citizens for whom the civil war was fought for higher values than the material. "Coat and conduct": a county tax for troop equipment and transport. "Nobles" English coins worth half a mark (6s. 8d.).
3. Milton alludes to some of Charles's attempts to extract funds without consent of Parliament.
4. Unjust.

life and fortunes to the church and commonwealth, we had not
now missed and bewailed a worthy and undoubted patron of this
argument. Ye know him I am sure; yet I for honor's sake, and may it
be eternal to him, shall name him, the Lord Brooke.[5] He, writing
of episcopacy, and by the way treating of sects and schisms, left ye
his vote, or rather now the last words of his dying charge (which
I know will ever be of dear and honored regard with ye) so full of
meekness and breathing charity that, next to his[6] last testament
who bequeathed love and peace to his disciples, I cannot call to
mind where I have read or heard words more mild and peaceful. He
there exhorts us to hear with patience and humility those, however
they be miscalled, that desire to live purely in such a use of God's
ordinances as the best guidance of their conscience gives them,
and to tolerate them, though in some disconformity to ourselves.
The book itself will tell us more at large, being published to the
world and dedicated to the Parliament by him who, both for his life
and for his death, deserves that what advice he left be not laid by
without perusal.

And now the time in special is by privilege[7] to write and speak
what may help to the further discussing of matters in agitation. The
temple of Janus[8] with his two controversial faces might now not
unsignificantly be set open. And though all the winds of doctrine[9]
were let loose to play upon the earth, so Truth be in the field, we do
injuriously by licensing and prohibiting to misdoubt her strength.
Let her and Falsehood grapple; who ever knew Truth put to the
worse in a free and open encounter? Her confuting is the best and
surest suppressing. He who hears what praying there is for light
and clearer knowledge to be sent down among us would think of
other matters to be constituted beyond the discipline of Geneva,
framed and fabricked already to our hands.[1]

Yet when the new light which we beg for shines in upon us, there
be who envy and oppose if it come not first in at their casements.
What a collusion is this, whenas we are exhorted by the wise man
to use diligence, *to seek for wisdom as for treasures early and late,*[2]
that another order shall enjoin us to know nothing but by statute?

5. Robert Greville (1608–1643), the second Lord Brooke, a general who died in battle
   while leading a parliamentary army. Milton refers to his *Discourse Opening the Nature
   of That Episcopacy, which Is Exercised in England* (1641).
6. I.e., Jesus' (John 14:27).
7. I.e., *cum privilegio,* the term found on a title page indicating the right to publish the
   book.
8. Roman god of gates, depicted with two heads looking in opposite directions ("controversial"). His temple was open in war time, shut in peacetime.
9. Alluding to Eph. 4:14.
1. Fashioned. "Discipline of Geneva": Calvinist doctrine, the model for Presbyterianism.
2. "If thou seekest her [wisdom] in silver, and searchest for her as for hid treasures" (Proverbs 2:4).

When a man hath been laboring the hardest labor in the deep
mines of knowledge, hath furnished out his findings in all their
equipage, drawn forth his reasons as it were a battle ranged, scattered and defeated all objections in his way, calls out his adversary
into the plain, offers him the advantage of wind and sun, if he
please, only that he may try the matter by dint of argument; for his
opponents then to skulk, to lay ambushments, to keep a narrow
bridge of licensing where the challenger should pass, though it be
valor enough in soldiership, is but weakness and cowardice in the
wars of Truth.

For who knows not that Truth is strong next to the Almighty? She
needs no policies, nor stratagems, nor licensings to make her victorious, those are the shifts and the defenses that error uses against her
power. Give her but room and do not bind her when she sleeps, for
then she speaks not true as the old Proteus[3] did, who spake oracles
only when he was caught and bound, but then rather she turns herself into all shapes except her own, and perhaps tunes her voice
according to the time, as Micaiah did before Ahab,[4] until she be
adjured into her own likeness. Yet is it not impossible that she may
have more shapes than one. What else is all that rank of things indifferent[5] wherein Truth may be on this side or on the other without
being unlike herself? What but a vain shadow else is the abolition of
those ordinances, that hand-writing nailed to the cross?[6] What great
purchase is this Christian liberty which Paul so often boasts of? His
doctrine is that he who eats or eats not, regards a day or regards it
not, may do either to the Lord.[7] How many other things might be
tolerated in peace and left to conscience had we but charity, and
were it not the chief stronghold of our hypocrisy to be ever judging
one another? I fear yet this iron yoke of outward conformity hath left
a slavish print upon our necks; the ghost of a linen decency[8] yet
haunts us. We stumble and are impatient at the least dividing of one
visible congregation from another, though it be not in fundamentals.
And through our forwardness to suppress and our backwardness to

3. Shape-shifting, oracular sea god, who speaks the truth only to someone who can successfully hold him, as Menelaus did (*Od.*, 4.412).
4. See 1 Kings 22:1–37. Having been urged by King Ahab's messenger "to declare good
   unto the king," Micaiah initially predicts the king's victory. When Ahab adjures him to
   speak the truth, he correctly predicts the king's death in battle.
5. Designating points of doctrine not set forth in scripture. Controversies arose over
   whether they could be prescribed by the church or should be left to the conscience of
   the individual Christian.
6. Colossians 2:14, on the abrogation of the ceremonial Mosaic law, including its dietary
   prohibitions. Earlier in the treatise, he connects dietary freedom with the right to read
   all manner of books.
7. Rom. 14:1–13.
8. Priestly vestments, condemned by the Puritans. Laud appealed to "decency" in imposing uniformity in the church.

recover any enthralled piece of truth out of the gripe of custom,[9] we care not to keep truth separated from truth, which is the fiercest rent and disunion of all. We do not see that while we still affect by all means a rigid external formality, we may as soon fall again into a gross conforming stupidity, a stark and dead congealment of *wood and hay and stubble*,[1] forced and frozen together, which is more to the sudden degenerating of a church than many subdichotomies of petty schisms.

Not that I can think well of every light separation, or that all in a church is to be expected *gold and silver and precious stones*. It is not possible for man to sever the wheat from the tares, the good fish from the other fry; that must be the angels' ministry at the end of mortal things.[2] Yet if all cannot be of one mind—as who looks they should be?—this doubtless is more wholesome, more prudent, and more Christian that many be tolerated rather than all compelled. I mean not tolerated popery and open superstition which, as it extirpates all religions and civil supremacies, so itself should be extirpate, provided first that all charitable and compassionate means be used to win and regain the weak and the misled; that also which is impious or evil absolutely either against faith or manners no law can possibly permit that intends not to unlaw itself. But those neighboring differences, or rather indifferences, are what I speak of, whether in some point of doctrine or of discipline which, though they may be many, yet need not interrupt *the unity of spirit*, if we could but find among us *the bond of peace*.[3]

In the meanwhile, if any one would write and bring his helpful hand to the slow-moving reformation which we labor under, if Truth have spoken to him before others or but seemed at least to speak, who hath so bejesuited[4] us that we should trouble that man with asking license to do so worthy a deed?—and not consider this, that if it come to prohibiting, there is not aught more likely to be prohibited than truth itself, whose first appearance to our eyes, bleared and dimmed with prejudice and custom, is more unsightly and unplausible than many errors, even as the person is of many a great man slight and contemptible to see to. And what do they tell us vainly of new opinions, when this very opinion of theirs, that none must be heard but whom they like, is the worst and newest opinion of all others and is the chief cause why sects and schisms do so much abound and true knowledge is kept at distance from us,

---

9. For the opposition of truth and custom, see the preface to *DDD*.
1. This quote and the next ("gold . . . precious stones"; next paragraph) name the different materials people bring to "God's building" (1 Cor. 3:10–13).
2. On the parable of the wheat and the tares, and on the angels as reapers, see Matt. 13:24–30 and 13:39.
3. Eph 4:3.
4. Initiated in Jesuitism.

besides yet a greater danger which is in it. For when God shakes a
kingdom with strong and healthful commotions to a general
reforming, 'tis not untrue that many sectaries and false teachers
are then busiest in seducing; but yet more true it is that God then
raises to his own work men of rare abilities and more than common
industry, not only to look back and revise what hath been taught
heretofore, but to gain further and go on some new enlightened
steps in the discovery of truth.

For such is the order of God's enlightening church, to dispense
and deal out by degrees his beam so as our earthly eyes may best
sustain it. Neither is God appointed and confined where and out of
what place these his chosen shall be first heard to speak. For he
sees not as man sees, chooses not as man chooses, lest we should
devote ourselves again to set places and assemblies and outward
callings of men, planting our faith one while in the old convocation
house and another while in the chapel at Westminster;[5] when all
the faith and religion that shall be there canonized is not sufficient
without plain convincement and the charity of patient instruction
to supple[6] the least bruise of conscience, to edify the meanest
Christian who desires to walk in the spirit and not in the letter of
human trust, for all the number of voices that can be there made;
no, though Harry VII himself there, with all his liege tombs about
him should lend them voices from the dead to swell their number.

And if the men be erroneous who appear to be the leading schismatics, what withholds us but our sloth, our self-will, and distrust
in the right cause, that we do not give them gentle meetings and
gentle dismissions, that we debate not and examine the matter
thoroughly with liberal and frequent audience, if not for their
sakes, yet for our own? Seeing no man who hath tasted learning but
will confess the many ways of profiting by those who, not contented
with stale receipts, are able to manage and set forth new positions
to the world. And were they but as the dust and cinders of our feet,
so long as in that notion they may yet serve to polish and brighten
the armory of truth, even for that respect they were not utterly to
be cast away. But if they be of those whom God hath fitted for the
special use of these times with eminent and ample gifts, and those
perhaps neither among the priests nor among the Pharisees, and we
in the haste of a precipitant zeal shall make no distinction but
resolve to stop their mouths because we fear they come with new

5. The Convocation, an assembly of bishops to deliberate on ecclesiastical matters, met in
   the Chapter House at Westminster. From 1643 to 1649, the Assembly of Divines,
   appointed by Parliament to restructure the church after the fall of episcopacy, met in
   Henry VII's chapel (mentioned at the end of the paragraph), also in Westminster.
6. Soften, mollify. "Canonized": embodied in canons (rules, laws, decrees), to be imposed
   by Parliament on the people.

and dangerous opinions (as we commonly forejudge them ere we understand them), no less than woe to us while, thinking thus to defend the Gospel, we are found the persecutors.

There have been not a few since the beginning of this Parliament, both of the presbytery and others, who, by their unlicensed books to the contempt of an *Imprimatur*, first broke that triple ice clung about our hearts and taught the people to see day. I hope that none of those were the persuaders to renew upon us this bondage which they themselves have wrought so much good by contemning. But if neither the check that Moses gave to young Joshua nor the countermand which our Savior gave to young John,[7] who was so ready to prohibit those whom he thought unlicensed, be not enough to admonish our elders how unacceptable to God their testy mood of prohibiting is; if neither their own remembrance what evil hath abounded in the church by this let of licensing, and what good they themselves have begun by transgressing it, be not enough but that they will persuade and execute the most Dominican part of the Inquisition over us,[8] and are already with one foot in the stirrup so active at suppressing, it would be no unequal distribution in the first place to suppress the suppressors themselves, whom the change of their condition hath puffed up more than their late experience of harder times hath made wise.

And as for regulating the press, let no man think to have the honor of advising ye better than yourselves have done in that order published next before this, that no book be printed unless the printer's and the author's name, or at least the printer's, be registered.[9] Those which otherwise come forth, if they be found mischievous and libelous, the fire and the executioner will be the timeliest and the most effectual remedy that man's prevention can use. For this authentic Spanish policy of licensing books, if I have said aught, will prove the most unlicensed book itself within a short while; and was the immediate image of a Star Chamber decree to that purpose made in those very times when that court did the rest of those her pious works, for which she is now fallen from the stars with Lucifer.[1] Whereby ye may guess what kind of state prudence, what love of the people, what care of religion or good manners there was at the contriving, although with singular hypocrisy it pretended to bind books to their good

7. Jesus tells John not to forbid others from acting in Jesus' name (Luke 9:49–50). See also p. 372, n. 1.
8. Many of the licensers were Dominican friars. "Let": obstruction.
9. Milton quotes from an earlier parliamentary order (January 1642) regulating printing.
1. Sirluck (YP 2:159) describes the Decree of Charles' Court of the Star Chamber in 1637 as "the most elaborate instrument in English history for the suppression of undesired publication; nothing was unforeseen except the determination with which it was defied." Milton compares the court's fall in 1641 with the fall of Lucifer (lit. "light bringer").

behavior. And how it got the upper hand of your precedent order so well constituted before, if we may believe those men whose profession gives them cause to inquire most, it may be doubted[2] that there was in it the fraud of some old patentees and monopolizers in the trade of bookselling; who, under pretense of the poor in their company not to be defrauded, and the just retaining of each man his several copy (which God forbid should be gainsaid) brought diverse glossing colors[3] to the House, which were indeed but colors and serving to no end except it be to exercise a superiority over their neighbors; men who do not therefore labor in an honest profession to which learning is indebted that they should be made other men's vassals. Another end is thought was aimed at by some of them in procuring by petition this order,[4] that having power in their hands, malignant books might the easier scape abroad, as the event shows.

But of these sophisms and elenchs of merchandise I skill not.[5] This I know, that errors in a good government and in a bad are equally almost incident,[6] for what magistrate may not be misinformed, and much the sooner if liberty of printing be reduced into the power of a few? But to redress willingly and speedily what hath been erred, and in highest authority to esteem a plain advertisement more than others have done a sumptuous bribe, is a virtue, honored Lords and Commons, answerable[7] to your highest actions, and whereof none can participate but greatest and wisest men.

THE TENURE OF KINGS AND MAGISTRATES (1649) If, according to Aristotle, *catharsis* is the purpose of tragedy, raising and then purging the emotions of pity and fear, then *The Tenure of Kings and Magistrates* is an anti-tragedy, in which a pitiless and fearless Milton attempted mightily to alienate his readers from those emotions. This was not an easy task, and one treatise, however compelling, could not accomplish it. England's unbroken chain of monarchs led many of his countrymen to question the legitimacy of the trial of Charles I. And that monarch's successful self-presentation as martyr and saint led even more of those countrymen Milton would later dismiss as "an inconstant, irrational, and image-doting rabble" (*Eikonoklastes*) to protest his execution on January 30, 1649. Finally, in March of that year, not the full and frequent Parliament but only the Rump—that is, Parliament purged of those who advocated compromise with Charles—

---

2. Suspected.
3. Misrepresentations; false colorings of the truth. "Copy": copyright.
4. In April 1643, the Stationers Company petitioned Parliament to restore to them control over the press that it lost when the Star Chamber fell.
5. Milton professes ignorance of fallacious and misleading arguments used for commercial advantage.
6. Likely to happen.
7. Corresponding. "Advertisement": notification of facts; admonition; warning.

abolished the office of kingship and founded a republic for the first and only time in British history. As Barbara Lewalski has noted, the overarching rhetorical purpose of *The Tenure* was "to support or at least accept the trial, the regicide, and the new commonwealth" (230).

Milton began writing the treatise during the trial and published the first edition two weeks after the execution. The longer second edition, printed here, is slightly less incendiary than the first, but even in this version it underscores Milton's status as the most radical and iconoclastic of the great English poets. The treatise may be as important for what it did as for what it said. It attracted the attention of Oliver Cromwell's Council of State, which appointed him its Secretary for Foreign Tongues, and thus it led to Milton's becoming the commonwealth's chief propagandist and justifier of the regicide (see Dzelzainis, ix).

Outrage over killing the king produced attacks, and Milton counterattacked. *Eikon Basilike* ("image of the king"), published soon after the execution and ostensibly written by the late king himself, was more likely ghost written by John Gauden, bishop of Worcester, a staunch royalist, who relied on Old Testament invective in his attack on the regicide, *Cromwell's Bloody Slaughter-House*, but who appropriated gentle New Testament verses in constructing an icon of a Christ-like Charles. The grossly sentimental *Eikon* was hugely popular, with thirty-five English editions published in 1649 alone, besides various foreign language translations. In his first commissioned publication as secretary, *Eikonoklastes* ("image or idol breaker or destroyer"), October 1649, Milton systematically undermines the *Eikon*, exposing the king's theatricality and feigned religiosity. Even more than the *Tenure*, it opposes sentimentality, attempting to alienate the emotions of readers who were already conditioned to connect the regicide with Christ's Passion. But it was at best merely a *succès d'estime*, with only two editions appearing during Milton's lifetime.

More than two learned counterattacks were required of Cromwell's secretary. Milton's *Pro Populo Anglicano Defensio* (*A Defense of the English People*), published in February 1651, answered the *Defensio Regia* (*Defense of Kingship*, 1649) by the immensely learned French humanist and philologist Claude de Saumaise (Salmasius), who was commissioned by royalists in exile to proclaim the illegality of the proceedings in England. And Milton's great *Defensio Secunda* (*Second Defense of the English People*, May 1654), answered the anonymous *Regii sanguinis clamor ad coelum adversus paricidas Anglicanos* (*The Cry of the Royal Blood to Heaven against the English Parricides*, 1649), for which the Church of England clergyman and religious controversialist Peter du Moulin was probably chiefly responsible.

A glance at *The Tenure's* title page, on the lawfulness of deposing "a tyrant, or wicked king," should indicate why Milton's defenses of England, which provoked immediate opposition, would later be taken up by revolutionaries in France and in the colonies across the Atlantic. Within the treatise, Milton goes further:

> since the king or magistrate holds his authority of the people both originally and naturally for their good in the first place and not his own, then may the people, as oft as they shall judge it for the best,

either choose him or reject him, retain him or depose him, though
no tyrant, merely by the liberty and right of free-born men to be
governed as seems to them best.

Milton's vigorous assertion in *The Tenure* that "all men naturally
were born free" spoke to the ideals expressed in the Declaration of
Independence. And his defenses of government by the people gained
the attention of John Adams and Thomas Jefferson. As early as the
1690s, Jean Barbeyrac, writing in the Huguenot diaspora, having been
expelled from a religiously unified France, frequently cited with approbation Milton's defenses of liberty and his separation of religion from
politics. Milton's views in *The Tenure* and in the treatises written while
secretary owe a great deal to his readings of the natural law theorists
Hugo Grotius and John Selden. Theoretically, the discovery of shared
moral rules in the natural, precivil state of humankind provides a basis
for relationships among human beings anywhere in the world. This is
in part what makes both thinkers pioneering contributors to international relations. Selden differs from Grotius in positing an external
source of natural law—that is, a universal divine positive law of perpetual obligation. Milton does the same in *The Tenure* when he bases
universal human freedom on scripture: "the image and resemblance of
God himself . . . born to command and not to obey."

The Tenure shares important characteristics with Milton's divorce
tracts: both the 1644 *Doctrine and Discipline of Divorce* and *The Tenure* begin by attacking custom, allied in the first with error and in the
second with "blind affections" (emotional attachments, prejudices). In
the *Doctrine*, hoping (futilely) that Presbyterian members of the Westminster Assembly, such as Herbert Palmer, who had justified defensive
war against the king, might understand the necessity for contingency
in domestic contracts as well as in political ones, Milton had insisted
on the propriety of dissolving bad unions: "He who marries intends as
little to conspire his own ruin as he that swears allegiance: and as a
whole people is in relation to an ill government, so is one man to an ill
marriage." Both treatises argue that covenants cannot bind against the
laws of nature and reason implicit in them, and both oppose the Solemn League and Covenant (1643), which the Presbyterians understood
as a contract to protect the king's life and office.

Perhaps the most important similarity between these treatises, and
the strongest evidence of Milton's debt to the natural law theory of
Grotius and Selden, is a monist hermeneutic of inclusiveness, strikingly different from the exclusivity of the early antiprelatical tracts.
One is permitted to remove a tyrant, according to all of the many authorities that Milton invokes: the mere law of nature understood even
by pagans bereft of the knowledge of God's expressed will; the Roman
Codex of Justinian, especially its discussions of freedom and servitude;
the prime authors among the Greeks and Romans, who celebrated the
heroism of those who murdered tyrants; the Mosaic law of the Jews,
who "had the knowledge of true religion," and whose heroes Ehud,
Samuel, and Jehu slew tyrants on the spot, without a trial; the gospel
of Christ, though here the examples are less striking; and the common

law of England, some of whose practitioners sat in the Rump Parliament, insisting on legal rather than regal rights.

Milton's refusal to make the same distinction as his Presbyterian opponents between foreign and domestic tyrants (the usurper Eglon, King of Moab, and a native ruler) points to a supranational perspective in the treatise that derives in large part from natural law theory: "For look how much right the king of Spain hath to govern us at all, so much right hath the king of England to govern us tyrannically." Milton's theme is universalist rather than nationalist: "Who knows not that there is a mutual bond of amity and brotherhood between man and man over all the world, neither is it the English sea that can sever us from that duty and relation." Indeed, alluding to the controversy regarding a single nation's rule over the high seas, Milton seems to prefer the Dutch scholar Grotius's classic argument for the free sea, *Mare Liberum*, over the rebuttal, *Mare Clausum*, by his countryman, whom he calls "our learned Selden," even though *our* means "our English," a scholar to equal or surpass the foreigners Scaliger, Grotius, and Salmasius. The person who in his youth signed his name "John Milton, Englishman" wrote in disillusioned old age, from a spirit of internationalism but also from sheer weariness, "One's country is wherever it is well with one." The *Tenure* represents a midpoint, proclaiming universalism while betraying a seventeenth-century Englishman's ordinary xenophobia:

> Nor is it distance of place that makes enmity, but enmity that makes distance. He therefore that keeps peace with me, near or remote, of whatsoever nation, is to me, as far as all civil and human offices, an Englishman and a neighbor; but if an Englishman . . . offend against life and liberty, . . . though born in the same womb, he is no better than a Turk, a Saracen, a heathen.

The diversity of Milton's sources corresponds to the diverse audience he intends to address, including the Council of State, Members of Parliament, officers of the New Model Army, and even possibly the Levellers. The last, despite enormous differences, shared with the Presbyterians the belief that killing the king would be wrong. If the first stated purpose on the title page is to justify deposing a tyrant, the second is more specific: to accuse of inconsistency, irresolution, and hypocrisy those Presbyterians who defied the king in the early 1640s but who would now protect him: "they, who of late so much blame deposing, are the men that did it themselves." Remembering that the cleric Herbert Palmer had attacked him as a divorcer, Milton singles out Palmer's *Scripture and Reason* (1643) for attack, citing specific militant passages that in effect had already deposed Charles. Indeed, when Milton asserts the universality of his argument against tyranny, he adds that it is "fetched out of the midst of choicest and most authentic learning . . . Mosaical, Christian, orthodoxal and, which must needs be more convincing to our adversaries, presbyterial." Alluding to the medieval theory of the king's two bodies—one mortal, the other infused with the divine right to govern— even though he would never have endorsed it, Milton argues that the Presbyterians have already killed the king. Since

the king is a name of dignity and office, not of person. . . . Then
they certainly who by deposing him have long since taken from
him the life of a king, his office and his dignity, they in the truest
sense may be said to have killed the king.

In *Paradise Lost,* defining the Christian heroism that will replace
Edenic virtue, the Miltonic bard disjoins power from goodness. His
rejection of heroic warfare (9.28–31) implicitly devalues the earlier account of angelic heroism and the Son's triumph over evil in the war in
heaven. He prefers Christ's "better fortitude / Of patience and heroic
martyrdom" (31–32). But in *The Tenure,* written in the heady days of
the king's trial and its aftermath, Milton celebrates virtue as strength
conjoined with goodness rather than as saintly ataraxia not of this
world. In this treatise he pronounces the struggle with King Charles
"worthy of heroic ages" and praises those members of Parliament who
are "endued with fortitude and heroic virtue." *The Tenure* celebrates
the "better fortitude" of executing justice rather than suffering martyrdom: future nations studying the actions of Parliament and the Military Council "henceforth may learn a better fortitude, to dare execute
highest justice on them that shall by force of arms endeavor the oppressing and bereaving of religion and their liberty at home." Milton is
alluding here to the penultimate psalm, a song of triumph:

> Let the high praises of God be in their mouth, and a two-edged
> sword in their hand; to execute vengeance upon the heathen, and
> punishments upon the people; to bind their kings with chains,
> and their nobles with fetters of iron; to execute upon them the
> judgment written: this honor have all his saints. Praise ye the
> LORD. (149:6–9)

These verses, surely interpreted as a defense of regicide, and possibly
alluded to in the most famous Miltonic crux, the "two-handed engine
of *Lycidas,*" oppose another psalmic verse, 51:4, crucial to royalist arguments that the king is accountable to God alone: "some would persuade
us that this absurd opinion was King David's, because in the 51 Psalm
he cries out to God, *Against thee only have I sinned*; as if David had
imagined that to murder Uriah and adulterate his wife had been no
sin against his neighbor, whenas that law of Moses was to the king expressly, Deut. 17, not to think so highly of himself above his brethren."
Milton submits David's "pathetical words of a psalm" to the judgment
of the Mosaic law limiting the king's privileges (Deut. 17), which furnishes "abundantly more certain rules to go by."
  Substituting fortitude and heroic virtue for pity and fear as well as
for patience and heroic martyrdom, *The Tenure* expresses an ethos
more Hebraic than either Hellenic or Christian. Indeed, even the treatise's New Testament examples pertaining to Christ express aggression
rather than love: his calling Herod "that fox" (Luke 13:32) and Mary's
revelation of her son's triumph: "He hath put down the mighty [Gr.:
dynastas] from their seats, and exalted them of low degree" (Luke 1:52).
Royalist propaganda comparing the patient martyred king with Christ

would have made any references to the Passion rhetorically fatal. (After the execution of Charles, royalists associated regicides with the Jews, as when Abraham Cowley helped spread the rumor that Cromwell intended "to sell St. *Pauls* to them for a Synagogue . . . to reward that Nation which had given the first noble example of crucifying their King.") As the deuteronomic law of divorce subsists at the heart of Milton's divorce tracts, Deuteronomy 17, on the limitations of royal prerogative, is a central text of *The Tenure of Kings and Magistrates*. Milton's arguments in both tracts bear on his insistence on the rich potentialities of the human spirit to reform the commonwealth.

The Tenure of Kings and Magistrates

PROVING, That it is Lawfull, and hath been held so through all Ages, for any, who have the Power, to call to account a Tyrant, or wicked **KING**, and after due conviction, to depose, and put him to death; if the ordinary MAGISTRATE have neglected, or deny'd to doe it.

And that they, who of late so much blame Deposing, are the Men that did it themselves. *Published now the second time with some additions, and many Testimonies also added out of the best & learned among Protestant Divines, asserting the position of this book.*

The Author, J. M.

LONDON, Printed by *Matthew Simmons*, nextdoore to the Gil-Lyon in Aldersgate Street, 1650.

If men within themselves would be governed by reason and not generally give up their understanding to a double tyranny of custom from without and blind affections[1] within, they would discern better what it is to favor and uphold the tyrant of a nation. But being slaves within doors, no wonder that they strive so much to have the public state conformably governed to the inward vicious rule by which they govern themselves. For indeed none can love freedom heartily but good men; the rest love not freedom but license, which never hath more scope or more indulgence than under tyrants. Hence is it that tyrants are not oft offended nor stand much in doubt of bad men, as being all naturally servile; but in whom virtue and true worth most is eminent, them they fear in earnest, as by right their masters; against them lies all their hatred and suspicion. Consequently, neither do bad men hate tyrants but have been always readiest with the falsified names of loyalty and obedience to color over their base compliances.

---

1. Emotional attachments; prejudices.

And although sometimes for shame, and when it comes to their own grievances, of purse especially, they would seem good patriots and side with the better cause, yet when others for the deliverance of their country, endued with fortitude and heroic virtue to fear nothing but the curse written against *Those that do the work of the Lord negligently* [Jer. 48:10], would go on to remove not only the calamities and thraldoms of a people but the roots and causes whence they spring, straight these men, and sure helpers at need, as if they hated only the miseries but not the mischiefs, after they have juggled and paltered[2] with the world, bandied and borne arms against their king, divested him, disanointed him, nay, cursed him all over in their pulpits and their pamphlets to the engaging of sincere and real men beyond what is possible or honest to retreat from, not only turn revolters from those principles which only could at first move them, but lay the strain of disloyalty, and worse, on those proceedings which are the necessary consequences of their own former actions; nor disliked by themselves, were they managed to the entire advantages of their own faction;[3] not considering the while that he toward whom they boasted their new fidelity counted them accessory, and by those statutes and laws which they so impotently brandish against others would have doomed them to a traitor's death for what they have done already.

'Tis true that most men are apt enough to civil wars and commotions as a novelty and for a flash hot and active; but through sloth or inconstancy and weakness of spirit either fainting ere their own pretenses,[4] though never so just, be half attained, or, through an inbred falsehood and wickedness, betray, oft-times to destruction with themselves, men of noblest temper joined with them for causes whereof they in their rash undertakings were not capable.

If God and a good cause give them victory, the prosecution whereof for the most part inevitably draws after it the alteration of laws, change of government, downfall of princes with their families, then comes the task to those worthies which are the soul of that enterprise to be sweat and labored out amidst the throng and noises of vulgar and irrational men—some contesting for privileges, customs, forms, and that old entanglement of iniquity, their gibberish laws, though the badge of their ancient slavery.[5] Others, who have been fiercest against their prince under the notion of a tyrant, and no mean incendiaries of the war against him, when God out of his

---

2. Equivocated. "These men": i.e., the Presbyterians.
3. In a secret treaty signed with commissioners representing the Scottish government, Charles had agreed to establish Presbyterianism for three years and to suppress the Independents.
4. Assertions of rights.
5. Milton despised the so-called Norman yoke and the "gibberish laws" in Norman French imposed on English culture and law by William the Conqueror.

providence and high disposal hath delivered him into the hand of
their brethren, on a sudden and in a new garb of allegiance, which
their doings have long since cancelled, they plead for him, pity him,
extol him, protest against those that talk of bringing him to the trial
of justice, which is the sword of God, superior to all mortal things, in
whose hand soever by apparent signs his testified will is to put it. But
certainly, if we consider who and what they are on a sudden grown so
pitiful, we may conclude their pity can be no true and Christian
commiseration but either levity and shallowness of mind or else a
carnal admiring of that worldly pomp and greatness from whence
they see him fallen; or rather, lastly, a dissembled and seditious pity,
feigned of industry[6] to beget new discord. As for mercy, if it be to a
tyrant, under which name they themselves have cited him so oft in
the hearing of God, of angels, and the holy church assembled, and
there charged him with the spilling of more innocent blood by far
than ever Nero did, undoubtedly the mercy which they pretend is the
mercy of wicked men, and their mercies, we read [Prov. 12:10], are
cruelties, hazarding the welfare of a whole nation to have saved one
whom so oft they have termed Agag, and vilifying the blood of many
Jonathans that have saved Israel; insisting with much niceness on
the unnecessariest clause of their Covenant[7] [wrested], wherein the
fear of change and the absurd contradiction of a flattering hostility
had hampered them, but not scrupling to give away for compliments,
to an implacable revenge, the heads of many thousand Christians
more.

Another sort there is who, coming in the course of these affairs
to have their share in great actions above the form of law or custom, at least to give their voice and approbation, begin to swerve,
and almost shiver at the majesty and grandeur of some noble deed,
as if they were newly entered into a great sin, disputing precedents,
forms, and circumstances, when the commonwealth nigh perishes
for want of deeds in substance, done with just and faithful expedition. To these I wish better instruction, and virtue equal to their
calling; the former of which, that is to say instruction, I shall
endeavor, as my duty is, to bestow on them; and exhort them not to
startle from the just and pious resolution of adhering with all their
strength and assistance to the present Parliament and army in the

6. On purpose.
7. A 1643 document intended to uphold the rights of Parliament. It and the "unnecessariest
clause" of the Solemn League required its signers to "preserve and defend the King's
Majesty's Person and authority." Agag was the wicked king of the Amalekites, ancient
Israel's most hated enemy. The prophet Samuel hewed him "in pieces" (1 Sam. 15:32–
34), and his last words appear ironically in a speech by fallen Adam (PL, 11.157–58).
Jonathan heroically vanquished the Philistine enemy only to be sentenced to death by his
father, King Saul, merely for tasting honey. His fellow Israelites rescued him (1 Sam.
14:1–45). "Niceness": foolishness, fastidiousness.

glorious way wherein justice and victory hath set them—the only warrants through all ages, next under immediate revelation, to exercise supreme power—in those proceedings which hitherto appear equal to what hath been done in any age or nation heretofore justly or magnanimously.

Nor let them be discouraged or deterred by any new apostate scarecrows[8] who, under show of giving counsel, send out their barking monitories and *mementoes*, empty of aught else but the spleen of a frustrated faction. For how can that pretended counsel be either sound or faithful when they that give it see not, for madness and vexation of their ends lost, that those statutes and scriptures which both falsely and scandalously they wrest against their friends and associates would, by sentence of the common adversary, fall first and heaviest upon their own heads. Neither let mild and tender dispositions be foolishly softened from their duty and perseverance with the unmasculine rhetoric of any puling priest or chaplain sent as a friendly letter of advice, for fashion sake in private, and forthwith published by the sender himself, that we may know how much of friend there was in it, to cast an odious envy upon them to whom it was pretended to be sent in charity. Nor let any man be deluded by either the ignorance or the notorious hypocrisy and self-repugnance of our dancing divines, who have the conscience and the boldness to come with Scripture in their mouths, glossed and fitted for their turns with a double contradictory sense, transforming the sacred verity of God to an idol with two faces, looking at once two several ways, and with the same quotations to charge others, which in the same case they made serve to justify themselves. For while the hope to be made classic and provincial lords led them on, while pluralities[9] greased them thick and deep, to the shame and scandal of religion, more than all the sects and heresies they exclaim against— then to fight against the king's person, and no less a party of his Lords and Commons, or to put force upon both the Houses, was good, was lawful, was no resisting of superior powers; they only were powers not to be resisted who countenanced the good and punished the evil.

But now that their censorious domineering is not suffered to be universal, truth and conscience to be freed, tithes and pluralities to be no more, though competent allowance provided, and the warm experience of large gifts, and they so good at taking them—yet now

---

8. E.g., William Prynne, author of *A Brief Memento* (1649), objecting to the deposition and execution of England's "*Lawful King.*"
9. Multiple church livings held by a single minister, a system upheld by the Presbyterians. The Westminster Assembly planned to organize English Presbyterians into provinces, which would be divided into classical assemblies, or "classes."

to exclude and seize upon impeached members,[1] to bring delinquents without exemption to a fair tribunal by the common national
law against murder, is now to be no less than Korah, Dathan, and
Abiram.[2] He who but erewhile in the pulpits was a cursed tyrant, an
enemy to God and saints, laden with all the innocent blood spilt in
three kingdoms, and so to be fought against, is now, though nothing
penitent or altered from his first principles, a lawful magistrate, a
sovereign lord, the Lord's anointed, not to be touched, though by
themselves imprisoned. As if this only were obedience, to preserve
the mere useless bulk of his person, and that only in prison, not
in the field, and to disobey his commands, deny him his dignity and
office, everywhere to resist his power but where they think it only
surviving in their own faction.

But who in particular is a tyrant cannot be determined in a general
discourse otherwise than by supposition; his particular charge, and
the sufficient proof of it, must determine that: which I leave to magistrates, at least to the uprighter sort of them, and of the people,
though in number less by many, in whom faction least hath prevailed
above the law of nature and right reason, to judge as they find cause.
But this I dare own as part of my faith, that if such a one there be by
whose commission whole massacres have been committed on his
faithful subjects, his provinces offered to pawn or alienation as the
hire of those whom he had solicited to come in and destroy whole
cities and countries, be he king, or tyrant, or emperor, the sword of
justice is above him, in whose hand soever is found sufficient power
to avenge the effusion and so great a deluge of innocent blood. For if
all human power to execute, not accidentally but intendedly, the
wrath of God upon evildoers without exception, be of God, then that
power, whether ordinary, or if that fail, extraordinary, so executing
that intent of God is lawful and not to be resisted. But to unfold more
at large this whole question, though with all expedient brevity, I shall
here set down, from first beginning, the original of kings, how and
wherefore exalted to that dignity above their brethren; and from
thence shall prove that turning to tyranny they may be as lawfully
deposed and punished as they were at first elected: this I shall do by
authorities and reasons not learnt in corners among schisms and
heresies, as our doubling divines are ready to calumniate, but fetched
out of the midst of choicest and most authentic learning, and no prohibited authors nor many heathen, but Mosaical, Christian, orthodoxal and, which must needs be more convincing to our adversaries,
presbyterial.

---

1. The army in 1647 impeached eleven members of Parliament for corresponding with
   the queen.
2. Rebels against Moses and Aaron, and thus against God (Num. 16:1–35).

No man who knows aught can be so stupid to deny that all men
naturally were born free, being the image and resemblance of God
himself, and were, by privilege above all the creatures, born to command and not to obey, and that they lived so—till from the root of
Adam's transgression falling among themselves to do wrong and violence, and foreseeing that such courses must needs tend to the
destruction of them all, they agreed by common league to bind each
other from mutual injury and jointly to defend themselves against
any that gave disturbance or opposition to such agreement. Hence
came cities, towns, and commonwealths. And because no faith in all
was found sufficiently binding, they saw it needful to ordain some
authority that might restrain by force and punishment what was violated against peace and common right. This authority and power of
self-defense and preservation being originally and naturally in every
one of them, and unitedly in them all, for ease, for order, and lest
each man should be his own partial judge, they communicated and
derived either to one, whom for the eminence of his wisdom and
integrity they chose above the rest, or to more than one, whom they
thought of equal deserving: the first was called a king; the other,
magistrates; not to be their lords and masters (though afterward
those names in some places were given voluntarily to such as had
been authors of inestimable good to the people) but to be their deputies and commissioners, to execute, by virtue of their entrusted
power, that justice which else every man by the bond of nature and of
covenant must have executed for himself and for one another. And to
him that shall consider well why among free persons one man by civil
right should bear authority and jurisdiction over another, no other
end or reason can be imaginable. These for a while governed well,
and with much equity decided all things at their own arbitrement, till
the temptation of such a power left absolute in their hands perverted
them at length to injustice and partiality. Then did they, who now
by trial had found the danger and inconveniences of committing
arbitrary power to any, invent laws, either framed or consented to by
all, that should confine and limit the authority of whom they chose
to govern them; that so man, of whose failing they had proof, might
no more rule over them, but law and reason, abstracted as much as
might be from personal errors and frailties. While as the magistrate
was set above the people, so the law was set above the magistrate.
When this would not serve, but that the law was either not executed
or misapplied, they were constrained from that time, the only remedy
left them, to put conditions and take oaths from all kings and magistrates at their first installment to do impartial justice by law—who,
upon those terms and no other, received allegiance from the people,
that is to say, bond or covenant to obey them in execution of those
laws which they the people had themselves made or assented to. And

this oft-times with express warning, that if the king or magistrate proved unfaithful to his trust, the people would be disengaged. They added also councillors and parliaments, nor to be only at his beck, but with him or without him, at set times, or at all times when any danger threatened, to have care of the public safety. Therefore, saith Claudius Sesell, a French statesman, *The parliament was set as a bridle to the king*; which I instance rather, not because our English lawyers have not said the same long before, but because that French monarchy is granted by all to be a far more absolute than ours. That this and the rest of what hath hitherto been spoken is most true might be copiously made appear throughout all stories heathen and Christian, even of those nations where kings and emperors have sought means to abolish all ancient memory of the people's right by their encroachments and usurpations. But I spare long insertions, appealing to the known constitutions of both the latest Christian empires in Europe, the Greek and German, besides the French, Italian, Aragonian, English, and not least the Scottish histories—not forgetting this only by the way, that William the Norman, though a conqueror, and not unsworn at his coronation, was compelled the second time to take oath at St. Albans ere the people would be brought to yield obedience.

It being thus manifest that the power of kings and magistrates is nothing else but what is only derivative, transferred, and committed to them in trust from the people to the common good of them all, in whom the power yet remains fundamentally and cannot be taken from them without a violation of their natural birthright; and seeing that from hence Aristotle and the best of political writers have defined a king him who governs to the good and profit of his people and not for his own ends, it follows from necessary causes that the titles of sovereign lord, natural lord, and the like are either arrogancies or flatteries, not admitted by emperors and kings of best note, and disliked by the church both of Jews (Isai. 26.13) and ancient Christians, as appears by Tertullian and others—although generally the people of Asia, and with them the Jews also, especially since the time they chose a king against the advice and counsel of God, are noted by wise authors much inclinable to slavery.

Secondly, that to say, as is usual, the king hath as good right to his crown and dignity as any man to his inheritance, is to make the subject no better than the king's slave, his chattel, or his possession that may be bought and sold; and doubtless, if hereditary title were sufficiently inquired, the best foundation of it would be found either but in courtesy or convenience. But suppose it to be of right hereditary, what can be more just and legal, if a subject for certain crimes be to forfeit by law from himself and posterity all his inheritance to the king, than that a king for crimes proportional should forfeit all his title and inheritance to the people—unless the people must be thought created all for him, he not for them, and they all in one body inferior to him single, which were a kind of treason against the dignity of mankind to affirm.

Thirdly, it follows that to say kings are accountable to none but God is the overturning of all law and government. For if they may refuse to give account, then all covenants made with them at coronation, all oaths are in vain, and mere mockeries, all laws which they swear to keep made to no purpose; for if the king fear not God (as how many of them do not), we hold then our lives and estates by the tenure of his mere grace and mercy as from a god, not a mortal magistrate—a position that none but court-parasites or men besotted would maintain. Aristotle, therefore, whom we commonly allow for one of the best interpreters of nature and morality, writes in the fourth of his *Politics*, chap. 10, that monarchy unaccountable is the worst sort of tyranny and least of all to be endured by free-born men.

And surely no Christian prince not drunk with high mind and prouder than those pagan Cæsars that deified themselves would arrogate so unreasonably above human condition, or derogate so basely from a whole nation of men his brethren, as if for him only subsisting, and to serve his glory, valuing them in comparison of his own brute will and pleasure no more than so many beasts, or vermin under his feet, not to be reasoned with, but to be trod on; among whom there might be found so many thousand men for wisdom, virtue, nobleness of mind, and all other respects but the fortune of his dignity, far above him. Yet some would persuade us that this absurd opinion was King David's, because in the 51 Psalm he cries out to God, *Against thee only have I sinned*; as if David had imagined that to murder Uriah and adulterate his wife had been no sin against his neighbor, whenas that law of Moses was to the king expressly, Deut. 17, not to think so highly of himself above his brethren.[3] David, therefore, by those words could mean no other than either that the depth of his guiltiness was known to God only, or to so few as had not the will or power to question him, or that the sin against God was greater beyond compare than against Uriah. Whatever his meaning were, any wise man will see that the pathetical words of a psalm can be no certain decision to a point that hath abundantly more certain rules to go by.

How much more rationally spake the heathen king Demophoön in a tragedy of Euripides than these interpreters would put upon

3. The sordid details of "Bathsheba-gate" can be found in 2 Sam. 17: David's adultery, the killing of pregnant Bathsheba's husband Uriah to cover up the adultery, and the massacre abetted by Joab to cover up the killing. Deut. 17 lists limitations on royal prerogative.

King David: *I rule not my people by tyranny, as if they were barbar-ians, but am myself liable, if I do unjustly, to suffer justly.*[4] Not unlike was the speech of Trajan, the worthy emperor, to one whom he made general of his prætorian forces: *Take this drawn sword,* saith he, *to use for me, if I reign well; if not, to use against me.* Thus Dion relates. And not Trajan only, but Theodosius the younger, a Chris-tian emperor and one of the best, caused it to be enacted as a rule undeniable and fit to be acknowledged by all kings and emperors, that a prince is bound to the laws, that on the authority of law the authority of a prince depends and to the laws ought to submit—which edict of his remains yet in the *Code of Justinian,*[5] Book 1, title 24, as a sacred constitution to all the succeeding emperors. How then can any king in Europe maintain and write himself accountable to none but God, when emperors in their own imperial statutes have written and decreed themselves accountable to law? And indeed where such account is not feared, he that bids a man reign over him above law may bid as well a savage beast.

It follows, lastly, that since the king or magistrate holds his authority of the people both originally and naturally for their good in the first place and not his own, then may the people, as oft as they shall judge it for the best, either choose him or reject him, retain him or depose him, though no tyrant, merely by the liberty and right of free-born men to be governed as seems to them best. This, though it cannot but stand with plain reason, shall be made good also by Scripture, Deut. 17.14: *When thou art come into the land which the Lord thy God giveth thee, and shalt say, I will set a king over me, like as all the nations about me.* These words confirm us that the right of choosing, yea of changing their own govern-ment, is by the grant of God himself in the people. And therefore when they desired a king, though then under another form of gov-ernment, and though their changing displeased him, yet he that was himself their king and rejected by them would not be a hin-drance to what they intended further than by persuasion, but that they might do therein as they saw good (1 Sam. 8), only he reserved to himself the nomination of who should reign over them. Neither did that exempt the king, as if he were to God only accountable, though by his especial command anointed. Therefore *David first made a covenant with the elders of Israel and so was by them anointed king* [2 Sam. 5.3], 1 Chron. 11. And Jehoiada the priest, making Jehoash king, made a covenant between him and the people (2 Kings 11.17). Therefore when Rehoboam, at his coming to the crown,

4. Euripides, *Heraclidae*, 423–24.
5. A collection of Roman law completed in 529, expanded in 534 to include the Code, the Digest, and the Institutes. It prevailed throughout western Europe. Theodosius the younger was a 5th-century Byzantine emperor.

rejected those conditions which the Israelites brought him, hear what they answer him: *What portion have we in David or inheritance in the son of Jesse? See to thine own house, David*. And for the like conditions not performed, all Israel before that time deposed Samuel, not for his own default but for the misgovernment of his sons.

But some will say to both these examples, it was evilly done. I answer that not the latter, because it was expressly allowed them in the law to set up a king if they pleased, and God himself joined with them in the work, though in some sort it was at that time displeasing to him, in respect of old Samuel, who had governed them uprightly. As Livy praises the Romans who took occasion from Tarquinius, a wicked prince, to gain their liberty, which to have extorted, saith he, from Numa or any of the good kings before, had not been seasonable. Nor was it in the former example done unlawfully; for when Rehoboam had prepared a huge army to reduce the Israelites, he was forbidden by the prophet, 1 Kings 12.24, *Thus saith the Lord, ye shall not go up, nor fight against your brethren, for this thing is from me*. He calls them their brethren, not rebels, and forbids to be proceeded against them, owning the thing himself, not by single providence but by approbation, and that not only of the act, as in the former example, but of the fit season also; he had not otherwise forbid to molest them. And those grave and wise counselors whom Rehoboam first advised with spake no such thing as our old gray-headed flatterers now are wont: "Stand upon your birthright, scorn to capitulate, you hold of God, not of them." For they knew no such matter, unless conditionally, but gave him politic counsel, as in a civil transaction.

Therefore kingdom and magistracy, whether supreme or subordinate, is called *a human ordinance*, 1 Pet. 2.13, etc., which we are there taught is the will of God we should submit to so far as for the punishment of evil-doers and the encouragement of them that do well. *Submit*, saith he, *as free men*. But to any civil power unaccountable, unquestionable, and not to be resisted, no, not in wickedness and violent actions, how can we submit as free men? *There is no power but of God*, saith Paul, Rom.13,[6] as much as to say, God put it into man's heart to find out that way at first for common peace and preservation, approving the exercise thereof; else it contradicts Peter, who calls the same authority an ordinance of man. It must be also understood of lawful and just power, else we read of great power in the affairs and kingdoms of the world permitted to the devil; for, saith he to Christ, Luke 4.6, *All this power will I give thee, and the glory of them, for it is delivered to me, and to whomso-*

---

6. Royalists often cited these New Testament verses (1 Peter 2, Rom. 13:1–2) to prove that human submission to royal authority is divinely ordained.

ever I will, I give it; neither did he lie or Christ gainsay what he affirmed; for in the thirteenth of the Revelation, we read how the dragon gave to the beast *his power, his seat, and great authority*, which beast so authorized most expound to be the tyrannical powers and kingdoms of the earth. Therefore St. Paul in the fore-cited chapter tells us that such magistrates he means as are not a terror to the good but to the evil, such as bear not the sword in vain but to punish offenders and to encourage the good.

If such only be mentioned here as powers to be obeyed, and our submission to them only required, then doubtless those powers that do the contrary are no powers ordained of God, and by consequence no obligation laid upon us to obey or not to resist them. And it may be well observed that both these apostles, whenever they give this precept, express it in terms not concrete but abstract,[7] as logicians are wont to speak; that is, they mention the ordinance, the power, the authority, before the persons that execute it; and what that power is, lest we should be deceived, they describe exactly. So that if the power be not such, or the person execute not such power, neither the one nor the other is of God but of the devil and by consequence to be resisted. From this exposition Chrysostom[8] also on the same place dissents not, explaining that these words were not written in behalf of a tyrant. And this is verified by David, himself a king, and likeliest to be the author of the Psalm 94. 20, which saith, *Shall the throne of iniquity have fellowship with thee?* And it were worth the knowing—since kings in these days, and that by Scripture, boast the justness of their title by holding it immediately of God, yet cannot show the time when God ever set on the throne them or their forefathers, but only when the people chose them— why by the same reason, since God ascribes as oft to himself the casting down of princes from the throne, it should not be thought as lawful, and as much from God, when none are seen to do it but the people, and that for just causes. For if it needs must be a sin in them to depose, it may as likely be a sin to have elected. And contrary, if the people's act in election be pleaded by a king as the act of God and the most just title to enthrone him, why may not the people's act of rejection be as well pleaded by the people as the act of God and the most just reason to depose him? So that we see the title and just right of reigning or deposing, in reference to God, is found in Scripture to be all one: visible only in the people and depending merely upon justice and demerit. Thus far hath been considered briefly the power of kings and magistrates: how it was

---

7. Of kingship in general, not of particular kings.
8. Even St. John Chrysostom (345–407), archbishop of Constantinople, whose homily was usually cited by royalists, makes the distinction to which Milton has just referred.

and is originally the people's, and by them conferred in trust only to be employed to the common peace and benefit, with liberty therefore and right remaining in them to reassume it to themselves if by kings or magistrates it be abused, or to dispose of it by any alteration, as they shall judge most conducing to the public good.

We may from hence with more ease and force of argument determine what a tyrant is and what the people may do against him. A tyrant, whether by wrong or by right coming to the crown, is he who, regarding neither law nor the common good, reigns only for himself and his faction; thus St. Basil[9] among others defines him. And because his power is great, his will boundless and exorbitant, the fulfilling whereof is for the most part accompanied with innumerable wrongs and oppressions of the people, murders, massacres, rapes, adulteries, desolation, and subversion of cities and whole provinces, look[1] how great a good and happiness a just king is, so great a mischief is a tyrant; as he the public father of his country, so this the common enemy. Against whom what the people lawfully may do, as against a common pest and destroyer of mankind, I suppose no man of clear judgment need go further to be guided than by the very principles of nature in him.

But because it is the vulgar folly of men to desert their own reason, and shutting their eyes, to think they see best with other men's, I shall show by such examples as ought to have most weight with us what hath been done in this case heretofore. The Greeks and Romans, as their prime authors witness, held it not only lawful but a glorious and heroic deed, rewarded publicly with statues and garlands, to kill an infamous tyrant at any time without trial; and but reason that he who trod down all law should not be vouchsafed the benefit of law. Insomuch that Seneca the tragedian brings in Hercules, the grand suppressor of tyrants, thus speaking:

> ————— —————*Victima haud ulla amplior*
> *Potest, magisque opima mactari Jovi*
> *Quam Rex iniquus*————— —————
> ————— —————There can be slain
> No sacrifice to God more acceptable
> Than an unjust and wicked king[2]————— —————

But of these I name no more, lest it be objected they were heathen; and come to produce another sort of men, that had the knowledge

---

9. In his *Commonplace Book* (*YP*, 1:453), Milton enters this distinction between a tyrant and a king offered by St. Basil the Great, bishop of Cappadocia (370–379): "the one considers at every point his own advantage, the other provides what is helpful to his subjects."
1. Consider.
2. Seneca, *Hercules Furens* 2.922–24.

of true religion. Among the Jews this custom of tyrant-killing was not unusual. First Ehud, a man whom God had raised to deliver Israel from Eglon king of Moab, who had conquered and ruled over them eighteen years, being sent to him as an ambassador with a present, slew him in his own house.[3] But he was a foreign prince, an enemy, and Ehud besides had special warrant from God. To the first I answer, it imports not whether foreign or native; for no prince so native but professes to hold by law, which when he himself over-turns, breaking all the covenants and oaths that gave him title to his dignity and were the bond and alliance between him and his people, what differs he from an outlandish[4] king or from an enemy?

For look how much right the king of Spain hath to govern us at all, so much right hath the king of England to govern us tyrannically. If he, though not bound to us by any league, coming from Spain in person to subdue us or to destroy us, might lawfully by the people of England either be slain in fight or put to death in captivity, what hath a native king to plead, bound by so many covenants, benefits, and honors to the welfare of his people; why he through the contempt of all laws and parliaments, the only tie of our obedience to him, for his own will's sake and a boasted prerogative unaccountable, after seven years' warring and destroying of his best subjects, overcome and yielded prisoner, should think to scape unquestionable, as a thing divine, in respect of whom so many thousand Christians destroyed should lie unaccounted for, polluting with their slaughtered car-casses all the land over and crying for vengeance against the living that should have righted them. Who knows not that there is a mutual bond of amity and brotherhood between man and man over all the world, neither is it the English sea that can sever us from that duty and relation;[5] a straiter bond yet there is between fellow-subjects, neighbors, and friends. But when any of these do one to another so as hostility could do no worse, what doth the law decree less against them than open enemies and invaders? Or if the law be not present, or too weak, what doth it warrant us to less than single defense or civil war? And from that time forward the law of civil defensive war differs nothing from the law of foreign hostility. Nor is it distance of place that makes enmity, but enmity that makes distance. He there-fore that keeps peace with me, near or remote, of whatsoever nation, is to me, as far as all civil and human offices, an Englishman and a neighbor; but if an Englishman, forgetting all laws, human, civil, and

3. Judg. 3:12–23.
4. Foreign.
5. Cicero's affirmation of a universal human society based on reason was cited in various contemporary works of natural law theorists, including those of Hugo Grotius and John Selden. They took opposite positions on the issue of the freedom of the seas, Grotius in *Mare Liberum* (The free sea), 1609, and Selden in *Mare Clausum* (The closed sea), 1635.

religious, offend against life and liberty, to him offended, and to the
law in his behalf, though born in the same womb, he is no better
than a Turk, a Saracen, a heathen.

This is gospel, and this was ever law among equals; how much
rather then in force against any king whatever, who in respect of
the people is confessed inferior and not equal; to distinguish therefore of a tyrant by outlandish or domestic is a weak evasion. To the
second, that he was an enemy, I answer, what tyrant is not? Yet
Eglon by the Jews had been acknowledged as their sovereign. They
had served him eighteen years, as long almost as we our William
the Conqueror, in all which time he could not be so unwise a
statesman but to have taken of them oaths of fealty and allegiance,
by which they made themselves his proper subjects, as their homage and present sent by Ehud testified. To the third, that he had
special warrant to kill Eglon in that manner, it cannot be granted,
because not expressed. 'Tis plain that he was raised by God to be a
deliverer, and went on just principles, such as were then and ever
held allowable, to deal so by a tyrant that could no otherwise be
dealt with.

Neither did Samuel, though a prophet, with his own hand abstain
from Agag, a foreign enemy no doubt; but mark the reason: *As thy
sword hath made women childless*,[6] a cause that by the sentence of
law itself nullifies all relations. And as the law is between brother
and brother, father and son, master and servant, wherefore not
between king, or rather tyrant, and people? And whereas Jehu had
special command to slay Jehoram, a successive and hereditary tyrant,
it seems not the less imitable for that.[7] For where a thing grounded
so much on natural reason hath the addition of a command from
God, what does it but establish the lawfulness of such an act? Nor is
it likely that God, who had so many ways of punishing the house of
Ahab, would have sent a subject against his prince if the fact in itself,
as done to a tyrant, had been of bad example. And if David refused to
lift his hand against the Lord's anointed,[8] the matter between them
was not tyranny but private enmity, and David as a private person
had been his own revenger, not so much the people's. But when any
tyrant at this day can show to be the Lord's anointed, the only mentioned reason why David withheld his hand, he may then, but not till
then, presume on the same privilege.

6. The prophet utters these words before hewing King Agag in pieces (1 Sam. 15:33).
7. One of the students of the prophet Elisha anoints Jehu as king and commands him to
destroy the house of Ahab, including his son Jehoram (2 Kings 9).
8. In his influential treatise of natural law, *De Jure Belli ac Pacis*, Hugo Grotius cites
David's sparing of Saul's life (1 Sam. 24:10) to support his argument for submission to
monarchs (1.4.7).

We may pass therefore hence to Christian times. And first our Savior himself, how much he favored tyrants and how much intended they should be found or honored among Christians, declares his mind not obscurely, accounting their absolute authority no better than Gentilism, yea, though they flourished it over with the splendid name of benefactors;[9] charging those that would be his disciples to usurp no such dominion, but that they who were to be of most authority among them should esteem themselves ministers and servants to the public, Matt. 20. 25, *The princes of the Gentiles exercise lordship over them*; and Mark 10. 42, *They that seem to rule*, saith he, either slighting or accounting them no lawful rulers, *but ye shall not be so, but the greatest among you shall be your servant*. And although he himself were the meekest, and came on earth to be so, yet to a tyrant we hear him not vouchsafe an humble word, but *Tell that fox*,[1] Luke 13. So far we ought to be from thinking that Christ and his gospel should be made a sanctuary for tyrants from justice, to whom his law before never gave such protection. And wherefore did his mother the Virgin Mary[2] give such praise to God in her prophetic song that he had now, by the coming of Christ, cut down *dynastas*, or proud monarchs, from the throne, if the church, when God manifests his power in them to do so, should rather choose all misery and vassalage to serve them and let them still sit on their potent seats to be adored for doing mischief?

Surely it is not for nothing that tyrants by a kind of natural instinct both hate and fear none more than the true church and saints of God as the most dangerous enemies and subverters of monarchy, though indeed[3] of tyranny. Hath not this been the perpetual cry of courtiers and court prelates? Whereof no likelier cause can be alleged, but that they well discerned the mind and principles of most devout and zealous men, and indeed the very discipline of church, tending to the dissolution of all tyranny. No marvel then if since the faith of Christ received, in purer or impurer times, to depose a king and put him to death for tyranny hath been accounted so just and requisite that neighbor kings have both upheld and taken part with subjects in the action. And Ludovicus Pius, himself an emperor, and son of Charles the Great, being made judge (Du Haillan is my author)[4] between Milegast, king of the Vultzes, and his subjects who

---

9. "The kings of Gentiles exercise lordship over them; and they that exercise authority upon them are called benefactors. But ye shall not be so: but he that is greatest among you, let him be as the younger" (Luke 22:25–26)
1. Herod.
2. "He hath put down the mighty [Gr. *dynastas*] from their seats, and exalted them of low degree" (Luke 1:52).
3. In truth.
4. In his *Commonplace Book* (*YP*, 1:454–55), Milton cites Girard du Haillan's account of Ludovicus Pius's approval of the people's deposing an insolent king.

had deposed him, gave his verdict for the subjects and for him whom
they had chosen in his room. Note here that the right of electing
whom they please is, by the impartial testimony of an emperor, in the
people. For, said he, *A just prince ought to be preferred before an
unjust, and the end of government before the prerogative.* And Con-
stantinus Leo, another emperor, in the Byzantine laws saith that *the
end of a king is for the general good, which he not performing, is but
the counterfeit of a king.*[5]

And to prove that some of our own monarchs have acknowledged
that their high office exempted them not from punishment, they
had the sword of St. Edward borne before them by an officer who
was called Earl of the Palace,[6] even at the times of their highest
pomp and solemnities, to mind them, saith Matthew Paris, the best
of our historians, that if they erred, the sword had power to restrain
them. And what restraint the sword comes to at length, having both
edge and point, if any skeptic will doubt, let him feel. It is also
affirmed from diligent search made in our ancient books of law that
the peers and barons of England had a legal right to judge the king,
which was the cause most likely (for it could be no slight cause)
that they were called his peers, or equals. This however may stand
immovable, so long as man hath to deal with no better than man:
that if our law judge all men to the lowest by their peers, it should
in all equity ascend also and judge the highest.

And so much I find both in our own and foreign story, that dukes,
earls, and marquesses were at first not hereditary, not empty and
vain titles, but names of trust and office, and with the office ceasing;
as induces me to be of opinion that every worthy man in Parliament
(for the word baron imports no more) might for the public good be
thought a fit peer and judge of the king, without regard had to petty
caveats and circumstances, the chief impediment in high affairs, and
ever stood upon most by circumstantial men.[7] Whence doubtless our
ancestors, who were not ignorant with what rights either nature or
ancient constitution had endowed them, when oaths both at coronation and renewed in Parliament would not serve, thought it no way
illegal to depose and put to death their tyrannous kings. Insomuch
that the Parliament drew up a charge against Richard the Second,
and the Commons requested to have judgment decreed against him,
that the realm might not be endangered. And Peter Martyr, a divine
of foremost rank, on the third of Judges approves their doings.[8] Sir

5. Another entry (under "King") in Milton's *Commonplace Book* (*YP*, 1:439), taken from
   Johann Leunclavius, *Jus Graeco-Romanum.*
6. Milton cites this ceremony as "an office to correct the K[ing]" in his *Commonplace
   Book* (*YP*, 1:447).
7. Distinguished only by the pomp and circumstance of their position.
8. In his *Commonplace Book* (*YP*, 1:455–56), Milton summarizes the commentary on Judg.
   3 of Peter Martyr (1499–1562), an Augustinian Monk who converted to Protestantism.

Thomas Smith also, a Protestant and a statesman, in his *Common-wealth of England*, putting the question whether it be lawful to rise against a tyrant, answers that the vulgar judge of it according to the event and the learned according to the purpose of them that do it.

But far before these days, Gildas,[9] the most ancient of all our historians, speaking of those times wherein the Roman empire, decaying, quitted and relinquished what right they had by conquest to this island and resigned it all into the people's hands, testifies that the people thus reinvested with their own original right, about the year 446, both elected them kings whom they thought best (the first Christian British kings that ever reigned here since the Romans) and by the same right, when they apprehended cause, usually deposed and put them to death. This is the most fundamental and ancient tenure that any king of England can produce or pretend to, in comparison of which all other titles and pleas are but of yesterday. If any object that Gildas condemns the Britons for so doing, the answer is as ready; that he condemns them no more for so doing than he did before for choosing such; for, saith he, *They anointed them kings not of God, but such as were more bloody than the rest.* Next, he condemns them not at all for deposing or putting them to death, but for doing it overhastily, without trial or well examining the cause, and for electing others worse in their room.

Thus we have here both domestic and most ancient examples that the people of Britain have deposed and put to death their kings in those primitive Christian times. And to couple reason with example, if the Church in all ages, primitive, Romish, or Protestant, held it ever no less their duty than the power of their keys,[1] though without express warrant of Scripture, to bring indifferently both king and peasant under the utmost rigor of their canons and censures ecclesiastical, even to the smiting him with a final excommunion, if he persist impenitent, what hinders but that the temporal law both may and ought, though without a special text or precedent, extend with like indifference the civil sword to the cutting off without exemption him that capitally offends, seeing that justice and religion are from the same God, and works of justice oft-times more acceptable? Yet because that some lately, with the tongues and arguments of malignant backsliders, have written that the proceedings now in Parliament against the king are without precedent from any Protestant

---

9. Milton frequently cites Gildas, the ancient British historian, and in his *Commonplace Book* (YP, 1:474) he quotes the first part of the following statement: "Kings were anointed, not by God, but as those who stood out as more fierce; and a little later they were slain by the anointers, not according to trial of the truth, and others more fierce were chosen."

1. Administering church discipline; alluding to the keys to the kingdom of heaven given to Peter: "and whatsoever thou shalt bind on earth shall be bound in heaven" (Matt. 16:19).

state or kingdom, the examples which follow shall be all Protestant, and chiefly Presbyterian.

In the year 1546, the Duke of Saxony, Landgrave of Hesse, and the whole Protestant league raised open war against Charles the Fifth their emperor, sent him a defiance, renounced all faith and allegiance towards him, and debated long in council whether they should give him so much as the title of *Cæsar*. Sleidan.[2] [book] 17. Let all men judge what this wanted of deposing or of killing but the power to do it.

In the year 1559, the Scotch Protestants claiming promise of their Queen Regent for liberty of conscience, she answering that promises were not to be claimed of princes beyond what was commodious for them to grant, told her to her face in the parliament then at Stirling that if it were so, they renounced their obedience; and soon after betook them to arms. *Buchanan Hist.* l. 16.[3] Certainly, when allegiance is renounced, that very hour the king or queen is in effect deposed.

In the year 1564, John Knox, a most famous divine and the reformer of Scotland to the Presbyterian discipline, at a general assembly maintained openly, in a dispute against Lethington[4] the Secretary of State, that subjects might and ought to execute God's judgments upon their king; that the fact of Jehu and others against their king having the ground of God's ordinary command to put such and such offenders to death was not extraordinary but to be imitated of all that preferred the honor of God to the affection of flesh and wicked princes; that kings, if they offend, have no privilege to be exempted from the punishments of law more than any other subject; so that if the king be a murderer, adulterer, or idolater, he should suffer, not as a king, but as an offender; and this position he repeats again and again before them. Answerable was the opinion of John Craig, another learned divine, and that laws made by the tyranny of princes or the negligence of people, their posterity might abrogate, and reform all things according to the original institution of commonwealths. And Knox being commanded by the nobility to write to Calvin and other learned men for their judgment in that question, refused, alleging that both himself was fully resolved in conscience, and had heard their judgments, and had the same opinion under handwriting of many the most godly and most learned that he knew

---

2. Johann Philippson, from whose *General History of the Reformation of the Church* Milton quotes in his *Commonplace Book*: "The German princes renounce their loyalty and their duty to the Emperor because of their religion, which he has tried to destroy."
3. George Buchanan's, *Rerum Scoticarum Historia* (1582). The Queen Regent is Mary of Guise, widow of James V and mother of Mary, Queen of Scots.
4. William Maitland of Lethington, who defended Queen Mary's decision to marry Henry Stuart Darnley, in opposition to the anti-monarchist arguments of the great Reformer John Knox.

in Europe; that if he should move the question to them again, what should he do but show his own forgetfulness or inconstancy. All this is far more largely in the *Ecclesiastic History of Scotland*, l. 4,[5] with many other passages to this effect all the book over, set out with diligence by Scotchmen of best repute among them at the beginning of these troubles, as if they labored to inform us what we were to do, and what they intended upon the like occasion.

And to let the world know that the whole church and Protestant state of Scotland in those purest times of reformation were of the same belief, three years after, they met in the field Mary their lawful and hereditary queen, took her prisoner yielding before fight, kept her in prison, and the same year deposed her. *Buchan. Hist.* l. 18.

And four years after that, the Scots, in justification of their deposing Queen Mary, sent ambassadors to Queen Elizabeth, and in a written declaration alleged that they had used toward her more lenity than she deserved; that their ancestors had heretofore punished their kings by death or banishment; that the Scots were a free nation, made king whom they freely chose, and with the same freedom unkinged him if they saw cause, by right of ancient laws and ceremonies yet remaining, and old customs yet among the Highlanders in choosing the head of their clans or families; all which, with many other arguments, bore witness that regal power was nothing else but a mutual covenant or stipulation between king and people. *Buch. Hist.* l. 20. These were Scotchmen and Presbyterians; but what measure then have they lately offered to think such liberty less beseeming us than themselves, presuming to put him upon us for a master whom their law scarce allows to be their own equal? If now, then, we hear them in another strain than heretofore in the purest times of their church, we may be confident it is the voice of faction speaking in them, not of truth and reformation—which no less in England than in Scotland, by the mouths of those faithful witnesses commonly called Puritans and Nonconformists, spake as clearly for the putting down, yea, the utmost punishing, of kings, as in their several treatises may be read, even from the first reign of Elizabeth to these times. Insomuch that one of them, whose name was Gibson,[6] foretold King James he should be rooted out and conclude his race if he persisted to uphold bishops. And that very inscription stamped upon the first coins at his coronation, a naked sword in a hand with these words, *Si mereor in me, Against me, if I deserve*, not only manifested the judgment of that state but seemed also to presage the sentence of divine justice in this event upon his son.[7]

---

5. Knox's *History of the Reformation of the Church of Scotland* (1644), book 4.
6. James Gibson had warned James VI in 1586 that he would share the fate of Jeroboam, who was rooted out for preventing the true worship of God.
7. Charles I.

In the year 1581, the states of Holland, in a general assembly at the Hague, abjured all obedience and subjection to Philip king of Spain, and in a declaration justify their so doing, for that by his tyrannous government, against faith so many times given and broken, he had lost his right to all the Belgic provinces; that therefore they deposed him and declared it lawful to choose another in his stead. *Thuan.*[8] l. 74. From that time to this, no state or kingdom in the world hath equally prospered; but let them remember not to look with an evil and prejudicial eye upon their neighbors walking by the same rule.[9]

But what need these examples to Presbyterians, I mean to those who now of late would seem so much to abhor deposing, whenas they to all Christendom have given the latest and the liveliest example of doing it themselves? I question not the lawfulness of raising war against a tyrant in defense of religion or civil liberty; for no Protestant church, from the first Waldenses[1] of Lyons and Languedoc to this day, but have done it round and maintained it lawful. But this I doubt not to affirm, that the Presbyterians, who now so much condemn deposing, were the men themselves that deposed the king, and cannot with all their shifting and relapsing wash off the guiltiness from their own hands. For they themselves, by these their late doings, have made it guiltiness and turned their own warrantable actions into rebellion.

There is nothing that so actually makes a king of England as rightful possession and supremacy in all causes both civil and ecclesiastical, and nothing that so actually makes a subject of England as those two oaths[2] of allegiance and supremacy observed *without equivocating or any mental reservation.* Out of doubt, then, when the king shall command things already constituted in church or state, obedience is the true essence of a subject, either to do, if it be lawful, or, if he hold the thing unlawful, to submit to that penalty which the law imposes, so long as he intends to remain a subject. Therefore when the people, or any part of them, shall rise against the king and his authority, executing the law in any thing established, civil or ecclesiastical, I do not say it is rebellion if the thing commanded, though established, be unlawful, and that they

---

8. Jacques Auguste de Thou (1553–1617), French statesman, diplomat, and historian.
9. Milton criticizes Holland, a Protestant Republic, for interfering on behalf of royalty and against its coreligionists by protesting the trial of Charles I.
1. The Waldensians were a Christian spiritual movement that actually began in the middle ages and, in the 16th century, joined the Genevan branch of Protestantism. In Sonnet XVIII, protesting their near annihilation in a 1655 massacre ordered by the Duke of Savoy, Milton emphasizes their purity of worship, which he believed dated from apostolic times.
2. Required of English citizens, instituted by Henry VIII to root out Roman Catholics, declared allegiance to the crown and the supremacy of the crown in the English church.

sought first all due means of redress (and no man is further bound to law); but I say it is an absolute renouncing both of supremacy and allegiance, which in one word is an actual and total deposing of the king and the setting up of another supreme authority over them.

And whether the Presbyterians have not done all this and much more, they will not put me, I suppose, to reckon up a seven years' story[3] fresh in the memory of all men. Have they not utterly broke the oath of allegiance, rejecting the king's command and authority sent them from any part of the kingdom, whether in things lawful or unlawful? Have they not abjured the oath of supremacy by setting up the Parliament without the king, supreme to all their obedience; and though their vow and covenant bound them in general to the Parliament, yet sometimes[4] adhering to the lesser part of Lords and Commons that remained faithful, as they term it, and even of them, one while to the Commons without the Lords, another while to the Lords without the Commons? Have they not still declared their meaning, whatever their oath were, to hold them only for supreme whom they found at any time most yielding to what they petitioned? Both these oaths, which were the straightest bond of an English subject in reference to the king, being thus broke and made void, it follows undeniably that the king from that time was by them in fact absolutely deposed, and they no longer in reality to be thought his subjects, notwithstanding their fine clause in the covenant to preserve his person, crown, and dignity, set there by some dodging casuist with more craft than sincerity to mitigate the matter in case of ill success and not taken, I suppose, by any honest man but as a condition subordinate to every the least particle that might more concern religion, liberty, or the public peace.

To prove it yet more plainly that they are the men who have deposed the king, I thus argue. We know that king and subject are relatives, and relatives have no longer being than in the relation. The relation between king and subject can be no other than regal authority and subjection. Hence I infer past their defending that if the subject, who is one relative, take away the relation, of force he takes away also the other relative. But the Presbyterians, who were one relative, that is to say, subjects, have for this seven years taken away the relation, that is to say, the king's authority and their subjection to it. Therefore the Presbyterians for these seven years have removed and extinguished the other relative, that is to say, the king;

3. Dating back to the Grand Remonstrance of November 1641, a list of grievances presented by Parliament to the king, which brought England closer to civil war.
4. Alluding to Presbyterian vacillation, as when they sided first with the Independent minority against Charles's proposals for an Episcopal settlement of the church; then with the Lords supporting it; and, a day later, with the Commons, rejecting it.

or, to speak more in brief, have deposed him, not only by depriving him the execution of his authority, but by conferring it upon others.

If then their oaths of subjection broken, new supremacy obeyed, new oaths and covenants taken, notwithstanding frivolous evasions, have in plain terms unkinged the king, much more then hath their seven years' war not deposed him only but outlawed him and defied him as an alien, a rebel to law and enemy to the state—it must needs be clear to any man not averse from reason that hostility and subjection are two direct and positive contraries and can no more in one subject stand together in respect of the same king than one person at the same time can be in two remote places. Against whom therefore the subject is in act of hostility, we may be confident that to him he is in no subjection; and in whom hostility takes place of subjection—for they can by no means consist together—to him the king can be not only no king but an enemy.

So that from hence we shall not need dispute whether they have deposed him, or what they have defaulted towards him as no king, but show manifestly how much they have done toward the killing him. Have they not levied all these wars against him, whether offensive or defensive (for defense in war equally offends, and most prudently beforehand) and given commission to slay where they knew his person could not be exempt from danger? And if chance or flight had not saved him, how often had they killed him, directing their artillery without blame or prohibition to the very place where they saw him stand? Have they not sequestered[5] him, judged or unjudged, and converted his revenue to other uses, detaining from him as a grand delinquent all means of livelihood, so that for them long since he might have perished or have starved? Have they not hunted and pursued him round about the kingdom with sword and fire? Have they not formerly denied to treat with him,[6] and their now recanting ministers preached against him as a reprobate incurable, an enemy to God and his church marked for destruction and therefore not to be treated with? Have they not besieged him and to their power forbidden him water and fire, save what they shot against him to the hazard of his life? Yet while they thus assaulted and endangered it with hostile deeds, they swore in words to defend it with his crown and dignity; not in order, as it seems now, to a firm and lasting peace or to his repentance after all this blood, but simply, without regard, without remorse or any comparable value of all the miseries and

5. Cut off from contact with supporters; converted his revenues to the uses of Parliament.
6. In January 1648, both Houses of Parliament voted "No More Addresses," which forbade further negotiation with Charles.

calamities suffered by the poor people, or to suffer hereafter, through his obstinacy or impenitence.

No understanding man can be ignorant that covenants are ever made according to the present state of persons and of things, and have ever the more general laws of nature and of reason included in them, though not expressed. If I make a voluntary covenant, as with a man to do him good, and he prove afterward a monster to me, I should conceive a disobligement. If I covenant not to hurt an enemy, in favor of him and forbearance and hope of his amendment, and he after that shall do me tenfold injury and mischief to what he had done when I so covenanted, and still be plotting what may tend to my destruction, I question not but that his after-actions release me; nor know I covenant so sacred that withholds me from demanding justice on him.

Howbeit, had not their distrust in a good cause and the fast and loose of our prevaricating divines overswayed, it had been doubtless better not to have inserted in a covenant unnecessary obligations, and words, not works, of supererogating[7] allegiance to their enemy; no way advantageous to themselves, had the king prevailed, as to their cost many would have felt; but full of snare and distraction to our friends, useful only, as we now find, to our adversaries, who under such a latitude and shelter of ambiguous interpretation have ever since been plotting and contriving new opportunities to trouble all again. How much better had it been, and more becoming an undaunted virtue, to have declared openly and boldly whom and what power the people were to hold supreme, as on the like occasion Protestants have done before, and many conscientious men now in these times have more than once besought the Parliament to do, that they might go on upon a sure foundation and not with a riddling Covenant in their mouths, seeming to swear counter almost in the same breath allegiance and no allegiance; which doubtless had drawn off all the minds of sincere men from siding with them, had they not discerned their actions far more deposing him than their words upholding him; which words, made now the subject of cavillous[8] interpretations, stood ever in the Covenant, by judgment of the more discerning sort, an evidence of their fear, not of their fidelity.

What should I return to speak on, of those attempts for which the king himself hath often charged the Presbyterians of seeking his life, whenas in the due estimation of things they might without a fallacy be said to have done the deed outright? Who knows not that the king is a name of dignity and office, not of person? Who therefore kills a

7. Making up by excess for the failing of another. The disputed clause in the Presbyterian Covenant asserts over-zealously a commitment to preserve and defend the king's person and authority.
8. Frivolously fault-finding.

king must kill him while he is a king. Then they certainly who by
deposing him have long since taken from him the life of a king, his
office and his dignity, they in the truest sense may be said to have
killed the king—nor only by their deposing and waging war against
him, which besides the danger to his personal life, set him in the
farthest opposite point from any vital function of a king, but by their
holding him in prison, vanquished and yielded into their absolute
and despotic power, which brought him to the lowest degradement
and incapacity of the regal name. I say not by whose matchless valor[9]
next under God, lest the story of their ingratitude thereupon carry
me from the purpose in hand, which is to convince them, that they,
which I repeat again were the men who in the truest sense killed the
king, not only as is proved before, but by depressing him their king
far below the rank of a subject to the condition of a captive, without
intention to restore him, as the Chancellor[1] of Scotland in a speech
told him plainly at Newcastle, unless he granted fully all their
demands, which they knew he never meant. Nor did they treat or
think of treating with him till their hatred to the army that delivered
them, not their love or duty to the king, joined them secretly with
men sentenced so oft for reprobates in their own mouths, by whose
subtle inspiring they grew mad upon a most tardy and improper treaty.[2] Whereas if the whole bent of their actions had not been against
the king himself, but only against his evil counselors, as they feigned
and published, wherefore did they not restore him all that while to
the true life of a king, his office, crown, and dignity, when he was
in their power and they themselves his nearest counselors? The
truth, therefore, is both that they would not and that indeed they
could not without their own certain destruction, having reduced him
to such a final pass as was the very death and burial of all in him that
was regal, and from whence never king of England yet revived but by
the new reinforcement of his own party, which was a kind of resurrection to him.

  Thus having quite extinguished all that could be in him of a king,
and from a total privation clad him over, like another specifical
thing, with forms and habitudes destructive to the former, they left
in his person, dead as to law and all the civil right either of king or
subject, the life only of a prisoner, a captive and a malefactor; whom
the equal and impartial hand of justice finding, was no more to
spare than another ordinary man; not only made obnoxious[3] to the

9. I.e., of Oliver Cromwell.
1. In May 1646, the Scottish chancellor, John Campbell, encountered Charles I, who was
   a prisoner at Newcastle-upon-Tyne.
2. The Treaty of Newport (fall 1648), rescinding "No More Addresses" and thus reopen-
   ing negotiations with the king.
3. Liable to punishment. "Specifical": a different species. "Habitudes": manner of being
   or existing, constitutions, dispositions.

doom of law by a charge more than once drawn up against him, and
his own confession to the first article at Newport, but summoned
and arraigned in the sight of God and his people, cursed and devoted
to perdition worse than any Ahab, or Antiochus, with exhortation to
curse all those in the name of God that made not war against him,
as bitterly as Meroz[4] was to be cursed, that went not out against a
Canaanitish king, almost in all the sermons, prayers, and fulmina-
tions that have been uttered this seven years by those cloven tongues
of falsehood and dissension, who now, to the stirring up of new discord, acquit him; and against their own discipline, which they boast
to be the throne and scepter of Christ, absolve him, unconfound
him, though unconverted, unrepentant, unsensible[5] of all their precious saints and martyrs whose blood they have so oft laid upon his
head: and now again with a new sovereign anointment can wash it
all off, as if it were as vile and no more to be reckoned for than the
blood of so many dogs in a time of pestilence; giving the most opprobrious lie to all the acted zeal that for these many years hath filled
their bellies and fed them fat upon the foolish people. Ministers of
sedition, not of the gospel, who, while they saw it manifestly tend to
civil war and bloodshed, never ceased exasperating[6] the people
against him; and now that they see it likely to breed new commotion, cease not to incite others against the people that have saved
them from him, as if sedition were their only aim, whether against
him or for him. But God, as we have cause to trust, will put other
thoughts into the people and turn them from giving ear or heed to
these mercenary noisemakers, of whose fury and false prophecies
we have enough experience, and from the murmurs of new discord
will incline them to hearken rather with erected minds to the voice
of our supreme magistracy,[7] calling us to liberty and the flourishing
deeds of a reformed commonwealth; with this hope, that as God was
heretofore angry with the Jews who rejected him and his form of
government to choose a king, so that he will bless us and be propitious to us who reject a king to make him only our leader and supreme
governor, in the conformity, as near as may be, of his own ancient
government; if we have at least but so much worth in us to entertain
the sense of our future happiness and the courage to receive what
God vouchsafes us: wherein we have the honor to precede other

---

4. In the Song of Deborah, the inhabitants of Meroz are cursed for failing to support
Barak in his battle against Sisera: "they came not to the help of the Lord against the
mighty" (Judg. 5:23). Ahab, king of Israel, was condemned by the prophet Elijah for
idolatry, the sins of his wife Jezebel, and the murder of Naboth and the seizing of his
vineyard (1 Kings 16:29–22:38). Antiochus IV, Epiphanes, ruled over the Jews and
brought idols into their temple. He was defeated by the Maccabees.
5. The modifier switches from Charles to Parliament. "Unconfound": restore.
6. Incensing.
7. Parliament, with a hint of divine sanction.

nations, who are now laboring to be our followers. For as to this question in hand, what the people by their just right may do in change of government or of governor, we see it cleared sufficiently, besides other ample authority, even from the mouths of princes themselves. And surely they that shall boast, as we do, to be a free nation, and not have in themselves the power to remove or to abolish any governor supreme or subordinate, with the government itself upon urgent causes, may please their fancy with a ridiculous and painted freedom fit to cozen babies; but are indeed under tyranny and servitude, as wanting that power which is the root and source of all liberty, to dispose and economize[8] in the land which God hath given them as masters of family in their own house and free inheritance. Without which natural and essential power of a free nation, though bearing high their heads, they can in due esteem be thought no better than slaves and vassals born, in the tenure and occupation of another inheriting lord, whose government, though not illegal or intolerable, hangs over them as a lordly scourge, not as a free government, and therefore to be abrogated. How much more justly then may they fling off tyranny or tyrants, who being once deposed can be no more than private men, as subject to the reach of justice and arraignment as any other transgressors. And certainly if men, not to speak of heathen, both wise and religious, have done justice upon tyrants what way they could soonest, how much more mild and humane then is it to give them fair and open trial—to teach lawless kings and all who so much adore them that not mortal man or his imperious will but justice is the only true sovereign and supreme majesty upon earth. Let men cease therefore out of faction and hypocrisy to make outcries and horrid things of things so just and honorable. Though perhaps till now no Protestant state or kingdom can be alleged to have openly put to death their king, which lately some have written, and imputed to their great glory, much mistaking the matter. It is not, neither ought to be, the glory of a Protestant state never to have put their king to death; it is the glory of a Protestant king never to have deserved death. And if the Parliament and military council do what they do without precedent, if it appear their duty, it argues the more wisdom, virtue, and magnanimity that they know themselves able to be a precedent to others, who perhaps in future ages, if they prove not too degenerate, will look up with honor and aspire toward these exemplary and matchless deeds of their ancestors as to the highest top of their civil glory and emulation; which heretofore, in the pursuance of fame and foreign dominion, spent itself vaingloriously abroad, but henceforth may learn a better fortitude, to dare execute highest justice on them that shall by

8. Conduct domestic management.

force of arms endeavor the oppressing and bereaving of religion and their liberty at home—that no unbridled potentate or tyrant, but to his sorrow, for the future may presume such high and irresponsible license over mankind, to havoc and turn upside down whole kingdoms of men as though they were no more in respect of his perverse will than a nation of pismires.[9]

As for the party called Presbyterian, of whom I believe very many to be good and faithful Christians, though misled by some of turbulent spirit, I wish them earnestly and calmly not to fall off from their first principles nor to affect rigor and superiority over men not under them; not to compel unforcible things, in religion especially, which, if not voluntary, becomes a sin; nor to assist the clamor and malicious drifts of men whom they themselves have judged to be the worst of men, the obdurate enemies of God and his church; nor to dart against the actions of their brethren, for want of other argument, those wrested laws and scriptures thrown by prelates and malignants against their own sides, which though they hurt not otherwise, yet taken up by them to the condemnation of their own doings, give scandal to all men and discover[1] in themselves either extreme passion or apostasy. Let them not oppose their best friends and associates, who molest them not at all, infringe not the least of their liberties, unless they call it their liberty to bind other men's consciences, but are still seeking to live at peace with them and brotherly accord. Let them beware an old and perfect enemy, who, though he hope by sowing discord to make them his instruments, yet cannot forbear a minute the open threatening of his destined revenge upon them when they have served his purposes. Let them fear, therefore, if they be wise, rather what they have done already than what remains to do, and be warned in time they put no confidence in princes whom they have provoked, lest they be added to the examples of those that miserably have tasted the event.

Stories[2] can inform them how Christiern the Second, king of Denmark, not much above a hundred years past, driven out by his subjects and received again upon new oaths and conditions, broke through them all to his most bloody revenge, slaying his chief opposers when he saw his time, both them and their children, invited to a feast for that purpose. How Maximilian dealt with those of Bruges,[3] though by mediation of the German princes reconciled to them by solemn and public writings drawn and sealed. How the massacre at Paris was the effect of that credulous peace which the French

9. Ants.
1. Reveal.
2. Histories.
3. In 1490, the emperor Maximilian took revenge on the oppressed inhabitants of the city of Bruges, who had risen up against him, captured, and imprisoned him.

Protestants made with Charles the Ninth, their king; and that the
main visible cause which to this day hath saved the Netherlands
from utter ruin was their final not believing the perfidious cruelty
which, as a constant maxim of state, hath been used by the Spanish
kings on their subjects that have taken arms and after trusted them;
as no later age but can testify, heretofore in Belgia itself, and this
very year in Naples.[4] And to conclude with one past exception, though
far more ancient, David, whose sanctified prudence might be alone
sufficient, not to warrant us only, but to instruct us, when once he
had taken arms, never after that trusted Saul, though with tears and
much relenting he twice promised not to hurt him. These instances,
few of many, might admonish them, both English and Scotch, not to
let their own ends and the driving on of a faction betray them blindly
into the snare of those enemies whose revenge looks on them as the
men who first begun, fomented, and carried on, beyond the cure of
any sound or safe accommodation, all the evil which hath since
unavoidably befallen them and their king.

I have something also to the divines, though brief to what were
needful, not to be disturbers of the civil affairs, being in hands better
able and more belonging to manage them, but to study harder and to
attend the office of good pastors, knowing that he whose flock is
least among them hath a dreadful charge, not performed by mounting twice into the chair with a formal preachment huddled up at the
odd hours of a whole lazy week, but by incessant pains and watching
in season and out of season, from house to house,[5] over the souls of
whom they have to feed. Which if they ever well considered, how little leisure would they find to be the most pragmatical sidesmen[6] of
every popular tumult and sedition! And all this while are to learn
what the true end and reason is of the gospel which they teach, and
what a world it differs from the censorious and supercilious lording
over conscience. It would be good also they lived so as might persuade the people they hated covetousness, which, worse than heresy,
is idolatry; hated pluralities and all kind of simony;[7] left rambling
from benefice to benefice, like ravenous wolves seeking where they
may devour the biggest. Of which if some, well and warmly seated
from the beginning, be not guilty, 'twere good they held not conversation with such as are. Let them be sorry that, being called to
assemble about reforming the church, they fell to progging and soliciting the Parliament, though they had renounced the name of priests,

---

4. Spain cruelly crushed a Neopolitan revolt in 1648, violating a formal pledge. Paris was
   the site of the massacre of Huguenots on St. Bartholomew's Eve in 1572. Belgia is in
   The Netherlands.
5. 2 Tim. 4:2 and Acts 20:20. "Chair": pulpit.
6. Meddlesome partisans.
7. Buying or selling ecclesiastical preferments.

for a new settling of their tithes and oblations; and double-lined themselves with spiritual places of commodity[8] beyond the possible discharge of their duty. Let them assemble in consistory with their elders and deacons, according to ancient ecclesiastical rule, to the preserving of church discipline, each in his several charge, and not a pack of clergymen by themselves to belly-cheer in their presumptuous Sion,[9] or to promote designs, abuse and gull the simple laity, and stir up tumult, as the prelates did, for the maintenance of their pride and avarice.

These things if they observe, and wait with patience, no doubt but all things will go well without their importunities or exclamations; and the printed letters which they send subscribed with the ostentation of great characters[1] and little moment would be more considerable than now they are. But if they be the ministers of Mammon instead of Christ, and scandalize his church with the filthy love of gain, aspiring also to sit the closest and the heaviest of all tyrants upon the conscience, and fall notoriously into the same sins whereof so lately and so loud they accused the prelates, as God rooted out those wicked ones immediately before, so will he root out them their imitators; and to vindicate his own glory and religion will uncover their hypocrisy to the open world and visit upon their own heads that *curse ye Meroz*, the very motto of their pulpits, wherewith so frequently, not as Meroz but more like atheists, they have blasphemed the vengeance of God and traduced the zeal of his people. And that they be not what they go for, true ministers of the Protestant doctrine, taught by those abroad, famous and religious men who first reformed the church, or by those no less zealous who withstood corruption and the bishops here at home, branded with the name of Puritans and Nonconformists, we shall abound with testimonies to make appear that men may yet more fully know the difference between Protestant divines and these pulpit-firebrands.

* * *

[Milton cites numerous religious authorities who assert the right of the people to overthrow tyrants, including Luther, Zwingli, Calvin, Bucer, Knox, and Paraeus. Where Luther, uncharacteristically, argues that popes and emperors, elected by the people, can also be deposed by them, Milton believes that this right applies as well to hereditary rulers:

---

8. Profit. "Called to assemble": the Westminster Assembly, commissioned by Parliament in 1643 to frame a church settlement. "Progging": begging.
9. Presbyterians held twice-weekly provincial assemblies in Sion College, London. "Belly-cheer": to feast luxuriously.
1. Capital letters on the title pages of their pamphlets.

Shall then so slight a consideration as his hap to be not elective simply, but by birth, which was a mere accident, overthrow that which is moral and make unpleasing to God that which otherwise had so well pleased him? Certainly not; for if the matter be rightly argued, election much rather than chance binds a man to content himself with what he suffers by his own bad election; though indeed neither the one nor other binds any man, much less any people, to a necessary sufferance of those wrongs and evils which they have ability and strength enough given them to remove.

Milton concludes his list with the Marian exiles William Whittingham, Christopher Goodman, and Dudley Fenner. According to Goodman,

When kings or rulers become blasphemers of God, oppressors and murderers of their subjects, they ought no more to be accounted kings or lawful magistrates, but as private men to be examined, accused, condemned and punished by the law of God; and being convicted and punished by that law, it is not man's but God's doing. C. x. p. 139.

By the civil laws, a fool or idiot born, and so proved, shall lose the lands and inheritance whereto he is born because he is not able to use them aright, and especially ought in no case be suffered to have the government of a whole nation; but there is no such evil can come to the commonwealth by fools and idiots as doth by the rage and fury of ungodly rulers. Such, therefore, being without God, ought to have no authority over God's people, who by his word requireth the contrary. C. xi. p. 143, 144.

Milton praises Goodman and others driven out from England during the reign of Mary Tudor, or Bloody Mary, 1553–58.]

These were the true Protestant divines of England, our fathers in the faith we hold; this was their sense, who for so many years laboring under prelacy through all storms and persecutions kept religion from extinguishing and delivered it pure to us, till there arose a covetous and ambitious generation of divines (for divines they call themselves) who, feigning on a sudden to be new converts and proselytes from episcopacy, under which they had long temporized, opened their mouths at length in show against pluralities and prelacy, but with intent to swallow them down both, gorging themselves like harpies on those simonious places and preferments of their outed predecessors as the quarry for which they hunted, not to plurality only but to multiplicity, for possessing which they had accused them, their brethren, and aspiring under another title to the same authority and usurpation over the consciences of all men.

Of this faction, diverse reverend and learned divines (as they are styled in the phylactery of their own title-page), pleading the lawfulness of defensive arms against this king in a treatise called *Scripture and Reason*,[2] seem in words to disclaim utterly the deposing of a king; but both the Scripture and the reasons which they use draw consequences after them which, without their bidding, conclude it lawful. For if by Scripture, and by that especially to the Romans, which they most insist upon, kings doing that which is contrary to Saint Paul's definition of a magistrate may be resisted, they may altogether with as much force of consequence be deposed or punished. And if by reason the unjust authority of kings *may be forfeited in part, and his power be reassumed in part, either by the parliament or people, for the case in hazard and the present necessity,"* as they affirm, p. 34, there can no Scripture be alleged, no imaginable reason given, that necessity continuing, as it may always, and they in all prudence and their duty may take upon them to foresee it, why in such a case they may not finally amerce[3] him with the loss of his kingdom, of whose amendment they have no hope. And if one wicked action persisted in against religion, laws, and liberties may warrant us to thus much in part, why may not forty times as many tyrannies by him committed warrant us to proceed on restraining him, till the restraint become total? For the ways of justice are exactest proportion. If for one trespass of a king it require so much remedy or satisfaction, then for twenty more as heinous crimes it requires of him twentyfold; and so proportionably, till it come to what is utmost among men. If in these proceedings against their king they may not finish by the usual course of justice what they have begun, they could not lawfully begin at all. For this golden rule of justice and morality, as well as of arithmetic, out of three terms which they admit, will as certainly and unavoidably bring out the fourth, as any problem that ever Euclid or Apollonius made good by demonstration.

And if the Parliament, being undeposable but by themselves, as is affirmed, p. 37, 38, might for his whole life, if they saw cause, take all power, authority, and the sword out of his hand, which in effect is to unmagistrate him, why might they not, being then themselves the sole magistrates in force, proceed to punish him who, being lawfully deprived of all things that define a magistrate, can be now no magistrate to be degraded lower but an offender to be punished. Lastly, whom they may defy and meet in battle, why may

---

2. In 1643, Herbert Palmer (1601–1647), a Church of England clergyman, collaborated with a number of other divines in writing *Scripture and Reason Pleaded for Defensive Armes*, which justified Parliament's "defensive" war against the king. Milton's page references are to this tract.

3. Punish.

they not as well prosecute by justice? For lawful war is but the execution of justice against them who refuse law. Among whom if it be lawful (as they deny not, p. 19, 20) to slay the king himself coming in front at his own peril, wherefore may not justice do that intendedly which the chance of a defensive war might without blame have done casually, nay, purposely, if there it find him among the rest? They ask, p. 19, *By what rule of conscience or God a state is bound to sacrifice religion, laws, and liberties, rather than a prince defending such as subvert them should come in hazard of his life.* And I ask by what conscience, or divinity, or law, or reason a state is bound to leave all these sacred concernments under a perpetual hazard and extremity of danger, rather than cut off a wicked prince who sits plotting day and night to subvert them.

They tell us that the law of nature justifies any man to defend himself, even against the king in person. Let them show us then why the same law may not justify much more a state or whole people to do justice upon him against whom each private man may lawfully defend himself, seeing all kind of justice done is a defense to good men as well as a punishment to bad; and justice done upon a tyrant is no more but the necessary self-defense of a whole commonwealth. To war upon a king that his instruments may be brought to condign punishment, and thereafter to punish them the instruments, and not to spare only but to defend and honor him the author, is the strangest piece of justice to be called Christian, and the strangest piece of reason to be called human, that by men of reverence and learning, as their style imports them, ever yet was vented.[4] They maintain in the third and fourth section that a judge or inferior magistrate is anointed of God, is his minister, hath the sword in his hand, is to be obeyed by St. Peter's rule[5] as well as the supreme, and without difference anywhere expressed; and yet will have us fight against the supreme till he remove and punish the inferior magistrate (for such were greatest delinquents) whenas by Scripture, and by reason, there can no more authority be shown to resist the one than the other, and altogether as much to punish or depose the supreme himself as to make war upon him, till he punish or deliver up his inferior magistrates, whom in the same terms we are commanded to obey and not to resist.

Thus while they, in a cautious line or two here and there stuffed in, are only verbal against the pulling down or punishing of tyrants, all the Scripture and the reason which they bring is in every leaf direct and rational, to infer it altogether as lawful as to resist them.

4. Expressed. "Instruments": persons used by an agent ("author") to accomplish his purposes. "Condign": deserved.
5. 1 Peter 2:13–14. Earlier in the treatise, Milton reads it as identifying monarchical rule as "a *human ordinance*," which, if evil, can be resisted.

And yet in all their sermons, as hath by others been well noted, they went much further. For divines, if ye observe them, have their postures and their motions no less expertly and with no less variety than they that practice feats in the artillery-ground. Sometimes they seem furiously to march on, and presently march counter; by and by they stand, and then retreat; or, if need be, can face about, or wheel in a whole body with that cunning and dexterity as is almost unperceivable, to wind themselves by shifting ground into places of more advantage. And Providence only must be the drum, Providence the word of command that calls them from above, but always to some larger benefice, or acts[6] them into such or such figures and promotions. At their turns and doublings no men readier, to the right, or to the left, for it is their turns which they serve[7] chiefly; herein only singular, that with them there is no certain hand right or left but as their own commodity[8] thinks best to call it. But if there come a truth to be defended which to them and their interest of this world seems not so profitable, straight these nimble motionists can find no even legs to stand upon, and are no more of use to reformation thoroughly performed, and not superficially, or to the advancement of truth (which among mortal men is always in her progress[9]) than if on a sudden they were struck maim and crippled. Which the better to conceal, or the more to countenance by a general conformity to their own limping, they would have Scripture, they would have reason also made to halt with them for company, and would put us off with impotent conclusions, lame and shorter than the premises.[1]

In this posture they seem to stand with great zeal and confidence on the wall of Sion, but like Jebusites, not like Israelites or Levites; blind also as well as lame, they discern not David from Adonibezek,[2] but cry him up for the Lord's anointed whose thumbs and great toes not long before they had cut off upon their pulpit cushions. Therefore he who is our only king, the root[3] of David, and whose kingdom is eternal righteousness, with all those that war under him, whose happiness and final hopes are laid up in that only just and rightful kingdom (which we pray incessantly may come soon, and in so praying wish hasty ruin and destruction to all tyrants), even he our immortal King, and all that love him, must of necessity have in abomination these blind and lame defenders of Jerusalem, as the soul of David

---

6. Puts in motion.
7. To serve one's turn is to satisfy one's needs.
8. Advantage, profit.
9. Onward march.
1. Quintilian's warning against rhetorically weak terminations was a cliché. Compare *Othello* 2.1.161, Desdemona to Iago: "O, most lame and impotent conclusion!"
2. Canaanite king, whose mutilation rendered him harmless as a warrior. The Jebusites were a tribe of Canaanites, dispossessed of Jerusalem by David. In the 17th century, the term referred to Roman Catholics.
3. Scion, offshoot (alluding to Christ).

hated them,[4] and forbid them entrance into God's house and his own. But as to those before them which I cited first (and with an easy search, for many more might be added) as they there stand, without more in number, being the best and chief of Protestant divines, we may follow them for faithful guides, and without doubting may receive them as witnesses abundant of what we here affirm concerning tyrants. And indeed I find it generally the clear and positive determination of them all (not prelatical or of this late faction sub-prelatical) who have written on this argument that to do justice on a lawless king is to a private man unlawful, to an inferior magistrate lawful; or if they were divided in opinion, yet greater than these here alleged, or of more authority in the church, there can be none produced.

If anyone shall go about by bringing other testimonies to disable these, or by bringing these against themselves in other cited passages of their books, he will not only fail to make good that false and impudent assertion of those mutinous ministers that the deposing and punishing of a king or tyrant *is against the constant judgment of all Protestant divines*, it being quite the contrary; but will prove rather what perhaps he intended not, that the judgment of divines, if it be so various and inconstant to itself, is not considerable,[5] or to be esteemed at all. Ere which be yielded, as I hope it never will, these ignorant asserters in their own art will have proved themselves more and more not to be Protestant divines, whose constant judgment in this point they have so audaciously belied, but rather to be a pack of hungry church-wolves, who in the steps of Simon Magus[6] their father, following the hot scent of double livings and pluralities, advowsons, donatives, inductions, and augmentations, though uncalled to the flock of Christ but by the mere suggestion of their bellies, like those priests of Bel whose pranks Daniel found out,[7] have got possession, or rather seized upon the pulpit as the stronghold and fortress of their sedition and rebellion against the civil magistrate. Whose friendly and victorious hand having rescued them from the bishops their insulting lords, fed them plenteously both in public and in private, raised them to be high and rich of poor and base, only suffered not their covetousness and fierce ambition (which as the pit that sent out their fellow-locusts hath been

4. In 2 Sam. 5:8, David calls any who will smite the Jebusites, whom his soul hates, "the chief and the captain."
5. Worth consideration.
6. The sin of simony, offering money for position and influence in the church, is named after Simon Magus, who offered the Apostles money for the power to impart the Holy Spirit by the laying on of hands (Acts 8:18–19).
7. In the apocryphal Book of Bel, Daniel exposes those corrupt priests who hoarded offerings intended by worshipers for their gods. "Advowsons": the right of presentation to an ecclesiastical living. "Donatives": livings or appointments. "Inductions": formal institution of a Presbyterian minister in his parish. "Augmentations": increases in a clergyman's stipend.

ever bottomless and boundless) to interpose in all things and over all persons their impetuous[8] ignorance and importunity.

THE READY AND EASY WAY TO ESTABLISH A FREE COMMONWEALTH Three poets—John Dryden, Andrew Marvell, and John Milton—walked together in Oliver Cromwell's funeral procession in September 1658. Young Dryden's first important poem, the *Heroique Stanzas* (1660), characterized the late Protector as a strong and wise leader. But after the Restoration, his *Astraea redux* (Justice brought back) portrayed Charles II as a second Augustus, and his poem *To His Sacred Majesty, a Panegyric on his Coronation* (1661) celebrated the Stuart monarchy that he would serve as laureate. Marvell had written the great *Horatian Ode upon Cromwell's Return from Ireland* (1650), as well as *The First Anniversary of the Government under O.C.* (December 1654), and he had assisted the blind Milton in his Latin secretaryship of Cromwell's Council of State. But in April 1660, he was elected to the Convention Parliament that recalled the Stuarts, and in July he was ordered to help in replying to a letter of congratulation on the Restoration.

Milton's *Ready and Easy Way* (first edition February 1660; revised and expanded second edition, reprinted here, March 1660) is the last signed treatise opposing monarchy to be published before the Restoration by a champion of the Good Old Cause. Already by April 4, 1660, a month before he entered London, Charles made known in the Declaration of Breda the conditions of his acceptance of the crown. Marvell was encouraged by his promise of "a liberty to tender consciences." But Milton could never have been bought off that way. He never wavered in his passionate and extreme opposition to monarchy. Other republicans objected to the crown's abuse of coercive power, but Milton rejected even its latent existence, observing in *The Tenure* that a people lacking the power of self-determination "can in due esteem be thought no better than slaves," even if their government is "not illegal, or intolerable."[1] His visceral abhorrence of monarchy is also evident more than twenty years later in *The Ready and Easy Way*:

> A king must be adored like a demigod, with a dissolute and haughty court about him of vast expense and luxury, masques and revels, to the debauching of our prime gentry both male and female.

What madness is it for them who might manage nobly their own affairs themselves, sluggishly and weakly to devolve all on a single person, and, more like boys under age than men, to commit all to his patronage and disposal who neither can perform what he undertakes, and yet for undertaking it, though royally paid, will not be their servant but their lord! How unmanly must it needs be to count such a one the breath of our nostrils, to hang all our felicity on him,

---

8. Violent. Rev. 9:1–3 describes locusts rising from the smoke of the bottomless pit.
1. See on this point Blair Worden's review of Quentin Skinner's *Hobbes and Republican Liberty*, in *The New York Review of Books*, July 16, 2009, p. 42.

all our safety, our well-being, for which if we were aught else but sluggards or babies, we need depend on none but God and our own counsels, our own active virtue and industry.

There is some continuity between the two treatises, since on the eve of the Restoration Milton raises some of the same concerns that vexed Parliament and much of the nation in the 1640s, including royal prerogative, martial law proclaimed by the king, and forced loans in the form of subsidies required by the sovereign to meet special needs. He prophesies the perpetuation of such disputes once monarchy is restored. But the situation in the interim regarding Parliament and the people has altered drastically. On February 21, 1660, General George Monck reinstated the Presbyterian Members of Parliament who had been excluded in Pride's Purge of 1648, which virtually guaranteed the return of the Stuart monarchy. And most of the people now favored the return of Charles II, so that Milton must argue that the minority can coerce the majority to accept liberty:

> Is it just or reasonable that most voices against the main end of government should enslave the less number that would be free? More just it is, doubtless, if it come to force, that a less number compel a greater to retain, which can be no wrong to them, their liberty, than that a greater number, for the pleasure of their baseness, compel a less most injuriously to be their fellow slaves.

It is a commonplace that for Puritans the identification of England and New England with biblical Israel as holy nations entering into a covenantal relationship with God was a thoroughgoing and comprehensive procedure. And in prose tracts of the early 1640s, Milton makes this identification frequently, as in this passage from the *Areopagitica*:

> The favor and the love of Heaven, we have great argument to think in a peculiar manner propitious and propending towards us. Why else was this nation chosen before any other, that out of her, as out of Sion, should be proclaimed and sounded forth the first tidings and trumpet of reformation to all Europe?

Here Milton alludes to Isaiah 2:3 ("out of Zion shall go forth the law [lit., "Torah"], and the word of the Lord from Jerusalem"), comparing England, as the first nation to hear the trumpet of Reformation, with Israel, the first nation to hear the divine word. But in *The Ready and Easy Way*, while still maintaining the biblical comparison, Milton regards with desperation and frustration his cowardly countrymen, who resemble the Israelites in the wilderness: backsliding ex-slaves, tired of their diet of manna and longing for the imagined delicacies they enjoyed in captivity and, fearful of the Canaanites God has commanded them to conquer, "choosing them a captain back for Egypt" (Num. 11:5–6; 14:4). In the treatise's same concluding paragraph, a weary Milton echoes the voice of Jeremiah (22:29) in his prophecy against monarchy: "Thus much I should perhaps have said though I were sure I should have spoken only to trees and stones, and had none to cry to, but with the prophet, O *earth, earth, earth!*"

In addition to rejecting majority rule, Milton would replace the full and free Parliament that his countrymen want with a single Grand Council whose members would be elected for life. He provides ancient models for such an aristocratic form of government:

> Therefore among the Jews, the supreme council of seventy, called the *Sanhedrim*, founded by Moses, in Athens that of *Areopagus*, in Sparta that of the ancients, in Rome the senate, consisted of members chosen for term of life and by that means remained as it were still the same to generations.

These two proposals are reliable indicators of the political situation rather than of Milton's rejection of true republicanism. The treatises that Milton wrote in 1659–60 might seem inconsistent with one another as well as increasingly elitist, but that is due in large part to the rapid changes in circumstance during this turbulent period. Milton is committed to maintaining commonwealth government and preventing monarchy at virtually any cost. As Barbara Lewalski has pointed out (in *Patrick*, 439), changing political alignments caused Milton to sound inconsistent, as when he located political power variously "in the people themselves, in the worthy few, and in the regenerate saints." As England edged ever closer toward monarchy, Milton adapted his arguments accordingly, trying to make the best of an increasingly dire situation. He knew that vesting power in a free and open Parliament would make the return of Charles II inevitable. The two most disturbing proposals in this treatise do not reflect Milton's ideal vision of republican government. Milton's willingness to offer new plans to supersede earlier ones in the face of new and worsening reality and to identify himself as the author of an anti-monarchical treatise at so dangerously late a date attest to his uncommon bravery and to a mental resilience that is less often remarked than his general intellectual power.

The readie and easie way to establish a free Commonwealth; and the excellence therof compar'd with the inconveniencies and dangers of readmitting Kingship in this nation.

The second edition revis'd and augmented.
The author J. M.
——— *Et nos
Consilium dedimus Syllæ, demus populo nunc.*[1]
London, Printed for the Author, 1660

Although, since the writing of this treatise, the face of things hath had some change, writs for new elections have been recalled, and the

---

1. Juvenal, *Satires*, 1: "And we have given counsel to Sulla, now let us give it to the people."

members at first chosen re-admitted from exclusion, yet not a little
rejoicing to hear declared the resolution of those who are in power
tending to the establishment of a free commonwealth,[2] and to remove,
if it be possible, this noxious humor of returning to bondage, instilled
of late by some deceivers and nourished from bad principles and false
apprehensions among too many of the people; I thought best not to
suppress what I had written, hoping that it may now be of much more
use and concernment to be freely published in the midst of our elections to a free parliament, or[3] their sitting to consider freely of the
government, whom it behooves to have all things represented to them
that may direct their judgment therein; and I never read of any state,
scarce of any tyrant, grown so incurable as to refuse counsel from any
in a time of public deliberation, much less to be offended. If their
absolute determination be to enthrall us, before so long a Lent of servitude they may permit us a little shroving-time[4] first wherein to
speak freely and take our leaves of liberty. And because in the former
edition, through haste, many faults escaped, and many books were
suddenly dispersed[5] ere the note to mend them could be sent, I took
the opportunity from this occasion to revise and somewhat to enlarge
the whole discourse, especially that part which argues for a perpetual
senate. The treatise thus revised and enlarged is as follows.

The parliament of England, assisted by a great number of the
people who appeared and stuck to them faithfulest in defense of religion and their civil liberties, judging kingship by long experience a
government unnecessary, burdensome, and dangerous,[6] justly and
magnanimously abolished it, turning regal bondage into a free commonwealth, to the admiration and terror of our emulous neighbors.
They took themselves not bound by the light of nature or religion to
any former covenant, from which the king himself, by many forfei-
tures of a latter date or discovery, and our own longer consideration
thereon, had more and more unbound us, both to himself and his
posterity; as hath been ever the justice and the prudence of all wise
nations that have ejected tyranny. They covenanted *to preserve the
king's person and authority in the preservation of the true religion and
our liberties;*[7] not in his endeavoring to bring in upon our consciences
a popish religion;[8] upon our liberties, thraldom; upon our lives,

---

2. General George Monck, the tyrant Sulla of the motto, controlled both the army and
the Council of State. In February 1660, he declared a commitment, which the will of
the people ultimately kept him from honoring, to "the Settlement of these nations
upon Commonwealth foundations."
3. Or: ere.
4. The keeping of Shrove-tide, which includes *Mardi Gras*, a time of confession and
carnival.
5. Quickly distributed.
6. Phrase taken from Parliament's resolution, February 1649, to abolish kingship.
7. From the Solemn League and Covenant of 1643.
8. Episcopacy.

destruction, by his occasioning, if not complotting, as was after discovered, the Irish massacre; his fomenting and arming the rebellion; his covert leaguing with the rebels against us; his refusing, more than seven times, propositions most just and necessary to the true religion and our liberties tendered him by the parliament both of England and Scotland. They made not their covenant concerning him with no difference between a king and a God; or promised him, as Job did to the Almighty, *to trust in him though he slay us*; they understood that the solemn engagement wherein we all forswore kingship was no more a breach of the covenant than the covenant was of the protestation before,[9] but a faithful and prudent going on both in the words well weighed and in the true sense of the covenant, *without respect of persons*, when we could not serve two contrary masters, God and the king, or the king and that more supreme law sworn in the first place to maintain our safety and our liberty. They knew the people of England to be a free people, themselves the representers of that freedom; and although many were excluded, and as many fled (so they pretended) from tumults to Oxford,[1] yet they were left a sufficient number to act in parliament, therefore not bound by any statute of preceding parliaments, but by the law of nature only, which is the only law of laws truly and properly to all mankind fundamental, the beginning and the end of all government; to which no parliament or people that will thoroughly reform but may and must have recourse, as they had and must yet have in church reformation (if they thoroughly intend it) to evangelic rules; not to ecclesiastical canons, though never so ancient, so ratified and established in the land by statutes which for the most part are mere positive laws,[2] neither natural nor moral: and so by any parliament, for just and serious considerations, without scruple to be at any time repealed. If others of their number in these things were under force,[3] they were not, but under free conscience; if others were excluded by a power which they could not resist, they were not therefore to leave the helm of government in no hands, to discontinue their care of the public peace and safety, to desert the people in anarchy and confusion, no more than

---

9. Parliament's protest against the levying of a Catholic army in Ireland (May 1641), which included a promise to maintain and defend both "the true reformed Protestant religion" and "His Majesty's royal person and estate." See Job 13.15: "Though he slay me, yet will I trust in him." "Solemn engagement": the oath of loyalty to the Commonwealth, "as the same is now established, without a King, or House of Lords," required of members of Parliament, October 1649.

1. Where Charles summoned royalists of both Houses to set up their own Parliament, January 1644. "Many were excluded": through the purging of members of Parliament hostile to the politicized New Model Army, December 1648 (Pride's Purge).

2. Mere statutory and artificial human law, in contrast to natural law based on universally accepted moral principles deriving from nature and reason, "God's law." "Evangelic rules": faith and charity, or belief and practice.

3. After Pride's Purge, excluded members of Parliament complained that the army controlled the commonwealth.

when so many of their members left them as made up in outward
formality a more legal parliament of three estates against them.[4] The
best-affected[5] also and best-principled of the people stood not num-
bering or computing on which side were most voices in parliament,
but on which side appeared to them most reason, most safety, when
the house divided upon main matters. What was well motioned and
advised, they examined not whether fear or persuasion carried it in
the vote, neither did they measure votes and counsels by the intentions of them that voted; knowing that intentions either are but
guessed at or not soon enough known; and although good, can neither make the deed such nor prevent the consequence from being
bad. Suppose bad intentions in things otherwise well done; what was
well done, was by them who so thought not the less obeyed or followed in the state; since in the church, who had not rather follow
Iscariot or Simon the magician, though to covetous ends preaching,
than Saul,[6] though in the uprightness of his heart persecuting the
gospel? Safer they therefore judged what they thought the better
counsels, though carried on by some perhaps to bad ends, than the
worse by others, though endeavored with best intentions.[7] And yet
they were not to learn that a greater number might be corrupt within
the walls of a parliament as well as of a city;[8] whereof in matters of
nearest concernment all men will be judges; nor easily permit that
the odds of voices in their greatest council shall more endanger them
by corrupt or credulous votes than the odds of enemies by open
assaults; judging that most voices ought not always to prevail where
main matters are in question. If others hence will pretend to disturb
all counsels, what is that to them who pretend not, but are in real
danger—not they only so judging but a great (though not the greatest) number of their chosen patriots, who might be more in weight
than the others in number; there being in number little virtue, but by
weight and measure wisdom working all things, and the dangers on

4. The Oxford Parliament of king, lords, and commons, as opposed to the Long Parliament, from which the king was excluded.
5. Republican term for adherents of Parliament against the king, a dwindling number.
   Milton needs to justify the power of the minority of Parliament over the majority. He
   also denounces the terms that the majority in the Long Parliament had been bent on
   concluding with Charles I in the later months of 1648—terms that were often referred
   to in the spring of 1649 as a possible basis for the restoration of Charles II.
6. As Saul, an ex-Pharisee of the strictest school, St. Paul before his conversion zealously
   persecuted Christians (Acts 8.1–3). In John 12.3–6, Judas Iscariot, who would betray
   Jesus for money, protests that the oil used to anoint Jesus' feet might better have been
   sold to relieve the poor. In Acts 8.9–23, Simon Magus ("the magician") offers to buy
   from the Apostles John and Peter the power to confer the Holy Ghost. Simony is traffic
   in sacred things.
7. The Rump Parliament and the army, accused of corruption, could still advance the
   cause of the commonwealth.
8. A Presbyterian majority in Parliament and in London wanted to continue negotiating
   with the king in the months before his execution. "Not to learn": already knew.

either side they seriously thus weighed. From the treaty, short fruits of long labors and seven years' war; security for twenty years, if we can hold it; reformation in the church for three years; then put to shift[9] again with our vanquished master. His justice, his honor, his conscience declared quite contrary to ours, which would have furnished him with many such evasions, as in a book entitled *An Inquisition for Blood*[1] soon after were not concealed; bishops not totally removed but left, as it were, in ambush, a reserve, with ordination in their sole power; their lands already sold not to be alienated but rented, and the sale of them called *sacrilege*; delinquents, few of many brought to condign punishment; accessories punished, the chief author above pardon though after utmost resistance vanquished, not to give but to receive laws; yet besought,[2] treated with, and to be thanked for his gracious concessions, to be honored, worshiped, glorified. If this we swore to do, with what righteousness in the sight of God, with what assurance that we bring not by such an oath the whole sea of blood-guiltiness upon our heads?[3] If on the other side we prefer a free government, though for the present not obtained, yet all those suggested fears and difficulties, as the event will prove, easily overcome, we remain finally secure from the exasperated regal power, and out of snares; shall retain the best part of our liberty, which is our religion, and the civil part will be from these who defer[4] us much more easily recovered, being neither so subtle nor so awful as a king reinthroned. Nor were their actions less both at home and abroad than might become the hopes of a glorious rising commonwealth; nor were the expressions both of army and people, whether in their public declarations or several writings, other than such as testified a spirit in this nation no less noble and well-fitted to the liberty of a commonwealth than in the ancient Greeks or Romans. Nor was the heroic cause unsuccessfully defended to all Christendom, against the tongue of a famous and thought invincible adversary; nor the constancy and fortitude that so nobly vindicated our

---

9. Driven to extremity. "Treaty": the unsuccessful Newport Treaty of 1648, in which Charles assented to parliamentary control of the militia for twenty years but only to the temporary, not permanent, abolition of Episcopacy and establishment of Presbyterianism. "Seven years' war": from 1642 (beginning of First Civil War) through 1648.
1. A royalist pamphlet (July 1649), arguing that Charles, acting in his politic rather than personal capacity, was not bound to the Newport Treaty.
2. Entreated. "Alienated": transferred. "Rented": for ninety-nine years, with Charles's proviso "that the Propriety and Inheritance of those Lands may still remain to the Church." "Called": by King Charles. "Delinquents": those who raised arms against Parliament. "Condign": fitting, deserved. "Chief author": Charles.
3. I.e., to be lenient toward Charles is to be complicit in the bloodshed he caused. Swearing by the Solemn League and Covenant to preserve and defend both true religion and the king's majesty are two incompatible obligations, according to Milton, since Charles assaulted the true religion and thus forfeited the right to be defended.
4. Delay. "Event": outcome. "Exasperated": enraged.

liberty, our victory at once against two the most prevailing usurpers over mankind, superstition and tyranny, unpraised or uncelebrated in a written monument,[1] likely to outlive detraction, as it hath hitherto convinced or silenced not a few of our detractors, especially in parts abroad. After our liberty and religion thus prosperously fought for, gained, and many years possessed (except in those unhappy interruptions, which God hath removed), now that nothing remains but in all reason the certain hopes of a speedy and immediate settlement forever in a firm and free commonwealth for this extolled and magnified nation, regardless both of honor won or deliverances vouchsafed from heaven, to fall back, or rather to creep back so poorly, as it seems the multitude would, to their once abjured and detested thraldom of kingship, to be ourselves the slanderers of our own just and religious deeds, though done by some to covetous and ambitious ends, yet not therefore to be stained with their infamy, or they to asperse the integrity of others; and yet these now by revolting from the conscience of deeds well done, both in church and state, to throw away and forsake, or rather to betray, a just and noble cause for the mixture of bad men who have ill-managed and abused it (which had our fathers done heretofore, and on the same pretense deserted true religion, what had long ere this become of our gospel and all protestant reformation so much intermixed with the avarice and ambition of some reformers?) and by thus relapsing to verify all the bitter predictions of our triumphing enemies, who will now think they wisely discerned and justly censured both us and all our actions as rash, rebellious, hypocritical, and impious, not only argues a strange, degenerate contagion suddenly spread among us, fitted and prepared for new slavery, but will render us a scorn and derision to all our neighbors. And what will they at best say of us, and of the whole English name, but scoffingly, as of that foolish builder mentioned by our Savior, who began to build a tower and was not able to finish it?[2] Where is this goodly tower of a commonwealth, which the English boasted they would build to overshadow kings and be another Rome in the west? The foundation indeed they laid gallantly, but fell into a worse confusion, not of tongues but of factions, than those at the tower of Babel; and have left no memorial of their work behind them remaining but in the common laughter of Europe. Which must needs redound the more to our shame, if we but look on our neighbors the United Provinces,[3] to us inferior in all outward advantages;

5. I.e., Milton's treatise. "Adversary": Claude de Saumaise (Salmasius), French polymath, whose attack on the regicides and the Commonwealth Milton answered in his great *Defence of the English People* (1651).
6. Luke 14:28–29: "For which of you, intending to build a tower, sitteth not down first, and counteth the cost, whether he have sufficient to finish it? Lest haply, after he hath laid the foundation, and is not able to finish it, all that behold it begin to mock him."
7. The Netherlands.

who notwithstanding, in the midst of greater difficulties, coura-
geously, wisely, constantly went through with the same work and are
settled in all the happy enjoyments of a potent and flourishing republic to this day.

Besides this, if we return to kingship and soon repent (as
undoubtedly we shall when we begin to find the old encroachments
coming on by little and little upon our consciences, which must
necessarily proceed from king and bishop united inseparably in one
interest), we may be forced perhaps to fight over again all that we
have fought, and spend over again all that we have spent, but are
never like to attain thus far as we are now advanced to the recovery
of our freedom, never to have it in possession as we now have it,
never to be vouchsafed hereafter the like mercies and signal assis-
tances from heaven in our cause, if by our ingrateful backsliding
we make these fruitless; flying now to regal concessions from his
divine condescensions and gracious answers to our once importuning prayers against the tyranny which we then groaned under; making vain and viler than dirt the blood of so many thousand faithful
and valiant Englishmen who left us in this liberty, bought with
their lives; losing by a strange after-game of folly all the battles we
have won, together with all Scotland as to our conquest, hereby
lost, which never any of our kings could conquer, all the treasure
we have spent, not that corruptible treasure only, but that far more
precious of all our late miraculous deliverances; treading back
again with lost labor all our happy steps in the progress of reformation, and most pitifully depriving ourselves the instant fruition of
that free government which we have so dearly purchased, a free
commonwealth, not only held by wisest men in all ages the noblest,
the manliest, the equalest, the justest government, the most agreeable to all due liberty and proportioned equality, both human, civil,
and Christian, most cherishing to virtue and true religion, but also
(I may say it with greatest probability) plainly commended, or rather
enjoined by our Savior himself, to all Christians, not without
remarkable disallowance, and the brand of gentilism[8] upon kingship. God in much displeasure gave a king to the Israelites[9] and
imputed it a sin to them that they sought one; but Christ apparently
forbids his disciples to admit of any such heathenish government:
The kings of the Gentiles, saith he, *exercise lordship over them; and
they that exercise authority upon them are called benefactors: but ye
shall not be so; but he that is greatest among you, let him be as the
younger, and he that is chief, as he that serveth.*[1] The occasion of

---

8. Heathenism. "Equalest": the justest.
9. See *Tenure of Kings and Magistrates* for discussion of 1 Sam. 8.
1. Luke 22:25–26; also Mark 10:32–45, as a response to James and John when they ask to
   sit next to Jesus in his glory.

these his words was the ambitious desire of Zebedee's two sons, to be exalted above their brethren in his kingdom, which they thought was to be ere long upon earth. That he speaks of civil government is manifest by the former part of the comparison, which infers the other part to be always in the same kind. And what government comes nearer to this precept of Christ than a free commonwealth; wherein they who are greatest are perpetual servants and drudges to the public at their own cost and charges, neglect their own affairs yet are not elevated above their brethren; live soberly in their families, walk the streets as other men, may be spoken to freely, familiarly, friendly, without adoration. Whereas a king must be adored like a demigod, with a dissolute and haughty court about him of vast expense and luxury, masques and revels, to the debauching of our prime gentry both male and female; not in their pastimes only but in earnest, by the loose employments of court-service, which will be then thought honorable. There will be a queen also of no less charge; in most likelihood outlandish and a papist, besides a queen-mother such already, together with both their courts and numerous train; then a royal issue, and ere long severally their sumptuous courts, to the multiplying of a servile crew, not of servants only but of nobility and gentry, bred up then to the hopes not of public but of court offices, to be stewards, chamberlains, ushers, grooms even of the close-stool;[2] and the lower their minds debased with court opinions, contrary to all virtue and reformation, the haughtier will be their pride and profuseness. We may well remember this not long since at home, or need but look at present into the French court, where enticements and preferments daily draw away and pervert the Protestant nobility. As to the burden of expense, to our cost we shall soon know it, for any good to us deserving to be termed no better than the vast and lavish price of our subjection and their debauchery, which we are now so greedily cheapening and would so fain be paying most inconsiderately to a single person;[3] who, for anything wherein the public really needs him, will have little else to do but to bestow the eating and drinking of excessive dainties, to set a pompous face upon the superficial actings of state, to pageant himself up and down in progress among the perpetual bowings and cringings of an abject people, on either side deifying and adoring him for nothing done that can deserve it. For what can he more than another man? who, even in the expression of a late

---

2. Chamber pot. "Outlandish": foreign, like Henrietta Maria, the French Catholic wife of Charles I and queen mother of Charles II, who would soon marry Princess Catherine of Portugal.
3. Republican parlance for king or protector. "Cheapening": bargaining over, bringing into contempt.

court poet, sits only like a great cipher[4] set to no purpose before a long row of other significant figures. Nay, it is well and happy for the people if their king be but a cipher, being oft-times a mischief, a pest, a scourge of the nation, and, which is worse, not to be removed, not to be controlled, much less accused or brought to punishment without the danger of a common ruin, without the shaking and almost subversion of the whole land; whereas in a free commonwealth, any governor or chief councilor offending may be removed and punished without the least commotion. Certainly then that people must needs be mad or strangely infatuated that build the chief hope of their common happiness or safety on a single person; who, if he happen to be good, can do no more than another man; if to be bad, hath in his hands to do more evil without check than millions of other men. The happiness of a nation must needs be firmest and certainest in a full and free council of their own electing, where no single person, but reason only, sways. And what madness is it for them who might manage nobly their own affairs themselves, sluggishly and weakly to devolve all on a single person, and, more like boys under age than men, to commit all to his patronage and disposal who neither can perform what he undertakes, and yet for undertaking it, though royally paid, will not be their servant but their lord! How unmanly must it needs be to count such a one the breath of our nostrils, to hang all our felicity on him, all our safety, our well-being, for which if we were aught else but sluggards or babies, we need depend on none but God and our own counsels, our own active virtue and industry. *Go to the ant, thou sluggard*, saith Solomon;[5] *consider her ways, and be wise; which having no prince, ruler, or lord provides her meat in the summer, and gathers her food in the harvest*—which evidently shows us that they who think the nation undone without a king, though they look grave or haughty, have not so much true spirit and understanding in them as a pismire;[6] neither are these diligent creatures hence concluded to live in lawless anarchy, or that commended; but are set the examples to imprudent and ungoverned men of a frugal and self-governing democracy or commonwealth, safer and more thriving in the joint providence and counsel of many industrious equals than under the single domination of one imperious lord. It may be well wondered that any nation styling themselves free can suffer any man to pretend hereditary right over them as their lord, whenas by acknowledging that right they conclude themselves his servants and his vassals, and so renounce their own freedom. Which how a

4. Zero.
5. Prov. 6:6, the commonwealth of the ants as nature's original republic.
6. Ant.

people and their leaders especially can do who have fought so gloriously for liberty; how they can change their noble words and actions, heretofore so becoming the majesty of a free people, into the base necessity of court flatteries and prostrations, is not only strange and admirable but lamentable to think on. That a nation should be so valorous and courageous to win their liberty in the field, and when they have won it, should be so heartless[7] and unwise in their counsels as not to know how to use it, value it, what to do with it or with themselves, but after ten or twelve years' prosperous war and contestation with tyranny, basely and besottedly to run their necks again into the yoke which they have broken, and prostrate all the fruits of their victory for nought at the feet of the vanquished, besides our loss of glory, and such an example as kings or tyrants never yet had the like to boast of, will be an ignominy if it befall us that never yet befell any nation possessed of their liberty; worthy indeed themselves, whatsoever they be, to be forever slaves, but that part of the nation which consents not with them, as I persuade me of a great number, far worthier than by their means to be brought into the same bondage. Considering these things so plain, so rational, I cannot but yet further admire on the other side how any man who hath the true principles of justice and religion in him can presume or take upon him to be a king and lord over his brethren, whom he cannot but know, whether as men or Christians, to be for the most part every way equal or superior to himself; how he can display with such vanity and ostentation his regal splendor so supereminently above other mortal men; or, being a Christian, can assume such extraordinary honor and worship to himself, while the kingdom of Christ, our common king and lord, is hid to this world, and such gentilish imitation forbid in express words by himself to all his disciples. All Protestants hold that Christ in his church hath left no vicegerent[8] of his power; but himself, without deputy, is the only head thereof, governing it from heaven; how then can any Christian man derive his kingship from Christ, but with worse usurpation than the pope his headship over the church, since Christ not only hath not left the least shadow of a command for any such vicegerence from him in the state as the pope pretends for his in the church, but hath expressly declared that such regal dominion is from the gentiles, not from him, and hath strictly charged us not to imitate them therein.

I doubt not but all ingenuous and knowing men will easily agree with me that a free commonwealth without single person or house of lords is by far the best government, if it can be had; but we have

7. Without courage. "Admirable": astonishing.
8. Earthly representative.

all this while, say they, been expecting[9] it and cannot yet attain it. 'Tis true, indeed, when monarchy was dissolved, the form of a commonwealth should have forthwith been framed and the practice thereof immediately begun, that the people might have soon been satisfied and delighted with the decent order, ease, and benefit thereof; we had been then by this time firmly rooted, past fear of commotions or mutations, and now flourishing; this care of timely settling a new government instead of the old, too much neglected, hath been our mischief. Yet the cause thereof may be ascribed with most reason to the frequent disturbances, interruptions, and dissolutions, which the parliament hath had, partly from the impatient or disaffected people, partly from some ambitious leaders in the army;[1] much contrary, I believe, to the mind and approbation of the army itself and their other commanders, once undeceived or in their own power. Now is the opportunity, now the very season, wherein we may obtain a free commonwealth, and establish it for ever in the land, without difficulty or much delay. Writs[2] are sent out for elections, and, which is worth observing, in the name, not of any king, but of the keepers of our liberty, to summon a free parliament; which then only will indeed be free, and deserve the true honor of that supreme title, if they preserve us a free people. Which never parliament was more free to do, being now called not as heretofore, by the summons of a king, but by the voice of liberty. And if the people, laying aside prejudice and impatience, will seriously and calmly now consider their own good, both religious and civil, their own liberty and the only means thereof, as shall be here laid before them, and will elect their knights and burgesses able men, and according to the just and necessary qualifications[3] (which, for aught I hear, remain yet in force unrepealed, as they were formerly decreed in parliament), men not addicted to a single person or house of lords, the work is done; at least the foundation firmly laid of a free commonwealth, and good part also erected of the main structure. For the ground and basis of every just and free government (since men have smarted so oft for committing all to one person) is a general council of ablest men chosen by the people to consult of public affairs from time to time for the common good. In this grand council must the sovereignty, not transferred but delegated only, and as

9. Waiting for.
1. In 1653, Cromwell dissolved the Rump Parliament, the remnant in power since Pride's Purge (1648) that had most strenuously opposed the king. Between 1658 and 1660, the struggle between the army leaders and Parliament led to three dismissals of that body.
2. For election to the new parliament in the name of the "Keepers of the Liberties of England" went out on March 16, 1660.
3. Disabling provisions set forth by the restored Rump Parliament in January and February 1660, barring royalists and Roman Catholics; nullified in March. "Knights": representatives to Commons from counties and shires. "Burgesses": representatives from towns, boroughs, and the universities of Oxford and Cambridge.

it were deposited, reside; with this caution, they must have the
forces by sea and land committed to them for preservation of the
common peace and liberty; must raise and manage the public revenue, at least with some inspectors[4] deputed for satisfaction of the
people how it is employed; must make or propose, as more expressly
shall be said anon, civil laws, treat of commerce, peace or war with
foreign nations; and for the carrying on some particular affairs
with more secrecy and expedition, must elect, as they have already
out of their own number and others, a council of state.[5]

And although it may seem strange at first hearing, by reason that
men's minds are prepossessed with the notion of successive parliaments, I affirm that the grand or general council, being well chosen, should be perpetual, for so their business is or may be, and
ofttimes urgent, the opportunity of affairs gained or lost in a
moment. The day of council cannot be set as the day of a festival
but must be ready always to prevent[6] or answer all occasions. By
this continuance they will become every way skillfulest, best provided of intelligence from abroad, best acquainted with the people
at home, and the people with them. The ship of the commonwealth
is always under sail; they sit at the stern, and if they steer well, what
need is there to change them, it being rather dangerous? Add to this
that the grand council is both foundation and main pillar of the
whole state; and to move pillars and foundations not faulty cannot
be safe for the building. I see not therefore how we can be advantaged by successive and transitory parliaments; but that they are
much likelier continually to unsettle rather than to settle a free
government, to breed commotions, changes, novelties, and uncertainties, to bring neglect upon present affairs and opportunities,
while all minds are suspense[7] with expectation of a new assembly,
and the assembly for a good space taken up with the new settling of
itself. After which, if they find no great work to do, they will make
it, by altering or repealing former acts, or making and multiplying
new, that they may seem to see what their predecessors saw not,
and not to have assembled for nothing, till all law be lost in the
multitude of clashing statutes. But if the ambition of such as think
themselves injured that they also partake not of the government,
and are impatient till they be chosen, cannot brook the perpetuity
of others chosen before them; or if it be feared that long continuance of power may corrupt sincerest men, the known expedient is,
and by some lately propounded, that annually (or if the space be

4. Auditors. "Delegated": by the people.
5. A council of state of thirty-one, including ten from outside the House of Commons,
   had been set up three times between May 1659 and February 1660.
6. Anticipate.
7. In suspense, suspended.

longer, so much perhaps the better) the third part of senators may go out according to the precedence of their election, and the like number be chosen in their places, to prevent the settling of too absolute a power if it should be perpetual; and this they call *partial rotation*.[8] But I could wish that this wheel, or partial wheel in state, if it be possible, might be avoided, as having too much affinity with the wheel of Fortune. For it appears not how this can be done without danger and mischance of putting out a great number of the best and ablest, in whose stead new elections may bring in as many raw, unexperienced, and otherwise affected,[9] to the weakening and much altering for the worse of public transactions. Neither do I think a perpetual senate, especially chosen and entrusted by the people, much in this land to be feared, where the well-affected either in a standing army or in a settled militia have their arms in their own hands. Safest therefore to me it seems, and of least hazard or interruption to affairs, that none of the grand council be moved, unless by death or just conviction of some crime; for what can be expected firm or steadfast from a floating foundation? However, I forejudge not any probable expedient, any temperament[1] that can be found in things of this nature, so disputable on either side. Yet lest this which I affirm be thought my single opinion, I shall add sufficient testimony. Kingship itself is therefore counted the more safe and durable because the king, and for the most part his council, is not changed during life. But a commonwealth is held immortal, and therein firmest, safest, and most above fortune; for the death of a king causeth ofttimes many dangerous alterations, but the death now and then of a senator is not felt, the main body of them still continuing permanent in greatest and noblest commonwealths, and as it were eternal. Therefore among the Jews, the supreme council of seventy, called the *Sanhedrim*, founded by Moses, in Athens that of *Areopagus*, in Sparta that of the ancients,[2] in Rome the senate, consisted of members chosen for term of life and by that means remained as it were still the same to generations. In Venice they change indeed ofter than every year some particular council of state, as that of Six,[3] or such other: but the true senate, which upholds and sustains the government, is the whole

---

8. The republican theorist James Harrington, a member of the Rota Club (*rota*, "a wheel"), proposed this in *Oceana* (1656).
9. Disposed.
1. Consistence, mixture.
2. A council with thirty members, all of them over sixty years of age. "Sanhedrim": the supreme legislative and judicial assembly of the Jews, derived from the seventy elders appointed by Moses (Num. 11:16–17). Milton was familiar with John Selden's admiring and immense three-volume study, *De Synedriis* (1650–55). "Areopagus": the supreme court of Athens. (See notes to *Areopagitica*.)
3. The Council of Six assisted the Doge. Its members served terms no longer than a year, but the Grand Council was permanent.

aristocracy immoveable. So in the United Provinces, the states-general, which are indeed but a council of state deputed[4] by the whole union, are not usually the same persons for above three or six years; but the states of every city, in whom the sovereignty hath been placed time out of mind, are a standing senate, without succession, and accounted chiefly in that regard the main prop of their liberty. And why they should be so in every well-ordered commonwealth, they who write of policy give these reasons: "That to make the senate successive not only impairs the dignity and luster of the senate but weakens the whole commonwealth and brings it into manifest danger; while by this means the secrets of state are frequently divulged, and matters of greatest consequence committed to inexpert and novice counselors, utterly to seek in the full and intimate knowledge of affairs past."[5] I know not therefore what should be peculiar in England to make successive parliaments thought safest, or convenient here more than in other nations, unless it be the fickleness which is attributed to us as we are islanders. But good education and acquisite wisdom ought to correct the fluxible[6] fault, if any such be, of our watery situation. It will be objected that in those places where they had perpetual senates, they had also popular remedies against their growing too imperious: as in Athens, besides Areopagus, another senate of four or five hundred; in Sparta, the Ephori;[7] in Rome, the tribunes of the people. But the event tells us that these remedies either little availed the people, or brought them to such a licentious and unbridled democracy as in fine[8] ruined themselves with their own excessive power. So that the main reason urged why popular assemblies are to be trusted with the people's liberty rather than a senate of principal men, because great men will be still endeavoring to enlarge their power, but the common sort will be contented to maintain their own liberty, is by experience found false; none being more immoderate and ambitious to amplify their power than such popularities, which was seen in the people of Rome, who at first contented to have their tribunes, at length contended with the senate that one consul, then both, soon after that the censors and praetors also should be created plebeian and the whole empire put into their hands; adoring lastly those who most were adverse to the senate, till Marius,[9] by fulfill-

---

4. Delegated.
5. Milton is translating from Jean Bodin's *De Republica* (1576). "Policy": government. "To seek": lacking.
6. Fluid. "Acquisite": acquired.
7. Overseers, magistrates.
8. The end. "Event": outcome.
9. Gaius Marius (157–86 B.C.E.), general, tribune of the people, was elected consul an unprecedented seven times. But his struggles against the patrician general and dictator Sulla (138–78 B.C.E.) tore the Roman Republic to pieces. "Popularities": democracies. "Both": i.e., two annually elected magistrates in ancient Rome who exercised

ing their inordinate desires, quite lost them all the power for which they had so long been striving and left them under the tyranny of Sylla. The balance therefore must be exactly so set as to preserve and keep up due authority on either side, as well in the senate as in the people. And this annual rotation of a senate to consist of three hundred, as is lately propounded, requires also another popular assembly upward of a thousand, with an answerable[1] rotation. Which besides that it will be liable to all those inconveniencies found in the foresaid remedies, cannot but be troublesome and chargeable, both in their motion and their session, to the whole land, unwieldy with their own bulk, unable in so great a number to mature their consultations as they ought, if any be allotted them, and that they meet not from so many parts remote to sit a whole year lieger in one place, only now and then to hold up a forest of fingers, or to convey each man his bean or ballot into the box, without reason shown or common deliberation; incontinent of secrets, if any be imparted to them; emulous and always jarring with the other senate.[2] The much better way doubtless will be, in this wavering condition of our affairs, to defer the changing or circumscribing of our senate, more than may be done with ease, till the commonwealth be thoroughly settled in peace and safety, and they themselves give us the occasion. Military men hold it dangerous to change the form of battle in view of an enemy; neither did the people of Rome bandy with their senate while any of the Tarquins[3] lived, the enemies of their liberty; nor sought by creating tribunes to defend themselves against the fear of their patricians till, sixteen years after the expulsion of their kings and in full security of their state, they had or thought they had just cause given them by the senate. Another way will be to well qualify and refine elections: not committing all to the noise and shouting of a rude multitude, but permitting only those of them who are rightly qualified to nominate as many as they will, and out of that number others of a better breeding to choose a less number more judiciously, till after a third or fourth sifting and refining of exactest choice, they only be left chosen who are the due number and seem by most voices[4] the worthiest. To make the people fittest to choose, and the chosen fittest to govern, will be to mend our corrupt and faulty education, to

---

supreme power after the abolition of monarchy. "Censors": officials who drew up the census of the citizens and supervised public morals. "Praetors": judiciary officers, subordinate to consuls.
1. Corresponding. "Propounded": i.e., by Harrington.
2. The popular assembly, known as the Prerogative, with 1,050 members, could vote only silently for or against the proposals debated in the smaller senate. "Lieger": resident, stationary. "Session": meeting; "motion": travel. "Chargeable": expensive.
3. Legendary kings of Rome, whose banishment in 510 B.C.E. led to the establishment of the republic. "Bandy": contend.
4. Votes. When county elections were indecorous, the side with the loudest voices won.

teach the people faith, not without virtue, temperance, modesty, sobriety, parsimony, justice; not to admire wealth or honor; to hate turbulence and ambition; to place every one his private welfare and happiness in the public peace, liberty, and safety. They shall not then need to be much mistrustful of their chosen patriots in the grand council, who will be then rightly called the true keepers of our liberty, though the most of their business will be in foreign affairs. But to prevent all mistrust, the people then will have their several ordinary assemblies (which will henceforth quite annihilate the odious power and name of committees)[5] in the chief towns of every county, without the trouble, charge, or time lost of summoning and assembling from far in so great a number, and so long residing from their own houses, or removing of their families, to do as much at home in their several shires, entire or subdivided, toward the securing of their liberty, as a numerous assembly of them all formed and convened on purpose with the wariest rotation. Whereof I shall speak more ere the end of this discourse; for it may be referred to time, so we be still[6] going on by degrees to perfection. The people well weighing and performing these things, I suppose would have no cause to fear, though the parliament abolishing that name, as originally signifying but the parley of our lords and commons with the Norman king when he pleased to call them, should, with certain limitations of their power, sit perpetual, if their ends be faithful and for a free commonwealth, under the name of a grand or general council.[7] Till this be done, I am in doubt whether our state will be ever certainly and thoroughly settled; never likely till then to see an end of our troubles and continual changes, or at least never the true settlement and assurance of our liberty. The grand council being thus firmly constituted to perpetuity, and still, upon the death or default of any member, supplied and kept in full number, there can be no cause alleged why peace, justice, plentiful trade, and all prosperity should not thereupon ensue throughout the whole land; with as much assurance as can be of human things that they shall so continue (if God favor us, and our wilful sins provoke him not) even to the coming of our true and rightful and only to be expected king, only worthy as he is our only Savior, the Messiah, the Christ, the only heir of his eternal father, the only by him anointed and ordained since the work of our redemption finished, universal lord of all mankind. The way propounded is plain, easy, and open before us, without intricacies, without the introducement

---

5. Local governing bodies for enforcing policies of assessing and collecting revenues, susceptible of abuse and therefore odious to the people.
6. Always. "Referred": deferred.
7. Milton considers *parliament* to be a "French word, a monument of our ancient servitude," the Norman Conquest.

of new or obsolete forms or terms, or exotic models—ideas that would effect nothing, but with a number of new injunctions to manacle the native liberty of mankind, turning all virtue into prescription, servitude, and necessity, to the great impairing and frustrating of Christian liberty. I say again, this way lies free and smooth before us; is not tangled with inconveniencies; invents no new encumbrances; requires no perilous, no injurious alteration or circumscription of men's lands and proprieties; secure that in this commonwealth, temporal and spiritual lords removed,[8] no man or number of men can attain to such wealth or vast possession as will need the hedge of an agrarian law (never successful, but the cause rather of sedition, save only where it began seasonably[9] with first possession) to confine them from endangering our public liberty. To conclude, it can have no considerable[1] objection made against it that it is not practicable, lest it be said hereafter that we gave up our liberty for want of a ready way or distinct form proposed of a free commonwealth. And this facility we shall have above our next neighboring commonwealth (if we can keep us from the fond conceit of something like a duke of Venice, put lately into many men's heads by some one or other subtly driving on under that notion his own ambitious ends to lurch a crown) that our liberty shall not be hampered or hovered over by any engagement to such a potent family as the house of Nassau,[2] of whom to stand in perpetual doubt and suspicion, but we shall live the clearest and absolutest free nation in the world.

On the contrary, if there be a king, which the inconsiderate multitude are now so mad upon, mark how far short we are like to come of all those happinesses which in a free state we shall immediately be possessed of. First, the grand council, which, as I showed before, should sit perpetually (unless their leisure give them now and then some intermissions or vacations, easily manageable by the council of state left sitting), shall be called, by the king's good will and utmost endeavor, as seldom as may be. For it is only the king's right, he will say, to call a parliament; and this he will do most commonly about his own affairs rather than the kingdom's, as will appear plainly so soon as they are called. For what will their business then be, and the chief expense of their time, but an endless tugging between petition of right and royal prerogative, especially about the negative

---

8. No House of Lords, made up of nobles and bishops.
9. In a fitting time. "Agrarian law": proposed by Harrington in *Oceana* to keep landed estates from exceeding a given value, the law would abolish primogeniture and set limits on land accumulation.
1. Worth consideration.
2. I.e., The powerful House of Orange, here a symbol of single-person government. "Fond conceit": foolish idea. "Lurch": steal. "Crown": expressing concern about a rumored move to restore Richard Cromwell as protector on the analogy of the doge of Venice.

voice,[3] militia, or subsidies, demanded and oft-times extorted without reasonable cause appearing to the Commons, who are the only true representatives of the people and their liberty, but will be then mingled with a court faction; besides which, within their own walls, the sincere part of them who stand faithful to the people will again have to deal with two troublesome counter-working adversaries from without, mere creatures of the king, spiritual, and the greater part, as is likeliest, of temporal lords, nothing concerned with the people's liberty. If these prevail not in what they please, though never so much against the people's interest, the parliament shall be soon dissolved, or sit and do nothing; not suffered to remedy the least grievance or enact aught advantageous to the people. Next, the council of state shall not be chosen by the parliament but by the king, still his own creatures, courtiers, and favorites; who will be sure in all their counsels to set their master's grandeur and absolute power, in what they are able, far above the people's liberty. I deny not but that there may be such a king who may regard the common good before his own, may have no vicious favorite, may hearken only to the wisest and incorruptest of his parliament; but this rarely happens in a monarchy not elective; and it behooves not a wise nation to commit the sum of their well-being, the whole state of their safety, to fortune. What need they; and how absurd would it be, whenas they themselves, to whom his chief virtue will be but to hearken, may with much better management and dispatch, with much more commendation of their own worth and magnanimity, govern without a master? Can the folly be paralleled, to adore and be the slaves of a single person for doing that which it is ten thousand to one whether he can or will do, and we without him might do more easily, more effectually, more laudably ourselves? Shall we never grow old enough to be wise, to make seasonable use of gravest authorities, experiences, examples? Is it such an unspeakable joy to serve, such felicity to wear a yoke? to clink our shackles, locked on by pretended law of subjection, more intolerable and hopeless to be ever shaken off than those which are knocked on by illegal injury and violence? Aristotle, our chief instructor in the universities, lest this doctrine be thought sectarian, as the royalist would have it thought, tells us in the third of his *Politics*[4] that certain men at first, for the matchless excellence of their virtue above others, or some great public benefit, were created kings by the people, in small cities and territories, and in the scarcity of others to be found like them; but when they abused their power, and gov-

---

3. Royal veto over parliamentary bills.
4. *Politics*, 3.9.7, which attributes the beginnings of monarchy to the scarcity of people in earlier times who excelled in virtue. Republicanism emerged when more people of equal virtue arose.

ernments grew larger, and the number of prudent men increased, that then the people, soon deposing their tyrants, betook them, in all civilest places, to the form of a free commonwealth. And why should we thus disparage and prejudicate[5] our own nation as to fear a scarcity of able and worthy men united in counsel to govern us, if we will but use diligence and impartiality to find them out and choose them, rather yoking ourselves to a single person, the natural adversary and oppressor of liberty; though good, yet far easier corruptible by the excess of his singular power and exaltation, or at best, not comparably sufficient to bear the weight of government, nor equally disposed to make us happy in the enjoyment of our liberty under him?

But admit that monarchy of itself may be convenient to some nations; yet to us who have thrown it out, received back again, it cannot but prove pernicious. For kings to come, never forgetting their former ejection, will be sure to fortify and arm themselves sufficiently for the future against all such attempts hereafter from the people, who shall be then so narrowly watched and kept so low that though they would never so fain, and at the same rate of their blood and treasure,[6] they never shall be able to regain what they now have purchased and may enjoy or to free themselves from any yoke imposed upon them. Nor will they dare to go about it, utterly disheartened for the future, if these their highest attempts prove unsuccessful; which will be the triumph of all tyrants hereafter over any people that shall resist oppression; and their song will then be to others, How sped the rebellious English? to our posterity, How sped the rebels your fathers? This is not my conjecture, but drawn from God's known denouncement against the gentilizing Israelites, who, though they were governed in a commonwealth of God's own ordaining, he only their king, they his peculiar people, yet affecting rather to resemble heathen, but pretending the misgovernment of Samuel's sons, no more a reason to dislike their commonwealth than the violence of Eli's sons was imputable to that priesthood or religion,[7] clamored for a king. They had their longing, but with this testimony of God's wrath: *Ye shall cry out in that day, because of your king whom ye shall have chosen, and the Lord will not hear you in that day* [1 Samuel: 8:18]. Us if he shall hear now, how much less will he hear when we cry hereafter, who once delivered by him from a king, and not without wondrous acts

5. Judge beforehand.
6. Even if they were willing to sacrifice as much blood and money to regain their liberty as they did to attain it.
7. 1 Sam. 2:12: "Now the sons of Eli were the sons of Belial; they knew not the Lord." "Gentilizing": asking to be ruled by a king like the surrounding pagan [gentile] nations (1 Sam. 8:19–20). "Peculiar": special.

of his providence, insensible and unworthy of those high mercies, are returning precipitantly, if he withhold us not, back to the captivity from whence he freed us. Yet neither shall we obtain or buy at an easy rate this new gilded yoke which thus transports us: a new royal revenue must be found, a new episcopal, for those are individual: both which being wholly dissipated, or bought by private persons, or assigned for service done, and especially to the army, cannot be recovered without a general detriment and confusion to men's estates,[8] or a heavy imposition on all men's purses; benefit to none but to the worst and ignoblest sort of men, whose hope is to be either the ministers of court riot and excess or the gainers by it. But not to speak more of losses and extraordinary levies on our estates, what will then be the revenges and offenses remembered and returned, not only by the chief person but by all his adherents: accounts and reparations that will be required, suits, indictments, inquiries, discoveries, complaints, informations, who knows against whom or how many, though perhaps neuters,[9] if not to utmost infliction, yet to imprisonment, fines, banishment, or molestation. If not these, yet disfavor, discountenance, disregard, and contempt on all but the known royalist or whom he favors will be plenteous. Nor let the new royalized Presbyterians persuade themselves that their old doings, though now recanted, will be forgotten,[1] whatever conditions be contrived or trusted on. Will they not believe this nor remember the pacification, how it was kept to the Scots;[2] how other solemn promises many a time to us? Let them but now read the diabolical forerunning libels, the faces, the gestures that now appear foremost and briskest in all public places as the harbingers of those that are in expectation to reign over us; let them but hear the insolencies, the menaces, the insultings of our newly animated common enemies crept lately out of their holes, their hell I might say, by the language of their infernal pamphlets, the spew of every drunkard, every ribald; nameless, yet not for want of license,[3] but for very shame of their own vile persons, not daring to name themselves, while they traduce others by name; and give us to foresee that they intend to second their wicked words, if ever they have power, with more wicked deeds. Let our zealous backsliders forethink now with

---

8. Land formerly owned by the king and the bishops, assigned during the interregnum to commonwealth supporters, would have to be relinquished at the Restoration. "Individual": indivisible.
9. Remaining neutral.
1. Despite their opposition to the execution of Charles I and their efforts to bring Charles II to the throne, the Presbyterians were still privately denounced by royalists for their earlier support of the rebellion and the commonwealth.
2. According to the terms of the Pacification of Berwick in June 1639, Charles promised the Scots autonomy in regulating civil and church affairs, but he broke his promise less than three months later.
3. Permission to publish; dissoluteness.

themselves how their necks yoked with these tigers of Bacchus, these new fanatics of not the preaching but the sweating tub,[4] inspired with nothing holier than the venereal pox, can draw one way under monarchy to the establishing of church discipline with these new disgorged atheisms. Yet shall they not have the honour to yoke with these, but shall be yoked under them; these shall plough[5] on their backs. And do they among them who are so forward to bring in the single person think to be by him trusted or long regarded? So trusted they shall be and so regarded as by kings are wont reconciled enemies; neglected, and soon after discarded, if not prosecuted for old traitors; the first inciters, beginners, and more than to the third part actors[6] of all that followed. It will be found also that there must be then, as necessarily as now (for the contrary part will be still feared), a standing army; which for certain shall not be this, but of the fiercest cavaliers, of no less expense, and perhaps again under Rupert.[7] But let this army be sure they shall be soon disbanded, and likeliest without arrear or pay; and being disbanded, not be sure but they may as soon be questioned for being in arms against their king. The same let them fear who have contributed money, which will amount to no small number, that must then take their turn to be made delinquents and compounders.[8] They who past reason and recovery are devoted to kingship perhaps will answer that a greater part by far of the nation will have it so, the rest therefore must yield. Not so much to convince these, which I little hope, as to confirm them who yield not, I reply that this greatest part have both in reason and the trial of just battle lost the right of their election what the government shall be;[9] of them who have not lost that right, whether they for kingship be the greater number, who can certainly determine? Suppose they be, yet of freedom they partake all alike, one main end of government; which if the greater part value not, but will degenerately forgo, is it just or reasonable that most voices against the main end of government should enslave the less number that would be free? More just it is, doubtless, if it come to force, that a less number compel a greater to retain, which can be no wrong to them, their liberty, than that a greater number, for the pleasure of their baseness, compel a less most injuriously to be their fellow slaves. They who seek nothing

4. Makeshift pulpit for street preachers; tub used in treating venereal diseases. Bacchus, the god of wine, was often depicted riding in a chariot drawn by tigers.
5. Tear up, whip.
6. Actors beyond the third act of a five-act drama.
7. Prince Rupert of Bohemia, grandson of James I of England, led the army of his uncle, Charles I, from 1642 until the close of the first civil war in 1646. At the Restoration he became a member of the king's privy council.
8. Delinquent royalists could redeem (compound) their estates by paying a sum of money set by Parliament.
9. Royalist supporters, as defeated enemies, have lost the right to vote.

but their own just liberty have always right to win it and to keep it
whenever they have power, be the voices never so numerous that
oppose it. And how much we above others are concerned to defend
it from kingship, and from them who in pursuance thereof so per-
niciously would betray us and themselves to most certain misery
and thraldom, will be needless to repeat.

Having thus far shown with what ease we may now obtain a free
commonwealth, and by it with as much ease all the freedom, peace,
justice, plenty that we can desire; on the other side, the difficulties, troubles, uncertainties, nay rather impossibilities, to enjoy these
things constantly under a monarch; I will now proceed to show
more particularly wherein our freedom and flourishing condition
will be more ample and secure to us under a free commonwealth
than under kingship.

The whole freedom of man consists either in spiritual or civil
liberty. As for spiritual, who can be at rest, who can enjoy anything
in this world with contentment, who hath not liberty to serve God
and to save his own soul according to the best light which God hath
planted in him to that purpose, by the reading of his revealed will
and the guidance of his holy spirit? That this is best pleasing to
God, and that the whole Protestant church allows no supreme
judge or rule in matters of religion but the Scriptures, and these to
be interpreted by the Scriptures themselves, which necessarily
infers liberty of conscience, I have heretofore proved at large in
another treatise;[1] and might yet further by the public declarations,
confessions, and admonitions of whole churches and states, obvious in all histories since the Reformation.

This liberty of conscience, which above all other things ought to
be to all men dearest and most precious, no government more inclinable not to favor only but to protect than a free commonwealth, as
being most magnanimous, most fearless and confident of its own
fair proceedings. Whereas kingship, though looking big, yet indeed
most pusillanimous, full of fears, full of jealousies, startled at every
umbrage,[2] as it hath been observed of old to have ever suspected
most and mistrusted them who were in most esteem for virtue and
generosity of mind, so it is now known to have most in doubt and
suspicion them who are most reputed to be religious. Queen Elizabeth, though herself accounted so good a Protestant, so moderate,
so confident of her subjects' love, would never give way so much as
to Presbyterian reformation in this land, though once and again
besought, as Camden[3] relates; but imprisoned and persecuted the

---

1. *A Treatise of Civil Power in Ecclesiastical Causes* (February 1659). "Infers": implies.
2. Shadow.
3. According to William Camden (1551–1623), in his *Annales* of the reign of Elizabeth,
   her counselors warned her that sedition would result from the alteration of church
   policy.

very proposers thereof, alleging it as her mind and maxim unalterable that such reformation would diminish regal authority. What liberty of conscience can we then expect of others far worse principled from the cradle, trained up and governed by Popish and Spanish counsels, and on such depending hitherto for subsistence? Especially what can this last parliament expect, who having revived lately and published the covenant,[4] have re-engaged themselves never to readmit episcopacy? Which no son of Charles returning but will most certainly bring back with him, if he regard the last and strictest charge of his father, *to persevere in, not the doctrine only, but government of the Church of England, not to neglect the speedy and effectual suppressing of errors and schisms*; among which he accounted Presbytery one of the chief. Or if, notwithstanding that charge of his father, he submit to the covenant, how will he keep faith to us with disobedience to him, or regard that faith given[5] which must be founded on the breach of that last and solemnest paternal charge and the reluctance, I may say the antipathy, which is in all kings against Presbyterian and Independent discipline? For they hear the gospel speaking much of liberty, a word which monarchy and her bishops both fear and hate but a free commonwealth both favors and promotes—and not the word only but the thing itself. But let our governors beware in time, lest their hard measure to liberty of conscience be found the rock whereon they shipwreck themselves, as others have now done before them in the course wherein God was directing their steerage to a free commonwealth; and the abandoning of all those whom they call sectaries, for the detected falsehood and ambition of some, be a wilful rejection of their own chief strength and interest in the freedom of all Protestant religion, under what abusive name soever calumniated.

The other part of our freedom consists in the civil rights and advancements of every person according to his merit: the enjoyment of those never more certain, and the access to these never more open, than in a free commonwealth. Both which, in my opinion, may be best and soonest obtained if every county in the land were made a kind of subordinate commonalty or commonwealth, and one chief town or more, according as the shire is in circuit,[6] made cities, if they be not so called already; where the nobility and chief gentry, from a proportionable compass of territory annexed to each city, may build houses or palaces befitting their quality; may bear part in the government, make their own judicial laws, or use these that are, and execute them by their own elected judicatures and judges without appeal, in all things of civil government between man and man.

---

4. In March 1660, the restored Long Parliament republished the Solemn League and Covenant with the Scots (1643), with its Presbyterian agenda.
5. As given.
6. According to size.

So they shall have justice in their own hands, law executed fully and finally in their own counties and precincts, long wished and spoken of, but never yet obtained. They shall have none then to blame but themselves if it be not well administered; and fewer laws to expect or fear from the supreme authority; or to those that shall be made of any great concernment to public liberty, they may, without much trouble in these commonalties, or in more general assemblies called to their cities from the whole territory on such occasion, declare and publish their assent or dissent by deputies within a time limited sent to the grand council; yet so as this their judgment declared shall submit to the greater number of other counties or commonalties, and not avail them to any exemption of themselves or refusal of agreement with the rest, as it may in any of the United Provinces,[7] being sovereign within itself, ofttimes to the great disadvantage of that union. In these employments they may, much better than they do now, exercise and fit themselves till their lot fall to be chosen into the grand council, according as their worth and merit shall be taken notice of by the people. As for controversies that shall happen between men of several counties, they may repair, as they do now, to the capital city, or any other more commodious, indifferent place, and equal[8] judges. And this I find to have been practiced in the old Athenian commonwealth, reputed the first and ancientest place of civility in all Greece: that they had in their several cities a peculiar,[9] in Athens a common government, and their right, as it befell them, to the administration of both. They should have here also schools and academies at their own choice, wherein their children may be bred up in their own sight to all learning and noble education, not in grammar only but in all liberal arts and exercises. This would soon spread much more knowledge and civility, yea, religion, through all parts of the land, by communicating the natural heat of government and culture more distributively to all extreme parts, which now lie numb and neglected; would soon make the whole nation more industrious, more ingenuous[1] at home, more potent, more honorable abroad. To this a free commonwealth may easily assent (nay, the parliament hath had already some such thing in design); for of all governments a commonwealth aims most to make the people flourishing, virtuous, noble, and high-spirited. Monarchs will never permit; whose aim is to make the people wealthy indeed perhaps and well fleeced, for their own shearing and the supply of regal prodigality; but otherwise softest, basest, viciousest, servilest, easiest to be kept under—and not only in fleece,

---

7. The lack of centralized power in The Netherlands sometimes led to deadlock.
8. Equitable, fair. "Indifferent": impartial.
9. Individual, distinctive.
1. Noble, generous.

but in mind also sheepishest; and will have all the benches of judicature annexed to the throne, as a gift of royal grace that we have
justice done us, whenas nothing can be more essential to the freedom of a people than to have the administration of justice and all
public ornaments[2] in their own election, and within their own
bounds, without long traveling or depending upon remote places to
obtain their right or any civil accomplishment; so it be not supreme,
but subordinate to the general power and union of the whole republic. In which happy firmness, as in the particular above mentioned,
we shall also far exceed the United Provinces, by having not as they
(to the retarding and distracting ofttimes of their counsels on
urgentest occasions) many sovereignties united in one commonwealth, but many commonwealths under one united and intrusted
sovereignty. And when we have our forces by sea and land either of a
faithful army or a settled militia in our own hands, to the firm establishing of a free commonwealth, public accounts under our own
inspection, general laws and taxes with their causes in our own
domestic suffrages,[3] judicial laws, offices and ornaments at home
in our own ordering and administration, all distinction of lords and
commoners that may any way divide or sever the public interest
removed; what can a perpetual senate have then wherein to grow
corrupt, wherein to encroach upon us or usurp? Or if they do,
wherein to be formidable? Yet if all this avail not to remove the fear
or envy[4] of a perpetual sitting, it may be easily provided to change a
third part of them yearly, or every two or three years, as was above
mentioned; or that it be at those times in the people's choice whether
they will change them or renew their power, as they shall find cause.

I have no more to say at present: few words will save us, well considered; few and easy things, now seasonably done. But if the people be so affected as to prostitute religion and liberty to the vain
and groundless apprehension that nothing but kingship can restore
trade, not remembering the frequent plagues and pestilences that
then wasted this city,[5] such as through God's mercy we never have
felt since; and that trade flourishes nowhere more than in the free
commonwealths of Italy, Germany, and the Low Countries before
their eyes at this day; yet if trade be grown so craving and importunate through the profuse living of tradesmen that nothing can
support it but the luxurious expenses of a nation upon trifles or
superfluities; so as if the people generally should betake themselves
to frugality, it might prove a dangerous matter, lest tradesmen should
mutiny for want of trading; and that therefore we must forgo and

2. Trappings.
3. Consent.
4. Ill-will.
5. The last major outbreak of plague was in 1625.

set to sale religion, liberty, honor, safety, all concernments divine
or human, to keep up trading: if, lastly, after all this light among us,
the same reason shall pass for current to put our necks again under
kingship as was made use of by the Jews[6] to return back to Egypt
and to the worship of their idol queen because they falsely imagined that they then lived in more plenty and prosperity, our condition is not sound but rotten, both in religion and all civil prudence,
and will bring us soon, the way we are marching, to those calamities which attend always and unavoidably on luxury, all national
judgments under foreign or domestic slavery. So far we shall be from
mending our condition by monarchizing our government, whatever
new conceit[7] now possesses us. However, with all hazard I have
ventured what I thought my duty to speak in season, and to forewarn my country in time; wherein I doubt not but there be many
wise men in all places and degrees, but am sorry the effects of wisdom are so little seen among us. Many circumstances and particulars I could have added in those things whereof I have spoken, but
a few main matters now put speedily in execution will suffice to
recover us and set all right; and there will want at no time who are
good at circumstances;[8] but men who set their minds on main
matters and sufficiently urge them, in these most difficult times I
find not many. What I have spoken is the language of that which is
not called amiss *the good old cause*; if it seem strange to any, it will
not seem more strange, I hope, than convincing to backsliders.
Thus much I should perhaps have said though I were sure I should
have spoken only to trees and stones, and had none to cry to, but
with the prophet, O *earth, earth, earth!*[9] to tell the very soil itself
what her perverse inhabitants are deaf to. Nay, though what I have
spoke should happen (which Thou suffer not, who didst create
mankind free; nor Thou next, who didst redeem us from being
servants of men!) to be the last words of our expiring liberty. But I
trust I shall have spoken persuasion to abundance of sensible and
ingenuous men—to some, perhaps, whom God may raise of these
stones to become children of reviving liberty; and may reclaim,
though they seem now choosing them a captain back for Egypt,[1] to
bethink themselves a little and consider whither they are rushing;
to exhort this torrent also of the people not to be so impetuous but
to keep their due channel; and at length recovering and uniting

6. In Num. 11:5–6, the wandering Israelites, tired of their diet of manna, long for the
   delicacies of Egypt.
7. Idea.
8. Subordinate details.
9. Jer. 22:29: "O earth, earth, earth, hear the word of the Lord."
1. The backsliding Israelites, fearful of the Canaanite tribes they have been commanded
   to conquer, ask for a captain to return them to Egyptian slavery (Num. 14:4).

their better resolutions, now that they see already how open and unbounded the insolence and rage is of our common enemies, to stay[2] these ruinous proceedings, justly and timely fearing to what a precipice of destruction the deluge of this epidemic madness would hurry us, through the general defection of a misguided and abused multitude.

2. Refrain from.

BIBLICAL SOURCES

Judges[†]

13

1: And the children of Israel did evil again in the sight of the LORD; and the LORD delivered them into the hand of the Philistines forty years.

2: And there was a certain man of Zorah, of the family of the Danites, whose name was Manoah; and his wife was barren, and bare not.

3: And the angel of the Lord appeared unto the woman, and said unto her, Behold now, thou art barren, and bearest not: but thou shalt conceive, and bear a son.

4: Now therefore beware, I pray thee, and drink not wine nor strong drink, and eat not any unclean thing:

5: For, lo, thou shalt conceive, and bear a son; and no razor shall come on his head: for the child shall be a Nazarite unto God from the womb: and he shall begin to deliver Israel out of the hand of the Philistines.

6: Then the woman came and told her husband, saying, A man of God came unto me, and his countenance was like the countenance of an angel of God, very terrible: but I asked him not whence he was, neither told he me his name:

7: But he said unto me, Behold, thou shalt conceive, and bear a son; and now drink no wine nor strong drink, neither eat any unclean thing: for the child shall be a Nazarite to God from the womb to the day of his death.

8: Then Manoah intreated the Lord, and said, O my Lord, let the man of God which thou didst send come again unto us, and teach us what we shall do unto the child that shall be born.

9: And God hearkened to the voice of Manoah; and the angel of God came again unto the woman as she sat in the field: but Manoah her husband was not with her.

10: And the woman made haste, and ran, and shewed her husband, and said unto him, Behold, the man hath appeared unto me, that came unto me the other day.

11: And Manoah arose, and went after his wife, and came to the man, and said unto him, Art thou the man that spakest unto the woman? And he said, I am.

12: And Manoah said, Now let thy words come to pass. How shall we order the child, and how shall we do unto him?

13: And the angel of the Lord said unto Manoah, Of all that I said unto the woman let her beware.

† The source of *Samson Agonistes*. From the King James Bible.

14: She may not eat of any thing that cometh of the vine, neither let her drink wine or strong drink, nor eat any unclean thing: all that I commanded her let her observe.

15: And Manoah said unto the angel of the Lord, I pray thee, let us detain thee, until we shall have made ready a kid for thee.

16: And the angel of the Lord said unto Manoah, Though thou detain me, I will not eat of thy bread: and if thou wilt offer a burnt offering, thou must offer it unto the Lord. For Manoah knew not that he was an angel of the Lord.

17: And Manoah said unto the angel of the Lord, What is thy name, that when thy sayings come to pass we may do thee honour?

18: And the angel of the Lord said unto him, Why askest thou thus after my name, seeing it is secret?

19: So Manoah took a kid with a meat offering, and offered it upon a rock unto the Lord: and the angel did wondrously; and Manoah and his wife looked on.

20: For it came to pass, when the flame went up toward heaven from off the altar, that the angel of the Lord ascended in the flame of the altar. And Manoah and his wife looked on it, and fell on their faces to the ground.

21: But the angel of the Lord did no more appear to Manoah and to his wife. Then Manoah knew that he was an angel of the Lord.

22: And Manoah said unto his wife, We shall surely die, because we have seen God.

23: But his wife said unto him, If the Lord were pleased to kill us, he would not have received a burnt offering and a meat offering at our hands, neither would he have shewed us all these things, nor would as at this time have told us such things as these.

24: And the woman bare a son, and called his name Samson: and the child grew, and the Lord blessed him.

25: And the Spirit of the Lord began to move him at times in the camp of Dan between Zorah and Eshtaol.

14

1: And Samson went down to Timnath, and saw a woman in Timnath of the daughters of the Philistines.

2: And he came up, and told his father and his mother, and said, I have seen a woman in Timnath of the daughters of the Philistines: now therefore get her for me to wife.

3: Then his father and his mother said unto him, Is there never a woman among the daughters of thy brethren, or among all my people, that thou goest to take a wife of the uncircumcised Philistines? And Samson said unto his father, Get her for me; for she pleaseth me well.

4: But his father and his mother knew not that it was of the Lord, that he sought an occasion against the Philistines: for at that time the Philistines had dominion over Israel.

5: Then went Samson down, and his father and his mother, to Timnath, and came to the vineyards of Timnath: and, behold, a young lion roared against him.

6: And the Spirit of the Lord came mightily upon him, and he rent him as he would have rent a kid, and he had nothing in his hand: but he told not his father or his mother what he had done.

7: And he went down, and talked with the woman; and she pleased Samson well.

8: And after a time he returned to take her, and he turned aside to see the carcase of the lion: and, behold, there was a swarm of bees and honey in the carcase of the lion.

9: And he took thereof in his hands, and went on eating, and came to his father and mother, and he gave them, and they did eat: but he told not them that he had taken the honey out of the carcase of the lion.

10: So his father went down unto the woman: and Samson made there a feast; for so used the young men to do.

11: And it came to pass, when they saw him, that they brought thirty companions to be with him.

12: And Samson said unto them, I will now put forth a riddle unto you: if ye can certainly declare it me within the seven days of the feast, and find it out, then I will give you thirty sheets and thirty change of garments:

13: But if ye cannot declare it me, then shall ye give me thirty sheets and thirty change of garments. And they said unto him, Put forth thy riddle, that we may hear it.

14: And he said unto them, Out of the eater came forth meat, and out of the strong came forth sweetness. And they could not in three days expound the riddle.

15: And it came to pass on the seventh day, that they said unto Samson's wife, Entice thy husband, that he may declare unto us the riddle, lest we burn thee and thy father's house with fire: have ye called us to take that we have? is it not so?

16: And Samson's wife wept before him, and said, Thou dost but hate me, and lovest me not: thou hast put forth a riddle unto the children of my people, and hast not told it me. And he said unto her, Behold, I have not told it my father nor my mother, and shall I tell it thee?

17: And she wept before him the seven days, while their feast lasted: and it came to pass on the seventh day, that he told her, because she lay sore upon him: and she told the riddle to the children of her people.

18: And the men of the city said unto him on the seventh day before the sun went down, What is sweeter than honey? and what is stronger than a lion? And he said unto them, If ye had not plowed with my heifer, ye had not found out my riddle.

19: And the Spirit of the Lord came upon him, and he went down to Ashkelon, and slew thirty men of them, and took their spoil, and gave change of garments unto them which expounded the riddle. And his anger was kindled, and he went up to his father's house.

20: But Samson's wife was given to his companion, whom he had used as his friend.

15

1: But it came to pass within a while after, in the time of wheat harvest, that Samson visited his wife with a kid; and he said, I will go in to my wife into the chamber. But her father would not suffer him to go in.

2: And her father said, I verily thought that thou hadst utterly hated her; therefore I gave her to thy companion: is not her younger sister fairer than she? take her, I pray thee, instead of her.

3: And Samson said concerning them, Now shall I be more blameless than the Philistines, though I do them a displeasure.

4: And Samson went and caught three hundred foxes, and took firebrands, and turned tail to tail, and put a firebrand in the midst between two tails.

5: And when he had set the brands on fire, he let them go into the standing corn of the Philistines, and burnt up both the shocks, and also the standing corn, with the vineyards and olives.

6: Then the Philistines said, Who hath done this? And they answered, Samson, the son in law of the Timnite, because he had taken his wife, and given her to his companion. And the Philistines came up, and burnt her and her father with fire.

7: And Samson said unto them, Though ye have done this, yet will I be avenged of you, and after that I will cease.

8: And he smote them hip and thigh with a great slaughter: and he went down and dwelt in the top of the rock Etam.

9: Then the Philistines went up, and pitched in Judah, and spread themselves in Lehi.

10: And the men of Judah said, Why are ye come up against us? And they answered, To bind Samson are we come up, to do to him as he hath done to us.

11: Then three thousand men of Judah went to the top of the rock Etam, and said to Samson, Knowest thou not that the Philistines are rulers over us? what is this that thou hast done unto us? And he said unto them, As they did unto me, so have I done unto them.

12: And they said unto him, We are come down to bind thee, that we may deliver thee into the hand of the Philistines. And Samson said unto them, Swear unto me, that ye will not fall upon me yourselves.

13: And they spake unto him, saying, No; but we will bind thee fast, and deliver thee into their hand: but surely we will not kill thee. And they bound him with two new cords, and brought him up from the rock.

14: And when he came unto Lehi, the Philistines shouted against him: and the Spirit of the LORD came mightily upon him, and the cords that were upon his arms became as flax that was burnt with fire, and his bands loosed from off his hands.

15: And he found a new jawbone of an ass, and put forth his hand, and took it, and slew a thousand men therewith.

16: And Samson said, With the jawbone of an ass, heaps upon heaps, with the jaw of an ass have I slain a thousand men.

17: And it came to pass, when he had made an end of speaking, that he cast away the jawbone out of his hand, and called that place Ramath-lehi.

18: And he was sore athirst, and called on the Lord, and said, Thou hast given this great deliverance into the hand of thy servant: and now shall I die for thirst, and fall into the hand of the uncircumcised?

19: But God clave an hollow place that was in the jaw, and there came water thereout; and when he had drunk, his spirit came again, and he revived: wherefore he called the name thereof En-hakkore, which is in Lehi unto this day.

20: And he judged Israel in the days of the Philistines twenty years.

16

1: Then went Samson to Gaza, and saw there an harlot, and went in unto her.

2: And it was told the Gazites, saying, Samson is come hither. And they compassed him in, and laid wait for him all night in the gate of the city, and were quiet all the night, saying, In the morning, when it is day, we shall kill him.

3: And Samson lay till midnight, and arose at midnight, and took the doors of the gate of the city, and the two posts, and went away with them, bar and all, and put them upon his shoulders, and carried them up to the top of an hill that is before Hebron.

4: And it came to pass afterward, that he loved a woman in the valley of Sorek, whose name was Delilah.

5: And the lords of the Philistines came up unto her, and said unto her, Entice him, and see wherein his great strength lieth, and by what means we may prevail against him, that we may bind him to afflict him: and we will give thee every one of us eleven hundred pieces of silver.

6: And Delilah said to Samson, Tell me, I pray thee, wherein thy great strength lieth, and wherewith thou mightest be bound to afflict thee.

7: And Samson said unto her, If they bind me with seven green withs that were never dried, then shall I be weak, and be as another man.

8: Then the lords of the Philistines brought up to her seven green withs which had not been dried, and she bound him with them.

9: Now there were men lying in wait, abiding with her in the chamber. And she said unto him, The Philistines be upon thee, Samson. And he brake the withs, as a thread of tow is broken when it toucheth the fire. So his strength was not known.

10: And Delilah said unto Samson, Behold, thou hast mocked me, and told me lies: now tell me, I pray thee, wherewith thou mightest be bound.

11: And he said unto her, If they bind me fast with new ropes that never were occupied, then shall I be weak, and be as another man.

12: Delilah therefore took new ropes, and bound him therewith, and said unto him, The Philistines be upon thee, Samson. And there were liers in wait abiding in the chamber. And he brake them from off his arms like a thread.

13: And Delilah said unto Samson, Hitherto thou hast mocked me, and told me lies: tell me wherewith thou mightest be bound. And he said unto her, If thou weavest the seven locks of my head with the web.

14: And she fastened it with the pin, and said unto him, The Philistines be upon thee, Samson. And he awaked out of his sleep, and went away with the pin of the beam, and with the web.

15: And she said unto him, How canst thou say, I love thee, when thine heart is not with me? thou hast mocked me these three times, and hast not told me wherein thy great strength lieth.

16: And it came to pass, when she pressed him daily with her words, and urged him, so that his soul was vexed unto death;

17: That he told her all his heart, and said unto her, There hath not come a razor upon mine head; for I have been a Nazarite unto God from my mother's womb: if I be shaven, then my strength will go from me, and I shall become weak, and be like any other man.

18: And when Delilah saw that he had told her all his heart, she sent and called for the lords of the Philistines, saying, Come up this once, for he hath shewed me all his heart. Then the lords of the Philistines came up unto her, and brought money in their hand.

19: And she made him sleep upon her knees; and she called for a man, and she caused him to shave off the seven locks of his head; and she began to afflict him, and his strength went from him.

20: And she said, The Philistines be upon thee, Samson. And he awoke out of his sleep, and said, I will go out as at other times before, and shake myself. And he wist not that the Lord was departed from him.

21: But the Philistines took him, and put out his eyes, and brought him down to Gaza, and bound him with fetters of brass; and he did grind in the prison house.

22: Howbeit the hair of his head began to grow again after he was shaven.

23: Then the lords of the Philistines gathered them together for to offer a great sacrifice unto Dagon their god, and to rejoice: for they said, Our god hath delivered Samson our enemy into our hand.

24: And when the people saw him, they praised their god: for they said, Our god hath delivered into our hands our enemy, and the destroyer of our country, which slew many of us.

25: And it came to pass, when their hearts were merry, that they said, Call for Samson, that he may make us sport. And they called for Samson out of the prison house; and he made them sport: and they set him between the pillars.

26: And Samson said unto the lad that held him by the hand, Suffer me that I may feel the pillars whereupon the house standeth, that I may lean upon them.

27: Now the house was full of men and women; and all the lords of the Philistines were there; and there were upon the roof about three thousand men and women, that beheld while Samson made sport.

28: And Samson called unto the Lord, and said, O Lord God, remember me, I pray thee, and strengthen me, I pray thee, only this once, O God, that I may be at once avenged of the Philistines for my two eyes.

29: And Samson took hold of the two middle pillars upon which the house stood, and on which it was borne up, of the one with his right hand, and of the other with his left.

30: And Samson said, Let me die with the Philistines. And he bowed himself with all his might; and the house fell upon the lords, and upon all the people that were therein. So the dead which he slew at his death were more than they which he slew in his life.

31: Then his brethren and all the house of his father came down, and took him, and brought him up, and buried him between Zorah and Eshtaol in the burying place of Manoah his father. And he judged Israel twenty years.

Psalms[†]

6

1: O Lord, rebuke me not in thine anger, neither chasten me in thy hot displeasure.

2: Have mercy upon me, O Lord; for I am weak: O Lord, heal me; for my bones are vexed.

3: My soul is also sore vexed: but thou, O Lord, how long?

4: Return, O Lord, deliver my soul: oh save me for thy mercies' sake.

5: For in death there is no remembrance of thee: in the grave who shall give thee thanks?

6: I am weary with my groaning; all the night make I my bed to swim; I water my couch with my tears.

7: Mine eye is consumed because of grief; it waxeth old because of all mine enemies.

8: Depart from me, all ye workers of iniquity; for the Lord hath heard the voice of my weeping.

9: The Lord hath heard my supplication; the Lord will receive my prayer.

10: Let all mine enemies be ashamed and sore vexed: let them return and be ashamed suddenly.

114

1: When Israel went out of Egypt, the house of Jacob from a people of strange language;

2: Judah was his sanctuary, and Israel his dominion.

3: The sea saw it, and fled: Jordan was driven back.

4: The mountains skipped like rams, and the little hills like lambs.

5: What ailed thee, O thou sea, that thou fleddest? thou Jordan, that thou wast driven back?

6: Ye mountains, that ye skipped like rams; and ye little hills, like lambs?

7: Tremble, thou earth, at the presence of the Lord, at the presence of the God of Jacob;

8: Which turned the rock into a standing water, the flint into a fountain of waters.

---

† Cf. with Milton's Psalm paraphrases.

Matthew[†]

From 20

LABORERS IN THE VINEYARD

1: For the kingdom of heaven is like unto a man that is an householder, which went out early in the morning to hire labourers into his vineyard.

2: And when he had agreed with the labourers for a penny a day, he sent them into his vineyard.

3: And he went out about the third hour, and saw others standing idle in the marketplace,

4: And said unto them; Go ye also into the vineyard, and whatsoever is right I will give you. And they went their way.

5: Again he went out about the sixth and ninth hour, and did likewise.

6: And about the eleventh hour he went out, and found others standing idle, and saith unto them, Why stand ye here all the day idle?

7: They say unto him, Because no man hath hired us. He saith unto them, Go ye also into the vineyard; and whatsoever is right, that shall ye receive.

8: So when even was come, the lord of the vineyard saith unto his steward, Call the labourers, and give them their hire, beginning from the last unto the first.

9: And when they came that were hired about the eleventh hour, they received every man a penny.

10: But when the first came, they supposed that they should have received more; and they likewise received every man a penny.

11: And when they had received it, they murmured against the goodman of the house,

12: Saying, These last have wrought but one hour, and thou hast made them equal unto us, which have borne the burden and heat of the day.

13: But he answered one of them, and said, Friend, I do thee no wrong: didst not thou agree with me for a penny?

14: Take that thine is, and go thy way: I will give unto this last, even as unto thee.

15: Is it not lawful for me to do what I will with mine own? Is thine eye evil, because I am good?

16: So the last shall be first, and the first last: for many be called, but few chosen.

* * *

[†] Allusions in Sonnets VII and XIX.

From 25

PARABLE OF THE TALENTS

* * *

14: For the kingdom of heaven is as a man travelling into a far country, who called his own servants, and delivered unto them his goods.

15: And unto one he gave five talents, to another two, and to another one; to every man according to his several ability; and straightway took his journey.

16: Then he that had received the five talents went and traded with the same, and made them other five talents.

17: And likewise he that had received two, he also gained other two.

18: But he that had received one went and digged in the earth, and hid his lord's money.

19: After a long time the lord of those servants cometh, and reckoneth with them.

20: And so he that had received five talents came and brought other five talents, saying, Lord, thou deliveredst unto me five talents: behold, I have gained beside them five talents more.

21: His lord said unto him, Well done, thou good and faithful servant: thou hast been faithful over a few things, I will make thee ruler over many things: enter thou into the joy of thy lord.

22: He also that had received two talents came and said, Lord, thou deliveredst unto me two talents: behold, I have gained two other talents beside them.

23: His lord said unto him, Well done, good and faithful servant; thou hast been faithful over a few things, I will make thee ruler over many things: enter thou into the joy of thy lord.

24: Then he which had received the one talent came and said, Lord, I knew thee that thou art an hard man, reaping where thou hast not sown, and gathering where thou hast not strawed:

25: And I was afraid, and went and hid thy talent in the earth: lo, there thou hast that is thine.

26: His lord answered and said unto him, Thou wicked and slothful servant, thou knewest that I reap where I sowed not, and gather where I have not strawed:

27: Thou oughtest therefore to have put my money to the exchangers, and then at my coming I should have received mine own with usury.

28: Take therefore the talent from him, and give it unto him which hath ten talents.

29: For unto every one that hath shall be given, and he shall have abundance: but from him that hath not shall be taken away even that which he hath.

30: And cast ye the unprofitable servant into outer darkness: there shall be weeping and gnashing of teeth.

* * *

Luke†

From 4

1: And Jesus being full of the Holy Ghost returned from Jordan, and was led by the Spirit into the wilderness,

2: Being forty days tempted of the devil. And in those days he did eat nothing: and when they were ended, he afterward hungered.

3: And the devil said unto him, If thou be the Son of God, command this stone that it be made bread.

4: And Jesus answered him, saying, It is written, That man shall not live by bread alone, but by every word of God.

5: And the devil, taking him up into an high mountain, shewed unto him all the kingdoms of the world in a moment of time.

6: And the devil said unto him, All this power will I give thee, and the glory of them: for that is delivered unto me; and to whomsoever I will I give it.

7: If thou therefore wilt worship me, all shall be thine.

8: And Jesus answered and said unto him, Get thee behind me, Satan: for it is written, Thou shalt worship the Lord thy God, and him only shalt thou serve.

9: And he brought him to Jerusalem, and set him on a pinnacle of the temple, and said unto him, If thou be the Son of God, cast thyself down from hence:

10: For it is written, He shall give his angels charge over thee, to keep thee:

11: And in their hands they shall bear thee up, lest at any time thou dash thy foot against a stone.

12: And Jesus answering said unto him, It is said, Thou shalt not tempt the Lord thy God.

13: And when the devil had ended all the temptation, he departed from him for a season.

* * *

† The source of *Paradise Regained*.

CRITICISM

ANTHONY HECHT

Lizards and Snakes[†]

On the summer road that ran by our front porch
   Lizards and snakes came out to sun.
It was hot as a stove out there, enough to scorch
   A buzzard's foot. Still, it was fun
To lie in the dust and spy on them. Near but remote,
   They snoozed in the carriage ruts, a smile
In the set of the jaw, a fierce pulse in the throat
Working away like Jack Doyle's after he'd run the mile.

Aunt Martha had an unfair prejudice
   Against them (as well as being cold
Toward bats.) She was pretty inflexible in this,
   Being a spinster and all, and old.
So we used to slip them into her knitting box.
   In the evening she'd bring in things to mend
And a nice surprise would slide out from under the socks.
It broadened her life, as Joe said. Joe was my friend.

But we never did it again after the day
   Of the big wind when you could hear the trees
Creak like rockingchairs. She was looking away
   Off, and kept saying, "Sweet Jesus, please
Don't let him near me. He's as like as twins.
   He can crack us like lice with his fingernail.
I can see him plain as a pikestaff. Look how he grins
And swinges the scaly horror of his folded tail."

GEORGIA B. CHRISTOPHER

Milton's "Literary" Theology in the Nativity Ode[‡]

"On the Morning of Christ's Nativity" is a veritable Milton sampler displaying the major ingredients of his esthetic of "the word."

† From *The Hard Hours* (New York: Atheneum, 1981), p. 30. From *Collected Earlier Poems* by Anthony Hecht, copyright © 1990 by Anthony Hecht. Used by permission of Alfred A. Knopf, a division of Random House, and by the Estate of Anthony Hecht.
‡ From Georgia Christopher, *Milton and the Science of the Saints*. Copyright © 1982 by Princeton University Press. Reprinted by permission of Princeton University Press.

Though the poem is generally conceded to be a product of puritan spirituality, it is still taxed for not being a sensuous *icon* on the grounds that "the doctrine of the incarnation cannot be expressed unless the artist can manage a flesh-and-blood baby."[1] Puritan spirituality, on the contrary, took God's word on the matter and proceeded on the assumption that God's actions could not be properly understood without the reportorial powers of language. They believed that the mysterious reach of language could connect, in a single moment, a grand historical deed, the God who performed it, and the motions of a human heart. In the Nativity Ode, as one might expect, Milton treats the Incarnation as a "speech act," and his poetic strategies belong in the category of *event* rather than *icon*. Milton is not giving instructions to a painter, but offering an elliptical narrative, a scenario for history, with the nodal points starred, as it were.

The Advent is announced immediately and linked to the Crucifixion and to its *interpretation* as a definitive legal transaction:

> The Babe lies yet in smiling Infancy,
>   That on the bitter cross
>   Must redeem our loss.

(16.151–153)

To excerpt a doctrinal pronouncement, however, is to distort a major excellence of the Ode, that is, the way in which doctrine serves as the armature of the poem without being homiletically importunate. Martz observes that the poem is really about the *effect* of the Incarnation, or Redemption.[2] The presence of the poet in Milton's epic, which has received the best critical attention of late, needs to be considered here.[3] The presence of the poet makes the Ode a dramatization of the Protestant "sacrament"—the verbal transaction in which "objective" Promise is implanted in consciousness, a transaction signaled here by a celebratory repetition of doctrine. The poet-swain establishes in the proem that the Ode itself is his verbal offering, and with it he proceeds to perform one of Luther's "heavenly works" and "join [his] voice unto the Angel Choir" (Proem 4.27). Despite Milton's headnote on how the poem came to him one Christmas morning, and despite the intimation that he speaks at the behest of the Holy Spirit ("From out his secret Altar toucht with

1. See, for example, John Carey, *Milton*, New York, Arco Press, 1970, p. 30; Ross, *Poetry and Dogma*, p. 190.
2. Louis L. Martz, *The Poetry of Meditation*, New Haven, Yale University Press, 1954, p. 165.
3. See Arnold Stein, *The Art of Presence: The Poet and Paradise Lost*, Berkeley, University of California Press, 1977.

hallow'd fire" [4.28]), the poet's inner motions are handled with extreme reticence. The Ode brilliantly bonds the poet-swain's subjective awareness to objective events; both his heart's motions and points of doctrine are presented as *events*. The revolution that grace makes in the consciousness of the poet is expressed in the familiar pastoral paradigm, according to which a swain's response to his beloved is described as a radical change in nature. This familiar paradigm from the Renaissance miscellanies has considerable numinous potential, though it often becomes a routine strategy for compliment. A fresh use of the paradigm, when Nature is made to embody the power of the beloved and the adoration of the lover in equal measure, usually evokes a sense of mystery. The paradigm had already been applied to Christ in a rudimentary way in English Christmas carols,[4] but Milton's use of it is extended and more sophisticated. Nature's response is first generalized by a personification:

> Nature in awe to him
> Had doff't her gaudy trim,
>   With her great Master so to sympathize.
>   (1.32–34)

Then individual aspects of nature display the kind of animate response that had been offered to many a Phyllis and Astrea during the preceding thirty years, the kind that Marvell was to lay at the feet of Maria in "Upon Appleton House":[5]

---

4. See, for example, Edmond Bolton's "The Sheepheards Song," in *England's Helicon*, 1600, 1614, ed. Hyder Edward Rollins, Cambridge, Mass., Harvard University Press, 1935, I, 132, ll. 24–31:
> After long night, vp-risen is the morne,
> Renowning *Bethlem* in the Sauiour.
>   Sprung is the perfect day,
>   By Prophets seene a farre:
>   Sprung is the mirthfull May,
>   Which Winter cannot marre.
> In *Dauids* Cittie dooth this Sunne appeare:
> Clouded in flesh, yet Sheepheards sit we heere.

5. Rosamund Tuve thought that the Nativity Ode would not have been considered a pastoral in the seventeenth century, despite the inclusion of shepherds, because "the basic metaphors of pastoral are absent" (*Images and Themes in Five Poems by Milton*, Cambridge, Harvard University Press, 1957, p. 42). The Nativity Ode, however, uses a pastoral paradigm common both to the Christmas carols of the miscellanies and to Marvell's sophisticated praise of Lord Fairfax's daughter in "Upon Appleton House":
> See how loose Nature, in respect
> To her, it self doth recollect;
> And every thing so whisht and fine,
> Starts forth with to its *Bonne Mine*.
> The *Sun* himself, of *Her* aware,
> Seems to descend with greater Care;
> And lest *She* see him go to Bed;
> In blushing Clouds conceales his Head.

> The Winds, with wonder whist,
> Smoothly the waters kiss't,
>   Whispering new joys to the mild Ocean,
> Who now hath quite forgot to rave,
> While Birds of Calm sit brooding on the charmed wave.
>   (5.64–68)

If we read the pastoral paradigm aright, Nature presents a simultaneous description of the swain's heart and of the power of his God—exactly the reverse of Adam's situation in *Paradise Lost*, where *real* nature needs a priest to offer up its praise. Once we see that pastoral Nature "speaks" intimately for the poet, the Ode does not appear nearly so remote and cold as sometimes claimed. The "foul deformities" and "guilty front" belong to the poet whose sins are now "covered" by snow. It is his heart to which "meek-ey'd Peace" and the (Turtle) dove descend from the clouds. Just as the grounds of Appleton House are transformed into a paradise when Maria comes, so the poet-swain's redeemed consciousness becomes a pastoral idyll. Milton's conspicuously original touch is to combine the halcyon days of Nature with the halcyon days of the Augustan Age—"No War, or Battle's sound/Was heard the World around" (4.53–54). This widening of the pastoral response to include history shows again how relentlessly the poem is organized by *event*, rather than by *pictura*.

Milton's second major strategy is likewise a dynamic one; from the very first, his stanza form, with its trimeter lines suggesting the folk meter of naïve English carols,[6] has linked musical and doctrinal apprehension. This association becomes explicit when he presents doctrine *heard* as the sudden change from silence to song. That the swain hears the unheard music of the spheres in the nativity *Gloria* is Milton's musical version of the Reformation *topos* that to have faith is to be let in on God's "secrets" of well-published doctrine. It is a brilliant stroke to present a system of doctrine with unoffensive succinctness by giving each tenet an auditory correlate. The morning

---

> So when the Shadows laid asleep
> From underneath these Banks do creep,
> And on the River as it flows
> With *Eben Shuts* begin to close;
> The modest *Halcyon* comes in sight,
> Flying betwixt the Day and Night;
> And such an horror calm and dumb,
> *Admiring Nature* does benum.

(*The Poems and Letters of Andrew Marvell*, ed. H. M. Margoliouth, Oxford, Clarendon Press, 1967, I, 79, stanzas 83–84).
6. See Martz, "The Rising Poet, 1645," in *The Lyric and Dramatic Milton*, ed. Joseph H. Summers, New York, Columbia University Press, 1965, p. 27.

stars in chorus, *Gloria in excelsis*, Satan's clanging chains, and the trump of doom invoke, respectively, the doctrine of Creation, the Incarnation, Redemption, and the Second Coming. This equation of musical with doctrinal apprehension helps to articulate the paradox of the Kingdom, which is difficult enough for verbal syntax and clumsy, if not impossible, in the visual arts. Angelic choruses easily knit together the once and future kingdom that

> now begins; for from this happy day
> Th' old Dragon under ground,
> In straiter limits bound,
> Not half so far casts his usurped sway.
> (18.167–170)

The anticipation of a remembered tune brilliantly conveys the conundrum of the Kingdom that is, has been, and is yet to be. Lest we miss the point, Milton invokes the circular structure of Vergil's Messianic Eclogue ("For if such holy Song/Enwrap our fancy long,/Time will run back, and fetch the age of gold" [14.133–135]), in order to amend Vergil's scheme ("no,/This must not yet be so"). Defining eschatology as musical repetition has the further advantage of giving doctrine the passionate esthetic coloring that it is said to lack in *Paradise Lost*. The place of eros in Reformation piety becomes clear when Milton describes an access of faith (*hearing* the word) as apprehending such music

> As never was by mortal finger struck,
> Divinely-warbled voice
> Answering the stringed noise,
> As all thir souls in *blissful rapture took*:
> The Air such *pleasure* loath to lose,
> With thousand echoes still prolongs each heav'nly close.
> (9.95–100, *author's italics*)

Milton's contrasting styles of reference are yet another way by which he gives the poem decisive movement. The divine Birth is treated in three brief notations (1.29–31, 8.85–92, and 27.237–244). In each case, the reference is simple and direct and itself takes on "semantic" value. After the conceited indirection of the first seven stanzas on nature's toilet, we turn once more to direct statement about the shepherds and the babe "kindly come to live with them below" (8.90), as if we were returning, after elaboration in a minor mode, to the key signature. In this way, the referential organization of the poem pits flirtatious obliquity against unambiguous directness—charm against truth—in a way that makes direct reference climactic, as it should be in a piety that defines grace as clarity

discovered. In the latter half of the poem, Milton announces his
view of the pagan gods as straw men,[7] rather than as unwitting
Christian oracles, and he conveys their insubstantiality as much by
style of reference as by auditory association—all those hysterical
"shrieks" and neurasthenic "sighs." The catalogue goes on with ever
more oblique and windy ways of proclaiming absence ("In vain [the]
Cymbals' ring" in Moloch's palace, nor is Osiris seen on "*Memphian*
Grove or Green,/Trampling the unshow'r'd Grass with lowings loud"
[24.214–215]), until the roll call of abdicating pagans seems to be all
encrustation, a piling up of epithets and entire lines having eccentric reference to a vacuum. Milton's strongest contrast in referential
style comes when he describes the sun at two figurative removes,
first through the civilized screen of bed curtains, and then *per con-
fusio* through the faeries' Moon-loved maze:

> So when the Sun in bed,
> Curtain'd with cloudy red,
>   Pillows his chin upon an Orient wave,
> The flocking shadows pale
> Troop to th'infernal jail;
>   Each fetter'd Ghost slips to his several grave,
> And the yellow-skirted *Fays*
> Fly after the Night-steeds, leaving their
>   Moon-lov'd maze.
>   (26.229–236)

Milton may not have intended to contrast "poetic" obfuscation with
the clarity of divine revelation, but we cannot miss how he tries "to
clothe the sun" with conceits, then follows it with a naked statement about the infant Son. The contrast in referential style makes
the child being put to bed seem very real:

> But see! the Virgin blest,
> Hath laid her Babe to rest.
> Time is our tedious Song should here have ending.
>   (27.237–239)

At last we are invited to look at the Advent as Nativity *scene*, and we
have a sense of journey completed as the goal of the Wise Men,
announced in stanza 5 of the proem, is finally *shown*. The last
stanza has the strongest visual appeal of any in the poem, and
Louis Martz observes that it is the kind that typically might begin a

---

7. Philip Rollinson, "Milton's Nativity Poem and the Decorum of Genre," *Milton Studies*,
VII, 180.

Catholic meditation.[8] Milton withholds any visual statement until its doctrinal import has been presented *and* apprehended, apparently valuing *pictura* as the Reformers did, that is, merely as a means of rhetorical emphasis. Milton, like Rembrandt, knew that the elimination of color and light gives unusual intensity to what remains. So it is here when *pictura*, though only the outline of a crèche, comes as a bold rhetorical stroke summing up, or "sealing," the promise of history and doctrine.

As if heeding Luther's caveats about substituting a tabloid response to the *scene* of Christ's birth and death, instead of "reading" its promise (*LW* 31.357), Milton avoids the risk of sentimentality by suppressing domestic detail. The tenderness in the final scene is all the more powerful because of its indirect, masculine expression: love is defined by how power is used. What the last stanza "reveals" is that all of God's power is concentrated upon loving, tender care. All the "hevenly sodiers," as Tyndale calls them in his version of Luke 2:15, are put to minding the baby:

> Heav'n's youngest-teemed Star
> Hath fixt her polisht Car,
>   Her sleeping Lord with Handmaid Lamp attending:
> And all about the Courtly Stable
> Bright-harness'd Angels sit in order serviceable.
>
>   (27.240–245)

In the Nativity Ode, Milton reveals his lifelong preoccupations—his understanding of God's love in terms of power and clarity, his description of faith as doctrine "heard," his view of doctrine as incipient history (and vice versa), and his belief in the momentous effects of God's speech. Milton later would abandon a pastoral view of history, would give the pagans their dark due, and would allow God's word to speak more on its own; but here his theology of the word proves no esthetic liability because he brilliantly uses musical association and pastoral paradigm as poetic "cover" for the naked word.

8. Martz, *The Poetry of Meditation*, p. 165.

STEPHEN BOOTH AND JORDAN FLYER

From Milton's "How Soon Hath Time": A Colossus in a Cherrystone†

This essay is essentially an appreciation of "How soon hath time," and the essay's thesis is that "How soon hath time" is a great poem—not only great in the metaphoric sense by which *great* means "very good indeed" but great in its literal sense: "big." That explains why the essay's title alludes to Samuel Johnson's dictum to Hannah More: "Milton, Madam, was a genius that could cut a Colossus from a rock; but could not carve heads upon cherrystones."[1]

> How soon hath time the suttle theef of youth,
> Stoln on his wing my three and twentieth yeer!
> My hasting dayes flie on with full career,
> But my late spring no bud or blossom shew'th.
> Perhaps my semblance might deceive the truth,
> That I to manhood am arriv'd so near,
> And inward ripenes doth much less appear,
> That som more timely-happy spirits indu'th.
> Yet be it less or more, or soon or slow,
> It shall be still in strictest measure eev'n,
> To that same lot, however mean or high,
> Toward which Time leads me, and the will of Heav'n;
> All is, if I have grace to use it so,
> As ever in my great task Masters eye.[2]

Most of what little critical attention this sonnet has received has gone to the last two lines. Reflecting on the poem in tranquility—or, more probably, reflecting on it in a sweat to demonstrate that it makes as much sense as it seems to make—one may come to several conclusions about the syntax of those two last lines, but the rhetorical rhythm of the poem they conclude, the rhythm of the lines themselves, and the 1645 and 1673 punctuations all present *All is as ever in my great taskmaster's eye* as an independent clause—a

---

† *From* Stephen Booth and Jordan Flyer, "Milton's 'How Soon Hath Time': A Colossus in a Cherrystone," *English Literary History* 49:2 (1982): 449–67, 266–467. Copyright © 1982 by The Johns Hopkins University Press. Reprinted with permission of The Johns Hopkins University Press.
1. *Boswell's Life of Johnson*, ed. George Birkbeck Hill and L. F. Powell, 6 vols. (Oxford, 1934–1950), IV, 305.
2. This is the 1673 text of sonnet 7 as given by Frank Allen Patterson in *Shorter Poems*, Volume I (1931) of the Columbia Milton, 18 vols. (New York, 1931–1938), p. 60. In our discussion of the sonnet we have casually modernized quotations from it—but only where to have done otherwise would have been confusing and wantonly pedantic (e.g., we say *Stol'n* for *Stoln*, *year* for *yeer*, and *ev'n* for *eev'n*).

clause that, by its physical position in the logic of the whole and by its tone of triumphant illumination, implies that its matter is just as self-evident as it is self-evidently just.

The strength of that implication probably derives from the effect the interrupting *if* clause has on one's understanding: *All is* promises a simplification, a sweeping statement that overrides and transcends the making of distinctions. The pause for qualification implies precision and logical thoroughness behind the grand assertion it interrupts. More importantly, the particular substance of the interrupting *if* clause suggests that the main clause is equally unimpeachable and, what is still more important, that its substance is as commonplace and as transparently obvious in its import as the *if* clause is—or, rather, as the *if* clause sounds. Moreover, the mere fact of interruption encourages a reader to *believe* whatever it is that finally comes to be asserted. As a necessity of accommodating the blind modification put forth by the *if* clause, a reader's mind is obliged to treat the first two syllables of the *All is* clause as if the clause were already complete—as if instantly apparent antecedents for *it* and *so* were already there to be modified. The interrupting *if* clause thus encourages a reader to come away from the poem assuming that he has in fact taken meaning from the main clause, that he understood what *All is as ever* meant at the moment in his reading when that clause emerged.

To say that is to say that it does not matter what the last two lines mean. The lines do not invite or require one to know what their obviously valid assertion asserts. A reader's experience of those two last lines is an effortless act of practical faith—albeit faith in the lines, rather than faith in the deity. The lines are not troublesome until and unless one attempts to determine their particular purport and to understand how these twenty syllables in this particular order can be seen to transmit that particular purport. The words and phrases relate in multiple pertinent ways to each other and to the rest of the poem they conclude—so many that the lines convince one of their truth without revealing what that truth is. That is a considerable accomplishment—and one urgently auxiliary to the grand, general indifference to mundane distinctions that is inherent in *All is as ever in my great taskmaster's eye*.

Although these last two lines of "How soon hath time" satisfy us and convince us of their justice without revealing their meaning, they are by no means meaningless. The lines are meaningful—meaningful both in the standard metaphoric sense of that word and in a peculiarly literal one. They are so full of meaning, indeed, that they cannot be meaningful in the sense of that word in which "meaningful" includes the capacity to deliver specific, logically coherent, isolatable ideational substance. Their special meaningfulness is apparent if one examines the paraphrases academic commentators—

under generic pressure to seek out and subdue imprecision wherever it may occur—have attempted. Such glosses have been of two general kinds. The first, as has been previously implied, responds to, and derives from, the logic of the poem-long line of thinking these final two lines conclude. The syntax of the sestet is such as to imply the summary or explanatory function for the last two lines of this particular Petrarchan sonnet that form foists on the final couplets of English-style sonnets. Thus, since the four preceding lines treat of something—*it*—that *shall be in strictest measure ev'n to* something else—*that same lot*, words and phrases in the last two lines that are capable of echoing the preceding four and are capable of making *it* and *that lot* specific ask to be taken as having done so. Lines 13 and 14 seem appositive to lines 9–12. *All is as ever in my great taskmaster's eye* presents itself as a coalescent syntactic unit that strains toward being understood to say that, in the terms by which God measures, it does not matter how soon or in what way a human life is productive— that "it's all the same to God." That reading is a bumptious variant on a paraphrase published by Donald Dorian: "All time is, if I have grace to use it so, as eternity in God's sight."[3] We suggest that that general sense is at least chronologically primary in one's experience of the poem—primary for two reasons. The first—that the verse rhythm, the rhetorical rhythm, and the 1645 and 1673 punctuations present *All is as ever* as an independent clause interrupted by modification in an *if* clause—has already been mentioned. The other, which may be merely autobiographical, is that that kind of paraphrase reflects and makes substantial what both of us remember to have been our first impression of the lines.

Although that interpretive paraphrase is probably just, it is not by any means adequate. For one thing, though that reading offers *All* as an antecedent for *it* in *if I have grace to use it so*, that reading does not accommodate *so*. Unless one understands it as a pronominal stand-in for the readily extrapolatable but inappropriately glib word "gracefully" or for the more reasonable "in accordance with the will of Heav'n" (a reading that requires several steps and a couple of splints), *so* is left to float meaninglessly.

So, what about a reading that does accommodate *so?* The poem itself provides one: all one has to do is decide to take line 14 as a gloss on *use it so.* The second of the two general kinds of gloss that have been generated from lines 13 and 14 does just that. For example, Kester Svendsen proposed this paraphrase (one that takes *ripeness* to be the antecedent for *it* in line 13, as it demonstrably—but

3. *Explicator,* 8 (1949–50), Item 10. Dorian's paraphrase presses the adverb *ever* into service as a substantive and rather improbably assumes that *All* is an ellipsis for "all time"—improbably because, since the preceding line personifies *Time,* the leap to conceiving of it as a measurable commodity is not invited.

not necessarily effectively—is in lines 9 and 10): "All that matters is whether I have grace to use my ripeness in accordance with the will of God as one ever in His sight" (*Explicator*, 7 [1948–49], Item 53). A. S. P. Woodhouse offered a significant variant: "All [that matters] is: whether I have grace to use it so, as ever [conscious of being] in my great taskmaster's [enjoining] eye" (*UTQ*, 12 [1943], 96; the brackets are Woodhouse's). Those paraphrases reflect demonstrably workable syntaxes, demonstrably available in the lines—but ones likely to solidify in a glosser's consciousness only as alternatives to previously frustrated efforts to get a satisfying reading for the more immediately evident "All is as ever" construction.

Be that as it may, the lines *do* imply reference to the human need to be mindful of the Santa-Claus-like perspicacity of an all-, and ever-, judging God. The lines include that idea, whether it is brought to gloss-induced prominence or not. That idea, after all, complements, and is implied in, the moral economics assumed in *if I have grace to use it so*—a moral economics that, on its face, presumes heavenly justice to follow a humanly comprehensible and predictable pattern—a pattern that must be assumed if the idea of moral obligation and determination to make proper use of one's time and talents is to make the easy, ready, theologically unassisted sense it traditionally makes. Moreover, even for a casual reader who does not spell out the syntactic relationship between *so* and line 14, that relationship is there and is included in the experience of the lines.

What one has here, then, is a pair of lines that persuade us of their validity and include in validation suggestively arranged materials for two propositions. Neither permits paraphrase—except in formulations that require prosthetic supplements and osteopathic manipulation and that still have unaccommodated bits and pieces left over. Neither proposition is complete enough to stand alone or, indeed, to be separated from the other.

That last is important. We said earlier that, for a reader free of obligation to gloss the lines, it does not matter whether he knows at all what particular truth it is to which he so willingly accedes at the end of the poem. We want now to argue that it does not matter what paraphrase a self-conscious, self-monitoring, reader accepts. When all is said and done, all the suggested readings are suggested by the poem, and all come essentially to the same thing.

Consider, by way of illustration, the fact that both Svendsen's gloss and Woodhouse's rest heavily on a casually assumed paraphrase in which *All is* becomes "All *that matters* is." That phrase is emblematic of the spirit of the "All is as ever" construction, but both of the paraphrases that inject it into line 13 read line 14 in a syntax that absolutely denies the phrase *as ever* its capacity to function as direct object of *is* in the preceding line. The introduction of the phrase "All that matters is" as a gloss for *All is* reflects a gesture of disregard for distinction undeniably present in the lines but denied by the syntax in which the paraphrasers choose to read it— denied by a syntax that is as undeniably present as the gesture is. Indeed, paraphrases of the sort Svendsen and Woodhouse provide are altogether just. We do, however, insist (a) that, in reading *All is* as "All that matters is," the paraphrasers violate the logic by which their paraphrases at large were determined, and (b) that that does not matter, and (c) that in violating their own logic the paraphrasers rise above the human limitation of which logic and our need for it are a desperate advertisement, and (d) that it is the poem that enabled them to make that temporary but marvelous advance beyond the mental frailty of lapsed humanity.

The poem, in fact, is a persuasive and stunningly effortless demonstration that a whole range of sub-lunary distinctions of the sort by which we maintain and define sanity need not matter. Everything already said about the last two lines goes to illustrate that proposition.

And the curious relationship between *If I have grace to use it so* and the assertion it (at least temporarily) modifies will illustrate that proposition further. For one thing, the *if* clause—just because it is an *if* clause and thus renders the truth of the interrupted assertion conditional—contradicts that assertion's spirit of sweeping absolutism; and, at the same time, the same *if* clause, by virtue of its ring of specifically Christian humility, contributes to the authority of the interrupted absolute.

Similarly, but in another dimension, the paradoxically comfortable relationship between the substantive particulars of the *if* clause and those of the *All is* clause enacts another dissolution of distinction, one that cannot be discussed without broaching a subject that, until now, we have meticulously avoided: the poem's relationship to the parable of the laborers in the vineyard (Matthew 20:1–16), and to the parable of the talents (Matthew 25:14–30).

In the second and more complete of the two Trinity-manuscript drafts of the letter in which he included a copy of this sonnet, Milton lays out the case for and against his present inactive, unproductive life of study. He refers to "that command in the gospell set out by the terrible seasing of him that hid the talent," but, he implies, he cares less about putting his gifts to immediate use than about being able to put them to worthy use—"not taking thought of being late so it give advantage to be more fit, for those that were latest lost nothing when the maister of the vinyard came to give each one his hire."[4]

4. *Familiar Letters*, ed. Donald L. Clark, Volume XII of the Columbia Milton (New York, 1936), p. 324.

Evidence that Milton associated the parables with the poem does not, of course, inform the poem, and—at least in the case of the parable of the vineyard—editors and commentators have persistently failed to recognize any such association in "How soon hath time." The association, however, is active in the poem and would be audible even if Milton's drafts of "Letter to a Friend" had not survived. Given the poem-long concern with achievement, lack of achievement, and relative time—and given the levelling implications of *All is . . . As ever*—and given the immediate contexts of the overtly religious concept of *grace* in the preceding line and of the implied reference to God evoked by the adjective *great*—the term *taskmaster*, here used to designate a being indifferent to distinctions between service begun early and service begun late, introduces specific allusion to the parable of the vineyard—an allusion that both assists in and justifies the assertion that all the distinctions that have previously been the poem's topics do not matter. Although much less overt than the allusion to the parable of the vineyard, the poem's allusion to the parable of the talents has been widely recognized. It too operates independently of the latterly discovered hint provided by the accidental survival of the Trinity drafts of the letter. The allusion derives from the word *use* in line 13 and acts only retroactively—set in motion as a result of the new, specifically Christian context the poem enters with the completion of line 14.

In one's experience of the poem, its allusions to the parables function as two among many actions whereby the sonnet increases its effective size and scope beyond the limits implied by its duration, tone, and narrowly private topic. We do not, however, want to imply that the poem is "about" the parables or that its effect upon a reader whose perception of the last two lines is colored by the Biblical references they imply is radically different from its effect on a reader to whom those references are inaudible. It was to avoid that implication that we delayed introducing the parables into this discussion. If one fails to hear echoes of the parable of the vineyard in the poem's final phrase, the "All is as ever" gesture still propounds the general philosophy for which the parable is locus classicus. Similarly, recourse to the idea of salvation by works—an idea inherent in the parable of the talents—is implied in any case by line 13, which—despite its pointed appeal to grace—does not ask to be understood as *if I have grace* would be understood if it stood alone, without *to use it so*. The completed *if* clause does not so much sound as if it is saying "God willing" as "If I behave myself"— although of course—and, given this poem's habitual incidental, insignificant self-contradiction, appropriately—if one thinks hard about the phrase, there is no way to deny that *if I have grace to use it so* does say "God willing."

If I have grace to use it so thus conflates—makes indistinct—wipes out the distinction between—two distinct kinds of seemly and traditional Christian humility—one that implies a theologically unsophisticated notion of free will and fits a moral economics in which one gets only earned rewards—and one, inherent in the mere presence of the idea of grace, that implies the metaphysical, supra-logical justice that prevails in the divine economy illustrated in the parable of the vineyard. Those two views of things are not compatible in ordinary, theologically unupholstered thought. But in *if I have grace to use it so* they lie together like lambs. Not only does the distinction between them not matter—as in fact it does not, once ministered to by theological explanations—the distinction disappears from one's consciousness, *actually feels* as if it does not matter. As the *if* clause by itself makes *grace* the easy bedfellow of mundane resolve, and as lines 13 and 14 make a similarly harmonious (and similarly improbably harmonious), pair that presents indistinction in action and makes us capable of taking it for granted, the whole poem has been doing similar things all the way through—and has been demonstrating and enacting the justice of the parable of the vineyard from the beginning.

One might with real but limited justice describe the poem as a sustained exercise in illustrating, imitating, and justifying the parable of the vineyard. In support of that proposition one might point to the action the parable itself takes upon the poem. All of the poem is informed by the parable of the vineyard, but it is not so informed all the way through. The reference to the parable does not enter the poem until the last phrase of the last line. The relation between the allusion and the poem is thus comparable to that of the last-hired workers to the workers that precede them in the vineyard. But that neat and gratifying line of argument assumes that the poem's efficacy depends upon the audibility of its reference to the parable—and thus limits and generally underestimates the poem's achievement. One does better to describe the poem as a fourteen-line illustration of the practicality of the *principle* propounded in the parable of the vineyard—a principle presented by the parable as specifically foreign to its poor human reader and beyond his capacity, but a principle which its reader's mind obeys effortlessly and necessarily as it acknowledges and dismisses one ordinarily meaningful distinction after another in its easy word-by-word, line-by-line progress through the syntax of "How soon hath time."

For example, before a reader arrives at the two relatively troublesome last lines, the experience of the poem has already included practical experience of the inconsequentiality and fluidity of the concept of location in time. From a speaker who has been bemoaning loss of youth, the first words of line 4—*But my late spring*—ask to be understood as "But my recently departed springtime," "the springtime that is past." Only the tense of the verb—*shew'th*—brings the sproutless spring back into the present (where *late* must mean "tardy").

Comparable processes occur during the lines immediately preceding the critically troublesome last two: *To that same lot, however mean or high, / Toward which Time leads me, and the will of Heav'n.* The last phrase arrives late—well after the point in the syntax where one might expect a second grammatical subject coordinate with *Time* to arrive; that striking tardiness both exhibits the work pattern of the belatedly-hired workers in the vineyard and anticipates the belated introduction of the first allusion to that parable into this poem in its last phrase. Because *and the will of Heav'n* is so unusually placed, it can, at least momentarily, present itself to a reader's understanding as grammatically parallel with *me*—as a second direct object of *leads* (Milton apparently acknowledged that possibility: in the otherwise unpunctuated copy of this sonnet in the Trinity manuscript, he troubled to put that copy's sole punctuation mark, a comma, between *leads me* and *and the will of Heav'n*).

Although the possibility for that momentary aberration can contribute to the density of the experience of the poem, it presumably can operate *only* momentarily and *as* an aberration because the idea of *Time* as director of *the will of Heav'n* is philosophically ridiculous. Yet, the mere fact of the logical openness of the syntax and its invitation to error can open the way to another auxiliary sense of lines 11 and 12—another sense auxiliary to the one in which *Time* and *the will of Heav'n* are cooperative co-leaders—one less inviting syntactically than the one in which *Time* led *the will of Heav'n*, and more inviting substantively. *The will of Heav'n* can be understood as parallel with *that same lot*—can be understood as a distant second object of *to* in an assertion that the speaker's destiny and *the will of Heav'n* are one and the same. *The will of Heav'n*, thus, is either the leader or the destination—and, of course, it does not matter which: both amount to the same thing.

In the course of lines 10–12, the action of the word *to* in the quantitative concept "even to" blends into the action of a near-synonym for a sense—"fully as far as"—that the words "even to" commonly carry but do not carry during lines 10 and 11 of this poem; the action of *to* in the "even to" construction blends into the action of *Toward* in *Toward which* in line 12. Thus, as one reads lines 11 and 12, a gesture of equation (*ev'n, / To that same lot*), becomes one of destination: *To that same lot, however mean or high, / Toward which Time leads me. . . .* In the process, moreover, the word *high*, used metaphorically in opposition to *mean*, reawakens in its literal sense and suggests arduous upward striving.

Also consider the miraculously undemanding conflation of two idioms in the phrase *in strictest measure ev'n* in line 10. The phrase simultaneously achieves focus on the idea of quantity (as the phrase "in measure even"—a phrase that says "equal in quantity"—would), *and* similarly exclusive focus on the idea of precision in the means and process of ascertaining quantity (as the phrase "in strictest measure"—a phrase that says "as measured by the most exacting standards"—would if it stood alone). Our point in asking such minute attention to the phrase is—once again—first, that the phrase both enlarges its logically probable capacity to communicate and makes the supra-logical achievement of comprehending it an effortless one—and, second, that the distinction between the two conflated phrases is real but here does not really matter.

For an analogous phenomenon of the poem, consider the opalescent activity within the first two lines where the verb "to steal" goes through a momentary and altogether insignificant metamorphosis. Since, at the beginning of line 2, one arrives at *Stol'n* immediately after the stealer—*time*—has been labeled a *thief*, one first understands it to be a transitive verb meaning "purloined"; the next three words of line 2 transform *Stol'n* into an intransitive verb: Time has *Stol'n on his wing*, has "travelled stealthily"; then, however, the concluding phrase of line 2—*my three and twentieth year*—presents a direct object for *Stol'n* and changes its sense back to "purloined."

We are, predictably, concerned about two qualities of that metamorphosis. The first is that it does not matter to the general purport of the line whether the verb is transitive and means "filched" (time steals youth), or is intransitive and means "moves stealthily" (time steals away); both amount to the same thing. As the syntactic flow of the sentence smoothed away an ordinarily perceptible distinction, so the two potential assertions of line one are ideational equals. The distinction between two kinds of stealing does not invite any conscious attention at all as one's mind moves across the sentence; a distinction is thus effectively lost in the syntax.

This poem habitually suggests incidental and gratuitous distinctions and just as incidentally neutralizes them. (In fact, it does that so often and in so many ways that the use of the word *habitually* is justified—even though the poem is only 118 words long.)

The second focus of our interest in the metamorphosis of *Stol'n* is as one of many means by which the poem comes to include more than its paraphrasable content can admit: the idea of time sneaking away unperceived is extra—is delivered by the line but at last not quite a logically demonstrable part of the line's syntactically delivered substance.

Both the related qualities we have pointed out in the first two lines recur profusely and multifariously in elements of the lines that follow.

Both the metaphoric images evoked by lines 1 and 2 employed the idea of motion in space; the traveller was the personified abstraction *time*. In line 3, days *fly* (helped by imped feathers from the idea of winged time in line 2). By line 6 it is the speaker who, in the verb *arrived*, is the traveller. And the distinction among Time the thief, days, and the speaker is a real distinction that does not really matter—either in our perception of the poem's progress or in fact. Each is a mere factor in a particular casually and arbitrarily selected way of thinking about the same fact.

In line 3, *hasting* is contextually identified as what OED observes it to be, a nonce adjective meaning "speeding," "hastening." But the next line introduces a botanic metaphor to which the botanic sense of *hasting* pertains: "early ripening."

Lines 5 and 6 work a change comparable to the one *Stol'n* undergoes in lines 1 and 2; they work a change on the botanical metaphors in line 4 where *bud* and *blossom* are atrophied extensions of a standard metaphoric use of *my spring* to mean "my youth." In lines 5 and 6, the idea of physical appearance—introduced in a word, *semblance*, that suggests specifically facial appearance—and the idea of visible signs of masculine maturity, infuse the solemnly poetic sprigs in quatrain one with appropriately gauche and appropriately petty suggestions of boyish despair over a relentlessly beardless chin. Then, with the standard metaphoric use of *ripeness* in line 7, the poem moves on as if it had never for a moment dallied with reference to the puerile anxieties of practical puberty.

Quatrain two, which takes up the distinction between appearance and reality, variously disables that distinction in the act of discussing it. Take, for example, what happens to the potentially—but at last not actually—key word, *semblance*. In line 5, at the moment of reading, *my semblance* is morally neutral and says only "my appearance," "the way I look." Then, when *semblance* turns out to be the grammatical subject of *might deceive*, the combination activates a sinister aura of deliberate sham in *semblance*. Such implication is always available to the word from its currency in designating appearances contrary to reality—"semblance of worth, not substance" (*Paradise Lost* I, 529)—but, until the entrance, midway through line 5, of the idea of deceit, the context excludes it—excludes it even though the "Perhaps . . . might" construction gives the line scheming potential that opens the way for the idea of purposeful, self-interested deception. And, no sooner does that idea emerge than it evaporates: the truth line 6 specifies—*That I to manhood am arriv'd so near*—offers no potential opportunity in which profitable deceit is possible; *semblance* subsides once again into the moral neutrality it had at first, and *deceive the truth* turns out capable of having been nothing more sinister than an idiomatically improbable synonym for "be misleading." Once again a distinction—here between kinds of appearance—turns out at last not to matter practically.

A larger and more impressive demonstration of the insignificance of distinctions occurs in the logical relationship between the first two lines of quatrain two and the second two. The quatrain presents a contrasting pair: outward appearance (lines 5 and 6) and inner truth (lines 7 and 8). But the two are linked by *And*, a word that implies a likeness between the matters it links and simple continuation of the train of thought to which it presents an appendage. If one follows the implied instruction of the conjunctive particle one must understand *doth much less appear* as "shows"—as "is perceptible to sense"—and see that lines 5 through 7 say that, as the speaker's physical appearance is such as to hide his age, so the fact of his intellectual and spiritual maturity is safely hidden by the fact that such invisible qualities are never available to the senses. No reader, however, is capable of following the instructions given by *and*: this is not a culture in which this speaker could reasonably be expected to want to hide *inward ripeness*. But any reader is altogether ready to entertain the kind of argument that would confound and confute charges of immaturity (and of lack of tangible achievement) by laying claim to inner maturity (and inner wealth). And—since the phrase *much less appear* carries traces of the traditional Christian-Platonic lament that spiritual worth is always undervalued as compared with material achievement (always "appears to be much less than" material achievement)—the words *And inward ripeness doth much less appear* do in fact make momentary allusion to unperceived, undervalued spiritual achievement and resources, do momentarily imply the line of argument they would signal outright if line 7 began with "But" rather than *And*.

Although the suggestions with which we have just credited line 7 are indeed present in it, they last only as long as the line does. Line 8, *That some more timely-happy spirits indu'th*, denies the word *appear* the capacity any longer to function as a synonym for "be visible." The modification line 8 provides for *ripeness* defines it as ripeness of a kind that is socially evident and as a quality possessed by the timely-happy spirits and not by the speaker. The only available sense line 8 leaves for *doth appear* is "makes its appearance," "arrives." And the two-line unit comes to have been substantively parallel with the lament in line 4: "My late spring shows no outward sign of maturity, and I show even less evidence of inward ripeness."

So—to say about the second quatrain what we have previously said about the other elements we have discussed—the quatrain delivers more substance than its final identity can hold; and the experience of reading the quatrain—a quatrain on the topic of distinction—is an experience in which the dissolution of distinction is (if the general silence of critics and annotaters is any evidence), so easy to accept that readers are not troubled by it even to the extent of forcing a paraphrase upon it.

Also consider the unmanageability of the altogether manageable ninth line—*Yet be it less or more, or soon or slow*—where the symmetry of the paired opposites *less* and *more* extends itself by rhythmic equation to *soon* and *slow*: as *less* and *more*, balanced on the conjunction *or*, are to one another, so, analogy suggests, are the first pair—*less or more*—to the second—*soon or slow*; the pairs themselves become a pair of units hinged on the conjunction that stands between *more* and *soon*. However, the identities as precise opposites that *soon* and *slow* have in this line are theirs only in, and because of, this line. *Soon* is ideational cousin to the neat opposite of *slow*, as *slow* is to the neat opposite of *soon*, but—though *slow* makes the line include "fast" and echo *with full career*, and though *soon* does the same for "late" and thus acts as an ideational echo of *late* in *my late spring*—*soon* and *slow* are not the idiomatic opposites they here convince us they are. The act of comprehending the line is thus an experience of understanding more than the line can reasonably be believed to hold (the experience of three pairs of alternates, not two: *less/more, soon/*"late," and "fast"/*slow*)—of understanding it in a casually perverse order (the two pairs balance undesirable [*less*] or desirable [*more*] against desirable [*soon*] or undesirable [*slow*])—and of understanding the words as two pairs, even though they are also and simultaneously four individual, logically equal, interchangeable alternatives ("be it A or B or C or D").

Moreover, the line—a line whose substance is a gesture of indifference to distinction, a line that says "it doesn't matter"—is, since in the act of dismissing distinctions it blurs the distinctions it dismisses—*also* a demonstration of the practicability of such dismissal. The line is an enabling act by which its reader becomes capable of thinking independently of distinctions, becomes superior to dependence on exactly the service all words—and comparative (and effectively comparative) adjectives in particular—exist to provide. What words are, after all, are distinction makers; they pander to the human mind, which ordinarily needs more assurance of distinction than is available in nature. The effortless experience of apprehending a line that dismisses distinction as trivial, and dismisses that idea via token representative distinguishers that are themselves rendered indistinct by the superior defining force of the line in which they appear is an altogether minor but altogether real experience of being actually, though temporarily, superior to the limitations of the human mind—superior in the way one would need to be not merely to *believe* that the wage scale in the Parable of the Vineyard is just but to understand its justice as confidently and easily as one does the humanly limited notion of "equal pay for equal work."

*   *   *

We have left * * * the matter of poetic contribution by semantic potential in words and phrases used in contexts that exclude its delivery in the paraphraseable content of a poem, to the end—and have come last to the most bizarre examples precisely because we wish to insist that such contributions are of the poem but that they weigh in it as—and only to the degree that—obviously non-signifying incidental relationships do—things like the rhyme between *wing*, the fourth syllable of line 2, and *spring*, the fourth syllable of line 4; and like the assonance and partial consonance between *grace*, the sixth syllable of line 13, and *great*, the sixth syllable of line 14; and like the ideational rhyme between *shew'th*, the rhyme word of line 4 (an *a* rhyme in the *a b b a* pattern of the octave), and *appear*, the rhyme word of line 7 (a *b* rhyme in that other, otherwise-established, coexistent pattern); and like the relation between the word *That*, the first word of line 6 where it is a conjunction, and the same word in the same position in line 8 where it is a relative pronoun; and like such habitual, habitually unobserved, everyday linguistic paradoxes as the one inherent in the stock phrase *much less* (line 7), or in the interaction between *more* modifying *timely* in line 8 and the noun-like *more* of *Yet be it less or more*, or between *some* in line 8 and *more*, its potential comparative ("some," "more," "most"), or between "some more" in *some more timely-happy spirits* and the standard noun phrase "some more."

Nonetheless, if it is firmly understood that these last substantively incidental phenomena are only that and are not here pointed out as potential clues to extrapolatable hidden meaning, it is reasonable to admit that, like all the other substantively extra actions of the poem, these trivial connections and fleeting, whispered invitation to frivolous mental detours swell the experience the poem gives its readers in exchange for the ninety seconds it takes from their lives. This sonnet is no *Paradise Lost*, but, for its size, it is colossal. None need ever wish it longer than it is.

DAVID NORBROOK

The Politics of *A Masque* [*Comus*]†

* * *

Not all Milton's early poems remained at the high prophetic level of the Nativity hymn. He experimented with ideas and poetic forms that would have been offensive to many Puritans. A taste for the worldly pleasures celebrated in 'L'Allegro', even down to attending Jonson's plays, was not unknown in the 1630s amongst some individuals who might be classed as Puritans.[1] But the question of Milton's relationship to the Caroline court, and to the legacy of Ben Jonson, was posed in a very direct form when he was invited to write a masque for the installation of the Earl of Bridgewater as Lord President of Wales in 1634. This was to be a major state occasion. Charles was strengthening the Council for the Marches in Wales in the face of a certain amount of local opposition, and the office of Lord President carried the full weight of royal approval for the new policies. Milton seems to have gained the commission for this masque because of his contacts with the Earl's family: he had already written an entertainment in honour of the Earl's mother-in-law, the Countess of Derby, who lived not far from Milton.[2] But the Ludlow commission raised far more ideological problems than the panegyric of the Countess, a venerable survivor from the Elizabethan era. The status of the court masque as symbol of anti-Puritan policies had recently been highlighted by William Prynne's *Histrio-Mastix*, a massive attack on the public theatre which did not spare aristocratic entertainments and contained what was held to be a glancing reference to Henrietta Maria's appearing in plays and masques. Women actors, in Prynne's view, were notorious whores.[3]

---

† From David Norbrook, *Poetry and Politics in the English Renaissance*, 2nd ed. (Oxford: Oxford University Press, 2002), pp. 233–52. Reprinted by permission.
1. Quarles's patron Sir Thomas Barrington, though a leading Puritan politician, supported the staging of plays and May-games: Martin Butler, *Theatre and Crisis 1632–1642* (Cambridge, 1984), 92–3. For a critique of my own and other arguments for the young Milton's radicalism see Thomas Corns, 'Milton Before "Lycidas"', in Graham Parry and Joad Raymond (eds.), *Milton and the Terms of Liberty* (Cambridge, 2002), 23–36.
2. In my first edition I followed Cedric C. Brown in dating *Arcades* to 1634, 'Milton's *Arcades*: Context, Form, and Function', *Renaissance Drama*, NS 8 (1977), 245–74 (255), but he has since revised the dating to 1632: Cedric C. Brown, *John Milton's Aristocratic Entertainments* (Cambridge, 1985), 47. My reading of *Comus* owed a great deal to Leah Marcus's work on Jonson, and for a reading very much complementary to this one see her *The Politics of Mirth: Jonson, Herrick, Milton, Marvell, and the Defense of Old Holiday Pastimes* (Chicago, 1986), ch. 6.
3. William Prynne, *Histrio-Mastix* (London, 1633), index, s.v. 'Women-Actors'. On the ways in which Prynne's attacks helped to politicize court culture, see David Howarth, *Images of Rule: Art and Politics in the English Renaissance, 1485–1649* (Houndmills,

He saw masques and revels as part of the general order of rituals and festivities which it was the duty of reformed Christianity to eradicate. Prynne's trial, in which he was accused of fomenting regicide, took place in the summer of 1634. He was punished with the loss of his ears. Milton's friend Alexander Gill had himself almost received this punishment in 1628 for circulating obscene libels against Buckingham; and in a recent attack on Gill Jonson had expressed the wish that he should be 'whipt, Cropt, branded, slit, neck-stockt': that he should receive a punishment as severe as that meted out to Prynne.[4] Milton would have hardly seen the issue as a simple quarrel between courtly civilization and Puritan philistinism.

The politics of masque-writing in 1634 was, however, further complicated by the fact that Jonson himself had fallen from favour and launched a bitter attack on masques. He had not composed any masques in the first few years of Charles's reign, perhaps because his relations with Buckingham were strained. In 1631 he had written two masques with Inigo Jones; but the architect was no longer used to collaborating with such a demanding partner, and they quickly quarrelled. Most masque texts were from now on provided by distinctly inferior poets; and in his 'Expostulation with Inigo Jones' Jonson attacked the empty show of masques which were nothing but painting and carpentry. In an entertainment commissioned by the Earl of Newcastle in 1634 he complained that '[r]ime will undoe you, and hinder your growth, and reputation in Court'. In 1632 a letter-writer expressed surprise on learning that Ben was still alive.[5] A Puritan treatise published after Charles's execution alleged that Jonson had been exiled from court and left to starve because of the king's ingratitude.[6] Significantly, his late plays show him moving towards the political rhetoric of the 'Spenserians'. He had not shared in the Spenserians' nostalgia for the Elizabethan age in James's reign, but now he began to imitate the Elizabethans closely. At a time when new fashions in courtly pastoral were being imported from France, he wrote a self-consciously English pastoral play, *The Sad Shepherd*, in which for the first time he adopted the Spenserian archaisms which he had earlier disdained. In *A Tale of a Tub*, a play set in Elizabethan times, the audience is reminded that John Heywood, the author of interludes in Henry VIII's reign,

1997), 247 ff. In the year of *Comus* the Inns of Court staged a masque, Shirley's *The Triumph of Peace*, to apologize for Prynne's misconduct; see Martin Butler, 'Politics and the Masque: *The Triumph of Peace*', *Seventeenth Century*, 2 (1987), 117–41.

4. *Ben Jonson*, ed. C. H. Herford and Percy and Evelyn Simpson, 11 vols. (Oxford, 1925–52, hereafter *H&S*), viii.410–11 (ll. 15–16).
5. Ibid. viii.402–6, i. 92.
6. Anon., *The None-Such Charles his Character* (London, 1651), 170. I owe this reference to Joseph Taylor.

is still alive, and in its structure the play recalls archaic dramatic and festive forms.[7]

Jonson's alienation from the court, however, was personal rather than ideological in motivation. Many of Charles's most controversial policies consisted in trying to translate into reality the political visions which had been dramatized in Jonsonian masques. Charles responded eagerly to the idea of a Britain in which political dissension had been banished and traditional social forms took on an aesthetic grace and harmony. In *Pleasure Reconciled to Virtue* Jonson had endorsed James's policy of defending rural sports; Charles had the book reissued. In *The Sad Shepherd* Jonson renewed his defence of rural traditions against Puritan attack, and rural games were commemorated in a royal entertainment of 1633.[8] Like James, Charles called on the nobility to return to the country and exercise their tra ditional duties of hospitality; court poets celebrated this theme in poems that echoed 'To Penshurst' and 'To Sir Robert Wroth'. Jonson's celebration of the peaceful Stuart forests received new relevance in 1634 when Charles announced substantial extensions of the traditional forest boundaries. James's policy of increasing ritualism in the Scottish church, celebrated in *Pleasure Reconciled to Virtue*, was followed through by Charles; Jonson wished him good fortune on his trip to Scotland in his 1633 entertainment. Where father and son differed was not so much in goals as in tactics: Charles had a stiffer sense of his royal dignity and was much less ready to compromise at the right moment, and his gestures of royal authority succeeded in arousing political alarm without gaining him loyalty. The tactlessness with which Charles handled Scottish problems was one of the major causes of the Civil War. Such a personality, shy, fastidious, always standing on ceremony, was likely to be ill at ease with someone as abrasive as Jonson.

Despite these personal differences, however, the masque form could be said to have embodied Jonson's world-view: his belief that transcendental religious truths had to be embodied in traditional rituals, that political ideals were dangerous unless identified with personal loyalties. The end of each masque united religious and

7. Anne Barton, 'Harking Back to Elizabeth: Ben Jonson and Caroline Nostalgia', *ELH* 48 (1981), 706–31. Martin Butler, 'Late Jonson', in Gordon McMullan and Jonathan Hope (eds.), *The Politics of Tragicomedy: Shakespeare and After* (London, 1992), 166–88, sees the late plays as closer to Newcastle's absolutism than to the politics of the Spenserian poets; for a constitutionalist reading see Julie Sanders, *Jonson's Theatrical Republics* (Houndmills, 1998), 144–79.

8. 'The King's Entertainment at Welbeck', *H&S*, vii.791–803. Jonson aligned himself with William Cavendish's programme of enlisting festivals against Puritan melancholy in his late entertainments, and also touched on the theme of agrarian rebellion, probably in response to the 'Western Rising' (below, n. 56), in *The Sad Shepherd*: see Julie Sanders, 'Jonson, *The Sad Shepherd*, and the North Midlands', *Ben Jonson Journal*, 6 (1999), 49–68.

political abstractions with the persons of the courtiers. Such a
world-view did imply limits on the poet's political autonomy: with
what authority could he lay claim to independence of established
institutions? Jonson had, in a sense, backed himself into a corner,
attacking all critics of the court as seditious malcontents when in
favour and finding himself impotent when out of favour. Jonson's
nostalgia for the Elizabethan age superficially resembled the disillu-
sion of the ageing Michael Drayton, whose last collection of
eclogues, *The Muses Elizium* (1630), evoked the glories of that age
in its title and in its 'golden' style. But even though Drayton had
patched up his old quarrel with Jonson, his reservations about the
masque form were more radical than his rival's. The Stuart masque
offered artificial aids to the imagination; it needed elaborate
machinery and spectacle to achieve its idealizing effects. In *The
Muses Elizium* Drayton drew a stark contrast between the 'golden
world' of his own imagination, a world evoking the glories of Elizabethan poetry, and the current state of the England of his day, ironically named 'Felicia', which had sunk into 'sordid slavery' and
neglected the Muses.[9] Partly because of his inhibitions about the
individual imagination, Jonson's poetry never makes such a stark
contrast between the inner world of the poetry and the public world.
Milton's mingling of pastoral and masquing conventions in *Comus*
indicates that he ultimately had more in common with Drayton
than with Jonson. And yet his attitude to Jonson's masques would
have been complex, for the older poet had consistently maintained
more artistic integrity than the younger masque-writers and had
ensured that poetic excellence was not completely sacrificed to
visual spectacle. Nor did the Spenserian tradition imply a complete
rejection of masques. Certainly the Spenserians, unlike Jonson,
tended to see religious truth as potentially independent of institutional embodiment: Milton was working within this tradition in 'On
the Morning of Christ's Nativity', where instead of celebrating a
particular court as the site of transcendent ideals he used the imagery of court masques to describe the final descent to earth of religious absolutes at the millennium. But throughout the Stuart period
there had been critics of the political content of court masques who
nevertheless did not reject the form itself: they wanted a 'reformation' of the masque, not its abolition. *Comus* is the most thoroughgoing 'reformation' of all; Milton both pays tribute to Jonson's art
and implicitly criticizes his politics.[1]

9. *The Works of Michael Drayton*, Ed. J. William Hebel, Kathleen Tillotson, and Bernard
   H. Newdigate, 2nd ed., 5 vols. (Oxford, 1961), 3:321–5; 5:223.
1. I am particularly indebted to John Creaser, '"The Present Aid of this Occasion": The
   Setting of *Comus*', in David Lindley (ed.), *The Court Masque* (Manchester, 1984), 111–
   34; see also David Norbrook, 'The Reformation of the Masque', in the same volume,

It seems something more than a coincidence that Milton should have chosen the name of Comus for the villain of his piece—a name which posterity has transferred to the whole masque. Jonson's masques of Comus, *Pleasure Reconciled to Virtue* and *For the Honour of Wales*, were not yet in print, but Milton's collaborator Henry Lawes had probably attended Jonson's recent royal entertainments, and would have been in a position to help him in research for the Ludlow masque; if Milton knew that Jonson had written a masque with Welsh associations he would have wanted to find out about it.[2] It cannot be proved that Jonson's Comus masques were a direct model, but the general strenuous didacticism of *Comus*, and the preponderance of text over spectacle, reflect Jonson's influence rather than current courtly fashions. On the other hand, the pastoralism of Milton's masque provided at least a superficial link with the queen's dramatic tastes, with what Prynne denounced as 'scurrilous amorous Pastorals'.[3] In these courtly pastorals, expensive scenic effects designed by Inigo Jones performed the somewhat paradoxical task of transforming the Banqueting House into a scene of rural simplicity. For one nostalgic royalist after the Civil War, pastoral drama was a symbol of the vanished culture of the Caroline era: Sir Richard Fanshawe dedicated to the young Prince of Wales his translation of Guarini's *The Faithfull Shepherd* with the claim that it presented 'a *Lantskip* of these Kingdoms . . . as well in the former flourishing, as the present distractions thereof'.[4] Milton's choice of the theme of chastity also had fashionable associations. After Buckingham's assassination and the king's rapprochement with his queen, much had been made of the married chastity of the royal couple. The Puritan Lucy Hutchinson later praised the 'temperate and chast and serious' Charles for banishing sexual excess from the court.[5] One of Sir William Davenant's masques centred on

94–110. On the politics of the Caroline masque see also Kevin Sharpe, *Criticism and Compliment: The Politics of Literature in the England of Charles I* (Cambridge, 1987); Butler, 'Politics and the Masque: *The Triumph of Peace*', 117–41; 'Politics and the Masque: *Salmacida spolia*', in Thomas Healy and Jonathan Sawday (eds.), *Literature and the English Civil War* (Cambridge, 1990), 59–74; 'Reform or Reverence? The Politics of the Caroline Masque', in J. R. Mulryne and Margaret Shewring (eds.), *Theatre and Government under the Early Stuarts* (Cambridge, 1993), 118–56. Sharpe stresses the political openness of Caroline court masques while Butler has become increasingly insistent on their ideological limits.

2. W. McClung Evans, *Henry Lawes: Musician and Friend of Poets* (New York, 1941), 31–2, 77, 97–8.

3. Prynne, *Histrio-Mastix*, 253; John G. Demaray, *Milton and the Masque Tradition: The Early Poems, Arcades, and Comus* (Cambridge, Mass., 1968), notes the resemblances between *Comus* and other Caroline masques but fails to emphasize the differences.

4. *A Critical Edition of Sir Richard Fanshawe's 1647 Translation of Giovanni Battista Guarini's Il Pastor Fido*, ed. William E. Simeone and Walter F. Staton, Jr. (Oxford, 1964), 5. On Caroline pastoral see John Harris, Stephen Orgel, and Roy Strong, *The King's Arcadia: Inigo Jones and the Stuart Court* (London, 1973).

5. *Memoirs of the Life of Colonel Hutchinson*, ed. James Sutherland (London, 1973), 46. Cf. G. F. Sensabaugh, 'Platonic Love and the Puritan Rebellion', *Studies in Philology*,

a 'Temple of Chaste Love'. But Davenant himself was sceptical about the new cult of chaste Platonic love, which easily developed, in its literary expressions, either into a blandness that had been lacking in Jonson's more robust poems and masques or into a titillating eroticism. Chastity had a special relevance to the Bridgewater family: three years earlier the Earl of Castlehaven, who had married Bridgewater's sister, had been beheaded for a series of brutal and exotic sexual crimes. Sir Henry Wotton had singled out Charles's punishment of Castlehaven as an example of the just morality he was imposing on the nation.[6] It is difficult to decide, however, whether this scandal would have made it more or less tactful for Milton to have chosen the theme of chastity. Perhaps more immediately to the point is that the leading role was to go to Lady Alice Egerton, a girl of 15; neither her sex nor her age would have made the choice of a more active central virtue appropriate. But this explanation, too, is not quite adequate: for Milton alters the conventional form of the masque to give his Lady an unusually prominent role. In his treatment of chastity he subtly revives some political and religious associations of that virtue which had been obscured by current fashions.

Only recently have critics recognized just how innovatory Milton was being in giving such a prominent role in a masque to a woman. Prynne's strictures against women actors were very topical in 1634. It was the Catholic queen who had encouraged play-acting by women, so that the topic was politically sensitive. The very act of giving a speaking part in a masque to any aristocrat was relatively new.[7] But Milton was not one to reject artistic innovations simply because of their unacceptable connotations; instead, he set himself to change those connotations, to make the innovation serve his

37:3 (1940), 457–81, and 'Love Ethics in Platonic Court Drama 1625–1642', *Huntington Library Quarterly*, 1 (1937–8), 277–304. Barbara K. Lewalski, 'Milton's *Comus* and the Politics of Masquing', in David Bevington and Peter Holbrook (eds.), *The Politics of the Stuart Court Masque* (Cambridge, 1998), 296–320 (310), argues that the Lady's celebration of chastity at the height of her reply to Comus, which is not found in the Bridgewater manuscript, may have been added as a specific retort to Davenant's *The Temple of Love*, which had strong Catholic associations.

6. Barbara Breasted, '*Comus* and the Castlehaven Scandal', *Milton Studies*, 3 (1971), 201–24; Sir Henry Wotton, *Reliquiae Wottonianae* (London, 1651), 150. Cynthia B. Herrup, *A House in Gross Disorder: Sex, Law and the 2nd Earl of Castlehaven* (New York, 1999), throws new light on this question by showing that this scandal was no mere family matter but had wide political ramifications, with those finding Castlehaven guilty of buggery including 'those most immediately dependent upon the King', while amongst those who retained doubts were several more independent figures, some of whom had opposed the forced loan (88).

7. These points are emphasized by Creaser, "'The Present Aid of this Occasion'", 117. On the feminist aspects of Caroline courtly entertainments see Erica Veevers, *Images of Love and Religion: Queen Henrietta Maria and Court Entertainments* (Cambridge, 1989).

own ideological purposes.[8] The parts which Henrietta Maria liked to play in court entertainments centred on concerns conventionally considered female, on love and intrigue. Lady Alice had taken part two years earlier in Aurelian Townshend's masque *Tempe Restor'd*, in which the queen and her ladies represented Beauty, while the king embodied the male principle of Heroic Virtue. Lady Alice was one of fourteen masquers representing Harmony; these ladies too were complimented for their beauty in the conventional language of love poetry. The masque arranged male and female virtues hierarchically; heroic virtue was ultimately superior because it appealed to the mind, whereas the queen embodied '*Corporeall* Beauty'. The masque presented this hierarchy of soul and body as smooth and harmonious, however: earthly magnificence became a living embodiment of the divine. At the end of the masque the evil enchantress Circe was so impressed by the splendour of the court that she abandoned her magic powers.[9]

Milton makes the relationship between virtue and physical appearance much more problematic, and challenges courtly notions of female virtue. In order to play her part effectively, Lady Alice would have had to develop qualities going far beyond the conventional aristocratic grace and deportment. She does not simply cling passively to her chastity, she justifies her position by appeal to a whole political philosophy—thus disconcerting Comus, who does not believe it to be a woman's role to think. The 'cavalier' poets had very clear and simple ideas about what women were for. But woman's conventional subordinate role was beginning to be challenged. A series of pamphlets in the second decade of the century had affirmed woman's dignity, defending Eve against the charges levelled at her by male theologians.[1] Before long, Puritan women in London were to be claiming a right to play a greater part in public affairs. The critical and rationalistic premises of Milton's own thought undermined many conventional justifications for the subordination of women. This very fact may have contributed to his later defensiveness on the subject of man's superiority. At the time

8. Jennifer Chibnall, '"To That Secure Fix'd State": The Function of the Caroline Masque Form', in Lindley (ed.), *The Court Masque*, 78–93, challenges simplified notions of the 'decadence' of Caroline masques, showing their artistic inventiveness.
9. *The Poems and Masques of Aurelian Townshend*, ed. Cedric C. Brown (Reading, 1983), 93–108; Brown demonstrates in his edition the close links between Townshend and the Bridgewater family (54–6). Sears Jayne, 'The Subject of Milton's Ludlow *Mask*', in John S. Diekhoff (ed.), *A Maske at Ludlow: Essays on Milton's Comus* (Cleveland, 1968), 165–87, speculates on ways in which Milton may have tried to Platonize Townshend's masque, and demonstrates the Neoplatonic associations of chastity; he does not, however, consider the more directly political aspects of the masque.
1. See, for example, Rachel Speght, *A Mouzell for Melastomus* (London, 1617), in *The Poems and Polemics of Rachel Speght*, ed. Barbara K. Lewalski (New York, 1996), 43–90. Spenser was invoked by such defenders of women as 'T.G.', *An Apologie for Woman-Kind* (London, 1605), sig. A4', and Daniel Tuvil, *Asylum Veneris* (London, 1616), 136–7.

of writing *Comus*, however, he may have been less defensive. Woman's equality and, indeed, superiority to men had already been proclaimed in a masque performed in 1618, at the height of the Jacobean controversy over women. Six female masquers, representing chastity and other female virtues, had been urged to

> know your Strength & your own Vertues see
> which in everie Several grace
> of the mind, or of the face,
> Gives women right to have Prioritie.
> Brave Amazonian Dames
> Made no count of Mankind but
> for a fitt to be at the Rutt.
> free fier gives the brightest flames;
> Menns overawing tames
> And Pedantlike our active Spirits smother.
> Learne, Virgins, to live free;
> Alas, would it might bee,
> weomen could live & lie with one another![2]

The end of the masque did not endorse this radical separatist position but did emphasize that men and women were equal.

The tone of this masque at Cole-Orton was playful, but there may have been a certain seriousness in the play. For the six male virtues were drawn from characters in *The Faerie Queene*, and the poet may have been responding to Spenser's questioning of conventional roles. Milton too may have been encouraged to rethink the conventional imagery of sexual relations by Spenser, whom he later described as 'sage and serious' (ii.516)—the adjectives with which the Lady praises virginity. Spenser's treatment of chastity had been influenced by the strong hostility to the old Catholic scheme of virtues in Protestant polemic. The chastity of monks and nuns was 'fugitive and cloister'd' (ii.515), and the artificial conditions under which it was maintained in the cloister led to hypocrisy and immorality. Bale had thundered against the falsity of the Roman cult of chastity. A century later Marvell was making similar points, rather more urbanely, in 'Upon Appleton House', where he contrasted the narrow-minded self-absorption of the nuns with Fairfax's active virtue and young Maria's learning. In *The Faerie Queene* Spenser had challenged convention by making his chief representative of Chastity an active, 'Amazonian Dame', Britomart. In *Comus* the Lady has to display her resourcefulness in unfamiliar and threaten-

---

2. This Cole-Orton masque, sponsored by Sir Thomas Beaumont, not the Earl of Essex as suggested in my first edition, is printed by R. Brotanek, *Die Englischen Maskenspiele* (Vienna, 1902), 328–37. ° ° °

ing surroundings. The Elder Brother's long speech in praise of chastity and beauty is fairly conventional in sentiment, and might almost have come from a Caroline court masque; what is extremely unusual is that his confidence in the magical power of these virtues proves to be exaggerated. The Lady's beauty and noble lineage do not make her miraculously immune. But she is given an opportunity to display her integrity and powers of argument. It could perhaps be argued that Milton is merely introducing a new set of stereotypes for ideal female behaviour; nevertheless, his rejection of courtly stereotypes is striking.

The Spenserian echoes in *Comus* are not confined to Book III. Comus in his palace with his enchanted cup is a male equivalent of Acrasia in the Bower of Bliss, and the opposition in Milton's imagery between the clear water of truth and the viscous liquid of intemperance probably owes something to Spenser's second book. Spenser's Acrasia is linked with Duessa, the wicked enchantress and antitype to the religious purity of Una. In a long tradition of apocalyptic literature, the temptations of idolatry had been represented as an enchanted cup; idolatry was defined as spiritual fornication, so that true faith became identified with chastity. In the Stuart period poets critical of the court had often drawn their imagery from Spenser's first three books. Under James the unchastity of the court had become notorious, providing a glaring contrast with the Virgin Queen who had been celebrated in a Petrarchan cult of Chastity. In his Spenserian satire *The Cuckow* Richard Niccols had shown the virgin Casta expelled first from the Bower of Bliss (James's court?) and then from Troynobantum (London?) and finally seeking refuge in Virgina (Virginia—a colony whose name recalled the Virgin Queen).[3] Other satirists drew on the imagery of Spenser's first book to signify their dislike of James's pacific foreign policy. William Browne had described the exile from court of the beautiful Aletheia in apocalyptic terms. The satirist John Day—an enemy of Jonson's—combined apocalyptic symbolism with 'faerie' legend in a satire written in the latter part of James's reign, describing how Error seduces Philosophos and his page Alethe with an enchanted cup and proceeds to entertain her captives with masques and antimasques. Time and Truth, Day implied, could not be found at court: lost time must be recovered elsewhere, with the aid of Industry.[4] By the 1630s, however, apocalyptic ideas were viewed

3. Hoyt H. Hudson, 'John Hepwith's Spenserian Satire upon Buckingham: With Some Jacobean Analogues', *Huntington Library Bulletin*, 6 (1934), 39–71 (62–5).
4. John Day, *Peregrinatio scholastica, Works*, ed. A. H. Bullen, 2 vols. (London, 1881), i. On the date see M. E. Borish, 'A Second Version of John Day's *Peregrinatio scholastica*', *Modern Language Notes*, 55 (1940), 35–9. One manuscript of this work—which was too politically sensitive to be published—was dedicated to William Austin, a great admirer of Spenser and a defender of women: see his *Haec homo* (London, 1637).

with more suspicion than ever at court. It is significant that the most overt revival of Spenserian symbolism in court entertainments of the 1630s came in 1636, when Princess Elizabeth's sons were on a visit to England and some courtiers hoped that the king would now declare war on Spain; a character named Britomartis appeared in an entertainment debating the issue of war.[5] In the previous reign Middleton had glorified apocalyptic Truth in a pageant for Sir Thomas Myddleton, a great sponsor of Protestant propaganda and Puritan lectureships in Wales; now the lectureships were being suppressed as seditious. Milton probably knew Middleton's apocalyptic satire *A Game at Chess*. In the opening scene a Catholic priest uses love-language similar to Comus's to try to tempt the chaste and Protestant White Queen's Pawn; his phrase 'the opening eyelids of the morn' reappears, with very different connotations, in *Lycidas*.[6]

Comus was performed on St Michael's Day, so that apocalyptic associations would have been appropriate; the phrase 'the sun-clad power of chastity' (l. 781), added in the 1637 edition, made such echoes slightly more explicit. The scene in which the Lady wanders in a dark and threatening forest recalls the Wood of Error at the start of *The Faerie Queene*. It is also reminiscent of a more famous dark forest, in the *Inferno*; it is interesting that when Milton was later charged by an opponent with loose living he declared that his reading in Dante and Petrarch had made him love chastity. These poets also, of course, provided authority for attacks on the Papacy. The foremost opponent of the apocalyptic tradition at the Stuart court had been Ben Jonson, and while it cannot be proved that Milton knew Jonson's masque of Comus, his handling of similar imagery seems to be pointedly different. One of Jonson's aims in *Pleasure Reconciled to Virtue* had been to defend royal ecclesiastical policy against Puritan as well as Catholic attacks, at a time when the new rituals the king was trying to introduce in Scotland were being denounced as idolatrous. Jonson had made his Comus, the repre-

Jonson linked Day and Middleton together as 'base fellows' (H&S, i.137); both had close connections with London Puritans. In the first edition I referred to marginalia in a copy of Browne's *Britannia's Pastorals* as being Milton's, but the attribution is rejected by John T. Shawcross, entry in William B. Hunter et al. (eds.), *A Milton Encyclopaedia*, 9 vols. (Lewisburg, Pa., 1978–83), v.74.
5. *The King and Queenes Entertainment at Richmond* (Oxford, 1636); ed. W. Bang and R. Brotanek, *Materialen zur Kunde des älteren englischen Dramas*, ii (Louvain, 1903), and see Martin Butler, 'Entertaining the Palatine Prince: Plays on Foreign Affairs 1635–1637', *English Literary Renaissance*, 13 (1983), 319–44; on Charles's apparent move towards a more militant policy about this time see R. M. Smuts, 'The Puritan Followers of Henrietta Maria in the 1630s', *English Historical Review*, 93 (1978), 26–45.
6. On Middleton's debt to 16th-century apocalyptic drama see Jane Sherman, 'The Pawns' Allegory in Middleton's *A Game at Chess*', *Review of English Studies*, NS 29 (1978), 147–59; on Milton and apocalyptic drama see Alice-Lyle Scoufos, 'The Mysteries in Milton's *Masque*', *Milton Studies*, 6 (1974), 113–42. * * *

sentative of riotous and disorderly festivity—and hence, in part, of idolatry—a relatively unformidable adversary. Hercules banished him and took back from him the cup he had 'abused'—on one allegorical level, a claim that elaborate ritual was a mere 'thing indifferent', idolatrous when abused but not intrinsically evil. Puritans feared that this argument, even if valid on a very general level, might be used to permit specific idolatrous practices to return to the church.

Milton's Comus is a much more dangerous figure than Jonson's. The reference to 'misused wine' (l. 47) may function as an allegorical reminder of the distinction between a tradition and its abuses, hence as a qualification of iconoclastic zeal; but the action of the masque emphasizes the formidable power of Comus the maker of false images, the immense danger of complacency in the face of idolatry. Comus' glass is broken but he is still on the loose at the end of the masque. If Milton did imitate Jonson's masque, he also implicitly criticized it. And in more general terms, his evocation of the apocalyptic tradition was a subtle reminder of the differences between the current cult of courtly chastity, sponsored by a Catholic queen, and older traditions. The closest he comes to a topical allusion is the Lady's indignant response to

> the sound
> Of riot, and ill-managed merriment,
> Such as the jocund flute, or gamesome pipe
> Stirs up among the loose unlettered hinds,
> When for their teeming flocks, and granges full,
> In wanton dance they praise the bounteous Pan,
> And thank the gods amiss. (ll. 170–6)

This opposition between literacy and traditional cultural forms is a characteristic Puritan emphasis. It is a distinctly odd sentiment to come from an aristocratic character in a masque, where it was more usual to find praise of the ruler in pastoral terms, as in Jonson's *Pan's Anniversary* (1620):

> PAN is our All, by him we breath, wee live,
> Wee move, we are.[7]

Jonson may have agreed with Newcastle that 'hinds' ought to be 'unlettered'. But the Lady's anxieties reflect the concern amongst Welsh Puritans that the Laudian regime was defending idolatrous sports at the same time as it was placing restrictions on the preaching of the Word.

7. *H&S*, vii.535, ll. 192–3.

Milton does not, however, reject dancing altogether. The rustics' sports turn out to be innocent; what the Lady has heard is the far more sinister sound of Comus' entourage. At the end of the masque there is dancing both by countrymen and by the Bridgewater children. But Milton, more than Jonson, and still more than current Caroline masque-writers, places the emphasis on moral struggle rather than courtly resolution. Only after Comus' rout and the Lady's release do the virtuous characters return to court; the dancing is a supplement to the main action rather than being, as in many masques, the central agent and instrument of virtue. *Comus* has often been accused of being undramatic. One answer to this charge is that masque conventions demanded the juxtaposition of moral absolutes rather than psychological realism. But most masques used spectacle to give dramatic force to the conflicts; in *Comus*, however, spectacle plays a less central part. Certainly there was scenery, and, within the limits imposed by the setting, it was probably fairly elaborate. What was original was the use Milton made of scenery. The setting for Comus' enchanted palace would have shown 'all manner of deliciousness'; but Comus, like Spenser's Archimago, is a creator of false images. He compares himself to Apollo, whose song made Daphne '[r]oot-bound' (l. 661)—organic imagery is less positive in Milton than in Jonson. The Lady must resist by an act of moral iconoclasm, refusing to be impressed by the 'magic structures' of his art. Precisely the same demand is made of the spectator. But the Lady is not even granted the power accorded to Spenser's Guyon of destroying this Bower of Bliss. Like many of Milton's Christian heroes, she is placed in a situation which is primarily one of passive resistance, a situation which is so far from conforming to standard notions of the heroic that it verges on the absurd. Immobilized in her chair, she is in a state almost as grotesque as Kent in the stocks in *King Lear*, a play that was on Milton's mind when he composed *Comus*. She can display neither the feats of strength granted to the men in conventional masques nor the courtly graces of the women.

What the Lady does have is the power of argument. She replies to Comus' speech of seduction with an indignant refutation of his arguments, attacking not only his immediate conclusions but his basic premises, his assumption that luxury and conspicuous consumption are natural. A more equitable distribution of wealth would bring society much closer to the order of nature than the traditional hierarchies. The Lady draws attention to the power of her language: she had not intended 'to have unlocked my lips' (l. 755) but her tongue must check Comus' pride. In a passage added in revision, Milton further developed the idea of the power of speech: if she really unfolded the whole mystery of virginity,

> the uncontrolled worth
> Of this pure cause would kindle my rapt spirits
> To such a flame of sacred vehemence,
> That dumb things would be moved to sympathize,
> And the brute Earth would lend her nerves, and shake,
> Till all thy magic structures reared so high,
> Were shattered into heaps o'er thy false head. (ll. 792–8)

The word 'unfold' hints at an apocalyptic unveiling, at a destructive force which the Lady is only just able to keep in check. But she does keep it in check, for reasons which remain, on a naturalistic level, slightly unclear. Comus continues to try to make her drink; only the brothers' arrival interrupts him, and they fail to capture him. Milton undermines the confidence in human self-sufficiency normally displayed in masques: *Pleasure Reconciled to Virtue* ended with praise of virtue as a perfect quality which refines herself 'by hir owne light' (l. 341), *Comus* with an acknowledgement that virtue may be 'feeble' (l. 1021) without divine aid.

Milton's presentation of the Lady's dilemma combines intense conviction about the power of language with a sense of absurdity and impotence. Here he was revealing his own view of his situation as a prophetic poet. A self-consciously youthful writer who had taken a vow of chastity, he was aware that he would seem ridiculous in the eyes of the world. By the solitary pursuit of learning, he had recently written, 'a man cutts himselfe off from all action & becomes the most helplesse, pusilanimous & unweapon'd creature in the [world], the most unfit & unable to doe that wch all mortals most aspire to[,] either to defend & be usefull to his freinds, or to offend his enimies' (i.319). His learning almost unmanned him.[8] But he was convinced that when he did eventually publish a major work it would have a powerful effect. The commission to write the Ludlow masque gave him an opportunity to put his learning to good use, but it also involved difficult compromises. For the first major public display of his skill he had to make his mark in a form that Puritans like Prynne regarded as inherently idolatrous: for Prynne theatres and masquing-halls were little different from temples to heathen idols. Milton was well aware that the true situation was more complex: Jonson had been able to make masques into moral statements. But he had had to pay a price: he often gained least recognition from the courtiers for his most serious efforts. *Pleasure Reconciled to Virtue*, arguably his most didactic masque, had not been well received. The problem of

---

8. John T. Shawcross, 'Milton and Diodati: An Essay in Psychodynamic Meaning', *Milton Studies*, 7 (1975), 127–63, uses such statements to argue that the young Milton (the 'Lady of Christ's') had passive homosexual tendencies. Milton's sense of 'weaponless-ness' may, however, have been conditioned by political more than 'psychodynamic' factors.

political compromise was of course an old one: in the *Utopia* Hythlodaeus had argued that serious philosophy—by which, in this context,
he meant social criticism—would never be welcome at court. More's
persona had replied by comparing an austere humanist who tried to
lecture princes to a figure in tragic attire interrupting a court comedy and quoting from a play which prophesied the destruction of the
old unjust order and prayed for a better one. More declared that such
a course would be too indecorous. But this was effectively what Milton did in *Comus*, though he skilfully kept just within the bounds of
decorum. More the writer, of course, had been less timid than his
persona, had given voice to Hythlodaeus as well as to counsels of
moderation. Milton greatly admired More and other utopian writers
like Bacon who could imagine 'better and exacter things, then were
yet known, or us'd'; but he believed that conservative Laudian bishops were unable to appreciate 'the largenesse of their spirits' (i.881).
At least one Caroline churchman and poet, John Donne, did in fact
admire the *Utopia* and found it highly relevant to the current situation. Beside the passage where Hythlodaeus denounced monopolies
and the application of political pressure to judges he wrote 'ship-
monie' on his copy; where Hythlodaeus complained that the king
was allowed to do all he wanted, Donne wrote 'criers up of yᵉ Kings
prerogative'. But Milton would have thought that the conduct of this
pillar of the Caroline church, preaching in praise of monarchy and
obedience in public while he scribbled his private doubts in the margins of his books, itself exemplified the intellectually narrowing consequences of authoritarianism.[9] In *Comus* he showed that he had the
courage of his convictions.

   The Lady's speech, in fact, came close to shattering the very
basis of the masque form: whatever its intellectual pretensions, the
masque was ultimately an exercise in the very kind of conspicuous
consumption she denounced. Austere criticisms were normally
voiced in court entertainments only by mean-minded Puritans who
failed to understand the value of magnificence. The Lady was
touching on issues that were currently sensitive: in the late 1620s
and early 1630s there had been extensive agrarian disturbances in
south-west England in protest against illegal enclosures. A Puritan
in the Forest of Dean was arrested in 1631 for inciting rebellion
by preaching universal equality.[1] The government took measures

9. John B. Gleason, 'Dr Donne in the Courts of Kings: A Glimpse from Marginalia', *Journal of English and Germanic Philology*, 69 (1970), 599–612 (601–2). New editions of
   Robinson's translation of the *Utopia* were in fact published in 1624 and 1639. The
   publisher, with no sense of irony, dedicated the translation to one of More's descendants, praising him for his birth and the magnificence of his estate.
1. Eric Kerridge, 'The Revolts in Wiltshire against Charles I', *Wiltshire Archaeological
   and Natural History Magazine*, 57 (1958–60), 64–75; Christopher Hill, *Change and
   Continuity in Seventeenth-Century England* (London, 1974), 18. The lecturer in ques-

against illegal enclosures and the disturbances died down; the anxieties they had raised, however, were still reflected in Davenant's masque *Britannia triumphans* (1638): Jones's designs included the figure of Jack Kett, leader of the 1549 uprising, amongst other rebels. The Lady's speech is studiedly vague and could be interpreted as compatible with aristocratic rule: she urges that 'every just man' should be given his due, which might imply distribution by geometrical rather than arithmetical proportion. She is, after all, a noblewoman, and one must assume that the earl's payment of Milton for the masque did not constitute wasteful extravagance. But her insistence on government by rational principles rather than reverence for traditional aristocratic values is more in the spirit of the *Utopia* than of current court literature.

The Lady's discourse is potentially anti-hierarchical in yet another way: a woman lectures a man on how society should be governed. Denied participation in conventional forms of public discourse, some women sought an outlet in prophetic utterance. Prophecies against Laud were circulating widely in the 1630s, but for a woman to claim prophetic inspiration was regarded as doubly subversive. One such prophetess, however, would have been very much on the Bridgewater family's mind. Lady Eleanor Davies had acquired a reputation for accurate prophecy after she foretold the doom of Buckingham. Though not radical in her social views, she was fiercely anti-Laudian, and in 1633, denied an outlet for her views in print by the censorship, she went to the Netherlands and had some of her writings printed there. A poem about Belshazzar's feast described the inevitable doom that awaited this evil monarch who held drunken feasts in a 'Banqueting-house' and encouraged idolatrous Sabbath revels.[2] The parallels with Caroline masques were obvious enough and were to be

---

tion, Peter Simon, indignantly rejected the charge of seditious speech and was released. He did admit to having preached that all were equal 'setting the Kings place and qualitie aside'. Whatever his intentions, it is possible that his parishioners missed his qualifications; the authorities were certainly jumpy about the 'western rising' of 1626–32 which spread through several parts of the midlands and west of England: Buchanan Sharp, *In Contempt of All Authority: Rural Artisans and Riot in the West of England, 1586–1660* (Berkeley and Los Angeles, 1980), 132–3 and *passim; Calendar of State Papers, Domestic Series, 1631–33,* 36. Like his precursor, Simon was a committed Puritan pitted against a strongly royalist 'dark corner of the land'; he became a strong supporter of Parliament during the Civil War: Ian Archer, *The History of the Haberdashers' Company* (Chichester, 1991), 80.

2. Lady Eleanor Audeley (she also used the names of Douglas and Davies), *Strange and Wonderfull Prophesies* (London, 1649), 3: this volume reprints a poem first printed in Amsterdam in 1633. On women and prophecy see Keith Thomas, *Religion and the Decline of Magic: Studies in Popular Beliefs in Sixteenth- and Seventeenth-Century England,* rev. edn. (Harmondsworth, 1973), 162–4. The burgeoning literature on women prophets includes Phyllis Mack, *Visionary Women: Ecstatic Prophecy in Seventeenth-Century England* (Berkeley and Los Angeles, 1992) and Hilary Hinds, *God's Englishwomen: Seventeenth-Century Radical Sectarian Writing and Feminist Criticism* (Manchester, 1996); on Lady Eleanor see Esther S. Cope, *Handmaid of the Holy Spirit: Dame Eleanor Davies, Never soe Mad a Ladie* (Ann Arbor, 1992).

gleefully pointed out by Lady Eleanor when she reprinted this poem
after the king had been executed outside the Whitehall Banqueting
House. When she returned from the Netherlands she was quickly
arrested for circulating such propaganda, and she brought further
punishment on herself by prophesying that Laud would die before
the year was out. Despite such inflammatory utterances, however,
she had friends amongst the great and famous; Elizabeth of Bohemia
herself, who was sympathetic to the apocalyptic world-view, had
pleaded her cause. Elizabeth pointed out that she was after all of
noble blood. She was in fact the sister of the notorious Earl of Castlehaven, whose cause she vehemently championed in her writings.
Unchastity was not the only charge that had recently been levelled
against Bridgewater's relatives by marriage: there was also the
offence of subversive prophecy. Lady Eleanor was still in prison
when *Comus* was performed. Milton's Lady makes no explicitly feminist points—she speaks only of every just *man*—and her prophetic
speech is no more a direct allusion to Lady Eleanor than the chastity
theme is a direct reference to Castlehaven. The fact remains that a
writer anxious to pay anodyne compliments would have steered clear
of all such topics; Milton highlighted points of political, social, and
religious tension. The Lady's speech with its iconoclastic philosophy
threatens to disrupt the courtly framework. Milton's only other dramatic work was to be a consciously anti-theatrical tragedy, *Samson
Agonistes*, which allegorically denounced the idolatry and aestheti-
cized politics of the Restoration and ended with the hero's bringing
down a 'theatre' on the spectators' heads.[3]

Some critics have found the Lady's iconoclastic discourse flat and
poetically uninteresting and have complained that Milton gives the
better poetry to Comus. The seduction speeches are certainly given
great power, putting the audience as well as the Lady to the test:
Milton does not deny that poetry is capable of making evil seem
beautiful. Closer reading of Comus' speeches, however, reveals the
care with which Milton indicates the limitations of his ideology.
There is no crude antithesis between art and bald moralization.[4]
Milton was to praise Spenser as 'a better teacher than *Scotus* or *Aquinas*' (ii.516), and the context in *Areopagitica* makes it clear that one
thing he valued in Spenser was his ability to try out new ideas, to step
outside conventional intellectual frameworks. Philosophers like
More and Bacon, who destroyed conventional idols and encouraged
intellectual progress, had more in common with poets than with

3. Nicholas Jose, *Ideas of the Restoration in English Literature 1660–71* (London, 1984),
   ch. 8.
4. Archie Burnett, *Milton's style: The Shorter Poems, 'Paradise Regained,' and 'Samson
   Agonistes'* (London, 1981), 41 ff.

conservative scholastics. The second brother praises 'divine philoso-phy' because it is

> Not harsh, and crabbed as dull fools suppose,
> But musical as is Apollo's lute,
> And a perpetual feast of nectared sweets,
> Where no crude surfeit reigns. (ll. 475–9)

The Lady's prophetic voice is so powerful because it is informed by this musical quality. Her song moves even Comus: the 'sweet madness' of his mother's Bacchanalian music lulled the senses and the pleasure it gave was deceptive. The Lady's song does not give less pleasure but merely a different and more permanent kind, a 'sober certainty of waking bliss' (l. 262). It gives 'resounding grace to all heaven's harmonies' (l. 242): the pun which fuses divine grace with the sophisticated art of the grace-note is characteristic.[5] On this elevated plane, pleasure and virtue can be reconciled.

But Milton's masque constantly returns to the idea that the power relations of the fallen world can distort artistic pleasure, that the arts can be turned to politically dubious ends. Throughout *Comus*, music and poetry are seen as essentially independent of the court, and more closely allied with natural forces. Already in *Arcades* Milton had almost overshadowed the courtly compliment by a long speech in which the Genius of the Wood described his kinship with the harmony of nature. In *Comus* music becomes a symbol of transcendence rather than courtly splendour. But Milton's view of the relationship between art and politics is extremely complex. The Spirit's pastoral disguise links him with current Caroline masque conventions, and indeed Lawes participated in court entertainments. He was also involved with music in the royal chapel. In the Civil War he was to side with the king. At moments *Comus* verges on becoming the first English opera, an art form which had emerged at Italian courts and depended on extravagant princely subsidy.[6] But Milton, in his younger days at least, did not reject artistic innovations simply because their patronage might be suspect. It was more constructive to look for the deeper potential of these innovations, to find in them an ideological significance that their originators might not themselves have recognized.

In a poem addressed to Lawes, Edmund Waller compared medieval music to ornate stained glass: the musical elaboration obscured

---

5. John Hollander, *The Untuning of the Sky: Ideas of Music in English Poetry, 1500–1700* (Princeton, 1961) 323.
6. For an interesting discussion of the social basis of opera see H. G. Koenigsberger, 'Republics and Courts in Italian and European Culture in the Sixteenth and Seventeenth Centuries', *Past and Present*, 83 (1979), 32–56.

the sense. Lawes's music, which respected the meaning of the words, was thus iconoclastic, stripping away ritual embellishment.[7] Puritans had long valued music as more spiritual, less immediately sensual than the visual arts, and they especially valued the ability to harmonize sound with sense. As has been seen, in Milton's early poetry the reform of music had taken on apocalyptic associations. Even after he and Lawes had parted company politically, Milton was still prepared to address to him a sonnet of warm praise for his music. The concluding allusion to Dante in this sonnet very subtly plays his sense of ideological difference from his old friend against a poignant awareness of their common artistic interests. Cromwell was personally fond of music, and Lawes was to provide some music in 1656 for an entertainment by Davenant which opened the way to opera performances. As a young man he had not been associated with violently anti-Puritan circles: he had gained his position at court through the patronage of the third Earl of Pembroke, a defender of the low-church tradition and supporter of Spenserian poets; he had set to music poems by Pembroke himself, his political ally Rudyerd, and William Browne.[8] He was also renowned for settings of the Psalms. One critic has argued that the 'haemony' which grows 'in another country', obtained from a 'leathern scrip' (ll. 625 ff.), represents the Word of God: as mediator between the actors in the masque and the divine truth, Thyrsis becomes a Protestant shepherd, in the tradition of prophetic literature rather than Italianate court pastoral.[9] His skill as a pioneer counts for more than his associations with a conservative environment: this musician who 'first taught our English music' the right procedure is a worthy partner for the young Puritan poet ambitious to achieve

> What never yet was heard in tale or song
> From old, or modern bard in hall, or bower. (ll. 44–5)

It was conventional for the devisers of masques to insert some kind of compliment to their own poetic, musical, or scenic skills. But if the 'magic' that effected the masque's resolution was in an immediate sense the creation of the court artists, it was ultimately a manifestation of the power of the royal patron, and this would be made very clear. In *Comus*, however, the magic is very firmly in the

7. *The Poems of Edmund Waller*, ed. G. Thorn Drury, 2 vols. (London, 1905), i.20. For an extensive discussion see Percy A. Scholes, *The Puritans and Music in England and New England* (Oxford, 1934).
8. Evans, *Henry Lawes*, 32, 37, 41; for more on Milton, Lawes, and Waller, see Norbrook, *Writing the English Republic: Poetry, Rhetoric, and Politics, 1627–1660* (Cambridge, England: 1999) 160–3.
9. Cedric C. Brown, 'The Shepherd, the Musician, and the Word in Milton's Masque', *Journal of English and Germanic Philology*, 78 (1979), 522–44; *Milton's Aristocratic Entertainments*, 104–15.

hands of musician and poet. It is the Spirit who tells the brothers how to free their sister; and the aristocrats bungle the attempt. This can be put down to their youth: the masque is an educational exercise in which paternal authority is delegated to the children's tutor. But in a conventional masque the Lady's final release would have been achieved by the sudden revelation of the virtue of the courtiers or the beauty of their ladies. In *Comus*, by contrast, the Earl of Bridgewater, the representative of royal and patriarchal authority, plays no part in the resolution of the action. There are many echoes of *The Tempest*, but here it is Ariel, not the Duke of Milan, who is in charge. The Lady is saved not by heavenly courtiers descending from above but by the river-goddess Sabrina rising from below. Though she has some courtly associations—she was a British princess in legend—Sabrina is essentially an image of the beauty and harmony of nature; and hence, through the association between water and prophetic song that runs through the masque, of music and poetry. She can save the Lady only if she is 'right invoked in warbling song' together with 'adjuring verse'. Her song is a virtuoso display of Lawes's monodic art, combining sensuousness with sharpness of phonetic outline. This regenerate art is not narrowly austere—Sabrina's waters are both symbols of chastity and agents of fertility, invoked by the shepherds—but its clarity and precision distinguished it clearly from the courtly wine and viscous liquors peddled by Comus, who ridicules the idea that we should '[d]rink the clear stream' (l. 721).

The opposition between clear water and courtly 'opiate' (Trinity MS, l. 729) is developed throughout the masque, and it draws on long-established conventions in the prophetic and apocalyptic traditions. It is, essentially, a distinction between discourse corrupted by association with idolatry and injustice and discourse which is able to break free of these constraints and mirror divine truth. In *The Advancement of Learning* Bacon consistently associated reformed learning with flowing water. Milton was to develop this imagery in his political writings: 'Truth is compar'd in Scripture to a streaming fountain; if her waters flow not in a perpetuall progression, they sick'n into a muddy pool of conformity and tradition' (ii.543). Bacon argued that the 'idols' of received ideas were a prime cause of the failure to understand the secrets of nature; as the apocalyptic revelation advanced, these idols would gradually be destroyed and full harmony with nature achieved. Puritans like Cartwright had accused those Anglicans who justified ecclesiastical traditions by appeal to the order of nature of a comparable idolatry: nature was not patterned after human institutions. In *Comus* the characters' relationship to nature becomes a sign of their moral state. The masque is pervaded with the 'faerie' lore which in the Spenserian

tradition had increasingly become associated with imaginative independence of the court. The Spirit can achieve perfect harmony with
his surroundings through his music: his songs have often 'delayed
The huddling brook'. His music can transform nature precisely
because he is willing to listen to nature, to subordinate his own personality to a wider universe, so that natural and artificial sounds
harmonize perfectly with each other, just as his monodic music
respects, and co-operates with, the sounds and meanings of language. Comus' music rudely shatters the silence of the nocturnal
landscape, whereas the Lady's song is sensitive to the atmosphere, it
floats 'upon the wings of silence' and makes Silence wish 'to be
never more Still to be so displaced'. Even Comus can respond to the
Lady's song, and the opening of his first speech is powerfully lyrical:
even evil can pay tribute to the divine order. In a similar manner, in
Book I of *Paradise Lost* (ll. 781–8) Milton was to make the fallen
angels suddenly dwindle in a simile comparing them to dancing
elves. But when he is in his palace Comus loses his sensitivity to
nature, which he sees as something to be appropriated, existing only
to 'please and sate the curious taste'. Beauty is 'nature's coin', a mere
exchange value. Even the silkworms are seen as labouring in 'shops'
to satisfy their customers. Beneath Comus' praise of nature's fertility there is a certain fear. Apocalyptic writers like Hakewill were
enthusiastically predicting a massive increase in the earth's abundance; Comus as courtier lacks a full responsiveness to the divine
measure and order of the universe, he fears that without human
intervention nature would be 'strangled with her waste fertility' (l.
728). She must therefore be consumed.[1]

  Comus is, of course, a perverter rather than a representative of
traditional aristocratic values; but there is a suggestion that the
traditional rural and courtly rituals which were held to mirror the
cosmic order in fact blunted awareness of deeper levels of cosmic
harmony. To construct a truly 'natural' order, based on conformity
to the divine pattern, it would be necessary to reverse the process:
rather than projecting conventional social hierarchies anthropo-
morphically on to the cosmos, and thus aestheticizing politics, it
would be necessary to listen with a new attentiveness to the voice of
nature. Milton was not advocating a simple primitivism: it needed
effort to improve human arts to the point where they became truly
natural, just as spontaneous oratory required more effort than par-
roting clichés, and religious worship which did away with traditional rituals placed more demands on the congregation than the

1. Cf. Ronald W. Hepburn, 'George Hakewill: The Virility of Nature', *Journal of the His-
   tory of Ideas*, 16 (1955), 135–50. On Cartwright and analogies from nature see now
   David Norbrook, 'Rhetoric, Ideology, and the Elizabethan World Picture', in Peter
   Mack (ed.), *Renaissance Rhetoric* (London, 1994), 140–64.

'dull Opiat' of 'the drone of one plaine Song' (i.691). Lawes's music demanded an unprecedented degree of musical skill which was itself the sign of a reawakening harmony with nature. It has been well said that *Comus* is 'a study in listening'. Sabrina must 'listen and save'; in the final speech mortals are urged to '[l]ist . . . if your ears be true' (l. 996).[2] Milton's poetry does of course draw on conventional symbolism to describe natural processes: Sabrina's chariot is thick set with rich jewels. But the chariot and jewels paradoxically seem to stray (l. 894), wandering in the perpetually flowing water and in the turns of Milton's artful syntax: static artifice is set against natural process.[3]

As Milton almost defiantly proclaimed by his title, the Ludlow *Maske* adhered to the orthodox conventions of the genre. But only just: the work keeps threatening to break out of its allotted boundaries. The end of the 1634 version was perhaps its most conventional feature, and this may be why Milton felt the need to change it before publication. Perhaps at Lawes's request, the 1634 ending was relatively simple.[4] The Spirit interrupted the courtly dancers, who were performing in front of a backdrop representing Ludlow Castle itself, in order to present the children's skill in dancing: they could emulate the 'court guise' of Mercury. After praising the children to the proud parents, and introducing a final dance, the Spirit gave a short concluding speech in praise of virtue. Mercury had made a similar speech at the end of *Pleasure Reconciled to Virtue*, calling on the masquers to re-ascend the hill of virtue. Despite this gesture of transcendence, however, this and all Stuart court masques celebrated the incarnation of divine qualities in the persons of the courtiers. King James was the god Hesperus, and the court with its beautiful ladies was the Garden of the Hesperides, a site of virtuous pleasure. In the Ludlow performance the Spirit began by descending from the Gardens of Hesperus to the masquing-hall. For the 1637 publication, however, Milton restored this passage to what was probably its position in the first draft, as part of the Spirit's concluding speech before he ascended to heaven, thus emphasizing transcendence rather than immanence. And he added two further passages which heightened the tension between the earthly and the heavenly. The Garden of Hesperus merged with the Garden of Adonis, which had been located above the normal action of Spenser's Legend of Chastity. To some extent this allusion mitigated the austerity of the masque's main action, serving as a reminder that sexual pleasure was not evil in itself. Spenser's

2. Angus Fletcher, *The Transcendental Masque: An Essay on Milton's 'Comus'* (Ithaca, NY, 1971), 166. Cf. John D. Cox, 'Poetry and History in Milton's Country Masque', *ELH* 44 (1977), 622–40.
3. Burnett, *Milton's Style*, 64–5.
4. Parallel texts of the different versions are provided by S. E. Sprott, *John Milton: A Maske: The Earlier Versions* (Toronto, 1973).

third book had contained a prophecy of its heroine's marriage, and
Milton would have shared Spenser's reservations about the traditional
cult of virginity. On the other hand, his dramatization of chastity had
permitted a sharp critique of aristocratic conventions. E. M. W.
Tillyard argued that the oblique allusion to marriage would be
appropriate to a masque: 'The setting is aristocratic; the Lady,
though but young, will one day be a great lady. She must take her
place in society and do what is expected of her.[5] But Milton, in
Comus, was not quite doing what was expected of a masque-writer;
and, as it turned out, the Lady did not do what was expected of
her—she did not marry until 1652.

The climactic allusions to marriage in the Spirit's speech are not
references to traditional secular festivities but to the apocalyptic
mystical marriage. His imagination moves 'far above' the Garden of
Adonis to a heavenly realm where Psyche is united with Cupid. This
myth was a conventional allegory for the union of the soul with heavenly love; it had become popular at the Caroline court. But it also
had apocalyptic associations, to which Milton delicately pointed.
Psyche had become a symbol of the true, Invisible Church, wandering in the wilderness; Milton's description of Psyche's labours as
'wandering' alludes to this idea and sets up an association with the
earlier scene where the Lady wanders in the dark forest. But Psyche
is now reunited with Cupid, the souls of the godly are with Christ.[6]
The traditional epithalamic imagery with which Milton celebrated
this union was in some ways a repudiation of asceticism. A famous
passage in Revelation 14: 3–5, told of a heavenly song that was audible only to the undefiled; Milton was emphatically to reject the
notion that this passage alluded only to virgins, as if marriage were a
defilement (i.892–3). Cupid and Psyche are to have offspring, the
'blissful twins' Youth and Joy (ll. 1009–10). This masque of chastity
ends with images of spiritual bliss which strongly imply that sexual
joy, and the joy of poetic composition, can share its nature. But not
only the births but the marriage itself will take place in the future:
like Foxe's *Christus triumphans*, Milton's masque ends on a note of
incompleteness. Secular time has been no more than an antimasque
for the apocalyptic unmasking. Meanwhile, Comus remains on the
loose, and it is essential to be vigilant in case he should attempt
'some . . . new device' (l. 940).

---

5. E. M. W. Tillyard, 'The Action of *Comus*', in Diekhoff (ed.), *A Maske at Ludlow*, 43–57
   (54).
6. Psyche appears in Foxe's *Christus triumphans*; for the true church as Psyche cf. one of
   Fairfax's eclogues: Godfrey of Bulloigne: *A Critical Edition of Edward Fairfax's Translation of Tasso's* Gerusalemme liberata, *Together with Fairfax's Original Poems*, ed. Kathleen M. Lea and T. M. Gang (Oxford, 1981), 665–75. On this myth at court see
   Graham Parry, *The Golden Age Restor'd* (Manchester, 1981), 196–7.

Despite its criticisms of aristocratic assumptions, *Comus* seems to have pleased the Bridgewater family. Milton had observed the conventional forms and his more oblique allusions were too subtle to be easily noticed. What was obvious was that this was a masque of unusual literary excellence, whose publication would therefore reflect credit on its noble patrons. And in 1637 it was published, with a dedication by Lawes to Bridgewater's heir, Viscount Brackley (the Elder Brother). But Milton added a Virgilian epigraph indicating that the work was coming to the light prematurely. Such professions were of course conventional; but Milton does seem to have felt that he had not yet found the right subject, that his verse needed to find a new direction. *Comus* represented a victory of personal integrity over public conventions, but a victory gained at the cost of extreme indirectness and of going against the grain of the form he had to use: even more than in Jonson's masques, humanist scholarship is disproportionate to the social occasion.[7] Milton did not put his name to the masque and seems to have made no effort to use his new connections to gain a place at court; he continued his programme of private study.

*   *   *

WILLIAM KERRIGAN

From The Root-Bound Lady in *Comus*[†]

The occasion for the entertainment now known as *Comus* was the presidency of John Egerton. But after the opening speech installs his "new-entrusted Scepter" within the cosmic hierarchy of government, the masque proceeds to celebrate his authority and his fitness to rule within the realm of domestic politics. Families, too, have

---

7. Interesting new evidence has come to light about the reception of *Comus*. In 1637 a masque of Comus was performed at Skipton in Yorkshire, the dwelling of Henry Clifford, Earl of Cumberland. The cast list makes it very unlikely that this was Milton's masque, but it does seem that the figure of Comus was a continuing focus for different ideological interpretations of the masque: Martin Butler, 'A Provincial Masque of Comus, 1636', *Renaissance Drama*, NS 17 (1986), 149–73. Clifford was a close friend of the absolutist-leaning Earl of Strafford, who was now patronizing James Shirley, author of another 1634 masque, and had also advised William Cavendish over his plans for court advancement; we might infer that the text would have offered a more positive image of Comus than Milton. A masque that seems to respond to *Comus* at a number of points was staged at Bretby in Derbyshire in 1640: a satyr exalts country simplicity over the court but is won round to the superior delights of courtly sports. The author, Sir Aston Cokayne, was a Catholic: *The Dramatic Works of Sir Aston Cokain*, ed. J.H. Maidment and W.H. Logan (Edinburgh, [1874]), 9–13.

† From William Kerrigan, *The Sacred Complex: On the Psychogenesis of "Paradise Lost"* (Cambridge, Mass.: Harvard University Press, 1983), pp. 22–37. Copyright © 1983 by the President and Fellows of Harvard College. Reprinted by permission of the publisher.

their rituals, and *Comus* is a ritual for the unification of a family, its plot derived from the actual journey of three children to the "wish't presence" (950) of their parents.[1] When the siblings arrive at the parental seat, they are certified as Egertons in the manner of a ceremony of investiture:

> Noble Lord, and Lady bright,
> I have brought ye new delight,
> Here behold so goodly grown
> Three fair branches of your own.   (966–969)

These "fair branches" belong to the family tree by merit as well as birthright. Unlike the herd of Comus, who "all their friends and native home forget" (76), the Egerton children have remembered their native home, and because they have not lost their "human count'nance" (68), they can in turn be remembered *at* their native home. The particular question decided en route to this reunion is whether the scepter of the Lord President commands obedience and legitimacy in the conscience of his daughter when she is, for a time, the captive of a tempter's magic. In line with the general movement from political to familial authority, the symbolism of virtue in *Comus* situates conscience at its origins in childhood.

Virtue bears its own "bright day," able to see in dark places, whereas vice "Benighted walks under the midday Sun" (381–384). The tempter cannot, his captive assures him, "touch the freedom of my mind" (663). "Love virtue, she alone is free" (1019). Such passages have the ring of ancient sentiment, a wisdom almost global, and we know before we check that maxims like these will have ricocheted through the diverse minds of Plato, Plutarch, Cicero, Seneca, and Augustine. But what is this wisdom about virtue and freedom that has flowed into Ludlow Castle from so many sources? Dancing in the night, the tempter clarifies his opposition:

> Rigor now is gone to bed,
> And Advice with scrupulous head,
> Strict Age, and sour Severity,
> With their grave Saws in slumber lie.   (108–110)

---

1. The element of familial ritual in *Comus* has been noticed by David Wilkinson, "The Escape from Pollution: A Comment on 'Comus,'" *Essays in Criticism*, X (1960), 34, and Barbara Breasted, "*Comus* and the Castlehaven Scandal," *Milton Studies* III, ed. James Simmonds (Pittsburgh: University of Pittsburgh Press, 1970), p. 211.

Breasted's argument, endorsed by Christopher Hill in *Milton and the English Revolution* (New York: Viking, 1977), pp. 43–44, asks us to suppose that the Egerton family, wishing to dissociate themselves from the obscene behavior of a notorious relative, first commissioned a masque on the subject of their sexual virtue, then excised from the performance text passages explicitly touching on this theme. Is this not having it both ways? If the theme *was* commissioned, nothing prevents us from assuming that the Egertons (or Lawes) knew their man.

Rigor, Advice, Age, and Severity are personifications of parental authority, ways in which an older generation transfers its "grave Saws" to a new generation. Now the parents of the world are in bed, eyes closed—or so the tempter thinks. "'Tis only daylight that makes sin," Comus continues, equating darkness with secrecy ("these dun shades will ne'er report") and light with tattletales ("the blabbing Eastern scout," "the telltale sun"). Daylight is the symbol of being observed by the older generation, exposed to the watch of their external authority. If an observed person harbors scenes of orgiastic disobedience within him, meditating all that he would do in the absence of his observer, then this man "Benighted walks under the midday Sun; / Himself is his own dungeon" (383–384). He lives invisibly, chained in the dungeon of his privacy, where there is no authority and he enjoys the indulgence of a perpetual midnight. Why does he behave, limiting himself to fantasy? The gaze of authority. But because he would not behave in its absence, the gaze of authority is his jailer.

Virtue has no jailer: it is its own. Acting without regard to external conditions, the same in public as when alone, the virtuous man has the authority within him, where it is always bright noon. "Virtue could see to do what virtue would / By her own radiant light, though Sun and Moon / Were in the flat Sea sunk" (373–375). He sustains the conditions of external observation in the well-lit privacy of his mind, keeping watch over himself: the daylight that literally constrains the evil man becomes, as a symbol, the definition of the virtuous man. He has consented to a tradition, and will in time take his place with Age, Rigor, and Advice. But the only way for someone to tell a free man from a constrained man, the virtuous from the vicious, is to let him out of his sight, which is why the midnight encounter with Comus permits the Lady to be recognized as a fair branch of the family tree. She has demonstrated that the "Noble Lord, and Lady bright" have been enthroned within her, a presence even in their absence.

The Masque of the Superego

Freud's theory of the superego is a continuation of the venerable wisdom informing the ethics of the masque. It seeks to explain how the regulation of desire, which begins for all of us in the scrutinies and restraints of external authority, metamorphoses into a self-regulating conscience, wherein the ego can accuse itself and impose the psychic punishment or self-aggression of guilt. The state of being revealed to us by the temptation myth achieves a formal organization in our lives through the turbulence of the oedipus complex. The love of the child, focused for the first time on a distinct object, encounters law;

all of the earlier conflicts between felt omnipotence and experienced finitude coalesce in this illegal wish. At the resolution of the complex, the two relationships of love and rivalry, desire and law, "are dissolved, destroyed internally and something novel, psychic structure, comes into being."[2] As a monument to the sacrifice of desire, formed primarily from an identification with the law-bearer, the superego establishes at the beginning of moral existence an intrinsic connection between an ideal and a prohibition. This is precisely the moral structure celebrated by the temptation myth: one becomes ideal by prohibiting oneself, by refusing and renouncing, by saying "no." The oedipal child is the first hero of temptation.

Certain features of *Comus* acquire a new lucidity when read from this perspective. No doubt there is a world of difference between an observed child listening to the grave saws of its elders and the luxuriously furnished conscience of the Lady, replete with myth, magic, religion, song, and the charm of divine philosophy; her parents have not gone to bed this night, and the very fact of the masque exonerates them from the charge of sour severity. Yet the symbolism of virtue, representing the mature state in terms of the primitive one, keeps this world of difference before us. The symbolism, furthermore, has its counterpart in the form of the masque, which represents concretely the etiology of conscience preserved in this symbolism.

The definitive character of the genre lies in its attachment to an ephemeral occasion. Art is embedded in event. In masques the relation of actor to role, usually incidental in the playhouse, is supplied (for some roles, at least) with a motive; fiction and occasion interpenetrate through winking allusions to the stage machinery (as in ll. 221–225 and 331–335) or to the nobility present, waiting for the plot to glide into the festive dancing of a party. Always original in his ways with genre, Milton has informed the special ontology of the masque with the life of an idea. For the parents of Alice Egerton look on from their thrones as an unacknowledged audience—as if absent, as if invisible—while the residue of their spectatorship in the mind of this child is being tried. "Eye me blest Providence," the Lady declares as she leaves with the false shepherd Comus (dark inverse of the Attendant Spirit, also disguised as a shepherd), knowing that she must act, like her author, "As ever in my great task-Master's eye" (Sonnet VII). In the darkness of the woods, seemingly, *no one would know*. But in fact everyone would know: the inward

---

2. Hans Loewald, "On Internalization," *International Journal of Psychoanalysis*, 54 (1973), 16. I have discussed theories about the genesis of the superego in "Superego in Kierkegaard, Existence in Freud," in *Psychiatry and the Humanities*, vol. 5: *Kierkegaard's Truth: The Disclosure of the Self*, ed. Joseph Smith (New Haven: Yale University Press, 1981), pp. 119–165.

gaze of conscience would see, the unacknowledged eyes of the parents would see, the invisible watch of providence would see. All of the stages of conscience—external and internal, secular and religious—are present at the exposure of her virtue, having become analogons of each other through a symbolic use of the nature of a masque.

Milton recovers in this way the primordial experience of conscience. The gaze and the light inside the virtuous mind of the Lady have been dismantled and reexternalized in her "Noble Lord, and Lady bright." Surely the most common metaphors for the vigilance of the superego are the sun and the eye, often merged in iconographical traditions—which is one of the cheaper lessons to be learned from a dollar bill. But what do we learn from these metaphors? Reflexivity, the great theme of philosophies of consciousness from Plotinus to Husserl, is binary. Self-awareness demarcates the boundary between me and not-me, setting the knowing ego against known objects. With the institution of the superego, however, a third term occupies our mental space, transforming self-awareness into the triangular structure of moral existence. Jonas' description of the choice that engraves its image is one instance of this transformation: the figure of authority has come to rest within us, sensed in the observation of our conduct and heard in the "call" of conscience. The sacrifice instituting the superego *does* leave an indelible impression, completing the structure of mind with a unique otherness—the burden of the law. This new reflexivity is not addressed to the ego as reason, determining objects in the realm of knowledge, but to the ego as will, determining itself in the realm of value. Its expansion and exploration occur in the symbolism of the sacred.

We could not speak feelingly of this otherness without making symbols of the scene of observation. It is a tendency of all symbolism to represent the higher by the lower, what is futural and mysterious by what is previous and overcome. The biblical vocabulary of evil, Ricoeur has shown, draws on the everyday facts of the spot, the weight, and the deviating path.[3] If we say "God is the sun" as a metaphor, this statement depends for its evocative power on our ability to imagine, and be moved by imagining, that God *is* the sun. Symbolism has a regressive component, an internal dynamic that pulls symbol and meaning back toward idol and image. It is not surprising, then, that the pattern we have discovered in the tropes

---

3. Paul Ricoeur, *The Symbolism of Evil*, trans. Emerson Buchanan (Boston: Beacon Press, 1967), esp. pp. 225–246. Owen Barfield develops a wide-ranging critique of idolatry from Levy-Bruhl's "collective representations (participations)" in *Saving the Appearances: A Study in Idolatry* (New York: Harcourt Brace, 1965): an idol is "a representation or image which is not experienced as such" (p. 110). Idolatry springs from an exclusively ontological interpretation of the "is" coupling two terms in a metaphor, which is why I suggest that the idol remains part of the internal dynamic of the symbol.

of virtue and the form of the masque will be found elsewhere in
Comus. But the representation of a complex or ideal state by a sim-
pler or earlier one is so predominant here that questions arise concerning the freedom of these symbols. To what extent is the
meaning of this work "root-bound," captive to a regressive movement from which there is no significant return? This question is
accentuated for a psychoanalytic reading, but many interpreters of
Comus have struggled in their own terms with a problem of this
sort. For at the center of the entertainment chastity narrows to virgin chastity, a state of the soul evolving from, and unable to detach
itself from, a precondition of the body.

Virginity's Logic

The theme of solitude leads directly to this lapse. It is already
ironic that the manifestation of virtue requires solitude, yet as we
learn from the brothers, this stipulation poses a more serious difficulty in the case at hand. Their exchange turns on two consequences of aloneness. The Younger Brother fears that his sister may
be in the "direful grasp" of "Savage hunger" or "Savage heat" (357–
358), vulnerable to rape. Somewhat obtusely, the philosophical
brother replies that his sister is not "unprincipl'd in virtue's book,"
taking solitude to be the prerequisite for moral trial and limiting
the consequence that worries his brother to a parenthesis (370).
When corrected, the Elder Brother offers his peculiar doctrine of
the "hidden strength" (416), the "complete steel" (421) and "arms of
Chastity" (440), symbolized in ancient myth by the bow of Diana
and the shield of Minerva; more than internal, chastity has the
kind of strength a savage would respect. This assertion arises solely
because the virtue at issue rests on virginity. A faithful, hopeful,
charitable, wise, prudent, courageous, patient, or temperate Lady
could not have her virtue snatched away by force: she could say to
her tempter, "Thou canst not touch the freedom of my mind" (633),
and that would be that. But the virtue of the Lady is not only in her
mind, and if it is to be tempted (as it must) in solitude (as it must),
then guardian forces not of this world must protect it from unchosen ruin (as they do).

   The moral logic of the masque's religious universe identifies virginity as a virtue of singular prestige:

>   Against the threats
> Of malice or of sorcery, or that power
> Which erring men call Chance, this I hold firm;
> Virtue may be assail'd but never hurt,
> Surpris'd by unjust force but not enthrall'd,
> Yea even that which mischief meant most harm

> Shall in the happy trial prove most glory.
> But evil on itself shall back recoil,
> And mix no more with goodness, when at last
> Gather'd like scum, and settl'd to itself,
> It shall be in eternal restless change
> Self-fed and self-consum'd; if this fail
> The pillar'd firmament is rott'nness,
> And earth's base built on stubble.   (586–599)

The Elder Brother places the trial of his sister in the context of a theodicy, for assuming that she is indeed virtuous, her captivity puts the moral direction of the universe on trial. His transition from the Lady's ordeal to the end of time, "when at last" the contraries will be disengaged, evil contained and virtue purified, is not at all gratuitous: the vulnerable base on which her virtue is built calls forth an intervention, a sign of the full theophany to come. Feeble to the degree that it rests on a bodily state, virginity makes heaven stoop. Its exemplars, when tried by force as well as fraud, will come into contact with transcendent beings.

As virginity is connected with heaven, so is it disconnected from nature. Like all tempters, Comus tries to appall his captive with the extremity of her virtue: how can you deny yourself this without denying yourself everything? So after his appeal to the positive benefits of his liquor has failed, Comus attacks the refusal itself. He accuses the Lady of advocating "The lean and sallow Abstinence" (709), and then, making explicit the sexual advance symbolized by the liquor, taunts her with the specific abstinence of "that same vaunted name Virginity" (738). The Lady can extricate herself from the blunt either/ or of the first charge by invoking the "holy dictate of spare Temperance" (767): to partake or not partake, that is *not* the question, but when, with whom, how much, what, and in what attitude. A symmetrical answer to the taunt of virginity would be chastity, widely believed in the Renaissance, especially among Protestants, to include marriage. As temperance to abstinence, so Protestant chastity to virginity. But the Lady refuses to voice even a hint of compromise with the second, specifically sexual charge of abstinence, and in a gesture that has provoked much critical debate, accepts the name given to her by her tempter. Her chastity is virginity, transvalued from a defective extremity to a "sublime notion and high mystery" (786).

Is the doctrine of virginity so strange that even critics who would prefer to treat literature as the storehouse of intellectual history must fall back on a biographical explanation? This is the conception of the problem that the most influential critic of the masque, A. S. P. Woodhouse, responded to. In his view, the Lady's reply, dramatically apt for the fifteen-year-old Alice, need not implicate the doctrines of the author in any way whatsoever. Woodhouse contended that Milton held chastity able to survive the marriage bed, but did not bother to make this "qualification" explicit: "Nor is it necessary, surely, for any rational mind, that he should."[4] I suppose there must be rational minds for whom the difference between living with or without sexuality amounts to a dispensable "qualification," and I suppose that these minds would not be changed by the fact that the five best poems written during the first half of Milton's life are "An Ode on the Morning of Christ's Nativity" (the Virgin Birth of a virgin God), "Il Penseroso" (a virgin goddess, whose literary tastes do not include the Hymen masques enjoyed by L'Allegro), *Comus*, and the two elegies for virgins, "Lycidas" and "Epitaphium Damonis." But to take the matter in context, Milton could have written a speech conveying both the Lady's allegiance to virginity *and* her awareness that Comus professes a concept of chastity as exaggerated and impoverished as his concept of temperance. The last words of the taunting Comus, "you are but young yet" (755), actually invite a reply of this kind, all but asking the Lady to concede a relationship between her sexual continence and her youth. Why did our notably contentious poet forbear in this instance? Was it his practice to pass up opportunities to correct his tempters? It is odd for a reader of *Comus* to hear that no rational mind could mistake the conventionality of the Lady's chastity, since she calls virginity and virginity alone a "mystery," "sage" as well as "serious," which presumably means that the virginity here professed is not, like temperance or quotidian chastity, a cardinal virtue derived from reason. The common ways of this world, we are told in the first speech of the masque, do not aspire toward "high mystery."

If we find something more esoteric in *Comus* than the trite allegory whose appreciation Woodhouse made into a test of our rationality and, in other places, our spirituality, we need not adopt the equally odd position of those who reason that, because virtue tightens into mystical virginity during the temptation scene, *Comus* is a disunified work.[5] As may be learned from the Platonic One, the Cartesian piece of wax, or the identity of any man, unity is a complex idea, arguably the most complex idea. Language such as "tied

4. A. S. P. Woodhouse, *The Heavenly Muse: A Preface to Milton* (Toronto: University of Toronto Press, 1972), pp. 72–73.
5. E. M. W. Tillyard asserts the disunity of *Comus* in *Milton* (New York: Collier, 1967), pp. 58–66: "The final impression I get from *Comus* viewed as a whole is that when Milton wrote it he was not inspired by any compelling mood to give it unity" (p. 64). Parker found the plot "flimsy, devoid of suspense, and lacking in dramatic unity" in *Milton: A Biography*, I, 130. Edward Tayler, whose discussion of the temptation scene is close to my own, also feels that "Milton's concern with extreme forms of chastity threatens the artistic integrity of *Comus*"—*Milton's Poetry: Its Development in Time* (Pittsburgh: Duquesne University Press, 1979), p. 137.

together," "linked," and "bound up" suggests an undercurrent of tyranny in commonplace descriptions of a unified text. I do not understand why conflicts of affect or proposition in a work should be prima facie evidence of "disunity," or if so, why disunity should be considered prima facie a flaw. To require of art that its ambivalences and ambiguities be "resolved" is to ask for a dangerous variety of aesthetic illusion—one set against life. We can try to update the neoplatonic *concordia discors* by insisting that conflicts become incorporated into the coherent sense of a text when and only when they are intentionally produced. But this type of solution, whose consequence is the division of literature into mature texts able to manage their own subversive tendencies and immature texts given over to biography and psychology, seeks to contain the idea of the unconscious prematurely. Conflict is inherent in coherence. Freud proposed that the concept of "no," emerging from primitive repression, makes judgment possible by allowing the repudiated to be thought without being repressed: intentional meaning, like psychic unity, depends on the achievement of contradiction (S.E. XIX, 235–239).[6] One may of course debate with Freud; those appealing to the self-sufficiency of intentional meaning should be doing precisely that. But *Comus* is a work about temptation—the myth of the heroism of "no"—and it seems reasonable to imagine that here, if anywhere, meaning will exude its own adversary.

Discussions about the success or failure of this work have been marked for some time by the adherence of both sides to an idea of coherence more suitable to symbolic logic than to symbolic literature. Enid Welsford adduced the standards of Ben Jonson to devalue *Comus*. Subsequent critics, who seem always to be rediscovering the masqueness of the masque, have been quick to dismiss her belief that Hymen is the presiding deity of the genre, which turns Milton into a Puritan at the Maypole, but they have not questioned seriously whether Jonson's prescriptive analysis of the form exhausts its possibilities. It would be highly improbable, perhaps a unique case in the history of literature, if Jonson had laid down The Rule for a good masque when he wrote of "one entire body, or figure . . . with that general harmony so connexed, and disposed, as no one little part can be missing to the illustration of the whole."[7]

6. Freud's insight was considerably advanced by the pioneering psycholinguistics of René Spitz, *No and Yes: On the Genesis of Human Communication* (New York: International Universities Press, 1956); Francesco Orlando explores some aesthetic implications of negation in *Toward a Freudian Theory of Literature*, trans. Charmaine Lee (Baltimore: Johns Hopkins Press, 1978).
7. See Enid Welsford, *The Court Masque* (Cambridge: Cambridge University Press, 1927), pp. 315–318, and for a sampling of criticism based on a Jonsonian view of the genre of the work, the well-known articles of Robert M. Adams ("Reading *Comus*"), Rosemond Tuve ("Image, Form, and Theme in *A Mask*"), and C. L. Barber ("*A Mask Presented at Ludlow Castle*: The Masque as a Masque"), all reprinted in John S. Diekhoff, ed., *A*

Working from this principle, critics have generally approached
Comus with something close to the following model of what would
constitute a perfect interpretation: find its theme, conceived of in
scholastic fashion as a single substantive, and then demonstrate that
the meaning of the masque is a set of mutually consistent predicates
for this nominated noun. If such a model guided the composition of
Comus, Milton deliberately chose to withhold predicates from the
moment at which his Lady, all the eyes of conscience upon her,
declares the magic substantive:

Thou hast nor Ear nor Soul to apprehend
The sublime notion and high mystery
That must be utter'd to unfold the sage
And serious doctrine of Virginity,
And thou art worthy that thou shouldst not know
More happiness than this thy present lot.
. . . Thou art not fit to hear thyself convinc't;
Yet should I try, the uncontrolled worth
Of this pure cause would kindle my rapt spirits
To such a flame of sacred vehemence,
That dumb things would be mov'd to sympathise,
And the brute Earth would lend her nerves, and shake,
Till all thy magic structures rear'd so high,
Were shatter'd into heaps o'er thy false head.
   Comus. She fables not, I feel that I do fear
Her words set off by some superior power. (784–789; 792–801)

At this critical juncture the Lady's theme is *only* a substantive; the
"whole," in Jonson's terms, is entirely missing to the illustration of
this "part." Her strength is "hidden" in the sense that a solitary
Lady does not appear to be a formidable foe, but also in the sense
that her doctrine of virginity remains undivulged, itself virginal, as
if speech this intimate would be equivalent to the sexuality her virtue forbids—the exhibition of the self to the other.

Although doubly hidden, the mere threat of strength's disclosure
proves its mettle, vindicating the architect of this pillared firmament.
Virginity is indeed a "vaunted name" in the masque: at no time in her
competent exposition of temperance did the Lady seem ready to
become an Orpheus ("dumb things would be mov'd to sympathise")
accomplishing the feat of a Samson ("Till all thy magic structures
rear'd so high, / Were shatter'd into heaps o'er thy false head"); the
doctrine of virginity, not the doctrine of temperance, is able to demonstrate that "earth's base" is not "built on stubble" by literally call-

Maske at Ludlow: Essays on Milton's Comus (Cleveland: Press of Case Western Reserve
University, 1968).

ing to its aid "the brute Earth." But what is the substance that would
lend this name, if uttered, its superior power? In order to couple
predicates of any kind to this unforthcoming theme, we must first
examine the cosmos whose laws protect the "happiness" of a virgin.

Wright and Arthos have confirmed the decisive influence of
Plato.[8] Inspired by the myth of the two earths in the *Phaedo*, Milton
set his trial in the cosmos of the Orphic tradition. The "daemon,"
as the Attendant Spirit is called in the Trinity MS., introduces the
masque with a severe contrast between "My mansion" and the "dim
spot" called "Earth," where frail and feverish men are "Confin'd and
pester'd in this pinfold" (I–II). This imagery strongly suggests that to
live at all is to have undergone the animal metamorphosis produced
by Circe and her son, for the archetype of their ability to transform a
man into "some brutish form" is the imprisonment of soul in body.
Virtue begins, as it has always begun in the Orphic cosmos, with the
gnosis of this estrangement, teaching us that we are the same as the
soul and other than the body. What the potion of Comus offers is the
familiar opponent of salvation in the many philosophies and religions
founded on this cosmology:

> And they, so perfect is their misery,
> Not once perceive their foul disfigurement,
> But boast themselves more comely than before,
> And all their friends and native home forget,
> To roll with pleasure in a sensual sty.   (73–77)

His crew have *forgotten*. They represent life in ignorance of the
difference.

Within Christian thought this Greek cosmos has usually been
interpreted by reference to the Pauline dualism of "flesh" and
"spirit." Here, as in *Paradise Lost*, the difference to be remembered is
inside the soul. Including passions and appetites, "flesh" is a diag-
nostic category in the pathology of the will; the body as a thing
belonging to an alien world of things becomes, not the dead fact

8. See B. A. Wright's annotations for the masque in his *Shorter Poems of John Milton*
(London: Macmillan, 1938), and John Arthos, *On "A Mask Presented at Ludlow's Castle"* (Ann Arbor: University of Michigan Press, 1954); "Milton, Ficino, and the *Charmi-
des*," *Studies in the Renaissance*, VI (1959), 261–274.
Sears Jayne's "The Subject of Milton's Ludlow *Mask*" (included in Diekhoff, *A
Maske at Ludlow*, pp. 165–187), proceeding at some distance from the language of the
masque, finds a neoplatonic allegory of the ascent of the soul by assuming that mythological allusions in Milton have the same significance they possess in the philosophy of
Ficino. One would think that the first test of the validity of such a reading is the coincidence between Ficino's philosophy and the philosophical passages in the masque
itself. But despite his astrological mysticism of the bodily spirits, Ficino never to my
knowledge proposes that the virtuous life will transform body into soul: the consistent
goal of his philosophy is to escape from the confinements of the flesh. So while *Comus*
has the look and feel of a neoplatonic cosmos, its central doctrine has no parallel in
Ficino.

against which the soul is known, but a symbol in moral psychology.[9] The virtue of temperance expounded by the Lady answers to this interpretation of the flesh. There is nothing wicked in needing to eat or in the food consumed, for wickedness can only arise in the volition of the soul. But the mystery of virginity she next announces can be associated with a partial reversion, felt elsewhere in the masque, from the Christian to the Greek dualism.

Descending from purity, the Attendant Spirit finds "rank vapors" and a "sin-worn mold." On this night "black usurping mists" (337) obscure the stars of his homeland. Given these allusions to the bad odors and thickened atmosphere of our pigsty earth, the "unhallow'd air" (757) of the enchanter's den, where the Lady rues the necessity of unlocking her lips to speak, seems the concentrated distillate of air itself. In Fulke Greville's haunting and truly Pauline sonnet on the terrifying fantasies we have in the dark, these hellish images "but expressions be of inward evils."[1] A "thousand fantasies" (205) beset the lost Lady of *Comus* and, as her brother assures us, a "thousand liveried Angels" (455) attend the chaste soul—an angel for every fantasy. Yet these superior powers appear to guard her, not from interior impurity, but from contamination by the tainted physicality of the world, "Driving far off each *thing* of sin and guilt" (456; my italics). These are not fantasies expressive of inward evil, but fantasies indicative of external danger. In the older conception of the difference, virtue was the soul's defense against the invasions of matter. This idea dominates the symbolism of *Comus*.

Before learning of the difference, an inhabitant of the Orphic cosmos will have drawn breath and eaten food, and unless virtue is suicide (as indeed it was for Sabrina), he will continue to do so. The one taint of the flesh subject to absolute denial is sexuality. Providing our fullest exposition of the sage and serious doctrine, the Elder Brother equates lust with the intrusion into the soul of an incarnate evil:

> So dear to Heav'n is Saintly chastity,
> That when a soul is found sincerely so,
> A thousand liveried Angels lackey her,
> Driving far off each thing of sin and guilt,
> And in clear dream and solemn vision
> Tell her of things that no gross ear can hear,

9. Ricoeur, *Symbolism of Evil*, pp. 279–305, 330–345. See also Leonard Eslick, "The Material Substrate in Plato," in Erson McMullin, ed., *The Concept of Matter in Greek and Medieval Philosophy* (Notre Dame: University of Notre Dame Press, 1963), pp. 39–54. The Orphic myth presumed to have given rise to Plato's philosophy is discussed by W. C. K. Guthrie, *The Greeks and Their Gods* (Boston: Beacon, 1954), pp. 305–353. Milton associates Circe with ignorance in Prolusion VII (CP I, 103).
1. *Caelica*, Sonnet C, in Geoffrey Bullough, ed., *Poems and Dramas*, 2 vols. (New York: Oxford University Press, 1945), vol. 1.

Till oft converse with heav'nly habitants
Begin to cast a beam on th' outward shape,
The unpolluted temple of the mind,
And turns it by degrees to the soul's essence,
Till all be made immortal: but when lust
By unchaste looks, loose gestures, and foul talk,
But most by lewd and lavish act of sin,
Lets in defilement to the inward parts,
The soul grows clotted by contagion,
Imbodies and imbrutes, till she quite lose
The divine property of her first being.
Such are those thick and gloomy shadows damp
Oft seen in Charnel vaults and Sepulchers,
Lingering and sitting by a new-made grave,
As loath to leave the body that it lov'd,
And link't itself by carnal sensuality
To a degenerate and degraded state.
    Second Brother. How charming is divine Philosophy!
                             (453–476)

The magic of the poetry is simply splendid: *lust, looks, loose, lewd, lavish, lets in, lose, lingering, loath, leave, lov'd,* and *link't* lead us to imagine that one consonant was given to the lolling tongue of man in order that his gross ear could be attuned to the death knell of the soul, then taken unawares by the redemptive chime of *charnel, carnal, charming.* Like a wish, this enchantment is intense enough to suspend unwelcome knowledge. For if the "unpolluted temple of the mind"—which means the body, in apposition to "th'outward shape"—becomes "the soul's essence," making "all" immortal, could there *be* any virgins in a graveyard? Milton first expressed his refusal of this fact in "On the Death of a Fair Infant":

    Yet can I not persuade me thou art dead
    Or that thy corse corrupts in earth's dark womb,
    Or that thy beauties lie in wormy bed,
    Hid from the world in a low delved tomb.   (29–32)

In the invented myth that opens this poem, death comes to a "Virgin Soul" (21) from sexual assault. *Comus* is a magic fortress to preserve the wish whose earlier formula was "can I not persuade me." Spiritual guardians make sexual assault impossible. Divine philosophy proves that, if we retain the virginity we are born with, the "divine property" of our "first being," our bodies will never "lie in wormy bed."

    Virginity being the supreme virtue, lust emerges as the supreme sin. In keeping with the pattern of regression we discovered first in the symbolism of conscience and now discover in the history of moral dualism, the Elder Brother represents the sin of unchastity by eating and drinking. Foreshadowing the liquor of the temptation scene, the act "most" opposed to chastity lets in, clots, and imbrutes. One can understand why, in the Orphic cosmos, virginity might present itself as a strategy of integrity. Let us suppose that, as the Elder Brother implies, body and soul are posed against each other as the profane against the sacred. Life would involve a constant warfare of the soul against the body, its inescapable other; linked to the contagion of profane flesh, regularly absorbing impure substance, the soul would be enmeshed in what Durkheim termed the most absolute dualism "in all the history of human thought."[2] Through choosing virginity, however, the soul can transform the brute condition of the body, moving flesh inside the shelter of its sacredness. Become "soul's essence," the virgin body is no longer other to the soul, and although the dualism persists, it has been happily resituated: a unified person confronts the profanity of the world across the boundary of the body. Hence the loss of virginity would institute the more divisive form of the dualism, consigning body to the "contagion" of a material world constantly brought inward to the seat of the soul by nourishment. Bad food, therefore, symbolizes sexuality.

The new partnership of soul and virgin body, through the ministrations of "heav'nly habitants," somehow bypasses the moment of death. In the passage of the *Phaedo* from which Milton drew his vision of the graveyard, Socrates says that "the soul which is deeply attached to the body . . . hovers around it and the visible world for a long time, and it is only after much resistance and suffering that it is at last forcibly led away by its appointed guardian spirit. And when it reaches the same place as the rest, the soul which is impure *through having done some impure deed, either by setting its hand to lawless bloodshed or by committing other kindred crimes which are the work of kindred souls*, this soul is shunned and avoided by all."[3] The Miltonic version replaces murder as the crime of lingering souls with the self-murder of lust. Socrates proves immortality before going to his death, but *Comus* positions this subject before sexuality, claiming through this shift to have abolished the death sentence for body as well as soul.

In a general way the emotions that underlie this wishful transposition of Plato are not obscure, nor were they obscure during the Renaissance—witness the semantic range of the word "death." Perhaps, as Frye has noted of the threatened virgins of romance, the loss

2. Émile Durkheim, *The Elementary Forms of Religious Life* trans. Joseph Swain (New York: Free Press, 1965), p. 53.
3. *The Collected Dialogues of Plato*, ed. Edith Hamilton and Huntington Cairns (New York: Pantheon, 1961), 108A-B (p. 89); my italics.

of virginity has meant for many people, male and female, a metaphorical death, a fall into the ordinary, a submission to the processes
of life that hurry us toward its end.[4] Christians have traditionally
represented salvation as a new virginal wholeness, a purification
through rebirth; to this extent, Woodhouse was right to argue that
virginity in *Comus* is an "illustration" and a "symbol" of chastity in
the order of grace.[5] But Milton's determinedly physical elaboration of
the sage doctrine does not permit the symbol to be detached from
the illustration. The argument of *Comus* is trying to include the
body, not just what the body means, in the order of grace. Its divine
philosophy asserts that only virginity can accomplish this inclusion,
producing a sublimation of the flesh "by degrees." Clearly the reverse
of Comus' transformation, this magical undoing of birth has a narrative echo in the "quick immortal change" (841) of Sabrina, "a Virgin
pure" (826). The water god revives her corpse by pouring "Ambrosial
Oils" into "the porch and inlet of each sense" (839–840).[6] Her perfect chastity, it would appear, has prevented the orifices that admit
the external world, whether as substance or as sensation, from
becoming "clotted." The symbolic significance of her myth is predicated, in some detail, on the fact of her virginity.

    According to divine philosophy, the "quick immortal change" of
the Sabrina myth will happen to the Lady "by degrees." More than
critics have realized, the opposition between a bestial and a virginal
physiology defines the alternatives presented during the temptation
scene. As there are spirits from the transcendent world that attend
aspiring mortals, so there are "spirits" in the blood that "Strive to
keep up" our "frail and feverish being." Comus wants the Lady to see
his "cordial Julep" as a simulacrum of lively blood able to produce
this liveliness, when imbibed, by sympathetic magic:

> See, here be all the pleasures
> That fancy can beget on youthful thoughts,
> When the fresh blood grows lively, and returns
> Brisk as the *April* buds in Primrose-season.
> And first behold this cordial Julep here,
> That flames and dances in his crystal bounds
> With spirits of balm and fragrant Syrups mixt.   (668–674)

---

4. Northrop Frye, *The Secular Scripture: A Study of the Structure of Romance* (Cambridge: Harvard University Press, 1976), pp. 81–86.
5. Woodhouse, *Heavenly Muse*, pp. 63–64.
6. Although she walks with "printless" feet, Milton's Sabrina has not, like Drayton's, dissolved into the stream—see my "The Heretical Milton: From Assumption to Mortal-
ism," *English Literary Renaissance* (hereafter *ELR*), 5 (1975), 133, n. 20. This
preservation of the integrity of a distinct and bounded body is consistent with psychoanalytic interpretations of virginity proposed later in this chapter.

The use of words such as "spirits" and "cordial" in the modern
vocabulary of alcohol derives from the belief, presumed in this passage, that intoxicants quicken the three kinds of spirits distributed
by the blood.[7] Like a Renaissance physician, Comus prescribes a
glass of dancing spirits to refresh his tired captive. Given the known
effect of this cordial, there is an implicit pun here on "animal spirits," and given the known desires of the tempter, betrayed in the word
"beget," it might not be untoward to remember that in the Galenic
tradition the pneumata of the blood distilled a potent essence known
as "seminal spirits."[8] But the Lady already contains a magic potion.
Were she to expound the doctrine of virginity, the internal effect
would be holy inebriation: the cordial that "flames and dances" in the
crystal cup of the magus has its sacred complement in her "rapt spirits" kindled "To such a flame of sacred vehemence." The last words of
Comus conclude this battle of opposed physiologies with the high
comedy of a projection:

> I must not suffer this, yet 'tis but the lees
> And settlings of a melancholy blood;
> But this will cure all straight, one sip of this
> Will bathe the drooping spirits in delight
> Beyond the bliss of dreams. Be wise, and taste.   (809–813)

He unmistakably diagnoses his own depression. Far from being
weighed down by unvivified spirits, hers is a sacred melancholy,
inflamed and enraptured like the "sad virgin" of "Il Penseroso." The
sage doctrine of the masque concerns a virginity ambitious enough
to have generated a quasi-science.

But the highest mystery of *Comus* is a symbol that questions the
efficacy and coherence of this doctrine. Because of the inexperience
of the brothers, Comus retains his wand, and he makes good apparently on his initial threat to render the Lady "as Daphne was, / Root-
bound." Her body is now inert; the lips that were reluctant to speak,
now locked indeed. "We cannot free the Lady that sits here / In stony
fetters fixt and motionless" (818–819). Wilkenfeld has analyzed brilliantly the symbolic character of movement in *Comus*, where the
freedom of virtue has a spatial correlate in rising, descending, and
dancing.[9] Disrupting this metaphorical structure, the temporary
paralysis of the Lady invites us to reinterpret the virtue we have
pieced together from philosophy and cosmology. Comus has restated
his diagnosis in the very flesh of his opponent. She never spoke the

7. Salvatore Lucia's *Wine and the Digestive System* (San Francisco: Fortune House, 1970)
   is an annotated bibliography containing classical and Renaissance items.
8. And not only in Galenism: see Allen Debus, *The Chemical Philosophy*, 2 vols. (New
   York: Science History Publications, 1977), II, 340–341, 353.
9. Roger Wilkenfeld, "The Seat at the Center: An Interpretation of *Comus*," in *Critical
   Essays on Milton from ELH* (Baltimore: Johns Hopkins Press, 1969), pp. 123–150.

mysterious doctrine. She will not speak again in the masque. Motion-less before us, her virgin body has become the emblem of itself, or half an emblem, an emblem without words, as if the doctrine and privileges and expectations of virginity had been reduced by the enchanter to nothing more than a stasis in the body, bound to their root. Within the artistic frame of *Comus*, the author of this subver-sive new symbol is the hero of the anti-masque, and its meaning need not be fettered by the divine philosophy that leads to Jove's court. We must not rush to the theologians: we are instead invited to "revise" the Lady, to look again at her virtue, submitting the temptation of the masque to a second and open critique. The issue of unified meaning arises at this point, but as it does, it ceases to be a question directed toward the pure formalism of meaning, dissolving into other and more pressing questions about the authenticity of the values intended in the work. Why should the Lady, having resisted her tempter and given proof of "some superior power" at her command, still be enchanted by the power of the wand? Is virtue *not* free? How strong is a virtue that would exchange the sexual life in order to gain a tinge of realism for the wish to be exempt from death? Might her paralysis at the scene of temptation symbolize her deliverance to the equal but contrary forces of law and desire? Has Comus exposed through symbolism a deeper knowledge of the high mystery than the one the Lady refused him?

On at least one occasion the foremost interpreter of *Comus* left evidence of his own uncertainty over the strength of its virtue. Mil-ton, toward the end of his travels abroad, placed two inscriptions beneath his name in the guest book of the Cerdogni family of Geneva: *Coelum non animum muto dum trans mare curro* (Though I travel across the sea, I do not change my mind with my skies); and the last words of *Comus*, "if virtue feeble were / Heaven itself would stoop to her."[1] His mind is steadfast in alien lands, unmoved by for-eign counsel, guarded by the impenetrable shield of its own "no," but if virtue feeble were . . . The symbol created by the enchanter hints that this uncertainty over the strength or self-sufficiency of virtue conceals and perpetuates the true problem. *Because* virginity *is* fixed and unmoved, strengthened by magical delusions, it is feeble. In the second stage of his poetic career Milton will also make a strength of weakness—of blindness. But the possibility of this stronger future lay in the affirmation of the antimasque.

* * *

1. See J. H. Hanford, *John Milton, Englishman* (New York: Crown, 1949), p. 98. This biographer assumed that, when abroad, Milton "made it his special mission to preach 'the sage and serious doctrine of virginity' and conspicuously to exemplify it, some-times . . . out of season" (p. 88).

WILLIAM HALLER

[Puritan Milton and *Lycidas*]†

After *Comus* Milton is at his studies, but he is also pluming his
wings for another poem. Something had happened to make him
reflect once more on the course he had chosen, to count the risks in
which his ambitions involved him, to take stock of himself and his
purposes as he had done several years before on his twenty-third
birthday. The result was *Lycidas*, Milton's most perfect expression
of faith in his own conception of priesthood and his most memorable polemic against those who had kept him from exercising that
priesthood in the English church.

Edward King had been a student with Milton at Cambridge, had
written verses, and had accepted the lot which Milton had rejected.
He was about to enter the church when he was drowned by shipwreck in the Irish Sea. His college friends went about preparing a
volume of poems in his memory. It does not appear that the personal bond between him and Milton was anything but slight and
casual, but he and his sudden death now assumed symbolic meaning for the poet who had been church-outed by the prelates. A little
more or less and he might himself have been Edward King. As it
was, he was asked to write an elegy for him. It was like writing an
elegy on himself, on the churchman he had decided not to be, still
more on the man the English church had lost by his decision.
These were the suggestions which he chose to invest with poetry.
He has to say: I was at Cambridge with this man; I might have been
Lycidas; we studied together; he is dead; such men are ill-spared;
he cannot have died; he has but gone to live a larger life. The commonplaces of mourning, lifted above commonplace by Milton's art
and personal convictions. The convention of pastoral elegy is cast
over the timeworn theme but not permitted to embarrass or obscure.
Arcady sets off Cambridge. English scenes are enriched by delicately
poised association with the land of shepherds. But all this artistry is
not employed for the exhibition of the writer's virtuosity or for the
enhancement of Cambridge or of King. The poem is Milton's personal confession of his effectual calling from God to be a poet, as
truly such as the testimony of any of the spiritual preachers, the confession of his calling and of his answering to the call by the dedication of his talents to service prompted by faith. The image carved in
a few lines in *Lycidas* is the same picture that appears in sonnet, in

† From William Haller, *The Rise of Puritanism*, pp. 321–23. Copyright © 1938 by Columbia
University Press. Reprinted with permission of the publisher.

letter, in Latin verse and in revolutionary pamphlet, the picture of Milton making a Miltonic poem or a sermon, whichever one chooses to call it, out of his own life. After the idyllic picture of college friendship with pastoral lament for the departed comes the question, why be a poet, why meditate the thankless muse?

> Were it not better don as others use,
> To sport with Amaryllis in the shade,
> Or with the tangles of Neaera's hair?

The right Puritan answer follows. He must be a poet because that best pleases God, not for sake of fame on earth, though that is but the last infirmity of noble minds, but fame in heaven.

Then the poet proceeds to do God and his church an immediate service. He may be called to meditate the muse, but nevertheless that church is to be condemned which will not take such men as he to be its ministers. St. Peter himself is brought on to condemn the prelates for church-outing Milton for sake of those blind mouths that creep and intrude and climb into the fold for their bellies' sake, shove away the bidden guest, and let the people go untaught or mistaught, 'swoln with wind and the rank mist they draw.' In two cryptic lines the dread voice speaks of smiting, and then ceases. We shall hear it again a little later, neither so cryptic nor so soon silent. Meanwhile the poet strews English flowers on Lycid's bier, invokes the vision of the fabled shores where his body lies, and again hears the angels singing.

> There entertain him all the Saints above,
> In solemn troops and sweet Societies,
> That sing, and singing in their glory move,
> And wipe the tears forever from his eyes.

Thus Milton in 1637 immortalized the zeal of the saints here below. Laud probably never heard of *Lycidas*, and the preachers had no real notion what manner of person they had in its author won to their cause. Yet there could hardly have been given more extraordinary evidence than that poem gave of the depth and sweep to which their influence had attained. The Puritan pulpit might temporarily be stilled, but it had done its work, done it thoroughly and well. By popularizing the Bible and the Puritan epic of the spiritual life, it had popularized an incomparable vocabulary for the expression of the people's discontent with the present and their hope for the future. In extending the range of its own popular appeal, it had fostered the press, and in giving such characters as Prynne a cause for playing the martyr, it had made the uses of publicity known to all. It had raised up such men as the two Goodwins and the other independents who were to prove the undoing of the dream of presbyterian reform.

It had opened the way to the irretrievable disruption of the church, to dissent and to the incipient democracy voiced by Lilburne. In Milton, finally, the cause of the Puritan preachers had enlisted a great literary genius, one who brought the idealism bred by the poetry and philosophy of Renaissance humanism to the support of Puritan revolutionary zeal in church and state. The performances of Prynne, Bastwick and Burton and of Lilburne, the dialectics of John Goodwin, and the appearance of *Lycidas* showed that revolution was ready to burst forth and that repressing preachers, cropping the ears of pamphleteers and church-outing idealistic poets could not stop it. Laud had but to give the occasion, and the upheaval would begin.

DONALD M. FRIEDMAN

Lycidas: The Swain's Paideia[†]

Lycidas has provoked debates and disagreements because so many of the questions it asks remain unanswered or receive inadequate or irrelevant answers; the experience of reading *Lycidas* is, I suspect, more like Milton's in writing it than is the case with most other poems. And it is an important part of Milton's central conception of his pastoral persona to show him in the midst of a roiling sea of uncertainty, anger, despair, and bewilderment. Out of these weltering moods come the challenges, the demands, the questionings of fate, the gods, the self, which constitute so much of the actual texture of the poem. Responses come from the gods, from nature, from the saints; but these responses—explanations and utterances meant to quiet and reassure—are not only often shown to be unhelpful but are actually ignored by the questioner. He seems to be neither informed nor reassured, but merely determined to go on with his frustrating pursuit of resolution.

However one views what once were called "digressions" in the poem, explanations of its structure and of the thematic interrelations of its parts lead inevitably to the idea of a poem based on a dynamic of conflict—sometimes between classical and Christian myth, sometimes between innocence and experience, but always between major principles of poetic allegiance which Milton is striving to reconcile. An important consequence for *Lycidas* of its pattern of successive impact and recoil is that it allows Milton to render the experience of the poem's speaker as one of active strug-

† From *Milton's "Lycidas": The Tradition and the Poem*, ed. C. A. Patrides (Columbia: University of Missouri Press, 1983). Copyright © 1983 by the Curators of the University of Missouri. Reprinted by permission of the University of Missouri Press.

gle. The pastoral persona is not swept up in the poem's large movements of debate and abortive harmonies; typically, he fights *against*
the knowledge that floods the serene "high Lawns"[1] of his mental
landscape in the hortatory voices of Phoebus and St. Peter. The
struggle is not carried on forensically; the inspired arguments are
not refuted; the lamenting shepherd simply sweeps, or tries to
sweep, them away, urging himself on through the disordered countries of his mind, while demanding all the time an explanation that
never comes. The further reach of Milton's skill, in this portrait of
a consciousness defending itself against the knowledge it knows to
be necessary and saving, is his ability to show us the gradual, very
gradual, growth of understanding that accompanies and emerges
from the tides of conflict which shape the surface and structure of
the elegy. The final consoling vision is neither conceived nor spoken from a predetermined position of revealed or human wisdom; it
does not follow from the elegist's understanding or from his role at
the beginning of the poem; nor is it a knowledge held in suspense,
a potentiality implicit in the pastoral and in the mind of the shepherd persona. Rather, it is a knowledge whose realization depends
from moment to moment on his ability to grasp and accept what
the experience of the poem is teaching him.

At each stage of this development in the persona, changes in
consciousness are reflected in the speaker's language as he challenges the fate that governs the pastoral elegy, and as he reacts to
the literary and religious doctrines that are given voice in the poem
to meet his challenges. Lowry Nelson, Jr., has described this process as "a kind of self-education";[2] it is not presented, however, as a
slow and unperturbed ascent of that "hill side" Milton speaks of in
Of Education, than which "the harp of *Orpheus* was not more
charming."[3] *Lycidas* is a dramatization of the first steps in the
ascent of that hill, which Milton calls "laborious indeed." Knowing
that as fallen creatures our element is "the perpetuall stumble of
conjecture and disturbance in this our darke voyage," Milton insists
also that "the darknes and the crookednesse is our own," that "our
understanding [has] a film of *ignorance* over it," is "blear with gazing on . . . false glisterings," "The very essence of Truth is plain-
nesse, and brightnes";[4] that men cannot perceive that essence is not
the result of mere inability, but of their active struggle not to accept
truth, a struggle carried on by human energies perverted in the

---

1. Milton's poetry is quoted from the edition by Merritt Y. Hughes (New York, 1957); his
   prose, from the Yale edition of his *Complete Prose Works* (1953 ff.)
2. *Baroque Lyric Poetry* (New Haven, 1961), 149.
3. *Of Education*, in *Prose*, 2:376.
4. *Of Reformation*, in *Prose*, 1:566.

service of self-deception, egotism, sloth, and the "frail thoughts" that would "dally with false surmise."

At the very beginning of the poem we are troubled by allusions to a past we know nothing of. "Yet once more," says the voice we do not yet know as the swain's. The events he recalls are never specified; they exist in the poem as symbolic gestures invoking, perhaps, previous exercises in the same formal genre, or simply other poems, or even other moments of crisis and loss in the putative history of the mourning shepherd. His address to the emblematic, honorific plants combines reverent apology and a grinding, reluctant distaste for his enforced task. We cannot help noting that the thoroughly conventional disclaimer of the traditional elegist—the pretense that he is unqualified to praise the subject of his elegy adequately—is here transformed into a trope that is both wider in reference and more intensely—almost crudely—personal than the tradition would seem to allow. This poet is unready, not because King's virtues are beyond his powers to celebrate (the phrase, "hath not left his peer," is strangely ambiguous in context), but because he has not yet arrived at a desired state of "ripeness." We are made to feel the force of his desire for that ripeness without being told in what it consists or how it will be recognized. With the pervasive obliquity of the opening part of the poem, the ideal state is defined for us largely by images of negation and qualification. Although the berries the swain comes to pluck are "harsh and crude," emblematic both of his unpreparedness and of the act he is forced to perform, the stressed rhymes also draw our attention to "never sere" and "the mellowing year," sounds that contradict the violence of the action in the foreground of the poem and set up a standard of permanence and serenity by which to judge what follows. In this way Milton begins to shape one of the fundamental patterns of the poem: the dramatic *events* we witness and hear described are rendered in a language that simultaneously suggests a reinterpretation of those events; the meanings the swain attaches to them are subsumed in larger and truer meanings that reveal themselves to him only as he submits to the apparently random course of his experience.

Another way to make much the same point is to observe that the voice we hear in the *ottava rima* coda, the voice that guides us to look back at the swain and to consider what he has said and learned during the recitation of *Lycidas*, is in control of the poem's diction from the beginning. He allows us and helps us to see more than the swain does, at the same time that we listen to the swain's speech. Thus, while we translate "forc'd fingers rude" and "Shatter" into perceptions of the speaker's pain and dissatisfaction, we also become aware that "the mellowing year" represents a reality that comprehends, and promises ultimately to justify, the particular "perturbations of the mind" that are being displayed. The symbolic plants that receive the swain's first address have their "season due"; that prophetic concept governs the development of the poem as it moves through many mis-apprehensions and false versions of that promised ripeness. Simi-larly, the first ten lines or so of the poem, as they insist on the idea of death and disruption that come too early, also create the necessary notion of "due season," the stable, knowable criterion by which maturity is judged. Thus the swain, in his very first words, speaks truer than he knows, and the language of pastoral begins to generate the terms of a redefinition of the pastoral mode.

If the pastoral key signature tells us immediately that the poem will have something to say about poetry itself, it is typical of Milton to embody that familiar idea in a sequence of passages ordered by the importance of *sound*. Thus, the "logic" of the opening fourteen lines of the poem says that the "bitter constraint" of Lycidas's death forces the swain to disturb the laurels of poetry prematurely *because* Lycidas was a singer and must not be left to the winds and waters without the "meed" of a mournful song. In the fictive world of Mil-ton's swain, silence is a threat, an unspeaking sign of death, disor-der, unnaturalness. So, when the muses are implored to "sweep the string," one strenuous activity of the poem is begun, the act of fill-ing the silence wrought by too early fatality with the music of the "Sphere-born harmonious Sisters, Voice and Verse"; and the neces-sary continuity of sound is established as the swain looks forward to the silence of his "destin'd Urn," hoping for the propriety of "lucky words" spoken for *him* by another poet.

Miss Tuve made much the same point, by her italics, when she remarked that "decay and disease . . . are 'such' as was the news of . . . loss, *to Shepherd's ear*."[5] But this ellipsis needs to be expanded; and the task is made light and easy by Milton's scrupulous insistence, in the early stages of the poem, on the figural importance of natural and artificial sound in the composition of the pastoral world. As the "eyelids" of the morn open to perceive the two shepherd-figures mak-ing their way onto the serene and fertile plains of youth and early, carefree song, the swain testifies to the quality of their common experience by remembering the sultry horn of the Gray-fly, and by showing us the power of their "Rural ditties" to stir the fauns and satyrs to dance, the excellence of the "glad sound" that could please those presumably sterner and better-trained sensibilities of "old Damoetas."

The momentary vision of delight that has passed, then, is sketched so that our familiar image of the pastoral landscape is suffused with

5. Rosemond Tuve, "Theme, Pattern, and Imagery in *Lycidas*," *Images and Themes in Five Poems by Milton* (Cambridge, Mass., 1957), pp. 73–111 185 ff.

minor harmonies and lively tunes, appropriate both to innocent immaturity and to its dawning and uncomplicated ambitions. We are then returned to a present transformed by a "heavy change," and denied the comfort, not of a promised future glory, but of the simplicities and satisfactions of a ravaged past. The bereaved shepherd is circumscribed both by events and by the limits of his understanding of them. One way in which the limits of that understanding are made clear is the variation Milton works on the conventional "pathetic fallacy"; the natural scene described by the swain does not mourn actively. The trees do not cast down their fruit, the ewes' udders do not wither, cattle do not refuse to drink, nor do any Libyan lions roar with grief, fountains do not dry up, nor does the earth give forth only darnels;[6] the "heavy change" is defined for us, rather, as the *absence* of a musical sound which once gave order, dancelike pattern, and pleasure to the natural world. The willows fan their leaves "no more" to Lycidas's songs, and the woods and caves mourn the dead shepherd with their "echoes" that can now only reverberate silence. Milton drives the point home unmistakably by having the lines rise in a rhythmic climax to the definition of all disruption and sorrow as a loss to the ear. And as a yet more refined intensification of his dominant idea, that loss is compared to the effect of *premature* death, the cutting-off of "weanling" herds, the "blasting" of flowers which put on their "gay wardrobe" in the earliest days of spring.

The lament thus takes us back to the tonality of the poem's opening lines, the bewildered and dismayed contemplation of an unexpected fate that has overtaken a poet whose youthful harmonies had given life and beauty to an appreciative world. At this point "denial vain and coy excuse" have been swept away not only by the necessary proprieties of elegizing a fellow poet but also by the "sight" of the scars his death has left on the charming and comfortable world sketched for us in lines 25–36. The movement of the entire elegy is rehearsed in the confrontation between the memory of that world and the undeniable present reality. The transformation has been worked, and the swain is trying to accommodate himself to its meaning. He defines what is by referring it to what has been, and can go no further than to realize that death has shown itself to be inimical not only to beauty and simplicity but to the potentiality of creation implicit in the figural poet. Still, it is the *shepherd's ear* that has been deprived, just as it had been the swain who was forced to shatter the laurel's leaves too soon.

And it is still that swain who is unable to grapple his mind to that reality for very long. His next thought, sanctioned by pastoral ele-

6. Cf. Moschus, *The Lament for Bion*; Virgil, *Eclogue V*; Castiglione, *Alcon*.

giac tradition, is to question the gods, to try to discover a complicity that will explain the death of Lycidas. He chooses the indigenous legendary figures, supposed to stand in a tutelary relation to bardic, prophetic poetry. But the attempt is abandoned as soon as it begins, not because the swain is too clear-sighted to place any faith in such Celtic nonsense, but because he knows that the great Muse, the mother of the true poet's guardian and genius—Orpheus—could do nothing to save her precious charge. Thus he exchanges one myth for another, but in that exchange he has moved toward the acceptance of an emblematic meaning larger than any he has yet acknowledged. "Universal nature did lament" Orpheus's death, and the contemplation of "his gory visage" effectively bars the reentrance to the world of "high Lawns" and "Rural ditties." Nor was it simply a silent and inexplicable act of fate that destroyed *this* myth; Orpheus's "enchanting" powers were drowned by the "hideous roar" of that "rout" whose type was the mad Bacchants but whose embodiments recur throughout human history. They are the forces that crush poetry and the sympathetic alliance with nature that generates it.

Having gone this far toward the recognition of a universal predicament, the swain cannot retreat unthinkingly into the reassuring formulas that had served him. Milton signals this by bringing his mind once again back to the present; but, as before, it is a present transformed by what he has learned in the lines that precede it. What was a memory of two brother poets "nurst upon the self-same hill" becomes an inquiry into the justification of the métier of poetry itself. Once the swain had recalled the pleasure and approval of the fauns and Damoetas; now he speaks of the "homely slighted Shepherd's trade." It is important to realize that nothing has been said in the poem to change our knowledge or opinions of the poet's calling; what the new characterization of poetry reflects is the swain's changing awareness. The atmosphere of pastoral ease and delight which surrounded the image of those glad sounds and care-free dances has been darkened by the memory of Orpheus's fate, and as a consequence the calling of poetry, which then seemed natural and unbidden, is now seen as burdensome and problematical. Furthermore, the swain's questioning of his own relation to his calling is not phrased in nostalgic terms, but clearly alludes to actual contemporary poets, fashionable styles, and immediate rewards. In short, the pastoral pretense begins to dissolve into a discussion of what it means to be a poet in England in 1637. The alternatives are set up in terms of effort and ease. The vision of *otium* usually associated with the pastoral tradition out of which Milton had fashioned the first picture of his youth at Cambridge is now transferred to the naturalists, the erotic poets who "sport with

Amaryllis in the shade"; and so the expressive figure of pastoral
poetry no longer remains unitary, but divides into true and false, or
at least worthy and slothful, song. And the former is attributed to
those who pursue their calling with "uncessant care," who "meditate" the muse "strictly." These are not the concepts of an untroubled shepherd piping "unpremeditated" tunes to an audience of
pagan hedonists; they reveal the grave dedication to a holy and
demanding art that has been observed in Milton's own youthful
writings. The question he asks himself is not simply whether one
kind of poetry is better than another, but whether the kind of
poetry he knows to be better is worth pursuing if his labors and his
achieved excellence are never to be given due praise.

However noble the Renaissance concept of fame may have been,
however different from its usual connotations of reputation and
public applause, Milton is at pains to show here that it is inadequate to the reassurance the swain is seeking. If it is the "last infirmity of Noble mind," it is nevertheless an infirmity. And the point is
underlined by the swain's hoping to "find" it, thinking to "burst out
into sudden blaze," thinking, in other words, of a spectacular, unexpected, almost unearned reward of glory and admiration. The very
terms belie the characterization of the poetic calling as a strict,
thankless, uncessant devotion to the highest standards of personal
and artistic integrity. The lines ring with ambition, and their passion is rendered even more compelling by the tight-lipped contempt
poured upon the "blind *Fury*" in the phrase, "slits the thin-spun
life." But this complex burst of energy is checked by the voice of
Phoebus, who replied to the swain's question by telling him that he
should expect fame only in heaven, that its plant, unlike the laurels
and myrtles, does not grow in mortal soil. The change of tense
breaks the time sequence that has been established in the poem
thus far and begins to suggest a mental past in which this examination has been carried on previously. It both clarifies some of the
implications hinted at by "Yet once more" and looks forward to the
coda in which Milton subsumes the entire experience of the swain
in his closing comment.

The deliberate blurring of the narrative line is Milton's way of
creating a fictive time in which the elegy exists, and it functions in
much the same way as the suggestive backward glance of the opening words of the poem. The discomfort we feel as a result of such
disorientation is a vital part of the experience of the poem, for it
reminds us in subtle ways that both the occasion and the statement
of *this* pastoral elegy vibrate between the poles of particularity and
universal meaning. The strained speculation through which the
swain forces himself enacts, but also reenacts, a mental history
through which Milton himself, and any serious poet, has lived

many times. And so he can immediately return to the waiting current of pastoral imagery, as his "Oat proceeds" in the present time
of the poem; the "higher mood" of Phoebus's speech, although it
necessitates a decorous invocation of the appropriately legendary
Arethusa and Mincius, does not disturb the flow of pastoral conventions in the swain's repertory. The procession of mourners,
which Milton might have found in elegies by Moschus, Castiglione,
Sannazaro, and others and in Virgil's Tenth Eclogue, carries us
back not only to the familiar traditions of the elegy, but also to the
questioning mood of the address to the nymphs in lines 50–55. It is
as if the swain has forgotten that both the inquiry into causes and
the notion of the protective muses have been discovered to be fond
dreams. But these figures—"the Herald of the Sea" and Hippotades—
come unbidden; the sea and the winds send their answer to questions unasked by the swain, as the classical deities of nature exculpate
themselves. The important point here is that what they have to say is
no answer to the underlying question about Lycidas's death: Even
Camus, the allegorical figure who recalls for the last time in the
poem the fading pastoral emblem of early life at Cambridge, brings
only another empty question; his venerable age and his aura of semi-
mystical wisdom cannot offer knowledge or resolution.

At this stage in the poem it seems as if the machinery of conventional pastoral has seized the initiative from the swain. With the
exception of the lines on the "perfidious Bark," which seem an
explanation *faute de mieux*,[7] he merely reports and describes; the
personal tones of anguish and bitterness diminish and are powerfully subdued by the angry, craggy denunciation voiced by St. Peter.

The conventional procession of mourners, then, erupts from
within, as the swain reports an incursion more violent and unas-
similable than any that have occurred thus far. The speech of
Phoebus might have been a version of any young poet's concerned
musings; but this diatribe, if only because of the many ways in
which it violates the rhetorical manners of the elegy, is meant to
make us feel that a power hitherto unacknowledged and untapped
by the swain's mind has now thrust into the fragile framework in
order to speak a truth that cannot be softened or distanced by literary technique. The point is made to the ear by a new vocabulary,
which includes the sounds and judgmental images of "flashy songs,"
"scrannel Pipes," and the "hungry Sheep" rotting "inwardly." This
is a language that has been only tentatively drawn upon in the lines
that spoke of the "homely slighted Shepherd's trade"; but it achieves
its full impact now, not simply by sound, but by the way it converts

---

7. See Michael Lloyd, "The Fatal Bark," *Modern Language Notes* 75 (1960): 103–9, for a
different reading.

the swain's defensive pastoral mode into a way of revelation. Peter
speaks of the same contemporary conditions the swain had deplored
in lines 64–69, but in his mouth the figure of the shepherd is no
longer an airy and elegant allusion to the life of art. While the
swain has been attempting to understand and control the implications of Lycidas's death for his own commitment to poetry, he has
been ignoring the significance of the young cleric's death for the
health of the English pastorate. Peter's speech reminds him of what
he has forgotten, but not in the solicitous manner of Phoebus.
Indeed, Peter does not even speak *to* the swain; he simply defines
what has been lost by describing the "corrupted clergy" that remain,
and foretells retribution. As at every marked turning point in *Lycidas* the bearing of the passage, its relation to the developing elegiac
pattern, is left unspecified. Milton provides no easy or obvious way
to decide what we or the swain are to understand from Peter's
speech; what is to be *done* is even more problematical.

This troubled indecision is underlined by the swain's response.
Peter's clarification of the true meaning of "shepherd" is referred to
as "the dread voice"; the swain acknowledges only a *sound* whose
harsh veracity has disrupted the orderly, plaintive, nostalgic gestures to which he is trying to attune his own thoughts. And so the
return to convention, as Peter's words have been more difficult to
accommodate than Phoebus's, is here more poignant, more detailed;
we may even say more desperate. The flower catalogue was as clearly
a standard part of the archetypal pastoral elegy as the mourning
procession; and we know from the Trinity manuscript that Milton
labored carefully over it, meaning it to stand for all similar attempts
to find respite from grief and bewilderment in the passive and
numerable beauties of a sympathetic nature. Alpheus and the Sicilian Muse are called once again into their mild and uncomplicated
relationship with the swain; they are asked to "call the Vales" and
ask them to cast their flowers on the imaginary "Laureate Hearse"
of the dead shepherd. This request, at least, is answered; for immediately the swain turns to address the "valleys low" himself, and his
imagination responds to the comforting "mild whispers" that issue
from the gushing brooks of this newly surmised landscape. The
flower catalogue sketches for us a *locus amoenus* quite different
from the remembered, autobiographical setting the swain described
initially. Here there are no "high Lawns," no gaily piped tunes, no
dancing pagan deities. Rather, in the extremity of shock wrought by
Peter's tirade, the swain conjures the healing and restorative landscape of the literary pastoral, as if the convention itself of the
flower catalogue had the power to wipe out the memory of what he
has just heard. No longer is he in full command of his chosen
poetic mode; no longer does he speak of King and himself as shep-

herds, assured of the stable meaning of that usage. Peter has bereft him of that simple and complacent equation, and he is driven back to its elemental, underlying pretense of an animate and empathetic nature. The swain tries, by exercising his command of an artificial literary mode, to grasp the consolation that may be distilled from it.

But the grasp is loosening even as it is attempted, for the very beauty of the things described is tempered and shadowed. The elaborate pastoral panoply that Milton draws, we must notice, is at the same time an indirect witness of its helplessness to stave off the effects of Peter's speech, if we conceive that as a new kind of statement, bringing with it a new kind of knowledge. The ambition and confidence adumbrated in the vision of shepherds' life on those high lawns of youth surrender to the mood of the flower catalogue. And that mood is attuned to the "valleys low" and their "mild whispers"; these lines are a demonstration of the pastoral's commitment to a life of ease, disengagement, even immaturity and a denial of responsibility. The flowers belong to the spring season, appropriate still to the theme of Lycidas's early death, but also to the stage of personal development in which the mind and spirit are shielded from the fierce, inevitable onslaught of destructive experience. The "swart Star sparely looks" on *this* pastoral scene; but it is impossible for the shepherd-poet who has faced the apparently random and indifferent harshness of life in the world to avoid emerging into the full blaze of that sun of maturity. The "wanton winds" may blow softly and playfully through these imagined dales, but the heights of poetic achievement that tempt the swain's "clear spirit" are buffeted by "every gust of rugged wings / That blows from off each beaked Promontory." The swain, the poet, the man can wander contentedly in the landscape of *otium* only so long as his mind can accept the literary mode as a real and satisfying substitute for the mode of active responsibility, in whose nature he has been instructed both by the death of Lycidas and by the words of St. Peter. Once the meaning of the true pastorate is understood, or even recognized, the low valleys must become an eternally desirable but finally uninhabitable region of the mind.

And so the magnificence, the brilliant detail, the lovingly fashioned colors and sounds of the flower passage must ultimately be dismissed as a "false surmise," and the swain must show, to himself as to us, that he understands the intrinsic meaning of the temptation he has overcome by exposing his motives with frank but tender honesty: "For so to interpose a little ease, / Let our frail thoughts dally with false surmise" (152–53). The sting is removed from the charge implicit in "false" by the conscious admission of the frailty of all human thoughts, among which the imagination of pastoral is one of the most beautiful and most fragile. Milton does not mute the notes of lingering nostalgia in these lines, but neither does he allow them to sound with transparent simplicity. The little ease supplied by this dimming glimpse of honied showers and vernal flowers is merely interposed between the acts of unillusioned contemplation that confront the truths of Peter's attack and the facts of King's death. The dalliance is interrupted brutally by the self-aware and resigned expletive, "Ay me!"; with the utterance of that brief appeal the swain is swept forward finally into the great concluding movements of the poem. Even syntax contributes to our sense of rising and climactic rhythm; we do not grasp the scope of "whilst" until nine lines later, when Michael is asked to "look homeward" while the body of Lycidas follows its uncouth path through the unfathomable waters. But "whilst" also looks backward to the flower passage, as the swain opens himself to the realization that the artistry he has devoted to the invocation of an "enamell'd" and animate nature has neither appeased his grief or confusion, nor stayed the flow of intractable experience, imaged here as the hurling of Lycidas's bones among the monsters of the unimaginable ocean depths. At this point the poetic imagination, in its role as a shaper of forms of language intended to soften, reinterpret, and give pattern to the formless succession of events we call experience, falters and proves to be inadequate. Milton tells us this, in one way, by juxtaposing the "fable" of Bellerus with the "great vision" of the guardian archangel; and the swain's response to his own discovery of the limits of his poetic power is to turn from lamentation and self-recrimination to prayer. He asks for no aid from the muses nor from symbolic rivers and fountains, for to do that would be to maintain the empty fiction of the centrality of the elegiac poet, to insist on the importance of the interpreting voice. Rather, he surrenders those illusory notions of competency, and in doing so surrenders as well the theme of the dead shepherd to the tutelary powers of St. Michael and the legendary dolphins. And that surrender is not entirely an act of conscious choice; he has been led to the discovery of Michael's guardianship by the current of imagination which, as it follows the dreadful vision of Lycidas's body lost beneath the sea, is brought back to the actual place at which knowledge stops, the Irish Channel, and to the actual presence of the "guarded Mount." Once again a question is answered, but not in an expected way. At the moment when the swain's consciousness of inability and ignorance is most profound, both ability and insight are *provided*; not because he has asked for them, but because he has admitted his lack.

The same pattern, the answer that comes unexpectedly and in terms that seem incomprehensible to the questioner, seems to me to govern the speech of consolation that follows the appeal to

Michael. The swain has given up the apparently fruitless task of demanding explanations from nature and the gods; his rending doubts about the worth and purpose of poetry have been stilled, if not satisfied. His ambitious sallies into the world of confusion and disappointment that surrounds the various pastoral attempts at order and intelligibility have been reduced to a single, painful speculation on the true whereabouts of the body of his dead friend. And that speculation is resolved, not by yet another voice from outside the frame of the elegy, but by the creation of a new voice for the swain. The first clear demarcation of that new voice is the fact that for the first time in the poem the swain addresses himself to a human audience.[8] He casts aside the obliquity inherent in speaking to muses, nymphs, laurels, and myrtles and turns to a silent group of fellow mourners whose presence we have not been allowed to suspect. And for the first time in the poem he neither questions, nor challenges, nor debates with himself, but simply *tells* what he knows to be true. It is crucial that we realize Milton forbids us to feel we understand how the swain has come to this knowledge of truth. The transformation he undergoes has nothing to do, in the poem, with a logical or sequential argument or demonstration; nothing he is told, nothing he hears, can account for his grasp of the new truth he promulgates to the listening shepherds. The transformation lies in the speech itself that we hear; and the effect of that speech depends as heavily on its function as on its content. The swain's consoling vision of Lycidas comforted in "other groves" is the only passage in the elegy which is directed to the enlightenment of men other than himself. It is neither a private revelation, as is Phoebus's lesson, nor a scarifying indictment of historical reality, as is Peter's; it is, precisely, an example of the service poetry performs which Milton described in *The Reason of Church-Government*, "to allay the perturbations of the mind, and set the affections in right tune, to celebrate in glorious and lofty Hymns the throne and equipage of Gods Almightinesse." It fulfills these tasks by embodying the obligations of the true pastor in poetry divinely inspired. It communicates saving truth in lines whose music is a reflection of the bright vision which is not the reward of study and preparation but of the proper rectification of the will. The swain's ability to speak the lines of consolation is Milton's dramatization of the infusion of grace.[9]

---

8. Lowry Nelson, Jr., makes much the same point in his *Baroque Lyric Poetry*.
9. William G. Madsen in "The Voice of Michael in *Lycidas*," *Studies in English Literature* 3 (1963): 1–7, argues that the consolation speech is delivered by the archangel Michael. For a number of reasons I find Madsen's argument unconvincing; most obviously, Madsen has difficulty in explaining why the *ottava rima* coda refers to the swain having sung the final verse paragraph, and is forced to divide the paragraph to allow for the swain's sudden reappearance in line 182; nor can he explain why Michael, alone of all

It is not an accident that these lines occur immediately after the
swain has reached the deepest levels of sorrow, self-abnegation,
and self-knowledge. Not until he has admitted to himself that the
noblest ideas of poetry he has held are but false surmises can he
receive the gift of true poetry which, as other critics have observed,
does not abandon the pastoral mode as a pagan fiction, but trans-
mutes it into a Christian mode of apprehending reality.[1] The classical idea of pastoral is not wrong, but incomplete; and in the poem it
serves not only as a conventional allegorical frame, but also as a
way of representing the incompleteness of mind and spirit that
handicaps all human endeavors that grow from an unexamined
assumption of the self-sufficiency of the imagination. The power of
this assumption has been demonstrated to us in *Lycidas* in many
ways: the serene complacency of the memories of the youthful
"high Lawns" of Cambridge; the bitter musings over the comparative rewards of Amaryllis and the "thankless Muse"; the strivings to
blot out the "higher mood" of Phoebus and the "dread voice" of
Peter by calling up the liquid sounds of Mincius and the Sicilian
Muses; the tapestry work of the flower passage; and the last,
despairing clutching at the little ease that all such surmises promise. In each case the inability, or the refusal, to face and accept the
inexplicable fact of death, the unbearable fact that dedication and
talent are not guaranteed recognition—in each case the swain's
struggle against the knowledge that will force him into maturity is
cast in the form of an attempt to maintain the flow of the pastoral
elegy. The conventions of the genre are used as examples of the
mind's defensive impulses; and while they reveal the swain's artistry, they also show the hollowness of that artistry when it is used
to falsify the reality that true poetry should embody.

Some years ago Michael Lloyd wrote a short piece to show that
the position of *Lycidas* in the volume known as *Justa Edovardo King*
was not without significance.[2] Lloyd does not comment on the fact
that, of all the poems in *Justa Edovardo King*, *Lycidas* is the only
pastoral elegy. Milton's choice of the genre must have appeared to
his contemporaries an act of conscious archaism, or an instance of
his scholarly traditionalism, or even a kind of homage to his
"teacher," Spenser. The death of a young shepherd serves as the
formal occasion and frame for the poem; but the death of a way of

the speakers identified specifically in the poem, is introduced without comment or
identification.
1. See Rosemond Tuve, "Theme, Pattern, and Imagery in *Lycidas*," in Patrides, *Milton's
Lycidas*, pp. 171 ff.; Jon S. Lawry, "'Eager Thought': Dialectic in *Lycidas*," in Patrides,
pp. 236 ff, and Isabel G. MacCaffrey, "*Lycidas*: The Poet in a Landscape," in Patrides,
pp. 246 ff.
2. "*Justa Edovardo King*," *Notes and Queries*, n.s. 5 (1958): 423–24.

conceiving the roles of poet and priest is the action that *Lycidas* truly imitates.

As in so many places in Milton's work, the death of an immature or inadequate idea is wrought by the incursion of a new kind of knowledge into a consciousness that wants to preserve its familiar sense of security, but cannot deny the power of truth to change its way of seeing the world. And in all those places Milton does not tell us *how* that change is accomplished; he shows us the results of the change. Adam never speaks about the *experience* of disobedience; what Milton shows us is the change in Adam's speech and behavior after he has eaten of the apple. Samson may speak of "some rousing motions" stirring within him, but the moment of regeneration occurs offstage, away from our view, and in silence. We are not privy to Christ's inner debates in *Paradise Regained*; we listen to the results of that debate as he turns Satan's questions and offers back against him, and we watch Christ's actions. Milton asks always that we learn from the contemplation of his heroes' deeds; and the implicit command is that we try to understand their inward spiritual progress by testing our responses to their situations against theirs. It is in this sense that Milton's major poems are didactic, as well as in the more limited sense of conveying knowledge or doctrine to his audience. The epics and the closet drama teach by submitting us to the experience of trial; they guide our rational understanding by the example of dramatic figures who undergo trial and are moved to act on what they learn in consequence.

Lycidas may, I think, be compared in some degree to these greater poems because the major instrument of its consolation is not the mere recounting of the swain's climactic vision of Lycidas's "large recompense," but the entire, complex process through which he both raises himself and is raised to the vantage point which grants him that vision. I have said that he delivers the consoling speech to the shepherds only after his imagination has surrendered its stiff self-will and allowed itself to follow the idea of Lycidas's corpse to the bottom of the sea. That surrender of the will elicits immediately the assurance of a corrective vision, which sees that Lycidas, "Sunk though he be beneath the wat'ry floor," is not dead because,

> So sinks the day-star in the Ocean bed,
> And yet anon repairs his drooping head,
> And tricks his beams, and with new-spangled Ore,
> Flames in the forehead of the morning sky.

Analogy as a means of discovering truth had been discredited in the progressive disarming of pastoral symbols and language; the equation of shepherd and poet, the swain had realized, does not suffice to explain or justify the true relationships between the poet and his world, or between the poet and the art to which he is called. What is at fault is not the idea of such relationships, but the misrepresentation of that idea inherent in the use of metaphor. Metaphor makes it seem that different realities can be fused by language; the swain realizes, however, that such fusion is brought about by the enlightened understanding, which uses language to reveal both differences and likenesses. And so in these lines the swain comes upon an analogy that brings into consonance the meaning of Lycidas's mortal tragedy, the psychic experience the swain himself is undergoing, and the traditional emblem of that power which guarantees the truth of the analogy and yokes all spiritual histories with their archetype, the "dear might of him that walk'd the waves." The elements of pastoral metaphor, which have been shown to be an incomplete picture of reality, are unfolded and exposed in a simile: "So sinks the day-star . . . So Lycidas." The swain now sees, controls, and explains an identity that exists in natural and supernatural phenomena, rather than in the literary language he has inherited.

Thus it is important to notice that, as a part of the elegy, the description of heaven's "other groves," "the blest Kingdoms meek of joy and love," is no less an imaginative fiction than the fields that first appeared "under the opening eyelids of the morn." Here, as there, are companionship, music, sunlight, and soothing liquids. The difference in our response to this setting is not accountable simply by the deliberately muted presence of Christ, but by the tone of the swain's speech. He speaks in a timeless present, describing firmly and clearly what is, not what once was or what is gone. And, finally, he takes upon himself the cloak of prophecy and tells Lycidas what is to come out of the grief and loss with which the poem began. Nor is the prophecy complete without a gesture toward the swain's newly found responsibility to all shepherds, to "all that wander in that perilous flood." The dead shepherd will receive the meed of creation as a tutelary "Genius," but the living poet is granted, and assumes, the charge of explaining the meaning of that uncertain journey to all men who will embark upon it.

To assume such a charge requires both humility and confidence, and the tone of the speech displays both. The poet knows that the "solemn troops, and sweet Societies" to which Lycidas has been assimilated "sing, and singing in their glory move," but the song itself is beyond his powers to imitate. Nevertheless, he accepts the burden, which must have been deeply vexing for Milton, of sustaining both the memory and the prophetic vision of that song in poetry which he knows to be only a shadow of its harmonious source. The combination of confidence and humility in his speech is exactly parallel to the ambiguous gifts of knowledge the swain accepts as he assumes the obligations of the true shepherd. The calling of priestly poetry confers special powers and special responsibilities. The swain as the grieving pastoral elegist had been conscious only of the talents that separated him from other men, even from other poets. Peter's speech had reminded him of the more important burdens of the pastorate; but his response was a retreat, even if momentarily, into the fictive world of beauty and *otium*. Now, with the acknowledgment of both his ability and his duty to speak of true Christian consolation to "woeful Shepherds" whose salvation lies partially in the power of his inspired voice, he is given a language adequate to the task he agrees to perform, a language both "answerable" and "in strictest measure ev'n" to the "lot" toward which time and the course of the elegy have led him.

We can recognize in Milton's works throughout his life—from Sonnet VII to *Samson Agonistes*—a grating tension between his will to create the proof of his singular powers and his will to believe that acts of poetic creation should be and would be prompted by "some strong motion" instilled in him by "Time . . . and the will of Heav'n." This tension is exhibited most clearly in Sonnet VII and in the figure of Samson; it is exposed and resolved in the invocations in *Paradise Lost*. But *Lycidas* is Milton's one attempt to dramatize the experience of that tension and to show how transcending it leads to the attainment of the poetic voice which alone can sustain the continuing act of creation which is the epic poem.

It is as a teacher, of course, that the swain speaks finally, and he teaches a truth that has not been uncovered by his reason in the course of the poem, but that has been borne in upon him by the action of the poem, as it responds to the guiding pressure of divine will. Milton is certainly playing on the word *uncouth* in the coda, for while the swain had been both uninstructed and unknown as he first laid his hands unwillingly upon the evergreen laurels, he is no longer ignorant. Nor, we are made to feel, will he be long unknown; the address we have just heard does not fit the characterization of a "*Doric* lay," and its majestic rhythms can be described as "warbling" only by the poet who knows fully how far his persona has traveled and what heights of wisdom and poetic brilliance he has attained. I find as much humor as serenity in the coda, because Milton is relying on our shocked rediscovery of the pastoral setting to remind us of the scope of the journey we have just undergone. We now find that the swain has been singing for the length of the imagined day, but that we have been raised out of the cycle of time in which we began; the magnificent, telling symbol of the "daystar" flaming "in the forehead of the morning sky" is once again simply the sun, now "dropt into the Western bay." The sensation is that of returning to a familiar, natural, real world; and we can appreciate the flourish of Milton's delighted skill when we remember that the reality to which we have been restored is the world of the literary pastoral, completely mastered and controlled by the poet whose voice we hear for the first time. This fiction has opened the way to a truth that can be expressed only in fictions; yet the discovery of that truth renders us, and the swain, forever unable to mistake fiction for what it is intended to represent.

That same discovery, the result of the process of self-education at the center of *Lycidas*, is, I think, the key to Milton's renovation of the conventional epic beginning, and to his successive re-creations of himself in the speakers of the several invocations in *Paradise Lost*. In the initial address to his "Heav'nly Muse," he defines her part in the process of writing the epic as assisting him to surpass the highest reaches of the classical epic, and to carry him toward the hitherto unattained excellences of Christian epic. I take that assistance to be conceived, at least in the first fifteen lines of the poem, as primarily stylistic. Milton asks the heavenly muse, in short, for the power to sustain a song that will tell man's history from the creation to the final triumph of Christ; to be more precise, he asks the muse to inspire and sustain a language the poet has already formed, during the patient and devoted years of study and practice.

But when he turns, in line 17, to what we may call the second invocation, we should be warned by his use of "chiefly" that Milton does not mean this to be the lesser request, an afterthought; quite the contrary. With that typical softening of focus that overtakes Milton's theological arguments as they move from *The Christian Doctrine* to *Paradise Lost*, the lines we are examining are addressed to a "Spirit" whose nature and rank are unspecified. But his function is clear and entirely consonant with the view of the Holy Spirit as the channel of saving knowledge. He is asked to "instruct"; the emphatic positioning of the word in line 19 is a sign that Milton is not simply appealing for the radical degree of knowledge demanded by *this* epic, but that he has also gone to the root meaning of the word, realizing that any human vessel, in order to contain such knowledge, must be remade. To follow the metaphor, he must be rebuilt, inherently constructed out of the knowledge infused in him by the Spirit. Thus, in another way Milton supports the notion, implicit in the Spirit's preference for the "upright heart and pure" "Before all Temples," that even the sanctity of Zion, the delight of the "Heav'nly Muse" whose aid he has so recently implored, is a less certain guarantee of prophetic truth than the actual regeneration of a soul by the truth conveyed by the Spirit.

The "great Argument" of *Paradise Lost*, of course, is truth—the truth of man's condition seen under the aspect of "Eternal Providence." In this opening invocation Milton prays for the kinds of assistance appropriate to the task of asserting that providence *while* revealing its justice to the audience of men. Although he places heavy emphases in the passage on his need for help, on that in him which is "low" and "dark," he speaks as if there is no doubt that, given the power to tell truth, he will inevitably succeed in the conjoint goal of creating assent to that truth. This air of untroubled confidence, which blends so unnoticeably with the suppliant tone of the invocation, may be accounted for, at least in part, by the fact that Milton chooses from the outset to implicate himself in the condition of the audience he is addressing. He speaks immediately of "our woe," looks forward to Christ's coming to "Restore us," and begins the narrative by referring to "our Grand Parents." This is not merely a variation of the familiar Miltonic device of "placing" the narrator and his listeners in the poem; it is also a declaration of Milton's solution to the unique problems facing a poet who chooses to sing to other men of divine and prophetic truths that no man can know simply by taking thought.

There are only the faintest suggestions of the garland and the singing robes in the figure of the poet Milton adumbrates in these lines. The grandeur and power of the epic role, qualities which had obsessed him in his youth, are muted and replaced by the weight of obligation he willingly assumes, his responsibility to "the chosen Seed." Milton's awareness of the change in his idea of the poet's role is shown, I think, in his deliberate identification of himself with Moses. The identity is asserted by the central term, *shepherd*, and through that term is extended to all the members of the line whose glory consisted in being burdened with the task of witnessing, explaining, justifying. In the consolation passage in *Lycidas* the swain had assumed a similar burden. But his audience were shepherds only by virtue of literary convention; the swain began as one of them and ended as a true shepherd, his state defined largely by his differences from them. Milton begins *Paradise Lost* in a voice that combines the hard-earned understanding of the swain and the stable, compassionate wisdom of the coda of *Lycidas*. That meaning of *shepherd* which is created by the long and intricate *agon* of *Lycidas* is the starting point of the epic. And once that meaning has been absorbed into the poet's idea of his relation to his subject, it leads unerringly to the massive, sustained, flexible, infinitely various union of sound and sense that is the music of *Paradise Lost*. Its keynote is the blending of humility and assurance that we hear in the first twenty-six lines, that incredibly exact rendering of the mind and impulses of a man praying to the Holy Spirit for gifts with which to instruct and solace his fellow men. In the climactic speech of consolation in *Lycidas* Milton drew a sketch for the full portrait he achieved in *Paradise Lost*.

MARY NYQUIST

The Genesis of Gendered Subjectivity in the Divorce Tracts and in *Paradise Lost*†

It appears that one can now speak of "third-wave feminism" as well as "post-feminist feminism." Like other labels generated by the historical moment to which they refer, these await a lengthy period of interrogation. But if they should stick, their significance will be associated with the variety of attacks mounted against Western bourgeois or liberal feminism over the past decade and a half. Now, as never before, what has to be contended with—precisely because it has been exposed in the process of contestation and critique—is the historically determinate and class-inflected nature of the discourse of "equal rights." The questions, equal with whom, and to what end? have been raised in ways that have begun to expose how, ever since the early modern period, bourgeois man has proved the measure. They have also shown how the formal or legal status of this elusive "equality" tends by its very nature to protect the status quo.

Because much academic criticism on *Paradise Lost*, especially that produced in North America, has been written within a liberal–humanist tradition that wants Milton to be, among other things, the patron saint of the companionate marriage, it has frequently made use of a notion of equality that is both mystified and mystifying. The undeniable emphasis on mutuality to be found in *Paradise Lost*—the mutual dependency of Eve and Adam on one another, their shared responsibility for the Fall—is for this reason often treated as if it somehow entailed a significant form of equality. Differences that in *Paradise Lost* are ordered hierarchically and ideologically tend to be neutralized by a critical discourse interested in formal balance and harmonious pairing. To take just one, not especially contentious, example, Milton is said to go out of his way to offset the superiority associated with Adam in his naming of the animals by inventing an equivalent task for Eve: her naming of the flowers. In this reading, Milton, a kind of proto-feminist, generously gives the power of naming to both woman and man.[1] The

---

† From *Re-Membering Milton: Essays on the Texts and Traditions*, ed. Mary Nyquist and Margaret W. Ferguson (New York and London: Methuen, 1987) pp. 99–127. Reprinted by permission.

1. For this, see Barbara K. Lewalski, "Milton and women—yet once more" (*Milton Studies*, 6, 1974, 8). Other defenses have been written by Virginia R. Mollenkott, "Milton and women's liberation: a note on teaching method" (*Milton Quarterly*, 7, 1973, 99–102); Joan M. Webber, "The politics of poetry: feminism and *Paradise Lost*" (*Milton Studies*, 14, 1980, 3–24) and Diane K. McColley, *Milton's Eve* (Urbana, University of Illinois Press, 1983). Generally speaking, an apologetic tendency is a feature of much North American academic literature on Milton.

rhetorical effectiveness of this point obviously depends in important ways upon the suppression of features suggestive of asymmetry. Left unquestioned must be the differences between Adam's authoritative naming of the creatures—an activity associated with the rational superiority and dominion of "Man" when it is presented by Adam, who in Book VIII relates to Raphael this episode of the creation story in the second chapter of Genesis—and Eve's naming of the flowers, which is revealed only incidentally in her response to the penalty of exile delivered in Book XI. In a speech that has the form of a lament for the garden she has just been told they are to leave, Eve's naming in Book XI appears in such a way that it seems never to have had the precise status of an event. It is, instead, inseparably a feature of her apostrophic address to the flowers themselves: "O flow'rs / . . . which I bred up with tender hand / From the first op'ning bud, and gave ye Names" (XI.273–7).[2] Here Eve's "naming" becomes associated not with rational insight and dominion but rather with the act of lyrical utterance, and therefore with the affective responsibilities of the domestic sphere into which her subjectivity has always already fallen.

In recent years, a remarkably similar critical current, intent on neutralizing oppositions, has been at work in feminist biblical commentaries on Genesis. Within the Judeo-Christian tradition, claims for the spiritual equality of the sexes have very often had recourse to Genesis 1.27, "So God created man [hā'ādām, ostensibly a generic term] in his own image, in the image of God created he him; male and female created he them."[3] This verse, which is part of what is now considered the Priestly or "P" creation account (Genesis 1–2.4a), has always co-existed somewhat uneasily with the more primitive and more obviously masculinist Yahwist or "J" creation account in chapter 2, where the creator makes man from the dust of the ground (thereby making hā'ādām punningly relate to hā'ādāmâ, the word for ground or earth) and woman from this man's rib. Within a specifically Christian context, the relationship between the two accounts has been—at least potentially—problematical, since 1 Timothy 2:11–14 uses the Yahwist account to bolster the prohibition against women taking positions of authority within the Church: "Let the woman learn in silence with all subjection. But I suffer not a woman to teach, nor to usurp authority over the man, but to be in silence. For Adam was first formed, then Eve. And Adam was not deceived, but the woman being deceived was in the transgression." Recently, in an effort to reconcile feminism and Christianity,

---

2. Quotations from Milton's poetry are from *John Milton: Complete Poems and Major Prose*, ed. Merritt Y. Hughes (New York, Odyssey, 1957).
3. Biblical quotations are from the King James version.

Phyllis Trible has tried to harmonize the differences between the
Priestly and the Yahwist creation accounts. Trible holds that the
exegetical tradition alone is responsible for the sexist meanings
usually attributed to the Yahwist creation story, which she renar-
rates using methods that are basically formalist.

More specifically, Trible argues that the second chapter of Genesis
tells the story not of the creation of a patriarchal Adam, from whom
a secondary Eve is derived, but the story of the creation of a generic
and androgynous earth creature or "man" to whom the sexually distinct woman and man are related as full equals. Throughout, Trible's
retelling is strongly motivated by the desire to neutralize the discrep-
ancy between the "P" and the "J" accounts by assimilating "J" to "P,"
which is assumed to recognize the equality of the sexes and therefore
to provide the meaning of the two creation accounts taken together
as one. Because "P" suggests the possibility of a symmetrical, nonhierarchical relationship between male and female, "J" is said by
Trible to tell the story of the creation of a sexually undifferentiated
creature who becomes "sexed" only with the creation of woman. The
simultaneous emergence of woman and man as equals is signalled,
she argues, when Yahweh brings the newly fashioned partner to the
previously undifferentiated *hā'ādām* or "man," who responds with
the lyrically erotic utterance: "This is now bone of my bones, and
flesh of my flesh: she shall be called Woman, because she was taken
out of Man" (Genesis 2:23) (in Trible's reading "taken out of" means
"differentiated from").[4]

Trible's revisionary and profoundly ahistorical reading is significant in large part because it has been so widely influential. Among
feminist theologians it would seem to have established a new orthodoxy. And it has recently been ingeniously elaborated for a secular
readership by Mieke Bal, who assumes with Trible that the commentator can, by an effort of will, position herself outside the traditions of masculinist interpretation; and that Genesis bears no
lasting traces of the patriarchal society which produced it.[5] Yet it is
far too easy to adopt the opposing or rather complementary view
that Genesis is a text inaugurating a transhistorically homogeneous
patriarchal culture. This is, unfortunately, a view that is frequently
expressed in connection with *Paradise Lost*. For in spite of the exis-

---

4. Phyllis Trible, *God and the Rhetoric of Sexuality* (Philadelphia, Fortress, 1978), 100–1.
   The discussion in chs 1 and 4 of this work revises and extends the influential "Depatri-
   archalizing in biblical interpretation" (*Journal of the American Academy of Religion*,
   16, 1973, 30–48). For a fuller discussion of some of the exegetical issues touched upon
   here, see an earlier version of this essay, "Genesis, genesis, exegesis, and the formation
   of Milton's Eve," in *Cannibals, Witches and Divorce: Estranging the Renaissance*, ed.
   Marjorie Garber (Baltimore, Johns Hopkins Press, 1987), 147–208.
5. Mieke Bal, "Sexuality, sin, and sorrow: the emergence of the female character (a reading of Genesis 1–3)" (*Poetics Today*, 6, 1985, 21–42).

tence of scholarly studies of Genesis in its various exegetical traditions, the view that the relationship of *Paradise Lost* to Genesis is basically direct or at least unproblematically mediated continues to flourish. And so, as a result, does an entire network of misogynistic or idealizing commonplaces and free-floating sexual stereotypes, relating, indifferently, to Genesis and to this institutionally privileged text by Milton, English literature's paradigmatic patriarch.

The notion of a timeless and ideologically uninflected "patriarchy" is of course vulnerable on many counts, not least of which is its capacity to neutralize the experience of oppression. I would therefore like to attempt to situate historically Milton's own appropriation of the Genesis creation accounts. In the process, I hope also to draw a preliminary sketch, in outline, of the genealogy of that seductive but odd couple, mutuality and equality. It is certainly not difficult to recognize the reading given Genesis by Trible and Bal as a product of its time. Especially in North America, the notion of an originary androgyny has had tremendous appeal to mainstream or liberal feminism. Taken to represent an ideal yet attainable equality of the sexes, androgyny is often associated metaphorically with an ideal and egalitarian form of marriage. A passionate interest in this very institution makes itself felt throughout Milton's divorce tracts, in which his interpretation of the two creation accounts first appears. Milton's exegesis, too, is the product of an ideologically overdetermined desire to unify the two different creation accounts in Genesis. Not surprisingly, at the same time it is representative of the kind of masculinist "mis"-reading that Trible and Bal seek to overturn. By emphasizing its historical specificity, however, I hope to show that it is so for reasons that cannot be universalized.

II

Milton appropriates these two texts, first in the divorce tracts and then in *Paradise Lost*, by adopting the radically uni-levelled or this-worldly Reformed method of reconciling them. For leading commentators such as Calvin and Pareus, the two accounts do not correspond to two stages in the creation of humankind, the intelligible and the sensible, as they do in an earlier, Greco-Christian tradition. Indeed there are not in their view two accounts in this sense at all but instead one story told in two different ways, once, in the first chapter of Genesis, in epitome, and then, in the second chapter, in a more elaborated form. Simplifying matters considerably, and using terms introduced into the analysis of narrative by Gérard Genette, one could say that in the view articulated especially cogently by Calvin and then elaborated, aggressively, by Milton, the *story* consists of the creation in the image of God of a single being supposed to be representative of humankind, Adam, and then the creation of Eve; the *narrative discourse* distributes this story by presenting it first in a kind of abstract and then in a more detailed or amplified narrative fashion. More specifically, the first two statements of Genesis 1:27, "So God created man in his own image, in the image of God created he him," are thought to refer to the creation of the representative Adam, told in a more leisurely and graphic fashion as a creation involving the use of the dust of the ground in the second chapter; while the concluding "male and female created he them" is taken to refer to the creation from this Adam of his meet help, Eve.

Echoing similar statements by Paraeus, Milton writes of the second chapter's narrative of Eve's creation for Adam: "This second chapter is granted to be a commentary on the first, and these verses granted to be an exposition of that former verse, 'Male and female created he them.'"[6] Yet the second chapter can have the status of a commentary in part because of the gaps, ambiguities, or troublesome suggestions to be found in the first. Commenting on the blessing of fertility in Genesis 1:28, for example, Calvin says that it is actually given to the human couple after they have been joined in "wedlocke," even though this event is not narrated until the following chapter.[7] As this indicates, for Protestant commentators, in so far as the rhetorically amplified second version is capable of interpreting and completing the account that comes before it in this way, it is the last creation account that tends to take precedence over the first.

If the Protestant exegetes Milton cites in his divorce tracts find the meaning of "male and female created he them" in the narrative of the creation of a help meet for Adam, they do so by reading that narrative ideologically, as proving that marriage, far from being what in their view the Roman Church would have it, a remedy prescribed for the spiritually weak, is divinely instituted, indeed recommended. That woman was created solely or even primarily for the purposes of procreation is the low-minded or "crabbed" (Milton's adjective) opinion the Protestant doctrine of marriage sees itself called to overturn.[8] Emphasizing, eloquently, the psychologi-

6. *Tetrachordon*, ed. Arnold Williams, in vol. II of *The Complete Prose Works of John Milton*, ed. Ernest Sirluck (New Haven, Yale University Press, 1959), 594. Subsequent references to this edition of *Tetrachordon* will appear parenthetically introduced by "*T.*" See David Paraeus, *In Genesin Mosis Commentarius* (Frankfurt, 1609), 267, 293.
7. John Calvin, *A Commentarie of John Calvine, upon the first booke of Moses called Genesis*, tr. Thomas Tymme (London, 1578), 47.
8. Margo Todd argues persuasively for the importance of relating Protestant to humanist views in "Humanists, Puritans and the spiritualized household" (*Church History*, 49, 1980, 18–34). For a discussion of the distinctively Puritan development of this ideology see William and Malleville Haller, "The Puritan art of love" (*Huntington Library Quarterly*, 5, 1942, 235–72); William Haller, "Hail Wedded Love" (*English Literary History*, 13, 1946, 79–97); see also John Halkett, *Milton and the Idea of Matrimony: A Study of the Divorce Tracts and "Paradise Lost"* (New Haven, Yale University Press, 1970), and James

cal needs sanctioned by the deity's words instituting marriage ("It is not good that the man should be alone," Genesis 2:18), the Reformers enable an emerging bourgeois culture to produce what has the appearance at least of an egalitarian view of the marital relation. The very phrase "meet for him" is said by Calvin to suggest in the Hebrew *kĕneged*, the quality of being "like or answerable unto" (*quia illi respondeat*) the man and to indicate vividly that psychological rather than physical likeness founds marriage as an institution.[9] Milton endorses this view when he takes the untranslatably expressive Hebrew "originall" to signify "*another self, a second self, a very self itself*" (*T* 600), and also when he has the divine interlocutor promise Adam, "Thy likeness, thy fit help, thy other self, / Thy wish, exactly to thy heart's desire" (*PL* VIII.450–1).

As has often been pointed out, in the divorce tracts Milton raises to unprecedented and undreamt of heights this early modern tendency to idealize the marriage bond. The extent to which he relies upon an implicit privileging of "J" over "P" (indeed, over the other texts he treats, as well) in order to do so has, however, not been commented upon. Milton's advocacy of a more liberalized interpretation of the grounds for divorce proceeds by countering the mean-spirited misinterpretations of scripture promulgated by scholastics and canonists.[1] On its more constructive front, it seeks to harmonize different and radically conflicting scriptural texts. The most taxing exegetical feat Milton has to perform is the reconciliation of Matthew 19:3–11, which suggests that remarriage after divorce is forbidden on grounds other than "fornication," and Deuteronomy 24:1–2, which Milton reads as sanctioning divorce for reasons of what we would now call incompatibility. *Tetrachordon*, the tract in

---

T. Johnson, *A Society Ordained by God: English Puritan Marriage Doctrine in the First Half of the Seventeenth Century* (Nashville, Abingdon, 1970). For a negative evaluation of the impact on women of the development of bourgeois marriage doctrine, see Linda T. Fitz, "'What says the married woman?:' marriage theory and feminism in the English Renaissance" (*Mosaic* 13, Winter) 1980, 1–22. For a wide-ranging, comparatist discussion of these socioeconomic and ideological changes as they affect the relations of the sexes, see the introduction to *Rewriting the Renaissance*, ed. Margaret W. Ferguson, Maureen Quilligan and Nancy J. Vickers (Chicago: University of Chicago Press, 1986), xv–xxxi.

9. Calvin, op. cit., 74. Latin cited from *Mosis Libri V, cum Johannis Calvini Commentariis* (Geneva, 1563), 19.

1. The political, legal and social contexts for Milton's tracts are discussed by Chilton L. Powell in *English Domestic Relations, 1487–1653* (New York, Columbia University Press, 1917), 61–100, and by Ernest Sirluck (ed.), vol. II of *Complete Prose Works*, 137–58. Milton's rhetorical strategies are examined by Keith W. Stavely, *The Politics of Milton's Prose Style* (New Haven, Yale University Press, 1975), 54–72, and by John M. Perlette, "Milton, Ascham, and the rhetoric of the divorce controversy" (*Milton Studies*, 10, 1977, 195–215). A relevant and illuminating study of the "crossing" of rhetorical, judicial and other discursive codes can be found in Pat Parker's "Shakespeare and rhetoric: 'dilation' and 'delation,'" in *Othello, Shakespeare and the Question of Theory*, ed. Patricia Parker and Geoffrey Hartman (London, Methuen, 1985), 54–74.

which Milton's skills as exegete are most on display, announces in its very title his determination to establish unity and sameness in the place of seeming difference and contradiction. Meaning "four-stringed," and thus referring to the four-toned Greek scale, *Tetrachordon* attempts to harmonize what on the title page are referred to as the "foure chief places in Scripture, which treat of Mariage, or nullities in Mariage." The first text given on the title page is "Gen. 1.27.28 compar'd and *explain'd by* Gen. 2.18.23.24" (*T* 577; my emphasis).[2]

The explaining of Genesis 1 *by* Genesis 2 is of multi-fronted strategic importance to Milton's polemical attack on existing English divorce laws, which don't properly recognize the spiritual nature of marriage. First and foremost, it permits Milton to exploit rhetorically the sexual connotations of "male and female," essential to the divorce tracts' central, most tirelessly worded argument, which is that neither sexual union in and of itself nor procreation is the primary end of marriage as originally constituted. Commenting directly on "Male and female created he them" in *Tetrachordon*, Milton states it has reference to "the right, and lawfulness of the mariage bed." When relating this text to its immediate context, he claims that sexual union is an "inferior" end to that implied by the earlier "So God created man in his own image, in the image of God created he him" (Milton's detailed exegesis of which I'll be coming back to later on) (*T* 592). As this suggests, a bi-polar and hierarchical ordering of the spiritual and physical dimensions of experience structures many of the exegetical moves in these tracts. The following commentary on "male and female" is fairly representative, and illustrates, in addition, the important role played by "J:"

> He that said *Male and female created he them*, immediately before that said also in the same verse, *In the Image of God created he him*, and redoubl'd it, that our thoughts might not be so full of dregs as to urge this poor consideration of *male and female*, without remembring the noblenes of that former repetition; lest when God sends a wise eye to examin our triviall glosses, they be found extremly to creep upon the ground: especially since they confesse that what here concerns mariage is but a brief touch, only preparative to the institution which follows more expressely in the next Chapter. . . .
>
> (*T* 592)

The divorce tracts seek to persuade the mind that doesn't want to creep upon the ground that it should be duly impressed with the fact that in Genesis 2:18 God himself speaks, revealing in no uncertain

2. For a discussion of the title, see the preface by Arnold Williams, *Tetrachordon*, 571.

terms what the end of marriage is: "And the Lord God said, It is not good that the man should be alone; I will make him an help meet for him." Expounding the true meaning of the earlier verse, "Male and female created he them," this verse declares "by the explicit words of God himselfe" that male and female is none other "than a fit help, and meet society" (T 594). Milton is willing to put this even more strongly. It's not just that we have here the words of God himself, expounding the meaning of an earlier text. God here actually explains *himself*: "For God does not heer precisely say, I make a female to this male, as he did briefly before, but expounding himselfe heer on purpos, he saith, because it is not good for man to be alone, I make him therefore a meet help" (T 595).

In Milton's exegetical practice, then, "J"'s narrative makes possible a spiritualized interpretation of the more lowly and bodily "male and female." Indeed, "J"'s narrative, understood as instituting a relationship primarily psychological, provides the very basis for the passages emphasizing mutuality to be found throughout the divorce tracts. The above citations don't begin to convey the eloquence with which Milton can celebrate the pleasures of a heterosexual union that is ideally—that is, on the spiritual plane intended by its divine institution—fitting or meet. And there are numerous other moments in these works where without rhetorical flourish mutuality is clearly asserted or implied. The woman and man of the marriage relation can, for example, be referred to as "helps meete for each other."[3] On a more practical level, and of direct relevance to the legal reforms he is proposing, is the statement Milton offers of his position when opening the first chapter of *The Doctrine and Discipline of Divorce*: "*That indisposition, unfitnes, or contrariety of mind, arising from a cause in nature unchangable, hindring and ever likely to hinder the main benefits of conjugall society, which are solace and peace, is a greater reason of divorce then naturall frigidity, especially if there be no children, and that there be mutuall consent*" (DDD 242). The explicit reference to "mutuall consent" here is matched or perhaps even deliberately introduced by the opening words of the subtitle appearing in both the first and second editions of this work: "Restor'd to the Good of Both Sexes, From the bondage of Canon Law, and other mistakes. . . ."

Yet much as the dominant discourse of the academy might like to celebrate this praiseworthy attention to mutuality, there are very few passages of any length in the divorce tracts that can be dressed up for the occasion. For over and over again, this laudable mutuality loses its balance, teetering precariously on the brink of pure abstrac-

---

3. *The Doctrine and Discipline of Divorce*, ed. Lowell W. Coolidge, vol. II of *Complete Prose Works*, 240. Further references will be introduced by "*DDD*."

tion. And the reason it does so is that it stands on the ground (to recall the play on *hā'ādāmâ*) of a lonely Adam who is not in any sense either ungendered or generic. It becomes clear, finally, that the concluding phrase of Milton's position-statement—"and that there be mutuall consent"—is not expected to stand up in a court of law. In the penultimate chapter of the second edition of *The Doctrine and Discipline of Divorce*, Milton states his view "that the absolute and final hindring of divorce cannot belong to any civil or earthly power, against the will and consent of both parties, *or of the husband alone*" (*DDD* 344; my emphasis). Even if this could, improbably, be attributed to a moment's forgetfulness on the part of an author busy revising and enlarging his original, it still wouldn't be able to pass itself off as an instance of simple self-contradiction. For as I hope to show, this particular assertion is also the self-consistent outcome of the deeply masculinist assumptions at work in Milton's articulation of a radically bourgeois view of marriage.

Time and again, the language of the tracts passes through the use of plural forms potentially inclusive of both sexes only to come to rest with a non-generically masculine "he." As the discussion up to this point has indicated, in so far as the story of Eve's creation from Adam's rib is thought to articulate the Protestant doctrine of marriage, it is not her creation *after* Adam *per se* that is so significant but her creation *for* him, to remedy his loneliness. The egalitarian sentiments expressed, sporadically, throughout the divorce tracts therefore cannot finally obscure Eve's secondary status as a "gift" from one patriarch to another. Created for Adam, Eve is, as Adam puts it in *Paradise Lost*, "Heav'n's last best gift" (V.19). Yet Eve is also, of course, created *from* Adam, as well as *for* him. And in Milton's view, as Adam's "likeness" Eve does not even have the status—to use Satan's description of "man" in *Paradise Lost*—of the Father's "latest," meaning most recent, "image" (IV.567). For by unifying the two creation stories in the way Reformed principles permit him to, Milton's exegesis makes possible the production of two ideologically charged and historically specific readings, contradictorily related: on the one hand an interpretation of "male and female" that psychologizes heterosexual union and dignifies marriage, and on the other an explication of "created man in his image" that tends to restrict the meaning of "man" to an individual Adam, from whom and for whom the female is then made.

It is important to put this exactly, for of course biblical commentators always claim that woman is also in some sense made in the image of God. Calvin, like Milton, however, locates the generic sense of "man" directly in the first and gendered man's representative status. Commenting on Genesis 2:18, "I will make him an help meet for him," Calvin responds to the question, why isn't the plural form "Let us make" used here, as it was in the creation of "man"?:

> Some think, that by this speach, the difference which is betweene both sexes is noted, and that so it is shewed, how much more excellent the man is, then the woman. But I like better of another interpretation, which differeth somewhat, though it be not altogether contrarie: namely, that when in the person of man, mankinde was created, the common worthinesse of the whole nature, was with one title generally adorned, where it is said, *Let us make man*: and that it was not needful to be repeated in the creating of the woman, which was nothing else but the addition and furniture of the man [quae nihil aliud est quam viri accessio]. It cannot be denied, but the woman also was created after the image of God, though in the seconde degree. Whereupon it followeth, that the same which was spoken in the creation of the man, perteineth to womankind.[4]

Milton's stridently masculinist, "Hee for God only, shee for God in him" in *Paradise Lost* obviously goes much further than Calvin in drawing out the masculinist implications of this hermeneutical practice, which forges an identity between the generic and the gendered "man." In *Tetrachordon*, too, Milton pursues the logic of this exegesis with a maddening and motivated precision. In his commentary on "in the image of God created he him," the intermediate statement of Genesis 1:27, he states that "the woman is not primarily and immediately the image of God, but in reference to the man," on the grounds that though the "Image of God" is common to them both, "had the Image of God been equally common to them both, it had no doubt bin said, In the image of God created he them" (*T* 589).

So it continues to matter that Adam was formed first, then Eve. As a further means of taking the measure of Milton's interest in this priority, I would now like to discuss three seventeenth-century texts more favourably disposed towards an egalitarian interpretation of Genesis. Although research in this area is still underway, it is safe to say that Milton could not but have known that questions of priority figure prominently in the Renaissance debate over "woman" we now know as the "Querelle des Femmes." In *A Mouzell for Melastomus, the cynicall bayter of, and foule mouthed barker against Evahs sex*, for example, one of the feminist responses to Joseph Swetnam's *The Araignment of lewd, idle, forward and unconstant women*, Rachel Speght appeals several times to the privilege assumed to be a property of firstness. Speght mentions that although it is true that woman was the first to sin, it is also woman

---

4. Calvin, op. cit., 72; *Mosis Libri V*, 18.

who receives the "first promise" that God makes in Paradise; she
argues that the dignity of marriage is proved by Jesus honouring a
wedding ceremony with "the first miracle that he wrought;" and
that the spiritual equality of the sexes is shown when after his Resurrection Christ "appeared unto a woman first of all other."[5]

In the restricted intellectual economy of the "Querelle," orthodox
views of male superiority are frequently countered by paradoxical
assertions of female superiority. Lastness is therefore placed in the
service of overturning firstness, as in Joan Sharpe's poetic defense of
women against Swetnam's *Araignment*, where it is claimed: "Women
were the last worke, and therefore the best, / For what was the end,
excelleth the rest."[6] Speght, however, deliberately avoids the use of
this kind of paradox. Like other Renaissance and Reformed commentators, preachers and courtesy-book writers, Speght places a
strong emphasis on marriage as involving the "mutuall participation
of each others burden." And this emphasis is sustained rhetorically
throughout the tract. For example, while accepting the conventional
view that woman is "the weaker vessel," Speght supplies a subtly
polemical reference to man as "the stronger vessel."[7] In deploying a
linguistic stress on balance and mutuality to neutralize hierarchical
oppositions, this young, early seventeenth-century Protestant may
very well be the most important unsung foremother of modern liberal feminist commentators on Genesis and on *Paradise Lost*.

Speght does not offer any programmatic statements on the relation of "P" to "J," nor does she attempt systematically to assimilate
one to the other. But like all feminist participants in the "Querelle
des Femmes," she assumes that Genesis 1:26 and 27 provide a clear
statement of the spiritual equality of the sexes. The passage in which
she briefly explicates Genesis 1:27 is distinctive, however, in its pro-
visional but decidedly revisionary reconciliation of the two creation
accounts: "in the Image of God were they both created; yea and to be
brief, all the parts of their bodies, both externall and internall, were

5. Rachel Speght, *A Mouzell for Melastomus, the cynicall bayter of, and foule mouthed
   barker against Evahs sex* (London, 1617), 6, 14, 16. Joseph Swetnam, *The Araignment of
   lewd, idle, forward, and unconstant women* (London, 1615). For further discussion of
   this controversy, see Coryl Crandall, *Swetnam the Woman-Hater: The Controversy and
   the Play* (Lafayette, Purdue University Studies, 1969), and Linda Woodbridge, *Women
   and the English Renaissance: Literature and the Nature of Womankind, 1540–1620*
   (Chicago, University of Illinois Press, 1984). The "Querelle des Femmes" has recently
   been studied by Joan Kelley, *Women, History and Theory* (Chicago, University of Chicago Press, 1984), 65–109. See also Ian Maclean, *The Renaissance Notion of Woman*
   (Cambridge, Cambridge University Press, 1980), as well as the discussion of "feminist
   polemic" in *First Feminists: British Women Writers, 1578–1799*, ed. Moira Ferguson
   (Bloomington, Indiana University Press, 1985), 27–32.
6. Joan Sharpe, chapter VIII of *Ester Hath Hang'd Haman: A Defense of Women, Against
   The Author of the Arraignment of Women* by Ester Sowernam, reprinted in *First Feminists*, 81.
7. Speght, op. cit., 4, 5.

correspondent and meete each for other."[8] By referring to both woman and man, and in relation to one another, the terms "correspondent and meete" ("correspondent" being, as modern commentators point out, a good translation of the Hebrew *kĕneged*) deftly unite the "male and female created he them" of the "P" account with the account in "J" of Eve's creation for Adam, which here, momentarily, loses its narrative identity. Speght's brief exegesis carefully preserves an emphasis on bodily fitness, while pointedly ignoring questions of chronology that might threaten the egalitarian statement.

At one point Speght refers to marriage as "a merri-age, and this worlds Paradise, where there is mutuall love."[9] The same celebratory word-play ("the very name whereof should portend unto thee merry-age") appears in a work published just two years before Swetnam's provocative tract, Alexander Niccholes' *A Discourse, of Marriage and Wiving*. Interesting for, among other things, its citation of lines from the Player Queen's speech in *Hamlet*, Niccholes' *Discourse* eulogizes the special pleasures of marital friendship in one of the very phrases used in *Tetrachordon*: the wife is "such a friend, which is to us a second selfe."[1] Niccholes' brief commentary on the two creation accounts differs significantly from Milton's, however. Appearing in the first chapter, "Of the First Institution and Author of Marriage," Niccholes' exegetical remarks follow the citation of Genesis 2:18 ("It is not good for the man to bee alone"):

> so the creation of the woman was to be a helper to the man, not a hinderer, a companion for his comfort, not a vexation to his sorrow, for *consortium est solatium*, Company is comfortable though never so small, and Adam tooke no little joy in this his single companion, being thereby freed from that solitude and silence which his lonenesse would else have bene subject unto, had there beene no other end nor use in her more, then this her bare presence and society alone: But besides all this, the earth is large and must be peopled, and therefore they are now the Crowne of his Workemanship, the last and best and perfectest peece of his handiworke divided into Genders, as the rest of His creatures are, Male and Female, fit and enabled *Procreare sibi similem* to bring forth their like, to accomplish his will, who thus blessed their fruitfulnesse in the Bud: Increase and multiply, and replenish the earth.[2]

In this passage, as in the divorce tracts, the two different creation accounts, presented in their "real" order of occurrence, are discussed

8. ibid., 11.
9. ibid., 14.
1. Alexander Niccholes, *A Discourse, of Marriage and Wiving: and of the greatest Mystery therein Contained: How to Choose a good Wife from a bad* . . . (London, 1615), 5.
2. ibid., 2.

as if each revealed a different end or benefit of the first institution.
And "J"'s narrative of the creation of a meet help for Adam, given a
strictly psychological and social interpretation, is given priority over
"P"'s. But Niccholes significantly omits any discussion of the creation of "man" in God's image. This absence permits the plural
"they" easily to take over, so that it is the (now happily united) first
man and woman alike who are "the last and best and perfectest
peece of his handiworke." Although Niccholes mentions that woman
was made both "for" and "out of" man, he maintains his emphasis on
mutuality by erasing any explicit or evaluative commentary on her
having been made *after* man, as well.

The commentary I would like to examine next is one produced
during the same period as the divorce tracts, that is, at the very time
when egalitarian issues of all kinds were being hotly contested, and
when women in the sectaries not only laid claim to their spiritual
equality with men on the basis of Genesis 1:27 and other texts, but
publicly proclaimed the extra-textual significance of this equality by
preaching and prophesying.[3] Unlike Speght's and Niccholes', the text
I turn to now belongs, officially, to the commentary genre. Issued in
association with the Westminster Assembly and published in 1645,
the annotations on Genesis in *Annotations Upon All the Books of the
Old and New Testaments* have not, to my knowledge, ever been studied.[4] Yet they shed an extraordinarily clear, not to say glaringly bright,
light on the distinctive and motivated features of Milton's exegesis.

An annotation on 1:26 takes up directly the question of the
meaning of the signifier "man" or "Adam." With reference to the
phrase "let them" (in "And let them have dominion over the fish of
the sea," etc.), the annotation states: "The word *man*, or the
Hebrew, *Adam*, taken not personally or individually for one single
person, but collectively in this verse, comprehendeth both male and
female of mankind: and so it may well be said, not *let him*, but *let
them* have dominion." Here the generic sense of *hā'ādām* is made
completely to override the gender-specific sense. To this end, the
use of the plural pronoun in the latter section of Genesis 1:26 is
privileged over the singular pronoun, used with reference to the
image ("in the image of God created he him"). This annotation

3. See the influential discussion by Keith Thomas, "Women and the Civil War sects" (*Past
and Present*, 13, 1958, 42–62). Phyllis Mack examines some female prophets and the
ways in which their activities were "limited by traditional beliefs about woman's passiv-
ity, her low social position, and her basic irrationality," in "Women as prophets during
the English Civil War" (*Feminist Studies*, 8, 1, 1982, 25). For a discussion of more
overtly political interventions, see Patricia Higgins, "The reactions of women, with
special reference to women petitioners," in *Politics, Religion and the English Civil War*,
ed. Brian Stuart Manning (London, Edward Arnold, 1973), 177–222.
4. *Annotations Upon All the Books of the Old and New Testaments . . . By the Joynt-Labour
of Certain Divines . . .* (London, 1645). For its insistence on the generic sense of Genesis "Man," the *Annotations* would seem to be indebted to the text ordered by the Synod
of Dort and published in 1637, later translated as *The Dutch Annotations Upon the
Whole Bible . . .* , tr. Theodore Haak (London, 1657).

alone therefore reveals a process of interpretation diametrically opposed to that at work in *Tetrachordon*, where, as we have seen, Milton seizes upon the difference between singular and plural forms in Genesis 1:26 and 27 to argue that only the gender-specific Adam is made immediately in the image of God.

What makes comparison of the *Annotations* with *Tetrachordon* possible and of crucial importance is that both accept the Reformed view of the relationship between the two creation accounts. Adam and Eve are said to be formed on the same, that is, the sixth, day, but their creations are presented first in chapter 1, where "their creation in the generall was noted with other creatures," and then again in chapter 2, where "in regard of the excellencie of mankind above them all, God is pleased to make a more particular relation of the manner of their making, first of the man, vers. 7. and here [vers. 22] of the woman." Yet as these words suggest, the *story* assumed by the *Annotations* is slightly different from Milton's, which starts unabashedly with a "man" taken personally or individually. The difference is fine, but extremely significant. Like Milton and other Protestant commentators, the *Annotations* rejects the view that male and female were created simultaneously, together with the view that both sexes were originally embodied, hermaphrodite-like, in a single being. "J"'s narrative ordering is respected, which means that woman was indeed created after man. But this is how the gloss on verse 27's "male and female" puts it:

> Not at once, or in one person, but severally; that is, though he united them in participation of his image, he distinguished them into two sexes, male and female, for the increase of their kinde: their conformitie in participation of Gods Image is clearly manifest by many particulars, for in most of the respects fore-mentioned, Annotation in ver. 26, the image of God is equally communicated to them both, and Eve was so like to Adam (except the difference of sexe which is no part of the divine image) in the particulars fore-mentioned, that in them, as she was made after the image of Adam, she was also made after the image of God: as if one measure be made according to the standard, an hundred made according to that, agree with the standard as well as it.

By associating differences between the sexes solely with reproduction, this comment seems to hearken back to a Platonically inflected division between the spiritual and the physical. The concluding analogy, however, shows this truly remarkable text grappling with hierarchically ordered notions of secondariness. Working with reference to the production of things in the form of commodities, the analogy attempts to take on the difficulties resulting from the view that man and woman were made "severally." And it tries to effect, on its own,

an egalitarian synthesis of "P" and "J." That man was first made in
the image of God is implicitly conceded. But that woman was made
"after" man becomes a statement referring not so much to an order
of temporality as to an order of materiality. Woman is made "after"
the image of Adam in the sense of being made "according to the standard" of the image of Adam. The analogy argues, by ellipsis, that
since Adam was himself really created "after" the image of God,
which is the original "standard," being created "after" Adam's image,
Eve is equally created "after" the image of God. Thanks to this highly
ingenious and polemically motivated analogy, Eve's being created
"after" Adam loses its usual sense of secondariness.

Read in the context of other learned Protestant biblical commentaries, this analogy has a jarring effect since, in exceeding by
ninety-nine the requirements of logic, it seems to testify to the contemporary phenomenon of the growth of mercantile capital. For
the sake of an egalitarian synthesis between "P" and "J," this work-
manly analogy tries to undermine not only a hierarchically inflected
logic of temporality but also the generally Platonic logic whereby
original is privileged over copy. It is true that man is still, quite literally, the "measure." And to give the analogy its force, woman is
placed in the position of being not the first commodity made "after"
this measure but rather the "hundred" that can be produced on its
basis. The logic deployed by the analogy from production insists,
however, that it is not really possible to measure any residual differences between the image of God, man, and woman. Of the great
variety of attempts made in the Renaissance and seventeenth century to come to Eve's defense, this must be the least chivalrous in
content, the most lacking in conventional grace or charm. But it
definitely does the job. And it certainly establishes, dramatically,
the possibilities open to Milton, which he rejected.

In rejecting a position like that of the *Annotations*, Milton implicitly takes what would seem, from another perspective, though, to
be a "progressive" stance, namely that the difference between
woman and man is not a simple matter of biology; that it is not a
difference of sex *per se*. In both *Tetrachordon* and *Colasterion* Milton rejects the view that Adam would have been given a male not a
female partner had companionship been the end of marriage. The
following passage from *Tetrachordon*, which comments on the all-
important "*It is not good for man to be alone*," suggests why Milton
would not want to imagine Eve's being created according to the
same "standard" as Adam:

> And heer *alone* is meant alone without woman, otherwise
> *Adam* had the company of God himself, and Angels to convers
> with; all creatures to delight him seriously, or to make him

sport. God could have created him out of the same mould a
thousand friends and brother *Adams* to have bin his consorts,
yet for all this till *Eve* was giv'n him, God reckn'd him to be
alone.

(T 595)

By specifying a desire that only "woman" can satisfy, and by associating that desire with a transcendence of sexual difference as vulgarly
understood, the divorce tracts seem almost to open up a space for the
category of "gender." Yet that this space is in no sense neutral can be
seen in the language with which friendship between men gets differentiated from the marital relation. In *Colasterion* Milton opposes
"one society of grave freindship" to "another amiable and attractive
society of conjugal love."[5] Elsewhere Milton can associate the marriage relationship with the need man has for "sometime slackning
the cords of intense thought and labour" (*T* 596); or he can refer to
the seeking of "solace in that free and lightsome conversation which
God & man intends in mariage" (*DDD* 273). It should go without
saying that man can have this need for companionship remedied,
can intend to enjoy "lightsome conversation" as opposed to "grave
freindship," only if woman is constituted as less grave, more attractive, more lightsome and more amiable than her male counterpart;
and if both she and marriage itself are associated with a world apart.

III

As has already been suggested, the priority bestowed upon Adam in
Milton's divorce tracts is not associated directly with the order of
creation. It tends, instead, to be inscribed in the divine words instituting marriage, "It is not good that the man should be alone; I will
make him an help meet for him" (Gen. 2:18). These words, which
Milton frequently refers to simply as "the institution," are in turn
often taken to gesture towards a prior loneliness or "rational burning" experienced by the first man, Adam. I have already argued that
the priority Milton gives "J" over "P" is inscribed indelibly in every
one of his major rhetorical and logical moves. In concluding this
discussion of the divorce tracts, I would like to show how consistently or systematically this priority is associated with the deity's
instituting words and thus, by implication, with Adam's needs.

It has not yet been mentioned that Matthew 5:31, 32 and Matthew 19:3–11, which together constitute one of the four texts
treated in *Tetrachordon*, and which appear unequivocally to forbid
divorce except for fornication, are susceptible to Milton's polemical

---

5. *Colasterion*, ed. Lowell W. Coolidge, vol. 2 of *Complete Prose Works of John Milton*,
739–40.

appropriation of them precisely because in chapter 19 Jesus is represented as quoting from Genesis. The relevant verses, cited by
Milton, are the following, verses 3–6:

> The Pharisees also came unto [Jesus], tempting him, and say-
> ing unto him, Is it lawful for a man to put away his wife for
> every cause? And he answered and said unto them, Have ye
> not read, that he which made them at the beginning made
> them male and female, And said, For this cause shall a man
> leave father and mother, and shall cleave to his wife: and they
> twain shall be one flesh? Wherefore they are no more twain,
> but one flesh. What therefore God hath joined together, let not
> man put asunder.

The two texts cited here are the now-familiar "male and female created he them" in Genesis 1:27 and "Therefore shall a man leave his
father and his mother, and shall cleave unto his wife: and they shall
be one flesh" (Gen. 2:24). Milton's strategy in commenting on the
verses from Matthew is to subvert their literal and accepted meaning by referring the citations back to the divine words of institution,
which, he points out, are *not*, significantly, quoted. Although the
tempting Pharisees, his immediate interlocutors, aren't worthy of
receiving this instruction, Jesus's intention, Milton argues, is to
refer us back to the uncited words of institution in chapter 2,
"which all Divines confesse is a commentary to what [Jesus] cites
out of the first, the *making of them Male and Female*" (*T* 649). The
instituting words are thus made to govern the manner in which
those cited by Jesus from chapter 1 are to be interpreted.

Also cited is Genesis 2:24, which Milton regards as spoken by
Adam. Yet Milton's exegesis has already determined that Adam's
speech too has meaning only with reference to the words of divine
institution. In the first part of Adam's speech ("This is now bone of
my bones, and flesh of my flesh: she shall be called Woman, because
she was taken out of Man," Gen. 2:23), Milton finds Adam referring
to and expounding his maker's instituting words, regarded as constituting a promise now fulfilled (*T* 602). By establishing a dialogic
relation between Adam's words and those of his maker, Milton can
argue that anyone who thinks Adam is in these words formulating
the doctrine of the indissolubility of marriage "in the meer flesh" is
not only sadly mistaken but guilty of using "the mouth of our generall parent, the first time it opens, to an arrogant opposition, and
correcting of Gods wiser ordinance" (*T* 603). It is the next part of
Adam's speech, however, verse 24, which is commonly thought to
be "the great knot tier," as Milton correctly points out: "Therefore
shall a man leave his father and his mother, and shall cleave unto
his wife: and they shall be one flesh." In Milton's view, *by* opening

with "therefore," this verse clearly indicates that Adam confines the implications of his utterance only to "what God spake concerning the inward essence of Mariage in his institution" (*T* 603). With reference to both parts of Adam's speech, Milton's position thus is that the deity's words are the "soul" of Adam's and must be taken into Adam's utterance if it is properly to be understood.

This is not, interestingly, the reading given these verses by Calvin, who assigns verse 23 to Adam, but draws attention to the interpretative choices open with regard to 2:24, for which three different speakers are eligible: Adam, God, and Moses. After a brief discussion Calvin opts for Moses, suggesting that, having reported what had historically been done, Moses in this passage sets forth the end of God's ordinance, which is the permanence or virtual indissolvability of the marriage bond.[6] For reasons that are obvious, Milton would want to reject this reading. By making Adam the speaker of this passage, Milton weakens its authority as a text enjoining the indissolubility of marriage. Since this is the very text cited by Jesus in Matthew, such an assault on its status as injunction is a decisive defensive move. But it is also more than that. For by assuming Adam to be its speaker, Milton also strengthens the contractual view of the first institution his exegetical practice implicitly but unmistakably develops.

That Milton's understanding of the first institution is implicitly both contractual and masculinist can perhaps be seen if his exegetical practice is compared with that of Rachel Speght. Towards the beginning of *A Mouzell for Melastomus*, Speght argues that Eve's goodness is proved by the manner of her creation:

> Thus the resplendent love of God toward man appeared, in taking care to provide him an helper before hee saw his owne want, and in providing him such an helper as should bee meete for him. Soveraignety had hee over all creatures, and they were all serviceable unto him; but yet afore woman was formed, there was not a meete helpe found for *Adam*. Mans worthinesse not meriting this great favour at Gods hands, but his mercie onely moving him thereunto: . . . that for mans sake, that hee might not be an unit, when all other creatures were for procreation duall, hee created woman to bee a solace unto him, to participate of his sorrowes, partake of his pleasures, and as a good yokefellow beare part of his burthen. Of the excellencies of this Structure, I meane of Women, whose foundation and original of creation, was Gods love, do I intend to dilate.[7]

6. Calvin, op. cit., 77–8.
7. Speght, op. cit., 2, 3.

Were Milton to have read Speght's tract, I suspect that midway through the first sentence here he would have discovered himself a resisting reader. The notion that God acted on Adam's behalf "before hee saw his own want" would have seemed highly provocative, if not downright offensive. Speght draws strategically on orthodox Protestantism's doctrinal emphasis on divine grace as radically transcendent, as an active principle utterly unconnected with human deserts. In the process, Adam becomes a passive recipient of a gift, meetness abounding, while Eve is subtly positioned in relation with her true "original," divine love.

By contrast, in the divorce tracts and, as we shall see, in *Paradise Lost* as well, Milton foregrounds an Adam whose innocent or legitimate desires preexist the creation of the object that will satisfy them. But this is to put it too abstractly. In Milton's exegesis, the significance of the gift—woman—passed from maker to man is determined by two speeches, first the maker's and then Adam's, precisely because these speeches are construed as a verbal exchange that is basically contractual. In Genesis 2:18 Adam's maker promises him that he will assuage his loneliness and provide him with a meet help; in 2:23 and 24, Adam accepts this gift by acknowledging it is exactly what was promised him, and then promises to honour it on these very grounds. Eve's status as a divinely bestowed gift is exploited polemically by both Speght and Milton. But unlike Speght's transcendent lord of love, Milton's veiled but systematic insistence on the contractual form of the first institution is produced by a Protestantism pressed into the service of an historically specific form of individualism, an individualism paradigmatically masculine, autonomous, articulate, and preternaturally awake to the implications of entering into relations with others.[8]

IV

One of the questions concerning *Paradise Lost* that this discussion of the divorce tracts has, I hope, made it possible to address is: why does Milton's Eve tell the story of her earliest experiences first, in Book IV? Why, if Adam was formed first, then Eve, does Adam tell *his* story to Raphael *last*, in Book VIII? An adequate response to

8. Catherine Belsey examines the development and representation of liberal-humanist "Man" in *The Subject of Tragedy: Identity and Difference in Renaissance Drama* (London, Methuen, 1985). Francis Barker suggestively locates in the seventeenth century the emergence of a distinctively bourgeois subjectivity; see *The Tremulous Private Body: Essays in Subjection* (London, Methuen, 1984). Jean Bethke Elshtain critiques the rise of liberal ideology in *Public Man, Private Woman* (Princeton, Princeton University Press, 1981), 100–46. For a discussion of the divorce tracts that sees them expressing an alienated bourgeois individualism, see David Aers and Bob Hodge in their very important "'Rational burning:' Milton on sex and marriage" (*Milton Studies*, 12, 1979, 3–33).

this question would require a full-scale analysis of the ways in which *Paradise Lost* articulates a putative sequential order of events or story with the narrative discourse that distributes this story. As a genre, epic is of course expected to develop complicated relations between a presumed chronological and a narrative ordering of events. But *Paradise Lost* would seem to use both retrospective and prospective narratives in a more systematic and motivated manner than does any of its predecessors, in part because it is so highly conscious of the problematical process of its consumption. I would like to argue here that *Paradise Lost's* narrative distribution of Adam and Eve's first experiences is not just complexly but ideologically motivated, and that the import of this motivation can best be grasped by an analysis aware of the historically specific features of Milton's exegetical practice in the divorce tracts.

This practice is crucially important to *Paradise Lost's* own use of the Genesis creation texts. In the case of the passage it most obviously informs, Raphael's account of the creation of "man" on the sixth day of creation in Book VII, certain features are intelligible only in the light of this historically specific context. If commenting on this passage at all, critics have tended to suggest that Raphael gives something like a heavenly, as compared with Adam's later more earthly, account of creation.[9] This doesn't, however, even begin to do justice to the intricately plotted relations of the "P" and "J" accounts in the following:

> Let us make now Man in our image, Man
> In our similitude, and let them rule
> Over the Fish and Fowl of Sea and Air,
> Beast of the Field, and over all the Earth,
> And every creeping thing that creeps the ground.
> This said, he form'd thee, *Adam*, thee O Man
> Dust of the ground, and in thy nostrils breath'd
> The breath of Life; in his own Image hee
> Created thee, in the Image of God
> Express, and thou becam'st a living Soul.
> Male he created thee, but thy consort
> Female for Race; then bless'd Mankind, and said,
> Be fruitful, multiply, and fill the Earth,
> Subdue it, and throughout Dominion hold
> Over Fish of the Sea, and Fowl of the Air,
> And every living thing that moves on the Earth.
> Wherever thus created, for no place
> Is yet distinct by name, thence, as thou know'st

9. J. M. Evans, *"Paradise Lost" and the Genesis Tradition* (London, Oxford University Press, 1968), 256.

> He brought thee into this delicious Grove,
> This Garden, planted with the Trees of God,
> Delectable both to behold and taste;
> And freely all thir pleasant fruit for food
> Gave thee, all sorts are here that all th' Earth yields,
> Variety without end; but of the Tree
> Which tasted works knowledge of Good and Evil,
> Thou may'st not; in the day thou eat'st, thou di'st;
> Death is the penalty impos'd, beware,
> And govern well thy appetite, lest sin
> Surprise thee, and her black attendant Death.
> Here finish'd hee.
>
> (VII.519–48)

Genesis 1:26–8 is here given in what is virtually its entirety. But the principal acts of Genesis 2:7–17 are also related: Yahweh's making of "Man" from the dust of the ground (2:7), his taking of this man into the garden of Eden (2:15), and his giving of the prohibition (2:16, 17). One could argue that even Milton's "artistry" here hasn't received its proper due, since this splicing economically makes from two heterogeneous accounts a single one that is both intellectually and aesthetically coherent.

Yet it does more, far more, than this. For Raphael's account removes any trace of ambiguity—the residual generic dust, as it were—from the Priestly account of the creation of *hā'ādām* or "man" in the image of God. This it does by a set of speech-acts unambiguously identifying this "man" with Raphael's interlocutor, Adam. The direct address in "he form'd thee, *Adam*, thee O Man / Dust of the ground" has what amounts to a deictic function, joining the representative "Man" to Raphael's gendered and embodied listener, who is specifically and repeatedly addressed here, while Eve (though still an auditor) very pointedly is not. It is clearly significant that these very lines effect the joining of the Priestly and Yahwistic accounts. By placing "thee O Man / Dust of the ground" in apposition to the named "Adam," it is suggested that this individualized "Adam" actually *is hā'ādām* or representative man and the punning *hā'ādāmâ* "ground," an identity that only the joining of the two accounts reveals.

The impression this joining creates is that the two accounts have always already been one in narrating the creation of Adam. The same cannot be said of Raphael's account of the creation of Eve, however. For in contrast (I would like to say something like "in striking contrast," yet it has not really been noticed) to the ingenious joining that takes place for the sake of Adam, Raphael refers to Eve's creation only in the statement immediately following, which is again, significantly, addressed to Adam: "Male he created thee, but thy consort / Female for Race" (529–30).[1] Outside of this meagre "but thy consort / Female for Race," Raphael's account does not otherwise even allude to the creation of Eve, although, as we have seen, other details of the narrative in the second chapter are included in it. Indeed, if we examine the matter more closely, it appears that the Yahwist account is made use of only up to and including Genesis 2:17 (the giving of the prohibition) precisely because Genesis 2:18 inaugurates the story of the creation of a help meet for Adam.

But of course the story of Eve's creation is not excised from *Paradise Lost* altogether, which is, presumably, why readers have not protested its absence here. It is told later, by another narrator, Adam. One of the effects of this narrative distribution is that in Milton's epic Adam's story comes to have exactly the same relation to Raphael's as in the divorce tracts and in Protestant commentaries the second chapter of Genesis has to the first: it is an exposition or commentary upon it, revealing its true import.[2] Yet the second telling can have this status only because it is Adam's. As my discussion indicates, Milton's argument in the divorce tracts rests on a radical privileging of "J" over "P" in the specific form of a privileging of the words of divine institution in Genesis 2:18. Had Milton interpolated the story of Eve's creation into Raphael's creation account, he would have had to record these words in the form of

---

1. If commented upon at all, the emphasis on procreation here is naturalized so that it becomes an expression of Raphael's character or situation. Aers annotates these lines by suggesting that Raphael is revealing a typically "distorted view of sexuality," *John Milton, "Paradise Lost:" Book VII–VIII*, ed. David Aers and Mary Ann Radzinowicz, *Cambridge Milton for Schools and Colleges*, ed. J. B. Broadbent (Cambridge, Cambridge University Press, 1974), 99. Halkett (op. cit., iii) points out that Raphael later (VIII.229–46) reveals that he was not present the day of Eve's creation. But since both are supposed to take place on the same "Day," Raphael's absence obviously cannot explain the different treatment given Adam's creation and Eve's in his account. I would argue that such character- and situation-related effects are part and parcel of the ideologically motivated narrative distributions examined here.

2. In emphasizing the lines of continuity between the divorce tracts and *Paradise Lost*, I am questioning the position developed by Aers and Hodge, who see *Paradise Lost* gesturing towards "a more adequate view of sexuality and the relationship between women and men" (op. cit., 4). Like other readers, Aers and Hodge stress the importance of the following speech, suggesting that in it "Adam makes the equation Milton did not make in his prose works, the crucial equation between mutuality, equality, and delight" (23):

> Among unequals what society
> Can sort, what harmony or true delight?
> Which must be mutual, in proportion due
> Giv'n and receiv'd.   (VIII. 383–6)

In my view, however, this produces a mystifying view of "equality," since what Adam is here rejecting is the society of creatures belonging to a different species; Eve is "equal" only in the restricted sense of being a member of the human species. Although I do not here explore the various tensions and contradictions of Milton's views on gender relations in *Paradise Lost*, I make an attempt to do so in "Fallen differences, phallogocentric discourses: losing *Paradise Lost* to history," in *Post-Structuralism and the Question of History*, ed. Derek Attridge, Geoff Bennington, and Robert Young (Cambridge, Cambridge University Press, 1987).

indirect speech (as he does the words of prohibition in lines 542–7) or else to have reproduced both the creator's speech and Adam's. In either case, the instituting words would have been displaced from their centres of authority. By transferring the entire narrative to Adam and by interpolating a dramatic colloquy into this narrative, *Paradise Lost* ensures the coincidence of narrator and auditor of the instituting words, of narrator and of the first man's instituting response. By dramatizing this commentary, this necessary supplement to Raphael's account, in the form of a colloquy narrated by Adam, *Paradise Lost* makes sure that the doctrine of marriage is both produced and understood by the person for whom it is ordained, just as in the divorce tracts it is the privileged male voice, Milton's, which expounds the true doctrine of divorce.

As the divorce tracts never tire of insisting, the true doctrine of marriage relates only to the satisfaction of that which the wanting soul needfully seeks. In *Paradise Lost* this doctrine is co-authored by Adam and the "Presence Divine," who work it out together. It is also communicated, formally, by the extraordinary emphasis placed on Adam's subjectivity, on his actual experience of desire. As Milton has masterminded the exchange, the divine instituting words come *after* Adam has been got to express his longing for a fitting companion (VIII.444–51), so that this longing has the kind of priority that befits the first man. Yet the longing is also clearly a rational burning. With its strong filiations to the disputation, the very form of the colloquy establishes that this desire is rational, and that merely reproductive ends are certainly not what Adam has in mind. Although procreation is referred to, it is presented as a kind of necessary consequence of the conjunction of male and female, but for that very reason as a subordinate end. Adam's language cleverly associates it with a prior lack, a prior and psychological defect inherent in his being the first and only man (VIII.415–25). The way Milton's Adam responds to the deity's formal presentation to him of his bride, Eve, is just as motivated. The Genesis 2:23–4 speech is cited, but only after it has been introduced in a way that joins it explicitly to the causes implicit in the deity's instituting words:

> This turn hath made amends; thou hast fulfill'd
> Thy words, Creator bounteous and benign,
> Giver of all things fair, but fairest this
> Of all thy gifts, nor enviest. I now see
> Bone of my Bone, Flesh of my Flesh, my Self
> Before me; Woman is her Name, of Man
> Extracted; for this cause he shall forgo
> Father and Mother, and to his Wife adhere;
> And they shall be one Flesh, one Heart, one Soul.
> (VIII.491–9)

This speech is presented as a species of spontaneous lyrical utterance ("I overjoy'd could not forbear aloud" (490)) and according to Adam is "heard" by Eve. Yet it is obviously addressed *not* to her but to her maker, who is thanked for the gift itself, but not until he has been praised for having kept his word. Before letting Adam commit himself to the project of becoming one flesh with Eve, Milton has to make it clear that Adam does so believing that the "Heav'nly Maker" has done what he has promised, that is, created a truly fit help.

Not only the placement of Adam's narrative after Raphael's but also its most salient formal features can thus be seen to be motivated ideologically, and to illustrate the causes joining the divorce tracts and *Paradise Lost*. Before turning to Eve, I would like to summarize the discussion so far by emphasizing that these causes are joined, and to man's advantage, both when "P" and "J" are united and when they aren't. By joining "P" and "J" as it does, Raphael's account specifies the gendered Adam of *Paradise Lost* as the "man" who is made in the divine image. By disjoining them, Raphael's account lets Adam himself tell the story of the creature made to satisfy his desire for an other self.

We can now, more directly, take up the question, why does heaven's last best gift tell her story first? One way of approach might be to suggest that had Eve's narrative of her earliest experiences appeared where "naturally," in the order of creation, it should have, that is *after* Adam's, *Paradise Lost* might have risked allowing her to appear as the necessary and hence in a certain sense superior creature suggested by what Jacques Derrida has called the logic of the supplement, undeniably set in motion by Adam's self-confessed "single imperfection." *Paradise Lost's* narrative discourse would seem to want to subvert this logic by presenting Eve's narrative first. And it seems to want to subvert it further by placing immediately *after* Adam's narrative a confession in which Eve's completeness and superiority is made to seem an illusion to which Adam is, unaccountably, susceptible. In this part of Adam's dialogue with Raphael, the language of supplementarity as artificial exteriority seems curiously insistent: Eve has been given "Too much of Ornament" (VIII.538); she is "Made so adorn for thy delight the more" (VIII.576) and so on.

Yet a displaced form of the logic of supplementarity may nevertheless be at work in the place of priority given Eve's narrative. For if Eve is created to satisfy the psychological needs of a lonely Adam, then it is necessary that *Paradise Lost's* readers experience her from the first as expressing an intimately subjective sense of self. From the start she must be associated in a distinctive manner with the very interiority that Adam's need for an other self articulates. Or to put this another way, Eve's subjectivity must be made available to the reader so that it can ground, as it were, the lonely Adam's articulated desire for another self. Appearing as it does in Book IV, Eve's narrative lacks any immediately discernible connection with the Genesis creation accounts on which the narratives of both Raphael and Adam draw. Its distance from Scripture as publicly acknowledged authority is matched by Eve the narrator's use of markedly lyrical, as opposed to disputational, forms. Set in juxtaposition to the rather barrenly disputational speech of Adam's which immediately precedes it in Book IV, Eve's narrative creates a space that is strongly if only implicitly gendered, a space that is dilatory, erotic, and significantly, almost quintessentially, "private."

In a recent essay, Christine Froula reads Eve's first speech thematically and semi-allegorically, as telling the story of Eve's (or woman's) submission of her own personal experience and autonomy to the voices (the deity's, then Adam's) of patriarchal authority. As the very title of her essay—"When Eve Reads Milton"—indicates, Froula wants to find in Milton's Eve if not a proto-feminist then a potential ally in contemporary academic feminism's struggle to interrogate the academic canon together with the cultural and political authority it represents. Milton's Eve can play the part of such an ally, however, only because for Froula the privacy of Eve's earliest experiences and the autonomy she thereby initially seems to possess are equivalent to a potentially empowering freedom from patriarchal rule.[3] Given the liberal assumptions of the feminism it espouses, Froula's argument obviously does not want to submit the category of personal experience to ideological analysis.

In attempting to give it such an analysis, I would like to suggest that Eve's speech plays a pivotal role, historically and culturally, in the construction of the kind of female subjectivity required by a new economy's progressive sentimentalization of the private sphere.[4] It is possible to suggest this in part because the subjective experiences Eve relates are represented as having taken place before any knowledge of or commitment to Adam. That is, they are represented as taking place in a sphere that has the defining features of the "private" in an emerging capitalist economy: a sphere

---

3. Christine Froula, "When Eve reads Milton: undoing the canonical economy" (*Critical Inquiry*, 10, 1983, 321–47). That Derrida's *Supplement* can productively expose motivated contradictions in the not unrelated field of Renaissance rhetorical theory is demonstrated by Derek Attridge in "Puttenham's perplexity: nature, art and the supplément in Renaissance poetic theory," in *Literary Theory/Renaissance Texts*, ed. Patricia Parker and David Quint (Baltimore, Johns Hopkins University Press, 1986), 257–79.

4. For a sharp analysis of the ways in which, among the upper classes, the development of an affective domestic sphere served to reinforce masculinist modes of thought, see Susan Moller Okin, "Women and the making of the sentimental family" (*Philosophy and Public Affairs*, 11, 1981, 65–88).

that appears to be autonomous and self-sustaining even though not "productive" and in so appearing is the very home of the subject. In Book VIII Adam recalls having virtually thought his creator into existence and having come up with the idea of Eve in a dialogue with his fellow patriarch. By contrast, Eve recalls inhabiting a space she believed to be uninhabited, autonomous, hers—but for the "Shape within the wat'ry gleam." It is, however, precisely because this belief is evidently *false* that it is possible to see this space as analogous to the "private" sphere, which is of course constituted by and interconnected with the "public" world outside it. Illusory as this autonomy is, inhabiting a world appearing to be her own would nevertheless seem to be the condition of the subjectivity Eve here reveals.

It has long been a commonplace of commentaries on *Paradise Lost* that a network of contrasts is articulated between Eve's narration of her earliest experiences and Adam's, the contrasts all illustrating the hierarchically ordered nature of their differences. Yet it has not been recognized clearly enough that while shadowing forth these bi-polar oppositions, Eve's narrative is supposed to rationalize the mutuality or intersubjective basis of their love. For by means of the Narcissus myth, *Paradise Lost* is able to represent her experiencing a desire equivalent or complementary to the lonely Adam's desire for an "other self." It is not hard to see that Adam's own desire for an other self has a strong "narcissistic" component. Yet Adam's retrospective narrative shows this narcissism being sparked, sanctioned and then satisfied by his creator. By contrast, though in Book IV Eve recalls experiencing a desire for an other self, this desire is clearly and unambiguously constituted by illusion, both in the sense of specular illusion and in the sense of error. Neo-Platonic readings of the Narcissus myth find in it a reflection of the "fall" of spirit into matter. Milton transforms this tragic tale into one with a comic resolution by instructing Eve in the superiority of spirit or, more exactly, in the superiority of "manly grace and wisdom" over her "beauty." But because this happily ending little *Bildungsroman* also involves a movement from illusion to reality, Eve is made to come to prefer not only "manly grace and wisdom" as attributes of Adam but also, and much more importantly, Adam as embodiment of the reality principle itself: he whose image she really is, as opposed to the specular image in which her desire originated.

To become available for the mutuality the doctrine of wedded love requires, Eve's desire therefore must in effect lose its identity, while yet somehow offering itself up for correction and reorientation. As has often been noted, Eve's fate diverges from that of Narcissus at the moment when the divine voice intervenes to call her away from her delightful play with her reflection in the "waters." We

have seen that in Book VIII Adam's desire for an other self is sanctioned by the divine presence's rendering of "It is not good that the
man should be alone; I will make him an help meet for him." When
the divine voice speaks to Eve, it is to ask that she redirect the
desire she too experiences for an other self:

> What thou seest,
> What there thou seest fair Creature is thyself,
> With thee it came and goes: but follow me,
> And I will bring thee where no shadow stays
> Thy coming, and thy soft imbraces, hee
> Whose image thou art, him thou shalt enjoy
> Inseparably thine.
>
> (IV.467–73)

Unlike the instituting words spoken to Adam in Book VIII, these
have no basis in the Yahwist creation account. Yet they are clearly
invented to accompany the only part of that account which Milton
has to work with here, the brief "and brought her unto the man"
(Gen. 2:22), which in Genesis immediately precedes Adam's words
of recognition. Marked inescapably by literary invention and
uttered by a presence that is invisible to Eve, the voice's words have
a curiously secondary or derivative status, at least compared with
those spoken to Adam. They seem indeed, fittingly, to be a kind of
echo of the divine voice.

In so far as it effects a separation of Eve from her physical image,
this word in a way echoes what Milton calls the creator's originary
"divorcing command" by which "the world first rose out of Chaos"
(*DDD* 273). But the separation of Eve from her image is not the
only divorce effected here. Before this intervention the "Smooth
Lake" into which Eve peers seems to her "another Sky," as if the
waters on the face of the earth and the heavens were for her indis-
tinguishable or continuous. The divine voice could therefore much
more precisely be said to recapitulate or echo the paternal Word's
original division of the waters from the waters in Genesis 1:6–7.
Before describing her watery mirror and her other self, Eve mentions "a murmuring sound / Of waters issu'd from a Cave"—murmurs, waters and cave all being associated symbolically with
maternality, as critics have pointed out. When the paternal Word
intervenes, Eve's specular auto-eroticism seems to become, paradoxically, even more her own, in part because it no longer simply
reflects that of Ovid's Narcissus. And when Eve responds to the
verbal intervention by rejecting not only his advice but also Adam,
"hee / Whose image" she is, preferring the "smooth wat'ry image,"
an analogical relationship gets established between female auto-
eroticism and the mother–daughter dyad. But—and the difference

is of crucial importance—this implicit and mere analogy is based on specular reflection and error alone. Grounded in illusion, Eve's desire for an other self is therefore throughout appropriated by a patriarchal order, with the result that in *Paradise Lost's* recasting of Ovid's tale of Narcissus, Eve's illusion is not only permitted but destined to pass away. In its very choice of subject, Milton's epic seems to testify to the progressive privatization and sentimentalization of the domestic sphere. That this privatization and sentimentalization make possible the construction of a novel female subjectivity is nowhere clearer than in Eve's first speech, in which the divine voice echoes the words originally dividing the waters from the waters, words which in their derived context separate Eve from the self which is only falsely, illusorily either mother or other.

This takes us to the very last feature of Eve's story-telling to be considered here. As has been suggested, Protestant exegetes consider Adam's declaration in Genesis 2:24, "This is now bone of my bones, and flesh of my flesh," to be part of the first wedding ceremony. A version of this ceremonial utterance appears in Adam's narrative and (highly abridged) in Eve's. In Genesis, this declaration follows "and brought her unto the man," a verse which is translated into action in both of *Paradise Lost's* accounts. Calvin, when commenting on this phrase, views the action from Adam's point of view, as involving the exchange of a gift: "For seeing Adam tooke not a wife to him selfe at his owne will: but tooke her whome the Lord offered and appointed unto him: hereof the holinesse of matrimonie doeth the better appeare, because we know that God is the author thereof."[5] Yet Milton is not alone in seeing this moment from Eve's point of view as well as from Adam's, for Diodati, commenting on "And brought her unto him," says: "As a mediator, to cause her voluntarily to espouse her self to Adam and to confirm and sanctify that conjunction."[6] In *Paradise Lost*, the story Eve tells stresses with remarkable persistence both the difficulty and the importance of Eve's "voluntarily" espousing herself to Adam. Many years ago Cleanth Brooks mentioned that Eve's speech in Book IV seemed to anticipate Freud's observations on the comparative difficulty the female has in the transition to adult heterosexuality.[7] But if it does so, it is in a context that constitutes female desire so as to situate the process of transition within competing representational media, within what is almost a kind of hall of voices and mirrors.

---

5. Calvin, op. cit., 76–7.
6. Annotation on Genesis 2:22 in John Diodati, *Pious and Learned Annotations upon the Holy Bible*, tr. (R.G.), 3rd edn (London, 1651).
7. Cleanth Brooks, "Eve's awakening," in *Essays in Honor of Walter Clyde Curry* (Nashville, Vanderbilt University Press, 1954), 283–5. Brooks says that to the student of Freud, Eve's psychology may seem "preternaturally" convincing; he also remarks that Eve is "charmingly feminine withal"!

This entire discussion of the relation between *Paradise Lost*'s ret-rospective creation narratives and the divorce tracts can therefore be put in the following, summary terms. If in Book VIII's recollected colloquy Adam is revealed articulating the doctrine of marriage, in Book IV's recollected self-mirroring Eve is portrayed enacting its discipline. Or to formulate this somewhat differently, by associating Eve with the vicissitudes of courtship and marriage, and by empha-sizing her voluntary submission both to the paternal voice and to her "author" and bridegroom, Adam, *Paradise Lost* can *first* present the practice for which Adam *then*, at the epic's leisure, supplies the theory. In doing so, *Paradise Lost* manages to establish a paradigm for the heroines of the genre Milton's epic is said to usher in. In the Yahwist's creation account, Adam may have been formed first, then Eve. But Milton's Eve tells her story first because the domestic sphere with which her subjectivity associates itself will soon be in need of novels whose heroines are represented learning, in struggles whose conclusions are almost always implicit in the way they begin, the value of submitting desire to the paternal law.

Of course the female authors and readers associated with the rise of the novel are not always willing to submit to this discipline. And in what is perhaps the most strongly argued critique of the institution of marriage to be written by a feminist before this cen-tury, "Milton" is prominently associated with the very ideological contradictions that get exposed. In *Reflections upon Marriage*, Mary Astell submits the notion of "subjection" to an analysis that is devastatingly sharp and in certain ways deconstructive, since she wants to undo the notion that subjection is synonymous with "nat-ural" inferiority. Arguing, even if with heavy irony, by means of the very rationalist and individualist principles that came to prevail during the Civil War period, Astell urges women who are consider-ing marriage to become fully conscious of the liberties they will have to surrender if they are to enter into this state of institutional-ized domestic subjection. Her wry reference to Milton is fairly well-known: "For whatever may be said against Passive-Obedience in another case, I suppose there's no Man but likes it very well in this; how much soever Arbitrary Power may be dislik'd on a Throne, not *Milton* himself wou'd cry up Liberty to poor *Female Slaves*, or plead for the Lawfulness of Resisting a Private Tyranny."[8]

8. Mary Astell, *Reflections upon Marriage, The Third Edition, To Which is Added A Pref-ace, in Answer to some Objections* (London, 1706), 27. Ruth Perry examines this work's political discourse in her recent biography, *The Celebrated Mary Astell: An Early English Feminist* (Chicago, University of Chicago Press, 1986), 157–70. See also Joan K. Kinnaird, "Mary Astell and the conservative contribution to English feminism" (*Journal of British Studies*, 19, 1979, 53–75); and see the discussion by Hilda Smith, *Reason's Disciples: Seventeenth-Century English Feminists* (Chicago, University of Illi-nois Press, 1982), 131–9.

As I have suggested, the appearance, at least, of Active-Obedience is far more important to *Paradise Lost* and to Milton's rationalism than this remark would suggest. Might an awareness of this be registered in Astell's reflections on Genesis in the supplementary "Preface"? Like other feminists writing from within the Christian tradition, Astell finds 1 Timothy 2:11–14, with its unambiguous assertion of the Genesis Adam's priority over Eve, exceedingly troublesome: she offers a rather laboured allegorical interpretation, and then adds the caveat that if the "Learned" don't accept it, it will be because "Learning is what Men have engros'd to themselves."[9] Though less defensive, her remarks on Genesis itself are no less acerbic. After mentioning, approvingly though tentatively, the opinion that "in the Original State of things the Woman was the Superior," Astell proceeds to this brilliantly savage rebuttal of the notion of woman's "inferior" secondariness:

> However this be, 'tis certainly no Arrogance in a Woman to conclude, that she was made for the Service of GOD, and that this is her End. Because GOD made all things for Himself, and a Rational Mind is too noble a Being to be Made for the Sake and Service of any Creature. The Service she at any time becomes oblig'd to pay to a Man, is only a Business by the Bye. Just as it may be any Man's Business and Duty to keep Hogs; he was not made for this, but if he hire himself out to such an Employment, he ought conscientiously to perform it.[1]

Like other feminist commentators, from participants in the "Querelle des Femmes" to Phyllis Trible and Mieke Bal, Astell here implicitly privileges "P" over "J." In overturning the view that woman was created "for" man, Astell, however, applies to the domestic sphere the historically determinate notion of contractual relations that Milton helps to articulate in his divorce tracts, political treatises and in *Paradise Lost*. With dazzling, Circe-like powers, Astell's analogy works to disabuse bourgeois "Man" of his delusions of grandeur. But in exploiting, however archly, a contractual notion of "Service," it also illustrates some of the hazards involved in the project—ongoing—of trying to call a spade a spade.

9. Astell, op. cit., Preface, a2, a3.
1. ibid., A2.

574

STANLEY FISH

Driving from the Letter: Truth and Indeterminacy in Milton's *Areopagitica*†

I

It has been some time since John Illo pointed out that Milton's *Areopagitica* has almost always been read as a classic liberal plea for "complete liberty." "The preponderance of English scholarship," Illo writes, "has drawn Milton into its own liberal centre, which claims a Western and ultimately an Attic heritage of universal freedom."[1] This is especially true in the twentieth century when the *Areopagitica* (through an irony its author would have understood but not appreciated) becomes a basic text supporting the ethic of disinterested inquiry, and Milton the revolutionary becomes a man with the ability "to look at social issues without using the glasses of sectarian theology, which . . . is very rare in this passionate time."[2] The commentator here is Harold Laski who writes with a host of others in a volume commemorating the three hundredth anniversary of *Areopagitica* and titled, significantly, *Freedom of Expression*. In this volume, Milton is not only the apostle of unrestrained freedom (precisely the *accusation* levelled at him by his contemporaries), he is also and "above all, a Humanist—the greatest representative in England of that movement which had abandoned the dogmatism of the middle ages and was seeking for a natural or empirical basis for its beliefs" (125). The same encomiast declares of the *Areopagitica*, "there is no encroachment on 'the liberty to know, to utter and to argue freely' which it does not . . . oppose" (122), apparently forgetting the encroachments it itself urges. Only the Dean of St Paul's, W. R. Matthews, is apparently aware of the fact that "Milton's conception of the nature of tolerable books was limited." "It appears," he says gently, "that many who have not recently read his book have an exaggerated notion of what he urges as reasonable liberty" (78).

That many, as Illo reminds us, would seem to include almost the whole body of Milton scholars. There have of course been exceptions: Illo himself, writing from the left, and Willmore Kendall,

† From *Re-Membering Milton: Essays on the Texts and Traditions*, ed. Mary Nyquist and Margaret W. Ferguson (New York and London: Methuen, 1987) pp. 234–47. Reprinted by permission.

1. John Illo, "The misreading of Milton," in *Radical Perspectives in the Arts*, ed. Lee Baxandall (Harmondsworth and Baltimore, 1972), 190, 189.
2. *Freedom of Expression: A Symposium Based on the Conference Called . . . To Commemorate the Tercentenary of the Publication of Milton's Areopagitica*, ed. Hermon Ould (1944; rpt Port Washington, 1970), 169.

writing from the right, have argued for a Milton less generous in his ecumenism, a Milton who is not above acts of exclusion and sharp judgment.[3] And Ernest Sirluck has given us a pragmatically political Milton who in the *Areopagitica* argues in several directions at once, hoping thereby to please the several constituencies whose support would be necessary for the revoking of the Act of 1643.[4] But by and large, in the writings and minds of most men and women, the *Areopagitica* remains what it was for those who celebrated it in 1944.

In what follows I would like to continue in the direction indicated by the work of Illo and Kendall and advance a series of theses even more radical (at least in terms of received opinion) than theirs. Specifically, I will argue that Milton is finally, and in a profound way, not against licensing, and that he has almost no interest at all in the "freedom of the press" as an abstract or absolute good (and, indeed, does not unambiguously value freedom at all); and that his attitude towards books is informed by none of the reverence that presumably led the builders of the New York Public Library to have this sentence from the tract preside over their catalogue room: "A goode Booke is the pretious life blood of a master spirit, imbalm'd and treasur'd up on purpose to a life beyond life."

Let us begin with that sentence and with the famous paragraph from which it comes:

> I deny not, but that it is of greatest concernment in the Church and Commonwealth, to have a vigilant eye how Bookes demeane themselves, as well as men; and thereafter to confine, imprison, and do sharpest justice on them as malefactors: For Books are not absolutely dead things, but doe contain a potencie of life in them to be as active as that soule was whose progeny they are . . . ; who kills a Man kills a reasonable creature, Gods Image; but hee who destroyes a good Booke, kills reason it selfe, kills the Image of God, as it were in the eye. Many a man lives a burden to the Earth; but a good Booke is the pretious life-blood of a master spirit, imbalm'd and treasur'd up on purpose to a life beyond life. 'Tis true, no age can restore a life, whereof perhaps there is no great losse; and revolutions of ages doe not oft recover the losse of a rejected truth, for the want of which whole Nations fare the worse. We should be wary therefore what persecution we raise against the living labours of public men, how we spill that season'd life of man preserv'd and stor'd up in Books; since we see a kinde of homicide may be thus committed, sometimes a martyrdome, and if

3. Willmore Kendall, "How to read Milton's *Areopagitica*" (*Journal of Politics*, 22, 1960, 439–73).
4. Ernest Sirluck, "Introduction" to *Complete Prose Works of John Milton*, vol. II (New Haven, 1959).

it extend to the whole impression, a kinde of massacre, whereof the execution ends not in the slaying of an elementall life, but strikes at that ethereall and fift essence, the breath of reason it selfe, slaies an immortality rather than a life.[5]

The first thing to say about this passage is that, detached from the literary idealism it apparently breathes, it is decidedly *un*Miltonic; first because it locates value and truth in a physical object, and second because the reverence it apparently recommends toward that object is dangerously close to, if not absolutely identical with, worship. The passage seems, in a word, to encourage idolatry, and that of course is exactly the purpose to which it has been often put when it has been cited as a central "scripture" in the "religion" of the book (the religion, that is, of humanism). This, however, is not Milton's religion. The center of *his* theology is the doctrine of the inner light and his entire career can be viewed as an exercise in vigilance in which he repeatedly detects in this or that political or social or ecclesiastical program one more attempt to substitute for the authority of the inner light the false authority of some external and imposed rule. It is in this spirit (a word precisely intended) that Milton makes a series of related arguments in the *Apology* (written only a year and a half earlier than the *Areopagitica*): he rejects set prayers in favor of "those free and unimpos'd expressions which from a sincere heart unbidden come into the outward gesture;" he rejects the rules of rhetoric and composition in favor of the "true eloquence" that inheres naturally in the speech of one who is "possest with a fervent desire to know good things, and with the dearest charity to infuse the knowledge of them into others;" he rejects any criticism of his own style that would measure it by some external decorum, and claims as a justification for his bitter, vituperative and even obscene words the spirit of zeal that moves him ("there may be a sanctified bitternesse against the enemies of truth") and he insists (in the most famous passage in the tract) that a true poem can only be written (and by implication read) by one who is himself "a composition and pattern of the best and honourablest things; not presuming to sing high praise of heroic men . . . unless he have in himselfe the experience and practice of all that is praiseworthy."[6] In this and every other sentence in the *Apology* Milton is continually alert to the danger of reifying some external form into the repository of truth and value.

5. John Milton, *The Tract for Liberty of Publication*, in *The Prose of John Milton*, ed. J. Max Patrick *et al.* (Garden City, 1967), 271–2. All references hereafter are to this text.
6. *Complete Prose Works of John Milton*, vol. I, ed. Don M. Wolfe (New Haven, 1953), 941, 949, 890.

In the first edition of the *Doctrine and Discipline of Divorce* (published in 1643) the form of the danger is no less than the Bible itself. Milton's scorn in this tract is directed at those who believe that the essence of the law is to be found in its letter, in the actual words of the text; these he calls "extreme literalists" and "letter bound men:" they display an "obstinate literality" and an "alphabetical servility:" and have made the text into "a transcendent command" that is "above the worship of God and the good of man."[7] This refusal to equate wisdom and truth with what is written in a book, even if the book is the Bible, will later lead him in the *Christian Doctrine* to reject the authority of the ten commandments because he follows the Pauline rule that "whatever is not in accordance with faith, is sin" which is something quite different, he points out, from holding that "whatever is not in accordance with the ten commandments, is sin."[8] And later still, this fierce anti-literalism turns into an even fiercer anti-literaryism as the Christ of *Paradise Regained* declares (in a passage that has given Milton's admirers fits) that the reading of books is "wearisome" (*PR* IV.322).

If we return from this brief excursion into Milton's other writings (and additional examples could have easily been adduced) to the *Areopagitica*, the paragraph that offers so extravagant a praise of books looks very curious indeed. It seems strange to hear Milton asserting that the spirit of a man can be abstracted from the conditions of its daily exercise and that the truth which finds an expression in varied and "unbidden" outward gestures can be so perfectly captured in one of those gestures that it can be "preserved" (in amber, as it were) between the covers of a book. And it is stranger still to find Milton displaying what he himself would describe as a papist idolatry of relics when he exalts the dead letter of a physical object ("imbalm'd" and "preserv'd" indeed) above the living labors of faithful men, and dismisses as "no great losse" the truth that perishes with a life, reserving for the loss of an "impression" or edition the vocabulary of homicide and massacre. It is almost as if he were writing an early draft of the sonnet on the Waldensians and had decided to begin that poem not with "Avenge O Lord thy slaughtered saints," but with "Avenge O Lord thy slaughtered books."

I do not, however, want to rest my case for the falseness of this passage on what Milton had previously written or on what he was later to write. My best evidence comes from those places in the *Areopagitica* itself where Milton gives voice to sentiments that undermine (if they do not flatly contradict) any argument for the

---

7. *The Doctrine and Discipline of Divorce*, in *The Prose of John Milton*, ed. Patrick, 183, 184, 164, 162.
8. *Complete Prose Works of John Milton*, vol. VI, ed. Maurice Kelley (New Haven, 1973), 639.

sanctity of books. Consider, for example, a sentence, some thirteen pages forward in the tract, that begins, "Banish all objects of lust." The phrase "objects of lust" is ambiguous between two readings; it can mean "banish all lustful objects," that is all objects that have, as a special property, the capacity to provoke lust; or it can mean banish all objects to which an already existing lust can attach itself. The attraction of the first reading is that it specifies a course of action that can be followed—let's get rid of these lust-provoking objects—while in the second reading the recommended course of action is self-defeating because it would require the banishing of everything. As it turns out, however, the second reading is the correct one:

> Banish all objects of lust, shut up all youth into the severest discipline that can be exercis'd in any heritage, ye cannot make them chaste that came not hither so.

> (297)

That is to say, chastity is not a property of objects, but of persons; and one can neither protect it nor promote it by removing objects from the world. Indeed, even if one went to the impossible lengths of removing all objects, the flourishing of lust and other sins would continue unabated, for, "though ye take from a covetous man all his treasure, he has yet one jewel left, ye cannot bereave him of his covetousnesse:" and with that "covetousnesse" as the driving force of his very being, such a man will populate the world—even if it is only the inner world of his imagination—with the objects of his desire, with the objects of lust.

It is easy to see how this line of reasoning fits into the case against licensing: in so far as licensing is urged as a means of combating sin, it is, as Milton says, "far insufficient to the end which it intends" (297), because sin does not reside in the objects licensing would remove. But, curiously, if this is a strong argument against licensing (and it is so strong that Milton makes it at least six times) it is equally strong as an argument against the alternative to licensing, the free and unconstrained publishing of books; for it follows that if men and not books are the source of sin, then men and not books are the source of virtue; and if sin will not be diminished by removing its external occasion, then virtue will not be protected by preserving its external representation. In short, the argument against licensing, which has always been read as an argument *for* books, is really an argument that renders books beside the point; books are no more going to save you than they are going to corrupt you; by denying their potency in one direction, Milton necessarily denies their potency in the other and undercuts the extravagant claims he himself makes in the passage with which we began. Whatever books are, they cannot be what he says they are in those ringing sentences, the preservers of truth, the life-blood of a master spirit, the image of God.

II

Why then does he say it? It will be the business of this essay to answer that question and we can begin by noting that at least on the local level he says it *in order* to move away from it. As the prose reaches the rapturous height of calling books an "ethereall and fift essence" and "the breath of reason it selfe," Milton suddenly checks its flight: "But lest I should be condemn'd of introducing licence, while I oppose licencing." This rhetorical flourish looks forward to the historical digression of the succeeding paragraphs, but for a moment it also refers backward to the license Milton has himself committed in transforming books, which are, after all, *only* objects, into the means and vehicle of grace. The moment passes quickly, almost before it has registered, but it is enough, I think, to cast the shadow of a qualification on what has just been said, a qualification we carry with us as we move into the brief history of "what hath been done by ancient and famous Commonwealths, against this disorder" (272).

By "this disorder," Milton means license, the supposed harm that follows from allowing books to be "as freely admitted into the world as any other birth" (281). It is this liberal practice, Milton tells us, that characterized the societies he is about to survey; and one would expect the point of the ensuing history to be that in these "ancient and famous commonwealths" the absence of licensing would have as one of its effects the flourishing of virtue; but it is an expectation that is disappointed by a history that never achieves so sharp a focus. Milton begins with what one would think would be his strongest example, the city of Athens "where Books and wits were ever busier than in any other part of Greece" (273); but rather than celebrating the benefits of this "busyness" he turns immediately to the measures taken by the Athenians to curtail it, and finds "only two sorts of writings which the magistrate car'd to take notice of; those either blazphemous . . . or Libellous." The tonal instability of this section is established immediately by "car'd to take notice of" which hesitates between an expression of approval for the magistrate's restraint and the suggestion that if he had been properly vigilant, he would have taken notice of *more*. When the survey turns from Greece to Rome the double argument continues as Milton simultaneously reports on the restraint exercised by magistrates who decline to license and describes the fruits of that restraint (or, more precisely, absence of restraint) in terms that call into question its wisdom. Is it, after all, a good or a bad thing, that the "naked plainness" of Lucullus and Catullus and the "wanton" poems of Ovid are allowed to do their work unchecked? This question is never asked in so many words, but Milton's judgmental vocabulary is continually implying it; and, moreover, there is nothing to counter the question on the other side, no instancing of books whose publication is causally related to a virtuous result. The only books Milton ever mentions are those that were allowed to appear despite the fact that they were impious or impudent or scurrilous or loose; it is this fact (established ever so casually but with a cumulative force) that dominates the history, a history which therefore makes the rather narrow and negative point that in a number of societies—some good, some bad, some cultured, some brutish— the absence of pre-publication licensing doesn't seem to have made very much difference at all.

Significantly, the lack of a difference goes in both directions; not only is it the case that what Milton will later call "promiscuous reading" did no particular harm; neither, at least on the evidence offered here, did it do any particular good. It seems in fact a "thing indifferent" not correlated in any observable way with the moral status of a commonwealth; and if licensing is thus indifferently related to the production or protection of virtue, so also are books, and the entire history becomes discontinuous with the encomium that introduces it.

It is only after the history has been concluded that Milton takes up the question it might have been expected to answer: "what is to be thought in generall of reading Books, . . . and whether be more the benefit, or the harm that thence proceeds?" (283). Earlier, when it seemed that what was or was not *in* books was going to be the issue, this would have been just the right question. Now, however, in the wake of the inconclusive account of Greek and Roman practice, the question sounds oddly, as if it were posed by someone who hadn't yet realized that the agenda it assumes—the agenda of separating the bad from the good in books—has more or less been abandoned. In these early pages the *Areopagitica* displays a curious inability to settle down and to pursue unambiguously the line of argument that was so strongly promised when books were the object of an apparently unqualified praise.

But then, almost before we know it, the tract takes a decisive turn and apparently stabilizes (at least for the moment) when Milton invokes a vision reported by Eusebius as he was debating with himself whether or not it was lawful to "venture . . . among" the "defiling volumes" of "hereticks." Milton identifies this second vision as one "sent from God" who speaks to Eusebius in these words: "Read any books whatever come to thy hands, for thou art sufficient both to judge aright, and to examine each matter" (285). "This revelation," as

Milton terms it, decides the issue by dissolving it, by transferring the question of value from books, of whatever kind, to Eusebius, who is "sufficient" in the strong sense of *self*-sufficient, capable by virtue (literally) of what is already in him of turning all that he reads into good. Lest we miss the point, Milton drives it home by supplementing the Eusebius citation from Thessalonians ("prove all things, hold fast to that which is good") with "another remarkable saying of the same Author: To the pure all things are pure," which is then immediately and powerfully glossed: "not only meats and drinks, but all kinde of knowledge whether of good or evil; the knowledge cannot defile, nor consequently the books, if the will and conscience be not defil'd." Indeed, books are even more "things indifferent" than meats, for while "bad meats will scarce breed good nourishment in the healthiest concoction," bad books "to a . . . judicious reader serve . . . to discover, to confute, to forwarn, and to illustrate." Of course, by the end of this sentence, there are no bad books, in the sense of books that can in and of themselves do harm; for all books, once they enter into the heart of the judicious reader, become the occasion and means by which that judiciousness is exercised and extended; but by the same reasoning, neither are there any good books, in the sense of books that can in and of themselves produce wisdom; for as Milton says within a few pages, if "a wise man like a good refiner can gather gold out of the drossiest volume . . . a fool will be a fool with the best book, yea without book" (291–2). The logic of this is inescapable and certainly supports the conclusion that licensing will bring no benefits; but it also supports a corollary conclusion that whatever we make available to a wise man will not be essential to his wisdom, for he will be wise with any book, "yea without book."

At this point the argument of the *Areopagitica* seems simply to have reversed itself. Where at first the question to be answered was whether the power in books will work for good or evil (a question directly related to the case for and against pre-publication licensing), by the time Milton declares that all things are pure to the pure the issue is no longer what is or is not in books, but what is or is not in persons; and consequently it has become a matter of indifference as to whether or not books are licensed, since, at least by the arguments that have so far been marshalled, the flourishing of *either* good or evil does not depend on books. From here there is a straight line to the sentence that begins "banish all objects of lust" (a recommendation that only makes sense if books are the source either of lust or of virtue) and ends by asserting that "ye cannot make them chaste that came not hither so."

But if the new point of the *Areopagitica* is that men and not books are the repository of purity, then it is a point that barely survives its own introduction; for within a page of saying that all things are pure to the pure, Milton also says that "we bring not innocence into the world, we bring impurity much rather" (288), and by saying that he immediately problematizes what had for a moment seemed to be a resolution (or a dissolution) of the dilemma initially posed, to license or not to license; after all it isn't much help to observe that purity is a condition of the heart if all of our hearts enter the world in a condition of impurity. This impurity is one of the reasons why licensing must be numbered among the "vain and impossible attempts" (291), but it is also a reason for something close to despair, since it leaves mysterious the process by which purity or even its near approximation can be achieved. If purity can be found neither in books, where it first seemed to reside, nor in naturally pure hearts, where the argument next seemed to place it, then it cannot be found anywhere.

That in fact turns out to be the right conclusion, but with a difference that redeems its negativity; for in the very same sentence that proclaims our congenital impurity Milton introduces us to its remedy: "Assuredly we bring not innocence into the world, we bring impurity much rather: that which purifies us is triall and triall is by what is contrary." If virtue is not to be found anywhere—either in a book or in an object, or even in a heart—it is because it must be *made*, and it can only be made by sharpening it against the many whetstones provided by the world, by "what is contrary." Not only does this give a positive direction to an argument that has for a while emphasized only what can*not* be done and what will *not* succeed; it also reanimates the question of licensing and makes it once again weighty; for if the emergence of virtue depends on the availability of materials against which it can be exercised, then it follows that the more materials the better, and that is why, after the tract has unfolded almost half its length, Milton can finally offer a coherent and non-contradictory argument against licensing; anyone who thinks that he can "remove sin by removing the matter of sin" is mistaken because sin is not a feature of the outer, but of the inner landscape and can only be removed (if that is the word) when that landscape is transformed; and since that transformation can only be accomplished by a continual exercise of the faculty of judgment, it is crucial that the judgment be supplied with occasions for its exercise; although it is offered as a way of promoting virtue, licensing will operate to eliminate the conditions of its growth by removing the materials on which growth can feed: "look how much . . . we thus expell of sin, so much we expell of virtue; for the matter of them is both the same" (297). Once again, then, books are declared to be absolutely essential to the maintenance of truth and virtue, not, however, because truth and virtue reside in books (as they were said to so many paragraphs ago), but because it is by (the indifferent) means of books that men and women can make themselves into the simulacrums of what no book could ever contain.

But this may seem a long way around the barn. If Milton had wanted to tell us (as he now tells us) that books are "necessary to the constituting of human vertue" (288)—as opposed to being the very essence of virtue—why didn't he just come right out and say so in the first place? The question is its own answer once one realizes that it amounts to asking why didn't he simply hand over the truth he wished us to have? To have done so, or, rather, to claim to have done so, would have been to claim for the *Areopagitica* the very capacity it denies to all other books, the capacity of being the repository of what no book can contain because it can only be written in the fleshly tables of the heart. In short, if the *Areopagitica* is to be faithful to the lesson it teaches, it cannot teach that lesson directly; rather it must offer itself as the occasion for the trial and exercise that are necessary to the constituting of human virtue; it must become an instrument in what Milton will later call "knowledge in the making" (321).

The tract performs this self-effacing office in two related ways. First it continually comments on its own inability to capture the truth that informs it. In the very first paragraph Milton reports that he is in the grip of a "power" within him that simply will not respect the decorums of the formal oration; and as a result he finds himself speaking with a "passion" (266) one does not usually find in a preface. A few pages later he makes a valiant attempt to monitor and control his discourse by "laying before" his readers the order of his arguments, but soon after he has concluded his inconclusive history he finds himself in danger of departing from that order and he catches himself up: "But I have first to finish, as was propounded" (283). He then gets himself back on track and is apparently proceeding according to plan, when suddenly he finds that he is already in the midst of making a point that was to have come later, finds, as he puts it, that the truth has prevented or anticipated him "by being clear already while thus much hath been explaining" (292). "See," he exclaims, "the ingenuity of Truth, who when she gets a free and willing hand, opens herself faster than the pace of method and discourse can overtake her" (292).

The image here is one that will loom larger and larger: it is of a truth that is always running ahead of any attempt to apprehend it, a truth that repeatedly slips away from one's grasp, spills out of one's formulations, and escapes the nets that for a moment promise to catch it. Here that net is the tract itself which is at this moment disqualifying itself as a vehicle of the truth it wants to convey; but at the same time and by the very same process, it is playing its part in the fashioning of another vehicle, the heart of the reader, who is the direct beneficiary of the *Areopagitica*'s failure, or, to be more precise, of Milton's strategy. That strategy is one we have been tracking from the beginning of this essay, and it involves encouraging the reader to a premature act of concluding or understanding which is then undone or upset by the introduction of a new and complicating perspective. As we have seen, this happens not once, but repeatedly. The result is, of course, disorienting, but it is also (or so Milton's claim would be) salutary, for in the process of being disoriented the reader is provoked to just the kind of labor and exercise that is necessary to the constitution of his or her own virtue. In this way, the tract becomes at once an emblem and a casualty of the lesson it teaches, the lesson that truth is not the property of any external form, even of a form that proclaims this very truth.

III

It is a strategy supremely pedagogical, and one that Milton both describes and names within the year in *Tetrachordon*, as he turns his attention to the manner of Christ's teaching. Milton is particularly struck by Christ's habit of breaking the external, written law in order to fulfill the law of charity; and he compares Christ's actions with the gnomic form of his precepts, and finds that both have the advantage of preventing his followers from too easily identifying the way of virtue with a portable and mechanical rule. "Therefore it is," says Milton "that the most evangelick precepts are given us in proverbiall formes, to drive us from the letter, though we love ever to be sticking there."[9]

   In the *Areopagitica* we are continually being driven from the letter, first from the quite literal letter of books, then from the letter as represented by the history of Athens and Rome, and then from the letter of a comforting, but finally too comforting, scripture ("to the pure all things are pure"). Of course all of these letters, along with others that could be instanced, are provided by the *Areopagitica* itself, which also provides the arguments that make them momentarily attractive; so that one of the letters the tract is driving us from is itself, as we are not allowed the comfort and false security of sticking to and with any of the formulations it presents in what is finally a self-cancelling sequence. By saying you won't find it there—in books, in history, in verses of scripture—the *Areopagitica* is also saying you won't find it here—in the pages of this tract—and finally saying that you won't find it, because you can only become it, which is what the tract in its small and self-sacrificing way is helping you to do.

9. *Complete Prose Works*, II.637.

It is a help the need for which is self-replenishing. That is, driving from the letter is a strategy that can have no end; for each time it succeeds it generates the conditions that once again make it necessary: the very act of demonstrating that truth and virtue do not reside "here" will always have the side-effect of suggesting that they will instead be found "there;" and at that moment "there" becomes a new letter from which we must then be driven. The only *positive* lesson that the *Areopagitica* teaches (a lesson it also exemplifies), is the lesson that we can never stop, and it receives a particularly powerful (although of course not definitive) formulation when Milton declares that

> he who thinks we are to pitch our tents here and have attain'd the utmost prospect of reformation that the mortall glass wherein we contemplate, can shew us, till we come to *beatific* vision, that man, by this very opinion, declares that he is yet farre short of truth
>
> (316)

By "here" Milton means both the present state of human knowledge and understanding and this particular moment in his own tract. Whatever place or object or condition holds out the possibility of rest and attainment has at that moment become a letter, the occasion for idolatry. Those who think of the Reformation as a finite program or agenda, as a series of steps at the end of which the job will have been done and the goal accomplished, make exactly the same mistake that is made by the proponents of licensing. The would-be licensers think that the moral life will be perfected when the landscape has been cleared of all objects of lust; the reformers think that the moral life will be perfected when, in accordance with the precepts of Zwingli and Calvin, we have divested ourselves of some of the trappings of popery. Licensing and the premature closure of a weak reformation are alike forms of a single temptation, the temptation to substitute for the innumerable and inconclusive acts that go to make up the process by which the self is refined and purified some *external* form of purification that can be mechanically applied. As I have argued elsewhere it is a temptation felt by every one of Milton's heroes (even the young Jesus of *Paradise Regained*)[1] and it is a temptation that Milton makes the readers of *Areopagitica* feel again and again as he beckons us forward in the name of a truth that always escapes his formulations and our straining apprehensions.

This pattern of seeking and *not* finding is most spectacularly displayed in those passages in which the nature of truth is the overt

---

1. See S. Fish, "The temptation to action in Milton's poetry" (*ELH*, 48, 3, Fall 1981, 516–31); and "Things and actions indifferent: the temptation of plot in *Paradise Regained*" (*Milton Studies*, 17, 1983, 163–85).

subject. As we first come upon it the assertion that a "man may be
a heretic in the truth" (310) seems available to a comfortable reading in which an independent truth can be held by a man in one of
two ways, either with personal conviction or simply on the strength
of what someone else—a pastor, a pope—had told him. Only the
first kind of holding is authentic, and as for the other, "the very
truth he holds becomes his heresie." But if the logic of this distinction is pursued the very notion of a truth that one can hold either
rightly or wrongly is problematized; for on the one hand, a truth
that has not been internalized is no longer the truth, and is merely
an empty letter; while on the other, a truth sincerely held cannot be
given a literal form such that it can be said that someone else is not
really holding "it." There is no "it" that is detachable from the holding or being held, and therefore no real sense can be given to the
phrase "a heretic in the truth." In so far as it seems for a moment to
have a sense it is itself one more letter—one more invitation to premature closure—from which we must be driven.

We are driven from it again in a sequence that begins with a
famous question: "Who ever knew truth put to the wors in a free
and open encounter?" (327). Here truth and falsehood are imagined as opposing armies—clearly distinguishable—who meet on a
battlefield. But as the military image is developed, its configura-
tions change. Rather than being a participant in the battle, truth is
suddenly the name of its outcome; the distinguishability of truth
from falsehood is not something with which we begin, but something we must achieve by marching out "into the plain" and trying
"the matter by dint of argument" (328). Truth in short has receded
from our view, but the rhetoric of the passage still allows us to
assume that she will once again come into focus if only we allow
"the wars of truth" to continue without prior restraint. The point is
made by a comparison of truth with Proteus, the notorious shape-
shifter and emblem of deception. Proteus, Milton reminds us,
would only appear in his own shape when he was bound; but in the
case of truth it is exactly the reverse; if you bind or constrain her,
"she turns herself into all shapes except her own" (328). The moral
is clear: "give her but room," allow those who claim to know her to
contend in the field, and she will soon be discernible. But that
moral becomes unavailable with the very next sentence. "Yet, it is
not impossible that she may have more shapes than one." But if she
has more shapes than one, then she has no shape, and is exactly
like Proteus, a figure who escapes every attempt to bind her, even
when that attempt takes the form of a carefully staged battle at the
end of which she is to emerge; and when Milton concludes this
sequence by declaring that "Truth may be on this side, or on the
other, without being unlike herself," the reflexive pronoun is an

almost mocking reminder that the object of our quest has never more escaped us than when we think to have it in view, and is *always* unlike herself.[2]

That object is held out as a lure and a temptation in still another passage, perhaps the most famous of all. It begins with a sad tale. Once upon a time, "Truth indeed came . . . into the world . . . and was a perfect shape, most glorious to look on;" but then "a wicked race of deceivers . . . hewed her lovely form into a thousand pieces" (316–17). One might say then that truth has receded from this story before it even begins; but all, it would seem, is not lost, for the dismemberment of truth has left us with a definite task, the task of "gathering up limb by limb" still as we can find them, the pieces of her body. "We have not found them all," says Milton, an observation that would seem preliminary to one more exhortation to continue in our search and not to pitch our tents here. But then he adds something much more devastating in its apparent finality: "nor ever shall doe, till her Master's second coming." This is at once the low point and the high point of the tract. It is a low point because it denies the possibility of *ever* achieving knowledge and thereby renders the search pointless, of no more efficacy than licensing; but it is the high point if we are able to apply the lesson the *Areopagitica* has repeatedly taught, the lesson that knowledge and truth are not measurable or containable entities, properties of this or that object, characteristics of this or that state, but *modes of being*, inward dispositions, conditions of a heart that is always yearning for new revelations. The search is only futile if we conceive of it as a search for something external to us, as a kind of giant jig-saw puzzle made up of pre-cut and prefabricated pieces; but if we think of the search as the vehicle by means of which our knowledge is "in the making" and our virtue is in the constituting, then it is always and already succeeding even when, as in this story, it is forever failing. We will indeed never find all the pieces of truth, but if we nevertheless persist in our efforts, when Christ finally does come "to bring together every joynt and member" each of us shall be one of them.

The moral, then, is not "seek and ye shall find," but "seek and ye shall become." And what we shall become in a curious Miltonic way is a licenser, someone who is continually exercising a censorious judgment of the kind that Milton displays when he casually stigmatizes much of Greek and Roman literature as loose or impious or scurrilous. This is the judgment, not of one who is free of

---

2. On its first appearance in the tract as a topic, truth is "compar'd in Scripture to a streaming fountain" (310). Even as it is introduced truth is twice removed, coming to us through the double mediation of writing (Scripture) and metaphor.

constraints, but of one whose inner constraints are so powerful that they issue immediately and without reflection in acts of discrimination and censure.[3] Ironically it is only by permitting what licensing would banish—the continual flow of opinions, arguments, reasons, agendas—that the end of licensing—the fostering of truth—can be accomplished; accomplished not by the external means that licensing would provide, but by making ourselves into the repository of the very values that licensing misidentifies when it finds them in a world free of defiling books. Books are no more the subject of the *Areopagitica* than is free speech; both are subordinate to the process they make possible, the process of endless and proliferating interpretations whose goal is not the clarification of truth, but the making of us into members of her incorporate body so that we can be finally what the Christ of *Paradise Regained* is said already to be, a living oracle (*PR* I.460).

To be a living oracle is to be a totally unified being, one whose "heart / Contains of good, wise, just, the perfect shape" (*PR* II.10–11). This, however, is the condition only of Christ; all other men exist at a distance from that which would make them whole, exist in that state of seeking and searching which for Milton marks at once the deficiency and the glory of this vale of tears. Like the moment of mortality, the moment of the *Areopagitica* is situated between two absent unities, one always and already lost, the other to be realized only in the absorption of those consciousnesses that now yearn for it. Although truth "indeed came once into her divine Master and was a perfect shape most glorious to look on," she has long since withdrawn, leaving us to the delusive attraction of those many shapes that would compel us in her name; and although she shall one day be reassembled "into an immortal feature of loveliness and perfection," that day is ever deferred and is only projected that much more into the future each time its dawning is prematurely proclaimed.

Meanwhile, man lives in the gap. Indeed, he *is* the gap, a being defined negatively by the union that perpetually escapes him, and which, once achieved, will mark the cessation of his separateness, his end, in two senses. The impurity we bring into the world is the impurity of difference, of not being one with God; yet it is because of that impurity that difference must not be denied or lamented but embraced. The temptation of idolatry, of surrendering ourselves to the totalizing claims of some ephemeral agenda, can only be resisted by the relentless multiplication of that which signifies our lack, the relentless multiplication of difference. We will be "wise in spirituall architecture" (322) only if we build with dissimilar—dis-

---

3. See on this point Henry Limouze, "'The surest suppressing': writer and censor in Milton's *Areopagitica*" (*The Centennial Review*, 24, 1 Winter 1980, *passim.* * * *

unified—materials: "there must be many schisms and many dissections made in the quarry and in the timber, ere the house of God
can be built." This allows us for a moment to assume that in time
the house of God will in fact be built, but this is exactly like the
assumption, so often encouraged, that the truth will finally emerge,
and it is immediately disappointed: "And when every stone is laid
artfully together, it cannot be united into a continuity, it can be but
contiguous in this world." The first half of this sentence increases
the expectation that the second half will report an eventual triumph ("when every stone is laid artfully together, the building will
be complete"), but the triumph is, as it has been so many times
before, deferred, and we are left with more of the same, that is,
with more difference, with side by side (in space and time) efforts
which do not cohere except in so far as they signify, in a variety of
ways, their own insufficiency and incompleteness. It is an incompleteness that must be at once lamented and protected; lamented
because it is the sign of our distance from bliss, protected because
as such a sign it is a perpetual reminder that bliss awaits us in a
union we can achieve (precisely the wrong word) only when we are
absorbed by another into a structure not made by hands.

* * *

LAURA LUNGER KNOPPERS

Paradise Regained and the Politics of Martyrdom[†]

> At the later end of the year 1648 I had leave given mee to goe to
> london to see my Father & during my stay there at that time at
> Whitehal it was that I saw the Beheading of King Charles the first;
> He went by our door on Foot each day that hee was carry'd by
> water to Westminster, for hee took Barge at Garden-stayres where
> wee liv'd, & once hee spake to my Father & sayd Art thou alive yet!
> On the day of his execution, which was Tuesday, Jan. 30, I stood
> amongst the crowd in the street before Whitehal gate, where the
> scaffold was erected, and saw what was done, but was not so near
> as to hear any thing. The Blow I saw given, & can truly say with a
> sad heart; at the instant whereof, I remember wel, there was such
> a Grone by the Thousands then present, as I never heard before &
> desire I may never hear again.   [PHILIP HENRY. DIARY][1]

The execution of Charles I followed nearly a decade of fighting in
print and with arms over the nature and limits of kingship.[2] The

† From *Modern Philology* 90 (1992), pp. 200–19. Copyright © 1992 by The University of
Chicago Press. Reprinted by permission.
1. Matthew Henry Lee, ed., *Diaries and Letters of Philip Henry* (London, 1882), p. 12.
2. For general accounts of Charles's life and death, see C. V. Wedgwood, *A Coffin for King
Charles* (New York, 1964); and John Bowle, *Charles I: A Biography* (London, 1975). On

revolutionary Independents had, with the support of the army, purged parliament and set up the High Court of Justice, which tried, condemned, and sentenced Charles. Both the trial and execution were public displays, designed to persuade the people that Charles was being justly punished for capital offenses against them. But the groan of the crowd as the king's head was severed from his body might have warned the revolutionaries of an audience not quite so tractable or convinced as they had hoped. In its response the audience demonstrated that the effects of punishment cannot be fully controlled by the mechanisms of exemplary power. The public display of punishment, dependent upon its audience, was immediately challenged and subverted by the discourse of martyrdom. The execution was followed shortly by the publication of *Eikon Basilike*, the "King's Book," which interpreted Charles's refusal to submit to the court not as obstinacy but as constancy, and his death not as just punishment for treason but as martyrdom. The cult of royal martyrdom which the *Eikon Basilike* initiated would meet with a determined and defiant opponent in John Milton. But, paradoxically, the royal martyr would not die.

I

Despite their victory over Charles in the field, the revolutionaries struggled in the trial and execution to win the ideological battle. On January 6, 1649, the Commons accused Charles of tyranny, treason, and murder, charging that he had "a wicked designe totally to subvert the antient and fundamentall lawes and liberties of this nation. And in theire place to introduce an arbitrary and tiranicall government . . . and hath prosecuted it with fire and sword, levied and maintayned a cruell warre in the land against the Parliament and kingdome."[3] The trial and execution were part of the dramaturgy of state, designed to convince its audience that the text of Charles's life must be read as treason, his death as "exemplary and condigne punishment." The court appealed to the rhetoric of justice and divine providence to supplement or, more accurately, occlude the force underlying the trial. John Cook, lawyer for the prosecution, described the proceedings as "the most Comprehensive, Impartial and Glorious piece of Justice that ever was acted and Executed upon the Theatre of England."[4] The High Court of Jus-

---

the civil war controversies, see Merritt Y. Hughes, intro. to *The Complete Prose Works of John Milton*, ed. Don Wolfe et al., 8 vols. (New Haven, Conn., 1953–82), 3:1–189.

3. "An Act of the Commons of England assembled in Parliament for erecting of a High Court of Justice for the Trying and Judging of Charles Steward King of England" (London, January 6, 1649), reprinted in *The Trial of King Charles the First*, ed. J. G. Muddiman (London, 1929), app. A, p. 193.

4. "King Charls, His Case, or an Appeal to all Rational men Concerning his Tryal at the High Court of Justice." (London, 1649), reprinted in Muddiman, ed., app. C, p. 234.

tice had not only a juridical but also a moral and theological function. Shifting among various Old Testament models by which their
actions could be interpreted and justified, the court fastened on the
notion of bloodguilt. According to Cook, they acted for a higher
court in trying and judging Charles, "whom God in his wrath gave
to be a King to this nation, and will, I trust, in great love, for his
notorious Prevarications and Blood guiltiness take him away from
us." In a drama that is allegorical and didactic, Charles "stands now
to give an account of his stewardship and to receive the good of
justice, for all the evil of his injustice and cruelty."[5]

By staging the trial as a public display, the regicides strove to
justify but also exposed to open challenge the legitimacy of their
cause. And Charles refused to play his given role. The king acted
out the part not of a penitent sinner, which would have confirmed
their case, but of a constant sufferer for liberty and truth. Refusing
to recognize the authority of the court, he continually exposed the
force which the display of justice attempted to cover: "it is not my
case alone, it is the Freedom and the Liberty of the people of
England; and do you pretend what you will, I stand more for their
Liberties. For if power without law may make lawes, may alter the
fundamental laws of the kingdom, I do not know what subject he is
in England, that can be sure of his life or any thing that he calls his
own."[6] Charles rewrites the script, recasting the regicides' justice
as a power which unlawfully threatens king and subject alike. As a
king betrayed and tried by his own subjects, not allowed to speak in
a court claiming justice, Charles soon found a more effective paradigm by which he could sustain and explain his case—that of martyrdom and, in particular, the royal martyrdom of Christ.

The scaffold as a theater for punishment, twinned with the public trial, shows the force of law and justice inscribed in the very
body of the condemned. Yet the display of the punished traitor
does not produce a single meaning.[7] Ironically, the Independents
themselves make Charles a martyr by trying and executing him
publicly. Charles's speech and demeanor during his trial and execution, fully reported and put into circulation, have unexpected consequences. On the scaffold, as during the trial, Charles refuses to
play his assigned role. No scaffold confession, acknowledging his
own guilt and the justice of the state which punishes him, is forth-
coming. On the contrary, Charles asserts his innocence and models
himself on the royal martyr, Christ. Like Christ, he forgives his

---

5. Ibid.
6. *A perfect Narrative of the whole Proceedings of the High Court of Justice, in the Trial of
the King* (London, January 20–27, 1649), in Thomas Bayly Howell, *A Complete Collection of State Trials*, 33 vols. (London, 1816–26), 4:998.
7. On the spectacle of punishment, see Michel Foucault, *Discipline and Punish: The
Birth of the Prison* trans. Alan Sheridan (New York, 1979).

enemies: "I have forgiven all the world, and even those in particular that have been the chief causes of my death. . . . I pray God forgive them." Claiming to die as "the Martyr of the people," Charles looks to a crown of martyrdom: "I go from a corruptible to an incorruptible crown, where no disturbance can be, no disturbance in the world." He bravely meets the execution which follows: "After a little pause, the King stretching forth his hands, the Executioner at one blow severed his head from his body, and held it up and shewed it to the people, saying, 'Behold the head of a Traitor.'"[8] But already the theater of punishment was crumbling.

In ceremonies of public execution the main character was the crowd, whose presence and belief was required for the performance. But the audience at Charles's execution was unreliable. Philip Henry reports that the soldiers, apparently fearing a negative reaction, immediately dispersed the crowd: "There was according to Order one Troop immediately marching from-wards charing-cross to Westm[inster] & another from-wards Westm[inster] to charing cross purposely to masker the people, & to disperse & scatter them, so that I had much adoe amongst the rest to escape home without hurt."[9] The audience did not cooperate in the official spectacle but sought another meaning, another kind of tragedy. A Royalist newspaper, *Mercurius Elencticus* (Tuesday, January 30), reports that the people rushed to buy relics of the dead king. For the people Charles was a martyr; for the soldiers he was a means of making money: "When they had murdered him, such as desired to dip their handkerchiefes or other things in his blood, were admitted for moneys. Others bought peeces of board which were dy'd with his blood, for which the soldiers took of some a shilling, of others half a crowne, more or lesse according to the quality of the persons that sought it. But none without ready money." The soldiers continued to profit: "And after his body was coffin'd, as many as desired to see it were permitted at a certaine rate, by which meanes the soldiers got store of moneys, insomuch that one was heard to say 'I would we had two or three more such Majesties to behead, if we could but make such use of them.'"[1] The soldier's wish would be granted, although not in the form he might have imagined. Charles would indeed reappear in the ensuing cult of royal martyrdom

---

8. Howell, 4:1138–41. A number of contemporary newspapers reported extensively on Charles's trial and execution, most following *A perfect Narrative* almost verbatim. These newspapers, dated in the Thomason tracts from January–February 1649, include *The Perfect Weekly Account, The Moderate Intelligencer, The Kingdomes Faithful Scout, The Kingdomes Weekly Intelligencer,* and *The Moderate.* Bruce Boehrer points astutely to the theatrical nature of Charles's execution in "Elementary Structures of Kingship: Milton, Regicide, and the Family," *Milton Studies* 23 (1987): 97–98.
9. Lee (n. 1 [p. 589]), p. 12.
1. *Mercurius Elencticus* (London, 1649), reprinted in *A History of English Journalism to the Foundation of the Gazette,* ed. J. B. Williams (London, 1908), app. A, p. 205.

which left the regicides and Cromwellian government with many
Charleses to confront, many new majesties to behead.

II

The publication of *Eikon Basilike* immediately after Charles's execution marked a new stage in the struggle between the monarch and
his foes. "Prayers and tears" would ultimately be more effective than
the weapons of warfare which had failed to make good the king's
cause, the discourse of martyrdom more effective than the spectacle
of treason. After the Restoration, the probable coauthor (or true
author) of *Eikon Basilike*, John Gauden, exulted in martial metaphor
over its publication: "When it came out, just upon the King's death;
Good God! What shame, rage and despite filled hys Murtherers!
What comfort hys friends! How many enemyes did it convert! How
many hearts did it mollify, and melt! . . . What preparations it made
in all men's minds for this happy restauration. . . . In a word, it was
an army, and did vanquish more than any sword could."[2] Although
much of the *Eikon Basilike* gives a detailed defense of Charles's
political actions and decisions, most compelling are its rhetoric of
piety and claim to a Christlike martyrdom for Charles that skillfully
adapts the precedent of John Foxe's "Book of Martyrs."[3] *Eikon Basilike* impresses Charles's story with the distinctive contours of Foxe's
martyrology as the king endures affliction, remains true to his conscience, and suffers the rage and malice of his enemies. But the
"King's Book" also conflates Charles's sufferings with Christ's, merg-
ing the Foxean portrait of the martyr with the rich and resonant
biblical and literary tradition of royal martyrdom. In so doing, *Eikon
Basilike* develops a powerful discourse for idealizing Charles and
stigmatizing his enemies.

Like the "Book of Martyrs," *Eikon Basilike* is self-consciously
concerned with defining and portraying true martyrdom. Charles
explicitly claims this status: "They knew my chiefest arms left me
were those only which the ancient Christians were wont to use

2. Quoted in introd., *Eikon Basilike*, ed. Philip Knachel (Ithaca, N.Y., 1966), p. xxxii.
Knachel discusses the vexed question of the authorship of the "King's Book" in this
introduction. All quotations from *Eikon Basilike* are from this edition and are noted
parenthetically in my text.
3. Foxe's *Acts and Monuments of these latter and perilous days, touching matters of the
church*, popularly known as the "Book of Martyrs," was first published in English in
1563 and frequently reprinted; after 1570 a copy was placed with the Bible in every
English church. On the enormous influence of Foxe, see William Haller, *Foxe's Book of
Martyrs and the Elect Nation* (London, 1963). The influence of Foxe on the *Eikon Basi-
like* is discussed by Florence Sandler, "Icon and Iconoclast," in *Achievements of the Left
Hand: Essays on the Prose of John Milton*, ed. Michael Lieb and John T. Shawcross
(Amherst, Mass., 1974), pp. 160–62; and John Knott, Jr., "'Suffering for Truths Sake':
Milton and Martyrdom," in *Politics, Poetics, and Hermeneutics in Milton's Prose*, ed.
David Loewenstein and James G. Turner (Cambridge, 1990), pp. 159–62.

LAURA LUNGER KNOPPERS

against their persecutors—prayers and tears. These may serve a good man's turn, if not to conquer as a soldier, yet to suffer as a martyr" (p. 47). And he denies martyrdom to his political opponents: "Some parasitic preachers have dared to call those 'martyrs' who died fighting against me, the laws, their oaths, and the religion established. But sober Christians know that glorious title can with truth be applied only to those who sincerely preferred God's truth and their duty in all these particulars before their lives and all that was dear to them in this world" (pp. 118–19). Charles claims the martyrs' constancy, commenting: "Here I am sure to be conqueror if God will give me such a measure of constancy as to fear him more than man and to love the inward peace of my conscience before any outward tranquility" (p. 38), for, "what they [my enemies] call obstinacy, I know God accounts honest constancy" (p. 138). Charles also prays: "*Give me that measure of patience and constancy which my condition now requires*" (p. 139). Such frequent references to conscience, patience, and constancy create a compelling portrait of Charles, the martyr-king.

While the "King's Book" portrays Charles as suffering and dying for the church as well as for the more strictly political cause of monarchy, the issues are inseparable because this martyr's truth is bound even more to an internal political power struggle than are those in Foxe's massive tome. While it would be naive to deny the political implications in Foxe's virulently anti-Catholic accounts of martyrdom, his Marian martyrs at least debate theological issues, albeit ones with political import—transubstantiation, purgatory and the penitential system (confession, indulgences, meritorious works), marriage of the clergy, and papal supremacy. *Eikon Basilike* appropriates and further politicizes the discourse of martyrdom, employing its rhetoric to interpret such specific events and points of dispute in the English civil war as "His Majesty's Calling This Last Parliament," "The Listing and Raising Armies against the King," "Their Seizing the King's Magazines, Forts, Navy, and Militia," and "The Various Events of the War: Victories and Defeats" (pp. vii–viii). But despite the increased attention to details of contemporary political events, Gauden (with Charles) is able to draw much more fully than Foxe had on the tradition of Christ as royal martyr. Foxe's own relationship to monarchy is complex if not problematic.[4] Foxe writes to support Elizabeth and the established church, to advise the queen in her destined role as true sovereign; yet the martyrdoms he most vividly and elaborately recounts are those of middle- and lower-class subjects under conformity proceedings mandated by another

---

4. For Foxe and the imperial tradition, see Janel Mueller, "Embodying Glory: The Apocalyptic Strain in Milton's *Of Reformation*," in Loewenstein and Turner, eds., pp. 15–16.

monarch—bloody Queen Mary. Although Foxe briefly recounts Christ's passion and crucifixion, he makes no real use of the reso- nant biblical and literary tradition of Christ as royal martyr. *Eikon Basilike* thus draws on and dramatically revises the Foxean tradition in its compelling portrait of the martyr-king.

Associations with Christ's sufferings, passion, and death resonate throughout the "King's Book," elevating Charles's cause and stigma- tizing his political enemies as traitors. "His Majesty's Retirement from Westminster" and his refusal to comply with parliamentary demands are presented as a choice of kingly martyrdom: "I will rather choose to wear a crown of thorns with my Saviour than to exchange that of gold, which is due to me, for one of lead" (p. 28). Foregrounding his divine type, Charles implicitly compares "Raising Armies against the King" with the crucifixion of a forgiving Christ: "*when Thy wrath is appeased by my death, O remember Thy great mer- cies toward them and forgive them, O my Father, for they know not what they do*" (p. 46). The "Troubles in Ireland" (in which the king stood accused of fomenting a Catholic uprising) are depicted in terms of Christ's suffering on the cross: "Therefore with exquisite malice they have mixed the gall and vinegar of falsity and contempt with the cup of my affliction" (p. 63). Similarly, the "Scots Delivering the King to the English" is compared to Judas's selling of Christ: "If I am sold by them, I am only sorry they should do it and that my price should be so much above my Saviour's" (p. 137).

Finally, in the "Meditations upon Death" which conclude *Eikon Basilike*, Charles moves from justifying specific actions to con- structing more fully the myth of the royal martyr by which his life and death may be interpreted. Charles refers to "those greater for- malities whereby my enemies, (being more solemnly cruel) will, it may be, seek to add (as those who crucified Christ) the mockery of justice to the cruelty of malice" (p. 174). Echoing Christ's words in the garden of Gethsemane, Charles professes willingness to accept the bitter cup: "*Thou givest me leave as a man to pray that this cup may pass from me; but Thou hast taught me as a Christian by the example of Christ to add, not my will, but Thine be done*" (p. 181). He claims conformity with Christ's martyrdom: "If I must suffer a violent death with my Saviour, it is but mortality crowned with martyrdom" (p. 179). And Charles is explicit in acknowledging that his martyrdom will be a paradoxical victory: "My next comfort is that He gives me not only the honor to imitate His example in suf- fering for righteousness' sake, (though obscured by the foulest charges of tyranny and injustice), but also that charity which is the noblest revenge upon and victory over, my destroyers" (p. 176). Like Foxe's martyrs whose constancy in burning at the stake astonished and amazed onlookers, and like Christ on the cross, to whom the

Roman centurion pays tribute, Charles will experience death but
no defeat.

III

The "King's Book" brilliantly subverted the exemplary power of the
state, recasting the public trial and execution of Charles as a drama
of suffering and martyrdom. Gauden's colleagues responded in
kind. The book initiated an outpouring of elegies and hyperbolic
laments on Charles the royal martyr.[5] Focusing on his final days
and his death, the martyrologies greatly elaborate the parallels
with Christ's passion and crucifixion, paying little attention to
details of the political struggle. Diverging from Foxe and elaborat-
ing on the *Eikon Basilike*, the martyrologies construct a full picture
of Charles as a uniquely royal martyr. For the first time, Charles is
given a sympathetic—even weeping—audience. The author of *An
Elegie Upon the Death of Our Dread Soveraign Lord King CHARLS
the MARTYR* is typical: "Com, com, let's Mourn; all eies, that see
this *Daie*, / Melt into Showrs, and Weep your selvs awaie: / O that
each Private head could yield a Flood / Of Tears, whil'st *Britain's
Head* stream's out His Blood."[6] Flouting state censorship, the martyrologies poignantly link Charles with Christ in his passion and
death, blackening the regicides with the powerfully resonant myth
of the crucifixion.

The martyrologies recast the alleged justice of Charles's public
trial and execution as a false, theatrical reenactment of Christ's trial
and crucifixion. [T]he bishop of Downe turns from the passion and
death of Christ "to present unto you another sad tragedy, so like
unto the former, that it may seem but *vetus fabula per novos histrio-
nes*, the stage onely changed, and new actors entred upon it."[7] *A
Deepe Groane Fetch'd* elaborates more fully on the tragic play:

> Such was their Bedlame Rabble, and the Cry
> Of *Justice* now, 'mongst them was *Crucifie*:
> *Pilates* Consent is *Bradshawes* Sentence here;
> The *Judgement hall's* remov'd to *Westminster*.
> Hayle to the Reeden Scepture the Head, and knee
> Act o're againe that Cursed Pageantrie.[8]

---

5. See Helen Randall, "The Rise and Fall of a Martyrology: Sermons on Charles I," *Huntington Library Quarterly* 10 (1947): 135–67.
6. *An Elegie Upon the Death of Our Dread Soveraign Lord King CHARLS the MARTYR* (London, 1649), n.p.
7. The Bishop of Downe, *The Martyrdom of King Charls I: Or his Conformity with Christ
in his Sufferings.* (The Hague, 1649; reprint, London, 1660), p. 16.
8. *A Deepe Groane Fetch'd At the Funerall of that Incomparable and Glorious Monarch,
Charles the First* (London, 1649), p. 3.

In this mock trial, Charles bears a unique resemblance to Christ. The Independents become the "Bedlame Rabble," Bradshaw takes the role of Pilate, and the trial at Westminster reenacts the "Cursed Pageantrie."

Focusing thus on the final days and hours of the king's life, elegies and sermons multiply links between the sufferings of Charles and Christ, much to the detriment of the king's accusers. *A Hand-Kirchife for Loyall Mourners* links the regicides with "Judasses," "Jewes and *Pilate*," while Charles is like Christ "in the temper of his sufferings, with so much meeknesse and fortitude, undauntedness of spirit, and submission to the will of God."[9] Similarly, *The Scotch Souldiers Lamentation* concludes, "There have beene many Martyrs, but no Martyr-Kings that I know of but my blessed Saviour Christ Jesus, and my late gracious Soveraigne Lord King Charles."[1]

In 1660, the martyrology tracts again proliferated with the restoration of the king's son, Charles II. But now the tragedy turns to tragicomedy, even to comedy; the king's murderers are banished from the stage and the new king installed in the leading role. Anthonie Sadler's *The Loyall Mourner* traces the developments of the past decade: "The King's Beheaded: and the Royall Crown's / Stript of *Monarchall* Rule: the Nobles down: / The Souldier sways the Judge: the Sword, the Law: / A Lawless Sword doth all the Kingdom awe." Suddenly now the play has changed:

> the Theater's new Hung,
> A Proclamation made, the Bells are Rung,
> The King's Receiv'd, Loyalties Return'd;
> All in a night, and welcome Formes Reform'd,
> Peace Crowns the Kingdome, *all* in each degree,
> Act *pleasant* parts, and play a Comedy.[2]

The triumphal return of Charles II and the punishment of those who had supported the regicide seemed to confirm the martyrdom of Charles I; the true church, afflicted under the republic, was now restored.

The publishing and republishing of the martyrologies and the *Eikon Basilike* thus had important political ramifications in Resto-

9. *A Hand-Kirchife for Loyall Mourners or a Cordiall for Drooping Spirits, Groaning for the bloody murther, and heavy losse of our Gracious King* (London, 1649), pp. 5–6.
1. *The Scotch Souldiers Lamentation Upon the Death of the most Glorious and Illustrious Martyr, King Charles* (London, 1649), p. 18.
2. Anthonie Sadler, *The Loyall Mourner, Shewing the Murdering of King Charles the First: Fore-shewing the Restoring of King Charles the Second* (London, 1660), pp. 2–3.

ration England. Like Foxe's "Book of Martyrs" dedicated to Elizabeth, the martyrologies implicitly or explicitly pointed to Charles II
as the true monarch about to restore the church. And also like
Foxe, the martyrologies instructed and guided Charles in the manner of establishing that church. The cult of the royal martyr exon-
erated the Anglican clergy, blackened the Independents, and
provided a text by which to interpret the display of the new, even
more theatrical Restoration monarchy. Even in their political victory, the Royalists seemed to retain firm control of the powerful
discourse of martyrdom.

IV

In publishing the text of Charles's trial and execution and allowing
the *Eikon* and the martyrologies to escape censorship, the Independents had seriously miscalculated the effects of the public execution.
Too late, the new government commissioned John Milton to answer
the "King's Book." Milton's *Eikonoklastes* (1649), although primarily
a point-by-point rebuttal of the *Eikon Basilike*, also recognizes the
cult of royal martyrdom which the "King's Book" had fostered. Milton rebukes the preachers who "howle in thir Pulpits" after the dead
Charles and he tries (futilely, in the event) to repel the rhetoric of
martyrdom with a combination of scorn and reason.[3] Milton attacks
the *Eikon Basilike*, first of all, by reversing the charges of stagecraft:
Charles's alleged martyrdom is false theatricality dependent on a
deluded and idolatrous audience.[4] The frontispiece of the *Eikon
Basilike*, which depicts a kneeling Charles about to exchange his
golden crown for a crown of thorns, aims, according to Milton, to
"Martyr him and Saint him to befool the people" (p. 343). The "conceited portraiture" of Charles is sleight-of-hand stage work, "drawn
out to the full measure of a Masking Scene, and sett there to catch
fools and silly gazers" (p. 342). Such "quaint Emblems and devices
begg'd from the Old Pageantry of some Twelf-nights entertainment
at *Whitehall* will doe but ill to make a Saint or Martyr" (p. 343). The
"King's Book" is to be rejected as false and theatrical: "Stage-work
will not doe it; much less *the justness of thir Cause*" (p. 530).

And yet the people are easy prey. Milton heaps scorn not only on
the royal actor but on his gullible, doting, idolatrous audience:
"The People, exorbitant and excessive in all thir motions, are prone
ofttimes not to a religious onely, but to a civil kinde of Idolatry in
idolizing thir Kings" (p. 343). The "King's Book" shows "what a mis-

3. *Eikonoklastes*, in Wolfe et al., eds. (n. 2 pp. 589–90), 3:365. Further references are
included parenthetically in my text.
4. For a fuller discussion of Milton's attack on theatricality in *Eikonoklastes*, see Lana
Cable, "Milton's Iconoclastic Truth," in Loewenstein and Turner, eds. (n. 13, above),
pp. 143–45; and David Loewenstein, *Milton and the Drama of History: Historical
Vision, Iconoclasm, and the Literary Imagination* (Cambridge, 1990), chap. 3.

erable, credulous, deluded thing that creature is, which is call'd the Vulgar" (p. 426). Charles will never "stirr the constancie and solid firmness of any wise Man" but will only "catch the worthles approbation of an inconstant, irrational, and Image-doting rabble" (p. 601). The people, like a "credulous and hapless herd, begott'n to servility, and inchanted with these popular institutes of Tyranny" are themselves witness to "thir own voluntary and beloved baseness" (p. 601).

Charles's claim to martyrdom, then, is false and theatrical; the people's responses to such a claim are idolatrous and deluded. Milton scornfully dismisses Charles's claim to a Christlike crown of thorns since Charles, unlike Christ, suffers for his own faults: "Many would be all one with our Saviour, whom our Saviour will not know. They who govern ill those Kingdoms which they had a right to, have to our Saviours Crown of Thornes no right at all. Thornes they may find anow, of thir own gathering, and thir own twisting . . . but to weare them as our Saviour wore them is not giv'n to them that suffer by thir own demerits" (pp. 417–18). According to Milton, Charles's self-promotion undermines his own cause since "Martyrs bear witness to the truth, not to themselves": "If I beare witness of my self, saith *Christ*, my witness is not true. He who writes himself *Martyr* by his own inscription, is like an ill Painter, who, by writing on the shapeless Picture which he hath drawn, is fain to tell passengers what shape it is; which els no man could imagin" (p. 575). Suffering or dying with constancy, Milton objects, does not make a martyr: "Lastly, if to die for *the testimony of his own conscience*, be anough to make him Martyr, what Heretic dying for direct blasphemie, as som have don constantly, may not boast a Martyrdom?" (p. 576).

In discounting Charles's suffering and emphasizing the truth for which genuine martyrs suffer, Milton implicitly revives the etymology of martyrdom—"witnessing." If Milton primarily focuses in *Eikonoklastes* on denying Charles the name of martyr, he also constructs his own text as a counterexample, a true martyr or witness to the truth before God and man. *Eikonoklastes* comes to counter the king's false claims to the truth, impelled by the king's "making new appeale to Truth and the World" and leaving "this Book," *Eikon Basilike*, "as the best advocat and interpreter of his own actions" so that "his Friends by publishing, dispersing, commending, and almost adoring it, seem to place therein the chiefe strength and nerves of thir cause" (p. 340). Milton will oppose the *Eikon Basilike* by "remembring them the truth of what they themselves know to be heer misaffirm'd" (p. 338). Milton insists that this truth needs no reinforcement but is simply sent out "in the native confidence of her single self, to earn, how she can, her entertainment in the world, and to finde out her own readers; few perhaps, but those few, such of value and substantial worth, as truth and wisdom, not respecting numbers and bigg names, have bin ever wont in all ages to be contented with" (pp. 339–40).

Yet Milton's truth, like the king's, is embedded in and shaped by seventeenth-century politics. When, as confuter of Charles, Milton claims to be part of the "sole remainder" or remnant selected by God "to stand upright and stedfast in his cause; dignify'd with the defence of truth and public libertie" (p. 348), he politicizes not only martyrdom but also the truth to which martyrs bear witness. Later in the work, he more radically conflates truth with justice and claims both were operative in executing the king: "either Truth and Justice are all one, for Truth is but Justice in our knowledge, and Justice is but Truth in our practice . . . or els, if there be any odds, that Justice, though not stronger then truth, yet by her office is to put forth and exhibit more strength in the affaires of mankind" (pp. 583–84). Writing thus, Milton hopes to "set free the minds of English men from longing to returne poorly under the Captivity of Kings, from which the strength and supreme Sword of Justice hath deliverd them" (p. 585). Like the Royalists, Milton strives to appropriate and deploy justice and truth for his political cause: once again, it is clear that such truth is a thing of this world, produced and defined in ideological struggle.

Central to *Eikonoklastes*, then, is Milton's rebuttal of Charles's claim to cap the Foxean tradition of martyrdom. To Charles's false, theatrical martyrdom, Milton opposes his own witness to the truth, a revised and reconstituted kind of martyrdom. Ironically, after the Restoration, *Eikonoklastes* itself suffered the traditional fate of a martyr—public burning by the common hangman. But Milton was left alive to contemplate and develop new modes of witness, of standing upright for the truth.

V

After 1660, although Milton's "left hand" no longer produced polemical prose, he continued his fight against kingship in the more allusive medium of poetry. *Paradise Regained*, seemingly so remote from contemporary political issues, is centrally concerned with depicting a Christ who cannot be associated with the Stuart monarchy. Milton's Son of God recalls the *Eikon Basilike* and the martyrologies of Charles I precisely to critique the claims of one who suffers for the preservation of an earthly monarchy.[5] If in *Eikonoklastes* Milton pri-

5. Recent critics have variously explored the political significance of *Paradise Regained*. Christopher Hill sees Christ as rejecting those things which led the revolutionaries astray; see his *Milton and the English Revolution* (New York, 1977), pp. 413–27. Andrew Milner argues that Christ's rejection of Satan's political offers reflects Milton's own quietism in face of the collapse of the Commonwealth (*John Milton and the English Revolution* [Totowa, N.J., 1981], pp. 167–79). Michael Wilding also finds quiet-

marily sought to rewrite the figure of Charles so as to deny him martyrdom with Christ, in *Paradise Regained* he strives, even more radically, to rewrite the meaning of martyrdom. Milton constructs a Son of God who embodies many of the characteristics of Foxe's martyrs—constancy in affliction, plain speaking of the truth, self-composure. Yet the Son is no martyr in the traditional sense employed by Foxe and elaborated by Gauden and the martyrologies; he is a victor who does not die to achieve his conquest. Rejecting the theatrical suffering and lachrymose exaltation of the recent English royal martyr, Milton reinvents in *Paradise Regained* the root sense of martyrdom as witnessing to the truth. *Paradise Regained* counters the Royalist appropriation of the discourse of martyrdom by radically rewriting both recent English political history and the centuries-old literary and cultural tradition of the royal martyr.

The long-standing problems of the poem are significant with regard to this revisionary project. The Son of God in *Paradise Regained* has been termed a "celibate detective," "heartless, prissy, or downright cold," a "peevish obscurantist," and an "inhuman snob."[6] The Son refuses to act or even to show any emotion. Faced with its spare style, austere setting, and paucity of action, readers have found the poem, as well as its hero, baffling and cold.[7] Even the most basic questions remain unsettled. Why this subject? Why not the crucifixion? Is there development? Does the Son learn anything? Is there a miracle atop the temple tower? Why does Satan fall astonished? Such cruxes are not resolved by classifying the poem as brief epic. Indeed, Milton's use of that genre is equally puzzling. Why no heroic action, figurative richness, poetic allusiveness, divine intervention?[8]

Viewing *Paradise Regained* as participating in the political discourse of martyrdom clarifies a number of these issues. Here epic action, narrative, and plot are circumscribed by the single action of the martyr who must speak the truth—repeatedly, constantly. The hero's actions consist precisely in his witness to the truth—speaking out, enduring fraud and force, standing upright to the

---

ism in the poem (*Dragon's Teeth: Literature in the English Revolution* [Oxford, 1987], pp. 249–53). David Quint argues that the poem challenges the Davidic claims of Charles I and II ("David's Census: The Politics of *Paradise Regained*," in *Re-membering Milton: Essays on the Texts and Traditions*, ed. Mary Nyquist and Margaret Ferguson [New York and London, 1987], pp. 128–47). My own essay, which implicitly counters the claims of quietism, is indebted to John Knott's brief but compelling discussion of *Paradise Regained* [n. 3, p. 595] pp. 166–68.

6. See John Carey, *Milton* (London, 1969), p. 137; Alan Fisher, "Why Is *Paradise Regained* So Cold?" *Milton Studies* 14 (1980): 206; and Northrop Frye, "The Typology of *Paradise Regained*," in *Milton: Modern Essays in Criticism*, ed. Arthur E. Barker (London, 1965), p. 439.

7. See, e.g., Fisher. For a challenge to this view, see Wayne Anderson, "Is *Paradise Regained* Really Cold?" *Christianity and Literature* 34, no. 4 (Summer 1983): 15–23.

8. For a full account of the history and nature of brief epic, see Barbara Lewalski, *Milton's Brief Epic* (Providence, R.I., 1966).

end. Divine intervention comes by way of the inward consolations which fortify martyrs. Epic allusiveness and figurative richness become Satanic snares, pitfalls to the plain and simple truth. While the Royalist tracts focus on the passion and crucifixion of Christ with only scant attention to the wilderness temptation as preparation for Christ's martyrdom, for Milton the temptation not only prepares for but essentially replaces the passion and crucifixion. Paradise is regained not by theatrical suffering but by an intellectual debate in the wilderness; the genre is not tragedy but brief epic, the protagonist not the crucified, kingly Christ but the constant, unmoved Son of God.

Unlike the Royalist martyrologies, *Paradise Regained* offers no physical suffering and death, no pathos, no public spectacle, no weeping audience. The poem is deliberately antitheatrical, or, rather, it links theatricality with Satan, who has a full complement of props, costumes, scenery, and dramatic ploys. While Satan seems to do all the acting, he also continually presses the Son to say or do something dramatically interesting.[9] The character of the Son—private, terse, unemotional—is the opposite of that of the king, who acts out a well-calculated pageant before a gullible audience. The Royalists may have the theater, but Milton has the truth.

The contemporary political discourse which linked Charles Stuart with Christ thus clarifies both Milton's choice and treatment of his subject in *Paradise Regained*. There is, to begin with, the simple, essential, but continually overlooked point that the hero of *Paradise Regained* is never called Christ. He is the "Son of God" (thirty-six times), the "Son" (fifteen times), "our Saviour" (eighteen times), "Jesus" (five times), "Messiah" (seven times), but never Christ, the one in whom the kingly line of David had been fulfilled.[1] Critics, however, invariably call this character Christ, thus coloring the character and poem with the sacramental associations of earthly kingship which Milton consciously avoided. The Christ of the Gospels is dramatically attractive as he suffers for others, forgives and prays for his enemies. The passion of Christ is central in the Gospels, and it was the language of the passion narratives which Charles so powerfully appropriated. Christ's passion takes place in the capital, Jerusalem; his agony in the garden, trial, condemnation, and carrying of the cross are all publicly accessible events. The Christ of the Gospels

---

9. From a different perspective, and without exploring the political implications, Stanley Fish has examined the antitheatrical nature of *Paradise Regained* in "The Temptation of Plot in *Paradise Regained*," *Milton Studies* 17 (1983): 163–85, and "Inaction and Silence: The Reader in *Paradise Regained*," in *Calm of Mind: Tercentenary Essays on "Paradise Regained" and "Samson Agonistes" in Honor of John S. Diekhoff*, ed. Joseph Anthony Wittreich, Jr. (Cleveland, 1971), pp. 25–47.
1. *John Milton: Complete Poems and Major Prose*, ed. Merritt Y. Hughes (Indianapolis, 1957). Further references are included parenthetically in my text.

does not eschew the notion of kingship, although he also states, paradoxically, that "My kingdom is not of this world" (John 18:36, King James Version). Charged before Pilate with claiming to be the king of the Jews, Christ simply replies, "Thou sayest it" (Matt. 27:11; Mark 15:2; Luke 23:3).[2] The passion of the gospel Christ is compelling because of the pathos he evokes as a figure tragically misunderstood and unjustly put to death. What Milton leaves out of a poem on paradise regained is, from this perspective, astonishing. In rejecting the passion narratives as models for telling how Christ regains paradise, Milton represses the main emphases of the Gospels—Christ misunderstood, suffering for others, redeeming humanity through his death and resurrection. The witness of Milton's Son of God counters and challenges the pathos and dramatic appeal not only of the martyred Charles but also of the Christ whom Charles imitates.

Suffering and death, the traditional marks of martyrdom, are invoked in *Paradise Regained*, but then only to be pushed beyond the margins of the narrative. God the Father explains the Son's future mission: "To conquer Sin and Death the two grand foes, / By Humiliation and strong Sufferance: / His weakness shall o'ercome Satanic strength / And all the world, and mass of sinful flesh" (1.159–62). The Son knows from the beginning that his claim to his promised kingdom will ultimately consist in a traditional martyr's witness: "my way must lie / Through many a hard assay even to the death, / Ere I the promis'd Kingdom can attain" (1.263–65). Satan, too, forecasts the Son's future suffering and death: "Sorrows, and labors, opposition, hate, / Attends thee, scorns, reproaches, injuries, / Violence and stripes, and lastly cruel death" (4.386–88). Rejecting an earthly kingship, the Son envisages his God-appointed mission thus:

> What if he hath decreed that I shall first
> Be tried in humble state, and things adverse,
> By tribulations, injuries, insults,
> Contempts, and scorns, and snares, and violence,
> Suffering, abstaining, quietly expecting
> Without distrust or doubt, that he may know
> What I can suffer, how obey? who best
> Can suffer, best can do; best reign, who first
> Well hath obey'd.
>   [3.188–96]

2. Christ's reply to Pilate in the Gospel of John is strikingly different: "Thou sayest that I am a king. To this end was I born, and for this cause came I into the world, that I should bear witness unto the truth. Every one that is of the truth heareth my voice" (John 18:37). Interestingly enough, while Milton's Son of God seems closest to this Christ, the Gospel of John has no temptation account. Milton seems to meld the Christ of the Gospel of John with the temptation episode found in the other Gospels.

While the Son's rejoinder to Satan here seems to refer to future martyrdom, his speech (which significantly omits any mention of the crucifixion) also strikingly describes the action of *Paradise Regained* itself. In a very material sense, the wilderness temptation—during which the Son is tried by "injuries, insults, / Contempts, and scorns, and snares, and violence" and responds by "Suffering, abstaining, quietly expecting / Without distrust or doubt"—substitutes for traditional martyrdom in Milton's poem. The Son's suffering here consists of endurance as he abstains from earthly political power. Martyrdom thus delineated can encompass all the faithful republicans in Restoration England (including those who do not bear the ultimate witness of death). In Milton's hands, the martyrdom of the Son of God becomes an inclusive condition, no longer unique and no longer linked with his kingship—or with that of Charles I.

Although the Son does not suffer death in *Paradise Regained*, he nonetheless shows throughout his temptations the constancy which centrally defines Foxean martyrs. This, however, has been perhaps his most frustrating and puzzling trait for readers. In response to Satanic temptations, the Son replies "sternly" (1.406), "with unalter'd brow" (1.493), "temperately" (2.378), "patiently" (2.432), "calmly" (3.43), "fervently" (3.121), "unmov'd" (3.386, 4.109), "with disdain" (4.170), and "sagely" (4.285). During the Satanic storm he is "patient" (4.420), "Unshaken" (4.421), and "unappall'd" (4.425). Satan names the trait that constitutes the Son's central defense when he rejects Belial's suggestion of a temptation involving women: "with manlier objects we must try / His constancy" (2.225–26). The simile which opens book 4 of *Paradise Regained* recalls the frontispiece to *Eikon Basilike* as well as Charles's claims (repeated by the martyrologies) of his constancy in faith through storms of popular rage: "[As] surging waves against a solid rock, / Though all to shivers dash't, th'assault renew, / Vain batt'ry, and in froth or bubbles end; / So Satan" (4.18–21).[3] Likewise, Satan later complains that he has found the Son "Proof against all temptation as a rock / Of Adamant, and as a Center, firm" (4.533–34). This constancy reaches its apex (literally and dramatically) in *Paradise Regained* in the temptation of the Tower, when the Son stuns Satan by the untheatrical action of standing still: "To whom thus Jesus. Also it is written, / Tempt not the Lord thy God; he said and stood / But Satan smitten with amazement fell" (4.560–62).

And yet, as Milton himself had argued in *Eikonoklastes*, such constancy is in itself insufficient. Milton wants to show that the Son of God, unlike Charles, is constant in his witness to the truth.

---

3. On the connection with *Eikon Basilike*, see Knott, p. 167.

The Son declares early in *Paradise Regained* that even as a child he felt himself "born to promote all truth, / All righteous things" (1.205–6). Military might allures him to subdue tyrannic power to these specific ends: "Till truth were freed, and equity restor'd" (1.220). By contrast, Satan is repeatedly defined in terms of falsehood. The Son reproaches Satan as "compos'd of lies / From the beginning, and in lies wilt end" (1.407–8). Later, he charges Satan: "For lying is thy sustenance, thy food. / Yet thou pretend'st to truth" (1.429–30). Even Satan praises (though guilefully) the Son's truthfulness: "Hard are the ways of truth, and rough to walk, / Smooth on the tongue discourst, pleasing to th' ear, / And tunable as Silvan Pipe or Song; / What wonder then if I delight to hear / Her dictates from thy mouth?" (1.478–82). This praise is blandishment offered as a response to the Son's characterization of himself in terms of truth:

> God hath now sent his living Oracle
> Into the World to teach his final will,
> And sends his Spirit of Truth henceforth to dwell
> In pious Hearts, an inward Oracle
> To all truth requisite for men to know.
> [1.460–64]

Truth, as embodied in the Son, becomes inward, not visible, not subject to display. Such a definition is politically charged, formed in a nexus of political struggle. Thus *Paradise Regained* dissociates truth from kingship, as the Son confirms his unlikeness to Charles by rejecting an earthly throne and redefining kingship: "But to guide Nations in the way of truth / By saving Doctrine, and from error lead / To know, and knowing worship God aright, / Is yet more Kingly" (2.473–76). Once the Son has definitively denied any association with earthly political power, the narrator concludes: "So spake *Israel's* true King, and to the Fiend / Made answer meet, that made void all his wiles. / So fares it when with truth falsehood contends" (3.441–43).

Finally, as opposed to Charles's false kingly witness, the Son's true witness is private. While Charles courts publicity as a martyr, publishing his meditations and seeking through theatrics to rouse the people, Milton's Son of God is alone in the wilderness. Milton moves his hero's public role—not only his suffering and death, but his entire ministry—beyond the poem's purview. Although it opens with the public baptism of the Son, the action then relocates to a private sphere. Unlike Charles, Milton's Son of God is found "tracing the Desert wild, / Sole, but with holiest Meditations fed" (2.109–10). Satan mocks the Son's circumstances—"Thou art unknown, unfriended, low of birth, / A Carpenter thy Father known, thyself /

Bred up in poverty and straits at home; / Lost in a Desert here and hunger-bit" (2.413–16)—and tempts him to seek fame: "These God-like Virtues wherefore dost thou hide? / Affecting private life, or more obscure / In savage Wilderness" (3.21–23). But the Son harshly rejects public acclaim, the "people's praise," in language which strikingly recalls Milton's earlier polemic against the "herd" in *Eikonoklastes*: "And what the people but a herd confus'd, / A miscellaneous rabble, who extol / Things vulgar, and well weigh'd, scarce worth the praise?" (3.49–51). The link with Milton's *Eikonoklastes* clarifies the otherwise puzzling severity of these lines. Milton's Son of God, unlike Charles, rejects popular fame because he witnesses not to himself but to God: "Shall I seek glory then, as vain men seek / Oft not deserv'd? I seek not mine, but his / Who sent me, and thereby witness whence I am" (3.105–7).

The human bystanders in *Paradise Regained* neither see nor hear about the Son's temptation in the wilderness. Andrew and Simon are disappointed and baffled by the Son's disappearance; nonetheless they summon up their faith: "But let us wait; thus far he hath perform'd, / Sent his Anointed, and to us reveal'd him, / By his great Prophet, pointed at and shown, / In public" (2.49–52). Mary is not present at the baptism but hears by report that her son, "Private, unactive, calm, contemplative" (2.81), has now been "acknowledg'd . . . / By *John* the Baptist, and in public shown, / Son own'd from Heaven by his Father's voice" (2.83–85). Apprehensive about her son—"But where delays he now? Some great intent / Conceals him" (2.95–96)—Mary too keeps faith: "But I to wait with patience am inur'd" (2.102). The poem hence provides a model for the faithful few in Milton's Restoration audience, as the poet conceived them and his hero alike. The Son's true witness never finds a human audience in the poem. After withstanding Satanic temptation, the Son simply goes home: "hee unobserv'd / Home to his Mother's house private return'd" (4.638–39).

Yet the Son is not wholly unobserved for he has, in the first place, a divine audience. God the Father explains that he is sending the Son

> That all the Angels and Ethereal Powers,
> They now, and men hereafter, may discern
> From what consummate virtue I have chose
> This perfect Man, by merit call'd my Son,
> To earn Salvation for the Sons of men.
>
> [1.163–67]

Satan too, of course, closely tracks the Son's witness and is ultimately stunned and defeated by it. Finally, the Son is not unobserved because Milton himself publishes as he textualizes the Son's "private" witness in the wilderness. The narrator will "tell of deeds / Above Heroic, though in secret done, / And unrecorded left through many an Age, / Worthy t' have not remain'd so long unsung" (1.14–17). In order to lodge his insistence that the true Son of God has no real earthly audience, Milton must speak to some earthly audience. This audience might be those few of "value and substantial worth" with whom, in *Eikonoklastes*, Truth is contented. For Milton, the very inaccessibility of *Paradise Regained* throughout its reception history, its lack of drama and popular appeal, would paradoxically confirm the truth of his discourse.

Paradise Regained thus inscribes a specifically Miltonic witness to the truth in the context of popular reaction to the crisis of Stuart monarchy. Charles's assimilation of himself to the Christ of the Gospels—suffering for the people and unjustly put to death—was so brilliantly successful that Milton could no longer use this discourse. In a number of ways *Paradise Regained* shares the mission of *Eikonoklastes*, but, instead of deconstructing the martyr King Charles, the poem deconstructs the Christ of the Gospels. *Paradise Regained* is not an orthodox work, no matter how much critics downplay its manifold difficulties. Milton's highly politicized redaction of the temptation of Christ in the wilderness, fully implicated in the contemporary politics of martyrdom, might be better named the (new) gospel according to John.

BARBARA K. LEWALSKI

"With New Acquist of True Experience": *Paradise Regained*[†]

Milton's last major poems, published together as a diptych, continue the educational project of *Paradise Lost*: to create imaginative experiences that will help readers gain moral and political knowledge, virtue, and inner freedom—the "paradise within" that is also the necessary precondition for gaining liberty in the public sphere. These poems enact the two forms of heroism pointed to in *Paradise Lost*: "Patience and Heroic Martyrdom" by Jesus tempted in the desert, and the defeat of "worldly strong" by one "deemd weak," the blinded Samson (*PL* 9.32; 12.567–8). Both the brief epic and the classical tragedy portray an isolated hero's hard intellectual struggle in dialogues and debates with a tempter or series of tempters. And for both heroes, the right understanding of

† From Barbara K. Lewalski; *The Life of John Milton: A Critical Biography* (Oxford: Blackwell, 2000), pp. 510–22 and notes. Reprinted by permission.

themselves, of their different callings, and of a large spectrum of moral and political issues, must precede the fulfillment of those roles. *Paradise Regained* is concerned primarily with the realm of attitudes and choices, *Samson Agonistes* with the realm of public duties and political action. Like *Paradise Lost*, both poems are deeply engaged with contemporary issues as well as with enduring human passions, desires, and fears.

Paradise Regained is a complement, not a sequel to *Paradise Lost*. Milton's only major sources are the few short verses in Matthew 4:1–11, Mark 1:12–13, and Luke 4:1–13 and the exegetical tradition pertaining to them; partly for dramatic effect Milton followed the Luke sequence (stones, kingdoms, tower) rather than the more often cited Matthew sequence. From this slender basis, he produced a narrative in four books, 2,070 blank-verse lines. Contemporary readers were no doubt surprised, as some modern critics have been, by Milton's choice of the temptation in the wilderness as subject rather than the Passion–Crucifixion narrative, and with his portrait of an austere, naysaying Jesus who discounts and refuses all worldly pleasures and goods.[1] But this choice of subject follows naturally from Milton's belief that self-knowledge and self-rule are preconditions for any worthy public action in the world. The temptation episode allows Milton to present Jesus's moral and intellectual trials as a higher epic heroism, as a model for right knowing and choosing, and as a creative and liberating force in history. As a political gesture, it allowed him to develop a model of nonviolent yet active and forceful resistance to the Restoration church and state. Also, this choice contests royalist representations of Charles I's trial and execution as a martyrdom imitative of Christ's Passion and death by presenting Jesus enacting the essential meaning of the term martyr—a witness to the truth. The unmoved Jesus standing firm against every temptation and trial invites association, not with Charles the royal martyr, but with Puritan dissidents subjected to harassment and persecution. The Jesus–Satan debates can also lead readers to think rightly about kingship, prophecy, idolatry, millenarian zeal, the proper uses of civil power, the place of secular learning, and the abuses of pleasure, glory, and power. Significantly, the poem's structure gives primary attention to the Messiah's kingdom and its relation to secular monarchies and their values, giving over Books Two and Three, and much of Book Four, to that issue. Milton's Jesus is the projection of his author in a teaching role, as he undertakes,

---

1. See, for example, Stanley Fish, "Inaction and Silence: The Reader in Paradise Regained," in Joseph A. Wittreich, Jr., ed., *Calm of Mind: Tercentenary Essays on Paradise Regained and Samson Agonistes* (Cleveland, Ohio, and London, 1971), 25–47; and Alan Fisher, "Why is Paradise Regained So Cold?" *MS* 14 (1980), 195–217.

By winning words to conquer willing hearts,
And make perswasion do the work of fear;
At least to try, and teach the erring Soul
Not wilfully mis-doing, but unware
Misled.   (1.222–6)

In the epic proposition and invocation the Miltonic Bard, who in
Paradise Lost had explored in four extended Proems his authorial
anxieties, difficulties, and choices, now adopts a curiously recessive
and objective stance throughout. The opening lines, the only time
in the poem when he speaks of himself or invokes the inspiring
Spirit, are marked by an easy, confident tone:

I who e're while the happy Garden sung,
By one mans disobedience lost, now sing
Recover'd Paradise to all mankind,
By one mans firm obedience fully tri'd
Through all temptation, and the Tempter foil'd
In all his wiles, defeated and repuls't,
And *Eden* rais'd in the wast Wilderness.
  Thou spirit who ledst this glorious Eremite
Into the Desert, his Victorious Field
Against the Spiritual Foe, and broughtst him thence
By proof the undoubted Son of God, inspire,
As thou art wont, my prompted Song else mute,
And bear through highth or depth of natures bounds
With prosperous wing full summ'd to tell of deeds
Above Heroic, though in secret done,
And unrecorded left through many an Age,
Worthy t'have not remain'd so long unsung. (1.1–17)

The line "inspire, / As thou art wont" suggests that his new confidence stems from his experience of the Spirit's aid in his long epic
and his sense of that aid continuing in this "prompted" song, which
would be "else mute." It may owe something as well to the greater
familiarity of the new locale—the fallen world of history, not the
eternal places. Here the Miltonic Bard records what happens, what
is said, what seems to be the case, but he does not often comment
on speeches and scenes as he did in *Paradise Lost*, having given over
the role of authoritative critic and judge to his hero, Jesus.

The epic proposition makes the rather startling claim that this
poem treats a vastly more noble and heroic subject than *Paradise
Lost*, whose hero conquers his enemy, regains the regions lost to
Satan, and establishes his own realm—in this, more like Aeneas
than like Adam. These opening lines allude to the verses, then
widely accepted as genuine, that introduce the *Aeneid* in most

Renaissance editions, supposedly announcing Virgil's movement from pastoral and georgic to an epic subject.[2] That echo and the reference to *Paradise Lost* as a poem about a happy garden suggest, with witty audacity, that Milton has now, like Virgil, graduated from pastoral apprentice-work to the true epic subject, the spiritual warfare and victory of Jesus. Also, several allusions to the Book of Job suggest that Milton is now carrying out a poetic project he imagined a quarter of a century earlier in the *Reason of Church-Government*, when he proposed Virgil and Tasso as models for a long epic and the Book of Job as a "brief model" (*YP* I, 813). This poem is in part shaped by the exegetical tradition that interpreted Job as epic, and also by the long tradition of biblical "brief epics" in three or four books, in Latin and in the vernacular literatures.[3]

Milton reworked and adapted epic conventions and topics to his unusual subject. He transformed the central epic episode, the single combat of hero and antagonist, into a three-day verbal battle, a poem-long intellectual and moral struggle. The poem begins *in medias res* with Christ's baptism. There are two Infernal Councils (held in mid-air rather than Hell because Satan has now gained that region), and a Council in Heaven in which God prophesies his Son's immediate and ultimate victory over Satan. Also, there are two transformed epic recitals—Christ's meditation about his youthful experiences and aspirations, and Mary's reminiscenses about the prophecies and promises attending the hero's early life—as well as a transformed prophetic vision in which the hero, instead of viewing his *own* destined kingdom as Aeneas does, sees and rejects all the kingdoms that are not his. There is an epic catalogue of the kingdoms of the World displayed to Jesus; a martial pageant of the Parthian warriors; and a few striking epic similes in Book Four, in which Jesus assaulted by Satan is compared to a winepress vainly attacked by buzzing bees, to a solid rock against which waves ineffectually beat, to Hercules conquering Antaeus, and to Oedipus overthrowing the Sphinx. Milton sets up the Jobean "brief epic" frame at the outset, as Satan in the character of "Adversary" wandering to and fro upon the earth comes upon another assembly, Christ's baptism, at which a

2. See the Loeb *Virgil*, ed. H. Rushton Fairclough (London and Cambridge, Mass., 1960), I, 240–1: "Ille ego, qui quondam gracili modulatus avena / carmen, et egressus silvis vicina coegi / ut quamvis avido parerent arva colono, / gratum opus agricolis; at nunc horrentia Martis / Arma virumque cano. . . ." (I am he who once tuned my song on a slender reed, then, leaving the woodland, constrained the neighboring fields to serve the husbandmen, however grasping—a work welcome to farmers: but now of Mars' bristling. Arms and the Man I sing.)
3. Among them are Sannazaro's *De Partu Virginis*, Vida's *Christiad*, and Giles Fletcher's *Christ's Victorie and Triumph* (1610), the second book of which treats Christ's temptation in the wilderness as Spenserian allegory. See Barbara K. Lewalski, *Milton's Brief Epic: The Genre, Meaning, and Art of Paradise Regained* (Providence and London, 1996), 3–129.

superlative hero is exalted by God as his champion.[4] Like *Paradise Lost* this poem also incorporates other genres into the epic frame: continuous dialogue in which Satan's inflated epic rhetoric is met by Jesus's spare answers; a pastoral grove where Satan presents a sensuous banquet and also the more refined and enchanting "Olive Groves of Academe"; a romance topos in which Jesus reprises the conventional situation of a young knight who meets his first tests in the wilderness before being recognized as champion or king; and angelic hymns at the beginning and end of the temptation sequence. But this poem eschews the soaring, eloquent style of *Paradise Lost* for one appropriate to this subject: more restrained, dialogic, and tense with the parry and thrust of intellectual exchange.

Milton's Arianism is central to this poem, allowing for some drama in the debate–duel between Jesus and Satan even though the reader knows that Jesus will not fall. In *Paradise Lost* Milton portrayed the Son in heaven as mutable and as sharing only such part of the divine knowledge and power as God devolved upon him at certain times. Here he portrays the incarnate Christ in accordance with *De Doctrina Christiana's* treatment of *kenosis* as a real emptying out of the divine knowledge and power the Son exercised in heaven, so that he is "liable to sin" and subject to death in both natures (YP VI, 438–40). The poem opens with Jesus in that situation: God describes him to the angels in almost Socinian terms: they now and men hereafter are to learn from the temptation episode "From what consummate vertue I have chose / This perfect Man, by merit call'd my Son, / To earn Salvation for the Sons of men" (1.165–7). Then, as Jesus withstands the several temptations, he gains, apparently by divine illumination, an ever more complete understanding of who he is and what he is to do.

The question of identity is the primary focus for the poem's tension, centering on the title "Son of God" bestowed in a special way upon Jesus at his baptism. As Satan later remarks, that title "bears no single sence." Revealing some feelings of sibling rivalry with Jesus, Satan declares, "The Son of God I also am, or was, / And if I was, I am; relation stands; / All men are Sons of God," and then indicates that one purpose of his temptations is to discover "In what degree or meaning thou art call'd / The Son of God" (4.514–20). In his first council a puzzled Satan recognizes that Jesus shows some glimpses of his Father's glory, but he cannot imagine that this humble man is one with the Son in Heaven: "His first-begot we know, and sore have felt, / When his fierce thunder drove us to the

---

4. See Job 1:6–12. The character Job is named on six occasions (*PR* 1.147, 369, 425; 3.64, 67, 95); the book is quoted twice (1.33–4, 368). And either the book or the tradition of commentary on it are alluded to on at least ten other occasions.

deep; / Who this is we must learn" (1.89–91). Jesus's meditation as he enters the desert shows that he also has no recollection of his former state. He has learned what he knows of himself as the promised Messiah from his mother's testimony and from reading the Prophets: that his birth was miraculous, that he is "King of Israel born" and will sit on David's throne; and that he is to work redemption for humankind through "many a hard assay even to the death" (1.254–66). But he does not yet understand the full meaning of the prophetic metaphors, or of the divine Sonship proclaimed at his baptism, or just what his "God-like office now mature" will entail (1.188). He is conscious of his limited human knowledge, being led "to what intent / I learn not yet, perhaps I need not know," but also of the guidance and ongoing illumination of the Spirit: "For what concerns my knowledge God reveals" (1.291–3). These uncertainties sometimes make for moments of emotional distress, as when the hungry Jesus experiences a hunger dream in the desert and questions, "Where will this end" (2.245). Or when Satan "inly rack't" voices his psychic desperation to have it over with, even though it means his destruction: "I would be at the worst; worst is my Port, / My harbour and my ultimate repose, / The end I would attain, my final good" (3.209–11).

In this poem Milton portrays a Satan who has degenerated from what he was in *Paradise Lost*; evil has further coarsened his nature, though he is still cunning, even brilliant. His advantage in the temptations is his direct observation of human motives and human weakness throughout history, which Jesus knows only through wide reading. But more than compensating for that is the divine illumination Jesus merits, leading him to understand the spiritual meaning of the scriptural metaphors and prophecies which the literal-minded Satan cannot fathom. The poem's action turns on a central paradox: Satan appears to do all the acting, dancing around Jesus in a fever of motion, trying one approach and one argument after another, while Jesus remains impassive and unmoved. Yet it is in Jesus's consciousness that real change takes place, as he progresses by somewhat uneven stages to full understanding, whereas Satan cannot resolve the puzzle about Jesus's Sonship and mission until his utter defeat and fall from the tower force realization upon him.

Milton creates epic scope in his brief epic by making the temptation episode encapsulate past and future history through typological reference and allusion. God sets these terms, describing Jesus to the angels as an "abler" Job and a second Adam who will win "by Conquest what the first man lost / By fallacy surpriz'd," and build a new Eden (1.151–5). God also declares that he is to lay down in the wilderness the "rudiments" (157) of his great warfare, epitomizing there the exercise of his office throughout history. The debates between Jesus and Satan make continual reference to commonly accepted Old Testament and classical figures of Jesus and the functions of his office—Moses, Elijah, Gideon, David, Job, Socrates. To these, Satan proposes counter-models—Balaam, Antipater, Caesar, Alexander, the schools of Greek philosophy—or else insists that Jesus must conform himself exactly to his types and thereby limit himself by the mandate of the past. Satan's temptations presume the classical notion of history as cyclical repetition—what has been must be again—whereas Jesus must learn to fulfill and subsume the types so as to redefine history as process and re-creation.[5]

The poem's complex structure develops several interrelated paradigms. At one level Jesus is the "second Adam" withstanding the temptations to which Adam and Eve succumbed, which were linked in the exegetical tradition of the "Triple Equation" to the root sins of humankind enumerated in 1 John 2:16: sensuality (in Protestant versions, distrust), avarice or ambition, and vainglory.[6] That paradigm is explored especially in the first temptation (distrust), and in the first three segments of the second: the sensual banquet, wealth and kingship, and glory. Related to this are the three kinds of lives Plato defines in *The Republic*: the sensual life, the active life, and (in the Athens temptation) the contemplative life. Also, temptations are addressed to the three functions of Christ's office: prophet or teacher (the first temptation); king, i.e. ruler and defender of his church and people (the offers of Israel, Parthia, Rome, and Athens); and priest, i.e. redemptive sacrifice and mediator (the storm and tower temptations).[7] Into all the temptations Milton inserts bold commentary on fraught contemporary issues.

Satan offers the first temptation—to turn stones into bread—in the guise of a shepherd "Following, as seem'd, the quest of some stray Ewe" (1.315), a parody of Jesus's role as good shepherd. The issues involve distrust—accepting the guidance of Satan—and also Jesus's role as prophet or teacher. Satan asks Jesus to accept him formally as a prophet (he gives oracles to the gentiles) and to grant him continued access, as God allowed the reprobate Balaam to prophesy and allows hypocrites and atheists to conduct religious rites at his altars. If Jesus were to accept him on these terms he would sanction that Puritan *bete noir*, the association of holy and profane together in the established church and the abuses it gave rise to both in the Laudian church and in the Restoration:

---

5. Lewalski, "Time and History in *Paradise Regained*," in *The Prison and the Pinnacle*, ed. Balachandra Rajan (Toronto, 1972), 49–81.
6. See Elizabeth M. Pope, *Paradise Regained: The Tradition and the Poem* (Baltimore, 1947).
7. Here as in *De Doctrina Christiana* (YP VI, 430–7) Milton conceives that office and its three functions as many Protestant exegetes do.

> Thy Father, who is holy, wise, and pure,
> Suffers the Hypocrite or Atheous Priest
> To tread his Sacred Courts, and minister
> About his Altar, handling holy things,
> Praying or vowing, and vouchsaf'd his voice
> To *Balaam* Reprobate, a Prophet yet
> Inspir'd; disdain not such access to me.   (1.486–92)

But Jesus pointedly refuses to sanction the parish principle and those abuses—merely observing that God, for the time being, permits them: "I bid not nor forbid; do as thou find'st / Permission from above; thou canst not more" (1.495–6). Claiming his own role as prophet, Jesus asserts the Miltonic—and radical sectarian—principle of the entire sufficiency of the internal Spirit's teaching, which makes authorized ministers superfluous:

> God hath now sent his living Oracle
> Into the World, to teach his final will,
> And sends his Spirit of Truth henceforth to dwell
> In pious Hearts, an inward Oracle
> To all truth requisite for men to know.   (1.460–4)

The issues in the long kingdoms temptation are focused by the expectation on all sides that Jesus will soon become an earthly king. Satan expects God to advance him in "the head of Nations . . . / Their King, their Leader, and Supream on Earth" (1.98–9). Jesus at first thought himself called "To rescue *Israel* from the *Roman* yoke, / Then to subdue and quell o're all the earth / Brute violence and proud Tyrannick pow'r, / Till truth were freed, and equity restor'd" (1.217–20). And the apostles, anticipating millenarian Puritans, imagine the moment at hand for the Messiah's kingly reign in Israel:

> Now, now, for sure, deliverance is at hand,
> The Kingdom shall to *Israel* be restor'd: . . .
>   God of *Israel*,
> Send thy Messiah forth, the time is come;
> Behold the Kings of the Earth how they oppress
> Thy chosen, to what highth thir pow'r unjust
> They have exalted, and behind them cast
> All fear of thee, arise and vindicate
> Thy Glory, free thy people from thir yoke.   (2.35–48)

Countering these expectations, Jesus clarifies what his kingship is to be in history. First, it is the kingdom within "Which every wise and vertuous man attains" (2.468): by his temperance and ethical knowledge Jesus defines that kingdom and offers a trenchant critique of the values and practices of secular monarchies. Second, it is his own spiritual kingdom, the invisible church, which he comes by stages to understand and explain. Finally, it is the millennial rule he will exercise in the distant future, over all realms and monarchs.

Satan offers the kingdoms temptations in the guise of a courtier bred "in City, or Court, or Palace" dispensing needful worldly advice to the rustic Jesus. First, a lavish and deceptive banquet invites the now-hungry Jesus to intemperance by its abundance of sensuous pleasures: "Alas how simple, to these Cates compar'd, / Was that crude Apple that diverted *Eve* (2.348–9). The scene evokes extravagant banquets at the Stuart courts: a table "richly spred, in regal mode"; dishes piled high with the noblest "Beasts of chase, or Fowl of game"; strings and woodwinds playing "Harmonious Airs" (2.340–62), and sexual objects suited to every preference—ladies fairer than those who tempted Romance knights and "tall stripling youths" fairer than Ganymede. Despite Satan's disclaimer, this banquet contains foods forbidden under the Law, to force Jesus either to accept those dietary prohibitions or dispense with them before the appointed time. Also, though presented as nature's free offering, it is quite literally the Devil's table, the very symbol of idolatry. Side-stepping all these intellectual traps, Jesus refuses the banquet as the gift of an evil giver, and lays claim himself, as nature's Lord, to all nature's goods.

To Satan's offer of riches as a necessary means to accomplish great deeds and gain a kingdom, Jesus responds with an extended critique of monarchy based in part on Plato and Aristotle. To Satan's examples of wealthy kings he opposes several Hebrew judges and Roman republican leaders who rose from poverty to greatness,[8] as well as "the shepherd lad" David (439) who became Israel's king. Rejecting "with like aversion" both riches and realms (457), he restates Milton's core political principle, that rule over the self is a better kingship and that without it a ruler is unfit to govern others: "Subject himself to Anarchy within, / Or lawless passions in him which he serves" (2.471–2). Like Aristotle, Jesus claims that it is more magnanimous to give or relinquish a kingdom than to assume one,[9] and then asserts the greater worthiness of his own spiritual kingship:

> But to guide Nations in the way of truth
> By saving Doctrine, and from errour lead
> To know, and knowing worship God aright,
> Is yet more Kingly, this attracts the Soul,
> Governs the inner man, the nobler part,
> That other o're the body only reigns,

8. Jesus cites the judges Gideon and Jeptha, as well as heroes of the Roman republic, Quintius, Curtius, Fabricius, and Regulus (*PR* 2.445–9).
9. Aristotle, *Nicomachean Ethics* IV.ii.1123b, trans. H. Rackham (Cambridge, Mass., and London, 1926). For Milton's praise of Queen Christina of Sweden for relinquishing a kingdom see *Defensio Secunda*, YP IV.1, 605–6.

> And oft by force, which to a generous mind
> So reigning can be no sincere delight. (2.473–80)

Next, Satan urges Jesus to seek glory and empire by emulating great warriors and world conquerors—Alexander the Great, Julius Caesar, Scipio Africanus, Pompey—and Jesus responds by redefining true fame and the acts that merit it. As in *Lycidas*, true fame is bestowed by God; it cannot emanate from the people at large, "a herd confus'd, / A miscellaneous rabble" (3.49–50). Nor does it rightly belong to conventional epic heroes, military conquerors, and empire-builders, who "rob and spoil, burn, slaughter, and enslave / Peaceable Nations" (3.75–7).[1] It pertains rather to "deeds of peace, by wisdom eminent," to Job who bore Satan's wrongs "with Saintly patience," and the wise teacher Socrates, "For truths sake suffering death unjust" (3.91–8). Emphasizing that Alexander and Caesar "must be titl'd Gods" and idolatrously worshipped (3.81–3), Milton has his hero castigate as "sacrilegious" all those—including by implication divine-right kings—who seek such glory, which to God "alone of right belongs" (3.140–1).[2]

With the line "But to a Kingdom thou art born, ordain'd / To sit upon thy Father *David's* Throne" (3.152–3), Satan turns the discourse from Jesus's own desires and values to the kingly role prescribed by his office. Typically, Satan takes literally the prophecy that Jesus is to reign as king of Israel, while Jesus redefines Israel to refer to the invisible church his spiritual kingdom, and his millennial kingdom to come. Holding up Judas Maccabaeus as a model of zeal and duty, Satan goads Jesus to seize his kingdom at once, and so free his country from "her Heathen servitude" (3.165–76) to Roman rulers who have violated God's Temple and God's Law. Jesus's answer applies to his historical situation and also to that of Milton's defeated Puritans. Its terms reprove radical millenarian expectation of Christ's imminent return as king, and repudiate Fifth Monarchist uprisings, such as Venner's 1661 rebellion. But they also urge continued expectation of and right preparation for that ultimate Millennial Kingdom by waiting on God's time and learning from present trials:

> What if he hath decreed that I shall first
> Be try'd in humble state, and things adverse,
> By tribulations, injuries, insults,

1. This tirade is reminiscent of Michael's denunciation of the Giants who sought fame by slaughter and conquest (*PL* 11.640–99).
2. For the echoes throughout this episode of Cicero, Seneca, and various Stoic–Christian texts denouncing Alexander and Caesar for seeking false renown conferred by the multitude and for the impiety of seeking divine honors, see Lewalski, *Milton's Brief Epic*, 236–41.

> Contempts, and scorns, and snares, and violence,
> Suffering, abstaining, quietly expecting
> Without distrust or doubt, that he may know
> What I can suffer, how obey?   (3.188–94)

Then Satan from a high mountain shows Jesus a massive parade of Parthian armaments and troops, insisting that he can only gain and maintain the throne of Israel and deliver the ten lost tribes enslaved in Parthian territory by conquest of or league with Parthia and its military might (3.357–70). This offer of the wrong means to establish Christ's kingdom alludes to that constant target of Milton's polemic, the use of civil power by Protestant magistrates to establish, defend, or maintain the church. Jesus insists that his spiritual kingdom, the invisible church, has no need whatever of "fleshly arm, / And fragile arms . . . / Plausible to the world, to me worth naught" (3.387–93). Nor will he need or want such arms to begin his Millennial reign, which was thought to follow soon after the return of the ten lost tribes to Jerusalem and their conversion. Jesus refuses this invitation because he cannot liberate those who enslave themselves by deliberate participation in idolatry: the terms also apply to the English who, as Milton put it in *The Readie & Easie Way*, chose them a Captain back for Egypt when they supported the Restoration of the monarchy and the Anglican church. But he holds out hope that God may—in his good time—call them back in repentance and freedom, the true precondition for the Millennial Kingdom:

> Should I of these the liberty regard,
> Who freed, as to their antient Patrimony,
> Unhumbl'd, unrepentant, unreform'd,
> Headlong would follow; and to thir Gods perhaps
> Of *Bethel* and of *Dan*? no, let them serve
> Thir enemies, who serve Idols with God.
> Yet he at length, time to himself best known,
> Remembring *Abraham* by some wond'rous call
> May bring them back repentant and sincere,
> And at their passing cleave the *Assyrian* flood,
> When to their native land with joy they hast.
>   (3.427–37)

At the end of Book Three Jesus is termed "*Israel's* true King" (3.441), having understood that his Millennial Kingdom cannot be precipitously installed, that his spiritual kingdom, the invisible church, can make no use of civil power, and that political liberation cannot be won for inner slaves. Yet by teaching people how to free themselves from religious and monarchical idolatry Christ's kingship has profound implications for political liberty.

Imperial Rome, with its splendid architecture, sumptuous banquets, and every manifestation of dominion and glory, incorporates all the previous attractions: "ample Territory, wealth and power, / Civility of Manners, Arts, and Arms, / And long Renown" (4.82–4). It is the great kingdom of "all the world" (4.105), described in terms appropriate to the reign of the degenerate and lascivious emperor Tiberius, but also inviting the usual Protestant associations of Rome with the Roman Catholic church, and that church with the great Antichrist in the Book of Revelation.[3] Rome's imperial palace evokes St Peter's basilica, with its "compass huge, and high / The Structure, skill of noblest Architects, / With gilded battlements, conspicuous far" (4.51–3), and its banquets with rare wines quaffed in rich vessels suggest the Mass. Satan's observation that "All Nations now to *Rome* obedience pay" (4.80) points to the danger to Protestant England from Charles II's suspected adherence to, or at least sympathy with, Roman Catholicism and the openly professed Catholicism of his brother and heir. Satan urges Jesus to expel the "monster" Tiberius from his throne and take the empire over, thereby freeing the Roman populace (and Israel as part of the empire) from their "servile yoke:" the defeat of the Roman papal Antichrist was commonly expected to inaugurate the Millennium. But Jesus refuses to free Romans who degenerately abandoned republican virtue and so are "Deservedly made vassel" (4.100), a refusal which extends to Roman Catholics enslaved to the pope and to English Anglicans and Puritans who have invited that danger by restoring the Stuarts. But he then prophesies, in metaphor, that his Millennial Kingdom will at last subdue all others:

> What wise and valiant man would seek to free
> These thus degenerate, by themselves enslav'd,
> Or could of inward slaves make outward free?
> Know therefore when my season comes to sit
> On *David's* Throne, it shall be like a tree
> Spreading and over-shadowing all the Earth,
> Or as a stone that shall to pieces dash
> All Monarchies besides throughout the world,
> And of my Kingdom there shall be no end:
> Means there shall be to this, but what the means,
> Is not for thee to know, nor me to tell. (4.143–53)

---

3. Cf. John Lightfoot's exegesis of the kingdoms' temptation: "The object that the Devill presented *Christ* withall in this spectacle, was Rome, her Empire and glory. For 1. That Empire is called by the very name of *all the world*, Luke 2.5. . . . When *Satan* cannot at the entrance of the Gospel perswade Christ by all the pompe at *Rome*, to do like *Antichrist*, he setteth up *Antichrist* at *Rome*, to bee an enemy to the Gospel in all the continuance of it:" *The Harmony of the Foure Evangelists*, 2 vols (London, 1644–7), II, 30–2.

The tree seems to refer to the power of his spiritual kingdom to transform all the earth; the stone refers to his Millennial Kingdom which will crush all earthly monarchies and their evils, according to the usual exegesis of the prophecy in Daniel 2:44. But Jesus refuses to say when or how his Millennial Kingdom will come, intimating that it will come when people are prepared for it, by internalizing and enacting in history the virtue and love of liberty his gospel promotes. At this point a sharp exchange between Jesus and Satan uncovers the unstated condition of these offers: worship of Satan, which is involved whenever any of these worldly goods are made into idols. In some ways this near-last poem reprises Milton's first major poem, the Nativity ode: in both the casting out of idols is the necessary precondition for the establishment of Christ's kingdom in this world.

Milton then contrives a still more striking climax. Satan presents Athens, the zenith of classical learning, poetry, and oratory, as the fount of the nonmaterial goods Jesus needs to achieve his own defined goals, though, significantly, he does not claim that learning is in his gift. The evocative description of pastoral delights in the "Olive Grove of *Academe*" recalls those delightful scenes of retired study in idyllic pastoral surroundings that the young Milton praised in *Il Penseroso*, Prolusion VII, and *Lycidas*:[4]

> See there the Olive Grove of *Academe*,
> *Plato's* retirement, where the *Attic* Bird
> Trills her thick-warbl'd notes the summer long,
> There flowrie hill *Hymettus* with the sound
> Of Bees industrious murmur oft invites
> To studious musing; there *Ilissus* rouls
> His whispering stream. (4.244–50)

The beauty of the passage indicates the continued attraction of retired study for Milton, but his hero (like Milton himself) resists that lure to continue his active work in the world. The harshness of Jesus's responses seems to reveal Milton's deep-seated anxieties around the issue of learning, for they apparently repudiate the classical learning that has been so important to Milton throughout his life. Classical philosophy is "false, or little else but dreams, / Conjectures, fancies, built on nothing firm" (4.291–2). The Hebrew poets are far superior to classical poets, who sing "The vices of thir Deities, and thir own" (4.340) and, once their "swelling Epithetes" are removed, are "Thin sown with aught of profit or delight" (4.343–5). And the Greek orators are far inferior to the Hebrew prophets in teaching "The solid rules of Civil Government" (4.358).

---

4. See B. Douglas Trevor, "Learned Appearances: Writing Scholarly and Literary Selves in Early Modern England" (dissertation, Harvard University, 1999), 298–368.

But Jesus recognizes that Satan's version of learning is tainted, and Milton challenges his readers to make similar discriminations. Satan is here an arch-Sophist, proposing universal knowledge not as a way to truth but as a means to power, glory, and pleasure: "As thy Empire must extend, / So let extend thy mind o'er all the world"; "Be famous . . . / By wisdom" (4.22–3). Satan praises Plato chiefly for the highly refined sensory delights of his pastoral retirement, Aristotle as the teacher of a world conqueror, Socrates for his great influence on later schools, Homer for the envy Apollo showed for his poem, Demosthenes for his ability to promote war—degrading the learning Athens represents even judged by its own humanist lights. Satan also seeks to undermine Jesus's unique role as spiritual teacher by insisting on the *necessity* of classical learning for the contemplative life he seems to favor, the attainment of the inner kingship: "These rules will render thee a King compleat / Within thy self" (4.283–4). He also insists that Christ's prophetic and kingly offices of teaching and ruling by persuasion require him to converse with and confute the gentiles in their own terms. Jesus, however, denies that the classical writers are sources of true wisdom. Having no knowledge of the Creation, Fall, and redemption by grace, they are "Ignorant of themselves, of God much more" (4.310), though he acknowledges and he has himself quoted their moral teachings, informed by the light of nature. Since Jesus's mission is to bring true wisdom into history he will not accept their lower knowledge as in any way necessary, though he may possess it: "Think not but that I know these things, or think / I know them not; not therefore am I short / Of knowing what I aught: he who receives / Light from above, from the fountain of light, / No other doctrine needs" (4.286–90). In this repudiation, Milton's Jesus reinforces for his church the position Milton defended in *The Likeliest Means to Remove Hirelings*, that learning is not necessary to ministers, who require only knowledge of scripture and the Spirit's illumination. Jesus's answer (and Milton's) does not repudiate learning as such, but flatly denies that it is *necessary* to virtue, salvation, or the accomplishment of God's work in the world. Also, in Jesus's refusal to value books above their users, we hear some echo of Milton's frequent disparagement of scholarly authorities, as he insisted on his own originality and authorial parity with other writers and teachers:

> However many books
> Wise men have said are wearisom; who reads
> Incessantly, and to his reading brings not
> A spirit and judgment equal or superior,
> (And what he brings, what needs he elsewhere seek)
> Uncertain and unsettl'd still remains,

> Deep verst in books and shallow in himself,
> Crude or intoxicate, collecting toys,
> And trifles for choice matters, worth a spunge;
> As Children gathering pibles on the shore. (4.321–30)

In the storm-tower sequence Jesus endures with patience the final test of the kingdom within—violence—which foreshadows his Passion and death, the fulfillment of his priestly office. The tower episode is contrived as the ultimate identity test: Satan supposes that by placing Jesus on the pinnacle of the Temple he will save himself by miracle if he is divine, while if he is merely human he will fall or else sin by presumption if he casts himself down expecting divine rescue. But as he calmly maintains the posture into which Satan has thrust him, his passion becomes an active conquest over Satan: he is preserved by God and at the same time, it seems, is granted a full awareness of his divine Sonship: "Tempt not the Lord thy God, he said and stood. / But Satan smitten with amazement fell" (4.561–2). As Milton presents it, these episodes have relevance for Puritan dissidents subjected to the storms and tempests of royalist oppression and invited, like Jesus, to read their plight as a portent of God's displeasure and their coming destruction. But the bright day that follows the storm and Satan's fall from the tower invite a different reading: as Christ's resurrection followed his Passion and his victory on the tower foreshadows his victory over Satan at the Last Day, so may those dissidents expect a better day—and in due time a victory—if they endure their trials patiently, avoid precipitous action, and develop their spiritual strength.

Jesus's victory is celebrated with an angelic banquet and a long hymn of praise that make explicit his identity with the Son in Heaven as the "True Image of the Father" (2.596), and also foreshadow the Millennium. The hymn, like the Father's speech at the outset of the temptation, indicates by shifts in tense and perspective that Jesus's victory is now complete, but that it is also just beginning. He has "now . . . aveng'd / Supplanted Adam" and "regain'd lost Paradise," but he is about to "begin to save mankind" (4.606–8, 634–5). Because Jesus now understands himself and has been exercised in all the "rudiments" or root concerns of his great warfare, he has already won the essential victory. But that victory must now be worked out in history, as others respond to his teaching and are thereby enabled to become virtuous and free. Only then will Christ's Millennial Kingdom come.

Milton ends the poem quietly. Like Adam and Eve wandering forth to begin the human history whose end Adam has foreseen, Jesus returns from the angelic celebration of the prophesied end to his human beginnings, to live out the history the temptation episode

foreshadowed: "hee unobserv'd / Home to his Mothers house private return'd" (4.638–9).

*   *   *

JOHN CAREY

A Work in Praise of Terrorism?[†]

September 11 and Samson Agonistes

The tragedies of September 11 and their consequences are far more
important than literature. Even to discuss them in a literary context
may seem trivializing. However, events in the real world inevitably
change the way we read. The Holocaust, to take an obvious example,
changed much of the Western canon. One text on which September
11 has an immediate bearing is Milton's *Samson Agonistes*, usually
interpreted as a work in praise of terrorism. Critics have traditionally
seen Samson's massacre of the Philistines as a mark of spiritual
regeneration, identifying it as Milton's fantasy-vengeance on his Royalist conquerors. Since Milton was a subtle-minded poet not a murderous bigot, this reading has always had its opponents. But it has
remained dominant, encouraged by the modern view of Milton as
primarily interested in politics and only incidentally a poet.

Reading Stanley Fish's *How Milton Works* last summer, I found
him strongly opposed to any adverse criticism of Samson's terrorist
attack:

> In the end the only value we can put on Samson's action is the
> value he gives it in context. Within the situation, it is an expres-
> sion, however provisional, of his reading of the divine will, and
> insofar as it represents his desire to conform to that will, it is a
> virtuous action. *No other standard for evaluating it exists* [Fish's
> italics]—this is what the reader learns when his attempts to
> apply other standards are frustrated—and no other explanation
> of it can be maintained without distorting the experience of the
> play. . . . Samson's act is praiseworthy because he intends it to
> be answerable to the divine will; whether it is or not, especially
> in the terms in which he conceives it, he cannot know, nor can
> we; and in relation to the problem of judging him as a moral
> being, whether it is or not does not matter.

If Fish meant this to be provocative he was, in my case, completely
successful. To me his viewpoint seemed monstrous—a licence for any

† From *The London Times Literary Supplement* (*TLS*), September 6, 2002, pp. 15–17.
Reprinted by permission.

fanatic to commit atrocity. Then came September 11, and in the weeks that followed I could not keep his words out of my mind. I still cannot. The events of that day seem like a devilish implementation of his arguments. The similarities between the biblical Samson and the hijackers are obvious. Like them Samson sacrifices himself to achieve his ends. Like them he destroys many innocent victims, whose lives, hopes and loves are all quite unknown to him personally. He is, in effect, a suicide bomber, and like the suicide bombers he believes that his massacre is an expression of God's will. Applying Fish's opinions about Samson to the events of September 11 we find that the action of the murderers was, in so far as they desired to conform to the divine will, "virtuous" and "praiseworthy", and *"no other standard for evaluating it exists"*. If this is truly what *Samson Agonistes* teaches, should it not be withdrawn from schools and colleges and, indeed, banned more generally as an incitement to terrorism?

But is it what *Samson Agonistes* teaches? Milton's drama is, in fact, a drastic rewriting of the Samson story. It calls into question Samson's motivation, and whether he has any divine sanction for his suicide attack. In the Book of Judges Samson prays for strength immediately before pulling down the Philistine building (Judges 16:28–30). Since he does acquire the necessary strength, it seems that God answers his prayer and is complicit in the slaughter. Of course, people may acquire unexpected strength from other sources than the godhead, especially when seized by passion or fanaticism. But the implication of the Judges account is that God is involved.

In Milton it is different. Crucially, Milton omits Samson's prayer, as narrated in Judges. The messenger reports that, before the catastrophe, Samson stood silently with his head bowed:

as one who prayed,
Or some great matter in his mind revolved.

Perhaps he prays, perhaps not. If he does pray, his prayer cannot be the same as the biblical Samson's. He does not need to pray for strength, for his strength has already returned, as the "stupendious" feats he has just performed to entertain the Philistine audience testify. The "rousing motions" that he felt earlier, when he agreed to accompany the Philistine officer to the theatre, have been interpreted by some critics as evidence that he is in the grip of some kind of divine guidance. But they may signal his purely human excitement about a glimpsed opportunity. They may mark the moment when it dawns on him that attendance at the Philistine theatre could open an ingenious way to his revenge.

In this final stage of the drama we cannot know what is going on in Samson's mind. Milton conceals it from us. Just before the catastrophe Samson tells the Philistine audience that so far he has performed feats they have devised. But:

> Now of my own accord such other trial
> I mean to show you of my strength, yet greater;
> As with amaze shall strike all who behold.

Some critics have seized on this as proof that Samson does not believe he is conforming to God's plan when he destroys the theatre. He acts, he implies, independently. But the argument is not conclusive. In context the phrase "of my own accord" merely distinguishes his next feat from the earlier prescribed ones. Besides, he is addressing his enemies, and is anxious not to alarm them lest they try to escape or intervene. Even if he did believe he was about to comply with the divine will by massacring them, it would be impolitic to tell them so at this point.

All through this last phase Milton hides Samson's thoughts and, for that matter, God's. When he destroys the theatre Samson may think he is carrying out God's will, or he may be following his purely human impulse to revenge. If he does believe he is carrying out God's will, he may be correct or he may be mistaken (as his father thinks he was mistaken earlier in attributing his marriage to "divine impulsion"). There is insufficient evidence to eliminate any of these possibilities.

The complications I have touched on have long been apparent to Miltonists, and Fish's book shows most of them are apparent to him. What is strange, given the text's indefiniteness, is his dogmatism. From where does he derive his certainty that "Samson's act is praiseworthy because he intends it to be answerable to the divine will"? Faced with the horror of Samson's crime, on what does he base his assertion that *"no other standard for evaluating it exists"* apart from the perpetrator's desire to perform what he takes to be God's intention? To most people common humanity supplies a *"standard for evaluating"* mass murder. Why does it not do so for Fish? As we have seen, Milton rewrites his biblical source, removing Samson's prayer and the consequent restoration of his strength. In the Book of Judges, these seemed to show that the slaughter was God's will. Their excision throws the question open. As Fish concedes, Milton's Samson cannot know whether his vengeance conforms to the divine purpose or not. But if he acts merely on the presumption that it does, as Fish seems to assume, then the lesson Milton's drama teaches is that if you suppose you have private access to God's mind, and act on the supposition, it can have hideous consequences. For many, both Christian and Muslim, that is a lesson of September 11 also.

Fish claims that unless we see Samson's action as virtuous we distort "the experience of the play". Of course, that experience must be different for each reader. But it would be a troubling reader who did not feel some qualms about the sentiments expressed fol-

lowing Samson's death. The grisly glee with which the Israelites
receive news of the atrocity found a match in the pictures screened
on British television in the immediate aftermath of September 11,
which showed people in Arab dress dancing for joy in the streets.
Particularly horrible is the satisfaction with which Samson's coreligionists contemplate the long-term effects of his murders. It is
not just that many have died. A bonus is that the grief will desolate
the lives of relatives and loved ones far into the future. Samson has,
his father rejoices, left the bereaved "years of mourning".

It is ignorance as well as hatred that allows the Israelites this
jubilation. They have not seen the deaths they celebrate. But Milton shows us the effect on one Israelite who has—the messenger.
When the din and clamour of the theatre's destruction are heard,
Samson's father Manoa, and those waiting with him, wonder what
has happened. It is suggested that maybe God has restored Samson's eyesight and he is making his way towards them "over heaps of
slaughtered". Manoa greets the idea with enthusiasm: "That were a
joy presumptuous to be thought".

Then, within ten lines, the messenger enters, desperately trying
to rid his mind of what he has seen:

> O whither shall I run, or which way fly
> The sight of this so horrid spectacle
> Which erst my eyes beheld and yet behold;
> For dire imagination still pursues me.

The effect is rather like that in Shaw's *Saint Joan* when the chaplain,
who has been eager to have Joan burnt, staggers in after the execution, shattered and unhinged by the sight and smell of her burning:

> You dont know: you havnt seen: it is so easy to talk when you
> dont know. You madden yourself with words: you damn your-
> self because it feels grand to throw oil on the flaming hell of
> your own temper. But when it is brought home to you; when
> you see the thing that you have done; when it is blinding your
> eyes, stifling your nostrils, tearing your heart, then—then—
> [*Falling on his knees*] O God, take away this sight from me!

Milton, like Shaw, shows the enormous gulf between theory and
practice, belief and action, words and reality. The contrast between
Manoa and the messenger is inalienably part of "the experience of
the play", and it does not cohere easily with Fish's insistence that
we have no alternative but to consider Samson's massacre "virtuous" and "praiseworthy", provided that he believes he has divine
sanction. In judging Samson as a moral being, according to Fish, all
we can ask is that he should intend his actions to conform to the
divine will. But why should we not expect a moral being to question

and assess the instructions he thinks he is getting from a supernatural agency? Why, if that agency seems to counsel mass murder, should a moral being conclude that it ought to be worshipped and obeyed? Fish's implication that "the experience of the play" should prevent us asking such questions amounts to a demand that, when reading a work of literature, we leave our brains outside.

All this, it is true, was discernible before September 11. But the events of that day have made it glaringly obvious. September 11 has changed *Samson Agonistes*, because it has changed the readings we can derive from it while still celebrating it as an achievement of the human imagination. In particular, Stanley Fish's verdict, quoted in my second paragraph, now belongs to a world we have outgrown.

SHARON ACHINSTEIN

Samson Agonistes and the Drama of Dissent[†]

In 1662, the Quaker Thomas Ellwood spent two months in a London prison without knowing the charge against him. He had been arrested soon after the great crackdown on religious nonconformists in August. At his appearance before the court, he was asked to take the oath of Allegiance to the restored Stuart monarchy and its episcopacy, a requirement newly enjoined by the Act of Uniformity. As a Quaker, Ellwood likely would resist taking the oath on grounds that he owed allegiance to Christ and not to the king. Ellwood did resist taking the oath on these grounds, but not before pursuing another line of argument. Rather, he insisted that his condition of being a prisoner prevented him from offering the oath freely. Here are his words: "I conceive this Court hath not power to tender that oath to me, in the condition wherein I stand." The court asked for clarification, inferring Ellwood was challenging their jurisdiction. Here is his reply:

> "Not absolutely," answered I, "but conditionally, with respect to my present condition, and the circumstances I am now under."
> "Why, what is your present condition?" said the Recorder.— "A prisoner," replied I.—"And what is that," said he, "to your taking or not taking the oath?"—"Enough," said I, "as I conceive, to exempt me from the tender thereof while I am under this condition."—"Pray, what is your reason for that?" said he—"This," said I, "that if I rightly understand the words of the statute, I am required to say that *I do take this oath freely*

† From *The Miltonic Samson*, ed. Albert C. Labriola and Michael Lieb, *Milton Studies* 33 (1997): 133–58. Copyright © 1997. Reprinted by permission of the University of Pittsburgh Press.

and without constraint, which I cannot say, because I am not a free man, but in bonds and under constraint. Wherefore I conceive that if you would tender that oath to me, ye ought first to set me free from my present imprisonment."[1]

Ellwood's response to his interrogators was to ask for the granting of his civil liberty so that the act of consent (or the withholding of consent) could be freely performed. He could not promise he would take the oath if he were freed, but, not being free, he was not able to take the oath: thus he challenged the conditions under which he was being asked to perform as a moral agent.

Ellwood, like Quakers and many others attempting to live conscientious lives in the Restoration, spent a good deal of time in and out of prison, wrangling with civil authorities, and in fear of further punishment. Yet Ellwood's exchange with the state authorities highlights the degree to which those living under persecuting religious conditions were aware of the larger philosophic stakes of their assent or dissent. Ellwood's act went beyond the questions commonly asked by those opposing conformity, questions concerning allegiance to state authority, and inversely, grounds by which to justify resistance to that authority. Ellwood's story raises an important philosophic point: allegiance to the state, and the verbal act of consent by which allegiance is signified, must be offered from a position of freedom to act. As Ellwood asks that the guarantee of civil liberty precede his acts of consent he makes a striking challenge to the culture of oppression: a counterdiscourse of civil—not strictly religious—right.[2]

I begin with Milton's pupil Thomas Ellwood in order to summon the terms in which I read *Samson Agonistes*, not to claim that Milton is a Quaker, but to open our eyes to a Restoration context of religious persecution of dissent.[3] In that context, the play may be seen as an exploration of the nature of, and conditions under which, moral

---

1. Thomas Ellwood, *The History of Thomas Ellwood* (London, 1885), pp. 157–58.
2. See Michael Walzer, *Obligations: Essays on Disobedience, War, and Citizenship* (Cambridge, Mass., 1970), p. xiv: "it is not enough, however, that particularly striking acts of consent be free; the whole of our moral lives must be free, so that we can freely prepare to consent." See also Don Herzog, *Happy Slaves: A Critique of Consent Theory* (Chicago, 1989), pp. 182–93.
3. A pre-Restoration date for the composition of *Samson Agonistes* is posited by W. R. Parker, "The Date of *Samson Agonistes* Again," in *Calm of Mind: Tercentenary Essays on "Paradise Regained" and "Samson Agonistes,"* ed. Joseph Anthony Wittreich (Cleveland, 1971), pp. 163–74. Restoration topical allusions have been analyzed by Christopher Hill, *The Experience of Defeat: Milton and Some Contemporaries* (New York, 1984), pp. 310–19; Blair Worden, "Milton, *Samson Agonistes*, and the Restoration," in *Literature and Society in the Stuart Restoration: Literature, Drama, History,* ed. Gerald Maclean (Cambridge, 1995), pp. 111–36; Nicholas Jose, *Ideas of the Restoration in English Literature, 1660–1671* (Cambridge, Mass., 1984), pp. 142–63; and Laura Knoppers, *Historicizing Milton: Spectacle, Power, and Poetry in Restoration England* (Athens, Ga., 1994). Other treatments of a Restoration *Samson* that bear on my own reading include David Loewenstein, "The Kingdom Within: Milton and the Politics of *Paradise Regained*," *Literature and History* III, no. 2 (1994): 82–83. On the interpretive issues concerning chronology, see Jonathan Goldberg, "Dating Milton," in *Soliciting Interpretation,* ed. Kathy Maus and Elizabeth Harvey (Chicago, 1990), pp. 199–222.

agents might perform acts of obligation. In Barbara Lewalski's elegant reading of this work, "the poem achieves . . . a brilliant mimesis of the confusions attending moments of political crisis and choice," yet I suggest that these are not just *any* moments of political crisis, but those supplied by a context of Restoration dissent, not solely by an abstract Christian paradigm, or by classical languages of tragedy. My terms are taken from Restoration discussions about obedience, compulsion, and coercion, and thus my critical emphasis turns away from the question of whether Samson can be considered a Christian hero, away from the critical debate over the nature of Samson's inspiration and regeneration. Samson, it is true, struggles for personal meaning over the course of the play, and the questions of inspiration and spiritual growth are vital to understanding the Christianity in the work; I hope to illuminate here obligations other than the spiritual ones Samson is also shown struggling to fulfill. Samson in the play seeks not to dishonor the following—"our God, our Law, my Nation, or myself" (1425): each element on this list of obligations counts. By immersing the play back into its Restoration context, where debates over toleration for dissenters focused precisely on these different realms of obligation, we shall see how this is so.[4]

Regardless of when the play was written, the fact remains that it was published in the autumn of 1670. What could the play have meant at that time? Historicist critics have looked to the author's biography to understand Milton's intentions—both to understand his choice of dramatic genre and his choice of topic. This historical approach has tended to allegorize the play either in terms of Milton's biography or in terms of the Puritan cause; Milton, like Samson, found himself blind, in prisons both literal and metaphoric during the Restoration; he, like Samson, was questioning his divine gifts: "What is strength, without a double share / Of wisdom" (53–54). Samson has been seen to represent the New Model Army, or the crushed Good Old Cause. *Samson Agonistes*, in this reading, is Milton's working out the meaning of that personal and national failure. Such a historical approach sees *Samson Agonistes* as Milton's way of writing a political tract for his times in poetry, a message for how one *ought* to behave by the exemplary (or negative exemplary) story of Samson's internal growth and final action, an action that resembles—or doesn't—that of the Christian paradigm of sacrifice.[5]

4. Barbara Kiefer Lewalski, "Milton's *Samson* and the 'New Acquist of True [Political] Experience,'" in *Milton Studies* XXIV, ed. James D. Simmonds (Pittsburgh, 1988), pp. 233–51. Joseph Wittreich reads *Samson Agonistes* as one of those "how-*not*-to live poems" in *Interpreting Samson Agonistes* (Princeton, 1986), p. 379. On tragedy, see Anthony Low, *The Blaze of Noon: A Reading of "Samson Agonistes"* (New York, 1974).
5. All citations to *Samson Agonistes* are from Merritt Y. Hughes, *John Milton: Complete Poems and Major Prose* (Indianapolis, 1957). All subsequent references to the play are from this edition and will be cited by line numbers in the text. On representations of

The historical questions I choose here, rather, are those raised by debates over Restoration religious dissent. During the winter and early spring of 1670, both houses of Parliament had discussed the merits of a bill against conventicles—an act that tightened persecution of dissenters when it went into effect. Following the passage of that bill in April, and with the adjournment of Parliament, there was a great crackdown on dissenters as well as civil unrest in London. That summer, during which Charles was pursuing his secret treaty with France, Samson Agonistes made it to the licenser, and its publication virtually coincided with the reconvening of Parliament in the fall. That Parliament early set as its task the reconsideration of the conventicles bill. The year 1670 also saw the publication of Samuel Parker's antitolerationist Discourse of Ecclesiastical Politie (followed of course by Marvell's parody, The Rehearsal Transpros'd, in 1672), as well as other important rebuttals; but I am concerned about Milton's philosophy, not merely his polemic. I posit the contemporary debate over Restoration nonconformity as a lens through which to understand the purpose of Milton's work. By illuminating Milton's local historical context, I hope to draw Milton into that larger philosophic conversation known as the liberal tradition.[6]

In short, I see Milton's Samson Agonistes as political theory. In this reading, I do not emphasize the ending of the drama, that final vengeful violence as the action offered for imitation.[7] Focus on the ending has skewed our understanding of the philosophic richness of the text. Is it a coincidence that this notorious missing middle is blotted out by the conservative Tory Samuel Johnson? In my reading, I shift attention away from the ending of the play and attempt to restore something of that missing middle. The ending does not fully answer the dilemmas Samson faces, dilemmas that offer occa-

---

Samson, see Christopher Hill, Milton and the English Revolution (London, 1977), pp. 435, 437, 441; Jackie DiSalvo, "'The Lord's Battels': Samson Agonistes and the Puritan Revolution," in Milton Studies IV, ed. James D. Simmonds (Pittsburgh, 1972), pp. 39–62; Mary Ann Radzinowicz, Towards "Samson Agonistes": The Growth of Milton's Mind (Princeton, 1978), p. 178.

6. On the bill against conventicles, see John Spurr, The Restoration Church of England, 1646–1689 (New Haven, 1991), pp. 57–61; Journals of the House of Commons IX; Journals of the House of Lords XII; Cobbett's Parliamentary History of England (London, 1808), vol. IV, pp. 444–47. On civil unrest, see Richard L. Greaves, Enemies Under His Feet: Radicals and Nonconformists in Britain, 1664–1677 (Stanford, Calif., 1990), pp. 154–59. David Masson, The Life of John Milton (London, 1880), vol. VI, p. 651, notes the play was licensed on 21 July but not entered into the stationers' registers until 20 September 1670. Parliament went into session on 24 October 1670; one of its topics was to establish a committee to inspect the April law against conventicles. See The Parliamentary Diary of Sir Edward Dering, 1670–1673, ed. Basil Duke Henning (New Haven, 1940), p. 7.

7. Hill, Milton, p. 446; likewise, Loewenstein, "The Kingdom Within," p. 83, argues that the 1671 volume lets the reader "decide which kind of revolutionary response—verbal duelling [Paradise Regained] or iconoclastic violence [Samson Agonistes] is more appropriate in an age of Royalist ascendancy." My rejoinder to Loewenstein is that by looking not only at the ending, we might find a third option: political theory.

sions for understanding moral action and political obligation, and whose resolution provides a context and ground for acting with responsibility to obligations. Barbara Lewalski has emphasized the imperfect and partial state of knowledge that attends Milton's moral choices, arguing that "the drama has demonstrated that political choices must be made and actions taken *in medias res*, in circumstances always characterized by imperfect knowledge and conflicting testimony. The thematics of true political experience in this work offers readers no definitive answers, but instead presents a process for making such choices in such circumstances."[8] By thinking about the persecuting conditions of Restoration Anglicanism, I see that the ending of *Samson Agonistes*—its final act of retributive violence—is not the only clue to its historical meaning. What would happen in the end was, for the dissenter, not the only problem; rather, what to do in the meantime was. How to define a conscientious life, how to live it, even under the yoke of arbitrary and cruel persecution, was the problem for dissenters. It is this context I see reflected in the play.

The middle of the play, as we shall see, does not satisfy readers with positive answers to difficult questions. Stanley Fish has powerfully argued that *Samson Agonistes* is an exploration of radical indeterminacy—it provokes our "interpretive lust," but its ultimate tease is in refusing to fulfill that lust with a climax of knowable meaning: "The only wisdom to be carried away from the play is that there is no wisdom to be carried away, and that we are alone, like Samson, and like the children of Israel of whom it is said in the last verse of Judges: 'and every man did that which was right in his own eyes'" (Judg. xxi, 25). What Fish manages to leave out is the verse immediately preceding this one: "In those days there was no king in Israel." He leaves out the fact that both verses have previously served as a refrain during the course of the Book of Judges; and that for those seeking to understand the nature of political sovereignty in seventeenth-century England, the Book of Judges provided many examples of righteous action. Figures such as Ehud, Deborah, Jephthah, and even Samson were favorites of those authors thinking about virtuous self-rule without kings—the republicans. Those lines that provide the compelling proof-text of radical indeterminacy for Fish also served as polemical ammunition in debates over toleration; for instance, the epigraph to Thomas Tomkyns's 1667 tract, *Inconveniencies of Toleration*, was "In those dayes there was no King in Israel, but every man did that which was right in his own eyes": the Judges passage was quoted in order to argue *against* toleration

8. Lewalski, "Milton's *Samson*," pp. 236, 248.

for dissenters. The plot thickens, as we locate Milton's words within the realm of the political, not just the personal or hermeneutical.[9]

I agree with Fish that *Samson Agonistes* raises many questions it cannot answer, but raising unanswerable questions is not the same matter as voicing hopelessness about arriving at meaning. Raising possibly unanswerable questions is in fact the essential art of political theory that takes asking questions seriously.[1] Milton's *Samson Agonistes* may be the most brilliant piece of political theory created in the seventeenth century if we think about political theory not only in terms of a discourse of abstraction, but also of contemplation, experience, and subjective experience. *Samson Agonistes* is all those—both humanistic and spiritual, secular and divine, philosophical and political; and it is very fine poetry. Contradictions and failures to arrive at meaning are its strengths, as it offers a political theory that leaves in the working-through of problems, links us to its hero, the individual struggling with questions fundamental to social existence. It is not a good book to turn to for answers, but it is one to turn to for questions. Those questions I see Milton asking belong to a long tradition of arguments over freedom and religious toleration, and ultimately concern citizenship, rights, and responsibilities. As political theory and not polemic, *Samson Agonistes* spurs us to thought—and for Milton, is not thought also a kind of action?

In what follows, I bring this dissenting context, where the nature and purview of the subject's rationality and freedom are central issues, to Samson's struggles to live under the external condition of enslavement. Samson strives against a regime that was compelling him to submit to its command to perform obedience, and he seeks to retain not only his dignity, but his obligations to his people and his God. In the middle sections of the play Samson examines the spheres of his obligation—to his father, his wife—but he also examines the nature of his own freedom to act. What we find is that freedom is not only an inner condition, but also a performance in the world. The focus here is on the final encounter in Samson's drama, the scene with the Public Officer, though further study can link the other scenes as well to a Restoration context. In the scene under scrutiny here, Samson performs a drama of dissent, specifically in the acts

9. Stanley Fish, "Spectacle and Evidence in *Samson Agonistes*," *Critical Inquiry* XV, no. 3 (1989): 586. On the book of Judges, see Christopher Hill, *The English Bible and the Seventeenth-Century Revolution* (New York 1993). Note that Tomkyns was the censor who balked at the "eclipse" passage of *Paradise Lost* and who approved the *Samson* volume for publication in the summer of 1670.
1. I am influenced by Richard Ashcraft, *Revolutionary Politics and Locke's "Two Treatises of Government"* (Princeton, 1986), esp. pp. ix–xi, which defends analyzing historical conditions as a way to understand political theory. In reaction against current "Cambridge school" methodology, see Joyce Appleby, "Ideology and the History of Political Thought," in *Liberalism and Republicanism in the Historical Imagination* (Cambridge, 1992), pp. 124–39.

where he contemplates his obligations, examines the moral conditions under which obligations may be performed, and takes action. The drama of dissent, as we shall see, is a drama of a liberal political subject, both deliberating and acting in a civil sphere.

I began this essay with Ellwood, not to argue that Milton was writing a biography of his friend or that Milton was a Quaker, but to set the dissenting dilemma before us. That dissenting dilemma was not solely one of faith: Where is God and how could He have let me down? But it was also: How can I live under conditions of oppression, persecution, and compulsion—conditions very like those Samson faced in prison? Though I claimed I would avoid allegory, of course I am using allegory: rather than representing a particular historical character or event, Samson represents a "type" of moral agent. The dissenting dilemma is a dilemma of free moral action under conditions that allow little or no room for freedom of moral action.

With religious dissent a chief domestic problem of the Restoration governments, the Restoration Anglican Church put the problem of compulsion in sharp focus. The Restoration had left unsettled the dispute over the nature of the English church, a dispute that some historians blame as the cause of the English civil war. The Restoration resurgence of religious and political tensions was a complex dynamic, one of national and international dimensions, and not just a reversal of civil war projects. Although Charles II's return had brought hopes for wider latitude for religious practices, these were undermined by the Anglican Royalist Cavalier Parliament, which pursued instead a policy of religious persecution in order to secure the goal of uniformity of religious practices. A strict penal code was put into place beginning in 1662 with the Act of Uniformity, and with other legislation of increasing severity over the next decade. This code and these laws were not based on simple prejudice nor were they random, but they reflected thinking about what made for an orderly nation.[2]

The conditions of Restoration dissent give us a context in which to place the philosophic defense of nonconformity, with its preoccupations with questions of obedience, conscientious action, slavery, and resistance. After 24 August 1662, London lost one third of its ministers. At least two thousand ministers, clergy, and lecturers were forced from their livings between 1660 and 1662. Most of these were moderate Presbyterians, who would have supported a

2. On compulsion, see B. Worden, "Toleration and the Cromwellian Protectorate," *Studies in Church History* XXI (1984): 199–233. On religious and political tensions, see Tim Harris, "Introduction: Revising the Restoration" in *The Politics of Religion in Restoration England*, ed. Tim Harris, Paul Seaward and Mark Goldie (Oxford, 1990), p. 10. On the Act of Uniformity, see Alan Craig Houston, *Algernon Sidney and the Republican Heritage in England and America* (Princeton, 1991), p. 122.

national church but were forced into separation by the requirements of the act. In one stroke, legislation created a class of dissenters. Historians estimate the number of dissenters after the Great Ejection to be well over one hundred thousand souls. The Act of Uniformity was followed by a series of intolerant legislation which reduced civil liberties and due process of law on a massive scale: nonconformists were prohibited from assembling and ministers were driven out of towns. These laws, collectively called the Clarendon Code, promised punishment by incrementally stiff fines, often steep to the point of ruin; nonconformists were also subject to searches of their homes without warrants and, in order to pay fines, to seizing of their property without trial: this often meant depriving a poor or middling sort of man with the tools of his trade. In the climate of suspicion regarding sedition, due process was invaded; those suspected of nonconformist activity could be arrested and found guilty on the basis of a reduced number of witnesses.[3]

Milton himself was intimately familiar with consequences of persecution of dissent. His own neighborhood, St. Giles Cripplegate, was an area of London nonconformist concentration, and there was controversy about its local church ministry through the early 1660s. Its nonconformist vicar, Dr. Annesley, was legally ejected and an Anglican royalist installed in his place.[4] Milton's neighbor and friend, the Quaker Isaac Pennington, was arrested in 1665 and his family turned out of their house; Mrs. Pennington took lodgings near Milton while her husband was in prison. And the prisoner Ellwood was Milton's pupil, asker of the famous question about the sequel to *Paradise Lost*.

This dissenting context intersects with *Samson Agonistes* in that key moment in the play where Samson is pressed to perform for the state an action we know offends his conscience. At this moment, he is asked to attend the Philistine feast; first he refuses, and then he assents. This sequence of events seems to be lifted out of the pages of the history of compulsion and finds meaning in dialogue with nonconformist deliberation—about freedom of performance of required acts. It raises, and works through, questions about the obedience a subject owes to a state authority, specifically with regard to religious compulsion. Critics have combed over this sequence in

3. On moderate Presbyterians, see Tim Harris, *London Crowds in the Reign of Charles II: Propaganda and Politics from the Restoration Until the Exclusion Crisis* (Cambridge, 1987), p. 63; Michael R. Watts, *The Dissenters: From the Reformation to the French Revolution* (Oxford, 1978), pp. 219, 227–38; Greaves, *Enemies Under His Feet*, p. 1. See also Richard L. Greaves, *Deliver Us from Evil: The Radical Underground in Britain, 1660–1663* (New York, 1986); N. H. Keeble, *The Literary Culture of Nonconformity in Later Seventeenth-Century England* (Leicester, Eng., 1987).
4. Harris, *London Crowds*, pp. 59, 66, 222. Masson perhaps misses the real attractions this dissenting climate may have had for Milton, and explains that Milton moved to Giles Cripplegate in order to seek quieter quarters (*Life* VI, p. 406).

order to find out what changes inside Samson's heart in order to understand the nature of his regeneration.[5] Yet this history and this discourse also frame Milton's exploration of the nature of Samson's freedom—his freedom to perform acts, and thus his obligations, in the play. *Samson Agonistes* is not solely a drama of the awakening of conscience with regard to God; it is the awakening of a political conscience as well.

In the text, the Public Officer demands Samson's attendance at a public festival:

> This day to *Dagon* is a solemn Feast,
> With Sacrifices, Triumph, Pomp, and Games;
> Thy strength they know surpassing human rate,
> And now some public proof thereof require
> To honor this great Feast, and great Assembly;
> Rise therefore with all speed and come along.   (1311–16)

Rites, triumph, pomp: all these recall the familiar language of idolatry in Milton, with a distinct whiff of antiroyalism, as critics have amply shown. Yet this feast commanded in *Samson* and its relation to the discourses of iconoclasm and antipopery are not merely topical allusions, cheap asides attacking the restored Stuart monarch. This description of what goes on at the Philistine festival, and the invitation, especially with its language of "public proof," recall the specific context of Restoration Anglicanism. Much of the Clarendon Code enjoined compelling "public proof" of conformity, as authorities enforced allegiance by significant public performances. This act required all ministers and teachers to adopt the new prayer book and to mark their "unfeigned assent and consent to the use of all things contained and prescribed in and by . . . the Book of Common Prayer" by St. Bartholomew's Day or face ejection from their posts. The act pertained not only to ministers, but to all manner of public speakers, including college students and schoolmasters.[6]

According to the act, it was not enough that ministers adopt the revised prayer book in their services; they also had to *perform*, as the words of the law require: to "openly and publicly before the congregation there assembled declare his unfeigned assent and consent" with words prescribed by the statute. The minister was required to use "these words and no other."[7] Failure to perform this public

5. Fish, "Spectacle and Evidence," p. 575, claims Samson's movement from "I cannot come" to "I will not come" is a backward movement toward the self-imprisonment of his own quest for certainty. My reading is much closer to that of Joan Bennett, *Reviving Liberty: Radical Christian Humanism in Milton's Great Poems* (Cambridge, Mass., 1989), pp. 134–37, who explores Samson's fulfillment of his different obligations in terms of rational faith.
6. J. P. Kenyon, *The Stuart Constitution, 1603–1688*, 2nd. ed. (Cambridge, 1986), pp. 353–56.
7. Kenyon, *Stuart Constitution*, p. 355.

action, that of reading a set script, would lead to stripping of his office. Thus accordance to the get-tough religious regime required not only passive obedience—the adoption of liturgical conformity by using the new prayer book—but also active obedience—public, active assent to the adoption thereof. Both gestures of obedience were displayed in a public spectacle.

The experience of living under this harsh legislation was painful for those now labeled nonconformists, and their reaction, it is important to remember, was not uniform. The very difficult decisions— whether or not to wear the surplice, whether or not to take the oath, whether to attend a now illegal religious meeting: how to live conscientiously under such religious persecution—created daily choices for the nonconformist, and resistance to this policy was widespread. The Baptist John Bunyan went to prison for disobeying these laws, and prisons filled with a vast number of Quakers. Most nonconformists, however, inhabited the more complex middle ground between total obedience to the state and total obedience to God: perhaps God was working through the state, they considered.[8]

In their justifications of religious compulsion, Anglican Tories appealed to civil order, fear of sedition, and the threat of yet another civil war; and Anglican divines found scriptural precedent for their rigor. As Benjamin Laney, bishop of Lincoln, put it, in defending the Uniformity Act in a sermon preached before Charles in April 1663, *"That our Liturgie or Common Prayer is a true Sacrifice to God. . . .* And to this I shall not *beg* the assent of those that like it not, but *require* it."* The key text authorizing such compulsion was the parable of Jesus' calling all to the feast (Luke xiv, 16–23). Samson's invitation to the feast honoring Dagon resonates with this situation. In Luke, chapter xiv, a lord bids a servant to invite others to come in for a supper, and when they do not come voluntarily, Jesus recounts that the lord says to the servant: "Go out into the highways and the hedges, and compel them to come in, that my house may be filled." Luke, chapter xiv, was thus a powerful symbol for those defending the policy of persecution. The archconservative Benjamin Laney used this text in a sermon preached before Charles in March 1664, "For our Saviour in the *Parable*, when the guests came not to the *banquet* at his invitation, commanded his servants to *compel them to come in*" (Luke xiv, 23;—glossed in margin). Compulsion to attend the "feast" here is thus a scriptural precedent that Milton must address. Milton's text asks us how such compulsion squares with freely given obedience.[9]

8. See Harris, *London Crowds*, pp. 65–71, for reaction of nonconformists. See also John Owen, *A Discourse Concerning Liturgies, and Their Imposition* (London, 1662).

9. Benjamin Laney, *Five Sermons* (London, 1669), pp. 14, 85. For the importance of the citation from Luke, and the uses made of it by Anglican royalists defending intolerance, see Mark Goldie, "The Theory of Religious Intolerance in Restoration England," in *From Persecution to Toleration*, pp. 331–68.

Against these defenses of compulsion came a range of responses, yet for nonconformists to question this policy was to consider the possibility of disobedience, and defenses of disobedience were dangerous to make in public, to say the least. Algernon Sidney was executed for making such a defense only in private. It is easy to understand why many nonconformists stayed far clear of defenses of resistance to the code. They spent their time, rather, portraying themselves as good subjects and citizens, simply following their consciences and asking to be let alone. These respondents worked out definitions of subjecthood that could include obedience to the crown but nonconformity in spiritual matters. John Owen, in a 1667 pamphlet, expressed allegiance to the king: "We own and acknowledge the power of the king or supreme magistrate in this nation . . . and are ready to defend and assist in the administration of the government in all causes, according unto the law of the land, with all other good protestant subjects of the kingdom."[1]

Yet High Church Anglicans liked to portray nonconformists either as noncitizens or as seditious. They saw nonconformist pleas for liberty of conscience as defenses of rebellion, as did the conservative Anglican apologist Samuel Parker: "These men are ever prepared for any mischief. . . . And there needs no other motive to engage their Zeal in any Seditious Attempt, than to instil into their minds the Necessity of a thorow Reformation. . . . And therefore, it concerns the Civil Magistrate to beware of this sort of People above all others, as a party, that is always ready form'd for any Publick Disturbance." The conservative Benjamin Laney, preaching to Charles at Whitehall in March 1661, argued that liberty of conscience was a dangerous thing for an orderly state: "If a man should be so unreasonable as to say, his conscience may be bound by himself, but not by any else . . . though the truth is, they bind none but themselves . . . and misleading the people into Faction, Sedition and Disobedience, to say no worse." Nonconformists sever the bonds of society and therefore cannot enjoy the privileges of freedom.[2]

In their own defense, however, nonconformists portrayed themselves as loyal citizens, struggling to maintain their livings, and they appealed, as Owen did, to charity. It was persecution, moreover, that might drive them to rebel. In contrast to Laney, the persecutor was made responsible for the breakdown of social ties. Nicholas Lockyer warned that "this unnatural severity tends either

---

1. John Owen, *The Grounds and Reasons on Which Protestant Dissenters Desire Their Liberty* (1667), in *The Works of John Owen*, 16 vols. (New York, 1850–1853), vol. XIII, p. 578. Owen also pursues the "good citizens" argument in *A Few Sober Queries Upon the Late Proclamation for Enforcing the Laws Against Conventicles* (1668), p. 10.
2. Samuel Parker, *A Discourse of Ecclesiastical Politie* (London, 1670), p. liii. See also Roger L'Estrange, *Toleration Discuss'd* (London, 1663); Laney, *Five Sermons*, p. 31.

to deter from known duty (in attending the Worship of God according to his Word) or from the Extremity, to provoke to Sedition, Tumult or Rebellion; necessitating thereby a falling either into the hands of God or Man." John Locke, in his 1667 *Essay on Toleration*, also claimed that nonconformity itself did not spawn disobedience; rather, harsh penalties imposed by the state did: "for force and harsh usage will not only increase the animosity but number of enemies. . . . if you persecute them you make them all of one party and interest against you, tempt them to shake off your yoke and venture for a new government." Rebellion, it was admitted, was a possible consequence of nonconformity, in the conservative argument, because nonconformity *was* rebellion, or, in the protolerationist argument, because persecution created conditions where rebellion was likely—or even was necessary—to occur.[3]

Yet what about the second part of the equation to consider, what powers or rights belonged to the subject? Thomas Ellwood's claims— that he could not even offer consent while under the conditions of imprisonment—lead in this direction. Milton, in *Samson Agonistes*, also offers an analysis of the subject's obligations that sorts with the public discourse of political argument during 1660s and 1670s. Milton directly engages with the philosophical discourse on toleration of nonconformity. Over the course of the play, Samson has a chance to address several spheres of political and social obligation, and in each encounter—with Manoa, Dalila, and Harapha—law is evoked to consider and settle competing claims. But in his final encounter, Samson considers the moral conditions that ground any attachment to law and under which compliance to law is at all possible.[4] In the scene with the Public Officer, Milton examines the meanings of compulsive state power from the vantage point of a discourse of civil liberty. Divine injunction is one, but not the only, source of political authority and knowledge in the play. There is, as we shall see, a counterdiscourse of civil liberty, specifically focusing on the liberty of the subject.

The discourse of slavery was used by seventeenth-century thinkers to think through the nature of sovereign authority and of liberty from the vantage point of the subject. Over and over in Milton's prose and poetry we find the author engaging with the topic of slavery—slavery, of course, was not one thing to Milton. In his long career he opposed many different kinds of slavery, from the spiritual

3. Nicholas Lockyer, *Some Seasonable and Serious Queries Upon the Late Act Against Conventicles* (London, 1670), p. 16; John Locke, *Essay Concerning Toleration* (1667), in *Political Writings of John Locke*, ed. David Wootton (New York, 1993), p. 207.
4. On Milton and Mosaic law, see Jason Rosenblatt, *Torah and Law in "Paradise Lost"* (Princeton, 1994); and Joan Bennett, *Reviving Liberty*, pp. 119–60, for detailed examination of the kinds of laws—Mosaic, Pauline, natural—that Milton adopts in *Samson Agonistes*.

tyranny of bishops, to the yoke of Presbyterian prelacy over conscience, to Charles I's suppression of his subjects, to those who
opposed liberty of conscience, to the self-enslavement of humans to
their lusts and passions, and the slavery of idolatry and popery.

Milton most often described the condition of people under the
returning Charles II by drawing upon the story of Exodus: the Jews
returning to bondage in Egypt. That analogy worked in two ways:
not only were the English slaves, but they were also subjugated to a
foreign power, with Egypt overlord to Israel. Milton himself merges
these two facets of slavery in his jeremiad, *The Ready and Easie
Way*; returning to monarchy is comparable to accepting "forein or
domestic slaveries."[5]

Milton returns to this theme in *Samson Agonistes*, where Samson
accepts responsibility for his own self-enslavement. But the play
also explores his duties as a literal slave to the Philistines when
Samson resists attending the Feast of Dagon. The Public Officer
asks him to examine his condition: "Regard thyself, this [refusal]
will offend . . . highly" (1333), asking Samson to take stock of his
condition: "Art thou our Slave, / Our Captive" (1392–93). Samson,
therefore, has no liberty to refuse. But Samson chooses to redefine
himself not by the external condition of slavery, but by the internal
liberty by which he knows himself to be fully human: "Myself?"
he answers, "my conscience and internal peace" (1334). Samson
here rejects the Public Officer's definition that he is a slave and
therefore has no power to refuse.

Though he defines himself by his inner state, Samson still suffers under two kinds of slavery: self-enslavement of his submission
to Dalila ("foul effeminacy held me yoked," 411); and slavery under
the Philistine conquerers. Internal slavery is more disgraceful than
the other kind, as Samson explains early on in the play when he
laments his condition:

> This base degree to which I now am fall'n
> These rags, this grinding, is not yet so base
> As was my former servitude, ignoble,
> Unmanly, ignominious, infamous,
> True slavery.   (414–18)

True slavery, as these remarks show, is to be complicit in one's own
enslavement, freely and willingly to contribute to the surrender of
one's own freedom, a republican concept of dependence.

Yet Samson's personal enslavement is connected to his outward
condition, and to the condition of his nation. As Samson remarks,
again sounding a republican note:

5. *Complete Prose Works of John Milton*, 8 vols., ed. Don M. Wolfe et al. (New Haven,
1953–82), vol. VII, p. 462, hereafter cited in the text as YP.

But what more oft in Nations grown corrupt,
And by thir vices brought to servitude,
Than to love Bondage more than Liberty,
Bondage with ease than strenuous liberty.   (268–71)

Samson invites comparison between his personal condition of self-enslavement and the national condition of Israelite subjection to Philistine rule.

The theme of self-enslavement was used often in the Restoration to describe English citizens' complicity in their loss of liberty under the restored Stuart monarch, especially in republican writing. By welcoming back the Stuart regime, English citizens were willingly reducing themselves to the condition of slaves, as the republican Algernon Sidney wrote in the mid 1660s: "God hath deliver'd us from slavery, and shewd us that he would be our King; and we recall from exile one of that detested race." In the last lines of his eleventh-hour appeal to his nation to oppose the return of monarchy, Milton also, and once again, evokes the myth of Exodus in the closing sentences of his *Ready and Easy Way* (1660), challenging his audience "to become children of reviving libertie; and may reclaim, though they seem now chusing them a captain back for *Egypt*" (YP VII, p. 463).[6]

Samson's story begins where *Ready and Easy Way* leaves off, with a man reduced to slavery because of an act of his own free will. Though it is important for the drama that Samson come to recognize his voluntary complicity in his own enslavement, the play also meditates on the consequences of slavery, not merely its causes. What is to be done given conditions of enslavement, once responsibility for that condition has been taken? That outward condition of slavery poses new questions, questions that a traditional republicanism perhaps cannot answer. Instead, those who sought to understand the rights of a slave or captive turned to other languages—those of Christian charity, mercantilism, or natural rights theories.[7]

Writers opposing religious persecution in the 1660s confronted the situation of coercive state authority and religious persecution by

6. On the discourse of slavery and republicanism, see Houston, *Algernon Sidney and the Republican Heritage*, chap. 3. On Milton and republicanism, see Nicholas von Maltzahn, *Milton's "History of Britain": Republican Historiography and the English Revolution* (Oxford, 1991); Blair Worden, "Milton's Republicanism and the Tyranny of Heaven," in *Machiavelli and Republicanism*, ed. Gisela Bok, Quentin Skinner, and Maurizio Viroli (Cambridge, 1990), pp. 225–46. Sidney, *Court Maxims* (1665–66), p. 203, cited in Jonathan Scott, *Algernon Sidney and the English Republic, 1623–1677* (Cambridge, 1988), p. 186.
7. Languages not found in J. G. A. Pocock, *Politics, Language, and Time: Essays on Political Thought and History* (Chicago, 1989), and *The Machiavellian Moment: Florentine Political Thought and the Atlantic Republican Tradition* (Princeton, 1975), which emphasizes historical precedent, law, and the principle of custom over natural rights in the early modern period. Richard Tuck discusses the radical appeal against slavery on grounds of inalienable rights in *Natural Rights Theories: Their Origin and Development* (Cambridge, 1993), p. 147.

likening it to slavery. The Presbyterian Nicholas Lockyer, for example, likened the severity of the Anglican orthodoxy to "much at that rate as *Pharaoh* dealt with the *Israelites*, when he required them to make Brick without Straw, and beat them to if they brought not the full tare." John Locke also used the metaphor of slavery to argue for a toleration for protestant dissenters in 1667: persecution will "bring this island to the condition of a galley where the greater part shall be reduced to the condition of slaves, be forced with blows to row the vessel, but share in none of the lading, nor have any privilege or protection." Those suffering under religious persecution, he argued, were not only subject to force, but they were also denied their rightful entitlements as citizens, being denied the benefits of their lading, the "privilege or protection." Under such conditions, protection is not offered as a reciprocal benefit of obedience: the essential social contract begins to tear. Dependence alone did not define slavery in this analysis; since a slave was denied reciprocal obligations of society, slavery put at stake a human's physical, moral, and civil status. Protection was not exchangeable for that kind of obedience: against a Hobbesian argument, Locke suggests here, liberty is not absolutely alienable.[8]

Compulsion and slavery were intolerable not only because of their physical consequences, but because of their assault on the will and on human rationality: the condition of compulsion denied the free operations of conscience and rationality that were necessary for faith to grow. As Charles Wolseley put it, "force upon men will never beget, or change Principles or Opinions. . . . When I have used rational su[i]table means to inform another, I ought to acquiesce . . . he that forceth me to a Religion, makes me hate it, and makes me think, there wants reason, and other evidence to evince it. Nature abhors compulsion in Religious things, as a spiritual rape upon the Conscience." A "spiritual rape" not only evokes the subjection to force, but performs a gender reversal as well: citizens become women victims. According to Wolseley, fear or slavish considerations cannot succeed in extracting a subject's accord; in fact, conversion under such compulsion is "an impossibility." As Quentin Skinner has argued, Hobbes in *Leviathan* sought to construct a polity in which coercion and liberty could be made consistent with one another. But in these attacks on compulsion, Wolseley and others denied that liberty and coercion could coexist. Hugo Grotius had attacked religious compulsion, and he put

8. Lockyer, *Some Seasonable*, p. 26; John Locke, *Essay Concerning Toleration* (1667) in *Political Writings*, p. 205; See also James Tully, *An Approach to Political Philosophy: Locke in Context* (Cambridge, 1993), pp. 287–91.

his finger on the same passage from the Bible, Luke, chapter xiv, offering a tolerationist interpretation: "as in that Parable the word *compel* argues nothing else but a vehement sollicitation." In opposing religious compulsion, Milton himself indirectly seems to reflect on the meaning of Luke xiv in his *Treatise of Civil Power* (1659): "We read not that Christ ever exercis'd force but once; and that was to drive prophane ones out of his temple, not to force them in" (YP VII, p. 268).[9]

As Samson ponders whether or not to attend the feast of Dagon, Milton explores active, voluntary compliance to obligations. Samson works through several thorny political questions as he settles his own inner peace specifically regarding the conditions under which moral action—whether compliance or disobedience—might take place. Samson first refuses the Public Officer's invitation to the Feast of Dagon, refusing on the grounds of Hebrew law, "our Law": "Thou knowest I am an *Ebrew*, therefore tell them, / Our Law forbids at thir Religious Rites / My presence; for that cause I cannot come" (1319–21). Note Samson's equation of "law" with "cause," an ambiguity we might well ponder. The adherence to Hebrew law is the reason Samson cannot come, that is, the explanation for his nonattendance. But Hebrew law is also a cause, perhaps like the Good Old Cause, in the sense of a prior political allegiance. His resistance to the Public Officer's message—and indeed to the state-authorized compulsion—is grounded in his self-definition, "I am an *Ebrew*," which signals two prior obligations: both his national allegiance to the Hebrew nation, and his allegiance to the law.[1]

I call attention to the collective ownership of this law; it is not "my vow"—his personal Nazarite commitment to God, broken and betrayed to Dalila—but rather law shared by Samson and other humans. Samson draws a distinction between these two realms of obligation, vouching that he will do nothing that will "dishonour / Our Law, *or* stain my vow of Nazarite" (1385–86; italics mine). Samson acknowledges the presence of this collective law—"our law"—over and against his personal vow. This distinction indicates that his

---

9. Sir Charles Wolseley, *Liberty of Conscience Upon Its True and Proper Grounds Asserted and Vindicated* (London, 1668), p. 29. See also Robert Ferguson, *A Sober Enquiry Into the Nature, Measure, and Principles of Moral Virtue* (1673), who stressed that compulsion removed a man's rational capacity (p. 175).

1. See Rosenblatt, *Torah and Law*, pp. 87, 125, which stresses Milton's reliance on John Selden. However, the Law of Nations was not necessarily identical to Jewish law, according to Selden: "The Law of Nations is what was . . . enjoined by God either on the remainder of mankind [after creation], at the same time as the Hebrews, or on some of mankind. . . . The Civil Law is that which was, or at least that which was held to be, the law for that particular Church or commonwealth of the Jews," in *John Selden on Jewish Marriage Law: the "Uxor Hebraica,"* trans. Jonathan R. Ziskind (New York, 1991), p. 33.

shared bonds with his people might present different kinds of
obligations.[2]

What is Samson's relation to these obligations? The answer to
this puzzle depends on a construal of how free he is to act. In his
first response to the officer, Samson adheres to these named laws
from necessity: "I cannot come." This begins his moral analysis.
First of all, his physical impediments keep him from behaving as a
moral agent: even Hobbes admitted that physical constraint or
impediment of motion was unliberty (*Leviathan*, chap. 21). Yet as
Samson reflects, he realizes that he "can" come—that is, he is
physically able to come—and he then ponders the meaning of his
action relative to the Philistine audience. What becomes clear to
him is that the Philistines will look at his performance as "sport,"
like those "Wrestlers, Riders, Runners, / Jugglers and Dancers,
Antics, Mummers, Mimics": as a performance, theatrical inauthen-
ticity (1324–25). Darkly, he reasons that it might not be the content
of his performance that counts; his powerlessness is itself a kind of
entertainment. Perhaps the command merely stages his moral position as a slave and their own power as masters: "Do they not seek
occasion of new quarrels / On my refusal to distress me more, / Or
make a game of my calamities?" (1329–31). Such action must be
resisted, not on grounds of necessity—for that would merely make
him a "slave" to his own law—but by a positive choice.

By analogy, obedience to law based upon necessity—a "cannot"—
denies freedom to choose to act. If he resists the invitation to
become the Philistines' puppet only to become God's puppet, Samson has not done any better; in either case, Samson would merely
be acting in a slavish and instrumental way: "he had bin else a meer
artificiall *Adam*, such an *Adam* as he is in the motions" (YP II, p.
527). Freedom, it turns out, is power to *choose* to act in accordance
with right. After considering this possible meaning of his performance he shifts the ground of his resistance from *necessary* obedience to Mosaic law to *voluntary* consent to that law. "I will not
come," Samson repeats twice. In the interim, he has imagined what
attendance at the spectacle means: it is not only to submit to being
the object of sport, but also to willingly ratify the compulsive power
of his oppressors. After these thoughts come his willed refusal, not
a compelled one: "Return the way thou cam'st, I will not come"
(1332). In his move from "cannot come" to "will not come," Samson
is growing to acknowledge the full responsibility of his own assent
to higher law; and he is coming to act as a voluntary agent, not a
slave, either to law itself or to the commands of an external captor.

2. Grotius, *Rights of War and Peace*, p. 172, too, draws a distinction between "oath" and
"vow"; a vow is a type of oath, "being made to God."

The language of necessity is transformed into a language of free choice.

Now armed with his voluntaristic sense of obedience, Samson asks whether he might then willingly obey the Philistine command. He could, perhaps, consent to the terms of his servitude:

> But who constrains me to the Temple of *Dagon*,
> Not dragging? The Philistian Lords command.
> Commands are no contraints. If I obey them,
> I do it freely; venturing to displease
> God for the fear of Man, and man prefer,
> Set God behind.   (1370–75)

Samson's understanding that "commands are no constraints" mirrors his previous move from "I cannot come" to "I will not come"; that is, it reflects an understanding that compliance with the law is voluntary, a free action of the will, and under his own responsibility.[3] Samson has come to see that submission to law or to command involves freely entering into an agreement to obey, through an act of the will. By acknowledging the voluntary basis of his compliance with law, Samson is fully able to understand that consent is essential for moral action—the classic liberal starting point. I recall Ellwood's response to his captors: no freedom implies no capability to offer consent. Samson finds, however, in this case, that his free consent to the Philistine command might offend God.

At this point, when Samson owns up to the voluntary nature of his compliance—to the Philistine commands, to the common laws of the Hebrews, and to his own personal commitments—he begins "to feel / Some rousing motions" (1381–82). He has recovered not only his personal pride, his connection to law and community, but also his moral center as a free agent.

Behind the Philistine command, however, is the threat of force. Does force foster conditions under which consent is possible? The play considers this question by addressing Samson's options. The Public Officer threatens to compel Samson to come to the feast; if Samson resists, "we shall find such Engines to assail / And hamper thee, as thou shalt come of force" (1396–97). What room is left for Samson's humanity under such a command? Is there a possible free answer to this question? Since Samson has begun to recognize the full range of his obligations, he refuses now not on grounds of prior obligation, but on moral ones; he refuses to be reduced to the moral

---

3. Such an understanding does not by necessity invoke antinomianism; it could, on the contrary, mirror an argument for occasional conformity; that is, the opportunistic conformity with Anglican ritual. Samson, unlike many nonconformists, rejects this logic, too, arguing like his contemporaries that he owed his allegiance to God, not to man's laws. See Thomas Corns, *Regaining Paradise Lost* (New York, 1994), 131.

status of a beast: "They shall not trail me through thir streets / Like a wild Beast" (1402–03). Samson has complained about his slavish status as that of a beast early on in the play: "O glorious strength / Put to the labor of a Beast, debas't / Lower than a bondslave!" (36– 38), but in that earlier case, beasthood was defined sheerly in terms of physical labor. To be a beast is to exert "strength without a double share / Of wisdom" (53–54), to lack rational powers.

Yet here, bestiality is also considered in light of its moral status. As Sir Charles Wolseley saw it, "Men are to be ruled over as Creatures, that have immortal souls to be chiefly cared for, and they are to be ruled over as such who have a special relation to God, and a homage to pay him, above all the rest of the world; a rule over men without some respect to this, would denominate Mankind into Brutes."[4] The difference between man and beasts is not sheerly human rationality, but also that "special relation to God"—a form of obligation.

The play asks, What are the moral conditions under which free consent may be offered? The Quaker Thomas Ellwood entertained this question in his own trial, resisting to perform the oath on the grounds that he could not freely and voluntarily be in a position to take a consenting action because he was in prison. I now take Ellwood's position in light of Samson's dilemma, when Samson ponders the topic of "absolute subjection": "Masters' commands come with a power resistless / To such as owe them absolute subjection" (1404– 05). Samson considers not only what he "owes" masters, but the moral conditions under which obligation is exacted. The masters, by enslaving Samson, have taken away his condition of freedom to consent and allow him no room for action according to free will. By removing occasions for Samson to exert his free will, the oppressors have denied him a fundamental right to be recognized as a human being and instead have reduced him to the moral status of a beast.

When Samson assents, "I am content to go" (1403), however, he signals his acceptance of responsibility for his actions to the officer and his friends, and confirms that he will perform as a morally free agent and not as a beast. The last episodes of the play show that the conscience must not only be free from self-enslavement, but also that action not derive from external compulsion. Rather, action must be self-motivated and "owned" in order for Samson to be open to contact with God. The law can *never* compel without removing human freedom; it merely offers occasion for accord and compliance.

Performing freely is not just thinking freely, and it is performance that is at the center of Milton's notion of consent. Dissent was a drama, in which preserving the inner realm of conscience alone was not enough to define human freedom; actions in public

---

4. Wolseley, *Liberty of Conscience*, p. 24.

mattered, for there was a link between opinion and action in non-conformist thought.[5] In *Truth and Innocence Vindicated*, John Owen remarked that liberty of conscience was not only an inner freedom: "if conscience to God be confined to thoughts, and opinions, and speculation about the general notions and notices of things, about true and false and unto the liberty of judging and determining what they are or no, the whole nature and being of conscience, and that to the reason, sense, and experience of every man is utterly overthrown. . . . Conscience . . . obligeth men to act or forbear accordingly" (Owen, *Works* 13: 442).

Conscience acts in the world. In nonconformist defenses of freedom of religion, because conscience involves both the inner and the outer moral life, external religious ritual must be undertaken with extreme attention to the ways it might bind conscience. As John Owen argued against the imposition of liturgies in 1662, "It is not about stinted forms of prayer in the worship and service of God, by those who, *of their own accord*, do make use of that kind of assistance, judging that course to be better than any thing they can do themselves in the discharge of the work of the ministry, but of the imposition of forms on others."[6] Occasional conformity—the practice of performing Anglican ritual yet withholding conscience's assent from the performance thereof—would not do in this scheme. Moral performance is freely consensual performance that reflects an internal obedience, "of their own accord." The word *accord* has at its root the word *heart*: "joining heart with." According is the action of joining the heart—inner—with an external performance.

What is the connection between the inner and the outer realms of action? External compulsion in religious matters mistook the outer for the inner, according to Wolseley: "this is as much to say, 'You may as well cure a man of the Cholick by brushing his Coat, or fill a mans belly with a Syllogysme'" (*Liberty*, p. 38). Earlier in Milton's career, it seemed that preserving the inner realm of freedom was sufficient for virtue: in the masque *Comus*, the Lady's defense against compulsion was to assert against her captor, "thou canst not touch the freedom of my minde" (663). Yet in *Samson*, inner and outer are closer together, as we see when the Chorus asks Samson why he resists attending the feast when he does not mind performing physical labor for his oppressors. Samson answers the Chorus that his resistance to attending the feast of Dagon is not in contradiction to his compliance to perform other acts for the state. His response upholds a distinction between civil and religious

5. On opinion and action, see Ashcraft, *Revolutionary Politics*, p. 65. *Truth and Innocence* in Owen, *Works*, vol. XIII, p. 442.
6. John Owen, *A Discourse Concerning Liturgies, and their Imposition* (1662), in *Works*, vol. XV, p. 21 (italics mine).

spheres of obligation: "Not in ther Idol-Worship, but by labor / Honest and lawful to deserve my food / Of those who have me in thir civil power" (1365–67). These lines reveal the conditions under which performance of his slave-labor is consensual: to earn his food, and to submit to conquest, to exchange protection for obedience. Idol worship is different, as there are no reciprocal obligations owed to the state in the case of religious worship.

The Chorus proposes, however, that Samson ignore the conditions of consent, and it suggests that Samson offers external compliance to the state's compulsion in religious worship—occasional conformity. He could do this without surrendering inner compliance, "where the heart joins not, outward acts defile not" (1368). This line echoes *Areopagitica*'s defense of freedom in defending publication of books: "to the pure all things are pure." But Samson rejects that inner and outer performances are so distinct: "where outward force constrains," he says back, "the sentence holds" (1369). By this statement, Samson seems to contradict the doctrine of inner purity that is the reserve of individual conscience, as sufficient to ground a moral life. And so, he rejects the Chorus' pleas for "occasional conformity." This seems to turn back from Milton's earlier positions concerning inner freedom as represented in *Comus* and *Areopagitica*. External action, how one "performs" in the world, matters. Samson's final action then is taken in this spirit of the only freedom left to him—willing compliance to God's laws, and as the voluntary exercise of his human power, "Of mine own accord."

When Samson finally consents to go to the feast, then, he is in a position to own his voluntary obligations. He claims that he will not do dishonor to "our God, our Law, my Nation, or myself" (1425). This list stands as a kind of declaration of obligation, in which each element establishes a realm of responsibility and a context for liberty. And these lines—the last Samson utters—establish an order in obligations one owes, starting from the most general to the most specific.[7] To John Selden's list of laws adumbrated at the opening of his great text, *Uxor Hebraica*—natural or divine law; Law of Nations, civil law—Milton adds a last sphere of obligation: "myself." Each term in this list is important, and the addition of the last term unequivocally posits a sphere of personal liberty and responsibility. This declaration of obligations signals that personal regeneration is predicated on, and *inseparable from* social regeneration, national regeneration, and political regeneration. Authentic

---

7. Irene Samuel, "*Samson Agonistes* as Tragedy," in *Calm of Mind*, p. 246, sees these lines as Samson's tragic monomania, his fatal flaw, yet the notion of a fatal flaw seems to negate a premise of free will. Hugh MacCallum, "*Samson Agonistes*: The Deliverer as Judge," in *Milton Studies* XXIII, ed. James D. Simmonds (Pittsburgh, 1987), p. 279, reduces the emphasis on these lines to two terms: self and God.

performance encompasses all these spheres of moral obligation: Samson finally "owns" his actions, as he has owned up to his full morally free nature, as he has owned up to the need for a consensual basis for a moral political society. With these recognitions, Samson has *chosen* to act like Samson; Samson himself is defined in relation to these realms of obligation: "*Samson* hath quit himself / Like *Samson*" (1709–10).

External slavery poses challenges for the oppressed, offering a range of responses from violent rage to despair. A possible consequence of slavery is hopelessness, and I do not mean to undermine the importance of the psychological resources the play seeks to draw upon. Despair is eased, however, by Samson's reuniting with his community, by his movement away from self—whether self-absorption or self-accusation—and toward fulfilling the social obligations that make Samson a member of the Israelite community. He is able finally to act on behalf of that larger community, once he has understood himself to be a fully free moral agent.

What kind of action, then, is the play offering for readers? Despite Milton's profound humanism in this work, there is also the apocalyptic and spiritual element—the matter of that violent ending, to say nothing of the companion piece, *Paradise Regained*. And yet I wish to gesture at some possible reconciliation between what has been largely a secular or civil discourse, and what is incontrovertibly a providential or even millenarian ending of the play, and that reconciliation takes place in a discussion of genre. Though the action of the play is clearly mental action, it is cast as dramatic action, specifically as tragedy. Greek tragedy in democratic Athens, it has been argued, was specifically a site for the exploration of the most important questions of political philosophy, and Milton allies himself with that tradition, despite important reservations. This drama is not intended for the stage, but it is not only mental action, action taking place within Samson's inscrutable mind. It is a series of choices taking place in a public forum, not only as Samson deliberates before a chorus of friends, but dialogically, as Milton's text unfolds before the audience of the play, an audience of separated, silent readers. Samson's final action can only take place after he considers, addresses, and fulfills all his obligations, and I find it crucial that he does so before others to whom he is bound by those obligations.[8]

Michael Walzer has suggested that "oppressed individuals rarely experience their oppression as individuals. Their suffering is shared,

8. Mary Ann Radzinowicz, "The Distinctive Tragedy of *Samson Agonistes*," in *Milton Studies* XVII, ed. James D. Simmonds (Pittsburgh, 1983), pp. 249–80, sees the play as a "philosophical tragedy" that replaces the drama of action, with its dramatic suspense, with intellectual conflict. See J. Peter Euben, "Introduction," *Greek Tragedy and Political Theory* (Berkeley, 1986), pp. 1–42.

and they come to know one another in a special way. . . . From this understanding obligations follow."⁹ In *Samson Agonistes*, Samson does not suffer alone. His entire nation, on whose behalf his final actions are taken, is also suffering. Samson has justified his earlier resistance to the Philistine lords by claiming it was action taken, with divine command, on behalf of his people: "I was no private but a person rais'd. . . . I was to do my part from Heav'n assign'd" (1211–17). The play leaves readers to contemplate the meaning of action so that their freedom is not lost. Only when Samson has recovered his full freedom is he capable of "acting" according to God's agency.

Milton has chosen the genre of drama and has represented Samson's obligations to his nation as a "part" assign'd from heaven. It is significant that Samson's obligations are acknowledged, voiced by him publicly, and worked through to their bloody conclusion before an audience—first of the Chorus and second of the community of readers. The Chorus serves to place Samson in a social context, even if he feels isolated. The Chorus watches his drama, offers remedies and suggestions, takes his side, suffers with Samson, experiences *com-passion*.

Co-suffering was the reason many nonconformists took up pens. The experience of ten years in prison was depicted by John Bunyan in *Grace Abounding to the Chief of Sinners* (1666) as a physical condition that offered the occasion for spiritual examination. But prison sitting also gave Bunyan a novel occasion for performing his duty to his people, by giving him the conditions necessary to write. As Bunyan claimed God told him, "I have something more than ordinary for thee to do." His writing was a form of living out that divine injunction, that his "imprisonment might be an awakening to the saints in the country." Suffering may have made him feel isolated, but Bunyan used it as an opportunity to unite with others.[1]

Samson's actions are his "own," in the sense that he has taken full responsibility for them, and yet they are enacted on behalf of his people, to whom he is connected by a common condition of suffering. The consequences of his final act are liberatory for others: "To Israel / Honor hath left, and freedom" (1714–15), Manoa rejoices, adding, "let but them / Find courage to lay hold on this occasion" (1715–16). Samson's final act is linguistically represented, it has been noted, in a bounty of metaphor and symbol: he is the thunderstorm, the evening dragon, the eagle, the phoenix (1691–1706). The symbols work to help the survivors explain and understand the power and thus appreciate the mystery of Samson's final act. They help to tell

9. Walzer, *Obligations*, pp. 51–52.
1. Christopher Hill, *A Tinker and a Poor Man: John Bunyan and his Church, 1628–1688* (New York, 1989), p. 107. John Bunyan, *Grace Abounding to the Chief of Sinners* (London, 1987), pp. 1, 94.

the story, since mimetic language itself cannot represent the mystery of Samson's action. The attempts by those left behind to seal meaning, however, are not futile. Rather, they represent an important aspect of public, or community obligation: finding stories and apt symbols through which to express, and to experience, collective identities. The messenger, Manoa, the Chorus, and the Semichorus all contribute to the telling, this accumulation of symbols and meanings and narratives. It is now up to the Israelites to "lay hold on this occasion" and perform acts of their own. Manoa's storytelling is one such act, and another is his sending for all his kindred to attend a funeral train, something that might have been forbidden before, but now, "*Gaza* is not in plight to say us nay" (1729). Telling the story itself, performing the play as a drama of the mind, is itself an action of suffering, of passion, of active memory. These actions are not a release from obligations, but rather an invitation to be obliged. Critics have argued that the ending of the play is a catharsis that serves as a moderation, tempering, or even removal of passions.[2] I am not sure about this quietistic understanding of catharsis. Samson confronts his obligations in a drama played out before the Chorus, his father, and an unseen community of readers. Milton throughout his late writing appealed to that unseen community, that "fit audience . . . though few." As a drama "never intended" for the stage, *Samson Agonistes* works to release "God's servants" from their bondage. Is Samson's final violence supposed to leech away their passion for freedom by moderating or lessening their love of it?

In my reading, Milton's voice in the debate over toleration was not merely consoling those under persecution that God would finally look after them by sending a deliverer, if they accepted responsibility for their previous failures. *Samson Agonistes* addresses problems dissent posed in the public sphere, problems that included such fundamental questions concerning liberty of consent as Ellwood was asking his interrogators. I do not agree with Samuel Johnson that the play has a beginning and an end, but no middle. My analysis looks at the middle as very important: it is, in fact, what is in the middle that matters. In that middle, the play investigates spheres of obligation and contributes to the Restoration conversation about political obligation, not only as an abstract philosophic discourse, comparable to theorizing by John Locke or Algernon Sidney, but as a matter to be worked through, performed.

If performance was part of Milton's intention, then, how are we to understand the catharsis at the end of the play? The protolerationist

2. John M. Steadman, "'Passions Well Imitated': Rhetoric and Poetics in the Preface to *Samson Agonistes*," in *Calm of Mind*, p. 187; Sherman Hawkins, "Samson's Catharsis," in *Milton Studies* II, ed. James D. Simmonds (Pittsburgh, 1970), pp. 211–30; and Radzinowicz, *Toward "Samson Agonistes,"* pp. 105–07.

Robert Ferguson describes freedom not as an emptying out, but a filling up: "when the *Saints* arrive at consummated purity, and are actually stated in glory, [do they] remain in a dubious suspention between Good and Evil, or in an equal propension to both? No! But though the liberty of our Souls be then dilated to its utmost dimensions, yet we shall from an eternal Principle steadily adhere to God." Freedom, and the condition in which humans might find grace, is not a moderate entity: "If the Essential *idea* of humane Freedom were an *aequilibrious* Disposition of the mind, then by how much holier a man becomes, by so much the less Free he is."[3] Could this conception of freedom help us to understand the combustion of civil and spiritual discourses? When passions are spent in *Samson Agonistes*, following this conception of freedom, I take it to mean that the full measure of liberty is felt, and with that, suffering, and the full scope of obligations. That is the position from which action may be taken. Samson has not *erased* his passion, but has allowed himself and his cosufferers to feel the full measure of it and thus to experience the extent of their liberty. Passion here I take not in the sense of immoderate emotions, but in the Greek sense of suffering. Suffering, understanding the moral consequences of the deprivation of external liberty as well as taking responsibility for self-enslavement, could be the precondition for a new moral awareness for those who choose to *suffer with*, to experience compassion. That catharsis is not an emptying out of passion, but an invitation for readers to attend to their own condition of persecution with courage, and to remember not to surrender even further their liberty.

Henry David Thoreau, in prison for refusing to pay his taxes, greeted his friend Emerson who was visiting him. With the famous question, Thoreau asked, "what are you doing out there?" *Samson Agonistes*, by asking its Restoration readers to witness the drama of deliberation, the sorting-out of personal and social obligation, challenges its readers to consider the conditions under which actions for liberty might be taken. It asks, "what are you doing out there?" It is the power of this text to provoke a robust response to that question.

JOHN ROGERS

The Secret of *Samson Agonistes*[†]

It is no secret that the problem of *Samson Agonistes* that has most consistently provoked Milton's critics is the question of the presence

---

3. Ferguson, *A Sober Enquiry*, pp. 275–78.
† From *The Miltonic Samson*, ed. Albert C. Labriola and Michael Lieb, *Milton Studies* 33 (1996): 111–32. Copyright © 1997. Reprinted by permission of the University of Pittsburgh Press.

of divine authority for Samson's final action, his destruction of both himself and the Philistine aristocracy at the festival of Dagon. As early as his 1651 *Defence of the English People*, Milton had raised the issue that would prove so central to his literary treatment of the story, the question of whether Samson's heroism "was instigated by God, or by his own valor."[1] Milton scholars have largely assumed that this query, which Milton had permitted to float unanswered in 1651, must have been given in *Samson Agonistes* a final, definitive solution. And it is the literary critical attempt to determine the content of that solution that has founded the conflicting schools of *Samson* criticism. The scholarly identification of the source of the "rousing motions" that impel Samson to tug and shake the pillars of the temple has established itself as a necessary labor for all the poem's critics: it is the task performed in the traditional assessment of Samson's divine authorization, as well as in the more recent revisionist evaluation of the hero's irrational, merely instinctive barbarity. I will not attempt here to adjudicate the conflict between these increasingly entrenched positions; I will pursue rather an understanding of the function of what all critical parties must concede to be the evident ambiguity of Milton's representation of Samson's final action. If the larger problem of the divine or instinctive cause of Samson's action presents itself as this poem's central interpretive riddle, then we might profitably approach the meaning of that riddle by way of its manifestation within the poem's own plot. I refer to the poem's explicitly narrativized mystery, of unquestionable interest to the fictional characters, to which Samson refers as his "capital secret": "in what part my strength / Lay stor'd, in what part summ'd" (394–95). The theological question of the instigating source of Samson's action finds a narrative embodiment in the question of the source and location of Samson's strength: whether that strength is literally "stor'd" in the "capital" part of Samson's body, his hair, or whether it is merely "summ'd" there, a divinely derived power that has its corporeal summation, or simple testamentary ornament, in the champion's glorious locks. I will examine the secret buried in the hero's body not necessarily as a secret whose positive content can finally be revealed, but one whose status *as* secret is central to the theological, and, I will suggest, the ideological, import of Milton's poem.

I

With its focus on the hero's "capital secret," *Samson Agonistes* muses over the same riddle worried by the Philistines in the Book of Judges, who in their desire to rein in Samson press Delilah to ascertain

---

1. *The Works of John Milton*, 18 vols., ed. Frank Patterson et al. (New York, 1931–40), vol. VII, p. 219. All subsequent quotations from Milton's prose will be cited by volume and page number from this edition.

"wherein his great strength lieth" (xvi, 5).[2] The writers responsible for the Judges text may have been a little puzzled themselves, as we will see, about the proper answer to this question. But at a central moment in the Judges version of the Samson myth, that puzzle finds a straightforward solution: Samson's great strength lies in his hair, and, as a consequence, according to Samson, "if I bee shaven, my strength will goe from me, and I shall be weake" (Judg. xvi, 17). But Samson's secret, however plain, retreats in *Samson Agonistes* to the occulted status it possessed for the Philistines. In its preliminary attempts to answer that riddle, Milton's poem points us toward the mythic location of Samson's bodily strength at the heart of the original folktale. Samson, for example, laments near the poem's beginning that God, "when he gave me strength, to show withal / How slight the gift was, hung it in my Hair" (58–59). And other characters, no less unenlightened, will continue throughout the poem to reproduce this physiological understanding of Samson's strength: the giant Harapha speaks of Samson's "boist'rous" locks (1164), and Manoa, after Samson's death, will praise "those locks, / That of a Nation arm'd the strength contain'd" (1493–94). But Samson comes to reject this archaic identification of his hair as the literal container of strength. Responsive to the Protestant, specifically Calvinist, discomfort with this key feature of the Samson myth, Milton follows the many biblical exegetes who felt compelled to qualify the tale's overwhelming suggestion of the bodily source of Samson's power.[3] Samson's strength had an immediate and ongoing source in the will of God, who perpetuated that strength daily only as long as Samson adhered to his Nazarite pledge. For the normative Calvinist annotators of the Geneva Bible, Samson loses his strength, then, "Not for the losse of his hair, but for the contempt of the ordinance of God, which was the cause that God departed from him."[4]

2. All scriptural quotations and marginal glosses are drawn from the Geneva translation, cited, unless otherwise noted, from *The Bible* (London: Robert Barker, 1608). Michael Lieb, *Sinews of Ulysses: Form and Convention in Milton's Works* (Pittsburgh, 1989), pp. 98–138, has argued for the importance of what he calls "the theology of strength" in *Samson Agonistes*. Discussing Samson's strength in the context of Milton's exchange with Salmasius, Lieb elaborates his thesis in his *Milton and the Culture of Violence* (Ithaca, N.Y., 1994).

3. For a description of the early modern reinterpretation of the source of Samson's strength, see Michael Krouse, in *Milton's Samson and the Christian Tradition* (Princeton, 1949), p. 75.

4. For a related argument for the nonphysiological cause of Samson's fall, see William Perkins, *The Workes of That Famous and Worthie Minister of Christ*, 3 vols. (London, 1608), vol. I, p. 752. William Gouge, *A Learned and Very Useful Commentary on the Whole Epistle to the Hebrewes*, 2 vols. (London, 1655), vol. II, p. 176, further amplifies the Genevan gloss: "*Samsons* hair being thus a sign of more than ordinary comeliness, purity and subjection, so long as, in testimony of his inward piety, that external Rite was observed, Gods Spirit continued his assistance to him, and gave that evidence thereof, his extraordinary strength. But when by a violation of that Rite be manifested his impure, disobedient and rebellious disposition against God, God took away his

It is the Reformer's elevation of the source of Samson's strength, from the self-contained body of the hero to the immediate will of an arbitrary God, that Milton not only inherits but actually incorporates into the narrative of his poem. If the hero can be said to develop over the course of *Samson Agonistes*, then one of the components of that "regeneration" is surely his accedence to the dominant Protestant reinterpretation of the source of his strength. That moment of conversion occurs in the confrontation with Harapha, who, as Michael Lieb has persuasively argued, "affords Samson the opportunity to reaffirm his faith in the true source of power, God Himself."[5] Teasing out the logical absurdity of the mythical location of strength in hair, Harapha dismisses what he calls Samson's "magician's art,"

> which thou from Heaven
> Feign'd'st at thy birth was giv'n thee in thy hair,
> Where strength can least abide, though all thy hairs
> Were bristles rang'd like those that ridge the back
> Of chaf't wild Boars, or ruffl'd Porcupines.   (1134–38)

Harapha's reductio here, his hyperbolic elaboration on the unlikely inherence of force in the lifeless excrescence of hair, however chafed or ruffled, presses Samson into a new understanding of the provenance of physical force.[6] He responds to Harapha's taunt with an unequivocal declaration of what the poem presents as its orthodox understanding of the hero's power:

> I know no spells, use no forbidden Arts;
> My trust is in the living God who gave me
> At my Nativity this strength, diffius'd
> No less through all my sinews, joints and bones,
> Than thine, while I preserv'd these locks unshorn,
> The pledge of my unviolated vow.   (1139–44)

His strength, Samson declares, is not localized magically in his hair, where, as Harapha seems rightly to have noted, "strength can least abide." God has instead diffused his strength at his birth throughout his entire body and preserved that strength on the condition of Samson's preservation of his Nazarite locks, since, as the

---

Spirit." Michael Lieb discusses Gouge's contribution to the theology of Samson's strength in *Sinews of Ulysses*, pp. 114–16.
5. Lieb, *Milton and the Culture of Violence*, p. 257.
6. Harapha appears here to reproduce the pained literalism of the Calvinist William Gouge, who is led in his 1655 *Learned and Very Useful Commentary*, vol. II, p. 175, to itemize the arguments against the inherence of strength in Samson's hair:
   1. Hair is no integral or essential part of the body: it is a meer excrement.
   2. It hath no stability in itself, as bones have: but is exceeding weak.
   3. Hair draweth strength out of a mans body, as weeds out of the ground.

Calvinist theologian William Perkins had explained, "God promised strength but with a commaundement, that [Samson] should be
a Nazarite to the end."[7]

This reorientation of the ontology of strength is sudden and, in
marking the point at which the hero relinquishes all claims for
the autonomy and integrity of his body, the most recognizable sign
that Samson has submitted himself to a new and uncompromising theocentric cosmos. This theological transumption draws even
more force from the poem's reassessment of the nature of the
"pledge" of Samson's "unviolated vow": there lies an assumption
throughout Milton's text that Samson's "pledge" is not simply, as the
Book of Judges and its Calvinist interpreters had assumed, his vow
to uphold the Nazaritical codes of bodily purity. His pledge, much
more abstractly, appears in this poem to have been a vow—one mentioned nowhere in Judges or the other texts on the Nazarite—not to
reveal the *secret* of his source of strength. Samson's failure, from the
vantage of this even more sophisticated formulation of the source of
his power, was not the simple violation of his pledge to keep his hair
intact. It was instead an act of "Shameful garrulity" (491), the disclosure of a divine secret for which the poem offers many synonymous formulations: Samson, we are told, exposed his willingness to
"divulg[e] the secret gift of God" (201), to "profan[e] / The mystery
of God giv'n . . . under pledge / Of vow" (377–78), "Presumptuously"
to "publish" "his holy secret" (497–98), to "unbosom[] all [his]
secrets" (879), to "commit[] / To such a viper [as Dalila] his most
sacred trust / Of secrecy" (1000–02).[8] To authorize this translation
of Samson's pledge from a vow of purity to a vow of secrecy, Milton
appears to have relied on the original meaning of the name for Samson's consecrated status. To be a Nazarite (from the Hebrew *nazir*,
"separate") is by definition to be secret (from the Latin *secretus*,
"separated," "hidden").[9] Milton would have found further justification for his treatment of Samson's pledge in the rhetorical elaboration of Nazaritic secrecy already performed in the Judges text. When
Samson's father Manoah presses to know the Angel of the Lord who
has announced the conception of his son, that mysterious angel
secretes the knowledge of his divinity from its human interpreters:
"Why askest you thus after my name, which is secret" (Judg. xiii,
18). The secrets withheld by the story's divine agents adumbrate the
secret Samson will need later to keep, and Milton locates in the

---

7. Perkins, *Workes* I, p. 752.
8. A related cluster of images, focusing not merely on secrecy but on silence, is composed
   of Milton's references to Samson's willingness to break the "Seal of silence" (50) and
   "violate the sacred trust of silence/ Deposited within" him (428–29).
9. I am grateful to Matthew Giancarlo for bringing my attention to some of the implications of *secret*'s derivation from *secretus*.

Scripture's silent coupling of reticent man and withholding God the secret of his hero's miraculous feats of strength.

In these curious reformulations of the pledge, the origin of Samson's strength is cleansed entirely of its association with the autonomous physical body and the self-willed bodily behavior of the hero. The God whose overwhelming power and inscrutability the hero must come to acknowledge in Milton's text is a silent, unsearchable God whose sacredness is founded on his secretness. This is a God whose outlines Milton was able to sketch, with varying degrees of intensity and commitment, throughout his career. In *Eikonoklastes*, Milton would condemn the man who "takes upon himself perpetually to unfold the secret and unsearchable Mysteries of high Providence" (V, p. 272). He would extend this protection of divine privacy to *Paradise Lost*, when the otherwise garrulous Raphael thinks to hesitate before "unfold[ing] / The secrets of another World, perhaps / Not lawful to reveal" (V, 568–70). And in *Christian Doctrine* Milton would praise not only those angels who do not *reveal* such secrets, but those "good angels [who] do not *look into* all the secret things of God" (XV, p. 107, emphasis mine). This God of secrets whom Milton would champion with disconcerting frequency is capable not only of withholding the rational justification of his actions from his subjects; he can also compel them, as he does with Samson, to keep some secrets of their own. This God, in other words, is the nominalist God of Calvin whom this same Milton, writing not as pious believer but as rational theologian, had spent so much of his career struggling to reject.

"Just are the ways of God," asserts the Chorus for a brief moment in a colloquy with Samson, "And justifiable to men" (293–94). This ringing declaration of divine justice, preceding with terrible irony a competing claim for God's transcendence of justice, law, and reason (307–25), does not surface here to announce this poem's commitment to theodicy. It works instead to remind us of the core Miltonic faith in divine accountability so ostentatiously absent throughout all the other lines of *Samson Agonistes*. The special status of this poem as the most puzzling work in the Miltonic canon is due in no small part, of course, to the antagonism between its predominantly nominalist theology and the explicit theology of rational justifiability that forms the basis of *Paradise Lost* and *De doctrina Christiana*. In spite of the momentary defenses of divine secrecy cited above, the logical foundation of those texts, in which Milton asserts the ways of God as publicly justifiable, cannot support such a phenomenon as a "holy secret." The incommensurability of Milton's *Samson* with the other late works has been both defended and denied in a number of ways. It has been variously argued, for example, that Milton actually came to embrace the

dread God of Calvin in his final poem; that he intended its embarrassing theology to be read ironically, the hero's final action subjected to the reader's condemnation; and that Milton succeeds in
converting Samson to his own anti-Calvinist, free-will theology
despite the theological recalcitrance evidenced everywhere by the
Chorus and even Samson himself.[1] My own contribution to the
solution of the theological mystery that surrounds this poem will
rest on an analysis of Milton's representation of that phenomenon
that proves so mysterious to the fictional characters themselves: the
secret connection between Samson's body and his strength.

In the confrontation with Harapha, Samson enjoys the poem's
sanction, at least provisionally, when he accedes to the Calvinist
displacement of all power and will onto the deity. But it is nonetheless important that Samson's claim for his strength's dependence on
the arbitrary judgment of a secretive God is not the poem's only
theologically creditable etiology of human power. Milton's poem
offers, if not a reasoned argument against, then at least a show of
rhetorical resistance to the orthodox demotion of Samson's hair to a
sign, rather than a source, of his strength. *Samson Agonistes* effects
this resistance by exploiting a potentially contradictory moment in
the Judges version of the ancient story of Samson. It is generally
accepted that the folktale on which the Samson tale is based focuses
on the magical powers embodied in the strong man's hair. The deuteronomic authors, however, long before their Calvinist successors,
superimposed upon the beginning and ending of the original story
the narrative of Samson's mysterious, "secret" conception and of his
Nazarite vow; they attempted to harness that myth of organically
magical human strength to a more seemly exemplum of the pious
man's virtuous submission to an arbitrary religious code.[2] The redactive authors did not, however, successfully remodel all of the story's
archaic mythical components. A particular narrative detail, one that
somehow escaped revisionary deletion, clings fast to the story's end

1. In response to Mary Ann Radzinowicz's argument for the consonance of *Samson Agonistes* with the rational theology Milton developed in *De doctrina Christiana*, in her
Toward "Samson Agonistes": The Growth of Milton's Mind (Princeton, 1978), William Kerrigan has argued for Milton's late voluntarist rejection of reason in "The Irrational Coherence of *Samson Agonistes*," in *Milton Studies* XXII, ed. James D. Simmonds (Pittsburgh,
1987), pp. 217–32; Joseph Anthony Wittreich Jr. makes the strongest case for the ironic
structure of the poem in *Interpreting Samson Agonistes* (Princeton, 1986); and Joan S.
Bennett performs a subtle dialectical synthesis of all these readings in *Reviving Liberty:
Radical Christian Humanism in Milton's Great Poems* (Cambridge, 1989), pp. 119–60.
2. Cuthbert Aikman Simpson, *Composition of the Book of Judges* (Oxford, 1957), identifies two successive hands in the Judges revision of the original tale. The earlier writer,
"J1," he argues, is responsible for the narrative of Samson's miraculous birth, while "J2"
"carried further the process, begun by J1, of depaganizing the legend by ascribing Samson's deeds of prowess to the energizing power of the 'Spirit of Jahveh,' and by explaining his uncut hair as being due to the fact that he was, by divine appointment, a
life-long Nazirite" (pp. 53–54). This "theological updating" is also discussed by John G.
Boling, *The Anchor Bible: Judges* (Garden City, N.Y., 1975), pp. 29–38.

in the Judges text; and this surviving remnant of the ancient tale can reasonably be said to erode any interpreter's insistence on God's absolute control over his champion's strength: "the haire of his head," we are told in the Judges narration, "began to grow again after that it was shaven" (xvi, 22).[3] The story's revisors, as we might expect, neglect to develop this folkloric thread that persists in investing magical power in the strands of Samson's hair. They move instead to subordinate Samson's potentially autonomous physical regeneration to the arbitrary will of God. Samson's strength is not officially returned until he makes his appeal, at the temple, for the renewed strength required at the story's end: "O God, I beseeche thee, strengthen me," Samson prays (xvi, 28). But the present text of the Bible retains nonetheless the ancient detail of the hair's regrowth. And while the revised tale soon goes on to imply God's voluntary agency in the re-empowerment of Samson, that startling sentence works inevitably to arouse suspicions of an alternative explanation for the explosion of power with which Samson concludes his life: Samson may well regain his strength for the simple and unexceptional reason that his hair, the only obvious source of his strength, grows back.

Quick to recognize the potentially dangerous theology embedded in this odd detail, the annotators of the Geneva Bible provide a marginal gloss for xvi, 22 that warns readers not to heed its narrative implications: "Yet had he not his strength againe till he had called upon God, and reconciled himself." Given Milton's reproduction of the generally Calvinist emphasis on the Nazarite pledge, we might reasonably expect Milton, too, to emphasize the scriptural focus on the deity's agency behind the massive power displayed at the temple. But nowhere in *Samson Agonistes* does Milton suggest, like the Geneva commentators or the Judges redactors before them, that the hero regains his strength when "he called upon God"; nor does Milton ever state, or even imply, that Samson at the temple, his head bowed either "as one who pray'd, / Or some great matter in his mind revolv'd" (1637–38), is requesting the return of his physical prowess. Milton's Samson, quite to the contrary, makes clear *before* his arrival at the temple that his body is already experiencing its resurgence of strength, which is "again returning with my hair / After my great transgression" (1354–55). If the poem can be seen anywhere to thwart its own acceptance of the orthodox Calvinist reading of the

3. John L. McKenzie, *The World of the Judges* (Englewood Cliffs, N.J., 1966), p. 156, argues that Judges xvi, 22 "shows how in popular tradition the connection between Samson's strength and his hair was magical. The Nazarite consecration has nothing to do with this conception, the original conception of the stories. When Samson's hair is long, his strength is proportionate to its length." Simpson, *Composition*, p. 63, notes this verse's inconsistency with the stress on "the immediate divine origin of Samson's strength." See also J. Alberto Soggin, *Judges: A Commentary* (Philadelphia, 1981), pp. 257–58.

Samson myth, it is surely in this unmistakable gesture of resistance
to the chronology of the return of the hero's strength. Violating the
explicit logic of cause and effect established by the deuteronomic
author of Judges 16, Milton has clearly and carefully unhinged the
return of Samson's strength from the critical moment at the temple.
Exploiting the embarrassing folkloric remnant left untouched by the
biblical writers, Milton loosens the official dependence of Samson's
power upon the arbitrary will of God. Manoa, a little later, will voice
a theological compromise when he conjectures that God has "*permitted / His strength again to grow up with his hair*" (1495–96; my
emphasis). But Manoa's invocation of divine permission, a theological
category Miltonic theology carefully distinguishes from direct divine
action, surely fails to crush Samson's personal strength beneath the
weight of God's omnipotence.[4] The realignment of Samson's
strength with the length of his hair, one discouraged both by the
redacted biblical text and its early modern Protestant exegetes, simply
removes divine power from the realm of arbitrary will and restricts
it to the far less exalted realm of ongoing and impersonal natural
process. This realignment begins as well to undermine any orthodox
location of Samson's strength in his obedient observance of a pledge,
whether that pledge is one of purity, secrecy, or both. Through this
inversion of the established chronology of the return of Samson's
strength, Milton, I believe it can be said, begins to undo the authoritative voluntarism to which Samson had acceded and reinvests
Samson's body as a viable, perhaps even noble, origin of power. In
this extraordinary complication of the mystery charging Samson's
boisterous locks, or what the poet himself had in 1642 called Samson's "puissant hair," Milton has forced the tale of Samson to reveal
a new secret.[5]

II

The puzzle of his own body, and of human bodies in general, teases
Milton's Samson in his magnificent opening monologue. In order to
understand the ultimate function of the competing ontologies of
heroic strength that mark this poem, I propose we turn to the first
corporeal riddle Samson addresses, the question of his sight. Much

---

4. Milton distinguishes between God's "permission" of sin and his direct causation of it in
   Works of John Milton XV, pp. 67–93. For a careful coordination of the modes of divine
   action represented in *Samson Agonistes* and *Christian Doctrine*, see Albert C. Labriola,
   "Divine Urgency as a Motive for Conduct in *Samson Agonistes*," *PQ* L (1971): 99–107.
   It should be noted that *Samson Agonistes* attempts nowhere to suggest, with William
   Gouge, in *Learned and Very Useful Commentary* II, p. 176, that Judges xvi, 22, points
   simply to a "sign," rather than a cause, "of the Spirits return unto him."
5. Milton, *The Reason of Church Government*, in *Works of John Milton* III, p. 276. In
   Eikonoklastes, *Works of John Milton* V, p. 257, Milton refers to the "strength of that
   Nazarites locks."

as Samson, Manoa, Harapha, and the Chorus are all concerned to
pinpoint the location of strength in a part of Samson's body, so also
the blind Samson questions the Creator's curious localization of
visual strength in the eyes:

> Since light so necessary is to life,
> And almost life itself, if it be true
> That light is in the Soul,
> She all in every part; why was the sight
> To such a tender ball as th' eye confin'd?
> So obvious and so easy to be quench't,
> And not as feeling through all parts diffus'd,
> That she might look at will through every pore?   (90–97)

In this surprisingly syllogistic analysis that questions the nature
and extent of visual sentience, Samson in lamenting his blindness
is clearly making a case for all the injustices that beset the human
organism. Scholars have identified a source for Samson's critique
here of the justice of the Creator's organization of the parts of the
body. The Latin Father Arnobius, whom Milton cites throughout
his career, had formulated perhaps the first version of Samson's
fascinating query: "From what kind of material have the inner parts
of men's bodies been formed and built up into firmness? . . . Why,
when it would be better to give us light by several eyes, to guard
against the risk of blindness, are we restricted to two?" Arnobius
does not, as these questions might lead us to suspect, proceed to
justify God's seemingly irrational organization of the "parts of
men's bodies." His perspective is not theodicial, but fideistic, as he
quickly moves to argue that Christ "bade us abandon and disregard
all these things . . . and not waste our thoughts upon things which
have been removed far from our knowledge."[6] With this final appeal
to the inaccessibility of divine wisdom, Arnobius may be responding to a similarly nominalistic argument in Paul, who issues a
related defense of the Creator's isolation of the senses in the body's
most vulnerable organs: "If the whole body were an eye, where were
the hearing? If the whole were hearing, where were the smelling?
But nowe hath God disposed the members every one of them in the
body at his owne pleasure" (1 Cor. xii, 17–18). The body has not
been organized, for either Paul or Arnobius, along lines rationally
accessible to human understanding. To yearn for the animate perceptivity of the "whole body," to question the reason behind the
awkward division of labor among the body's parts, is to pursue a

---

6. Arnobius, *Seven Books of Arnobius Against the Heathen*, in *The Ante-Nicene Fathers:
Translations of the Writings of the Fathers down to A.D. 325*, ed. Rev. Alexander Roberts
and James Donaldson (Grand Rapids, Mich., 1987), vol. VI, pp. 456, 457. See Terence
Spencer and James Willis, "Milton and Arnobius," *N&Q* CXCVI (1951): 387.

dangerous critique of God's secrets. The Pauline and Arnobian formulas for the limitations of human understanding, and the corollary acceptance of the illogical manner in which "God disposed the members . . . in the body," are of course only two of countless precedents for this poem's pietistic demotion of reason and rational divinity. Milton calls on the entire tradition of such fideism when producing Samson's claim, uttered just a few lines before his querulous account of visual percipience, "I must not quarrel with the will / Of highest dispensation, which herein / Haply had ends above my reach to know" (60–62).

This rehearsal of *Samson's* proto-Calvinist, nominalist filiations is, at least, one way to define the theological parameters of Samson's startling inquiry—one no doubt close to Milton's heart—into the scandalous irrationality of the organization of the human body. But it is not, I think, the only way to understand the function of the poem's opening speech. Given the explicit interest this text has exhibited in the contradictory accounts of the constitution of Samson's body, we should not be surprised to discover that Milton may be alluding to more than just the pious fideism of an Arnobius or a Paul. He can also be seen to tap another, no less authoritative, response to the recognition of the illogical organization of the body's members. Milton may have found in the Gospel of Luke what seemed a rejection of Paul's sanguine acceptance of God's demarcation of the frail human organism "at his owne pleasure."[7] Far from acquiescing to the erratic logic of divine pleasure, Luke suggests that the "whole body" of the enlightened believer might actually be capable of vision: "The light of the body is the eye: therefore when thine eye is single, then is thy whole body light" (Luke xi, 34). Read literally, Luke's contribution to the theology of the body's members offers a more attractive perspective on the limitations of ocular vision. This is in fact the compensation the blind Milton himself requested in the second invocation in *Paradise Lost:* "So much the rather thou Celestial Light / Shine inward" (III, 51–52). But where Milton the blind bard was seeking the traditional internal illumination of the Spirit, his Samson has in mind a far more radical illumination that fills with sensible light the actual physical body. Far from courting blasphemy by quarreling with the will of highest dispensation, Samson might actually have a scriptural sanction for his fantastic desire that sight, like feeling, could be "diffus'd" "through all parts . . . / That she might look at will through every pore."

---

7. J. B. Broadbent notes this parallel with Luke in *Milton: Comus and Samson Agonistes* (London, 1961), p. 42.

If Milton was, as I suspect, more than casually interested in alternative modes of physical vision, he would not have needed to rely solely on Scripture for the authorization of Samson's imaginative investment in a more perfect body. There were seventeenth-century natural philosophers no less interested than Samson in the possibility of the homogeneous dissemination of percipience throughout the human organism. The natural philosopher Margaret Cavendish, whose affinity with Milton's own science I have described elsewhere, asserts the astonishing idea that the human body does in fact already enjoy a panorganismic capacity for perception: "though Man, or any other animal hath but five exterior sensitive organs, yet there be numerous perceptions made in these sensitive organs, and in all the body; nay, every several Pore of the flesh is a sensitive organ, as well as the Eye, or the Ear."[8] Few of Cavendish's philosophical contemporaries would have concurred that man, at least as his body is presently constructed, can look at will through "every several Pore of the flesh." But the physician William Harvey had argued, in his *De motu cordis* of 1628, that other creatures, whose bodies were less complexly organized than man, did possess this ideal state of homogeneously diffused organic sentience. In his celebrated revelation of the circulation of the blood, Harvey digresses to discuss those remarkable creatures—he calls them "Plant animals"—in whom he can distinguish no "distinct and separate" organs, whether heart or otherwise: "such as are *Palmer-worms* and *Snails*, and very many things which are ingender'd of putrefaction and keep not a *species*, have no *heart*, as needing no impulsor to drive the nutriment into the *extremities*: For they have a body *connate* and of one piece, and indistinct without members." Animals, like worms and snails, that are "ingender'd of putrefaction and keep not a species"—born, in other words, of spontaneous generation—are for Harvey constituted of "one piece, and indistinct without members." Their crucial vital functions are not consigned to the "tender ball" of a vulnerable organ like the heart, "for instead thereof they use their whole body, and this whole creature is as a *heart*."[9]

Far from a dangerous critique of the way in which "God disposed the members every one of them in the body," the question Samson forwards concerning an ideal state of total-body percipience touches upon a reasonable form of bodily organization that may, if we credit Harvey, actually have a basis in at least some corners of

8. Margaret Cavendish, *Philosophical Letters: or, Modest Reflections Upon Some Opinions in Natural Philosophy by the Thrice Noble, Illustrious, and Excellent Princess, The Lady Marchioness of Newcastle* (London, 1664), p. 112. I develop the connection between Milton and Cavendish in *The Matter of Revolution: Science, Poetry, and Politics in the Age of Milton* (Ithaca, N.Y., 1996).
9. William Harvey, *De motu cordis* (London, 1628); quoted here from the first English translation, *The Anatomical Exercises of Dr. William Harvey* (London, 1653), pp. 93–94.

the creation.[1] In *Paradise Lost*, Milton himself had indulged Samson's fantasy of a body that escaped the vulnerable hierarchies of human corporeal order. Samson, the man "with a strength / Equivalent to Angels" (342–43), in many ways simply reproduces the desire for the angelic body that charges Milton's epic:

> For Spirits that live throughout
> Vital in every part, not as frail man
> In Entrails, Heart or Head, Liver or Reins,
> Cannot but by annihilating die;
> Nor in thir liquid texture mortal wound
> Receive, no more that can the fluid Air:
> All Heart they live, all Head, all Eye, all Ear,
> All Intellect, all Sense, and as they please,
> They Limb themselves, and colour, shape or size
> Assume, as likes them best, condense or rare. (VI, 344–53)

Unlike the "cumbrous flesh" of humans, the angelic body is "uncompounded," not a compound of separate elements, but constituted by a single, homogeneous "Essence pure" (I, 424–28). Unlike "frail man," whose capacity for perception has been organized entirely into distinct and therefore vulnerable organs, angelic bodies are not "Vital" exclusively "In entrails, Heart or Head, Liver or Reins" (VI, 345–46). Like the bodies of palmerworms, they are "indistinct without members," embodying in their entirety the function of one vital organ as fully as any other. No less "all Heart" than Harvey's glorious "Plant animals," Milton's angels also live "all Eye," embodying Samson's powerful desire to "look at will through every pore" in a perpetual act of enlightened perception.[2]

To voice a desire, as Samson does, for an uncompounded, homogeneously constituted body is also to voice a call, as Harvey, Cavendish, and a number of Milton's monistic contemporaries did, for a new ontology of bodily matter. Like the ingeniously embodied angels of *Paradise Lost*, Samson's fantasized body functions, in fact, as a narrative extension of Milton's own radical ontology of substance, the theological doctrine, worked out at such length in chapter 7 of the first book of *Christian Doctrine*, of the inseparability of the body and soul. There Milton puts forward what may be the most conceptually daring of all his theological heresies: "Man is a living being,

---

1. There may in fact be more physiological wisdom than theological despair behind Samson's strange invocation of vermicular perception: fearing he has become "Inferior to the vilest . . . / Of man or worm," he expresses in his blindness an envy of what Milton may well have believed to be the panorganismic perceptiveness of worms: "the vilest here excel me, / They creep, yet see" (73–75).
2. William Kerrigan offers a psychobiographical reading of the vision-endowed bodies of Milton's angels in *The Sacred Complex: On the Psychogenesis of "Paradise Lost"* (Cambridge, Mass., 1983), pp. 211–12.

intrinsically and properly one and individual, not compound or separable, nor, according to the common opinion, made up and framed
of two distinct and different natures, as of soul and body, but that
the whole man is soul, and the soul man, that is to say, a body, or
substance individual, animated, sensitive, and rational" (XV, p. 41).[3]
By declaring the whole man "animated" and "sensitive," Milton is
not here proposing the visual percipience of every inch of human
flesh. But this exuberant definition of the monistic human frame
seems at the very least a wishful account of the mortal human body,
in which, as Milton knew, the organs of sensation and reason are all
too easily sundered from the vulnerable body and rendered lifeless.
Milton's monistic declaration does, however, in stressing the absolutely uncompounded nature of divinized human flesh, read as a
fairly accurate abstraction of the bodies of Milton's angels, and the
body embraced in fantasy by the blind, disgruntled Samson.

Samson, as we have seen, had arrived in his confrontation with
Harapha at an understanding of his strength that began to approach
the ideal of homogeneity implicit in the philosophy of monism: his
physical force was now to be seen as "diffius'd . . . through all [his]
sinews, joints and bones." But that equitably diffused strength was
nonetheless, within Samson's new orthodox conception of God's conditional bestowal of physical strength, contingent on divine favor. In
the monistic theological analogue of that diffusion of strength, and
in the monistic body for which Samson yearns at the poem's beginning, the dissemination of vital virtue throughout the entire human
animal is never contingent upon the approving nod of a secretive
God of Judgment. It is the unconditional prerogative of being human.
When the monistic God of *Christian Doctrine* breathed "that spirit
into man," and "moulded it in each individual, and infused it
throughout" (XV, p. 39), he created a being whose inalienable divine
properties could never be subject to divine arbitration.

Stephen M. Fallon has argued correctly that one of the most
notable puzzles of the doctrinal component of *Samson Agonistes* is
its failure to "fit the picture of the mature Milton's philosophy of
substance."[4] It would in fact be impossible to assimilate Samson's
soul, which dwells "Imprison'd now indeed, / In real darkness of the
body" (158–59), to the otherwise enlightened world of Miltonic
monism.[5] Except for the counterfactual fantasies we have heard

---

3. It will be apparent in what follows that I have not fully assented to the argument for the
   non-Miltonic authorship of *Christian Doctrine* forwarded by William B. Hunter, in
   "The Provenance of the *Christian Doctrine*," with comments by Barbara Lewalski and
   John Shawcross, *SEL* XXXII (1992): 129–66.
4. Stephen M. Fallon, *Milton Among the Philosophers: Poetry and Materialism in Seventeenth Century England* (Ithaca, N.Y., 1991).
5. Consider, for example, Milton's unqualified denunciation, in *Christian Doctrine*, of the
   segregation of body from soul implied by *Samson's* Chorus: "that the spirit of man

Samson voice, the dominant theological tenor of *Samson Agonistes* is aggressively dualist, so much so, in fact, that Fallon is led to argue that Milton must have begun composition in the 1640s, before his formal elaboration of the monistic thesis. But *Samson Agonistes*, I think we can see, is nothing if not conscious of the doctrine of monism or its far-reaching conceptual implications. This poem, to be sure, resists forwarding the explicit monistic argument Milton carefully framed for the pages of *Christian Doctrine* and *Paradise Lost*. But this doctrinally secretive poem does open itself up to a suppressed theory of monism, not by means of careful Ramistic argument—that was the purpose of the theological treatise—but by means of the dialectical interplay of dualist argument and monistic figure. Through the potentially more potent vehicle of the explosive rhetorical figure Milton establishes the priority of his monistic materialism over what he could not help but think to be the conceptual tyranny of the Calvinist structure of divinity.

It is necessary now to determine the end for which *Samson Agonistes* incorporates so many hidden signifiers of Milton's radical ontology of matter. I propose we examine the purpose of the poem's monism by means of Milton's echo of a passage from his theological treatise. Samson, we remember, had begun his questioning of the confinement of sight "To such a tender ball as th' eye" with this opening condition: "if it be true / That light is in the Soul, / She all in every part" (91–94). In the *Christian Doctrine*, the Miltonic source for Samson's metaphysical construction, Milton employs this same conditional proposition to found one of his wilder conclusions concerning the materiality of the soul: "If the soul be equally diffused throughout any given whole, and throughout every part of the whole" ("si anima est tota in toto, et tota in qualibet parte"), then the human soul, he reasons, can only be "communicated to the soul by the laws of generation," imparted to the child by means of the generative seed of the parent, "or at least of the father" (XV, pp. 47–49). No passage of Scripture, Milton argues at considerable length, can "prove that each soul is severally and immediately created by the Deity" (XV, p. 49). The human soul is not "created daily by the immediate act of God"; it is the product rather of the "power of matter" itself (XV, pp. 43, 49). The "power which had been communicated to matter by the Deity" at the Creation is itself capable of generating the human soul, without any direct activity from an intervening God (XV, p. 53). Milton is willing elsewhere in the treatise to grant the premise of divine omnipotence. But the elaborate

---

should be separate from the body, so as to have a perfect and intelligent existence independently of it, is nowhere said in Scripture, and the doctrine is evidently at variance both with nature and reason" (XV, p. 43).

argument that constitutes the bulk of Milton's theology of divine power works more often than not to restrict the exercise of that omnipotence to the initial moment of Creation, permitting all other acts of generation to proceed by a more or less inviolable principle Milton calls the "general law of creation" (XV, p. 53). The rigorous theological argument for monism, to which Samson alludes in his opening monologue, forms the intellectual means by which Milton defends himself against the seemingly inescapable doctrine of omnipotence, and the awkward, Calvinist notes of voluntarism with which that doctrine seems so often to resound. Miltonic monism, by distancing the human soul from the creating deity, establishes a set of judicial restraints on divine power. Like his own rebel angels in *Paradise Lost*, for whom the theses of monism and omnipotence are logically incompatible, Milton writes often, in his theological prose as in his poetry, as one of those "who while they feel / Vigor Divine within them, can allow / Omnipotence to none" (VI, 157–59).

I have attempted to demonstrate a way in which *Samson Agonistes* depicts its hero pressing for a monistic philosophy of substance that the poem's dualist ontology cannot support. I have not yet accounted for the purpose behind Milton's systematic opposition of incompatible derivations of Samson's strength and incompatible ontologies of matter. What might be the function of Samson's fantasy of corporeal perfection in this poem which, by means of its Chorus, works otherwise to resign itself, in humble obedience, to the "unsearchable dispose" of the secretive Maker? By way of answering this question, I propose we enlist the help of a recent avatar of Samson's oppositional fantasy of the homogeneous body's panorganismic perceptivity. One of the most intriguing aspects of the critical philosophy of Gilles Deleuze and Félix Guattari has been the obscure theoretical entity they style the "Body without Organs."[6] Using as their model a schizophrenic's delusional belief in an entirely organless, limbless, but nonetheless vital human body, Deleuze and Guattari posit the fantasy of this Body without Organs as a "de-organized," nonhierarchical mode of being—one admittedly impossible fully to cultivate or even imagine—that functions as an immanent conceptual domain necessary for the successful subversion of almost any established authority. Like Samson in his opening monologue, Deleuze and Guattari forward the most exuberant formulation of this desire for organlessness in the halting form of a question:

6. The central discussions of the Body without Organs appear in Gilles Deleuze and Félix Guattari, *Anti-Oedipus: Capitalism and Schizophrenia*, trans. Robert Hurley et al. (Minneapolis, 1983), pp. 9–16; and *A Thousand Plateaus: Capitalism and Schizophrenia*, trans. Brian Massumi (Minneapolis, 1987), pp. 149–66.

Is it really so sad and dangerous to be fed up with seeing with
your eyes, breathing with your lungs, swallowing with your
mouth, talking with your tongue, thinking with your brain,
having an anus and larynx, head and legs? Why not walk on
your head, sing with your sinuses, see through your skin,
breathe with your belly: the simple Thing, the Entity, the full
Body, the stationary Voyage, Anorexia, cutaneous Vision, Yoga,
Krishna, Love, Experimentation.[7]

The fantasy of "cutaneous Vision" and the massive percipience of
"the full Body" is not, of course, geared to any straightforward
expansion of physiological possibility. The intimately experienced
external forces that seem to have "organized" the human organism
work to signify for Deleuze and Guattari all the forms of hierarchical order and categorization that determine the operations of power
in every facet of human existence. The impossible but necessary
attempt to dismantle the hierarchical conception of the organized
bodily self must precede any attempt to dismantle the forces of discursive authority they identify as "state philosophy," or ultimately to
dismantle, they suggest, the state itself.

   In a gesture that might remind us of the peculiarly Calvinist universe of *Samson Agonistes*, Deleuze and Guattari telescope all of the
world's allied and unallied loci of authority into a single, demoniz-
able embodiment of arbitrary power they call the "judgment of
God." It is by means of the wicked "judgment of God" that the frail
organs of the human body seem to have been disposed and organized so irrationally and arbitrarily. The individual's oppositional
fantasy of the Body without Organs, or, as they come to denote it,
the "BwO," is

   opposed to the organism, the organic organization of the organs.
   The *judgment of God*, the system of the judgment of God, the
   theological system, is precisely the operation of He who makes
   an organism, an organization of organs called the organism,
   because He cannot bear the BwO, because He pursues it and
   rips it apart so He can be first, and have the organism be first.
   The organism is already that, the judgment of God.[8]

The hypothetical God forwarded by Deleuze and Guattari "cannot
bear the BwO" because the individual's capacity to imagine a Body
without Organs can unleash a subversive power so antihierarchical
that it undermines God's entire system of judgment; it renders the
fiction of a hierarchical cosmos governed by an absolutist deity
irrelevant, inoperative. The fantasy of the Body without Organs

7. *A Thousand Plateaus*, pp. 150–51.
8. Ibid., pp. 158–59.

facilitates an escape from the constraining network of the psychic, social, and political relations that present themselves as ineluctable truths, as facts as seemingly unimpeachable and inalterable as the order and function of the organs in the body created by God.

In their rhapsodic meditations on the Body without Organs, Deleuze and Guattari have opened themselves to the same type of criticism to which Samson, in his plaintive question concerning bodily organization, is vulnerable: the vision of the Body without Organs is without question a Utopian vision, a fantasy that could not possibly be instituted to effect meaningful change. But the theoretical construct of the undifferentiated body seems nonetheless to be forwarded by the French theorists as if it were something approaching a useful tool for progressive political and social action. If a comparison of Milton's "uncompounded" monistic body and the "BwO" of contemporary French philosophy is warranted, the connection is due surely to the curious faith Deleuze and Guattari share with Milton in the potential political implications of the monistic fantasy of the de-organized body. The utopian theorizations of Deleuze and Guattari read today as a cultural byproduct of the rebellion against the state in the Paris of 1968, much as the disestablishmentarian logic of Milton's monism is at least in part an intellectual response to the recentralized state in the years of the Stuart Restoration. *Samson Agonistes*, as I have noted, often seems committed to its restoration of the ontology of dualism that Milton himself had rejected, along with monarchic tyranny, well before the poem's composition. But there is a way in which this poem suggests, much like the texts of Deleuze and Guattari, that there exists a conceptual interdependence between the hierarchical logic of a dualist philosophy and the hierarchical logic of political oppression.[9] If Samson is compelled to end his days in a Philistine prison house, it is possible that a chief agent of oppression is his culture's intellectual propensity for dualism, the Chorus' belief that the soul "dwells" "Imprison'd . . . / In real darkness of the body" (158–59). By means of this rhetorical coordination of the political imprisonment of Samson with a dualist metaphysics of body and soul, Milton attributes to the misguided theology embraced by Samson and the Chorus a chief responsibility for their subjection to their Philistine oppressors.

9. This conceptual interdependence of physiology and politics was felt perhaps most keenly by early modern Calvinists. According to the commentators in the Geneva *New Testament* (London, 1602), p. 85[v], Paul in 1 Corinthians xii, 17, rejects the image of the Body without Organs in order to dissuade the Corinthians from the political belief that "all should be equall one to another": "And that no man might finde fault with this division as unequall, hee addeth that God himself hath coupled all these [separate bodily parts] together." I discuss some of the discursive ties binding natural and political philosophy in *Matter of Revolution*, pp. 1–16.

In his preface to *Christian Doctrine*, Milton explained that he had devoted himself to his formal theology "because nothing else can so effectually wipe away those two repulsive afflictions, tyranny and superstition" (VI, p. 118). Milton does not in that treatise articulate with any specificity how a new monistic theology can wipe away the affliction of tyranny. But Deleuze and Guattari supply a useful elaboration of the way in which a thesis of monism can function as a displaced discursive counter to what may seem to be the excessively organized and inextricably intertwined bodies of a tyrannical Church and a tyrannical state. Christopher Hill has argued persuasively that the philosophy of substance Milton develops late in his life had an origin in the poet's partial, sometimes submerged political sympathy with the Levelers, Diggers, and Ranters, radical political groups of the 1640s and 1650s whose theorists, especially Overton, Lilburne, and Winstanley, were among the first in England to propose the monistic heresy.[1] In Samson's hesitant invocation of the monistic body Milton proposed in *Christian Doctrine*, we can hear, I think, a powerful, if brief, reengagement of the radical egalitarian utopianism of the poet's earliest forays into political speculation.

III

I turn now to the poem's problematic ending because it is here that the full implications of the contradictions concerning Samson's body, and especially the fantasy of the Body without Organs, make themselves known. Milton, much to the dismay of many of his critics, resists concluding his poem with the easily apprehended gestures toward divine voluntarism that characterize so much of the Chorus' discourse. Refusing to submit desire and instinct to the compelling, transcendent forces of the deity, Samson articulates his astonishing decision to attend the forbidden festival as if it were the consequence of a gradual physiological process: "I begin to feel / Some rousing motions in me which dispose / To something extraordinary my thoughts" (1381–83). The traditional reading of *Samson Agonistes* has identified those "rousing motions" as providential; the revisionist reading has deemed them unauthorized and purely instinctive; and some analyses, those with which I am most sympathetic, have described them as both.[2] But the agential ambiguity

1. Christopher Hill, *Milton and the English Revolution* (Harmondsworth, 1977), pp. 317–33.
2. Albert C. Labriola discusses the divinity of the "rousing motions" in "Divine Urgency as a Motive for Conduct in *Samson Agonistes*," pp. 106–107. For a dialectical reading of motivation in *Samson*, see Edward Tayler, *Milton's Poetry: Its Development in Time* (Pittsburgh, 1979), pp. 105–22; and especially John Guillory, "The Father's House: *Samson Agonistes* in Its Historical Moment," in *Re-membering Milton: Essays on the Texts and Traditions*, ed. Mary Nyquist and Margaret W. Ferguson (New York, 1987), pp. 148–76.

raised by these "rousing motions" is not necessarily a sign of absolute theological indecipherability. The central point of overlap between Samson's idiosyncratic sensation of motion and Milton's rational theology occurs at the theologically loaded adjective "extraordinary." In *Christian Doctrine*, Milton had clung to a residual orthodox belief in God's miraculous powers of intervention, naming God's capacity for voluntary intervention his "extraordinary providence" ("providentia Dei extraordinaria"), which is that power "whereby God produces some effect out of the usual order of nature" (XV, p. 95). Here, however, as if to shake off forever the vestiges of voluntarism that had shackled the argument of *Christian Doctrine*, Milton shifts this loaded adjective, "extraordinary," from God to God's creature, as if in imitation of the devolution of power at the heart of Milton's monistic account of Creation. The verb that names Samson's apprehension of these motions, "feel," locates this new knowledge of rousing motions in the space of the monistically divinized body, as "feeling" is that sense which is neither irrationally segregated to a vulnerable organ or subject to whimsical conditions, being definitively, as Samson stated in his opening speech, "through all parts diffus'd."

Samson had begun the poem with his yearning invocation of the monistic body, and it is just this image of a divinely infused Body without Organs that reappears after Samson's climactic act of destruction. In the poem's final and most elaborate burst of rhetorical energy, Milton recalls the promise of compensatory percipience made by Luke that Samson, at the beginning of the poem, had questioned:

> But he though blind of sight,
> Despis'd and thought extinguish't quite,
> With inward eyes illuminated
> His fiery virtue rous'd
> From under ashes into sudden flame,
> And as an ev'ning Dragon came,
> Assailant on the perched roosts,
> And nests in order rang'd
> Of tame villatic Fowl. (1687–95)

In an extraordinary succession of similes, Milton characterizes Samson, the destroyer at his end of the "Lords and each degree . . . sit[ting] in order" (1607), as "an ev'ning Dragon" who has assailed the "nests in order rang'd / Of tame villatic Fowl." The being who had raged against the arbitrary ordering of sight and strength in the fragile receptacles of eyes and hair wreaks vengeance on the social and institutional manifestations of those irrational forms of order. "With inward eyes illuminated," Samson moves not only to destroy the irrationally organized body that had left him open to a punitive blindness and impotence; nor merely to destroy the carefully organized Philistine aristocracy, sitting in order of each degree; but to destroy the entire principle of arbitrarily determined organization, manifested throughout the bodily, religious, social, and political fabric of experience. Creating for himself, through suicide, an extravagantly literal Body without Organs, Samson strikes a blow at all the injustices perpetrated by that Deleuzian bogey, the judgment of God.

It is only at this point, once Milton has represented the destruction of the evils of order and organization, that he allows himself to indulge in a daringly liberated figuration of the redeemed being who thrives in the new organless, de-organized cosmos. The Chorus' shocking figure of the phoenix soars from the destruction of all the principles of hierarchical organization that Samson has crushed at the end of his life:

> Like that self-begott'n bird
> In the *Arabian* woods embost,
> That no second knows nor third,
> And lay erewhile a Holocaust,
> From out her ashy womb now teem'd,
> Revives, reflourishes, then vigorous most
> When most unactive deem'd.   (1699–1705)

We must take seriously, I think, the admonition of Dr. Johnson, who had written in *The Rambler* that "the grossest error" in *Samson Agonistes* "is the solemn introduction of the phoenix in the last scene."[3] In spite of Johnson's astute disapproval of what he must have adjudged the phoenix's theological impropriety ("it is so evidently contrary to reason and nature"), commentators have most typically attempted to demonstrate the decorous piety of Milton's comparison by invoking the association of the phoenix with the Crucifixion. But Milton's adjective here, "self-begott'n," can only with great difficulty be applied to the Son of God, whose "begetting" by the Father was such a consequential event in *Paradise Lost*. Milton's focus on that mythical bird's capacity for spontaneous generation reminds us, of course, much more of Satan than the Son, the Satan who boasted to Abdiel in heaven that the angels were "self-begot, self-rais'd, / By their own quick'ning power" (V, 860–61). William Harvey, in the passage from *De motu cordis* cited above, had identified those vermicular bodies without organs as beings born of spontaneous generation who "keep not a *species*," knowing no second or third. It is as

---

3. Samuel Johnson, *Works of Samuel Johnson*, 10 vols, ed. H. W. Liebert et al. (New Haven, 1969), vol. IV, p. 379.

if Milton here, revisiting the debate in heaven between Abdiel and Satan, were making a conceptual leap as fantastical as Harvey's. This final explosive figure seems almost to sanction Satan's claim that the angelic Body without Organs exists by right outside the arbitrary judgment of God. Milton's daring affirmation in *Samson Agonistes* of what may have been the grossest theological error in all of *Paradise Lost*—the heresy of angelic self-begetting—is not, of course, a rejection of the Creator of the monistic universe Milton described in *Christian Doctrine*.[4] It is a rejection, instead, of the theological voluntarism that had structured *Samson*'s dominant conception of God. Milton's image of the phoenix refigures Samson's "regeneration," which for the Chorus could only be the product of arbitrary divine will, as a process we might with justice call "spontaneous regeneration." The image of the phoenix suggests the possibility that Samson's alteration is the consequence less of divine impulsion than of the forces inhering, by right of divine Creation, within the inescapably physical, already divinized self.

We can discern the usurpation enacted here of a Calvinist voluntarism by Milton's own Arminian monism if we examine the function of one of the poem's most important words. As critics have noted, the "rousing motions" behind Samson's inscrutable change of heart are felt again when Milton writes of Samson, "His fiery virtue rous'd / From under ashes into sudden flame." Looking ahead to the image of the phoenix, Milton's loaded verb "rous'd" can be seen to retain a strong element of its original meaning, which was "to shake the feathers" or "to ruffle." But while Milton's verb does gesture ahead to the imminent figure of the phoenix, it is first and foremost the verb that names Samson's own action in his final moments at the temple: "but he though blind of sight . . . / His fiery virtue rous'd." In this more proximate alliance, the verb *rouse* here activates a closely related variant of its original meaning, which, when used intransitively of hair, meant "to stand on end." The satanic hero of Shakespeare's *Macbeth*, for example, recalls near the end of that play a time at which the hair on his skin "would . . . rouse and stir / As life were in 't" (5.5.12–13).[5] This crucial verb of material self-motion, with its roots in the autonomous activity of hair and feathers, returns us inevitably to that most intransigent element of the original Samson myth, the inherence of strength in the matter of his hair. We are reminded of the "rousing motions" that had earlier impelled Samson to attend the festival, and we are led, retrospectively, to identify the origin of those motions in the monistic bodily self. Although the implicit grammatical agent of

4. I defend the value of Satan's heresy in *Matter of Revolution*, pp. 122–29.
5. *The Riverside Shakespeare*, Gen. Ed. G. Blakemore Evans (Boston, 1974), p. 1337.

that rousing was left in that phrase deliberately unclear, Milton's "rousing" cannot help but draw upon some of the autonomous virtue and power it possessed in his *Areopagitica*, in which that word was definitively aligned with the immensely liberatory strength inhering in Samson's hair: "Methinks I see in my mind a noble and puissant nation rousing herself like a strong man after sleep, and shaking her invincible locks" (IV, p. 344).

The ending of *Samson Agonistes* will no doubt always remain the most secretive element of this secretive poem, because Milton has so steadfastly resisted submitting the great conceptual problems of his poem to his own high standards of rational, argumentative discourse. As if to compensate for the fateful loquacity of his hero, Milton refrains from violating "the sacred trust of silence" deposited deep within the Samson story. Instead of tearing down the structure of voluntarism by means of intellectual argument, as he had throughout most of *Christian Doctrine* and *Paradise Lost*, Milton permits his final poem to undermine that oppressive theology by means of subversive metaphor. The phoenix invoked in *Samson Agonistes* is, as we have noted, self-begot. But Milton's particular figuration of that phoenix has risen from the ashes of an earlier image in the poem, the far more traditional, sacrificial representation of Samson's miraculous beginnings. At the annunciation of Samson's birth, "an Angel . . . all in flames ascended / From off the Altar, where an Off'ring burn'd, / As in a fiery column" (24–27). This self-immolating angel (who in Judges had kept his name a "secret") declares at the poem's opening Samson's heavenly paternity and announces the cruel, voluntarist theology of sacrifice that marks Samson at birth as an adherent to the arbitrary Nazaritic code. But in the concluding reappearance of this image of fiery ascension, the figure of the self-begotten phoenix, Milton works to release his hero from the debt immense of heavenly paternity. It is as if Samson were born again, self-quickened this time by the divine vigor of his own body, into the noninterventionist monistic universe Milton had in his other poetry and prose claimed as his own. The positive valuation given the fantastic freedom of self-begetting announces the poem's magical, perhaps impossible, desire to escape once and for all the dualist and voluntarist theology in which it would seem to be imprisoned. Instead of marshaling a final argument, in his final poem, against an inimical theological system, Milton simply watches it go up in smoke.

John Milton: A Chronology[†]

1534	Act of Supremacy, by which King Henry VIII assumes full authority over the Church of England.
1558–1603	Reign of Queen Elizabeth I. Presbyterians at work to extend the Reformation in England.
1603–25	James VI King of Scotland, reared as a Presbyterian, rules England as James I.
1608	December 9, Milton born in London.
1609	The Pilgrims (left-wing Puritans) settle in Leyden.
1611	Authorized (King James) Version of the Bible published.
1616	Death of Shakespeare.
1620	Pilgrim Fathers land (Plymouth Rock). Milton enters St. Paul's School about this time.
1625	Milton enters Christ's College, Cambridge. Charles I crowned.
1628	Charles grants Petition of Right, agreeing not to tax without consent of Parliament or imprison without due process.
1629	Milton graduates B.A. in January; at Christmas writes "On the Morning of Christ's Nativity." King Charles dissolves Parliament.
1632	Milton graduates M.A.; begins six years' residence with his parents in the country, first in Hammersmith, later in Horton. William Laud, opponent of Puritanism, appointed Archbishop of Canterbury.
1632–37	Milton studies the history of western civilization: history, philosophy, literature, religion, political theory, geography, astronomy, mathematics, music, etc. Writes "L'Allegro," "Il Penseroso," *Comus*, and "Lycidas."
1637	Milton's mother dies.
1638–39	Milton travels in Italy.
1638	Charles Diodati dies.

† From John Milton, *Paradise Lost*, ed. Scott Elledge, 2nd ed. (New York: Norton, 1993). Copyright © 1993, 1975 by W. W. Norton & Company, Inc. Used by permission of W. W. Norton & Company, Inc.

1640	Milton settles into a house of his own in Aldersgate Street in London, a few blocks from his birthplace, and begins to tutor his two nephews. Completes *Epitaphium Damonis*, a 219-line pastoral elegy, in Latin, in memory of his friend Diodati.
1641–42	Milton publishes five tracts urging that the Church of England reform itself by reducing its monopolistic, tyrannical power over the religious lives of the people.
1641	Archbishop Laud impeached and imprisoned.
1642	Civil War begins. Milton marries Mary Powell, whose family supports the king and the hierarchical Church of England. She leaves her husband two months later and returns to her parents, near Oxford, a stronghold of Royalists.
1643–45	Milton publishes four tracts urging that divorce on grounds of incompatibility be allowed.
1644	In response to learning of (unsuccessful) efforts to prevent publication of his *Doctrine and Discipline of Divorce*, Milton publishes *Areopagitica*, against censorship.
1645	Mary Powell Milton returns to her husband. Battle of Naseby; victory of Cromwell and his New Model Army. Milton moves to large house in Barbican; continues to teach school in it till 1647.
1646	Publication of *Poems of Mr. John Milton*. Birth of daughter Anne. The Powells flee from Oxford and take refuge with Miltons in London.
1647	John Milton, Sr. dies. Milton gives up teaching and moves to smaller house in High Holborn.
1648	Birth of daughter Mary.
1649–53	The Commonwealth.
1649	January: Charles I executed. February: Milton's *Of the Tenure of Kings and Magistrates* published. March: Milton appointed Latin Secretary to Council of State at an annual salary of £248 14s 4½d; moves to an apartment in Whitehall.
1651	Milton's *Pro Populo Anglicano Defensio* published. Son, John, born. Milton becomes totally blind; moves to a house nearby in Petty France, Westminster.
1652	May 2: Daughter Deborah born. May 5: Mary Powell Milton dies. June 16?: Son, John, dies.
1653–58	Oliver Cromwell Lord Protector.
1654	*Defensio Secundo* published.
1656	November 12: Milton and Katherine Woodcock married.

1657   October 19: Daughter Katherine born.

1658   February and March: Katherine Woodcock Milton and infant daughter die. September: Cromwell dies; Richard Cromwell Lord Protector till Restoration.

1660   February: *Ready and Easy Way to Establish a Free Commonwealth* published. May 29: Charles II enters London as king. Milton goes into hiding in Bartholomew Close. June 16: order for Milton's arrest and for the burning of his pamphlets. Sept.–Oct.: Milton arrested, put in custody, and soon discharged; rents a house in Holborn, near Red Lion Fields.

1660–65   Milton writes *Paradise Lost*.

1661   Moves to house in Jewin Street.

1663   February 24: Milton and Elizabeth Minshull married.

1665   During the Great Plague in London, Milton lives at Chalfont St. Giles, Buckinghamshire. The house still stands.

1666   Great Fire in London.

1667   *Paradise Lost*, in ten books, published by Mrs. Mary Simmons and her nephew Samuel, next door to the Golden Lion, in Aldersgate Street, a building that had escaped the fire. Milton is paid £5 upon delivery of the MS and another £5 when the first edition of thirteen hundred copies is sold.

1671   *Paradise Regained* and *Samson Agonistes* published.

1669 or

1670   Moves to Artillery Walk, Bunhill Fields.

1674   Second edition of *Paradise Lost* published, in twelve books. November 8?: Milton dies of gout; buried in St. Giles, Cripplegate.

Selected Bibliography

• indicates a work included or excerpted in this Norton Critical Edition

Biographies

Campbell, Gordon. *A Milton Chronology*. London: Macmillan, 1997.
Darbishire, Helen, ed. *The Early Lives of Milton*. London: Constable, 1932.
French, J. Milton, ed. *The Life Records of John Milton*. 5 vols. New Brunswick, N.J.: Rutgers University Press, 1949–58.
• Lewalski, Barbara K. *The Life of John Milton: A Critical Biography*. Oxford: Blackwell, 2000.
Masson, David. *The Life of John Milton: Narrated in Connexion with the Political, Ecclesiastical and Literary History of His Time*. 7 vols. London, 1881–94; rpt. Gloucester, Mass.: Peter Smith, 1965.
Parker, William Riley. *Milton: A Biography*. 2 vols. Oxford: Clarendon, 1968; rev. Gordon Campbell, 1996.

Criticism

Achinstein, Sharon. *Milton and the Revolutionary Reader*. Princeton, N.J.: Princeton University Press, 1994.
• ———. "*Samson Agonistes* and the Drama of Dissent." *Milton Studies* 33 (1966): 133–58.
Allen, Don Cameron. *The Harmonious Vision: Studies in Milton's Poetry*. Baltimore: The Johns Hopkins University Press, 1954.
Barker, Arthur E. *Milton and the Puritan Dilemma, 1641–1660*. Toronto: University of Toronto Press, 1942.
———. ed. *Milton: Modern Essays in Criticism*. New York: Oxford, 1965.
———. "The Pattern of Milton's Nativity Ode." *University of Toronto Quarterly* 10 (1940–41): 167–81.
Bennett, Joan. *Reviving Liberty: Radical Christian Humanism in Milton's Great Poems*. Cambridge, Mass.: Harvard University Press, 1989.
Boesky, Amy. "The Maternal Shape of Mourning: A Reconsideration of *Lycidas*," *Modern Philology* 95 (1998): 463–83.
——— and Mary Thomas Crane, eds. *Form and Reform in Renaissance England: Essays in Honor of Barbara Kiefer Lewalski*. Newark: University of Delaware Press, 2000.
• Booth, Stephen, and Jordan Flyer. "Milton's 'How Soon Hath Time': A Colossus in a Cherrystone," *ELH* 49 (1982): 449–67.
• Carey, John. "A Work in Praise of Terrorism? September 11 and *Samson Agonistes*." *TLS*, September 6, 2002, 15–17.
Chaplin, Gregory. "'One Flesh, One Heart, One Soul': Renaissance Friendship and Miltonic Marriage." *Modern Philology* 99 (2001): 266–92.
• Christopher, Georgia. *Milton and the Science of the Saints*. Princeton, N.J.: Princeton University Press, 1982.

Corns, Tom. "Milton's Quest for Respectability." *Modern Language Review* 77 (1982): 769–79.

Diekhoff, John S., ed. *A Maske at Ludlow: Essays on Milton's 'Comus.'* Cleveland, Ohio: Case Western University Press, 1968.

Elledge, Scott, ed. *Milton's "Lycidas": Edited to Serve as an Introduction to Criticism.* New York: Harper & Row, 1966.

Empson, William. *Milton's God.* 2nd ed. London: Chatto & Windus, 1965.

Entzminger, Robert. *Divine Word: Milton and the Redemption of Language.* Pittsburgh, Pa.: Duquesne University Press, 1985.

• Fish, Stanley. "Driving from the Letter: Truth and Indeterminacy in Milton's *Areopagitica*." In Mary Nyquist and Margaret W. Ferguson, eds. *Re-Membering Milton: Essays on the Texts and Traditions.* London: Methuen, 1987. 234–54.

———. *How Milton Works.* Cambridge, Mass.: Harvard University Press, 2001.

———. "What It's Like to Read *L'Allegro* and *Il Penseroso, Milton Studies* 7 (1975): 77–99.

Fixler, Michael. *Milton and the Kingdoms of God.* London: Faber, 1964.

Fletcher, Angus. *The Transcendental Masque: An Essay on Milton's 'Comus.'* Ithaca, N.Y.: Cornell University Press, 1972.

• Friedman, Donald M. "*Lycidas*: The Swain's Paideia." In C. A. Patrides, ed., *Milton's 'Lycidas': The Tradition and the Poem.* Columbia: University of Missouri Press, 1983. 281–302.

Frye, Northrop. "The Typology of *Paradise Regained*." *Modern Philology* 53 (1956): 227–38.

Grossman, Marshall. *"Authors to Themselves": Milton and the Revelation of History.* Cambridge: Cambridge University Press, 1987.

Guibbory, Achsah. *Ceremony and Community from Herbert to Milton: Literature, Religion, and Cultural Conflict in Seventeenth-Century England.* Cambridge: Cambridge University Press, 1998.

———. "'The Jewish Question' and 'The Woman Question' in *Samson Agonistes*: Gender, Religion, and Nation." In Catherine Gimelli Martin, ed. *Milton and Gender.* Cambridge: Cambridge University Press, 2004. 184–203.

Guillory, John. "Dalila's House: *Samson Agonistes* and the Sexual Division of Labor." In Margaret W. Ferguson, Maureen Quilligan, and Nancy J. Vickers, eds. *Re-Writing the Renaissance: The Discourses of Sexual Difference in Early Modern Europe.* Chicago: The University of Chicago Press, 1986. 106–22.

———. "The Father's House: *Samson Agonistes* in Its Historical Moment." In Mary Nyquist and Margaret W. Ferguson, eds. *Re-Membering Milton: Essays on the Texts and Traditions.* London: Methuen, 1987. 148–76.

Halkett, John. *Milton and the Idea of Matrimony: A Study of the Divorce Tracts and Paradise Lost.* New Haven, Conn.: Yale University Press, 1970.

• Haller, William. *The Rise of Puritanism.* New York: Columbia University Press, 1938.

Haskin, Dayton. *Milton's Burden of Interpretation.* Philadelphia: University of Pennsylvania Press, 1994.

Herman, Peter C., ed. *Approaches to Teaching Milton's Shorter Poetry and Prose.* New York: Modern Language Association of America, 2007.

Hill, Christopher. *Milton and the English Revolution.* London: Faber, 1977.

Hollander, John. *The Figure of Echo: A Mode of Allusion in Milton and After.* Berkeley: University of California Press, 1981.

Jebb, Richard. "*Samson Agonistes* and the Hellenic Drama." *Proceedings of the British Academy* 3 (1907–08): 341–48.

Kahn, Victoria. *Wayward Contracts: The Crisis of Political Obligation in England, 1640–1674.* Princeton, N.J.: Princeton University Press, 2004.

Kendrick, Christopher, ed. *Critical Essays on John Milton.* New York: Hall, 1995.

———. *Milton: A Study in Ideology and Form.* London: Methuen, 1986.

Kermode, Frank, ed. *The Living Milton: Essays by Various Hands.* London: Routledge, 1960.
———. "Milton in Old Age." *Southern Review* 11 (1975): 513–29.
• Kerrigan, William. *The Sacred Complex: On the Psychogenesis of "Paradise Lost."* Cambridge, Mass.: Harvard University Press, 1983.
Knoppers, Laura Lunger. "Milton's *The Readie and Easie Way* and the English Jeremiad." In David Loewenstein and James Grantham Turner, eds. *Politics, Poetics, and Hermeneutics in Milton's Prose.* Cambridge: Cambridge University Press, 1990. 213–25.
• ———. "*Paradise Regained* and the Politics of Martyrdom," *Modern Philology* 90 (1992): 200–219.
Lewalski, Barbara K. *Milton's Brief Epic: The Genre, Meaning, and Art of "Paradise Regained."* Providence, R.I.: Brown University Press, 1966.
———. "Milton's *Samson* and the 'New Acquist of True [Political] Experience.'" *Milton Studies* 24 (1999): 233–51.
———. "*Samson Agonistes* and the 'Tragedy' of the Apocalypse." *PMLA* 85 (1970): 1050–62.
Lieb, Michael, and John T. Shawcross, eds. *Achievements of the Left Hand: Essays on the Prose of John Milton.* Amherst: University of Massachusetts Press, 1974.
———. *Milton and the Culture of Violence.* Ithaca, N.Y.: Cornell University Press, 1994.
———. "'Our Living Dread': The God of *Samson Agonistes*." *Milton Studies* 33 (1996): 3–23.
Loewenstein, David. *Milton and the Drama of History: Historical Vision, Iconoclasm, and the Literary Imagination.* Cambridge: Cambridge University Press, 1990.
——— and James Grantham Turner, eds. "The Kingdom within: Radical Religious Culture and the Politics of *Paradise Regained*." *Literature and History* 3 (1994): 63–89.
———. *Poetics, Politics, and Hermeneutics in Milton's Prose.* Cambridge: Cambridge University Press, 1990.
MacCaffrey, Isabel G. "*Lycidas*: The Poet in a Landscape." In Joseph H. Summers, ed. *The Lyric and Dramatic Milton.* New York: Columbia University Press, 1965. 65–92.
Marcus, Leah S. "Justice for Margery Evans: A 'Local' Reading of *Comus*." In Julia Walker, ed. *Milton and the Idea of Woman.* Urbana: University of Illinois Press, 1988. 66–85.
———. "The Milieu of Milton's *Comus*: Judicial Reform at Ludlow and the Problem of Sexual Assault." *Criticism* 25 (1983): 293–327.
———. *The Politics of Mirth: Jonson, Herrick, Milton, Marvell and the Defense of Old Holiday Pastimes.* Chicago: University of Chicago Press, 1986.
Martin, Catherine Gimelli, ed., *Milton and Gender.* Cambridge: Cambridge University Press, 2004.
• Norbrook, David. *Poetry and Politics in the English Renaissance.* 2nd ed. Oxford: Oxford University Press, 2002.
———. *Writing the English Republic: Poetry, Rhetoric, and Politics, 1627–1660.* Cambridge: Cambridge University Press, 1999.
• Nyquist, Mary. "The Genesis of Gendered Subjectivity in the Divorce Tracts and in *Paradise Lost*." In Mary Nyquist and Margaret W. Ferguson, eds. *Re-Membering Milton: Essays on the Texts and Traditions.* London: Methuen, 1987: 99–127.
——— and Margaret W. Ferguson, eds. *Re-Membering Milton: Essays on the Texts and Traditions.* London: Methuen, 1987.
Orgel, Stephen. *The Illusion of Power: Political Theater in the English Renaissance.* Berkeley: University of California Press, 1975.
Patrides, C. A., ed. *Milton's Lycidas: The Tradition and the Poem.* 2nd ed. University of Missouri Press, 1983.

Patterson, Annabel. "That Old Man Eloquent." In Diana Trevino Benet and Michael Lieb, eds. *Literary Milton: Text, Pretext, Context*. Pittsburgh, Pa.: Duquesne University Press, 1994. 24–44.

Prince, F. T. *The Italian Element in Milton's Verse*. Oxford: Clarendon, 1954.

Quint, David. "David's Census: Milton's Politics and *Paradise Regained*." In Mary Nyquist and Margaret W. Ferguson, eds. *Re-Membering Milton: Essays on the Texts and Traditions*. London: Methuen, 1987. 128–47.

——. "Expectation and Prematurity in Milton's Nativity Ode." *Modern Philology* 97 (1999): 195–219.

Radzinowicz, Mary Ann. *Milton's Epics and the Book of Psalms*. Princeton, N.J.: Princeton University Press, 1989.

Rajan, Balachandra. *The Prison and the Pinnacle: Papers [on] Paradise Regained and Samson Agonistes*. London: Routledge, 1973.

Revard, Stella P. *Milton and the Tangles of Naera's Hair: The Making of the 1645 Poems*. Columbia: University of Missouri Press, 1997.

• Rogers, John. "The Secret of *Samson Agonistes*." In Albert C. Labriola and Michael Lieb, eds. *The Miltonic Samson. Milton Studies* 33 (1966): 111–32.

Rosenblatt, Jason P. "The Angel and the Shepherd in *Lycidas*." *Philological Quarterly* 62 (1983): 252–58.

——. "Samson's Sacrifice." In Amy Boesky and Mary Thomas Crane, eds. *Form and Reform in Renaissance England: Essays in Honor of Barbara Kiefer Lewalski*. Newark: University of Delaware Press, 2000. 321–37.

——. *Torah and Law in "Paradise Lost."* Princeton, N.J.: Princeton University Press, 1994.

Rushdy, Ashraf H. A. "Standing Alone on the Pinnacle: Milton in 1752." *Milton Studies* 26 (1990): 193–218.

Sacks, Peter M. "Milton: *Lycidas*." *The English Elegy: Studies in the Genre from Spenser to Yeats*. Baltimore, Md.: Johns Hopkins University Press, 1985.

Shifflett, Andrew. *Stoicism, Politics, and Literature in the Age of Milton: War and Peace Reconciled*. Cambridge: Cambridge University Press, 1998.

Shullenberger, William. *Lady in the Labyrinth: Milton's "Comus" as Initiation*. Madison, N. J.: Fairleigh Dickinson University Press, 2008.

Skinner, Quentin. "John Milton and the Politics of Slavery." *Visions of Politics II: Renaissance Virtues*. Cambridge: Cambridge University Press, 2002.

Spitzer, Leo. "Understanding Milton." In Anna Hatcher, ed., *Essays on English and American Literature*. Princeton, N.J.: Princeton University Press, 1962.

Stein, Arnold. *Heroic Knowledge: An Interpretation of "Paradise Regained" and "Samson Agonistes."* Minneapolis: University of Minnesota Press, 1957.

Summers, Joseph H., ed. *The Lyric and Dramatic Milton: Selected Papers from the English Institute*. New York: Columbia University Press, 1965.

Teskey, Gordon. *Delirious Milton: The Fate of the Poet in Modernity*. Cambridge, Mass.: Harvard University Press, 2006.

Turner, James Grantham. *One Flesh: Paradisal Marriage and Sexual Relations in the Age of Milton*. Oxford: Oxford University Press, 1987.

Tuve, Rosemond. *Images and Themes in Five Poems by Milton*. Cambridge, Mass.: Harvard University Press, 1957.

Vendler, Helen. "John Milton: The Elements of Happiness." In *Coming of Age as a Poet: Milton, Keats, Eliot, Plath*. Cambridge, Mass.: Harvard University Press, 2003.

Welsford, Enid. *The Court Masque*. Cambridge: Cambridge University Press, 1927.

Wilding, Michael. *Dragon's Teeth: Literature in the English Revolution*. Oxford: Clarendon, 1987.

Wittreich, Joseph A. Jr., ed., *Calm of Mind: Tercentenary Essays on "Paradise Regained" and "Samson Agonistes."* Cleveland, Ohio: Case Western University Press, 1971.

——. *Interpreting "Samson Agonistes."* Princeton, N.J.: Princeton University Press, 1986.

Woodhouse, A. S. P. "Notes on Milton's Early Development." *University of Toronto Quarterly* 13 (1943–44): 66–101.

Worden, Blair. "Milton, *Samson Agonistes*, and the Restoration." In Gerald MacLean, ed. *Culture and Society in the Stuart Restoration: Literature, Drama, History.* Cambridge: Cambridge University Press, 1995. 111–36.